W9-BTK-320

AUTHOR'S NOTE

This is, in essence, a true story. However, the reader should know that due to the nature of events, I have changed several names and altered a few identities. This was done at the request of those persons directly involved, or their families, or the police of many nations. I do not believe it disturbs the integrity of the book.

It is impossible to thank the hundreds of people who co-operated with me by sharing time and information, but I want specifically to express my appreciation to the police of India, Thailand, Nepal, Iran, Turkey, Hong Kong, and Greece. Interpol headquarters in Paris was also courteous and helpful.

Last, as I conducted interviews in a dozen different languages including such exotic tongues (for me) as Hindi and Urdu, any errors in translation, if they exist, should be considered benign ones.

SERPENTINE

**A TRUE STORY . . .
A BYZANTINE TALE OF DECEPTION,
TERROR, AND EVIL**

"THE MOST BIZARRE TRUE-CRIME NARRA-
TIVE SINCE THE MANSON STORY *HELTER
SKELTER* . . . GROTESQUE, BAFFLING, AND
HYPNOTIC." —*San Francisco Chronicle*

"A MASSIVE UNRAVELING OF ONE OF MOD-
ERN HISTORY'S MOST NEFARIOUS DRUG AND
ROB MEN . . . A LOVER AND KILLER WHO
ROAMED ACROSS ONE THIRD OF THE EARTH.
. . . THOMPSON IS A DOGGED REPORTER AND
TIRELESS DETECTIVE AND, MOST OF ALL, A
KEEN OBSERVER OF HUMAN NATURE."
—*Houston Chronicle*

"COMPULSIVE READING . . . ALIVE . . . THE
BOOK UNRAVELS LIKE FICTION, BUT AFTER-
WARD HAUNTS THE READER LIKE THE DOCU-
MENT IT IS." —*The Plain Dealer* (Cleveland)

Also by Thomas Thompson

HEARTS
*RICHIE
*LOST!
*BLOOD AND MONEY

*available from Dell

SERPENTINE

THOMAS THOMPSON

A DELL BOOK

For my parents—
and all the parents who wait—and wonder.

"Coincidence, if traced far enough back, becomes inevitable."

—*Inscription on a Hindu temple near New Delhi and quoted by Carl Gustav Jung*

On a July noon in 1978, Judge Joginder Nath entered his modest courtroom in Old Delhi to make known his long-awaited decision. His chamber was thronged, in a state of agitation, each person present having passed through a gauntlet of soldiers with fixed bayonets on their rifles and a commando squad of police trained in judo. During an hour or two of last-minute suspense, while the judge attended to paper work in his office, the monsoon rains had assaulted the city, the courthouse roof sounding as if the gods were dancing amid a million penny nails. But now, as the judge cleared his throat and requested silence, the torrents stopped, abruptly, as if even the gods wanted to hear the end of the story.

For more than a year Judge Nath had presided—refereed was perhaps a better word—over a murder trial both tempestuous and bizarre, one that contained enough sex and betrayal and intrigue to fill the darkest scenario. But it was larger than that. Beyond the massive borders of India, blood had spilled over many countries in Southeast Asia, blood attributed by police to the principal defendant.

Over a period of several months in late 1975 and early 1976, tourists had been found slain, their corpses strangled and stabbed and burned and drowned, from the paradisical beaches of Thailand to the awesome slopes of the Himalayas to beside the holy river Ganges. Police of half a dozen Asian nations finally affixed the number of deaths at twelve—although one Delhi detective suspected the total could double—and perhaps double again.

The murders were savage, seemingly totally at random. Capricious. Inexplicable. Cruel pranks of fate. The victims, Americans and Europeans, had come to the East on varied personal missions, none knowing that beyond a certain bend in the road was waiting the agent of their deaths.

"Would the defendants please rise?" asked Judge Nath, peering through thick glasses at the two men and a woman. He seemed troubled, his face worn and melancholy. Perhaps it was because what he was about to say would neatly wrap up one murder, but it contained no answer to the most important question of all. *Why?* Why did these deaths occur? Why did these lives collide?

PROLOGUE

The threat of still another familial war with Pakistan and a swelling moon the hue of lemon topaz hung in contradiction over the capital of India on this torpid autumn evening in late October 1971. The government of Indira Gandhi had ordered a blackout, but in Delhi the stubs of candles flickered like massed stars, and the embers of street braziers glowed like cats' eyes.

The old part of the city was electric with tension and passion. If India had her way, the nuisance of East Pakistan would no longer squat like a malignant tumor on the shoulder of the subcontinent. One quick war, as swift as the slash of a great sword, would sever the squalid Moslem annex and transform East Pakistan into Bangladesh. It would be a new nation, but one as obedient and docile toward India as an adopted pup..Indira Gandhi knew that she had little to fear from Pakistan, but nonetheless she directed her country to gird for war. One hundred miles to the south of Delhi, camouflage netting and bales of straw swaddled the Taj Mahal for the first time in three centuries. But like a veiled woman, her beauty was not concealed, only transformed into an unmistakable silhouette of mottled bronze.

As this night began, another woman was in torment at Delhi's Ashoka Hotel, a sprawling pink palace set down in gardens of orchids and bougainvillaea, a structure larger than many Indian villages and built by Nehru with uncharacteristic extravagance. He had ignored the criticism, for he wished to celebrate the new India and provide a house of reception for the world leaders who would come to see what Britain had surrendered.

The woman, who called herself La Passionara, decided to defy the blackout. No degree of international tension could interfere with her toilette on this of all nights. She could not risk making up her face by candlelight. Drawing the heavy drapes, she cursed the thought of war and turned on a soft light. It was time to dance. In rose water and jasmine she bathed, rubbing oil of sandalwood onto her body, seeking to knead away the tightness in her legs and the knots of muscle. For her face, she selected a whitish base and powder, calculating that it would enhance not only her dark eyes—enlarged with a half moon of kohl and glistening from a drop of glycerine—but also the crimson silks she wrapped about her slender body. She envisioned how they would float like ethereal clouds, provided the cretinous stagehand (actually the busboy) remembered to switch on the electric fan for the finale. On her arms she heaped antique bracelets of filagreed ivory, and about her neck she placed her one real treasure, a necklace from the Moghul dynasty, of hammered gold, with enameled plaques of the gods in erotic play. It was a gift from an admiring maharaja whose grandmother had worn the piece to kneel in London before Victoria and Albert.

When she was done, La Passionara rose from her dressing table and swirled happily about the room, catching fragments of her reflection in the mirrors and brass lamps. "I *am* beautiful," she reassured herself by custom, "because I am a dancer." Like Isadora Duncan, she considered herself torn from the breast of Terpsichore. But when she stopped, and switched off the forbidden lights, and began the long walk down the hotel corridor to an elevator that would drop her one floor to the Club Rouge et Noir, La Passionara was assaulted by cross-currents, besieged by emotions beyond normal stage fright. Would anyone even come to see her dance with all this stupid talk of war? Would the hotel management permit the spotlight? Even though she had personally begged the vice-president in charge of entertainment, pleading tearfully that one lonely beam of stage light would not summon the warplanes of

Pakistan, and even though he had smiled and bowed and promised, she knew that nothing was ever certain in India until it happened. Why were these forces working against her, menacing what could be the turning point of her life? If all went well—she hardly dared think it, suspecting somehow that karma was teasing her—there would be no more performances for diplomatic wives in embassy auditoriums, no more cultural centers where her fee was a cup of tea and a piece of stale raisin cake, no more hotel managements that booked her into claustrophobic, smoke-shrouded cellars from Ankara to Lahore and then requested, after her first performance, that she make the act more—hemming and hawing here—more *provocative.* I am not a cabaret dancer, I do not take my clothes off, she had always snapped at the Philistines, summoning hauteur. I am an *artiste,* a student of the Kalakshetra school of dance. I am a museum of classical music and movement. I am keeper of the flame, seeking not to stir man's blood, but his heart, perhaps even his soul.

Now, finally, a decade of frustration might be swept away in a single hour. The portal of opportunity had reared abruptly in her path. She had fought her way past other, less dedicated supplicants to the head of the line. Gulping deep breaths, she stood behind the screen near the cash register, hearing masculine talk in the gloom beyond. Indian men rarely brought their women to night clubs. The night before, in this very spot, she had waited after the performance, perspiration drowning her face, straining to hear if the desultory applause would sustain a second bow. And then the waiter had brought her the silver tray. On it rested a calling card with exquisite engraving. On the front, discreetly, was printed, "J. Lobo, Director, The Casino at Macao," and, following an arrow to its back, "I admire your dancing. Can we discuss a possible engagement at my casino? Perhaps tomorrow night? *À bientôt.*"

Each time she read these words, La Passionara was filled with fear and the promise of power. The man who wrote them was out there now, at this moment, somewhere in the blackness. Who was he? Where was he sitting? Please, she prayed, please let him sit next to a well-mannered table, not to a collection of boors who would cackle and slurp while she danced. It does not matter, she reassured herself. Mr. Lobo will know that the dances are dedicated to *him*. She kissed his message and smuggled it within the red silks at her breast, hiding it next to her pounding heart. Then she sent a silent plea to Isadora Duncan, her idol and imagined patron—watch over me tonight!—hearing the drums and tambura announce her entrance.

At this moment, in the old section of Delhi, in a far more modest hotel in a serpentine alley near the Red Fort, the man who called himself Lobo was also dressing with care, as was his custom. He chose a shirt of Egyptian cotton, and a tie of muted gray by Sulka. His suit was Cardin, tailored to accommodate his wide shoulders, small waist, and muscular thighs. On his wrist he placed a Lucien Piccard watch, and in his pocket he put Dunhill's slimmest gold lighter. He cast but a hurried glance at the shadowy reflection that met his eyes in the candlelit bathroom mirror, for he had no need to confirm his appearance. Long ago he had learned its appeal and marketability. But for a moment he did smile. Lobo! The name was selected by caprice, but it suited him. With great brown eyes flecked with yellow and resting atop ridges of cheekbones that flared up like wings, he did indeed resemble a wolf, or a panther, for his legs were slim and built with grace and power. At first meeting, most people would take this man to be an Asian, but then, as acquaintance deepened, undertones of Europe came into play. He was a mélange of East and West, a small man, five feet eight at most, but he emitted messages of raw sexuality. The possibility of brutality was scarcely hidden, his hands rough and strong and eminently capable of snapping the bones in a neck. He bespoke danger, but it came wrapped in couturier jackets and very tight pants. He held appeal for most women, particularly those who shuddered at, yet secretly cherished, the element of risk. Not quite thirty years old, he had been merchandising this body for most of his adult life, and tonight was very important.

Hurrying out into the darkened quarter, Lobo ignored the sleeping bodies of the poor, wrapped in gray blankets as thin as an old woman's skin, and huddled against the shops of Chandni Chowk bazaar like sacks of grain delivered carelessly in blackness. The streets, chaos under normal conditions, were tonight madness. The blackout had raised the collective blood pressure of the people: taxis raced more insanely with blue paint splashed over their headlights, rickshaw drivers pedaled recklessly in and out of slumbering cows and huddles of men on street corners screaming hatred of Moslem Pakistan. Martial music swam from open windows; half-naked children dueled with sticks. In the silver market, merchants nailed boards over their shopwindows and slept with their best wares locked to their bodies. Placards of Indira Gandhi, wrinkleless, looking like a film star or a madonna, were held aloft by the mobs, bobbing like the saints on feast days in Rome. They screamed her name and her legend, "Indira is India—India is Indira!" Before the night would be over, scores of Moslems would be slain, many by neighbors of a lifetime, and their blood would flow in the ancient streets.

Lobo cursed, for he could not find a taxi. All he could engage was a "putt-putt" and, thrusting twenty extravagant rupees into the driver's hand, rode in less than splendor to his rendezvous with great fortune. On the way, he put aside his anger and replaced it with calm. His head could not contain impurities, else the plan might spoil. He remained serene while the three-wheeled motor scooter fought its way out of the fetid and lunatic embrace of Old Delhi and into the startling quiet and decorum of the new city, through the Delhi Gate, into a completely different place of wide boulevards, lavish embassies, traffic roundabouts redolent with the scent of marigolds, and great villas guarded by dour men with carbines at their shoulders. At this point in his journey, Lobo must have felt his pulse quickening. Meditating for a moment, drawing on Jung and Nietzsche—a symbiotic relationship and one that always nurtured him—Lobo summoned peace again. He would have it no other way. Though his life to this point had been one of outrageous exremes, his fortunes leaping and falling like the line of an electrocardiogram, Lobo was certain that tonight began an ascendancy.

When he entered the Ashoka Hotel by a side entrance, La Passionara was already halfway through her program. But Lobo did not hurry to the Club Rouge et Noir. His stroll was leisurely, a tourist promenading through the hotel's shopping arcade, pausing only briefly at the Rajasthan Emporium to note that it was closed. One candle in the corridor threw a faint glow against the display window, but even in the burnished shadows Lobo could see a tray of brilliant gems—sapphires, rubies, diamonds, golden bracelets; necklaces and figurines of rare ivory, spilling out over forest green velvet as if a sultan had emptied his treasure box to tempt a princess.

In a corner of the hotel's vast lobby, Lobo found a chair and slumped down. And waited. He was still there when La Passionara completed her final number, ecstatic that the spotlight was embracing her, that the fan was billowing her silks, that even the musicians seemed caught up in the fervor of her dance in homage to Lord Shiva, her hands entwined like serpents, her body in combat against the demons, an imaginary fire consuming all but her.

But when she was finished and had managed to squeeze an unprecedented three bows from the few dozen people in the room, Mr. Lobo did not present himself, nor send another card, nor invite her to his table. Disappointment chewed at her as she waited behind the screen, wondering if she should take a table in expectation of his summons. But that seemed brazen, inappropriate, for, she reasoned, a genuine *artiste* should be encountered presiding over a doting claque of admirers, tasting champagne, accepting compliments, dispensing *bons mots*, perhaps even unable to find a place at her altar for a man who did not keep appointments. Finally, dejection becoming humiliation, La Passionara returned to her room, stripped off her makeup, changed into an old robe, and was well into a tantrum when a soft rap sounded at her door. It was midnight. Frightened, La Passionara chose not to respond. The rap came quickly again. "It is Lobo," said the voice outside.

"You are much younger than I thought," said Lobo, when his quarry finally opened the door, after promising her it was of no importance that she was unprepared for visitors. "The lighting in the club is very bad. It makes you look ten years older."

La Passionara frowned, then blessed the candlelight of

her room. "And you," she said, bidding her caller to sit, "you are much younger than I had imagined." La Passionara decided at this moment to play the scene coquettishly. Throughout the day she had rehearsed variations, from an imperious grandness to show business hip. Now that Lobo was in her room, she was not sure how to deal with him. He could not have been much more than twenty-five, she surmised, although with Oriental men it was difficult to affix age. And he walked with the grace of a dancer; La Passionara could always tell when a body was well tuned and controlled. But it was his face that held fascination. Lobo wore the caste of Asia, his skin was antique gold, but in alternating moments he seemed completely Western, like a man holding up different masks. Whatever, he was sexy and he knew it. She would flirt with him, but she would not let him any closer than the sound of a merry laugh.

For a few moments they studied one another. Then Lobo broke the spell. He smiled broadly. It was difficult, he began, to address her as La Passionara. Could he know her real name? "Of course," she answered quickly, preparing to hand out one of many stage names she had used in her career. But there was something about Lobo that denuded her. He would know if she was lying. She felt compelled to tell the truth. "Esther," she said. "Esther Markowitz. Of New York."

"Manhattan?" asked Lobo.

"Brooklyn," confessed Esther.

"Esther is a beautiful name," said Lobo. "Do you speak French?"

She nodded dumbly. She had lived two years in Paris. But why did this Asian man from Macao wish to speak French?

He preferred it. It was "the language of negotiation."

For half an hour they conversed in French. Esther fell easily into her biography, how she studied ballet as a child, how, after failing an audition with a minor dance company, she fled in despair to Europe. In Paris she studied with one of those ferocious women from the Ballets Russe de Monte Carlo who smoked black cigarettes and carried an ebony cane to rap shins and ankles. In Madrid, on holiday, she had become enamored of flamenco and studied it, becoming so accomplished that she appeared "on the best stages of Madrid, Rome, Paris, and London." As she talked, Esther used the same florid language she did in interviews, on the rare occasion when a newspaper sent a reporter to speak with her.

Lobo listened attentively, then presented his view of the woman before him. He found La Passionara to be an exciting performer with the potential to become an international star. But her act, as currently presented in the Club Rouge et Noir, did not flatter her. Esther agreed. Absolutely! The conditions here were primitive. What Lobo envisioned was to present La Passionara as the star of a new international revue on the stage of his casino in Macao. Choreographers, set designers, lighting experts, a full orchestra, a troupe of dancers—all would be engaged to support her. Expenses be damned! Perhaps, he mused, perhaps she could combine Spanish flamenco with the classical dances of India. If the act were successful, as he was certain it would be under his tutelage, then La Passionara could undertake a world tour with his management. Hong Kong, Tokyo, Beirut, Paris, New York! He had contacts in Las Vegas.

Suddenly, abruptly, Lobo rose and took his leave. He would see Esther again tomorrow night, after her show. So absorbed was she in the fantasies that danced in her head, Esther did not notice Lobo studying her room, mentally marking its dimensions, stepping calculatedly on the carpet to measure its pile. Then he was gone. For a long while Esther Markowitz remained in delicious semishock, half expecting that moment of crushing disappointment when a dream ends and consciousness returns to wash it away.

When it was almost 2 A.M., Esther, unable to sleep, wrote a hurried letter to her fiancé, a guitarist working in Tokyo. The exciting news poured from her pen, cautioning that she was still crossing her fingers, but fairly certain that she was on the threshold of international celebrity. "I am trying not to get excited," she wrote, "but it would be fun to go to Macao and earn 'plenty' of money. How I love you! And the Chinese man, Lobo, said he would be glad to hire you to accompany my flamenco!" Later this

letter would become one of the most important documents
La Passionara ever wrote.

The first thing she did upon arising the next afternoon
was to telephone the vice-president in charge of entertainment at the hotel and yell that the atrocious lighting in the
Club Rouge et Noir made her look a decade older. No
wonder that the audiences had been small and, to an
extent, unappreciative. Had she known the harsh spot was
turning her into a crone, she would never have set foot
in such a place. Two weeks remained in her engagement,
and if the hotel did not wish to duel with her agents and
attorneys, then best it find a soft and flattering pink gel to
illumine her dance.

The rest of the day she spent trying unsuccessfully to
reach her fiancé by telephone in Tokyo. "It is urgent," she
shouted at the operator, and in truth it was, for Esther
had no idea what to pry from Lobo's purse as salary.
There was no agent, no attorney, no one to counsel her.
She was a woman alone in the East, now jumpy and wildly
nervous, wondering if she could even get through her next
performance.

A second midnight had come and gone, and Esther was
once again jilted—and consumed by disappointment. Lobo
had not attended either of her two performances. Now that
she at least knew what he looked like, she could peer
through the cracks of the screen and eye the audience. He
was not there! He had not even made a reservation with
the maître d'. Nor was there a message in her box at the
reception desk. What an infuriating man! Morosely she
washed her face of makeup and patted on cold cream,
wondering if the cosmetics she was forced to purchase
here in the East were causing the crinkle marks about her
eyes and the darkening pockets beneath them, or was it
the thirtieth birthday, unwelcome but due in a few months?
She took a Valium and was almost asleep when the telephone beside her bed rang urgently. At first she thought
it was the long overdue call to Tokyo. But then came the
sensuous voice of Lobo, speaking apologetically, his manner both soothing and seductive. Could he come to her

room to conclude the arrangement? Esther refused, worried
that she might thus annoy him, but unwilling to receive a
man of Lobo's stature in nightgown and cold cream. But
it *must* be tonight, countered Lobo. He was leaving Delhi
on one of those infernal flights that always seemed to
depart from the capital of India between 2 A.M. and dawn.
Finally Esther agreed, hanging up and flying to the bathroom to redo her aging face.

When the soft rap at the door came this time, Esther
opened it promptly, discovering not one but two young
men. The first was Lobo, dressed less elegantly for this
meeting, in work pants and turtleneck. Beside him stood
an attractive but somber young blond man. He was introduced as Pierre, a *copain* from Paris. He was carrying a
small canvas bag that appeared to be heavy. Were there
fat contracts inside?

For several minutes, Esther plied Lobo with questions
—the size of his stage, the condition of his dressing rooms,
the time she would need for rehearsal, the necessity of a
substantial orchestra. She inquired about everything except
money, having decided that it would be more shrewd to
wait for his offer. Her plan was set. When Lobo revealed
the kind of salary he was thinking about for his new star,
La Passionara would pronounce it penurious. He would
counter with more, she would pretend to be insulted, perhaps even show him the door. But finally, in her fantasy,
they would agree, and the rest would be champagne.
Esther had played this scene more or less non-stop all
day long.

But after a time, she began to notice that Lobo was
restless, his answers vague, his eyes studying not her, but
her hotel room. Was she boring the young impresario?
Offending him? "Excuse me," Lobo said abruptly, "may
I use your bathroom?" Esther gestured toward the door,
remembering that the toilet was a jumble of cosmetic jars,
spilled white face powder, and towels wadded in balls on
the floor. Lobo would think she was a slovenly person.
"I'm afraid it's rather a mess," she called out, adding that
under normal conditions she had a dresser to keep things
neat. The hotel management had refused to provide her
with one.

Left momentarily alone with the new blond Frenchman,

Esther studied his face. He had not uttered a word since entering the room. Esther attempted a warming smile, but his countenance in return was cold and unyielding. She tried to draw him out. He was from Paris? Pierre nodded. How long had he been in India? A shrug.

Getting nowhere, Esther grew uneasy. Where was Lobo? What was he *doing* in the bathroom? Why didn't he come out? Several minutes had passed. She had heard the toilet flush. His business must be done in there. She rose and lit another candle, wanting to turn on the lights but afraid these men would find her disrespectful of India's emergency blackout. The soft new glow revealed more of Pierre's thin face. On his cheek, a jagged, cruel scar ran from beside his eye to beneath his chin, as if marking a dangerous road on a map. He touched it, knowing that Esther found it fascinating, his finger lightly tracing its course. And for the first time he smiled, empty and false.

"Please sit down, Esther," came the voice of Lobo. He emerged from the bathroom and went to the dancer and touched her shoulder. In his fingers was strength. Esther dared not even draw back when his hand moved to stroke her naked neck. She looked up at Lobo, standing over her, and she knew at this moment that there was more to their meeting than an appreciation of her art. "Esther, it is time to tell you that I have a secondary proposition," said Lobo, crouching before her until their eyes were level. She did not want to look at him yet found it impossible to turn away. His eyes were like magnets that locked her. Slowly, theatrically, Lobo raised his hand and held before La Passionara a fistful of golden objects that glittered in the candlelight, throwing off sparks that danced in his horn-rimmed glasses. For a moment, Esther thought selfishly that Lobo was paying her tribute, offering jewels before the negotiations commenced. Then she realized that this man was clutching *her own* bracelets and the precious antique necklace. Obviously he had found them in the bathroom. Now he held them like a hypnotist.

India, he began, sounding like a tour guide, was a land rich in gems. Sapphires, rubies smuggled from Burma, topaz as big as doorknobs and less than ten cents a carat. Did Esther know that? She nodded. Often she had spent afternoons prowling the bazaars, searching for old ivory bracelets, or smoky gray sapphires with a star that appeared mysteriously when held at just the right light.

Lobo lectured briefly on the nature of gems, then suggested to Esther that when she traveled to Macao, she could bring stones with her. There was money to be made. At least four thousand dollars. Now Esther was totally confused. "I don't understand," she said honestly. Lobo was quick with enlightenment. He needed someone, a courier, who could transport gems discreetly from India to various distant cities, someone to whom customs officials would pay scant attention.

"You want me to smuggle jewelry?" gasped Esther incredulously. Lobo nodded. A great many respectable people did just that for him, he continued. Esther shook her head vigorously. "Well, not me," she said. Even if she were inclined to conceal contraband in her luggage—and she most certainly was not—she would be the most unsuitable courier that Lobo could possibly engage. "As a child I turned beet red every time I told a fib," she informed him. Any customs officer would read guilt writ large across her face.

Quickly Esther assessed her predicament. First there had been an engraved calling card on a silver tray, then a fascinating young impresario in a French-cut suit, now they had become two dangerous men in her room, one importuning her to become a smuggler, the second standing immobile like a lance waiting to be thrown. In indignation, Esther rose and went for the telephone. Lobo made himself a roadblock. His face was now a threatening storm.

"Is there really a casino in Macao?" she asked, her voice much meeker than she had intended it to be. Lobo nodded, steering her back to the chair.

"Unfortunately," he answered, "my only connection with it has been to lose great sums of money there at baccarat."

Esther began to weep. Why were these men in *her* room?

"Because you have the good fortune to be a resident of Room 289," said Lobo. "A very nice room."

"I hate this room," said Esther truthfully. She had pleaded with the Ashoka management to give her a chamber nearer the elevator, so that she did not have to walk the length of a football field in full makeup and

costume for her descent to the main floor and the Club
Rouge et Noir. The reply to her complaint had been
brusque. Her contract called for 2,000 rupees for a
month's dancing, plus room and board. It did not specify
which room.

"It is a *very* nice room," emphasized Lobo. Had Esther
ever wondered who lived beneath her? Lobo tapped lightly
with his foot against the carpet. As a matter of fact, agreed
Esther, she had, particularly on the nights when she rehearsed to dance flamenco and warmed up by stamping
her heels against the floor. She had expected a call of
complaint. But none ever came.

Lobo went directly to the point. Directly below Room
289 was the Rajasthan Emporium, an elegant shop containing some of the most desirable jewelry in India. For
two months, Lobo had studied the layout of this hotel,
even spending a week in residence. The plan was not an
impulsive one. It was, he revealed, the creation of half a
dozen colleagues in his profession. Already several thousands of dollars had been lavished on this night, ranging
from air tickets from Hong Kong to Teheran and back,
on special equipment, even on the calling cards which
Lobo had commissioned in a sudden change of direction.
The original scheme had been for him to personally rent
Room 289, but when the hotel management assigned it
to the night club dancer, then new arrangements were
dictated.

"If you want, blame it on karma," suggested Lobo.
"Fate brought us together in this room." And now fate
was giving La Passionara a very simple role to play. There
were no lines of dialogue to learn. All she had to do was
sit on her bed and remain absolutely silent. Midway through
the explanation, Esther noticed that Lobo was now holding a gun—small, black, gleaming in the candlelight. She
could not stop staring at it, wondering if it was a toy,
but somehow knowing it was not. Dialogue from cheap
theatrics rained on her ears. *We don't want to hurt you,
Esther. Nothing will happen to you if you stay quiet,
Esther. If you cry out, Esther, it might be tragic. We are
both black belts in karate, Esther.* Dimly, Esther looked
at Lobo's proffered hands, observing that the knuckles
were enlarged, the edges of the palms toughened and

calloused. She nodded. She believed. "We don't want to hurt your legs, Esther," whispered Lobo. "Then you could not dance again."

"I promise," said Esther, whimpering. "Please don't hurt me."

She watched as Lobo nodded and gestured at Pierre to begin the work. First the canvas bag was opened and a walkie-talkie pulled out. Lobo pressed a button, murmured something, received a staccato barrage of static in response. There were two accomplices in the hotel, warned Lobo, positioned near the room as lookouts. If Esther entertained aspirations of escape, she should know that these men would be waiting for her.

Then Lobo paced off several steps, paused beside the bathroom door, peeled back a corner of the carpet, and nodded at Pierre. The blond man took out a pneumatic drill and assembled it. He wrapped blankets about the contraption and handed it to Lobo.

"Within three to five hours," said Lobo, "provided you remain very quiet, we will be done." The scheme was bold: they intended to drill a hole large enough for the slim bodies of Lobo and Pierre to drop from Room 289 to the jewelry store below. There, presumably, they would fill their sacks with jewelry and—thanks to war fever—make an easy exit in the blackout. But hardly had the drilling bit begun to chew against the floor when Lobo grew worried about the noise. Cursing, he shut it off to study another way to muffle the machine. At that moment Esther intruded. Boldly. Somewhere in the depths of her fear she had relocated the haughty air of La Passionara.

"Do you really like my dancing?" she demanded.

Lobo looked up from his labor and smiled. Not untenderly. But he shook his head. "I haven't had the pleasure," he said. "Perhaps another day."

At that, La Passionara began to laugh, softly at first, then building to wild crescendo, drunk for a moment on the irony, rolling about her prison bed on the precipice of hysteria. Only when Lobo started toward her with his palm quivering like a just sprung trap did she stop, wondering whether she would go mad before the sun rose, or before they killed her.

Book One

CHARLOT

CHAPTER ONE

Behind bamboo screens, in the charity ward of the Catholic hospital in Saigon, lower-class women in final labor screamed. They beseeched their gods and cursed their bellies and received small solace from the nuns who always found out which girls had no legal husbands and whose sins should thus be reprimanded by Mother Church. It was April 1944. The room swam in thickest heat. The women, most of them very young, lay in pools of sweat and listened to their fears and to the crackling of an electric storm that hurled bolts of lightning at the hospital. Everything stank. The bed that contained Song was filthy when they brought her to it, and now, after two days of trying to squeeze the child from her thin frame, it was a battlefield.

Song suffered in silence. The pain was second nature now and screaming did not soften it. She envied the other girls who had come to this room and endured the contractions and the sharp tongues of the nuns and were wheeled away. Presumably they were holding babies now in contented arms, the progeny of war. One girl was pregnant with the baby of a Japanese naval captain, part of the invading force that had seized Indochina in 1940 as easily as plucking a mango from a tree. Of course, this captain could not marry Song's friend—not until the war was done and the Japanese possessed the entire world—but the fortunate creature would live in a nice apartment near the

river and have a servant to send out for sweets and cigarettes.

Song congratulated her friend and prayed for the infant
when they took her away. She also held the hand of a
frightened girl not yet fifteen who carried a Frenchman's
seed, but in her solicitude was a tinge of envy that Song
knew was shameful but that she could not conceal. Many
of her friends had French lovers, and all of them were
well treated. They bragged of going to Paris one day when
the war was over, and although Song had no real understanding of where Paris was located, she comprehended
that it was a prize. Certainly the French men were the most
handsome in Saigon, be they soldiers or civil servants, even
though during these war years they bowed lower than their
masters, the Japanese. A delicate balance existed between
the French, who in theory owned the country, and the
Japanese, who so easily had conquered it. Those French
who swore allegiance to the Vichy government were permitted to stay and operate Saigon's bureaucracy—just as
they had done for almost half a century. Thus, in the port
which had become the busiest in Asia, Japanese warships,
bearing the rising red sun nuzzled next to French cargo
vessels, a strange and tenuous marriage.

Waves of excruciating new pain swept over Song in her
fortieth hour of labor and she cried out, fearful that death
had come to take her. She tore off the thin and dirty sheet,
arching her naked back as high as it would go, putting a
strand of her own hair between her teeth to bite on. One
of the nuns came upon hearing the terrified girl and put
her hand on Song's belly and said the baby would soon
appear.

"Who is the father?" demanded the nun. In her agony,
Song shook her head in refusal. She did not want to tell.
"God is punishing you," said the nun. "God does not make
it easy for the fornicator. God wants you to suffer for
breaking the commandments." With that, the nun went
away to find the doctor, muttering all the way about country girls who come to Saigon and stain the laws of God.

It had not been in Song's scheme of things to be in this
bed, trapped by an unwanted new life. She had left her
village in the wetlands when she was not yet fifteen, over
the protests and warnings of her family. Saigon was evil,

lectured her mother. Her prophecy was that Song would find nothing there but pain and disgrace. The mother had even crept into her daughter's room and clipped off her toenails and, at dawn, threw them into the cooking fire. When dark green smoke rose from the flames, Song's mother pronounced it to be an omen. Song was not dissuaded—her mother could find an omen in the way a bird sang or a stalk of corn grew. Defying her family, she walked more than a hundred kilometers to Saigon, refusing every oxcart that offered her a ride. On her journey she fortified herself by reassurances that there was more to life than balancing a harness with twin water buckets on her shoulders, or crouching in rice paddies to pull the weeds and staying ever alert for the tiny serpents that lived in the muck and bit farmers' ankles. From her earliest years, Song had been told she was bright with an ability to learn. Everyone also said she was pretty, with long, shining black hair and a cheerful air. It must be true, she told herself, for now she was outside the perimeters of her village, and men who had never seen her before were slowing their carts and stopping on the road to flirt and tease. For the first time, Song felt the promise of power that was in beauty.

Within a few days, Song found a job washing melons for a merchant who sold to restaurants. She was one of a thousand women who worked in the open air vegetable market, most of whom were old and wrinkled and hidden beneath cone-shaped straw hats that blocked the sun. Song knew she stood out, bare-headed, getting to the stand before sunrise and arranging the shining fruit in such graceful displays that the French chefs always praised her. They flirted, too, and at *that* Song laughed and looked boldly back at them, even though she could not speak their language. One day an old Vietnamese man who owned a popular cafe bought melons and asked Song if she would like to better herself. Would she not prefer to wear silk instead of black cotton pajamas, and work inside, in a cool place, rather than under the tropical sun? He offered her a job as waitress, and though Song would have preferred that he was French, she accepted.

Before a year had passed, Song had managed diplomatically to resist the old gentleman's occasional lunges and had learned the abacus well enough to become cashier. She sat by the doorway, directly in front of a large window that she filled with plants, and she wore bright silk dresses and put fresh blossoms in her hair. The men who ate in the restaurant usually found an excuse to linger beside the cashier when they paid the bill, and the proprietor did not object. He knew that Song was more of an attraction than his noodles and spicy beef wrapped in lettuce, particularly now that he often substituted diced rat as wartime filling.

In the summer months of 1943, Song came to notice a foreign man who dined alone each night in the restaurant. He was tall and rather fair and handsome. Song was unable to discern his nationality. All she knew was that he was not Oriental and that he stole glances at her throughout his meal. But when he paid his bills, he never spoke, other than to smile and murmur "thank you" in broken Vietnamese. For a time, Song assumed the man was French, but when she addressed him in the new language she was learning from customers, he could not answer. One evening he paid his bill and thrust a package at Song before he hurried away. When she opened it, Song discovered an exquisite gown and a note, painstakingly printed in French, asking her to go for a boat ride on the Dong Nai River. When he returned the next night and took his customary table without daring to look at the cashier, Song sent over a note. "Thank you so much," it read. "Yes." His cry of joy was heard over the entire restaurant.

On their first date, Song learned that her admirer was an Indian in his early forties from a town near Bombay. He was a tailor who lived in Saigon and both lived and worked in one room. The machine on which he sewed was an old one, operated by a foot pedal, but from it emerged dress whites for officers and soft, pretty blouses for their women. He worked from before sunup until it was too dark for his eyes to see the stitches. It was his plan to build this one-room operation into a thriving business, then branch out with affiliated shops in Saigon, perhaps Hong Kong and other capitals if the war ever ended. One day, the tailor promised, he would be rich.

Life in one cramped room was not what Song had dreamed of when she left her native village, nor had she ever found Indian men to be particularly appealing. But there was something in the tailor's old-fashioned passion for work, and his ambition, and his almost adolescent infatuation for her that touched Song. Within a few weeks, she moved into the room and became the mistress of a man whose name was impossible for her to pronounce: Hotchand Bhawnani Sobhraj. He brought her white orchids and sweet oranges and gold buttons.

Not long thereafter, the tailor's mood swung abruptly. He was not at all happy when Song told him that she was pregnant. Nor was he convinced that he was the father, because, as he heatedly reminded Song, she flirted with every man who came to the restaurant. *That* was no longer a problem, yelled Song in angry retort, because she had just been fired. The proprietor threw her out upon learning that the girl who had always rejected his attentions had succumbed to the sweet talk of an impoverished tailor— and a foreigner at that. Mr. Sobhraj, as she called him, reluctantly permitted his pregnant mistress to stay in his room, but during the final months of her gestation, each day was acrimonious. As her belly swelled, Song hated the tailor and the seed he had planted.

The doctor who attended her in the labor room was kind, with a caring face, and he assured Song that everything was normal. But as the anesthetic seeped into her, Song felt desperation and she beseeched the physician to pay attention. Surely the baby was deformed! It did not want to come out of her womb. If it was a monster, she wanted it destroyed. And she did not want to know. Just tell her that the child was born dead. Every mother has such fears, soothed the doctor. Put those thoughts out of your head. But Song had heard bombs exploding during her pregnancy! And even though she had always pressed her hands to her stomach to let the baby know that she would protect it from harm, Song had come to believe that the unborn infant had been affected by the tumult of war. Just before she fell into unconsciousness, Song wished that she had possessed more courage when, early in her pregnancy, she had gone to an abortionist and watched the old woman mix a foul potion of secret herbs and laxatives.

Song had run out of the hut before the glass was offered
her.

She had not tasted a drop, and now it was too late.

A son was delivered precisely at midnight, and the
miracle of squawling new life softened even the scolding
nun when she placed the baby in Song's exhausted arms
and instructed her how to nurse. "He is perfect," said the
nun, "all thanks be to God." The next day, Song washed
herself and the baby and put a blossom in her hair. She
waited for the tailor to come, having sent him a message
that their son awaited his father. But Mr. Sobhraj did not
visit the hospital, nor was he receptive when Song and the
baby soon thereafter arrived at his shop. He made one
thing clear before he would grant them admittance: he
was not admitting paternity of this child, nor would he
accept responsibility for its upbringing. Those were his
conditions. Song was too tired to argue.

At the end of World War II, the Japanese left Saigon,
to be replaced by a British occupation force. But the country enjoyed little peace. Less than a fortnight after the
Japanese surrendered in August 1945, Ho Chi Minh seized
control of Hanoi in the north and proclaimed that his coali-
tion of nationalist rebels—called the Viet Minh—would
soon unite a country so long ravaged and abused by foreign
colonial powers.

Song knew little of politics, nor did she care, but she
heard stories of new violence in the city. Buildings owned
by the French blew up from time to time, and once she
saw two bloated bodies floating in the Saigon River. Mr.
Sobhraj assured her that such events were not important,
better that she concentrate on learning how to sew button-
holes and measure inseams. This she accepted until the
morning that she dressed up her infant son in a new linen
shirt and trousers that the tailor had sewn and took him
in a taxi to visit a girl friend. The little boy was called
Gurmukh, an Indian name that Mr. Sobhraj had come up
with, although the child had no official identity. Wartime
records had been poorly kept, and aside from an entry in
a hospital record, the baby did not exist in the eyes of the
transitional government. Song did not particularly like the

name. Gurmukh was strange-sounding and hard to pronounce, but it stuck.

When the taxi stopped for a traffic light in a section of
Saigon she did not know, the doors were suddenly yanked
open by Vietnamese men holding guns. They dragged Song
and her baby out of the taxi, ignoring the mother's screams
and passing the child between them like a soccer ball. Then
one of the men pressed a rough cloth smelling of fumes
against Song's nose. Before she blacked out, she saw another man putting a blindfold over her baby's eyes, wide
with fear.

The men were Viet Minh partisans and by nightfall they
had delivered a ransom note to Sobhraj the Tailor. Kidnap-
ing was common in Saigon in 1945, particularly against
foreigners whom the Viet Minh felt were intruders and
should contribute toward cleansing the country of alien
powers. The ransom note demanded $10,000, and inside
the envelope was a scrap of the linen shirt that the baby
had worn. It was torn and wet and flecked red.

Several years later, in a letter written to a friend, Sobhraj the Tailor remembered his predicament. "I could not
have raised $1,000," he wrote, "much less $10,000. And
I was afraid to go to the police because my visa to work
in Saigon had always been a problem. It happened that
one of my customers was a British officer. I was sewing
him a suit of white linen. When he came to get it that
night, I told him of what had happened to my wife and
the boy. He rounded up a group of his soldier friends,
some Americans, too, I believe, and they raided the house
where the kidnapers were living, and they freed Song and
Gurmukh. I made all of the brave men—eight of them, I
recall—a new suit to thank them, even though I have
often thought it would have better for the Viet Minh to
keep Song."

Mother and son had been held hostage for three days
before rescue came, sustained only by sips of water and
a few spoonfuls of cold rice. Afterwards when she told
the story, Song was reassured by friends and family that
the baby was too young to be seriously affected by the
experience. But she wondered, particularly when the boy
woke up screaming for years thereafter in the middle of
the night. It was also difficult for her to forget the tailor's

attitude upon her deliverance from kidnapers. Sobhraj had lectured her, suggesting that Song had perhaps brought the abduction on herself the way she dressed in sexy clothes and painted her lips and toes the same lacquer red. People must think she is a prosperous night club hostess, with a rich patron.

The boy now became witness to a year of increasing anger and accusation as Song and the tailor destroyed their relationship. Song discovered a letter that indicated her lover had another woman (perhaps a legitimate wife, although he would not admit it) back in India, where he went once or twice a year on extended visits. When she confronted him with this discovery, the tailor fired back with his accusations—principally that Song was seen now and then in the cafes of Saigon, drinking wine with French soldiers. How many secret lovers did *she* have? "How did this country girl become a bad woman so quickly?" wrote Sobhraj to his cousin in Bombay. "She spends all of her time painting her nails and her face and cares nothing about me or Gurmukh. She also gambles."

Before the child was two, his mother packed up all of her gowns, each sewn by her lover, and moved out on an afternoon when the tailor was worshiping at a Hindu temple. That night, Sobhraj went to a cafe, ordered an uncharacteristic bottle of champagne (for as a Hindu he rarely drank) and announced to the other customers that he was celebrating the successful removal of a tumor.

Song found a small apartment in another section of Saigon, far from the tailor, and there she took stock. At twenty-four, her beauty was at its peak. Men had not stopped looking at her on the street. But she was not ready for another love affair, having spent three mostly unhappy years in a tailor's bed, contending with his jealousy, stinginess, and tirades. What she wanted was fun, a commodity slowly returning to Saigon. She wanted to dance and laugh with the French soldiers. She wanted to be admired. But she also had a son to raise, and she needed money. The thought occurred that perhaps she could find another job as cashier in a restaurant, or open her own dress shop if someone would plant seed money. Some of her girl friends were working as "hostesses" in night clubs, but Song held herself above prostitution. Her best friend,

Ky-li, argued that there was a clear difference between a woman whose business was selling her sex for money and a woman who wore beautiful clothes to a dance club and made men happy—and accepted an occasional generous gift as a token of gratitude. Song agreed that this was true, but the peril was that it might lead to another full-time relationship, and she did not want another demanding man in her life. Oh, someday she would find another one and marry him. Until then—and she swore this to God on her knees—she would devote her life to finding work and caring for Gurmukh.

The resolution was unhappily broken when, a few weeks after leaving the bed and board of Sobhraj the Tailor, Song discovered that she was once again pregnant. And by her calculation, the only man who could have accomplished this was Sobhraj. In despair she sobbed bitterly on the shoulder of her friend Ky-li. Her life was in ruins. Why were the gods so vengeful? Two children, no money, no job, no husband, no prospects. Her mother's prophecy was fulfilled. There was no option save a shameful return to the village and a life bent over the rice paddies.

Ky-li had no tolerance for her friend's plight. The answer was simple. Find a new man. And quickly. Premature births are not difficult to explain, particularly when a male is blinded by love.

With fervor Song descended upon nocturnal Saigon, not so much in search of a husband as to cram as many memories into her life before the second—and condemning—child arrived. She danced at the Club Paradis, sipped cocktails at the Hôtel Caravelle bar, accepting an occasional necklace or bolt of silk from an admirer out to win her favor. These she sold to pay the rent and buy food for Gurmukh. The little boy, approaching three, was troublesome. During the day, he played quietly at the foot of his mother's bed while she slept late. But when darkness neared, and Song put on her perfume and her bright dresses, Gurmukh shrieked, fearful of being left alone even though an old woman nearby looked in on him from time to time. The worst nights were when the child locked himself around his mother's legs and threw tantrums that echoed after her when she clattered onto the street in her spike heels. When she returned, late, the little boy was

usually still awake, fresh tears dammed up and ready to
spill. Once he took scissors and cut up her best dress.

Many men admired Song and made lascivious proposi-
tions, but she always made it clear that her sex was not a
commodity. She was in a period of transition, looking for
another avenue for her life to follow. A French corporal
was persistent in his attentions, but when Song revealed
that she had a three-year-old son, the suitor withdrew
hastily. Then, on the very afternoon that she spent an hour
on her knees in the cathedral, praying that God send only
a modest blessing to improve her lot, she stopped for coffee
at an outdoor cafe. At a nearby table was an interesting
Frenchman. He was tall, erect, proud of a carefully trained
mustache, and—it had to be a miracle!—an officer.

Alphonse Darreau was a fortuitous catch for Song, the
kind of man who, once his commitment was made, kept
it. Even when Song cautiously revealed that she was
already the mother of one illegitimate son and carried another baby in her womb, Lieutenant Darreau was not
troubled. His love had begun the moment he first saw this
lovely girl at the outdoor cafe, and nothing could damage
it. On September 15, 1948, they were married, and shortly
thereafter he legally accepted paternity of Song's second
child, Anne-Marie, a daughter. But he declined to give
his name to the boy, Gurmukh, who cursed him and Song
for uniting their lives. At four, his tongue was already
nourished by street talk and he spoke in the argot of the
hustlers.

Lieutenant and Madame Alphonse Darreau took a spacious apartment near the military building where he
worked in the legal section. At long last Song was content,
surrendering all of her notions to be an independent
woman of business. Instead she embraced domesticity. On
the walls she hung pictures of the Catholic saints, and she
studied French diligently so that she could converse intelligently and grammatically when Alphonse invited his
fellow officers home for dinner. On these nights she had
to shut up Gurmukh in his room, for the child was a
hellion. Once he tore the brass buttons from his stepfather's uniform. He would not accept his mother's attempted persuasion that they were fortunate to have the
French officer around. Gurmukh chattered incessantly

about his *real* father, conjuring fantasies that the tailor
would one day swoop into the house and rescue him from
a foreign stepfather. The truth was something else. Sobhraj
the Tailor never even called Song to inquire about the boy.
He seemed less interested in him than in the price of sew-
ing-machine bobbins.

Problems with the child grew alarmingly. Gurmukh rebelled against toilet training, promising Song that he would
try to do better but waking up each morning on soaked
sheets. It would continue until he was well into his teens,
a cry for attention that was not understood by the mother.
Her response at such infantile behavior was a whip.

When the police brought Gurmukh home one day in
custody and said he was suspected of stealing a bicycle,
Song crossed herself, promised the officers she would deal
strictly with the boy, and then locked him in his room.
For a time, she heard her son's wails of repentance from
behind the door. Then silence. When Song unlocked the
door to check, a switch quivering in her hand should it
be needed, the room was empty. Gurmukh had vanished,
the curtain fluttering in the breeze from an open window.
For several days the little boy was gone, and although
Song was modestly worried, summoning an occasional
moist eye, she rebuked herself for not feeling more distraught. The house was pleasingly quiet without Gurmukh's mischief and tantrums.

Then came a call from Sobhraj the Tailor. He was
annoyed. Did Song realize that her son had made his way
across the city of Saigon, broken into the shop, and hidden for two days behind bolts of cloth, peeping through
a crack and silently watching his father sew? When
Sobhraj heard a noise and pushed the bolts apart, he discovered the son he had not seen—probably had not even
thought of—for a long time. Upon his discovery, Gurmukh
embraced his father hungrily. He begged permission to
stay. He hated his mother. She whipped him. He hated
his stepfather. "Please," cried the child, "please let me
live with you."

Unmoved, Sobhraj scooped up his son and delivered
him to Song, depositing him at the door with the warning
not to try that again. Not only was such a prank dangerous—Saigon's streets were perilous—but its goal was out

of the question. The tailor had other responsibilities now, a new woman, a child on the way. Gurmukh must accept what life had dished out to him, and the conditions in Song's house were certainly better than most anywhere else in Saigon. The French knew how to live well.

As punishment, Song tied the runaway to his bed, his arms and legs lashed to the bedposts, freeing him only when he swore tearfully never to flee the house again.

In 1949, Lieutenant Darreau received abrupt orders of transfer back to France. A military transport ship was leaving Saigon in two weeks, and he had to be on it, with his family. The news was ecstasy to Song. Her French was workable now, and in the urgent days of packing and telling friends and family goodbye, Song found time to study fashion magazines from Paris. She imagined herself in full skirts with petticoats and small hats clamped on the back of her with artificial fruits and flowers growing profusely on the brim.

The initial reaction from her son was grief. Upon learning that he would be moving halfway around the world to a country whose language he could not speak, Gurmukh cried for days, sobbing that he would never leave Saigon. Song tried reasoning, but, when the tantrums continued, turned deaf ears and coldly informed the child that, like it or not, he was going, and if necessary he would be tied up and put in the ship's cargo with the luggage.

Then Lieutenant Darreau came home with troublesome news. A serious problem of legality had arisen with Gurmukh, who had no passport and no identifying documents. His birth certificate, if one existed, could not be found, and as he was illegitimate, Gurmukh was not allowed to travel on his mother's passport. Lieutenant Darreau had investigated the possibility of accepting legal guardianship of the youngster, but this required hiring lawyers, possibly a court hearing, and certainly many weeks if not months.

"The sad truth is that this boy does not legally exist," said Lieutenant Darreau, "nor can he leave the country."

In despair, Song studied the problem. Her own family, still in the wetlands, was poor and unable to accept another mouth to feed. The government orphanage was notorious for abuse of children. The only alternative short of abandoning Gurmukh to the streets was to leave the boy with his natural father. But how could she persuade Sobhraj the Tailor to accept such responsibility? Song dressed modestly, made her face distraught, and humbly knocked on the tailor's door. Beside her, very happy, was Gurmukh, scrubbed and well dressed.

In the years since they had lived together, Sobhraj had prospered. The tailor now had quarters thrice the size of the old room, and there were several customers waiting for fittings. Two seamstresses worked efficiently at new electric sewing machines. Sobhraj came forward and greeted Song warily. On his hand was a diamond ring.

Like a supplicant, Song pleaded. The situation was critical. The only fair and just solution, she ventured, was for the child's natural father, the man who conceived him, to offer shelter for a few short months. It would take no longer than that for Lieutenant Darreau's lawyer to cut through the bureaucracy and establish a legal identity for the child. When that was accomplished, then money would be sent for Gurmukh's passage to France.

The tailor was not receptive to the plan. Not at all. He threw up an array of reasons why the notion was impossible. To begin, the boy would cost money. Food. Clothes. Song nodded in agreement. Naturally she would contribute financially to the child's upkeep. Money was not the only problem, continued the tailor. Gurmukh was troublesome, impossible to discipline.

The reason, suggested Song, was that he loved his father more than anything in the world. The tailor was the center of his son's universe. Why else would he run away so often and try to live hidden amid bolts of cloth?

While the tailor summoned strength to refute Song's petition, Gurmukh ran as if cued into the room and locked his arms about his father's waist, sobbing like a man condemned. After a time the tailor nodded, reluctantly muttering that perhaps it was time the lad learned a trade. Quickly Song hurried out of the shop and ran for the French lieutenant, fearful that the tailor would change his mind.

CHAPTER TWO

When Mao Tse-tung swept into Nanking in 1949 with his People's Liberation Army and conquered China, spreading Communism over the world's most populous country, an immediate beneficiary was Ho Chi Minh's revolutionary movement in nearby Indochina. Within a few months, arms began pouring in from China's new government—and the French were suddenly on the defensive. The Viet Minh devastated French positions along the Chinese border and pushed toward Hanoi in 1950.

In Paris, the stunned Quai d'Orsay ordered new troops to Indochina to deal with the Viet Minh nuisance. Thus did Lieutenant Alphonse Darreau find himself once again posted to Saigon. It was 1952. More than three years had passed since Song left her firstborn son behind with the tailor. The legal papers necessary to establish the child's identity had fallen into a bureaucratic crack somewhere, and after a time Song had abandoned her never too enthusiastic promise to import the child to France. A letter or two had crossed the world between Song and Sobhraj the Tailor, but there had been little news concerning Gurmukh other than that he was healthy, intelligent, and mischievous.

Song must have been relieved not to have another child at her feet, for there were now three others—the daughter by the tailor whom Lieutenant Darreau had legally adopted, and two new ones, a boy and a girl. From the day she married the Frenchman, Song had been pregnant almost continuously. And still another child, her fifth, was moving within her when she returned to the land of her birth.

Nonetheless, when Song established a new family household in Saigon at the French officers' enclave, she felt sufficient maternal stirrings to investigate the growth and development of Gurmukh. The boy was almost nine by now, and Song anticipated a joyful reunion with a son who surely had changed into an obedient, hard-working, and disciplined youngster under the direction of his real father.

Considerable change had indeed taken place in the household of Sobhraj the Tailor. He had taken a new lover, a sharp-tongued Vietnamese woman named Sao, and their union had been fertile. Three new babies had appeared in three years, and a fourth was on the way. Sao was a severe woman who disliked Gurmukh from the first day she laid eyes on him. The youngster was a constant live-in reminder of the tailor's love affair with Song—and consequently a threat to Sao's security. To compensate, she treated the stepson cruelly—scolding, whipping, criticizing, usually behind the tailor's back. Like any child, Gurmukh responded with even more rebellion, particularly since he was beginning to understand that as far as the official world was concerned he did not legally exist. And rather than bend under Sao's switches, the boy ran wild, refusing to work, plotting schemes against his stepmother, usually out on the streets, running with a gang of older boys, sometimes missing—but not being missed—for weeks at a time.

When Song, piously dressed but with a calculated Parisian flair, knocked on the door of Sobhraj the Tailor, Sao opened the door and studied her contemptuously. No, she did not know where Gurmukh was on this day. Perhaps in jail. Maybe he had run away for good. Whatever, the boy was nothing but trouble. He did not take after his father, said Sao, insinuating that the genes of wildness came from another source. Gurmukh was a liar, a thief, and dangerous to the younger children of the house. Once Sao had caught him carrying a knife, and he had also fashioned some sort of handmade gun that fired pebbles

with speed and accuracy. With that, Sao slammed the door
and did not open it when Song knocked again in annoyance.

Her face streaked with tears and anger, Song hurried
home and told Lieutenant Darreau the disturbing news.
"Then we must find him," said the Frenchman. Immediately he and Song descended on the streets of Saigon,
dispensing coins like candy to buy information as to Gurmukh's whereabouts. The child was eventually discovered
living in the ruins of a building bombed by the Viet Minh.
He was the leader of a pack of Dickensian urchins who
lived by their wits, hustling tourists and foreign soldiers,
stealing food to eat and to sell. They all carried gleaming
knives and none was over twelve.

Lieutenant Darreau took pity on the skinny, dirty
youngster and told Song that they could probably find
room at the table for one more mouth. And, suggested
Darreau, the only thing that could alter Gurmukh's behavior was to give him his identity, those government
documents that make a person's place on earth somehow
more permanent.

After months of slogging through the courts, of bribing
lawyers, of obtaining Sobhraj the Tailor's enthusiastic
signature on a court order that (1) acknowledged the
tailor's paternity of the boy Gurmukh, and (2) permitted
him to relinquish parental responsibility for his upbringing
to Lieutenant Alphonse Darreau, a tribunal in Saigon on
January 10, 1953, decreed that this child was the legal
custody of the French officer and his wife. Only one loose
string remained uncut: Darreau refused at the last minute
to award his name to the boy, even though he had routinely
done so for the daughter conceived by the tailor and now
living in the Frenchman's household. At this point, a clerk
in the tribunal held up his hands in bewilderment. *Something*, somebody's name had to be written down on the
transfer of guardianship. Another hurried meeting was
arranged with the tailor. Finally an accommodation was
reached. The child was to be officially named Hotchand
Bhawnani Gurmukh Sobhraj.

Lieutenant Darreau would not tell Song why he withheld his surname from Gurmukh, and she did not press
him. Perhaps even then he felt an omen.

* * *

France's position in Indochina worsened, and soldiers who normally filed papers and typed reports were thrown into combat. Lieutenant Darreau volunteered for front line duty and, as Song lighted candles in the cathedral for his safe return, fought to retain territory near Saigon that was threatened by the Viet Minh. The first few excursions were inconsequential, but then came the day when the lieutenant was brought home on a stretcher. His injury was not physical, but mental. He was in severe shell shock and his face was white and blank, save for enormous pain in eyes that had always been gentle. When Song found his hospital bed, he stared at her as if she was a stranger, unable to speak, his only gestures a continual throwing of his hands against his ears to blot out the screaming assaults of bombs that exploded inside his head. Some fragile piece of the lieutenant's psyche was devastated by war, and he would be tortured for the next three decades. The decent, caring young officer who had taken pity on Gurmukh and rescued him from the streets was from this day on a withdrawn, silent man whose landscape was silence and who had little or no further interest in anything save the pains that clamped his head in a vise that would never loosen. "I am in continuing pain," he would tell Gurmukh years later. "There are days when the pain has subsided enough so that I can function, but most of the time the slightest noise is cymbals crashing at my ears."

Orders came for Lieutenant Darreau to return to France for recuperation. He would be permitted to take his family, indicating that there was little likelihood of ever being posted to Saigon again. This time, Gurmukh could go. When Song told the now ten-year-old youngster, Gurmukh was at first ecstatic, bragging to his friends about the good fortune. But as the time neared for departure, the child began to balk. He did not want to leave his native country. In the last weeks of packing, Gurmukh often ran away, and Song always knew where she could find him—at the tailor's shop, hiding, some need being filled within the boy by just being close to his real father. Usually the tailor was not aware that a child was hiding and watching him, for he had forbidden the boy from ever coming near.

Years later, Gurmukh wrote a letter to a friend and recalled this time in his life:

"I look back and I can't explain it," he said. "My stepfather was a kind man who was good to me, even after his injury, but I did not want him. All I wanted was to be with my *real* father. My own flesh! I felt emptiness without him, something that I missed . . . Even when my mother would find me after I had run away, and tied me up with ropes, I didn't mind her prison for I felt I was suffering on behalf of my father.

"On the day we were supposed to leave for France, I was confused. I had not slept the night before. I kept telling myself that when the morning came, I would run away and hide until the boat left. But just before dawn, I dozed off, and it was in a half-sleep that my mother took me away from my country and my father. I never really forgave her . . ."

Mother France soothed the pains in Lieutenant Darreau's head sufficiently for the military to award him a comfortable assignment—a post in Dakar, capital of French West Africa and a torrid city so Francophile that it was known as "South Paris." French was the language, the cuisine, the life style. And Lieutenant Darreau was given a villa so enormous that the rooms were never counted. Outside spread a lime and ocher garden, where an occasional wild root hog could be found dozing under the acacia tree, or a brilliantly colored serpent curled in the sun. Lieutenant Darreau needed a large home, for Song delivered herself of two more children. By 1956, there were seven youngsters at the table, Gurmukh being the oldest, the shrewdest, but, always, the outsider. He was the stepchild, the one with the name that sounded like a bullfrog belching.

Song, who adjusted to the lush life quickly and spent languid afternoons resting under mosquito netting and sipping *vin blanc*, or evenings playing poker, reminded her son constantly of how lucky he was, plucked off the streets of Saigon and whisked across the oceans to this great mansion in Dakar. Lieutenant Darreau, rarely able to work a full day because the pains had returned, often threw tantrums at the dinner table, shrieking that seven children were noisier than seven platoons, not to mention the cost of filling so many stomachs, his eye often stopping in mid-lecture on Gurmukh, as if to say, "And this one is not even my own blood." On an occasional day, the lieutenant was a martinet, dispensing military orders to his household, posting schedules on the kitchen wall of chores to be performed by the children, inspecting their rooms like a commander. And when something went awry, the one on whose shoulders usually fell the blame was Gurmukh. "You are the oldest," preached Lieutenant Darreau, "and you should set the example for the other children. But you are more trouble than all of the others combined."

Gurmukh did not mind the scoldings; they rained off his back like water on oil. But he hated and feared the more frequent days when his stepfather would suffer a renewal of the head pains and a blanket of silence had to fall over the villa. Children walked on tiptoes and spoke in whispers, the servants disappeared, dogs stopped barking. Song stayed in bed trying out new cosmetics on her face. And all worried that some tiny noise would rouse the lieutenant and cause him to stagger from his room like a senile grandfather, shouting curses and threats. Into the vacuum of parental leadership stepped Gurmukh, who found from the other children the attention and devotion that he could not obtain from his mother and stepfather. He set up headquarters in a cave near the villa, and deep in the recesses Gurmukh kept his treasures—candles, toys, and clothes for masquerades. Dressing up as somebody else, and putting a mask over his face, these were Gurmukh's pleasures. "We are in Ali Baba's cave," he told his half-brothers and sisters. There were not forty thieves, only one. Gurmukh had brought to Africa the street knowledge of Saigon, and by the time he was twelve, the boy was well known to the police of Dakar as one of the city's more accomplished shoplifters. Each Christmas, Gurmukh conducted a private party in the cave, commanding all to dress with glitter and imagination, then handing out expensive—and carefully chosen—gifts. They were all stolen. "It's as easy as catching butterflies," Gurmukh told his favorite half-brother, André, eight years younger but already a startling carbon copy. "Someday I will teach you."

André adored his half-brother, and as he was only 4

years old, he did not understand that they were the seeds of different men and the same woman. All André knew was that Gurmukh knew how to solve problems, how to slip into the cinema without paying (and smuggle in at least three others as well), that he knew a river where a hippo lived and although no one ever actually saw the beast it did not dampen the pack's enthusiasm for regular hunting expeditions with sticks and pebbles. Most of all, André appreciated Gurmukh's confidence, his control of any situation, his lack of fear. Gurmukh did not look upon parents and adults as fearsome towers of authority, rather as equals, sometimes subequals to manipulate.

He was also a clown, a gifted one who made the children laugh. After a clandestine evening at the cinema, Gurmukh assembled his half-brothers and sisters in the cave, ordered them to close their eyes, then burst forth in baggy pants, oversized shoes, derby, walking cane, and a mustache drawn with charcoal. "Charlot!" screamed the youngsters as Gurmukh waddled and minced about a makeshift stage, as André shined a stolen flashlight on the star. He loved their applause, and he loved the name, so much that he directed everyone to call him Charlot. Thus when a priest at the French school in Senegal pointed out to Song that her son had never been formally baptized, she agreed to the rite, and to a new Christian name. In 1959, when her son was fifteen years old, his name was entered into the records of the church as Charles Gurmukh Sobhraj—although to her patriotic thinking the name "Charles" was more of an homage to De Gaulle than to The Little Tramp.

Despite his obvious brightness and talent, Charlot made mediocre grades at school. His report cards contained testimonial to the boy's potential. "Has extraordinary abilities," wrote one teacher, "but he is lazy, stubborn, and accepts no discipline." Another teacher admired his capacity for language—by the age of twelve, Charlot could already speak French, Vietnamese, English, and a little Hindu from his real father. "This boy learns so quickly that it is a scandal how poorly he behaves in class," the teacher cautioned.

Outside the family, Charlot's best friend was the son

of a Wolof tribesman who lived in a nearby native village. The boy, Sarak, was the son of a minor chief, his mother being one of six wives. Between Charlot and Sarak was the bond of mutual insecurity, since neither was certain what his place in the family structure was or would be. Whatever, Charlot used the African boy as a deputy.

Once Sarak was caught redhanded stealing canned goods from a Dakar market. The manager questioned the boy, who quickly broke down and tearfully confessed that he was but the agent of Charlot and was doing as ordered. Dismissing Sarak with a scolding, the store manager rushed to Charlot's home, waking Song from her afternoon nap. Her son was a thief, raged the manager. Where was he? Song was not surprised by the accusation, and she went in search of Charlot. "There are so many rooms in this house," she muttered, "so many places to hide." Together they searched the huge villa, finally reaching the basement, where a large packing crate caught the grocer's eye. "With your permission?" he said, picking up a crowbar. Song nodded, nervously.

The boards of the crate were pulled away, revealing three layers, like a cake. On the bottom layer was Sarak, the chief's son, trembling and tearful. The center layer contained a stash of canned goods and articles stolen from many stores. And on the top, regally grinning, proud, was Charlot.

"Did you take these things?" demanded Song after the grocer had left with his goods and accepted a small bribe. "No, Mama," answered Charlot.

"But the black boy said he was only doing what you told him," she pressed.

Charlot nodded. "There are always fools who will do what I tell them to," he said, with a strength to his adolescent voice that Song would never forget.

Song grew weary of Charlot's larcenies and pranks. A mild discipline was announced. Each afternoon following school, Charlot was expected to sit beside his mother's bed, fan her to sleep, and remain there in utter silence for the duration of her three-hour nap. At first Charlot was secretly delighted with the punishment, reporting faithfully, drawing the drapes to make the room dark, preparing a cold lemonade, fanning his mother tenderly, crooning to her, sometimes stroking her arm with a feathery touch until she fell asleep.

But one afternoon Song awoke to find a police inspector looming over her bed, demanding to know the whereabouts of her oldest son. Right here, murmured Song, searching for consciousness and looking about the room. Charlot was gone. Later she would learn that in recent days Charlot had grown weary of attending his mother and had waited until she fell asleep, then slipped out and enjoyed two hours of freedom before returning in time for the awakening at dusk. On this afternoon, Charlot had climbed out the second-story window, slid down a thick vine, found his pal Sarak, and gone in search of a cooling swim. They chose a reservoir and Charlot was annoyed because the water level was low. The policeman informed Song that her son had broken into the maintenance station, twirled flood locks, and brought on a substantial flood. When the torrents of water rushed into the reservoir, Sarak had almost drowned.

Charlot denied everything, but he was sentenced by Song and the French lieutenant to more severe discipline. New locks were put on his door that opened only from the outside, and bars installed on the window. Occasionally Song tied him to the bedposts with rope. But Charlot bore his punishment stoically, even managing to escape like Houdini from the ropes and locks to tend to important matters, and this made him all the more heroic in the eyes of the other children. They all believed Charlot possessed exceptional powers.

One very dark night, when Charlot and André, his adoring half-brother, were returning home from the cinema, their route took them past a kiosk where candies and fruit were sold. It was closed, boarded up tight for the night. Charlot told André to stand lookout while he broke in. Hiding behind a nearby tree, André watched as Charlot filled a sack with candy. In mid-theft, André heard a whistling man approaching and, as the figure neared, realized that it was the kiosk's owner. Charlot heard him, too, and he froze, his body half in, half out of the kiosk window. The owner walked directly past his place of business, eyed it casually, and continued on, not noticing that a thief was dangling out of his window.

Later, walking home, happily stuffing candies into their mouths, André told Charlot that he had been terrified when the owner suddenly appeared. "I thought he was going to catch you," said the younger boy. Charlot shook his head vigorously, as if the notion was unthinkable and foolish. "I can make myself invisible," he said, "when I want to." André believed him. And when he told the others, they did, too. André always believed Charlot—and would in later years—even when both became adults, when the resemblance between them was almost that of identical twins, even when Charlot almost destroyed his half-brother's life.

CHAPTER THREE

In Paris, Charles de Gaulle presided over the dismantling of France's colonial empire. Sometimes it was accomplished only in the wake of blood, tragedy, and humiliation—the epitaph of Dienbienphu. Then again, France withdrew elsewhere with a reasonable diplomatic grace, as she demonstrated in leaving her territories in West Africa, realizing that these new black nations would retain ties both in language and commerce. By the thousands, French soldiers, teachers, and civil servants returned home to Europe.

When Alphonse Darreau heard the news, it mattered little one way or another. His condition had deteriorated, and he cared little where he lived. Transferred to Marseilles on limited duty, he would remain on the military payroll for some time, although most of his waking hours were spent in search of a civilian doctor who could assuage the pains that continued to pound within his head. He became a tragic figure, jumping from hospital to clinic, a sheath of tattered medical documents in his trembling hands, trying somehow to find peace. He moved his family from the great villa in Dakar to a small and cramped yellow house in a working class district of Marseilles where Song tried to cheer the drab rooms by pinning up bright fabrics on the walls and sewing satin pillows of crimson and peacock blue.

If Charlot had been troublesome in Dakar, he was to become a family disaster in France. Nearly sixteen, he had severe psychological problems that went unnoticed or untreated by his parents. He was still a bed-wetter, a plea for attention that was still interpreted by Song as disobedience and childishness. He lied so frequently that it was more or less family policy not to believe anything he said. He either seemed to hate his mother or else to put her into a figurative closet of which only he had the key. When a woman friend would knock at the door of the little yellow house to visit with Song, or when some male friend would arrive to escort her to the poker games she loved, Charlot was there to threaten the visitors. "My mother is not home and besides she hates you," he said, when in truth Song was in her bedroom squeezing into a brightly colored gown and screwing ruby earrings into her lobes. And when Song emerged dressed and ready to go out, Charlot would fall to his knees and squeeze his mother's legs and beg her not to leave, just as he had done as a tiny child in Saigon.

In December 1959, Charlot was escorted home one afternoon by two Marseilles policemen who told Song the familiar news that the boy was trouble. He had been caught standing outside a department store and trying to sell Christmas cards, with a novel technique. If an elderly customer ignored him, or walked away without showing interest in his wares, the boy produced a gleaming knife which he held menacingly in his hands while continuing with his patter.

Song drew in her breath. Had anyone been hurt?

The policemen shook their heads. But people had been frightened by the knife. Song turned with anger to Charlot and glared at him. In response, the boy placed an imaginary knife to his throat and asked—silently—if Song wished his sacrifice.

"Enough!" cried Alphonse Darreau, rising from his sickbed and declaring that the boy he had adopted was impossible and dangerous to the welfare of his own blooded offspring. Husband and wife quarreled deep into the nights, arguing whether to throw the boy out, or ask the state to put him in an institution, or send him back to the East. At church, Song asked her priest for counsel and he recommended that Charlot be placed in a strict Catho-

lic boarding school where young men were trained to be
farmers. Tuition was inexpensive, hardly more than what
it would cost to feed and clothe a boy at home. It sounded
fine to Darreau, as long as Charlot vacated his premises
immediately.

When Song told her firstborn child that he was being
sent away to Catholic boarding school, Charlot listened
without expression, then ran out of the house. He was
absent for three days, brought home finally by a *flic* who
said the skinny fifteen-year-old had been caught hiding
near the docks, apparently planning to sneak aboard a
freighter.

Song shouted at her son. What was he trying to accomplish?

"I want to live with my real father," answered Charlot
defiantly. "*He* loves me. I am sure of that."

Song locked the boy in his room until he could be sent
away. She also informed him the truth of the matter:
Sobhraj the Tailor had not inquired about his son in
almost five years. Sobhraj the Tailor had not sent a single
franc to put bread in his son's mouth. Sobhraj the Tailor
had more children than he could count. What made
Charlot think the matter of love was relevant?

That night, the other children heard Charlot weeping
and called out one word over and over again: *Papa.*

From the day he went away to the agriculture school,
Charlot was known as Charles, and he so instructed his
family and friends. It was as if his expulsion to the country was a rite of passage to manhood and he wished no
reminders of the adolescent life in Dakar.

He tried to escape three times from the priests, the first
only two days after he arrived. Charles had managed to
run only as far as the nearest village when one of the
priests stopped him. The second came when he fell from
a tree and injured his leg. The doctor at the school infirmary telephoned Song in Marseilles to report the minor
hurt, only to discover that she and the French officer had
gone to Saigon on a family visit. When Charles was told
the news that his mother had returned to the Orient, he
wailed and screamed, believing that he had been abandoned. Before the leg was fully mended, Charles hobbled

out of the clinic and disappeared. The priest-doctor of the
school sent Song a telegram which she received upon her
return to Marseilles: "CHARLES RAN AWAY FRIDAY NIGHT.
SEARCH IN PROGRESS." A letter of amplification was also
waiting:

> Chère Madame:
> After we questioned his comrades at school, we
> learned that Charles had been talking for some time
> about going to Saigon to find his real father. He had
> been disciplined in the past few days and that probably
> hurried his decision. He told a friend it was his in-
> tention to find a ship and embark at the end of Easter
> vacation. The port authorities there have his descrip-
> tion. I think Charles will be found soon—as I have
> checked and there will not be a boat leaving for
> Vietnam in several weeks.

A few nights later, in April 1960, just after his sixteenth
birthday, Charles was unmasked trying to slip aboard a
freighter while wearing the clothes of a merchant seaman.
Only his slight stature betrayed him, for he almost convinced the arresting port officer that he was a child of the
sea who had put out on ships for a decade.

The farming school did not want to take Charles back,
but as it was near the end of the school year, Song begged
the fathers to keep him. The priests had her permission,
assured Song, to do *anything*, including tying the boy up
to forestall further disobedience. Years later Charles would
tell of the time when they tried to turn him into a farmer:
"Actually it wasn't too bad . . . I was at the point of
getting interested in books and ideas—but the priests made
me spend too much time cleaning out the stables. I have
often wondered what would have happened if I could
have pursued what I was on the edge of doing—plunging
into the library . . . But there is just so much horseshit a
boy can shovel . . ."

Before two months passed, Song received an urgent midnight call from the school. Charles was gone again. "I
don't care," she found herself saying. "Let him run. My
husband and I want to turn him loose."

This time Charles was reasonably successful in his flight. He made his way to Marseilles and stowed away in the hold of a ship bound for Djibouti, East Africa, not quite sure where that particular place was, but content that it was far from France and perhaps on the ocean highway to the East. His plan was to find another ship in Africa, one that would bear him secretly across the world to Saigon, where his real father would be waiting with welcoming, warming arms. In his pocket were but a handful of francs and no identification, but in his head was stubborn determination. Several nights out, just after the ship had passed through the Suez Canal, Charles was caught trying to steal the passport and papers from the trousers of a sleeping seaman. For the rest of the journey, Charles reposed in a makeshift brig, no one heeding his angry protests that if the captain would only cable his rich and doting father in Saigon, then money would be instantly sent to pay for the passage.

When the ship arrived in Djibouti—the ancient trading center and camel market on the sloping east shoulder of Africa—the company's business manager sent a telegram to Sobhraj the Tailor requesting 450 francs for the voyage from Marseilles to Africa, and seeking instructions on what to do with the youngster. No answer. Then the maritime company officials demanded that Charles reveal the name of his mother in France. Stubbornly he refused. Only when exasperation reached the point where the officials threatened to turn Charles over to the local African police with the suggestion that he be jailed for fraud did the boy bitterly spit out Song's name and address.

"What in the name of God do you want?" cried Song when she fetched her son from the freighter upon its return to France. "We have done everything we can for you, and you give us back disgrace." Beside her, Alphonse Darreau was trembling with rage. "You give me more pain than the war," he shouted. "I want you out—go away and leave us alone!"

That night, Charles found his mother crying softly, mourning a life gone sour. She was almost forty, and though her almond face retained most of its dark beauty, scant else was of comfort. True, she had traveled far from the rice paddies of Indochina, but now all that Song could enter on her ledger of assets were a husband, ill and grouchy, and seven babies that had grown in her womb and now overwhelmed her. In her private moments—how few they were!—she envied Charles. She, too, thought now and then of slipping onto a boat and returning to Vietnam, abandoning all responsibility, wondering if her village was ravaged by the continuing war, wanting nothing more than to sit beside her own mother and feel the caress of rough hands she could barely remember.

Charles knelt beside his mother and touched her wet cheeks. "Do you love me, Mama?" he asked softly.

"Yes," she finally said, after a time, wondering why it took so long to bless this firstborn child, knowing the affirmation was not altogether true.

"I love you, Mama," he went on. "I will show you. You will see."

In her agony, Song formed one more plan. In Paris, among the Vietnamese refugee community, Song had friends, many of whom were in the restaurant business. She arranged for Charles to become a kitchen worker; a distant cousin had agreed to give him a room. Charles balked, but Song was unbending. Either the boy accept the discipline of hard work, else his family would forever wash their hands of him.

Thus for a few months toward the end of 1960, Charles worked at first one restaurant, then another in Paris. He did not last long in any job, for he loathed the dreary protocol of a French kitchen, peeling and chopping vegetables, cleaning crusted sauces from dirty dishes, mopping floors, dodging the wrath of temperamental chefs. Then he was hired by La Coupole as a busboy, his duties principally being the daily polishing of the silver platter covers that kept the chef's culinary creations hot. When Charles telephoned Song in Marseilles to tell her of the new job, she congratulated him, pointing out that La Coupole was a celebrated restaurant whose patrons were rich and famous.

The trouble was, thought Charles as he hung up, he had no access to the rich and famous customers, being trapped in a steaming kitchen and made to wear an absurd and towering chef's hat under which his ears stuck out like semaphore flags. Sometimes he crept to the doorway and caught glimpses of the elegant restaurant as large as an airplane hangar. La Coupole was a mecca, particularly at midnight, for *tout Paris*, the clubhouse where fashions were born and money displayed and blue jeans sat next to Givenchy. "My problem," said Charles years later, recalling these forbidden sights glimpsed through swinging doors, "was in getting from the kitchen to one of those tables. I knew I would sit there someday—the trouble was, I couldn't wait."

One night a waiter found Charles peeling vegetables and said a customer had asked for him by name. Who? wondered Charles. The waiter shrugged: the customer had not identified himself. Some man dining alone. Seemed prosperous. Well dressed. Foreign. Charles approached the chef and asked for permission to enter the sacred dining hall. The answer was: Be quick about it.

Making his way through the crowded room, Charles approached the table and noticed that the customer was indeed eying him attentively. He rose, and Charles admired his well-cut suit and silk tie. "Gurmukh?" said the man tentatively. Charles was confused. No one had called him by that hated name for years.

The man held out his hand in greeting. "I am Sobhraj," he said. Charles broke, rushing to his father, his chef's hat falling from his head as he buried himself in the tailor's strong arms and sobbed. He always knew his father would rescue him.

Not precisely. Sobhraj the Tailor was in Paris as part of an around-the-world trip, combining vacation with business. In the years since he had casually surrendered his son to Song and the French officer, the tailor had grown wealthy. His one-room shop was now three separate stores, scattered along a better shopping district in Saigon. He employed several tailors, seamstresses, and he had customers who made special stop-offs in Saigon just to order one of his custom-made suits. A modest exporting business was in its infancy, and he had been in the United States to discuss marketing. Upon reaching Paris, he had telephoned Song in Marseilles and after a braggadocio conversation in which he could not resist informing his old mistress of his good fortune, the tailor learned that his son was working in Paris.

Curiosity, nothing else, had brought him to La Coupole. But his son's joy touched the tailor. They spent the next several days together, each revealing what the years had wrought. An enthusiastic guide, Charles proudly showed his father around Paris, speaking from time to time in four different languages, poised, intelligent, and dutiful. "I think," said Sobhraj, "that you can become more in life than a waiter."

Oh, how Charles agreed! He hated his work, but his mother and stepfather had forced him into it. He spun tales from *Oliver Twist*—a cruel home life, unloved, yanked out of school and hurled into an adult world of fourteen-hour workdays, laboring in a kitchen so hot that the fluids evaporated from his body and made him weak and as thin as a celery stick.

Moved by his son's plight, Sobhraj made a proposition. He asked Song for permission to take Charles home to Saigon, where he would train the lad in the clothing business, pay him an adequate salary, and perhaps, just perhaps, one distant day the boy would inherit a piece of Hong Kong Tailors—H. Sobhraj, Importers, Inc.

There was no hesitation. Song felt as if she had won the national lottery. Immediate permission rushed from her lips. But she pointed out that the boy did not have legal citizenship, not even a passport from any country. He had always traveled as a piece of family baggage among the possessions of Darreau. Then Sobhraj would make everything legal. He found a lawyer in Paris to draw up a *contrat de travail* which spelled out the conditions:

WORK CONTRACT BETWEEN H. SOBHRAJ AND ALPHONSE DARREAU, CONCERNING THE BOY CHARLES:

I will pay the cost of his trip from Paris to Saigon, and I will pay him a monthly salary of 7,000 Vietnamese piastres.

After three years, I will give to Charles Gurmukh

Sobhraj a 6-month vacation to spend in Vietnam or
France, as he prefers.

In case Charles wants to go to France on this
vacation, I will also pay for the cost of that trip,
and back to Saigon.

In case Charles does not work out in Saigon, I
will pay his way back to France, provided he com-
pletes one solid year of work.

Both men, father and stepfather, signed the document
with flourishes. Then Sobhraj went to the French passport
office and obtained, with considerable difficulty, a safe-
conduct travel document good only for one-way travel
from France to Vietnam. It was the tailor's plan to obtain
Indian citizenship for the boy at the consul in Saigon.
With a reputable businessman like Sobhraj vouching for
the youngster, there should not be any question as to his
eligibility.

"I am in heaven," wrote Charles to Song just before
leaving Paris. "My dreams are answered. My father loves
me and my life begins anew. A miracle!" It was the
spring of 1961 and he was seventeen years old.

But miracles are fragile, and a long time coming. When
Charles arrived in Saigon, he found that once again he
was an appendix. The tailor's wife, Sao, had delivered
four children to Sobhraj. Moreover, the tailor now no
longer concealed the fact that he had another wife in
India, who had presented him with five children, usually
as souvenirs of his infrequent visits to the homeland.
Charles counted up one day and figured that he had six
half-brothers and sisters back in Marseilles, and nine more
in the East. He was one child out of sixteen and the only
one who had been thrown back and forth between Song
and Sobhraj like an unwanted ball.

Immediately Sao took Charles aside and hissed the rules
of her household to him. His welcome was slim: she had
more than enough to handle with the care and feeding of
her own brood, and if Charles wished to stay he must fend
for himself, obey his father, and not get in anybody's way.
Charles hated her. In later years he recalled that Sao
always had a stick at arm's length and the slightest mis-

step could bring it crashing onto his backside. One day Charles took it away from Sao and snapped it and tossed it into her face.

The tailor posted a rigid work schedule. Charles was expected to rise before the sun, sweep away the scraps of cloth from the day before, clean and oil the sewing machines, wash the windows, prepare tea, and be ready to welcome customers at 9 A.M.—including translation of their wishes and measurements if they spoke French. Duties did not end until long after sundown, when the streets of Saigon were crowded with girls on promenade and music drifted out of every cafe. Once when the tailor and his son were strolling along a boulevard, Sobhraj noted a gaggle of young women and lectured on the danger therein. "Women are basically evil," he always said. "There are only a few valuable ones, but they are as hard to find as a good diamond." He warned Charles not to "mess up" his life by becoming entangled with bad women.

Within a few weeks, Charles took to slipping away from work early, then not showing up at all. The police came one day to tell Sobhraj that a boy who had no papers but who represented himself as the tailor's son was in jail on suspicion of car theft. Sao shrieked that she knew such grief and dishonor would come to her house. She knew it the moment the tailor foolishly brought this delinquent boy back from France. He was diseased—and he would surely infect her children as well. She had heard that Charles caroused in the cabarets and gambling dens of Saigon, with painted women draped about his pockets.

Sobhraj the Tailor shushed his harping wife. He was not yet ready to give up on Charles. Enough guilt had been harbored in his heart over the years for having signed away his son to a Frenchman. At the Hindu temple in Saigon where Sobhraj prayed, he experienced a revelation. Clarity enveloped him. He ran to find a priest for counsel. The whole problem with Charles—and the holy man concurred—was that the young man simply did not know who he was nor where he belonged. He possessed no roots, no security, no feeling of membership in either a family or a national culture. The priest suggested that Sobhraj arrange citizenship for his truant son. "That is exactly what I plan to do," said Sobhraj.

He summoned the boy. At seventeen, Charles was a handsome young man with broad, muscled shoulders and the slimmest of waists. The tailor had much to tell. He had spent frustrating days at the Indian Consulate in Saigon, trying to obtain a passport and citizenship papers. But it had not been as easy as he had anticipated. India's government would not bestow citizenship unless Charles spent a minimum of one year on Indian soil during which he had to become fluent in an Indian language. Therefore, the tailor had decided to send his son on one final journey—to Bombay. There he would go to a nearby village and spend the necessary year with distant cousins. Charles threw up his hands in dismay.

"Papa, I must tell you that I am in love with a Vietnamese girl named Tra, and if you make me leave, both she and I will die of heartbreak," said Charles theatrically. The tailor dismissed the prophecy. His son would only be in exile for one year, and during that time it would be possible to make at least one visit, perhaps two, back to Saigon. The Indian cousins were not wealthy, but they were respectable and hard-working, weavers of cheap cloth used in inexpensive saris.

Panic grew and swept over Charles. He cried out that he was being abandoned *again*, the latest verse in his life anthem. Sobhraj shut his ears to all of this and booked passage for India.

When the youth disembarked at Bombay, he was caught in a swarm of beggars, clutching at his arms and begging rupees. Sharp odors swam into his nostrils. He found a taxi and gave an address and learned that the village of his cousins was more than an hour from the sophistication of Bombay, in a poor suburb near Poona. The great hotels and apartment houses that overlooked the sea and that had seemed to welcome the youngster quickly disappeared in clouds of choking dust as the taxi carried Charles into rural India, where 85 per cent of the population lives.

The house of his cousins was not a house by Charles' definition—rather a one-room factory, perhaps twenty feet square, in which more than a dozen adults and uncounted children worked and ate and slept. Space is not wasted in India. A worktable in the day became a hard bed at night. The cousins spoke only Urdu, language of the Moghuls, and Charles could understand but a random word. He was expected to sleep on the ground and eat vegetarian meals, balls of mashed peas and potatoes fried in grease and set floating in fiery sauces. Everyone ate with their hands, dipping chunks of *nan*, the flat bread, into the foul liquids. Water dribbled from a rusty pipe that was the fountain of life for the entire village—when it flowed. Toilets were open trenches, running into bamboo groves where cobras sometimes waited.

Twice Charles tried to escape from his country cousins. Working his way to Bombay, he sneaked aboard a freighter bound for Saigon and was thrown off immediately. A few days later he snaked up a rope after midnight and found a place to hide in another freighter's cargo chamber. This time he was not discovered until the boat docked at Saigon, his arrest caused by his inability to resist running to a railing and watching the city of his father come into view.

Sobhraj the Tailor went to the port with anger and peeled off 245 francs to pay for his stowaway son's passage. He was not entirely surprised, as a letter had recently come from his relatives saying that Charles was arrogant, ungrateful, disobedient, and probably dishonest, for a small amount of money had coincidentally vanished upon his leave-taking. Sobhraj lashed his son with certain facts:

Item One: Charles had only a temporary visitor's permit valid for six months in Vietnam, and that time was almost gone. It could not be renewed. Without proper papers, Charles could be arrested and jailed.

Item Two: The only solution was to spend the required year in India so that a passport and citizenship could be obtained.

Item Three: Nobody in the entire world gave a damn about Charles Sobhraj, certainly not his fancy mother in France.

Item Four: The tailor had no more money or patience to waste on a youth who did not appreciate efforts made in his behalf.

"I have sent my son back to Bombay for the last time," wrote Sobhraj to his cousins. "If he does not stay there and obtain his citizenship, then let the demons take him!"

CHAPTER FOUR

The S.S. *Laos* docked at Bombay in March 1962, the slumbrous time of India when the subcontinent cooks under a torturous sun that will not relent until the June monsoons drench the steel-hard earth and cause steam to rise like water thrown on an overheated skillet. One passenger was not permitted to disembark. A letter of explanation was promptly mailed to Saigon.

"Dear Mr. Sobhraj," wrote the maritime company's Bombay representative, "The immigration authorities in Bombay have refused to let your son, Charles Gurmukh, get off the *LAOS* because he does not have proper papers or a passport. The *LAOS* will be in port here seven weeks, sailing on July 2 for Marseilles. Your son informs us that you will cable funds required to send the boy back to Saigon the next available ship. Please advise immediately."

Waiting impatiently, Charles was condemned to spend several days in the fourth-class quarters, a chamber that rode below the waterline and that reeked of vomit and clammy walls. Every day he asked anyone who passed by in a uniform if his father had responded to the letter. And every day the answer was negative. Finally someone took pity and ordered the young man transferred to the Port of Bombay jail, which was at least better than waiting on the oven-like ship. In the fourth week of his detainment, a telegram arrived. It was terse. "Cannot raise further funds. Send Charles Gurmukh Sobhraj to his mother in Marseilles. Signed: H. Sobhraj." When the commandant of the port summoned Charles and read the cable, he burst out crying. "It's not true," insisted Charles. "There's a mistake. My father is a wealthy man and he loves me."

The commandant shrugged. There was no mistake. Unless money was received from somebody to pay further passage on the *Laos* from India to France, then the only alternative was to turn the matter over to the Bombay police. Charles would be jailed as a stowaway and a stateless person. Already the youngster knew enough of bureaucratic India to realize that this would take months if not years to straighten out, and in the meantime he would rot in a Bombay jail. His fellow prisoners had told him that a twenty-year sentence would not be unusual.

"Am in desperate trouble," cabled Charles collect to Song. "Please send money for passage from Bombay to Marseilles. I beg you to help your loving son. Please, please. In the name of God." At the same time, the shipping company wrote a letter of explanation to Song, revealing that the French Consul was touched by the young man's plight and had agreed to give him a three-month visa for entry to France. But unless Song cabled 661 new French francs for passage, and an additional 379 francs to pay for one of Charles' stowaway ventures from Bombay to Saigon earlier in the year, then the boy would be charged as an illegal alien and would face the courts of India.

In Marseilles, Song did not show the telegram to her husband, for she knew that he would refuse to spend another centime on his stepson. She put the documents in her jewelry box, the temptation being to ignore them. But at night she could not sleep, thinking of her firstborn child in an Indian jail. Then two more cables arrived, both desperate, their tone indicating that Charles was standing on the gallows and only his mother could bribe the hangman and forestall execution. That did it. Song sold two of her rings and, together with a few hundred francs she kept hidden to finance her love of gambling, cabled passage to Bombay. "I expect you to pay me back," she wrote. "We are poor people and you have caused us more trouble and money than all the other children combined. This is the last help I will ever give you."

* * *

When Charles disembarked in Marseilles, he ran to the telephone and called his mother, full of filial devotion and gratitude. From the depths of his misery in Bombay, then across the Indian Ocean and through the Suez Canal into the Mediterranean—and home, Charles had resurrected his mother in his mind and painted her in the colors of a saint. He now wanted to erase the years of antagonism between them. He knew now that *she* was his anchor, not the tailor in Saigon who had hired him as a slave and who had expelled him to the degradation of an Indian village.

But Song's arms were not flung wide to embrace the prodigal son. She was cool on the telephone. Yes, she was glad that Charles was safely back in Marseilles. But no, she could not offer the boy a bed in her cramped home. Her husband was once again ill, at this moment in another hospital. The situation was such that Charles could not re-enter the family structure, for it was fragile enough already. Darreau demanded that the house remain silent as a crypt at all times, and Charles brought out the noisy worst in the other children. But, keep in touch, suggested Song in brush-off, and repay the money as quickly as possible. It was bread snatched from the mouths of his half-brothers and sisters.

Charles' situation was precarious. His visa was good only for ninety days, and the French consul in India had warned him that under no conditions could it be extended. And he had no money. But in order to find work, Charles needed not only a *permis de séjour*, permitting him to live in France, but a *permis de travail*, a work permit given to an alien, a difficult document to obtain. It the autumn of 1962, Charles worked for several restaurants along the waterfront, earning as little as five francs a day because he had no papers and was thus in the category of Algerian immigrants who flooded the city and rarely found employment more enriching than sweeping leaves from gutters with brooms made of sticks. Seldom did Charles last more than a day or two before an angry *hauteur* spewed from his lips and caused immediate termination. "I speak four languages and have traveled over much of the world," he snapped at one restaurateur. "My father is a millionaire in Saigon and you want me to clean out toilets for fifty centimes an hour!"

In November, his ninety-day visa expired, Charles was foolish enough to steal a car parked outside a cathedral in Marseilles and take a young woman on a joyride. They drove along the Riviera, stopping to view the jeweled lights of Cannes from a winding mountain road, then turning north toward Grasse, the city where Queen Victoria spent winters and where roses, jasmine, and bitter orange blossoms are cultivated to form the great perfumes of France.

En route, Charles was stopped for speeding, which led to an arrest for car theft and for being in France without proper papers. Sentenced to six months in prison, Charles was to be expelled from the country after completion of the jail time. Charles served his first prison sentence in an orderly manner, working in the kitchen of an old prison near Grasse. "It was really no worse than working for my father," he would later say. "And it wasn't a total waste. I learned karate and Italian."

On the day he was released, Charles was told that the court was giving him thirty days to put his affairs in order before deportation. He would then be placed aboard a ship leaving Marseilles and forever banished from France. Once again he turned to his mother, who had not known of her son's imprisonment. Nor did he tell her now, only that the immigration bureaucracy had trapped him like an innocent forest animal and he now had no place to go. His notion, explained Charles, was to leave voluntarily, slipping across the border into Italy. There he would wait until his case died from lack of attention, and there he could obtain documents that would enable him to return to France. He needed to borrow a few hundred francs for the journey. "I want to stay in France," he pleaded with Song. "I *am* French. You made me French."

Quickly Song shook her head. She had no more money to spend on her son. He had not paid back the sum she had sent to retrieve him from the Bombay port police. The boy would soon be twenty, he was a man, he must handle his problems alone. Charles' mood turned dark. He accused his mother of never having loved him. Song, unbending, showed Charles the door. She would not see him again for more than a decade, not until he had become one of the most famous men in a world whose

boundaries stretched from Paris to Hong Kong. And on
that distant day, she would crawl on her knees until they
were bloody. And then she would ask God to kill him.

Charles hitchhiked to Paris, where he lost himself easily
in the Vietnamese community, thousands of refugees having streamed into the city after France withdrew from
Southeast Asia. Among them Charles moved unnoticed for
months, drifting from one cheap hotel room to another,
working a night or two washing dishes, always keeping
an urgent eye open for the random policeman who might
question him for the most minor infraction and set in
motion his expulsion from France. The tightrope on which
he walked was extremely shaky. Dazzled by the temptations of the Champs-Élysées and Boulevard St. Germain,
where the young girls strolled and stirred his passions,
Charles had no money to pursue them. Worse, he had no
carte d'identité, a vital document in a time when the streets
of Paris were heavily patrolled by police in search of
terrorists and their *plastique* bombs being detonated to
oppose De Gaulle's withdrawal from Algeria. Christmas
Eve, 1963, was passed in the backroom of a Vietnamese
cafe near Montparnasse, playing dice with old men who
stripped him of everything he had, even the coat that his
father had sewn for him in Saigon. After midnight, he
dared walk openly along the quais beside the Seine, feeling that the police would be benevolent on this holiday
morning. It was bitterly cold; he was in despair. He cursed
the tailor in Saigon, who surely at this moment was stuffing goose into his stomach; he cursed his mother in Marseilles and the sick, carping soldier that she had married.
Never had he felt so alone. "I was a sack of garbage," he
would later say. "My family put me outside and waited
for the truck to take me to the dump."

Just before dawn, Charles found himself on a narrow,
cobblestoned street near the École des Beaux-Arts. The
shopwindow of a fancy foods grocer who sold *pâtés* and
puréed chestnuts and elaborate fruit tarts caught his eye.
He looked at the expensive temptations for a while, then
picked up a stone and threw it into the window. Reaching
inside, he scooped up a box of chocolates and a cold
quiche and a bottle of champagne. Then he ran quickly

toward the river, where he found a secluded place, and there he crammed the rich food into his mouth and drank the wine. He slept. But as dawn neared and the bells of Notre Dame called worshipers to Christmas mass, his stomach churned and he vomited into the river.

Charles fell in with a Vietnamese hoodlum who had been operating in Paris for a few years. He called himself Romain, and he set about educating his naïve younger countryman in the street life. Necessary immediately was further instruction in karate, which Charles had only begun to learn in the Grasse prison. There was more, far more to karate than breaking boards, tutored Romain. That was for night clubs. Karate was a philosophy, the way a man could both defend himself and at the same time emit auras of strength, like a child guarded by a watchdog. Charles studied the origin of martial arts in the ancient monasteries of Tibet. The monks of those days traveled once a week down the mountain paths to a village for provisions. En route, bandits lay in wait to rob them. The head monk, Daruma Taishi, studied the problem and created a method of self-defense that would protect, not kill. Nature was his teacher and inspiration, and the monk devised defense postures in which the human emulated nature—the praying mantis, the lion, the snake, the pine tree. In his book was a passage that Charles memorized: "Only when one can face death without fear can one face life." Another passage caught his attention. It decreed that the student of karate must develop a mind like a pool of water. When the water is absolutely still and calm, the moon is reflected perfectly, in all its beauty. But when a pebble is thrown into the water, the moon is distorted, broken, fragmented. The analogy was easy for Charles to understand. He had spent too much time railing at the injustices of his young life, when what he should have been doing was shoving these extraneous grievances aside and concentrating totally on whatever was at hand.

Romain's trade was minor crime—an occasional robbery-at-knife-point of a passenger in a Métro station late at night, shoplifting, car stripping. It was his intention that Charles become his right-hand man. But he could not risk employing an apprentice thief who had no identity papers and was thus in continual jeopardy of arrest. To remedy this, Romain led Charles one night to a secluded house on the outskirts of Paris where new lives were for sale. In a workshop lived an old Oriental man with a face of pale ivory. He spread out his wares. A student visa? Five hundred francs. *Carte d'identite?* Eight hundred fifty francs. Passports? What nation? The old man reached into a locked box and picked up dozens of passports, letting the small leatherette booklets dribble through his hands. The prices ranged from 1,000 francs for a poorly altered Swiss to 5,000 for a fresh new United States of America. On a side table, Charles noticed an array of precision tools, small needle punches, pots of ink and dye, a stack of assorted photographs, even fake visa stamps from many countries. "Who do you want to be?" whispered Romain, as Charles shook his head in bewilderment. He had never been *anyone,* and now was the opportunity to become a hundred different men.

In a six-week period in the early spring of 1964, Charles committed—by police count—eleven different robberies, most of a petty nature, trying to amass enough money to buy an identity. He stole a woman's coat from a restaurant, a suitcase from a train station, a sewing machine, 164 packages of cigarettes, a purse, a knife, a bit of change from a merchant's cashbox. The goods he sold at flea markets, his goal being 3,000 francs for a passport. Perhaps he would have reached it had he not become enamored of a pretty young Parisienne whom he took for a ride in a stolen car. Driving too fast on the Autoroute du Nord, Charles was stopped. He reached for the registration papers, knowing that they were in the glove compartment. But the policeman instead asked for his *carte d'identité* and all Charles could thrust forth was a stolen certificate of high school graduation that he had found, and to which he had sloppily attached his photograph from a vending machine. For a few unsuccessful moments, Charles tried to pass himself off as an instructor at the Sorbonne.

The judge of the Tribunal de Grande Instance de la Seine held the police report in his hands and lectured the thin young Oriental man standing white-faced before him. It was the judge's considered opinion that the streets of

Paris were no longer safe, due greatly to the flood of foreigners streaming in from former French territories in
Africa and Asia. Examples must be set. The citizens must
be protected from outlaws who imported the savagery of
foreign cultures to the City of Light.

Charles pleaded that he stole food because he was
hungry. He stole clothing because he was cold. He tried to
make the judge understand what it was like to be a stateless person, born during a war, reared by parents who
neither loved him nor wanted him. None of this touched
the magistrate. Did this defendant steal a car because he
was hungry? Did he rob a grocer because he was born
illegitimate? Did he forge a certificate of matriculation
because he was unloved?

Charles Sobhraj was sentenced to three years in Poissy
Prison. The enormity of the punishment did not really
settle on him until he was led manacled from the courtroom. Then his mind began to spin and he whirled, prepared to scream curses on the unfeeling judge. But at
that moment he remembered the Tibetan monks, and he
commanded his mind to become as still as the pool of unmolested water. He would endure this. He would not even
give the bastards the pleasure of seeing him weep. With
that he smiled serenely and nodded obediently and walked
in chains toward his destiny.

CHAPTER FIVE

In the 16th Arrondissement of Paris, bastion of the rich and the pretenders, there lived at this moment a proper young gentleman named Félix d'Escogne, elder son and heir to a substantial family holding in forestry. His flat, near enough to the Auteuil racetrack to hear crowds cheer the blooded horses, contained a few good pieces of art, mostly of Eastern origin, worn but real Persian carpets, shelves of books on philosophy and biography, and a record player whose needle rarely touched anything more tumultuous than Debussy. Nearing forty, he was shy, unmarried, though he appreciated the companionship of women, and employed as a young executive in the computer division of a conglomerate. He had a boyish, almost babyish face that was aging suddenly, and his clothes were usually rumpled from lack of attention. He was like a favorite house slipper, a cherished uncle, a solid and dependably comfortable easy chair. Uncommonly, for the French are not an especially charitable people, he was also imbued with a social conscience. For generations his family had recognized the duty of the privileged to share a portion with the needy, though normally it was accomplished by discreet contributions that did not soil the hands.

Félix, however, preferred to labor personally and his special interest was the penal system. One day each week he assumed the role of *visiteur*, a volunteer who is admitted to prisons and permitted to help the inmates with letter writing, minor personal needs. Most important, he provided an attentive ear for men who needed one.

His accreditation was at Poissy Prison, the ancient and ugly prison of Paris that had, centuries before, been constructed as a convent, later seized during the French Revolution, enduring home for most of France's most notorious criminals including several Nazis of World War II. "It is a horror," said Félix after his first few visits there. "One enters the place and chills pass through the bones like stepping into a cellar. Each moment I am inside, I am repelled." It was a place where time stopped two centuries ago, where there was no attempt at rehabilitation, where the business of each unfortunate man locked inside was survival, little else.

Poissy had several sections—one for the chronically ill, another for the maniacally dangerous, still another for those prisoners—usually foreigners—that the authorities did not know what to do with. Charles fell into this category, mixed in with a hundred men in a communal ward during daylight hours, locked into a chicken coop of a cell at night, large enough for only one. Discipline fell just short of perverse cruelty. Prisoners were not allowed to make a "home" out of their cells by tacking up family photographs or keeping a box of personal possessions. During the day, when the men were in the common room, guards liked to "inspect" individual cells and tear them apart. Radios were not permitted, nor newspapers; even letters were ruthlessly censored and often withheld.

In the fall of 1966, Félix paid a visit to Poissy after returning from a holiday in Yugoslavia. There he had visited the families of several prisoners and had hand-carried letters. His courtesies were received with such outpourings of emotion and gratitude that now, as the cruel fortress came once again into his view, he shuddered for the men inside. When he passed through the thick, massive gates and waited in the entrance lockup for an escort to the deeper regions, a guard appeared to compliment him. The Yugoslavian prisoners had all but enshrined him with their praise. "You did so well with the Serbs and Croats," said the guard, "perhaps you would like to take on a Vietnamese? One has been asking for a *visiteur*."

Down a long, dank hall, footsteps echoing on stones

laid before Louis XVI, Félix found the visitors' chamber
and waited. He would one day remember the next moments in detail:

"Presently my eyes beheld a frail, frightened, yet arrogant young Oriental boy with ears sticking out to here. He
sat down on the bench and stared at me. In fact, he tried
to stare me down—or frighten me. After a while I said,
'Look here, are we playing a game?' Still more staring.
I glanced at my watch. Only thirty minutes were allowed,
and twenty of them were gone. I said, 'I don't care to wait.
It doesn't seem likely to get any friendlier.'" Félix rose
and started to rap on the door for the guard outside to
unlock it.

At that point Charles cried out, "Wait!" He had been
studying Félix to determine if he could be "trusted."

And?

"I don't know," said Charles. "I've made the wrong
decision too many times."

Félix asked how he could be of help.

Words rushing out now in torrents, Charles asked Félix
to act as mediator in negotiating a *rapprochement* with
his father in Saigon. In Charles' continually shifting loyalties, the pendulum had swung from his mother back to the
tailor once more. During almost two years of imprisonment, in the insomnia of his chicken coop, the revelation
had come that he loved only his father and wanted his
support. It was his intention to finish his prison sentence
and then return to Vietnam, if the tailor would help him
get travel papers and agree to accept him.

"Does your father know all this?" asked Félix.

Charles shook his head and answered softly. No. He
had not heard from his father in almost five years.

Now Félix was confused. Surely Charles did not expect
him to fly off to Saigon, where a war was intensifying, and
extend a son's love to a tailor? Charles smiled—appealing-
ly, noted Félix—and shook his head. No. Not now. All he
wanted was Félix to continue visiting him in prison and
as the time passed they would become better acquainted.
Once Félix knew and understood the complex history of
Charles' life, then perhaps he could be a family peacemaker.

Time was up. Félix took his leave. But not before

Charles intoned a pretentious little epilogue. "In my body flow two rivers," he said. "They are the East and the West, and they are separate, never joining."

Eyebrows raised, Félix gratefully bolted for fresh air.

Félix encountered a priest in Poissy who served as one of the chaplains. The two men were friends and occasional conspirators, smuggling uncensored mail in and out on behalf of the prisoners, and filling shopping lists of needed items like soap and stationery. The priest knew that Félix had seen Charles Sobhraj, and he had words of caution. Charles would try to "overwhelm" Félix. He would attempt to "take command" of the *visiteur*'s life.

In the year just past, the priest had obtained—at Charles' directive—books on theology, philosophy, palmistry, yoga, essays by Voltaire, plays by Molière. And as he read them, Charles made up enormous long lists of words he did not understand and was continually soliciting the chaplain for definitions. They had quarreled vigorously over the relative virtues and defects of Christianity vs. Buddhism. Charles had asked for—and received—a chess set, and not only had he taught himself the game, he quickly became the ranking master in his section. "He has a mind like an anteater, sucking up every scrap of information he can obtain," remarked the priest. And the letters! "The man can go through a tablet of writing paper in a day or two. I think he became an expert at chess just to win money for stamps."

The priest and the *visiteur* shook hands and walked in their separate directions—Félix toward the sweet air of Paris gilding for a Saturday night, the priest toward the chapel, where he would pray for the men in society's cages. The next time they met, the young clergyman reminded himself, he must caution Félix against Charles' adroitness in lying. He was a champion at *that*, too. So much so that the priest wondered if the prisoner even knew the difference between truth and fantasy.

On the next visiting day, Charles leaped up when Félix entered the room, his eyes as happy as if he were welcoming a classmate at a school reunion. Immediately Charles seized control and began to outline the course of their

friendship. If Félix were to understand him, then Félix
must know his biography, which Charles was prepared to
deliver, in installments. Wondering what in God's name
he was getting into, Félix settled back. For the next several Saturdays, Charles delivered his life story as an expert
monologist, theatrical in the telling, raising his memories
at moments to the category of Greek tragedy with the
forces of nature and the gods united against an illegitimate
child born of parents who did not want him. And more
often than not, there were lies, or, as Félix charitably
reasoned, alterations in character analysis. One week
Song was a whore, parading around Saigon in tight-ass
dresses, painted like a denizen of Pigalle, men panting in
her wake. The next, she became a madonna, clasping
Charles to her breast, murmuring lullabies, squeezing a
favored place for him in the French lieutenant's crowded
rooms. Sobhraj the Tailor alternated from a tyrannical
brute whose sadistic switches rained bruises and welts on
the boy's tender skin to a gentle, religious holy man whose
every utterance should have been carved in stone.

And the letters! Charles began writing the moment
Félix left each Saturday, as he was usually interrupted in
mid-anecdote by the guard's knock, and they continued
daily, often two or three each day. Scrawled in a cramped
hand, filled with grammatical errors, they were nonetheless remarkable—spiced with quotations from Freud and
Nietzsche and Jesus Christ and Lord Buddha. In the main
they were repetitious plunges into the waters of introspection, mixed with continual thanksgiving for the new friendship. Very soon Félix came to realize that he was to be
more than a *visiteur*. "Every day I thank God for sending
you in answer to my prayers," wrote Charles. "You are
my brother, my lover in the purest sense that men can
have for one another, my father, my salvation . . . All my
life I have desired a contact that was not only 'social'
according to the laws of society, but 'human.' Man to
man. Human to human. I think this is in our stars . . .
P.S. The next time you come, please bring me anything
by Jung. I have not read him, but I know I will like him."

After a few months, Félix understood the priest's caution about being "overwhelmed" by Charles, and he deliberately skipped two Saturdays. Then Félix wrote his

demanding young prisoner friend a letter, commenting
that he never knew when Charles was "playing games" or,
more crucially, when he was telling the truth. "There is a
continuing tone of self-pity and bathos of which I am
growing weary," wrote Félix.

By return post, express, came an enormous letter from
Charles with alternating layers of anger, fear, threatened
suicide, and worship. "Please do not abandon me like
everyone else," he implored. "You are the most important
factor of my life. I know I dream too much and take leave
of reality. But I swear to you I am perfectly aware of
reality. After all I have endured, after all the sordid paths
I have traveled, don't you think I recognize reality? True,
there is a certain flexibility in my mind that wants to
escape now and then through a fanciful spirit. I come back
on earth only when it is necessary. But this gives me
strength. I am not a 'double personality.' Don't worry . . .
Ah, Félix, perhaps I am just a simpleminded person who
is condemned to the slag heap of life. Perhaps I am re-
tarded. On the other hand, perhaps I can touch your soul.
Perhaps I can make my mark on the world."

Félix gave in and resumed his Saturday visits. The subject of Sobhraj the Tailor was discussed and dissected
regularly. How should he be approached? How should the
news be broken that his son was in prison and desperate
to have the tailor send love and, one day, enough money
to fetch him back to Saigon?

The drama captured Félix's imagination. It did not seem
possible that a human being could exist in modern times
without some country awarding him citizenship. If Charles'
father was indeed Indian, and he seemed to be, then
surely that nation's government would accept him. Félix
took the matter to the Indian Embassy in Paris, presenting
Charles' dossier and a life history which he and the youth
had prepared together. It was a bare bones account of
Charles' war-time birth, early life, and enforced odyssey
over half the world. A polite consular official studied the
file and asked for time to check further. When Félix returned, the answer was negative. If Charles Sobhraj had
been born on Indian soil, then his citizenship would have
been assured. But since there was no birth certificate, and
no recommendation from the Vietnamese Government,

then nothing could be done. As he spoke, the consul's face darkened, as if he were venturing into a fearful, forbidden landscape. Then he abruptly ended the meeting, begging the press of work.

Félix was also troubled. Was something the matter?

The consul gestured to the dossier. "This man," he said, "someday he will meet his destiny in India." He almost shuddered, as if receiving a mystical foretaste of the prisoner's future. Félix wanted to know more. He began a question, but the consul cut him off. "Please," ordered the consul, "I cannot explain it. But I feel it."

On his business letterhead, Félix wrote an eloquent letter to Sobhraj the Tailor. He did not hide the truth. The tailor's son was in Poissy Prison, serving a long sentence for robbery and theft. But Félix believed there were extenuating circumstances. Could any other chapter have been expected in a biography so assaulted by unusual forces? "I think you will find that he is a changed young man," wrote Félix. "He is highly intelligent, he has spent his time in prison reading everything he can get his hands on, currently he is taking a course in law. He loves you very much, and he is deeply sorry for whatever trouble he caused you." Félix let it go at that. He did not think it politic to raise the matter of Charles' desired return to Saigon and the need for the tailor to send money.

Together, Félix and Charles waited impatiently for an answer. Every Saturday, Charles' first question was, "Did my father write?" and for three months the answer was a sorrowful shake of the head. Fearing the letter had gotten lost, Félix wrote twice more. Still no reply was sent.

Disappointment turning easily into anger, Charles wrote a letter of passionate denunciation to the tailor.

Dear Papa:

It's really too sad that you are my father, that I was born of your flesh. Why is it sad? Because when a father has a son, he has the duty to love him, educate him, then help that son build a future. In all history, isn't that the traditional duty of a father? But you, you pray to God, and you go to your temple, but where is your conscience? If you have one, it must be heavy.

You gave birth to a son, and you ignored him, left him worse than a dog, worse than the lowest beast . . . You are not my father anymore. I renounce you. Live in your abundance, eat your rich food like a lion. As for me, I only ask for water and bread. They fortify me every day and give me that strong will to strengthen me and harden my goal. I want to make you *suffer,* suffer again and again, like a man with cuts all over his body. I will make you regret having failed the duties of a father. Fortune I will have— even without you. It will help me to pile stones on your head.

You will remember and you will regret having ignored me all these years. I have stayed more days of my life in prison than out, and the fault is yours . . . I want this to live in you like a cancer . . . One day you will take notice of me, but by then it will be too late . . . Charles.

He slipped the letter to Félix and asked him to mail it— unread. It was the most important letter he had ever written, said Charles, an exorcism. Félix was troubled by the unconcealed raw hatred on the young prisoner's face.

On the last visiting day before Christmas, 1966, Félix hurried into Poissy with gifts for Charles. He watched contentedly as his demanding new friend discovered some sweets, a new box of writing paper, books on English drama and American literature, and a world atlas. Even though books were not allowed in prison, Charles had somehow managed to persuade the guards to give permission. "There's one thing more," said Félix routinely, casually handing over a letter festooned with foreign stamps and exotic cancellations.

Charles held the long-awaited letter from his father tightly, but he could not bring himself to open it. "What does it say?" he asked. "I don't want to read it."

Don't be childish, ordered Félix. Read it. And read it all. Don't stop in the middle, for the sun comes out at the end after a minor squall. Sobhraj the Tailor had delivered himself of a rambling summation of his son's history, including a harsh memoir of Charles' abortive return to Saigon under the work contract: "While he was here, he had some girl friends, he stole many things from home and sold them on the street to enjoy the girls. Once he took the automobile and made an accident for which I had to pay $200. I criticized him every time, but he was too young and he thought his father was rich." In 1964, the tailor went on, he had cabled Song in Marseilles to tell her that he would be in Paris again and would like to see his son. Song claimed she did not know his whereabouts. At that time, Charles was conducting his crime wave that concluded with his Poissy incarceration.

At this, Charles was touched. His father had come again to Paris to see *him!* If he had only known the tailor was in Paris, then perhaps he would not have been waltzing about the city stealing coats and cigarettes and briefcases at knife point. The letter was concluded with a fatherly sigh: "Since you tell me in your letters that Charles is a good boy now and wants to come to Saigon, it is all right with me, if we can overcome the problem of passport and nationality . . . But I do want to know just what is his idea in returning here. I don't like people who wander around the girls all the time. Man must work and earn and get married and stand on his own feet."

But Charles' elation at finally receiving the letter quickly turned to gloom. Fate had played a perverse trick. The bitter letter of damnation he had written was probably in the tailor's hands by now, and any inclination he might have had to help his son was surely washed away. Félix had one more Christmas gift. "I didn't mail this," he said, handing over Charles' letter to his father.

"I thought you might want to reconsider what you said."

Charles threw his arms around Félix and wept, joyously.

CHAPTER SIX

"I didn't know your mother lived in France," said Félix during one of his Saturday visits with Charles. It was the dead of winter, 1967, and the prison walls were as cold as ice. The two men huddled under blankets. In his last letter, the tailor had mentioned Song in Marseilles.

"I was afraid to tell you," said Charles. Had Félix known at the beginning that his star prisoner had a flock of relatives on French soil, then perhaps he would have spent his visiting privileges on another, less well-connected inmate. But now that the news was out, and convinced that their relationship was cemented, Charles was not only willing but anxious for Félix to meet his exotic mother. "Go see her the next time you are in the South of France on holiday," suggested Charles. "Ask her anything you want. She will confirm all that I have told you."

Soon thereafter, Félix planned to go to Marseilles and informed Charles that he would call Song. Quickly a letter rushed from Charles' pen to Félix. "You are at last going to see my mother," he wrote. "She will tell you things about my youth that I did not want to tell you. They are not pleasant to remember. It's not that I do not believe in your ability to understand them, they are simply memories that cannot come from my mouth. Any happiness I have had in my life has always been short—and I am afraid your friendship will be the same. I am always waiting for the return of unhappiness. It always comes back to me."

Félix telephoned Song from Paris, introduced himself as a friend of Charles, and said he would visit her in a couple of days. He did not reveal that the young man was in prison. Presumably Song did not know, for Charles had not enjoyed contact with her for more than two years.

When Félix rang the bell at the lemon-colored villa on the outskirts of Marseilles, the door was opened by a hauntingly familiar copy of Charles. It was André, the half-brother who had worshiped "Charlot" from their young years together in Dakar. Charles was eight years older, but they could have passed for twins. André showed the visitor to the living room, a cramped salon with vibrant splashes of color and eclectic décor. Perfume and incense made the air almost sickly sweet. Stuffed teddy bears and kittens were tossed on sofas and chairs. The walls were covered with polychromatic paintings of the saints and on an end table rested the three monkeys who would not hear, see, or speak evil. Several family photographs spilled from shelves and tables, but there was not a single memento of Charles, the lost son.

"This is my mother, Madame Darreau," said André, gesturing toward Song, a frightened-looking woman in her mid-forties who was clinging fanatically to a faded youth. Her dyed hair was an unbelievable black, cut in the bangs of Cleopatra, and her slit skirt was glued to her thickening body. She sat on the edge of a daybed that was occupied by a man in pajamas, seemingly in distress. "And this is my father," continued André.

Félix was taken aback. The man on the daybed seemed more vigorous than Charles had described him. Younger, too. The former French officer, now retired and a semi-invalid, surprisingly took command of the meeting, firing questions at Félix as if interrogating a suspect. Who are you? What is your business? What do you want from us?

Félix responded patiently to each inquiry, his courteous nature and wholesomeness filling the room with legitimacy. He explained his role of *visiteur* in Poissy, thus his meeting with Charles. Song gasped and crossed herself. *"Mon Dieu,"* she said, "I knew it would happen." From his bed, Darreau directed Félix to tell more about the prison. The detailed account indicated that Félix was truthful, that he had considerable knowledge about the law and its violators.

Suddenly Darreau leaned forward and whispered in Song's ear. She nodded in agreement. The sick man then sprang spryly from his bed and extended his hand. "I'm sorry," he said. "I'm afraid we've played a little trick on you." The man was an impostor, a detective from the Marseilles police. Madame Darreau had called and asked for protection. She knew that Charles had friends in the Paris underworld, and she was afraid that Félix might be one of them with plans to rob her. Félix threw back his head and laughed. The wolf was impersonating Little Red Riding Hood's grandmother. This whole family was more than a little eccentric.

Beyond its curiosity value, the visit to Song was valuable to Félix because it gave him a notion of how to obtain a legal identity for Charles. Since Song was legally wed to a former French military officer, perhaps there was some way for Charles to slip through a loophole into the family unit. But at a government office in Paris, Félix received a brusque *"Non."* Just as he was about to leave, dejected, the clerk asked him to wait. Finding a lawbook, the clerk pored over it, stopping finally at a section that seemed relevant.

Was this Charles Gurmukh Sobhraj born on Vietnamese soil at the time when it was called French Indochina? Félix nodded.

Was this man's mother a natural born citizen of French Indochina? Again, a nod.

The clerk spoke guardedly. There existed a rarely invoked clause that pertained to citizens of French Indochina who had to evacuate that country after France's withdrawal. Such persons were entitled to full French citizenship, provided they established permanent residence in France.

Suddenly everything was easy. Félix engaged a lawyer, collected assorted documents and travel papers from Song, then went before a civil tribunal. The judge studied the criminal record of Charles and commented that he was not precisely the kind of citizen that France desired.

Nevertheless, as this man's mother was a legitimate citizen of what was once a French colonial territory, then her issue was entitled to membership in the community of Napoleon, Rousseau, and Voltaire.

"I was holding my breath through it all," said Félix, when he told Charles the extraordinary news. The prisoner sat numbly on the visiting room bench, slowly shaking his head in disbelief. Almost twenty-five years old, he at last possessed what most men are given the moment they are born—a legal identity. Félix intruded on Charles' happiness. There were two strings attached. First: Charles would not be permitted to live within the city of Paris for a restricted period after release from prison, due to the several crimes he had committed there. Second: Charles would be liable for service in the French military, like all the sons of the country.

At that, Charles grimaced. He had no desire to spend two more years in another kind of prison. Félix suggested that he not worry. Everything was at least a year away. Charles must complete his prison sentence before any new bridges would be crossed. With emotion, Charles threw his arms around Félix. "I don't know what to say except 'thank you,' " he said weeping. "I promise never to let you down, Félix. I feel my life is finally beginning."

Another year crept by, Charles counting the days until late 1968, when he would be eligible for release. He used the time productively. Continuing to study, he taught himself German so that he could more fully comprehend Nietzsche, the philosopher of whom he had become enamored. "It really is true that nature divides the strong and the weak," he wrote. "There are people who are weak from the moment they leave their mother's breast. They are condemned. I believe I am in the category of the strong."

And he wrote letters. Flowing from his cell in astonishing numbers, he slipped most of them out of prison through the good offices of the chaplain, or Félix. From the confines of his cell, Charles planned his future life. He took elaborate measurements of his body and dispatched them to Saigon, requesting his father to sew half-a-dozen new suits, enclosing a photo of the modish fashion cut from a French magazine. "They should be ready for the day of freedom," he told his father. Several times a week he wrote anew to Félix, analyzing and reanalyzing himself in the light of some new notion born in the reading of his philosophy books. "*Cher Félix*," he wrote on May 10, 1968, "I have put myself on the couch, and here is a psychoanalysis of the patient: Subject is naturally sensual, but he is also intellectual and spiritual, and these go counter to his nature. The sensual vs. the spiritual, a struggle as old as time and destined to continue! Subject went through his first love, which was not satisfying. This love was only in the heart, not physical. Now, when subject has relations with a woman, he throws up an 'auto defense' to think bad things about the woman. An unconscious fear of new rejection (like his mother). Hmmmmm . . . an interesting case, don't you think?"

Félix knew little of Charles' reputation inside prison and his relationship with the other prisoners. But from time to time, there were splinters of troubling news. In his first year inside Poissy, Charles had been a loner, spending his time reading and writing, occasionally practicing karate with studied showmanship to keep homosexuals away from him. Then Charles was seen in clusters of foreign prisoners, usually Oriental, men whose dossiers contained crimes ranging from murder to trafficking in narcotics and stolen passports. Tactfully Félix suggested that such liaisons were perilous to a man who professed to be on the side of love, God, and reality. "I play chess with them," said Charles testily. "I'm not a student sitting at the feet of master criminals."

And when Charles was given French citizenship, a certain cockiness and arrogance were demonstrated, as if he were finally a member of the fraternity and could safely criticize its bylaws. A colleague in his section committed some minor infraction and was denied his daily ration of milk as punishment. Charles felt the man was ill, and in need of the nourishment of milk, so he shared his. When the generosity was discovered, the guards responded by cutting off Charles' milk as well. Promptly Charles fired off a letter to the director of the prison in which he elevated the matter to the category of Dreyfus:

Dear Mr. Director:

I write to protest your judgment of me. When I get a just punishment, I will do it without protest. But when I am given a punishment based on reports that are unjust, a flagrant injustice, I protest. I protest!

Even though I am in a low position in your eyes, I demand justice, the justice of human understanding, a humanity that every being in society should have. To punish me by taking away my milk ration just because I shared my milk with a friend in detention (who really needed it) is unfair! It was a gesture of solidarity on my part, nothing more. I find this action totally normal, even if I have a condemnable past in society.

I discussed this with the chaplain, and he gave me comfort. But I believe you are only trying to repress us, not to rehabilitate us. Ours is a miserable state. What is your role in this place? To drown us? Or to try and help us get a future, a tomorrow in society?

The report against me says my cell is kept in bad condition. The guards destroy it and then blame me. I will accept no further injustices! From now on, if you do not take my punishment away, I will not eat. I will *die* unless you repair these injustices.

When an acceptable response did not come from the director, Charles proclaimed a hunger strike. Coincidentally he had been reading a biography of Gandhi, and he now cast himself in the role of martyr, his body wasting away in the name of humanity and justice. He sat squat-legged in his cell, meditating, chanting, refusing to acknowledge the taunts and curses of the guards. When the strike continued for several weeks, Charles growing so weak that he could not even walk to the visitors' room to see Félix on Saturdays, his friend sent word to him that he was behaving like a fool. His cause was undeniably just, said Félix, but if he did not kill himself from malnutrition, he would risk an extension of his sentence for bad conduct, and when and if he were ever released, he would have to go directly to a hospital to see if doctors could save what little was left.

Charles requested that the French press interview him,

but when no reporter came, and when everyone seeeemed to lose interest in his drama, and when he began lapsing into unconsciousness, he declared on the forty-fifth day of the hunger strike that his purpose had been accomplished. He had illumined a dark place. His milk was resumed.

In the last few months of his imprisonment, Charles wrote bitterly of his Poissy experience. "I've stopped having illusions about 'humanity' and the life in prison," he told Félix.

"The guards! Instead of trying to help prisoners rehabilitate themselves, *au contraire* they only push you lower in the dirt. The ones who do not want to be rehabilitated, the ones whom society fears, these are the guys that the guards give good reports on—just to get them out of here fast. And as soon as they get out, then society suffers. Don't speak to me ever of justice and reform. Sooner or later, they are back inside, back 'home.' And they get the best treatment. Guards, you see, respect 'Fame,' even when it is the fame of a garbage pile.

"Have I told you what it is like between prisoners, the life here? There should be solidarity, to help each other. But they eat each other up like wolves. I live in a jungle. Even though you have seen much and heard much, it is only half reality. For the total, one has to live in hell . . .

"Ah, but don't think I'm suicidal. What gets me through each day is intelligence. My only weapon here is intelligence. It lifts me above the others. The strong man is the smart man, not the man who is muscle-bound. No fall can break a man like me . . ."

On the day of his release from Poissy, Charles was met by Félix, who walked with him out of the bleak prison into the brilliance of a spring morning in Paris. Félix was full of cheering news. Three suits of hand-tailored clothing were at this moment en route from Sobhraj the Tailor in Saigon. Several job interviews were lined up. And there was a party this very night to which Charles was invited.

Charles stiffened, fingering the work clothes and ill-fitting jacket that were his legacy from Poissy. Would the party guests know about his past?

"Not unless you tell them," answered Félix. "Nobody has to know anything. The past is past. It means what it says."

Charles rode silently in the taxi, drinking in the splendors of Paris, marveling, Félix assumed, at how quickly he could leave the confines of an ancient prison and within minutes be on the way to a friend's apartment in the most favored *arrondissement*.

Something else was on his mind. Would there be girls at the party? Félix smiled and nodded. There would be many girls. Nice girls. Not the kind who quote a price and then lead a customer up a narrow staircase in Pigalle. "Then I cannot go," Charles said. "I look like a *clochard*." Félix ordered the taxi to stop outside a men's boutique, and that Charles should go in and pick out something to wear. It would be a loan.

With concealed fear, Charles stood before the boutique, like a child gawking at a police parade. Skinny, his yellowish skin pale from the sunless years of Poissy Prison, he seemed bereft of the necessary courage to enter. Félix felt a twinge of sympathy. His friend was twenty-four years old, but he did not know how to buy a pair of pants.

They were late to the party because Charles spent most of the day in an elaborate rite of cleansing and grooming— scrubbing away the smell and feel of prison. He found a barber to sculpt his hair *à la mode*. He rummaged through Félix's closet searching for underclothes and socks. Finally he put it all together, and when he emerged, Félix was astonished. A transformation had occurred. Gone was the malnourished youth who had stood trembling before a men's boutique. In its place was an elegant young man in a well-tailored blazer and flared trousers. His shoes gleamed like polished brass. He seemed to the manner born, an habitué of *tout Paris*, his face a mask of sophisticated arrogance. "I am ready," said Charles. "Tonight I am newly born.

The two men drank a toast and hurried to the party, Félix feeling rather like a shabby cousin from the provinces, tagging along as a shadow. Indeed, Félix was a bit poorer on this night than he had been when the sun rose. Charles' splendid new clothes cost $350, which Félix would never see again. And in Charles' pocket was a handful of coins, which he had "borrowed"—without asking– from a hidden box in the closet. They were gold. Charles liked the way they clinked and felt in his pocket— and their sense of permanence.

CHAPTER SEVEN

The cultural shock of leaving prison in the morning and attending a crowded, noisy party that very night was at first too much, even for Charles. He clung to Félix's coat-tails like a child hanging onto a parent the first day of school. His bravado was gone. Three years within the cruel walls of Poissy had robbed Charles of social graces— or so Félix assumed.

Then the girl arrived.

Charles noticed her immediately, watching intently as she threaded her way through the crowd, laughing, accepting wine, teasing, earning compliments, and rejecting overtures. She had long chestnut hair with streaks of honey, and her eyes were pale blue. "Who is she?" whispered Charles. Félix smiled. Her name was Hélène. But he counseled Charles not to waste his time. Hélène was freshly on the rebound from an unhappy love affair with a man who was half Vietnamese. "I don't think she would like to know another Oriental man this quickly," said Félix. But if Charles heard the caution, he did not acknowledge it. He was transfixed by the vision before him. It was, Félix would remember, rather like a stage play in which the lights dim on all characters but two. "An extraordinary moment," Félix would recall. "From the moment their eyes first met, Hélène was lost. She no longer had control of her life."

When Charles learned her name, he pronounced it melodiously and led the young woman to a corner of the apartment. There they sat and mooned, as if they had been

lovers from previous lives, murmuring words dipped in
sugar and wine. Charles spoke with the language of his
letters—florid, romantic, a little silly. Hélène was mes-
merized. A simple girl from a suburb of Paris, she was
barely twenty years old, the child of a butcher and his wife.
Her world was solid bourgeois, her horizons extending only
from her parents' home to an office in Paris where she
filed papers and performed office work for a financial investment company. She rode the Métro to and from work,
purchased skirts and sweaters at Prisunic, dutifully went
to mass and confession, avidly read *France Dimanche* and
grew tearful over Queen Saroya's failure to bear the Shah
of Iran an heir. Now, suddenly, here was a man sitting
beside her with the blood of the Orient and the manner
of a *Parisien*—the son of a Vietnamese millionaire, or so
he said—whispering about a cafe in Dakar he would take
her to someday, quoting poetry written by a Moghul king
of his favored lover. Later in this evening, Charles began
reading Hélène's palm, an art he had learned "from an old
gypsy woman."

"Do you believe in destiny?" asked Charles.

Hélène nodded hesitantly. She had never really thought
about it before, being firmly planted in the garden of the
Catholic church.

"It's good that you do," said Charles. "For destiny will
make it impossible for you to escape from me."

Félix would one day look back on the ensuing months
after the lovers met as a tumultuous series of images. Their
sum was chaos. One day Charles was a man, the next a
child. At breakfast he would babble about honesty, it
being the "foundation" of his relationship with both Félix
and Hélène. But by nightfall, he would have stolen a tape
recorder from a relative's home, or bought clothes knowing that he had no funds to pay Félix when the bill arrived.
When Félix took the couple out for dinner, as he did frequently, Charles insisted on a restaurant of grand standing, and once there he chose dishes with no regard for
price and ate from the plates with no manners, food falling from his mouth as he gazed at the wondrous Hélène.

Félix made appointments for job interviews; Charles
failed to keep them. Félix came home from work and dis-

covered that his apartment had been tossed about like a
salad—books pulled down from library shelves and pages
dog-eared, phonograph records stripped of their jackets
and left exposed in the sun to warp, clothes fallen from
hangers in pursuit of something to match Charles' fancy
of the moment. It took but a few weeks for Félix's patience
to snap and he directed Charles to find lodging on his own.
The role of prison *visiteur* did not entail permanent adop-
tion of a demanding son. Dutifully, if a little petulantly,
Charles found a small flat near Hélène's home. But Félix
was no more successful in ridding himself of Charles than
is a man in expelling a chronic pain that appears in the
bones with each change of the weather. At 3 A.M. the
front door often burst open—somehow Charles always
managed to find a key, even when Félix changed the locks
—and songs of passion and love would fill the bedroom,
hymns to the glory of Hélène.

When the growing nemesis turned up at Félix's door to
borrow a thousand francs, the older man refused. He had
a substantial stack of due bills from Charles already, and
indications were that they could never be cashed. Charles
was behaving impetuously and expensively, charged Félix.
Unless Charles found legitimate work, unless he erected
fences around his life that would contain his destructive
behavior, then Félix would prefer not to see him again.

"Ah, Félix, you are right, you are always right," agreed
Charles. He was "ashamed" of his behavior, his only excuse
that he had been trying to redeem three lost years. From
the ages of twenty to twenty-four, he had reposed in Poissy
Prison. "They took the most vital years of a man's life
away from me," said Charles.

Félix found vents for his steam. *They* took nothing, he
said. Charles put himself in prison. And the way he was
conducting his life, it would not be a stunning surprise to
see his return. "That will never happen," said Charles. "I
will not permit it."

Briefly Charles worked as salesman for a fire extinguisher
company, long enough to order and receive beautifully
engraved business cards, of which Frenchmen are so fond.
He pressed them eagerly into the palms of everyone he
met. Often Félix caught him caressing the card, rubbing

his finger over the name raised in type, relishing the illusive permanence and membership in society that the cards brought. "When this young man actually worked, he was a good salesman," an official of the company later told Félix. "He was good at meeting people, at presenting our line of merchandise. He brought in business." But Charles was incapable of stringing together eight solid hours of work. Either he overslept, or he was sick, or he claimed to have gotten lost on the streets of Paris. He took advances from petty cash and never paid them back, he borrowed money from the secretaries who spent a disproportionate amount of their time watching his panther body prowl the office. When the company dismissed him, some of the women employees complained.

Another side of Charles existed which Félix knew nothing about, though later, when he learned, he was not surprised. The presence of Charles Sobhraj in Paris had not gone unnoticed by several of the *copains* with whom he had dwelled at Poissy. One of them, a Spaniard named Porto, a grotesque giant with half his face scarred from a pot of boiling olive oil that a whore in Barcelona had thrown at him, asked Charles to join three men who were committing occasional robberies. Nothing major. Nothing dangerous. They were not overly greedy. It was difficult to encounter a prosperous-looking man, preferably elderly, in a Métro station late at night where the sight of Porto's hideous face and the flash of a Basque knife were enough to convince most anyone to surrender wallet and watch. Their most successful score had been the recent robbing of a baker, alone in his shop at closing time. They earned eight hundred francs for this quick and neat caper.

Charles smiled and murmured congratulations. But eight hundred francs split three ways was minuscule reward for a risk that could bring a half century behind Poissy's walls. As police would one day reconstruct the association, Charles offered a counterproposal. From his pocket he pulled a felt-tip pen and a piece of paper and quickly sketched the diagram of a large apartment. This, said Charles, was the home of a wealthy Paris lawyer who lived on the Avenue Foch and who had recently given a reception to which Charles had somehow gained entrance. While present, he made careful notes of possible entrances and exits, of closets that contained fur coats and dressers that nested jewel boxes. Porto stared with openmouthed fascination. This was the blueprint to a possible fortune!

Seizing the paper, like snatching bread from a starving man's mouth, Charles folded it up. How much would such a document be worth to Porto & Co.? The thief stammered. Charles elected to help him. The blueprint would cost precisely fifty per cent of the proceeds. And that was *all* Charles was selling. He would not participate in the actual burglary. And to guarantee that the profits were split equitably, Charles demanded a deposit of five thousand francs in advance. Refundable, of course, should it fail to reap the anticipated rewards. Many other opportunities existed in the same area of endeavor, said Charles, tantalizingly going no further. It was his intention, police later learned, to obtain blueprints of homes belonging to prominent people whose lives had brushed his—judges, attorneys, psychiatrists, prison officials. A dash of private and expensive revenge.

Hélène did not know that the man who sent roses to her home and office several times a week, and who smothered her with kisses and poetry, was also a man who had spent three years in prison and was now negotiating with three ex-convicts to form a liaison dedicated to burglarizing some of the major residences of Paris. Had she been told this, she would not have believed it. Her lover was a man who walked with her on warm summer nights along a thin island in the middle of the Seine where they held one another tightly and watched the tourist boats prowl the river, accordion music floating across the water. Her lover sent telegrams at sunrise proclaiming his love. Her lover sent express letters to her office, and at lunch she read them until they were etched on her heart. "Eternal woman, little girl, you are mine," read a typical one. "I simply cannot bear the hours we are not together. I toss in my bed unable to sleep, summoning portraits of you that fill the walls of my room. There *is* a god, *chérie,* and he sent me to you."

Whenever Hélène inquired about his past, Charles invented romantic adventures, set halfway around the world and therefore impossible to dissect or disapprove. At given

moments, he asked Hélène to believe that he was an actor
in Indian films, a Saigon businessman, and a student of
the law. His ambition was to become a lawyer and he was
investigating the faculties of France to find the most challenging one for his intellect.

And always, from the roses at dawn to the midnight
embrace, he pressed her for marriage. Hélène demurred as
best she could. It was not that she disliked the idea of
spending the rest of her life in the arms of Charles Sobhraj;
it was simply that more time had to pass. Her family was
bedrock bourgeois, methodical people only once removed
from the soil, intolerant of impulsive behavior. Her answer
to Charles' importunings was: Give me more time. We've
known each other only a few months. Beyond that, she
was fearful of telling her parents about the demanding new
man in her life. On the one occasion when Hélène cautiously allowed Charles to fetch her at home—normally
they rendezvoused at cafes or at Félix's apartment—her
father stared at the Oriental-looking young man like a
diner presented with a spoiled fish. On his best behavior,
Charles spoke trivially of the Paris summer, of Charles de
Gaulle, and of his stepfather in Marseilles, who at this
moment was transformed into one of France's greatest
war heroes. The meeting went well until Charles complimented the butcher on his suit of clothes, approaching the
older man and fingering the cloth approvingly. He remarked that it would be an appropriate garment for "a
ceremony."

"If you mean a wedding ceremony," gruffed the butcher,
"then it is out of the question." Later Charles complained
to Félix about his prospective father-in-law's "insensibility."
Félix remarked that he did not blame Hélène's father at
all. Charles was holding the girl in his hands like a just
caught bird.

"But if I don't hold her," said Charles, "she will fly
away. Then I would kill myself." Félix sighed, long since
bankrupt of appreciation for adolescent love talk.

Porto spent several days raising 5,000 francs and with
his *copains* hatched a plan both primitive and basic. He
would pay Charles for the blueprints, then return in the
dead of night, slice his throat, retrieve the money, commit

the burglary, and spend the rest of his life wrapped in silk. He took the Métro to Charles' apartment and learned from the concierge that his quarry was out for the evening.

It was early August 1968. Charles picked up Hélène in a sports car that he had "borrowed from a friend." They drove leisurely to Deauville, where Charles planned an evening at the casino. En route, he spoke of a new urgence to his desire for marriage. Very soon he would be leaving for the Far East. His father was dangling an alluring partnership in an import-export business in Saigon. This news would have been a revelation to Sobhraj the Tailor, for he had written recently a letter to Félix declaring that under no conditions would he welcome his son to Saigon. The war there was intensifying, Lyndon Johnson was sending in what seemed to be tens of thousands of new soldiers every month, business was unpredictable. But most important, wrote the tailor, "I do not trust my son. His mother did not bring him up right."

Charles pleaded with Hélène. "I cannot leave Paris without you," he said. And once again Hélène begged for more time. She was working on her father, but the situation was complicated. Her mother had a failing heart. A family confrontation might kill her.

At the Deauville casino, Charles gambled recklessly, Hélène hovering behind him, fascinated by men and women in Paris *couture* who with seeming boredom won and lost thousands of francs. By mid-evening, Charles had run a stake of a thousand francs up to six thousand, half a year's wages for Hélène. "Stop, *chéri*," she whispered. He hissed her quiet. His face was so rapt that for the first moment since they met she felt like an intruder. Within half an hour, Charles lost his stake, even the fifty francs in Hélène's purse that she had pinned to the lining like any good French girl.

On the drive back to Paris, Charles was morose. He blamed Hélène for his losses. No wonder that his luck soured; his head was confused by Hélène's dalliance with his heart that he was lucky to escape with the clothes he was wearing. Angrily he shoved the accelerator to the floor, the car rocketing along the *autoroute* toward Paris. A light mist was falling, turning the pavement into glass.

Hélène begged Charles to slow down, but his answer was to snap on the radio with deafening music to drown out her fearful cries. "All right, you win, I'll marry you," she finally shouted. And with that, Charles laughed and lifted his foot from the pedal. At the moment he noticed the police car behind him, siren screaming.

Swearing, Charles pushed the accelerator down again, turning off the *autoroute*, twisting through the quiet peace of a sleeping village, losing control, clipping a fence, spinning end over end until the crushed little car came to shuddering rest in a newly plowed potato field.

When the police hurried in, guns drawn, to arrest this dangerous fool for stealing a car, speeding, reckless driving, and having a stolen permit, they discovered Charles holding a young woman, trying to kiss the blood from her face, weeping like a bereaved old woman, his howls protesting the fates that smote him.

Porto waited in an alley near Charles' apartment until midnight, then he found a cafe and drank red wine until he passed out and the owner threw him into the street.

CHAPTER EIGHT

The sentence was eight months, in a prison at Rouen, with an attendant comment from the judge that probably he was being too lenient. On the bench was a now thickening dossier for Charles Sobhraj. Someone, a policeman or a court official, had scrawled in warning red letters across the twenty-four-year-old felon's name, "*EXTREMEMENT DANGEREUX.*"

Hélène appeared at the hearing, a thin scar on her temple as the only souvenir from the accident. It did not mar her fresh beauty; she told the judge that she loved Charles and held no grievance against him and planned to marry him as soon as the matter was settled. Her soft voice and poised manner impressed the judge, as did the presence of Félix, who once again came to the aide of Charles despite his better judgment that it was time to lock his doors. With money from his own pocket, Félix engaged a psychiatrist who, after consultation with Charles, wrote an encouraging report.

"Fascinating case," remarked the psychiatrist. "Obviously there is a psychological deformity of image here that could bring on psychopathic states. This has not yet happened. The boy is intelligent—highly so—and I believe that psychotherapy could help him, if not cure him."

Félix greatly assisted the therapist by presenting his own "psychological profile." Knowing that it would take months to properly analyze Charles—"He is the most adroit liar you will ever encounter," warned Félix—the prison *visiteur* prepared his own lay observations. They were compelling and accurate:

—"Who is Charles Sobhraj? Why has he failed? Why does he wreck his life? Why one disaster after another?

—"Charles is a human being with paradoxical qualities. He has an intuitive intelligence, fast comprehension, an ability to cultivate his mind. Yet he is introspective in a morbid way. He is pessimistic, often worried, doesn't trust people easily, hides a very real lack of confidence in himself, has a tormented nature.

—"He exploits one hundred per cent the weaknesses of those around him. Is capable of the blind fidelity of the Asiatic. Is hungry for money and success, considering these to be noble ambitions.

—"He has a small conscience, if any. His vanity is extreme, with a passionate desire to be liked, but he never admits any vulnerability. He possesses the sentimentality and sexuality of Don Juan, in the pathological sense of the term. Is capable of politeness, but calculatedly so. Impulsive and aggressive.

—"His life is a history of running away. His explanation is that he is trying to find a better life in a better atmosphere, but of course he is really running away from himself. Wants people to feel sorry for him. He is a judge administering punishment to himself, trying to make his friends and family feel sad and sorry.

—"A brilliant actor, he is a *poseur extraordinaire,* always running away from reality."

All of this was placed before the judge, who perused it and then announced that he was not impressed by the character of the defendant. Indeed, were it not for the support shown by Hélène and Félix, he would make the sentence more severe than eight months.

As a guard led Charles away in manacles, Hélène burst out of the spectator section and was permitted an embrace. "I will wait for you," she whispered. "I will be a nun until the moment of your freedom." The sentence was retroactive to the night of the accident. It was now mid-December, 1968, and Charles would be free by late spring.

Charles shook off the girl's embrace. He did not need her "pity." She ran after him to explain the difference between love and pity, but for the moment it was too late.

Engulfed in a sea of guards and prisoners, Charles was carried away like a bobbing cork, quite small, very insignificant.

Petulant letters began arriving at Félix's mailbox. Their tone was whining self-pity. Charles felt he was being unfairly treated by persecutive authorities. Félix decided it was time to hold a mirror up to Charles or, to use his metaphor, "lance the boil." He wrote back a letter that slashed and ripped, calculated to shock the young prisoner into a more stable behavior pattern.

"Perhaps you will shred this letter in rage," wrote Félix at the beginning of 1969. "If so, too bad . . . One of the problems with you is that you are always engaged in morbid introspection. Morbid! Oh, an occasional intimate self-analysis is valuable. Everybody speaks to himself now and then; everybody steps aside to take a close look at oneself. I wonder what you see? This time you *must* look at the dirt. You cannot hurry past it any longer. I won't let you. I am here to make you see it.

"Charles, Charles, to be sure everybody leads something of a double life. But you lead God knows how many different lives and won't take cognizance of it. You seem incapable of sacrificing, even though you talk about it sometimes. You let yourself be guided by random impulse, and it is going to take you down to catastrophe . . .

"I want all these shocks to be the point of beginning for something new in your life. Only then can you really say 'I love Hélène.'

"Until then, I cannot believe you. Are your feelings perhaps twisted? Are you capable of real love? Or do you just hang onto someone in despair?"

Prisoners often go berserk in the agony of their confinement, but after receiving Félix's letter, Charles performed an act of violent disintegration that would be remembered for years in Poissy. Drawn by the cries of neighboring inmates, guards rushed down the corridor to discover Charles ripping apart his cell, pulling the cot out of the wall even though it was fastened with steel pins, shredding the thin mattress, tearing out chunks of plaster and rock from the walls. He tore off his clothes, stripping

naked on the bitterly cold winter night. In his hand was
Félix's letter, crumpled and wet with tears, and when the
guards seized him to lead him to *cachot*—solitary—he
tore up the letter and ate it rather than surrender it to
authority.

For fifteen days, Charles reposed in solitary, brooding
over the image that Félix had drawn. Upon his return to
a new cell, Charles wrote back. None of the baroque
romanticism that marked his previous letters was used.
Charles threw Félix out of his life like a man putting out
the cat.

"Do not ever worry about me again," wrote Charles.
"Do not concern yourself with what I will do when I get
out, or about my psychological makeup. Do not waste
another breath on me. Now I and I alone will direct the
destiny of my life . . . I will make my decisions, when and
where and how I want to—and not how *you* want. I
assure you that I am not the prisoner of an 'outraged
vanity' as you once suggested. Rather I am perfectly calm
and lucid and confident. From you, now and forever, I
want no help, no contact, no material assistance. Not a
centime! Nor will I ever set foot in your house for one
minute.

"On the day I leave prison—for the last time, incident-
ally—Hélène and I will become man and wife. The future
is ours. Please stay out of our lives forever!"

Promptly Félix fired back, professing sarcastic delight
at Charles' new independence. How happy he was that
Charles was "healed" and possessed of enough confidence
to write such a "deep" and "revealing" letter.

"It shows your true side," wrote Félix. "The same side
you have displayed to your father, your stepfather, and
to all those who care about you . . . I do as you wish, I
leave you! Build the life that you want. Let us presume
that it will be successful. Age will help, maybe even the
hate and aggressiveness that you demonstrate so often will
replace the same feelings you have for yourself . . . Whatever, you finally reveal yourself to be a *petit salaud*."

The term translates "little bastard."

The few months that remained of his sentence were
used productively. Charles took a course in French law

and wrote several eloquent papers, one of which merited a "Provocative! Well done!" from the instructor. A fellow prisoner asked Charles why he was so enamored of the law, as he had but a few months to serve. There was no need to act as jailhouse counsel in appeals or further trials. Charles smiled. "In order to break the rules, you must know them," he answered, using a comment that he would make many times in years and places yet to come.

And each night, *each* night, Charles poured out an overwhelming love and need for Hélène:

My dearest—

From the depths of my cell, I hear the other prisoners crying every night. Darkness is the lonely hour. Darkness is the moment when a man holds on the tightest to keep from going insane. I would be one of them were it not for you, for the memories that live in my heart.

What a joy you are, what a marvel, what a wonder . . . I have just received your last letter, with three photographs enclosed. Do you know which one I prefer? Oh, little girl, you surely know. It's the pose of you in the bathing suit, with all the perspectives of your beautiful body revealed. Let's close our eyes and dream, dream, dream that we are lying next to one another. I must have your beautiful love until the last breath of my life, and then beg God to live it all over.

God will protect our love, for it is an act of purity and perfection. I can see that you are making yourself beautiful for me when I return. I will find a beautiful little woman, so perfect that she will be like a deity, a goddess who dares present herself in front of me.

Hélène did not find her lover's words to be more overripe than penny novels. She treasured each, stuffing large stacks of correspondence in her purse and reading them on the Métro and during her lunch hour. Now and then a friend at the office would ask Hélène to accept a blind date, but she always refused, having invented the excuse that her fiancé was in the military and deserving of her unwavering fidelity. In her mind, Hélène was a war widow,

and from the trenches came words from her hero that
stirred passion. "You are so beautiful that I am fighting
a terrible enemy—jealousy! I worry each moment that
another man will take you away before I come back.
Hélène! Do you know what I would do, if I could, this
very moment? I would lock you up in a golden cage, plant
flowers around it, and wrap you in silk until I return."

For the last two months of his sentence, Charles had
few visitors, Félix being banned by letter from ever seeing
him again. Hélène traveled to Rouen when she could in-
vent an excuse that would fool her parents. They still did
not know she was in love with a prisoner. Two other
"friends" visited Charles regularly, a pair of Oriental men
who presented themselves as relatives from Vietnam. As
they pretended to speak little French and always dressed
as impoverished immigrants, prison authorities accepted
their credentials. In truth, police would later discover, one
of them was Vietnamese, a former street friend of Charles
when both hustled as youngsters in Saigon. The other, an
older man with but two teeth in his mouth, both gold, and
a stomach the equal of Buddha, was believed to be a resident of Hong Kong and who counted among his accomplishments the murders of five men. His name was Ling
and each time he visited Charles he brought a container
of stew in an insulated jug. In return, he was permitted
to reclaim an empty jug from the week before whose contents had been gratefully devoured. But as soon as he left
the prison and was in a safe place, Ling eagerly removed
the false bottom of the jug and found the compactly drawn
blueprint of a home in Paris worth burglarizing. The plans
suggested possible approach and escape routes. When
Charles neared the end of his sentence, he had almost
fifteen thousand francs being held in escrow by Ling, proceeds of theft by proxy. Police believed that as many as
four major burglaries were committed by the strange gang;
its head in prison, its arms on the street.

On becoming twenty-five years old in 1969, Charles had
a woman who loved him, and money waiting. But he
wanted more. He wanted Félix back as the anchor of his
ship. On May 29, 1969, Charles wrote and beseeched his
patron to forgive him:

Only 23 more days until freedom! I count every minute. I look back on eight lost months, wasted months, months of falling down, months of thinking about a destroyed future, months of remembering a lost friendship of irreplaceable value. I need you, Félix . . .

I want to confess my ungratefulness, so that I will not leave behind in your mind the image of an ungrateful person. With your blessing, Hélène and I will build our lives. We will find the joy and happiness that is due us. And to reclaim your friendship, I promise to put aside the superficial, the lies, and the cheating. Your son, Charles.

Reading the latest in what seemed the two thousandth letter from Charles, Félix on this occasion was not stirred by any feeling save *déjà vu.* He had heard this song before. He therefore did not travel to prison on the day Charles was released, nor did he accept an invitation to join the couple for a celebratory dinner. Félix was determined not to play the role of surrogate father anymore, nor was he interested in being the maypole around which Charles and Hélène danced. Fortunately, the court was his ally, for a condition of the prisoner's release was that he not set foot within the city limits of Paris, where he had committed robberies and consorted with known criminals. But the directive did not forbid the telephone, and Félix could not escape. It rang day and night. Nothing had really changed. Charles' life had no more apparent purpose than the route of a firefly, but he felt it vital to tell Félix each time he applied for a job, each time he was rejected, each time he realized—usually at two in the morning—how much Félix had changed his life. Once, near dawn, grouchy and worn, Felix yelled into the telephone, "Cut me loose, Charles! I am not your brother, I am not your father. You have no more notion of how people behave toward friends than a street dog."

Abruptly Charles vanished for a few months, Hélène with him, and into Félix's life fell wondrous peace. An occasional postcard drifted in now and then—"We are in Madrid at the Hotel Ritz. Business and love fill our days.

Charles and Hélène." Or, "Won a little last night at the
Casino de Monte Carlo. Wish you were here to bring us
more luck. Love, Charles and Hélène." Félix wondered
not only how Charles could afford travel of first-class
character, but, more pertinently, how he even obtained a
passport, trailing as he did a substantial criminal record.
It would turn out that Hélène was not exactly sure either,
because her questions were always met with protestations
of titanic love, with shushing fingertips to her lips, with
vague unfinished explanations that he was amassing capital
for business and a marital nest egg.

With the arrival of Paris's brilliant autumn, Felix opened
his door to find Charles and Hélène on the step. The order
prohibiting his presence in Paris had been lifted, said
Charles. Félix suspected otherwise, but for the moment
he was genuinely glad to see the young couple. On their
faces was the glow of love. They were expensively and
fashionably dressed. And Hélène bore on her finger a diamond and ruby ring. They told Félix they would marry on
an October afternoon at a mayor's office in Paris. "Congratulations to you both," cried Félix as he embraced them.
But how had Hélène persuaded her father?

"We did not *ask* him for permission," answered Charles.
"We *told* him. This beautiful woman is an adult, and an
adult makes her own decisions."

And so they were wed, in a simple civil ceremony that
was memorable principally for the best man's nervousness.
Félix fretted that the presiding mayor might ask Charles
for his *permis de séjour,* the residence permit, absence of
which might send the bridegroom back to jail before the
ink dried on the marriage license. Félix knew that Charles
did not possess one legally, but he did not know that
Charles had purchased a counterfeit document on the very
day he bought his navy blue wedding suit. Whatever, the
mayor did not ask for it, he only beamed and blessed the
couple, and the winds of love blew softly. The day was
perfect. Even Song, bejeweled and eye-catching, traveled
to Paris, and at the reception she was a center of attention.
Sobhraj the Tailor was absent, even though Charles had
sent his father a telegram and had spent several days trying to call Saigon. Hélène's father filled the parental gap.

Toasting the couple, dancing with Song, filling his belly with champagne, the butcher seemed as happy as any man in the room.

The newlyweds leased a small apartment in a suburb south of Paris where, for a few months, they lived lives outwardly respectable, decorous enough for the blessing of a country friar. While Hélène commuted to Paris each day and worked as a file clerk, Charles found odd jobs in restaurants and read books on philosophy and law. He was becoming a serious student of Jung and often kept Hélène awake at night interpreting words like "anima" and "animus" and "synchronicity." Jung made exceptional sense to Charles, particularly the philosopher's contention that meaningful events in a person's life are not necessarily traceable to specific causes. Rather they occur in different lives and different places, but at the same time. "It's like the bumper cars that people ride at fairs," said Charles. "Each person had a different reason for coming to the fair, and each person had a different reason for choosing to buy a ticket and ride one of the cars. And each person chose to bump into another car at a certain moment. Why?"

Whatever had lured Charles on his mysterious visits to Spain and Monte Carlo was apparently forgotten, for on the few occasions that Félix dined with the couple in their flat—furnished neatly with castoffs from friends—the subject did not arise. The talk was of happiness, of Hélène's growing prowess as a cook, of their desire for a child. When Félix took his leave one evening, warm and content from a meal of *pot-au-feu* and a new Beaujolais, Hélène walked with him a way toward the train station, reassuring the old friend of Charles' new sense of responsibility and permanence. All it took were marriage and the knowledge that someone needed him and loved him, said Hélène. Félix blessed them both, almost envying the marriage, for he had never found a woman to whom he could commit his life.

Just as he took his leave, Félix could not resist asking Hélène if any of Charles' old prison friends had turned up, perhaps trying to lure him back into a dangerous line of work.

Hélène did not like the question. She hedged. Yes, a few had come around, particularly one dreadfully fearsome Spaniard with a huge scar across half his face. But she had sent them away, and as far as she knew, Charles was not seeing them.

On the train ride back to Paris, Félix felt almost patriarchal, realizing that he had played matchmaker and was someday going to be rewarded with a godson. "Our first boy will be named Félix," Charles had promised at dinner.

Then, abruptly, either by coincidence, or synchronicity, or the caprices of fate, or from the forewritten and inescapable script of destiny, a series of small shocks unsettled the tenuous earth on which Charles walked. They would not have interrupted the progress of a normal man, and indeed, when Félix looked back and analyzed them, every one seemed minor. But their sum was awesome. They set in motion an odyssey that would sweep over half the world, launch a journey that would bring Charles into collisions with unimagined lives and destinies. And snuff out dreams not yet even born.

CHAPTER NINE

On a fine spring morning in 1970, Charles learned that Hélène would deliver their first child by year's end. And on that very afternoon, the government of France informed Charles that his presence was needed in the military service for a minimum of eighteen months. With panic, Charles telephoned Félix. How could these events have dovetailed? How could he abandon Hélène with his seed growing within her? Why did the military even want him, his past being what it was? "You were happy enough to be granted citizenship by this country," lectured Félix. "Now you must pay for it."

Félix promised to look after Hélène, who, after all, was not exactly being thrown out into the cold. She lived near her parents and could visit them daily if she wished, she would continue working, Charles would earn enough money to keep his wife in maternity clothes and pay the obstetrician.

"I don't believe the Army will want me very long," grumbled Charles ominously. He did report for induction, as ordered, but he did not last more than several weeks before a medical discharge was granted. One of his brother soldiers, a farm youth named Serge from a town in the Midi, recalled Charles' brief moments in the military. "Every day he was either sick—or acting crazy," said Serge. "The guy was incredible. He was able to make his face turn pale and his temperature go up the moment the doctor put the thermometer in his mouth. He convinced them he had a bleeding ulcer. Maybe the doctors knew he was acting, but they also reasoned he was more trouble—and expense—than he was worth."

Charles rushed home to Hélène and fretted that his wife was being attended by a suburban doctor rather than the chief of obstetrics at Paris's finest hospital. Perhaps that was one of the reasons he went to visit his sister Leyou, married now to a man who owned a restaurant in Paris. He begged for employment. Perhaps that was also the reason that, once engaged as a waiter, he stole 6,000 francs from his sister's purse and lost every centime the same night at the Casino d'Enghien near Paris. Furious, Leyou reported the theft to the police, ignoring her half-brother's pleas to retract the accusation. "I was just trying to get enough money to buy Hélène the best doctor in France," he swore. He promised to pay her back, twicefold. Leyou, unmoved, refused. She intended to prosecute Charles. If he wished to steal from other people, that was his own business. But when he behaved larcenously toward his own blood, then no pity was due.

Once again Félix made the now familiar visit to Charles in jail, and this time he found his young friend hysterical. The theft was stupid, wept Charles, but it was not really of criminal intent, only a "loan." He had intended to pay back his sister before she even discovered the loss. But fate had cursed the cards dealt him at baccarat. "I swear that I will never go near a casino again," promised Charles. The promise was not necessary. Félix suspected that the court would ban Charles from admission to gambling establishments, considering his record.

Already Charles had scribbled a legal brief of sorts. He thrust it into Félix's hands, begging him to act as conciliator with the judge and with his half-sister. In lawbooks, Charles had found numerous cases wherein the injured party agreed to drop charges in return for complete financial restitution. Félix sighed. Why did Charles make such demands on his life? And, more appropriately, why did Félix agree to help him? "Because," answered Charles, "you are the only one in the world who can help me. And my wife. And little Félix." Little Félix? The unborn son whose father, if not pried loose from the vengeance of an angry sister, would enter the world under direst conditions.

Félix went to Leyou and convinced her to withdraw the charge, a substantial down payment from his own pocket helping his petition. Then he went before the court in a pretrial hearing and one more time preached a sermon on behalf of Charles. The judge agreed to release Charles provisionally, but unless the money were repaid in full, the charge would be reinstituted. And if Charles Sobhraj as much as spat on the sidewalk, he would face the wrath of justice.

But the paramount event of the early summer of 1970 was neither Charles' brief career in the Army nor his wife's pregnancy, nor the contretemps with his half-sister. It was the sudden arrival in Paris of Sobhraj the Tailor, whom Charles had not seen for almost a decade, since he was banished from Saigon and put aboard a ship bound for Bombay.

When the tailor, now elderly, arrived at Orly Airport, he was surprised to see a striking young man in sleek clothing and dark glasses rush to him with open arms, crying, "Papa!" Charles hugged his father fiercely and wiped tears that spilled from beneath his glasses. The tailor, a man who rarely showed emotion, managed to extricate himself from the overwhelming embrace. He wondered how Charles knew which flight to meet. Before he had left Saigon, Sobhraj had written his son a vague letter, saying that he was beginning another round-the-world trip and might spend a day in Paris around June 25. "I have met every flight," answered Charles. "I would sleep on the floor of the lobby if it meant having my father with me in Paris. Come, my wife is waiting for us."

Sobhraj the Tailor was fêted like a sultan. Dinner the first night was at Maxim's, and on his plate was a gold watch. Hélène was gloriously pretty, dressed in an expensive new gown, her beauty enriched by the soft pink glow of the restaurant's famous light that flatters any woman. "It was Hélène's idea," insisted Charles, squeezing his wife's hand under the table so that she would not spoil the small lie about the watch. Later, when they were alone, Charles produced a sapphire ring for his wife, saying that it was a wedding gift from the tailor. The older man was too shy to present it himself, informed Charles, and would be embarrassed if she even mentioned it. When

Félix heard the story of the lavish gift exchange, he knew immediately what Charles was up to, clandestinely buying his father's approval of a new daughter-in-law, and gilding the father's image in the eyes of his wife. Félix also wondered where Charles obtained the money to buy a gold watch and sapphire ring—but he dared not ask.

Chauffeured limousines bore the tailor about Paris; fresh flowers filled his hotel room. When, after two days, Sobhraj announced his intention to leave for Geneva, Charles insisted on driving him there. "Nothing is too good for my father," said the son.

In a rented car, they set out for Geneva, and immediately the tailor noted a certain tenseness that played around the face of Hélène. Her husband dominated every conversation, talking expansively of an import-export business he planned to inaugurate, waving around a checkbook that seemed to have thousands on deposit. Every time Charles spun his tales of money and success, Hélène was stricken. En route, Charles impulsively stopped at a jewelry store outside Paris and invited his father and bride to pick out a trinket, anything that caught their eye. Both declined any further demonstrations of love and generosity, but Charles selected a gold watch band and a Swiss watch priced at 3,800 francs. When he wrote a check to pay, the saleswoman refused to accept it. The day was a Saturday; banks were closed. The account could not be verified. But Charles put on a dazzling show, convincing her that he was a fan of quality. Would he write a bad check in front of his wife, expectant with child, and his father, distinguished visitor from the East? Of course not, agreed the clerk. She took his check.

Later on the journey, when Charles was washing his hands at a roadside restaurant, Hélène broke down. A simple girl, she was unable to act out charades as professionally as her husband. She told her father-in-law that Charles spent the week prior to the tailor's arrival in frantic pursuit of money. He sold their furniture, some clothing. Strange and disturbing men called at their apartment after midnight with hidden parcels. Their bank account was not only overdrawn but closed. The check Charles gave the jewelry store was worthless. The entire outpouring of gifts was meant to impress the tailor, and it was fabricated out of nothing. Their brief months as husband and wife had been troubling. Charles was a compulsive gambler with a temper that could flare into violence. But even with all of this, she still loved him and hoped to change him.

The tailor shook his head in despair. "Let me tell you something," he said. "You are married to a Number One Crook." The father had recognized the dark side of his son when the child was barely able to walk. Perhaps it was his fault, perhaps it was Song's, perhaps it was the judgment of the gods. His advice was to get out fast. "My son is a destructor," he said.

The rest of the journey to Geneva was strained and mostly silent. Upon arrival, the tailor suddenly found an excuse to change his itinerary and fly directly back to Saigon. New war headlines from Vietnam made his story plausible. At the airport, Charles clung tightly to his father until the tailor disappeared down the ramp to the plane. And then he called out, "I love you! I will see you soon in Saigon! We will be one family again!"

Félix owned an old MG sports car whose speedometer had twice reached a hundred thousand kilometers. It was his intention to sell it to Charles for the token sum of a hundred francs, for it was hardly worth trading in. When Charles returned from Geneva and asked to borrow the car for one afternoon to fetch a table, Félix agreed routinely. He never saw his car again. By nightfall, the ancient MG was speeding out of Paris, south, bearing Charles, his distraught wife, and their few remaining possessions. Their first destination was Greece, where Charles had a contact he needed to see, then a left turn toward the East. He planned to drive ten thousand miles across half the world, over the muddy ruts of rural Turkey, through the deserts of Iraq and Iran, into the awesome emptiness of Afghanistan, dodging the Himalayas, plunging across a corner of India, into Thailand, Cambodia, and finally Vietnam. He would not be turned away by his father again.

A flurry of letters crisscrossed the world, with Félix finding himself in the middle of many voices clamoring as to the whereabouts of Charles and Hélène. Leyou called regularly, shrieking for the return of her stolen 6,000 francs. Coincidentally, French police built a case around the worthless checks that Charles passed to purchase tribute for his father. He was sentenced to one year in prison, in absentia. Plus permanent expulsion from France. Hélène's parents were devastated, her mother stricken with worsening heart disease, her father threatening to telephone the Sûreté if necessary to obtain the return of his pregnant daughter. To all of them Félix could respond honestly, "I have no idea where they are. If I hear anything I will let you know."

Then, in a matter of a few days at the end of summer, 1970, two letters arrived, and the picture became clear—and ironic. The first was from Charles, postmarked September 11, mailed from Delhi but written somewhere along the way. "Forgive me," wrote Charles to Félix, "I didn't have the courage to tell you that I was leaving, knowing it would make you sad. And if I had seen you, I could not have kept my decision to leave France . . . Please understand that I only wanted to break with my awful past—and not with you. I can never forget those years when we worked together and you pulled me out of the mud where I was mired, how you helped me find myself, my being, my potential, how you brought me happiness and joy I had never known before. I know now that my destiny is here, in the East. Hélène and I are going on to Saigon, where I will join my father . . .

P.S. The car served us well. No mechanical problems. It's like you had whispered inside the engine and told it to take us to India. Only problem was going through Turkey—1,500 kilometers of bad road, dirt, rocks, and a wife who kept throwing up."

Hardly had Félix pressed the letter into the folder where he kept Charles' mountain of correspondence when a letter arrived from Sobhraj the Tailor. He, too, had received a letter from Charles—somewhere along the road —and, not knowing where to send his answer, he had chosen Félix. It seemed that the tailor was prepared to stand at the city limits of Saigon with a rifle to bar admission to his son and daughter-in-law.

"If you hear from them," wrote Sobhraj, "please tell them they are not welcome at my home. If they come to

me, I will be the first man to inform the French Consul
General here in Saigon and they will be arrested and sent
to France . . . My son does not know truth from lies, nor
good from evil.

"My friend Félix, have you heard the fable of the blind
boy who was sitting on a big rock near a pond where other
boys were swimming? This boy could hear the others
laughing and singing and having races with one another.
A priest passed by and saw the blind boy sitting so lonely.
He took pity on the boy and prayed to the Mighty God to
give the boy sight so that he could swim too. And God
answered the prayer and gave the boy sight. He jumped
into the pond and beat all the other boys at their races
and pushed some of their heads under the water and
caused them to drown. Those left alive were frightened
and they ran away. Then the boy with the new eyes came
out of the water and asked the priest to swim with him.
The priest refused and prayed a new prayer—that God
should make the boy blind as he was before. God once
more answered the prayer and took away the light. Then
God said, 'I saw that this boy was dangerous for others
and therefore I took away his eyes.'

"Félix, do you see the moral? You should have done the
same thing with Charles. You should have let him stay in
prison rather than fight for his freedom. That was your
great mistake. You thought he would be good when he
was freed. He begged you and you believed him and took
pity on him. And now the result of your mercy will be the
blood of the innocents . . ."

Book Two

THREE WOMEN

CHAPTER TEN

South of Los Angeles, edging the Pacific, small towns hug the sand like mussels clamped to rocks. They spill into one another, like the bleeding colors of Madras cloth, and it is difficult to know when one is left and another is entered. The landmarks are the same—a taco stand in Huntington Beach is scarcely different from a taco stand in Redondo Beach, and the same can be said by and large for the children. They are beautiful, the young of Southern California's beach communities. Their heads are bleached gold by the sun, their bodies are lithe and coppery, they are for a few blessed moments graceful creatures who dance on the sand and wash in the sea, with no more commitment required than the duration of foam left behind by a crashing wave.

On Cabrillo Beach, below San Pedro, in early 1970, the boys strapped themselves to wings of crimson and yellow and glided off cliffs, sailing insolently over those youths balanced on surfboards. The girls, at whom most of this spectacular endeavor was directed, pretended indifference, clustered instead about transistor radios. They listened and sang along with "Angel Baby." They oiled their bodies and toasted in the sun. They combed their hair. They puffed on cigarettes, legal and otherwise. They laughed and flirted and waited—although few if any could answer what for.

One of the memorable girls of Cabrillo Beach that season was, on occasion, Jennifer Maria Candace Bolliver.

Jennie. Everyone knew her. Everyone liked her. She was petite in a forest of young women, standing barely five feet tall. And she was different, a little "off center," as she described herself. When the other girls obeyed the dictum that feminine hair must be long, lank, ironed on a board and the color of sand or wheat, Jennie chopped hers off, affected kinky curls, and dyed it all flaming red, like the strawberry wine passed around at beach parties. Her body was full and well curved, more like an hourglass than a surfboard, and her "black tan" was widely admired, olive skin kept gleaming year round. Her friends chose terms of effervescence to describe Jennie. She "bubbled." She "sparkled." She "lit up dark rooms." She was a "bell ringing in a mission tower." When Jennie was very young, her father called her "penny candy," for she was scarcely bigger than a peppermint stick. Later, her grandfather dubbed her "T.T.," for "tizzy tosser." Jennie's temperament was quickly aroused.

In the anonymity of her beach town, Jennie was unique, for she was not totally committed to the mating dance of the sand. Or to much of anything, for that matter. She transferred her loyalties from one social caste to another, never taking full membership in any. The surfers knew her and liked her and sought to have her grace their "woodies," those ancient station wagons with paneled sides weathered gray by sea and salt. But then, so did the cheerleaders and the "smarts" and the class officers, even the "low riders," those tough and pretending-to-be-tough youths whose ladies wore razor blades in their beehives and who cruised Highway 1 in lowered '55 Chevies with tumbling dice and dancing dolls on the dashboards. Jennie was comfortable in street talk, but then again she often preferred to sit content and alone in her room, reading poets as disparate as Auden, Ferlinghetti, and Omar Khayyam. Ordered in the tenth grade to write a composition about her community, Jennie began: "My town is a melting pot—Italians, blacks, snobs, wetbacks, purples, freaks, hoods, slobs—and me."

A hidden and unspecific hunger chewed at Jennie, and she was unable to find lasting nourishment in any of her divergent "crowds." But no one suspected it. Jennie thought she was the only girl who had to wear masks at

the age of sixteen to make people think she was normal—
and happy.

She was the firstborn child of a deep sea diver named
Ralph Bolliver and his wife Sandra, a grocery checker/
part-time manicurist. The father was a vigorous man with
strong arms tattooed in hearts, crosses, and mermaids. He
smelled strongly of the sea, and he could hold his daughter
over his head with one hand, until she could touch the
ceiling. When Jennie was young, he took the child on his
boat a time or two, but she was frightened and clung to
his legs so tightly that he was unable to tend to his duties.
When Jennie grew older, she remained afraid of the water
—be it ocean or swimming pool—a curious phobia for a
child who grew up within sight of the Pacific. She would
only go to the edge, no farther. Once, when she was in
her late teens, on an evening when she was deeply stoned
on mescaline and lying on harem pillows in a duplex in
Venice, California, Jennie remarked on her fear. "I think
I must have gone down on the *Titanic* a couple of lives
ago. I don't even like to *drink* water."

One reason, perhaps, was that the ocean symbolized her
father's long absences from the series of frame houses that
the Bolliver family occupied in a nomadic trail up and
down the West Coast. When Ralph was away, Jennie had
to deal directly with her mother, Sandra, a sullen woman
who smoked three packs of cigarettes each day and who
continually complained of being tired. She was as gray
in mood as the smoke that curled about her. There were
three children to raise, and never enough money, and a
husband more often gone than home, and two jobs that
kept her occupied from before the sun until after the dark.
By twelve, Jennie was housekeeper and substitute mother
to the other children. She was expected to return promptly
from school, clean house, prepare dinner, and then stand
by as witness to the intensifying quarrels between Ralph
and Sandra. Once she recalled them vividly in conversation
with a girl friend: "They were real knock-down-drag-outs.
. . . And then I would have to bring Mama a Valium and
sit with her until she went to sleep—and remember to lock
the front door from the inside so Daddy couldn't get back
in the house."

When Jennie entered her teens, the marriage broke, Ralph departing for Canada to nurse his wounds, Sandra finding a new husband in the construction business and moving to Texas. Grudgingly Jennie endured a few lonely months in Texas, fended off her father's attempt to transfer her to a workers' camp in the wilds of Canada, finally achieved what she really wanted—a return to California. "I want to finish school there," she pleaded with her mother. "I want a place to go back to for reunions." In her sophomore year of high school, Jennie settled in with her grandparents, they being a peg-legged fisherman named Cap and his red-haired wife Maggie. Home again, on familiar turf, Jennie moved quickly to seize some kind of identity and independence. She renounced the Catholic Church of her childhood, informing her saddened grandparents that religion held no more appeal for her. She rebelled at any hint of grandparental authority, refusing to obey curfews or perform dictated chores in the house. Her grades plunged. "I remember when you were unhappy if you got less than an A in any subject," complained Maggie. "You were Little Miss Perfectionist. Now you come in my house reeking of marijuana smoke and you're either asleep or playing that damned rock music so loud my eardrums hurt."

Maggie knew barely half of it. For most of her sixteenth year and considerably beyond, Jennie was stoned. But hardly unique. Marijuana in 1970 was as common among the young of her town as cola. It was smoked en route to school, on the grounds, and on the way home. Jennie was stoned in class, at the beach, standing outside movie theaters waiting to see *Fantasia* or the last half of *2001: A Space Odyssey*. It was no secret. Drugs were as integral to the youth culture of the beach as bikinis and troubadors. America's attention was focused on drugs during the 1960s, for they seemed a clue to the mobs of children cursing LBJ and trying to stop a war. But when a new decade began, drugs faded from public cognition, not because they were less used, but because the media had tired of them. Jennie did not limit herself to grass: she used mescaline, LSD, cocaine if some friend was prosperous, amphetamines, barbiturates, even a snort or two of heroin. She also sold drugs, not being a dealer on any grand scale, but merely a participant in the established custom of one kid selling a lid of marijuana to another —and making a couple of dollars' profit. Once, at a party, a boy held out a fistful of assorted pills and Jennie ate them all. "I'll try anything once," she said. "That's my motto." Within an hour she had passed out and slept for two days in a friend's garage while Maggie frantically combed the neighborhood. Her best girl friend, a lush creature two years older than she named Carmen, would one day recall these shadowed moments of Jennie's young life:

"For a time there was Sunshine Acid from Berkeley, so strong you could lick a tab and 'get off,' and then still sell it if you were able to function . . . You could buy anything you wanted if you had the money—and money was no problem. Jennie spent her lunch money on drugs, or her clothes money, or the money her grandmother gave her to go to the movies. Or she sold five tabs of acid at a dollar fifty each and got one free as commission. And if all else failed, there was always somebody who would share. The whole point of doing drugs was to do them with friends and share the experience."

Carmen was also Jennie's guide into the playing fields of sex. One night, when the two girls were at a slumber party, with eyelids rimmed red and heavy from grass, Jennie revealed that she was still a virgin, at sixteen and a half years old, making the admission sound like a secret disease. It must have been a difficult confession, as Carmen loomed sexy and widely experienced with men. She smiled, rather tenderly. "My first time was not until I turned eighteen," she said, "and it was with a guy I didn't really give a damn about. It just seemed I had waited long enough." Carmen had a piece of advice for her younger friend: wait for, if not marriage, the moment when Jennie really loved someone. "If the first time is the product of love, then sex will always be beautiful," counseled Carmen. Jennie threw her arms around her friend and said, "You're so right. I'm going to wait. I want everything to be beautiful."

But a few weeks later Jennie called Carmen in tears. She had not heeded the advice. Jennie had succumbed to the exhortations of a lifeguard; their pallet had been a blanket in the back of his station wagon. The experience was humiliating. Not only had it been quick and furtive and painful, a highway patrolman had driven up in mid-coitus and shined a spotlight on the young lovers.

Hearing distraught guilt, Carmen rushed to Jennie's house. "It's all right," she soothed. "The world's not over. There'll be better ones and worse ones. Just look at it this way. The pressure's off." From there, Jennie handled sex as casually as her peers. She said "yes" or she said "no" depending upon the currents of the moment. Birth control pills were not difficult to obtain, certainly not in a community where sleeping pills were as easily purchased by youngsters as aspirin. And, helpfully, the two girls became friends with an older boy named Cope, who was a little past twenty and who worked, fortunately, for a small pharmaceutical house. He was the candy man, pills jiggling in his pockets, always available for trips up, or trips down, or trips into a psychedelic world of exploding color and fragmented mood. Moreover, Cope was an experienced traveler into various Southern California schools of weird-ness, hypnotism being his vogue of the moment when he met Carmen and Jennie. The girls declared passionate interest in being hypnotized, and Cope agreed. At his apartment, a one-room studio in Santa Monica with no furniture save pillows and more candles than on the altar of any given Catholic church, Cope directed Jennie and Carmen to remove anything "binding"—belts, bras, shoes, glasses. Then they stretched out on pillows and obeyed Cope's dictum of absolute silence and concentration. "Now start to concentrate on my two fingers," he said, holding them like a narrow V before his bearded face. His voice was gentle, reassuring. When the experiment was over, Cope was eager for their reaction. Carmen pronounced it disappointing; she was aware of everything said and done. "So was I," agreed Jennie, "but it was beautiful. I felt a glow all around my body. I felt warm and content, like being wrapped in a baby blanket."

The three—Cope, Jennie, Carmen—formed a secret soci-ety to accommodate their interests, meeting regularly to discuss their hypnotic experiences. Cope taught the girls how to perform self-hypnosis and they practiced it each day. When Maggie wondered what three young people were doing in her house, sitting on the living room sofa and staring into space as if their heads had been emptied of sense, Jennie answered patiently, "It's got nothing to do with anything bad, Grandma, it's just something we're studying. We're all searching."

"Searching for what?" asked Maggie wearily.

"For ourselves," said Jennie.

Often the girls slept over at one or the other's home, and traditionally they put themselves "under" for several moments before surrendering to sleep. "We could lose time, space, and sometimes see in all directions at once," remembered Carmen, who treasured these moments, particularly for the "vibrations" she received from her friend. "Jennie's spirit was more tangible when we did self-hypnosis. Jennie was warm, female, loving, giving. God must have had his eye on her. There are no lukewarm spirits— only good and evil. In Jennie there was good—shining, radiant good."

Maggie and Cap, relieved their home no longer contained drugged children, were good-humored about their entranced granddaughter. For a few months, Jennie was quiet and gentle. "Drugs don't interest me anymore," Jennie told someone on the telephone, while Maggie overheard. "I don't even drink coffee or tea. Nothing can interfere with what I'm learning about myself."

Then two events occurred within one week that brought an end to hypnotic fascination. At a party in Marina del Rey, the Los Angeles suburb that houses singles and the nautically inclined, Jennie met a USC medical student who began speaking of hypnotism and its possible key to the locked doors of past lives. Listening attentively, Jennie had an interesting question: If a person dies, and the body is cremated, what can possibly be left to reincarnate? Do the ashes and bits of bone form new tissue, and, if so, what happens to those powdery remains of a corpse kept in a crypt or a bronze jar on someone's mantel? The student shrugged. He had no answer. Presumably, if one went along with the notion of reincarnation, it occurred by utilizing something intangible, some cell or seed or genetic particle that contained a person's entire life experience—a "diary," as it were—and passed on to the next life. But hidden in the subconscious.

"Hypnotize me," begged Jennie. "I'm a classic subject."

The medical student demurred. He did not perform party games. Besides, an element of danger might be present.

"Just for fun," pleaded Jennie. "See if you can take me back to another life. Beyond the womb." She was hard to turn down. Jennie was vivacious, persuasive, and so enthusiastic as she neared seventeen that usually she got her wish. The aspiring doctor and his subject went into a bedroom and locked the door. Jennie stretched out on the bed and the student routinely began regressive hypnosis, noting that the girl fell immediately into a deep hypnotic state. He asked a few questions, leading her carefully back to a well-remembered twelfth birthday party, then to the age of six and the first day of school, through the painful memory of a fall from a playground swing at three. With each step into her past, she winced.

"Have you always been called Jennie?" he asked. On the bed, Jennie stirred uneasily. A shudder passed across her body. The hypnotist pressed. Did she ever have another name? Could she remember it?

"No," said Jennie firmly. "Not now . . . I don't want to . . . I'm very thirsty." Then her eyes, which to this point had been obediently closed, flew open in terror and she stared wildly at the hypnotist. But she seemed to be looking *through* him not *at* him. The student was rattled by the serious turn that had come to the experiment. He asked once again if she ever had another name.

"Stop!" cried Jennie. "Stop pushing!"

"Can you remember before you were born?"

"Why should I tell you, my prince," answered Jennie, coyly. "You know my names are all secret." She began to cry, softly, her eyes filling with tears. Then she nodded, almost imperceptibly. And she said, "Yes." A few moments of silence passed. "I am called . . ." Jennie suddenly spoke in a voice several notes lower than her regular pitch, and it was strange—tinged with a guttural foreignness. She said a few more words, either nonsensical or of another language. With that, the student wisely elected to terminate the experiment. He commanded Jennie to leave her trance. When she returned to the present, Jennie rose immediately and left the room, running out of the apartment. She did not speak of the experience until years later, when she was more sophisticated in the land of the unanswered and unexplained. And then all she said was, "I saw things that night I shouldn't have. I couldn't breathe. I felt like I was drowning . . ."

Whether frightened, or confused, or simply thrown into territory that had no road map, Jennie compensated by abandoning psychic exploration, and returned to drugs. She refused to see her regular friends for a long time, filling her dance card instead with delegates from the junk pile. Jennie ran wild, as if fleeing from an approaching storm. Her appearance, which up to now had been merely colorful and in the mode of her friends, now turned to emulation of Janis Joplin in an opium den. On her nose Jennie perched granny glasses. Her hair grew out long and natural, but with infrequent washing and care, its natural shade of ash blonde turned to mouse gray. She put a gold slave bracelet on her upper arm (and set something of a school fashion), draped brilliantly colored bedspreads from India about her waist and called them skirts, found shawls at thrift shops, wore lace-up boots from the Gay Nineties, festooned more junk jewelry about her neck and arms and fingers than would be worn by any fortune-teller at a PTA carnival. "I don't know who or what you're trying to be," decided Cap, her grandfather, "but you look like what we used to scrape off the bottom of boats."

Joined by drugged sisters in the same costumes, Jennie and her crowd camped out in Maggie's living room, smoking joints openly and defying infuriated commands to vacate the premises. Maggie could be a salty woman if she desired—a half century of marriage to a sailor had influenced her vocabulary—but the rain of curses she unleashed brought back only goofy smiles and an occasional "Right on, sister!" On a day when Maggie discovered Jennie and another girl sitting like zombies in the living room, clearly in the throes of a powerful drug, oblivious to all, the grandmother physically jerked her ward by the seat of her bedspread and propelled her into a bedroom, slamming the door. Then Maggie, steaming, ordered the second girl out of her house forever. But the stoned young woman refused to budge, staring defiantly. On her face was a smile that Maggie took to be malevolent. Promptly she found the telephone and pointedly called the police, in clear earshot of the disturbing girl. Maggie spoke agitatedly to the narcotics division, listened quietly, stammered a response, hung up in despair. Later that night she reported to Cap that the police told her that nothing could be done. "Can you believe it?" groused Maggie. "The cops said, 'Just try and get the girl out of your house, but don't let her get hurt because she could sue you.'" Maggie threw up her hands in despair. "What kind of world has this become? I can't kick a drug addict out of my own house because she might sue me."

Jennie began to travel dark streets. Mecca for the young and disenchanted was the Sunset Strip in Hollywood, and though it was fifty miles from where she lived, Jennie had only to hold out her thumb and transportation could be obtained. Once there, she found birds of all feathers, most using false IDs to enter the discotheques and palaces of rock music, sashaying up and down the aorta of neon fantasy, or just lounging on the curb in front of Filthy McNasty's nightclub, "laid back," as the vogue called it. And if she needed currency, it was not difficult to earn. One Sunday morning, Jennie awoke groggy in a motel room near the Hollywood Bowl. Beside her, still sleeping, was a plumpish man well past forty whose bald head had infant hair transplants that seemed like struggling weeds in the desert. She loathed him, even though he had paid her thirty dollars for the night beside his heavy body. Creeping to the dresser where his pants were thrown, Jennie found his wallet and started to take the rest of his money. But the first thing she encountered was a color photograph of the man, standing beside a melancholy woman with unhidden pain in her eyes, and two small, impeccably groomed girls. They posed in front of a story-book house, probably in the Valley, with a peach tree erupted in glorious blossom. Jennie stared at the picture for a long time, feeling the sense of family that it contained, then she put the wallet back in its place, kissed her trick lightly on the forehead, and left.

At home, the situation grew more tense and ugly. Jennie's behavior would have been difficult for any parent to handle, but for Maggie and Cap, two generations removed, it was beyond a frame of reference. On a night when Jennie emerged unsteadily from her room, her eyes streaked with red, her hair in electric shock, her breasts promising to fall from a transparent and unbuttoned blouse, Maggie tried tenderness. She embraced Jennie and said emotionally, "I love you so dearly, but I don't know how to handle this new Jennie. Tell me what to do, honey. I'm old and I don't understand what you're doing to yourself."

Jennie feigned astonishment. "I'm the same person I always was, Grandma." Her mouth was glazed, her words disconnected. "You're simply imagining things. I'm just modern."

On another night, grandmother and granddaughter worked themselves into a yelling match, climaxed by Maggie ordering Jennie not to leave the house. Arrogantly, Jennie opened the front door and started outside. "If you go out that door," warned Maggie, "then don't bother to come home." The ultimatum was a common one in Jennie's town. It could be heard on any night, in a thousand households. Jennie's response was a smirk. Maggie rushed to the door and did not hesitate. She slapped her grand-daughter—hard, across the face. Then the old woman broke down and sobbed. "I'm so sorry," she said. "I've never done that before. I just couldn't think of anything else." With a glimmer of understanding, Jennie nodded, but then she was gone, down the sidewalk, disappearing into a battered car at the curb whose occupants were yelling at her to hurry, and whose music could be heard, Cap reasoned, miles out to sea.

Maggie was at the point when she was preparing to call the Los Angeles County juvenile authorities and implore them to take custody of her granddaughter, when Jennie's real mother turned up once again and announced that she was taking the troublesome girl to Seattle. Naturally Jennie balked at the idea of leaving home and friends, but there was no room for negotiation. Sandra, her mother, gave her two options: Seattle or the juvenile home.

Once ensconced in Eeattle, Jennie began running around the same old track. At a rock concert she took LSD, then removed her blouse and danced topless in the aisle until two policemen arrested her, scolded her, and told her that what was tolerated in L.A. was not appreciated in Seattle.

She took to shoplifting minor items, notebook paper, for example, and told her new friends that she was "liberating" such goods and fighting "capitalist oppression," although it is doubtful Jennie had any notion what the potent phrase meant. When all maternal counsel was rebuked, Sandra threw her out, and for a few nights Jennie found herself on the cold, damp streets of Seattle. Someone led her to someone else, and eventually Jennie found shelter in an informal foster home operated by a black man named Prince, whose white wife, Samantha, was reportedly a witch, or at least the dozen youngsters who lived in the old, gabled white frame house said so. The house had garrets and hidden corners behind stairwells where secret conversations could be held, or quick urgent couplings.

Jennie was not popular among the wards of Prince during her first weeks in residence. She was arrogant, temperamental, rude. When boys in the home asked her out on dates, she refused haughtily, pretending instead to be going steady with a university philosophy major. In truth her only friend was a thin, equally lonely eighteen-year-old black boy whom she had met on the street during her homeless period in the Queen Anne district. His name was Claude, and since neither of them had any money, their dates consisted of window-shopping and sitting above the lake, speaking of music and witchcraft.

One night, watching Jennie streak like a comet through the gabled house, Prince stopped her and led her to one of the secret places for a talk. He knew little of her background, save that she was one of a forgotten number of youngsters who had been cast out of broken homes and were trying to survive. Pleased to be asked, Jennie delivered a marathon biography. Prince listened patiently to the cocky recollections, undermined as they were by loneliness and insecurity. He told her that she was not unique. Jennie was no more or less abused than any of the kids who had drifted in and out of his house in recent years. And those who blamed their parents as an excuse to embrace drugs and sex—with no more commitment than soldiers on a weekend pass—were common in Prince's eyes.

"Have you ever loved anybody?" he asked gently.

Jennie thought on this and shook her head negatively.

In her early teens, she had waited weekly for love to arrive, but lately she had not fretted much over its absence.

Prince said he was not surprised. "And the reason is," he suggested, "you don't believe in *anything*. A dog believes in his master. A whore in her pimp. A priest in his bishop. A man in his woman. You'd better grab something to hold onto, or you're gonna be sucked under."

On her seventeeth birthday, Jennie was given a surprise party by the kids in the house, who found her more agreeable after the long conversation with Prince. Jennie broke down. She cried as she opened gifts as random as a string of amber worry beads, a peacock feather, a roach clip, a book of Rosicrucian philosophy. A girl named Katie gave her a diary. "I love you all," wept Jennie. "You're my family now. I'm sorry I've been such a pain in the ass."

By the time ice cream and cake were served, Jennie's stomach was pitching. She put it down to the excitement of the night, and too many glasses of wine. But during the party, she rushed to the bathroom and was sick.

Several weeks would pass before Jennie wrote her first entry in the diary, not until she had recuperated from the abortion of a two-month-old fetus growing within her. The fee was seventy-five dollars and she borrowed it from her friends. They comforted her and assured her that the decision had been the right one. She was not even sure who the father was. All of this she told her diary. Then she wrapped her amber worry beads around the book, put it beneath her pillow, and despite the pain, slept very soundly.

CHAPTER ELEVEN

When it was over, and assemblages could be made, and the story followed, a swami in India was asked to comment on a curious coincidence. With more than two billion people on earth, why did destiny choose two young women from the same state, California, to play principal roles? And what is destiny, anyway? The wise man, who lived beside the Ganges and drank of its sulfuric water each day, and who, it was said, could make his body spin like a falling meteor and cause slivers of fire to dance on the holy river and leap out as bidden to play around his fingertips, smiled. "Each life is a strand in the rope of mankind," he said, "and only the gods know how and when one strand will entwine with another. That is the best definition of destiny I can give to you."

Her name was Annabella, and it suited her, sounding like music. She was a "many splendored child" in the eyes of her mother, and "a blessing of joy and happiness" to her father. The parents, whose names were Dick and Jane, could have posed for the cover of a government booklet promoting the American dream. Annabella, their only child, was born in 1946, the year in which computers first appeared, in which Winston Churchill pronounced the phrase "Iron Curtain," and in which post-war babies were counted in such record numbers that it was a cause for naïve rejoicing.

The California of Annabella Tremont was far removed

from the hedonistic beach world of Jennie Bolliver. Annabella was reared in the middle of the state, a place rich with fruit and wine, with softly rolling hills and a sense of permanence. Victorian houses bespeak the flavor of New England. Families trace ancestors back to centuries past when Spaniards arrived; a settlement was thriving near San Jose when the Declaration of Independence was being signed in Philadelphia. Few more lovely pieces of earth can be found, and after hard storms, rainbows arch and fall into the valley where Annabella grew. When she became a woman, Annabella studied Eastern religions, and she came across a passage that caught her attention. "Some people believe that an unborn baby *chooses* its parents," she told her mother. "If that is true, then I chose wisely."

Dick Tremont worked for a utility and made twenty-five dollars a week when his daughter was born, a year after his discharge from the Coast Guard. He was a quiet, hardworking man with strong shoulders and hands, and intelligence that removed him from the outdoors that he loved into an executive job that he only tolerated. In middle age, he still looked as if he preferred hard labor to dictating letters. A dignity emitted from Dick Tremont, an old-fashioned courtliness, a respect for all men. He was a perfect counterbalance to Jane, whose Italian blood gave her not only dark beauty but a temperament in concert.

They had planned a large family, but Annabella was the only child that Jane was able to carry full term. No matter. From the moment of her birth, Annabella was the altar at which her parents worshiped. She was dark, like her mother, with deep, large eyes of brown that matched her hair. The early years were unremarkable, save for the grace with which she lived them. Annabella was the child who got the most valentines in her class, who was invited to every birthday party, who issued calm orders to her friends that were always obeyed, who read books, painted pictures, composed poetry and music. Clearly she was marked as special. The diseases of childhood rarely lingered, as if she was beyond their curse. "Annabella was not only the most beautiful little girl I ever saw," remembered a teacher, "she had enormous potential. When the other kids had trouble remembering that if you mix red and blue you get purple, Annabella could name six

shades of purple. How many eight-year-olds know the
word *mauve?*"

It must not be construed that Annabella was the baby
goddess of daintiness and saintliness, for she burst across
the wooded fields near the fine home that Dick built,
animals trailing after as if in a parade. She found rocks
that looked like jewels in fast-running streams, and the
wings of butterflies held her attention like masterworks
in a museum. When she tumbled out of trees, she came
up laughing; even the dirt on her face was artful. Hers
was the good life, the American promise. There were no
shadows. No dark corners were permitted in the house.
Surely she was heiress to a future of rich reward.

Now, looking back, Jane well remembers the moment
that her daughter's life changed. It is as clear to the mother
as the portrait of Annabella that hangs like a shrine over
the fireplace, the child in white lace, two favorite poodle
dogs sitting obediently in her lap. There are confused
moments when Jane cannot grasp *why* everything happened the way it did, but there is no quarrel in her mind
over *when* it all began.

When Annabella was ten, her mother surrendered to
the exhortations of her father, Carlo, who had begged
since the child was nine for the privilege of showing the
child the old country. Italy! Carlo insisted that his granddaughter could not wait any longer before she understood
the land of her maternal origin. Tradition must be honored.
Relatives must be introduced. Feasts must be laid in outdoor restaurants beside the sea, under lattice arbors of
grapes and roses. In her heart, Jane felt the little girl was
too young to plunge into the volatile land of her forebears,
none of whom spoke more than broken English. But Carlo
was persistent, warning that he was old and his heart was
rusty, and his death would be impossibly melancholy if
he could not show his American grandchild the beauty of
la vita italiana.

Finally, sighing, Jane sent her daughter off to Italy for
three weeks. It would be more than three months before
Annabella returned to California, and on that day, Jane
would know that irrevocable change had taken place.

The family album bears witness to Annabella's happy
initiation into Italy. Photographs show the little American
girl posing happily in front of Carlo's old stone house in
Forte dei Marmi, its façade covered with climbing roses
and geraniums. In others, old women in black throw
eager arms around their distant relative, blowing clouds
of garlic and olive oil through a few gold teeth. Oddly,
a "European look" had already come to Annabella, as if
it was meant for her to discard the manner of middle California and put on the robes of Northern Italy. In every
picture, Carlo was proud and expansive. He was a little
old man with a stomach crowded with pasta and wine,
with eyes merry and bleary. His hair was as white as the
marble in nearby Carrara, where four centuries earlier
Michelangelo had personally chosen the stone for his
David. Carlo had worked in the quarry until his lungs
could no longer tolerate the glistening powder that rose
in clouds from the explosions of dynamite that pried
marble from its place. Now he was retired and had
nothing but time, time to show Annabella where he had
worked when he was young and strong, time to stroll with
her on the Italian Riviera, time to stop and eat shrimp in
tomato and garlic sauce, time to sit in the surf and feel
the warm sea that bathed the feet of emperors, time to
visit the tombs of family ancestors, time to tell Annabella
the story of the cowardly fascists who tumbled so easily
to the ranting of Mussolini—and how Carlo led a band
of courageous partisans.

Between Annabella and Carlo grew the special relationship that can exist between the very old and the very
young. When the old women of the town tried to share
the child, Carlo shooed them away. He cared for her as
if she was Victor Emmanuel's daughter. Annabella awoke
each morning in the stone cottage and smelled delicious
odors rising from the kitchen—breakfast rolls with cheese
hot and runny baked inside, steaming chocolate with milk
taken from a neighbor's cow a half hour before sunrise,
fresh grapes and apricots, a little glass of red wine with
a spoonful of sugar on special occasions. The agreed-upon
three weeks disappeared quickly, before Annabella could
even learn the names of her third and fourth cousins. Carlo

telephoned across the ocean to his daughter and begged Jane for an extension. When she wavered, Annabella grabbed the telephone and shouted, "*Buon giorno*, Mama, I'm learning Italian!" Jane sighed and agreed. "Grandpa's kidnaped our child," she told Dick, but he laughed and saw no peril in an extension.

One afternoon Annabella burst into the stone cottage to wake Carlo from his post-luncheon nap. It was time for their daily walk. Something was wrong; an eerie silence bespoke it. Annabella found her grandfather crumpled beside his bed, his face leaden and drained of color, an arm outstretched for help. The other hand pressed against his heart. Carlo tried to smile as Annabella rushed to him. His breath came in one last rattle, and then he died.

The experience was profound for Annabella, discovering her beloved grandfather in his last moments, then staying for the funeral and mingling her tears with the villagers who had known Carlo for almost eight decades. On the day she left Forte dei Marmi, Annabella insisted on going alone to the grave, where she placed a bouquet of wild daisies and climbing roses on the fine marker of white marble from Michelangelo's quarry. She had seen the stone all summer, propped up against a work shed, not knowing that Carlo had selected it personally. The child stood beside the marker for a long while, sorrowing that the quickening chill of autumn had taken away her perfect summer.

Annabella returned to California and was changed, somber now, speaking only Italian. "I *am* Italian," she told Jane, who was disturbed over the transformation. "I sent away a ten-year-old American girl," she told Dick, "and back comes an adult Italian woman." But time passed, and the years blurred, and Annabella was once more Americanized, even though she often begged her mother for a return to Italy. By the time Annabella was in high school, she could not have been distinguished on sight from her sister cheerleaders who swirled in ecstasy over football heroes and knew the words to every Elvis Presley song. But Jane saw more, she knew that her daughter was on a holding pattern, that the die was cast, that the day would come when she would leave the valley. And then —Jane knew it in her heart—she would never come back.

* * *

When Annabella was graduated from high school, her parents gave her a second trip to Europe. This time Jane went along, ostensibly to visit the relatives in Italy but to keep an eye on her daughter as well. At the end of the designated month, Jane had to return home, where her job as a bookkeeper was waiting. "I can't go back, Mama," said Annabella. It was not a request, rather a statement of fact. Jane did not even argue with Annabella; she only insisted that her daughter stay in constant touch and to telephone collect if a problem arose. Back home, Dick complimented his wife on her decision. "I know it was hard for you to do," he said, "but let her wander. Let her get it out of her system. It's her life, not ours." Besides, her money would run out before very long, predicted Dick.

He was wrong. Annabella stayed two years in Europe and the Middle East, always finding temporary work to sustain her wanderlust. She sold rugs at a tourist shop in Athens at the foot of the Acropolis; she worked as a nurse's aide in Madrid emptying chamber pots and dressing wounds—and reading Hemingway; she sold *Herald Tribunes* in Paris, she taught English in Istanbul. It was the mid-1960s, and everywhere could be found nomadic young Americans, drifting through the season of discontent. In California, Jane was on edge. She wrote Annabella letters several times a week, all variations on a continuing theme: Come home.

"I want her back," said Jane to her husband. "She's my only child."

"And mine, too," said Dick. "But she's grown and we have no right to conduct her life for her. A person should be allowed to do what she wants, as long as she's not hurting anyone else."

Annabella returned to California in 1966, when she was twenty. Her beauty was remarkable, skin tanned dark gold from the Mediterranean sun, hair long and lustrous. She complained about the several extra pounds attributable to the pasta of Italy and the sauces of France, but she was, in truth, voluptuous. She now spoke fluent Italian, good French and Spanish, passable Greek. "I'm one of those people who can pick up languages quickly," said Annabella. "When I go back, they'll help me get work."

Jane was stunned. Go *back*? "But this is your home."

Annabella nodded gently. She embraced her mother. "Maybe I can explain it this way," she said. "Right now, this minute, I am in and of this country. But I am not a part of it."

But home is seductive, as is a country whose telephones work, whose toilets flush, whose appetites can be sated by boulevards of hamburgers and California supermarkets with produce so tempting it could be put in the Museum of Modern Art. Annabella's intention to stay only long enough to earn money for a return to foreign shores fell victim to *la vita americana*. Oh, she never woke up on any particular morning and announced that she had changed her mind, but with each passing week, then month, then year, the mother felt her heart beating more contentedly.

Resuming her education, Annabella became interested first in art, then medicine. Her rationale was that she could learn a hospital discipline that would be valuable for employment in Europe. Her junior college grades were good enough for admission to Stanford, where she studied X-ray technology. The classroom was stimulating, but when she was deemed sophisticated enough to transfer knowledge to actual hospital endeavor, a sore disenchantment took over. Among those who worked in the X-ray section of a hospital near San Francisco, Annabella found little or no great calling. It was a job, nothing else, like a petty office rife with feuds, jealousies, and goldbricking. At the end of a shift, technicians often ducked into the toilet to avoid a mangled patient being wheeled down the hallway, for fear it would add an unpaid-for half hour to the schedule. One morning Annabella discovered a minor leak in an X-ray machine that had the possibility of growing dangerous—to patients and staff. When her superior refused to act, Annabella went to the department head; he thanked her and did nothing. "I've discovered I don't really like doctors," Annabella told a girl friend the day she quit in despair. "Doctors have this attitude that says, 'I am a god, and if I make a mistake that is okay.' But this is wrong. Gods make mistakes."

When she had first returned from the long odyssey abroad, Annabella encountered a social gap. She had difficulty adjusting to the new crop of young men in her town. The year she had left home, 1963, the boys were barbered and tailored and the thoughts in their heads were traditionally American—combining sex, apathy, and ambition. Now, with a president assassinated in Dallas and the streets filling with hirsute youth in patched jeans crying defiance of an immoral war, questioning the foundations of their nation, Annabella felt alien. She dated infrequently. Conversation was difficult. Two years away and she knew not what to say. Then she ran into a boy from her high school.

Jimmy was his name, and how he had changed. Annabella vaguely remembered him as a kid interested in agriculture and sports. Now he was a shaggy young man with a blond mustache that drooped like sagging parentheses. He played melancholy songs on a guitar that was permanently strapped about his shoulders. As yet there was no purpose in his life that Annabella could discern, but in his manner was an encompassing gentleness, a *sweetness* that had only recently come to American men. Jimmy had a job of sorts, in landscaping, but it was only a means of minimal support. His needs were modest. He required enough money to buy guitar strings and a lid of Colombian when it was around, and half-gallon jugs of wine to take on long hikes into the wilderness where he told Annabella the name of every tree and flower.

"I've fallen in love," Annabella told her mother after dating Jimmy several months. "I didn't want it to happen, and I didn't think it would happen. But it has—and we want to get married." Jane was frankly surprised at her daughter's choice. She had not expected a young woman as worldly as Annabella to discover love with a man who had no more ambition than a sunflower. Jane expressed these thoughts to Dick, but she never told Annabella. "My daughter is also my friend," said Jane, "and I must accept her decision."

The wedding was lovely, though difficult to reach for those not comfortable in the outdoor life. The couple chose a stone quarry for their altar, in the lime and tan hills near San Jose. They recited their own marriage vows, simple, dedicated to love and mutual respect. The word "obey" was, of course, deleted. The bride worn an antique wedding gown of cream lace with a Spanish mantilla that

rose in a tower behind her dark hair. Jimmy had on a tan
leather suit and an open shirt, because, try as he could, he
was unable to affix a tie around his neck. The groom
played a serenade on his guitar for Annabella, and there
was dancing amid fountains of red wine and platters of
fruit and cheese. "I love this woman!" Jimmy cried tri-
umphantly. Annabella told Jane later that she had such a
good time at the wedding that she wanted to do it all over
again. She wished that Carlo had been there to lead the
dancing.

The newlyweds set up housekeeping in a log cabin on
a thirty-acre tract of heavily wooded land on a mountain-
side near their town. From their windows could be viewed
pine trees as sentinels, and the light that filtered through
the branches was golden. The cabin became a home for
animals—dogs, cats, an occasional coyote, goats, whatever •
creature that wandered by and elected to stay for a while.
Annabella and Jimmy often awoke to find their quilt
crowded with small critters, others sprawled on the hooked
rug that the lady of the house had made to spread on the
wide, rough plank floor.

For a time, Annabella busied herself playing house,
immersed in domesticity. She saw herself as a pioneer
wife, sewing curtains, making pottery, growing vegetables,
raising chickens, milking goats. Periodically, Jimmy worked
as a gardener, but he preferred to stay at home restoring
antiques and watching Annabella efficiently run the house.
When Jane visited several months into the marriage, she
felt that Annabella was becoming more mother than wife,
Jimmy more child than husband. But, she reasoned, relationships have worked on a script stranger than that. One
thing that did bother her was Jimmy's increasing use of
alcohol. He had moved from wine to stronger spirits, and
Jane saw that her daughter bit her lip when Jimmy reeled
toward the kitchen for a new drink, or sometimes passed
out in his chair beside the fireplace.

At this point, destiny sent another player onto the stage,
who at first proved a welcome diversion for Annabella.
He was an Indian youth, from Bombay, newly come to
town as an exchange student. Annabella's father, Dick,
encountered the boy, whose name was Sanjoy, at work,

liked him, discovered he lacked a place to live while he was employed over the summer, invited him home for dinner. Annabella was always pleased to meet someone from a foreign country; she liked Sanjoy immediately. He was a handsome youth approaching twenty, smart, something of a hustler, and consumed with ambition, a quality far more easy to tend in America than in India. Already he was dressing in jeans, trying to fit in words like "cool" and "right on" into his sentences. But they seemed as awkward as a temple dancer attempting rock and roll.

With their large home quiet and empty after the departure of Annabella to marriage and the log cabin, the Tremonts asked Sanjoy if he wanted to move in for the summer. The invitation was happily accepted, and quickly an intimate and rewarding friendship developed between the visitor and Annabella, their bond being his *foreignness*. The lawyer's son from Bombay represented a link to the world out there, the one which Annabella sorely missed at the cabin in the woods. She was lonely. Friends had not only been few, but comfortable chiefly in conversation that encompassed music and pop psychology. The relationship between Annabella and Sanjoy was never sexual, not even a hint thereof. From the beginning, neither had the slightest interest in the other romantically, developing instead into a "brother-sister" feeling, stronger, perhaps, than lovers.

Annabella took charge. She suggested that Sanjoy wash all the grease out of his hair and introduced him to a blow dryer. She took him to flea markets where secondhand jeans could be bought for two dollars. They ate hamburgers and gossiped and stopped for tea. An eager listener, Annabella wanted to know everything about India, encouraging her friend to speak of harems and holy men and the caste system that will segregate India despite a hundred laws to ban it. With six hundred million people, Sanjoy told her, there must be social regimentation. Identities are hard enough to come by in any culture.

When Sanjoy went back to college in the fall, one hundred dred miles down the coast near San Luis Obispo, Annabella suffered depression. It showed in her face. Jimmy saw it, too, using the innocent affection as ammunition in quarrels, suggesting that his wife was more emotionally committed to Sanjoy than she let on. At this, Annabella flared and shot back angry denials. But as Jimmy's accusations continued, she chose a course of silence, even when her husband drifted into the cabin past midnight and either threw up on the bathroom floor or spun into the bedroom ripe for a fight. Annabella told a girl friend that a caste system was now operative between her and Jimmy. Annabella preferred classical music but deferred to Jimmy's enchantment with acid rock. She liked to speak of art; he fell conversationally asleep if a name like Raphael arose at his dinner table. She went back to Stanford, taking a few courses in literature and psychology. Jimmy thought it not only time-consuming—the drive was an hour either way—but wasteful of the money it took to buy gasoline for their Volkswagen. And if Annabella really spoiled for a fight, all she had to mention was her passion for travel, of returning to Forte dei Marmi, or perhaps even India, where Sanjoy regularly invited her. "*This* is our home," answered Jimmy to all suggestions that the two might venture out of their nest. "We aren't going anywhere."

That's true, thought Annabella. Unchallengeably true.

There came the night when Annabella invited Sanjoy to bring a date to the cabin for dinner. She wanted it to be special. From a book in the library she copied down the recipe for *tandoori* chicken, spending three days marinating the fowl in honey, yoghurt, and spices, then popping it into an extremely hot oven to seal the juices. Vegetables were steamed in the scents of cumin and curry powder, and pita bread was as close as she could come to the *nan* that Sanjoy enjoyed in Bombay. With disinterest, Jimmy watched the preparations, and on the night of the feast appeared roaring drunk. He had wrecked the VW a week before, and on this important night chose to describe the accident in clinical detail. His wife and guests listened with polite boredom. Jimmy spilled his wine, put his food in his mouth and it fell out when he talked. The chicken was undercooked, he said, the vegetables smelled suspicious. Finally, Annabella ran to the kitchen to hide her tears. Sanjoy tried to make peace by saying that Indian food took some getting used to, that Annabella's was the most authentic he had eaten since leaving Bombay.

Presently Jimmy fell asleep on a pile of pillows, his dogs

snuggling at his body. The evening crept to an awkward close. When he said goodbye, Sanjoy hugged Annabella and whispered his continuing invitation to join him on a trip to India, with or without her husband. The next day Annabella called a girl friend and swore her to secrecy and said she might soon accept the offer. She had played the dutiful wife in the woods for a very long run; putting some space and distance into a rotting marriage did not seem inappropriate.

Clandestinely they planned their trip. Both had to tread carefully, for if Jimmy even suspected, there would surely be a wrenching drama. "I love Jimmy very much," Annabella told her friend Sally, "but I don't know if I can play mother to him the rest of his life. He's a little boy. A dear little boy at times. But he hasn't grown up and doesn't show signs of ever doing it." Sally, a practical sort who had a master's degree in English literature but who now made wall hangings, suggested marriage counseling. That had been tried already, said Annabella. Jimmy had broken two appointments, and when he finally showed for the third, he was tight and giggled the whole hour.

One autumn night in 1973, Annabella sat with her parents in their home, talking quietly in front of a roaring fire. It was crisp and in the nearby mountains snow was expected. Annabella tried to be cheerful, but she was not successful; Jane saw through her daughter's charade like a person trying to smile away a migraine. Then the telephone rang intrusively and Dick went to answer it.

His face was pale and tight when he returned. He stammered, and both women sensed that something was terribly wrong. "I don't know how to tell you this except to say it quickly," he began. Earlier on this night, Sanjoy and three college friends had been at a party in San Luis Obispo. Much wine had been drunk. One of the youths was a pilot and owned a private plane. He suggested a joyride to show Sanjoy the splendors of California's coastline by night.

"And?" urged Annabella, trying to hurry her father.

And the four boys got into the plane and prepared to take off. The night was wretched. From the sea, fog was rolling in to endanger visibility. The plane lifted off the

ground, but it stayed aloft only moments before falling
back onto the runway. An explosion! Fire rushed over the
little craft and devoured it. The boys were trapped in a
crematorium.

Sanjoy? Annabella's hand flew to her mouth.

With enormous sadness, Dick shook his head and turned
away. Sanjoy died instantly. The fire incinerated all of
them. It took hours to find enough flesh for identification.
Annabella moaned like one of the old women in Italy,
collapsing and surrendering to grief. She wept like she had
not done since the morning long ago in the stone cottage
where Carlo had died with his arm outstretched to her.

The tragedy forged temporary peace in the marriage.
For several months the young couple lived quietly in their
cabin. Regularly Jimmy swore off drinking, and though it
rarely lasted more than a few days, alcohol did not seem
to dominate his life. Sober, he was a brilliant artisan and
a devoted lover. Annabella marveled at her husband's
talent in restoring furniture. He possessed the same dedi-
cation for work that she had observed among certain craftsmen of Italy and Greece. If the truce held between them,
Annabella speculated about opening an antique store to
sell Jimmy's lovingly refinished pieces.

"Are you happy?" asked her friend Sally one day in a
visit to the cabin.

"I suppose so," answered Annabella. "If you define
happiness as the lack of unhappiness."

But wars, be they between nations or men and women,
break out over an accumulation of grievances stored up
over the years. Thus it was with Annabella and Jimmy,
who found themselves in full fury again within months.
Jimmy's position was that his wife was a snob, a pretentious one at that, with a roving eye and intolerance for
the quiet and basic life. Roaring back, Annabella charged
that her husband was a child, an alcoholic child who was
destructive and vengeful. Three wrecked automobiles
rusted this minute in junkyards as testimony to his dangerous nature.

Jimmy wouldn't buy it. His wife *drove* him to drink;
she so tormented his head that he had bad luck on the
highway; his wife cast spells on him—consciously or other-

wise. Alcoholics always have excuses, countered Annabella. They fought. They flung furniture at one another. They screamed until their throats were raw. They cried and hugged and promised and broke apart to curse anew.

In the end, on a fevered midnight when all the animals barked and jumped about nervously in the combat zone, the couple agreed to separate. But it was Jimmy who moved out, taking refuge in his own mother's house. "That's beautiful!" shouted Annabella with sarcasm. "*You* go home to Mama." Staying behind in the cabin, Annabella nursed her anger. She nailed the windows shut and put new locks on the doors so that Jimmy could not gain admittance. Often she lay in her bed in the chilled darkness and heard him pounding at the cabin, the dogs yelping joyously at his unsuccessful homecoming.

After a few months of separation, Jimmy telephoned and pleaded for a meeting. He had straightened himself out, or so his sales talk went. He was in a therapy group, and there he had recognized his immaturity and coincidental dependence on alcohol. His voice was earnest. Against her better judgment, Annabella gave in. But any "meeting" would have to take place on neutral ground, and she would bring along her friend Sally as moral support.

The three dined with strain and talked around the issues. In mid-meal, Jimmy ordered a bottle of wine to celebrate the reunion. He saw Annabella's look of anxiety, and he soothed her. "It's only for a toast," he insisted. But he drank most of the bottle himself, then another half bottle, and excused himself twice to go to the men's room, where, Annabella assumed, he was nipping at a pint that showed suspiciously in his jean jacket.

Afterwards, in Annabella's Honda, driving in the nearby town of Santa Cruz, Jimmy began to cry. He begged to go home. "That's where I'm taking you," said Annabella. "To your mama's."

"No, honey," pleaded Jimmy, trying to grab the wheel and change direction. "I mean *our* home. Just for one night. You'll see. It'll be wonderful." In the back seat, Sally watched the scene with great discomfort. She had recently broken up with her lover, and the unpleasantness was an echo of what she had gone through. Annabella put up with her husband's pleadings for a few more minutes, then stopped at a traffic light and extricated herself from Jimmy's lurching embrace. "I will let you come home when you stop drinking," she said. "And I mean *stop*. Once and for all. Period. Not until then."

Jimmy took his wife's face in his hands and held it tenderly. "I really love you," he said softly. Then, abruptly, he opened the car door, jumped out, and ran down a dark street. Annabella watched him disappear. The light turned to green and she drove on. She shrugged. She was used to theatrical scenes like this. Besides, it was a wet Saturday night and people acted crazy on wet Saturday nights.

But she slept poorly and the next day began to worry. Jimmy's parents answered her telephone inquiry. No, they had not heard from their son since yesterday; they assumed he was with Annabella. Hanging up, she quickly canvassed all of their friends. It was a very long Sunday. Annabella stayed at her parents' home, some unexplainable force keeping her away from the cabin in the woods. On Monday afternoon, Annabella asked her father to accompany her to the cabin. She had decided that Jimmy was surely there, holed up, probably passed out. If her suspicions were true, she would need Dick to help get him out.

When father and daughter arrived at the clearing, an eerie silence hung over the forest. The animals were outside, but strangely silent. Light filtered gray and leaden through the pine trees. Her heart constricted. Things were out of balance. They opened the front door and went inside. They saw Jimmy right away. He was lying on the floor, face pressed against the rug that Annabella had made. One arm was outstretched in a futile cry for help. Jimmy was dead, his stomach full of barbiturates.

A psychiatric resident at the hospital was summoned to Annabella's bed to treat her depression—so severe that sedatives failed to give her rest. The doctor's counsel was for the young woman to stop blaming herself. The words did no good. And when Sally came to comfort her friend, Annabella turned her head to the wall and refused to speak. She was consumed by guilt. She felt like an agent of death.

CHAPTER TWELVE

She came here often, alone, to the palisades of the St. Lawrence, to a special place where she could sit in silence and feel the presence of history and the promise of something more, over there, just out of reach. Across the powerful river, a haze often rises from the water and shrouds Quebec City, where mossy cannons guard the ghosts of medieval walls like the sentinels of Elsinore. In the late afternoon, the sun drives out the gray and transforms cathedral spires into towers of silver and fire. But having meditated on these wonders, she dutifully turned her back and accepted the banality of life in a hard and ugly little town called Lévis.

Here, where once Iroquois and Huron war parties fought Cartier and Champlain, where Americans under the command of Benedict Arnold vaingloriously failed to drive out the British, forests were hewn in the twentieth century and fertile land bulldozed to build a bleak community void of charm save its position on the riverbank and its view of a great city. A visitor newly come to Lévis might imagine that some demented urban planner tore out great chunks of America-at-its-worst and grafted them onto this place of history. The blight was cement plants—trailer parks— cut-rate motels—shopping centers with parking lots big enough to accommodate third-rate carnivals—sulfurous smoke—and potholes to savage tires.

The young woman who sat beside the river was named Marie-Andrée Leclerc, and hers was a predicament of poignance. Huddled on her bench, biting river winds whipping about her, she watched the ferryboats prowl from one bank to the other. How simple it is to board the ferry, pay the dollar, and a quarter of an hour later set foot in a city where Roosevelt and Churchill twice met, where the rhythm is that of modern France yet the architecture and narrow cobbled streets left over from centuries past, where sleek people read *Paris-Match* and linger three hours over dinner and speak of Montego Bay and a place to have a Citroën best tuned.

Marie-Andrée was more than fifteen minutes and a dollar away from the seduction of Quebec City. Her horizons stopped at river's edge. In her heart she wanted desperately to cross the river and find a place behind the Citadel's ancient walls. But it had taken Marie-Andrée twenty-eight years just to get this far. And she knew her chances of ever leaving Lévis were between slim and meager. She was small-town in every way, and she accepted it. When a woman nears thirty, dreams are replaced by reality. Or should have been.

Twenty miles deeper inland was the place where Marie-Andrée was born and reared, a farming village called St. Charles de Bellechasse, snuggled in a valley of rolling hills and taking about a minute and a half to drive through, even if one slows to glance at the church and graveyard. Two forces dominated village life—the Catholic church and the Canadian Pacific Railway—and both were important in the home of Augustin Leclerc. He was a conductor for the railroad, a job of some prominence in a town of 1,500 people. Once he had been a strong and strapping lad with thick wavy hair and an ambition to claim, or at least see, the world. Then he fell in love with the local belle, a merry young girl named Marie-Paule. She was short and tended toward plump, he was tall and soon to turn gaunt save his round belly.

Dutiful Catholics, Augustin and Marie-Paule produced six children—four girls and two boys—and though each birth was cause for rejoicing in the Leclercs' neat but modest frame house on the street grandly called Avenue Royale, slowly died the conductor's dream of shedding the anonymity of life in a place so small it was not on the map. Augustin's hair turned gray and he looked old before it was time. So did his wife, although she retained an infectious laugh and a sweet face that resembled that of the actress Spring Byington. The color to describe them, their lives, their town, was gray. The church was gray and so were the tombstones adjoining. The Couvent des Soeurs, founded in 1878, had only ivory lace curtains that flapped in the windows of the classrooms to relieve the bleakness. "There was no spice, no fun, and nothing to do in St. Charles," once recalled Marie-Andrée, "but there was love in our house and at the time it seemed enough."

Marie-Andrée was the third child, the classic one in the middle who had to scrap for an identity. Of the four daughters, she was the most slender, with a sharp, pinched face and a pointed nose that her spectacles could not get a grasp on. They always slid down the slope and gave her, even as a teen-ager, the look of a careless older woman. Three of the Leclerc girls shared the same bedroom in the house, and though Marie-Andrée was the quietest, the one to whom least attention was paid, she was the most romantic, concealing *Madame Bovary* under her pillow and staring at her face in the mirror to search desperately for latent beauty. On holidays, she signed gift cards to her father "From Marie-Andrée, *la plus belle.*" The name stuck and became something to mock. Her sisters and brothers took to calling her "La Plus Belle" and she did not recognize the tint of derision, so happy was she to be ranked— by self-acclaim—as the most beautiful. Only when some of the farm boys in the village began leaping out and making grotesque faces and yelling, *"Embrasse-moi, La Plus Belle,"* did Marie-Andrée understand. And suffer mortification.

After that, she decided the only thing open to her was to become a Carmelite nun, reasoning that a life of sacrificing prayer, locked away from the world as the bride of Christ, would fulfill her needs. There was, moreover, an air of the exotic about Carmelites. Once the commitment was made, it meant total withdrawal from the world. One of the families in the village had a relative in the severe order, and when the nun was visited in the convent, she could be glimpsed only behind bars, shadows over her face, serenely blessing her kin and lingering but for a few moments. Marie-Andrée read about the Carmelites and discovered that a sister in the order begins her day at 3 A.M. by flinging herself to the cold stone floor in front of the Cross and spending three hours in silent prayer. Thus was the girl discovered one morning at sunrise, face down, arms outstretched like a dutiful nun, but asleep on the kitchen floor. When it was established that Marie-Andrée was not ill, only rehearsing her life plan, the others laughed and teased so relentlessly that she put aside her calling.

Marie-Andrée was intelligent—the nuns traditionally wrote praise on her report cards—and she had tiny shoots of ambition that might have flourished under different cultivation. She entered the convent's oratory competition and won not only the village prize but a regional one as well. Her trophy became an icon in the Leclerc living room, a symbol of potential escape from the banality of her world. With that triumph, Marie-Andrée spoke of becoming an actress, or perhaps a political leader with a seat in the Quebec provincial government. She devoured biographies of Sarah Bernhardt and Jeanne d'Arc. As she neared eighteen, her father realized that the plainest and quietest daughter was perhaps the one who held most promise, with the potential to push beyond the limits of St. Charles de Bellechasse. From the early years, Augustin had taken Marie-Andrée for occasional rides on the train, on short runs that went from no place to nowhere.

Now, recognizing her abilities, the conductor spoke with great feeling of his own lost youth. Trains go everywhere, he told Marie-Andrée. Trains go to Quebec City, to New York, to the bottom of the world, and around it as well. Find one, he said. Don't settle for a short run to oblivion.

But not long thereafter, Augustin's heart, which had been pumping blood through narrowed arteries, began to fail, and he was forced into semi-retirement. He moved his family to Lévis, where better doctors were available. Their new home was a larger but drab house, half of an old duplex a block or two from the St. Lawrence, with a peeling, painted gray front porch on a street that seemed for the old and forgotten, like a terminal patient waiting to die. Inside, his wife made little attempt at decorating, most of the money having to go for Augustin's heart medicines and food for six children. The only spots of color were the gold frames of family pictures, the Sunday china in a corner curio cabinet, and pictures of the saints and the Virgin who ruled the rooms.

What hopes Marie-Andrée nurtured of attending college were put away by her father's illness. Instead she chose a year's course at a school that taught young women how to be medical secretaries. With a certificate, she found work at the Clinique d'Orthopédie, only a few blocks from home. Though she wanted to find a place of her own, Marie-Andrée remained at home, the dutiful French daughter, bound by the powerful apron strings of the French matriarchy. She did not move out until she was twenty-eight, and then only to a small apartment a block or so down the street, the *same* street, knowing that if a day went by without checking in at home, she best have a good explanation for her mother.

Life in Lévis was as predictable and ordinary as a boiled egg. Each morning she rose at six, prayed for a quarter of an hour, read her Bible, brushed her long and attractive brunette hair, which by twenty-one had already contained rude strands of silver, dressed in something simple, a wool skirt and sweater of modest cut and color, stopped at her parents' home for coffee and to inquire about Augustin's health, then walked ten minutes cross town to the gray and grim-looking clinic where her desk was in an office below the sidewalk level with a view of people's passing feet. Her route to work and home was along streets lined with elderly maples, past aging houses with gingerbread trim that once, perhaps, had color and cheer but that had long since become gray veterans. Few of them even had flowers. The only two "landmarks" in her path were Benoit Fourrures, where the mannequins in the window fitted in perfectly, being old and weary despite the minks and seal-skin they offered on yellowing forms, and the Hôtel Dieu, a hospital whose planners obviously had to eliminate any architectural embellishment and which loomed like the most anonymous government office building.

She dated rarely, due not only to the shortage of eligible young men in the town—those with ambition or ability early on crossed the river to seek fortunes in Quebec City —but because she could not deny the mirror. She was plain. And shy. And condemned.

Now and then some man would ask her to go cross-country skiing, or to the Grand Theater across the St. Lawrence. But the rare night out in the city was tempered by the realization that when the play was done, when she had only begun to sip the wine, there was a ferry to catch and, on the next morning, a return of despair. Mostly she was alone, spending her private moments reading, or trying to play a guitar that she bought in a reckless moment of abundance. "I never saw a girl with more pain in her face," said a neighbor woman. "She was like a little animal caught in a trap, and she didn't know how to find the way out." Her reputation in Lévis was that of a diligent, frillless young woman, dutiful to family and church, probably virginal, and blessedly unlike those youth across the river who, emulating Americans, stuffed their bodies with drugs and treated sex casually. "Marie-Andrée is a good daughter," everyone told her mother. And when she heard the compliments, Marie-Andrée murmured gratitude, even though the words fell on an empty heart.

An automobile became a symbol of escape. If she could earn enough money to buy one, then perhaps it would be liberation for short trips away from home. Then, who knew? She found a second job, moonlighting as a waitress in the Marie-Antoinette Restaurant, a chain operation whose Lévis branch was on the main highway and which required its female employees to wear butterscotch plaid uniforms with lace caps and white nurses's shoes. Marie-Andrée worked so hard that she grew painfully thin and dark circles appeared under her eyes. But within a year she had the down payment for a green Pinto. The achievement was remarkable in Lévis, and now everyone complimented the Leclercs on their thrifty and industrious daughter.

But she was not allowed to enjoy it very long. Soon after its purchase, Marie-Andrée started to leave a store where she had been shopping and as she pushed the glass door to exit, it broke, showering shards over her like rain and driving slivers deep into her left knee. She fell in bewilderment, her leg torn open and bleeding. Rushed to the same hospital that she had passed each morning and afternoon of her adult life, Marie-Andrée was told she had suffered a dropped foot. The doctors explained that the glass had cut into the peroneal nerve that runs down the back of the leg and controls the muscles that make the toes curl up. When it is damaged, ordinarily a person must drag the foot all the way to the grave. Surgery might succeed in repairing or transferring the muscles, but Marie-Andrée refused. "I am going to walk again," she said, "I refuse to be a cripple."

Her spunk and determination were remarkable. More than a year of therapy was required. She learned to push the toes and ball of her foot up, and if it required tens of thousands of times, then so be it. Her younger sister, Denise, drove the Pinto to the hospital parking lot and positioned it so that Marie-Andrée could look down and see another great goal in her life that had been achieved.

Two years after the accident, she was walking normally, save for a slight limp that came when she was tired. The scars on her knee faded to white but she knew they were there, she felt everyone looked at them as they would at a man with a goiter. Victor in a remarkable test of courage, Marie-Andrée nonetheless fell back emotionally to the shyness of her teens. She clamped a serious expression on her face and took a position in the corner, where the other wallflowers of life were huddled. For ten long years she worked at the clinic, typing medical reports on arthroplasty and anterior cervical fusion and lumbar laminectomy. She helped patients with their crutches and sometimes drove them home in her beloved Pinto. Her life was work and family and mass and sitting on the riverbank, alone, wondering why life had elected to pass her by.

Then a man came into her routine and stayed there, wedged like a piece of bread caught in the throat. His name was Bernard and he was a kind, decent fellow whose body was plump and whose head was fast losing its hair and whose talk usually concerned his work as a bookkeeper with some government economics office. He was not the man of her dreams, but he was the only one ringing her doorbell. They dated for two or three years, drifting toward marriage like water running out of a tub. One date for a wedding was set, then canceled by mutual consent. When the subject arose again, Marie-Andrée said, with difficult candor, that she was not altogether certain she loved Bernard. Her friend smiled. Nor was he sure of a need for her. It was simply that everybody in Lévis expected them to wed, the medical secretary and the bookkeeper. They went together well, like a gray suit and a black tie.

One night in the spring of 1975, the couple sat in the gloom of the Tahiti Lounge adjoining the Marie-Antoinette Restaurant, where Marie-Andrée had so long ago worn the butterscotch uniform. They sipped at rum drinks and listened to Hawaiian music. In Lévis, the Tahiti Lounge was as fanciful an escape as was available. Bernard, as solid and foursquare as the church's foundation, suddenly produced a tempting and wicked idea. Why not go away together on a long holiday, to someplace in the sun? Besides having a good time, they could determine once and for all if there was enough compatibility to make a marriage.

If ten friends had been asked to predict Marie-Andrée's response, each would have surely said, "No." Cautious, suspicious of impulse, Marie-Andrée considered for several minutes. Then she shook her head in enthusiastic agreement. "Yes," she whispered. "Oh yes!" For days they voyaged through guidebooks and travel brochures, scanning the Caribbean and imagining tanned bodies and warm nights. But Marie-Andrée was not content. Having agreed to a trip she knew was totally outside her normal boundaries, she suggested to Bernard that the Caribbean was too predictable. If she were going to risk the collective gossip of Lévis, if she were going to spend a substantial sum of money—after the accident she had collected ten thousand dollars in a lawsuit and had hoarded it like a dowry—then she demanded enough memories to last a lifetime.

Bernard was game. What did she have in mind? Marie-Andrée had been spinning the globe in her head all day. "India," she answered. "The Taj Mahal. Bangkok." All those places whose names excite the imagination and which seem forever out of reach. "All right," agreed Bernard. He, too, was ready for a plunge into strange currents.

Later, Marie-Andrée would marvel at the blur of the next weeks. In no time at all, the couple made reservations, informed their employers, cautiously told their families, obtained passports, bought hot weather clothing, and never once faltered at the enormity of their adventure.

"No one really thought we would go through with it,"

said Marie-Andrée when the plane left Montreal and began its awesome circle of the world. In her purse was a new Canadian passport, bearing the photograph of a young woman with tumbling, dark shiny hair, bright eyes, and a look of great expectation. She had taken her glasses off for the picture, and on the day that the passport came, she gazed at it proudly and squeezed it to her heart.

There could be no denial. Marie-Andrée Leclerc was twenty-nine years old, and she was leaving home with a man—and she was finally beautiful.

Book Three

CHARLES
AND
HELENE

CHAPTER THIRTEEN

Their odyssey was first noticed, fittingly, on the island of Rhodes, where once Julius Caesar studied oratory, at the easterly edge of Homer's wine dark sea. Since antiquity, the citizens of Rhodes have endured those who came to plunder, and the arrival of Charles Sobhraj in a semi-stolen sports car with a nauseated and pregnant wife in tow did not find its place in histories that marked the assaults of Cassius, Demetrius, and Philip of Macedonia. But police will long discuss the bizarre events of an early September morning in 1970. For a few hours it seemed that Rhodes had been invaded by a horde of criminals, when, as it would turn out, there was only one.

The first to complain was the manager of the Plaza Hotel, who appeared at the police station to make complaint against a guest who had disappeared during the night without paying his bill of eight thousand drachmas. While the officer in charge was taking the details, the manager of a car rental agency burst in, furious, to accuse a customer of abandoning a hired car without paying the charges, also several thousand drachmas. The young officer directed the rental agent to wait his turn. Within minutes arrived the director of the casino at Rhodes, agonizing over having accepted a worthless check for five thousand French francs from a customer who had lost heavily at baccarat. He was told to take third place in the complaining line.

Then, as topper, a dazed Englishman named Converse

staggered into police headquarters, both hands holding an aching head, groggy from a long and enforced sleep. He was pale and trembling and with gratitude accepted a glass of thick sweet coffee. His story cleared matters up considerably. The night before, said the Englishman, he had been at the casino of Rhodes and had met an interesting young man with Oriental blood and a stunning French wife. They were by far the most striking couple in the casino. "Yes, yes, that's *him!*" interrupted the casino director.

The policeman held out his hands to shush everyone. The "Oriental-looking man" and his wife, who had hair the color of honey and a shy, clinging manner, were sitting at the bar when Converse stuck up a conversation. The man introduced himself as Charles something and he was moaning over a substantial loss at the baccarat table. Converse had been more fortunate at roulette and foolishly bragged of winning. When the casino closed, the Englishman and the couple went to a nearby cafe for a nightcap. Two sips into his drink, Converse felt dizzy. Then his world turned dark.

When he awoke in his hotel room the next morning— an hour before coming to the police station—Converse discovered he had been robbed of several thousand drachmas, his passport, forty-five British pounds in cash, two hundred British pounds in traveler's checks, and an Olympic Airways ticket for London. By noon, police had determined that the same man had cheated the hotel, the car rental agency, the casino director, and had slipped a drug into Converse's nightcap. And the man, it would be charged, was Charles Sobhraj.

In the room where Charles and his wife had stayed at the Plaza Hotel, police found a curious-looking set of sticks, looking like sawed-off broom handles. Obviously great care had been paid to shaping them, but the investigators were baffled as to their purpose. At that moment the chambermaid entered the room with some pieces of writing paper that she had found in the wastebasket. Each was liberally stamped with official-looking entry and exit visas for Greece. Closer examination revealed that they were forgeries, made from impressions carved into the ends of the sticks. Police theorized that Charles had either purchased the "visa sticks" or else carved them himself, an elaborate undertaking particularly since they were in the Greek language.

The hotel switchboard records showed that Charles had made long-distance calls in abundance—seven to Saigon, three to Calcutta, and a dozen to Paris. The operator assumed Mr. Sobhraj was an important man, for he spoke in several different languages and always shouted at her to complete his calls more quickly. Digesting all of this, Greek police teletyped all airports and border crossings to be on the alert, but by this moment the objects of their attention were already in Turkey, motoring toward Istanbul.

It is doubtful that Hélène knew what was going on. A few weeks later, her parents in Paris received a cheery postcard postmarked Rhodes: "Chers Mama and Papa— We are in Greece having a lovely holiday. Charles is working hard on business, meeting people and making contacts. I have been seeing famous places like the site of the Colossus of Rhodes. The baby will be born in November. Probably in Saigon. Everything is fine. We send our love."

Later a Greek court sentenced Charles Sobhraj to one year in prison on various charges of fraud and theft. The conviction was *in absentia*.

They arrived in Delhi by train, having sold the valiant MG at the Pakistan border to a camel trader for three thousand rupees. The monsoon season was ending and the capital of India sweltered under a blanket of verdant heat. Steam rose from the pavements and in the air was a sweet smell like that of rotting fruit. Now in the seventh month of pregnancy, Hélène was in good health, though frazzled by the exhaustive three-month drive from France. She was also apprehensive, for she had not visited an obstetrician in several weeks, save a hotel doctor in Afghanistan who was summoned in the middle of a frightening night when Hélène experienced what she thought were premature contractions but which turned out to be a gassy stomach.

Charles promised they would stay in Delhi long enough for the baby to be born before proceeding to Saigon. But at the *poste restante*—where international travelers traditionally receive mail—several letters were waiting that

plunged him into a foul mood. Félix had written, passing
on the news of Charles being sentenced in Paris to one
year in prison for bad checks. Enclosed was a letter from
Charles' father, the tailor, who threatened to notify authorities if the wandering couple turned up on his door-
step. There was another letter from Hélène's parents,
which told of a disturbing visit from an Interpol investigator, something about a series of crimes in Rhodes. Surely
it was a case of mistaken identity, wrote the butcher and
his wife. But probably Charles would want to notify Interpol that his name was being slandered.

Gratefully, for she was not privy to the letters, Hélène
fell into bed and slept two days and nights while her husband conducted "business" in Delhi. Then, suddenly, he
appeared at her bedside, rousing her from a deep sleep,
announcing that they must leave immediately for Bombay.
Hélène protested feebly, but already she knew that her
arguments had less influence on her impulsive husband's
erratic dashes than would be a cry at a storm to stop raging.

The morning express for Agra bore the couple to the
city of the Taj Mahal, where Charles wanted to show
Hélène the exquisite tomb built from love. But as they
pushed their way through the swarm of guides and beggars
who infest the entrance plaza, through the great terra cotta
arches into the grounds, and finally to the steps that commence a series of reflecting pools that led like sym-
metrically placed jewels to the great monument, Hélène
almost swooned from the blistering heat. Her stomach,
heavy now, began to pitch. But Charles did not notice his
wife's discomfort, so busy was he rattling on about the
history of the Taj and at the same time scrutinizing tourists
as carefully as a carnival pitchman measures a customer's
weight and height. Hélène found a bench and sat down,
mopping her soaked face with the hem of her skirt. She
tried to appreciate the beauty before her eyes, but instead
for a berserk moment wondered if she was about to give
birth here, in the gardens of the world's most famous work
of art.

A few days later, at the first light of a new sun on the
morning of November 15, 1970, Hélène was delivered of
a healthy baby daughter in Bombay's finest hospital. The
new father was theatrically ecstatic, filling his wife's room

with flowers and sobbing at her breast. The child was named Shubra, a Hindu word for "purity," and she was blessed with dark curly hair, her mother's eyes, and a hint of the Orient in her caste. On the hospital record, in the blank marked "father's occupation," Charles wrote "Businessman." Which, in a sense, was true. Indeed he did have a new business, one that was ingenious, profitable, and illegal. More than one Indian detective would marvel not only at its audacity but at the enormous amount of work involved to make a dishonest rupee.

As he was young, only twenty-six, and handsome, and seemingly sophisticated, and from Paris, and having a chic wife, Charles moved easily into Bombay's international colony. It would become a pattern of his life that he always looked for French people to "befriend" in exotic places, they tending to embrace anyone who speaks the tongue of Voltaire among the savages. In Bombay he found immediate acceptance, even popularity at the Alliance Française. The associate director, Monsieur Mannet, offered the attractive émigré and his wife and baby a guest apartment, at modest rent, until Charles could find something more suitable. For three months, Charles lived as guest of Mannet and coincidentally was admitted to teas, cocktail parties, and official receptions for various dignitaries. Madame Mannet was always pleased to have Charles and Hélène at her soirées, for they added a flavor of cosmopolitan Paris. From daily readings of the important national newspapers of India, and *Newsweek,* and *Time* and *Le Monde,* and the *Paris Tribune,* Charles' conversation was *au courant.* "He could speak to a cabinet minister or a film star or a guru," observed Madame Mannet. "He was a very fitting guest. And his wife was very attractive and well spoken."

Years later, when official attention was turned to analysis of the kaleidoscope that was Charles' life, a lawyer in New Delhi became familiar with what the dashing Frenchman was really up to as he glided confidently through Bombay's social waters.

The lawyer, whose name was Rupinder Singh and who would one day become an important figure in the case of Charles Sobhraj, remembered:

* * *

Charles was brilliant and hard-working. Before he came to India he studied the laws of this country and discovered some flaws. He made use of them. In Bombay, there were many wealthy people who wished to drive European or American automobiles. These were scarce and extremely expensive. A Chevrolet could cost $25,000 if obtained legally, and only then after a very long wait and eternal red tape.

Through his contacts in the diplomatic world, Charles met many film stars and business executives who wanted cars and did not care how they were obtained. Charles would take an order for, say, a Mercedes, and request a $2,000 deposit in some hard currency like Swiss francs. He would then fly to Teheran, purchase a stolen Mercedes that had been driven there from Europe where it was picked off some Paris street. By now, new ownership papers had been created, and Charles became the 'legal' owner. He then drove the car across Pakistan, and into India at a place where few questions are asked, particularly if one's outstretched hand has a few large bills in it. Proceeding to Bombay, Charles would enter the city and go to a garage where he and a mechanic stripped the Mercedes of its radio, air conditioning, spare tire, and most of the vital innards. Then, just barely able to drive it, Charles took the wounded car to a forest outside Bombay where he staged a minor wreck, a fender bash or something like that. He then called police and reported the car stolen. Pretty soon the police would find it, notify Charles, and he would curse and sigh and consign it to an auction dealer to sell as junk. Of course Charles would know the day and moment it was to be auctioned, and he would put in a secret bid in the name of his customer, buy the car for peanuts, put all the equipment back in, repair the fender, transfer the papers, and sell it for $20,000. All perfectly legal. I believe he accomplished this at least five or six times.

His profits were such that Charles was able to lease a new apartment, on a fashionable street near the best beach with a spectacular view of the Bay of Bombay. For the early months of 1971, to be asked there was an invitation highly coveted.

While Charles prospered, his wife suffered. The sophisticated people she met at cocktail parties were of no help to her disposition when she was left alone—and Charles was absent more often than not. He refused to tell her where he was going, what he was doing, or when he would return, blaming it all on the press of "business" and assuring Hélène that his labor was meant to enrich her life— and theirs. India assaults the senses of any newcomer, and Hélène was afraid to leave her apartment, even if she could have found a babysitter trustworthy enough to care for Shubra. The young Frenchwoman spoke only Spanish besides her native tongue, neither of much communicative value in a bewildering country where hundreds of dialects are heard and where English, peculiar-sounding English at that, is the "official" language.

"Oh, Camille," she wrote to a friend in Paris, "everything here is *so* confusing. The cleaning woman belongs to some strange caste and wears gauze over her mouth so she won't accidentally swallow a gnat and kill it. I just point to things I need done. Nobody understands me . . . My beloved husband travels on business most of the time . . . Shubra is beautiful and my salvation. If I didn't have my adorable daughter, I would be very unhappy . . ."

New Year's Eve, 1971, Hélène was alone with the baby in her Bombay apartment, weeping, gazing out at the Indian Ocean, wondering where her husband was this special night. She tried to telephone her parents in Paris, but the operator said it would take at least two days to get through. She was a prisoner of loneliness; waves of self-pity washed over her.

On this night, Charles was at the casino of Macao, playing baccarat. Over several weeks of gambling, he was successful and in mid-January returned to Bombay with his pockets full of pacifying treasures—a gold necklace and ruby for Hélène, a petite string of pearls for Shubra, barely two months old. He had one more surprise. Apologizing for his erratic behavior since he had imported his wife to India, Charles announced a reward for her patience. They would leave soon for Hong Kong on a

royal holiday—a suite at the Mandarin Hotel, a Mercedes
limousine to fetch them at the airport, dinner aboard one
of the floating restaurants in the harbor of Aberdeen amid
the orderly chaos of a thousand junks. He was very close
to nailing down a "major deal" in Hong Kong. With some
associates, Charles would open a restaurant-boutique-disco-
theque, and after it was successfully launched, the plan
was to duplicate the clubs in a dozen world capitals from
Hong Kong to Paris. They would all be called Chez
Charles, and he wanted his wife to supervise the décor.

But even as the exhilarated Hélène busied herself packing and anticipating two weeks in a lavish hotel suite with
her seldom seen husband, Charles vanished again. He
simply walked out of the apartment to attend to "business,"
promised to return in an hour, and then sent a telegram
from Iran. "Urgent business Teheran. Hilton Hotel. Back
soon." In anger Hélène wrote immediately to Teheran, but
the letter was returned. Then came a crackling, middle-of-
the-night call from Charles, who was in Kabul, Afghanistan, another cable from Istanbul, a call from Karachi.
For several weeks, Charles crisscrossed Asia, blowing back
and forth like the trade winds. Hélène's diary, which later
would fall into police hands, revealed her desperation:

> February 20, 1971: *Waiting for my husband with
> impatience.*
> February 21—*I am a bit worried. Where is he?*
> February 22. *I am more than worried.*
> February 23. *I am very anxious.*
> February 24. *God help me and my baby. Where is
> our Charles? Please send him back to me.*
> March 4. *Finally news! My beloved is on his return
> journey.*
> March 12. *At last he is here! My heart sings!*
> March 14. *Despair. Gone again. Bombay to Hong
> Kong. Now we die a little until he returns.*

In April, Charles did take Hélène to Hong Kong on
the promised trip. They dumped Shubra in the care of
a Frenchwoman in the Bombay diplomatic community,
promising they would return from a much-needed holiday
in no more than a week. But when three weeks passed,

and the parents had not returned, the baby-sitter grew anxious. She wrote, called, and sent telegrams to the Mandarin Hotel in Hong Kong, but there was no response. After six weeks, worried that the young couple had met foul play, she asked the French Consul in Bombay to launch a search. Promptly Charles showed up at her door, all apologies, charming, asking if the sitter could take care of the baby just a few more days. "I refused," the French-woman told authorities later. "I told Mr. Sobhraj that if he left this poor child with me another day, I would turn her over to the police." With that, Charles thrust a small cassette tape recorder into the poor woman's hands as full payment for six weeks of child care, took his baby daughter, and hurried away.

En famille, they spent the summer months of 1971 in Hong Kong, where Hélène at first reveled in a life of hotel luxury, with room service obediently bringing the infant meals, and boutiques crowded with beautiful silk blouses and jewelry that could be charged to the hotel account. Silks at her breast and jade at her neck could not, however, conceal the disturbing signs that her marriage was collapsing. Charles never told her what he was doing in Hong Kong, nor would he answer her pleas to let her participate in his work, and, most critically, he was in-different to her sexual hunger. When he was away "on business," Charles wrote hugely romantic letters to his wife, remembering moments of passion, anticipating new ones yet to come. But upon his physical return to Hélène, he usually murmured about his fatigue, kissed the baby, and fell asleep on his side of the bed without even an arm outstretched to pillow his wife's frustration. If Hélène initiated talk of sex, and the lack thereof, he snapped, "You are more woman than mother—I knew it!" To which Hélène shot back, "I can be both, can't I?"

But the answer, in Charles' abnormal reasoning, was no. He wanted the madonna, not the whore; the Great Mother, not the Bad Woman. Each woman who came into his life was compared subconsciously to Song, the mother for whom he held complex love-hate. And if that woman passed muster, as Hélène apparently did, and was tempo-rarily awarded the role of maternal goddess, then she could not hope to last very long in the pantheon.

In June, Charles moved his wife and daughter to a hotel in Macao, where he could be nearer to the casino and not have to take the commuter hydrofoil from Hong Kong. He directed Hélène to wear her most stylish gowns and jewels and to hover in glamour behind his gambling chair, perhaps bringing him good fortune or, more pointedly, enhancing his desired image as an exotic international player who was at home in Monte Carlo or London and who was thus entitled to substantial deference and credit at this end of the world. Hélène performed her role well; she knew that the men in the casino looked at her approvingly. But on the nights when she wearied of posing as an *objet d'art* and returned to the hotel room, Charles did not even note her absence, so consumed was he with the lure of the cards.

"I won twenty-two thousand dollars last night," whooped Charles one near-dawn, showering bank notes onto his wife's groggy body. But two weeks later, he was loser by more than thirty thousand dollars. The jewels disappeared from Hélène's case, sold to pay gambling losses, even his daughter's pearl necklace. When Hélène beseeched her husband to stop playing baccarat, he swore at her. She had no sympathy. She was selfish. She put him in such a foul mood that it was no wonder he lost at cards. What else could he have expected from a girl who was reared in the sticks outside Paris? He would have dispatched her back to Paris a long time ago were it not for the baby. "I'm looking for a new mama for Shubra," he often taunted, "and when I do . . ." The sentence always dangled, menacingly. Finally Hélène had enough and wrote her parents a desperate letter, asking them to cable air fare home to Paris.

Back came a prompt answer. The butcher and his wife could not afford to send money. Their counsel was for Hélène to go to the French Embassy and ask for help. When she read the letter, Hélène knew the advice was sound but realized that she dare not risk presenting herself to French authorities. Already Charles had moved her and the baby out of one hotel in the middle of the night, without paying the bill, and now another simmering manager was calling her room several times a day demanding payment. "My husband is away for the day," she had learned to say, haughtily. "Upon his return, the bill will be settled promptly." If Hélène went to the French Embassy, perhaps they would discover her part in fraud and call the Hong Kong police. Scenarios of peril are not difficult to imagine in a city where intrigue seems to wait behind every door.

In mid-June, abandoned at the Lisboa Hotel in Macao, Hélène was at nadir. The baby would not eat and was too thin. Hélène could not shake dysentery. There was no money, and room service rarely bothered to deliver her orders. When a telegram came from Charles saying he was at a hotel in Delhi and would be there several more weeks, Hélène felt panic. Then came a cabled money order with enough to tide her over a short while. While she waited for her husband to return, Hélène began writing letters, pouring out bewilderment, pain, and pleas for a change. These would one day become part of police files in Delhi and Paris, giggled over by secretaries and translators, and revealing the frustration of a young woman who felt like a piece of left luggage.

On one single day, June 20, 1971, Hélène wrote four desperate and impassioned letters to Charles, her tears actually falling on the pages and staining them. In each she pleaded for him to return and rescue his wife and daughter from "the psychological hell of Macao." She revealed her sexual frustration over the weeks, sometimes months, of sleeping alone. She speculated that he was in the arms of other women while in pursuit of his mysterious "business" affairs. She begged him to abandon his gambling, his "violence" toward her, his dreams of great wealth. All she and the baby wanted, wrote Hélène, was for Charles to be with them; a thatched hut on a beach would serve as well as a palace. And in a poignant postscript to the fourth letter, written after midnight, Hélène cried out, "Help us, Charles! In the name of God, remember that *you* put us in this prison."

CHAPTER FOURTEEN

As Hélène suffered the twin demons of loneliness and sexual rejection, Charles was planning a robbery of such audacity and theatricality that a ballad would be sung on the streets of Delhi to mark it. According to his own statement made later to police, the seeds were sown in Macao when his luck turned bleak and the cards dealt him in baccarat refused to total the winning combination of nine. When his losses soared past $40,000, and the casino refused further credit, and the eyes of the pit bosses began to narrow and harden, Charles said he was approached by an Englishman offering sympathy. Polished and highly respectable-looking, the man called himself Maurice. He wore both a pinkish face and an attitude of complete serenity, as if earthquakes were only fissures to step across. He laid on a few names of mutual interest, including that of Porto, the scarred Spaniard, whose affinity for tempestuous women had finally resulted in a fatal stab wound to his abdominal aorta. Porto had bled to death in an alleyway near Pigalle. Charles murmured his sympathy, upon which Maurice suggested it was wasted. "Porto was planning to kill you, did you know that?" asked Maurice. Charles sighed. He did not appreciate violence.

Maurice proposed to engage Charles as subcontractor for a major robbery which was, for all intents and purposes, already worked out. It would require skill, agility, a flair for drama; it would *not* require harm to anyone, if orders were followed. The rewards were potentially enormous. When Charles agreed, Maurice advanced him enough money to get the casino goons off his back, these being men who make IOU collectors in Las Vegas appear almost godly. Moreover, Charles gathered, Maurice was well enough connected in Macao circles to offer his word as collateral for repayment of the gambling losses.

The summer months of 1971 were crowded with travel, logistics, and shopping. In Delhi, Charles and Maurice lived lavishly at the Oberoi-Intercontinental under assumed names while the Ashoka Hotel and its jewelry stores were scrutinized. They left in the middle of the night without paying the bill, Charles having learned how to abandon an inexpensive suitcase and a few dispensable items of clothing in a hotel room so as to keep chambermaid suspicion from being aroused. In Teheran, Charles would later testify, he purchased a pneumatic drill, flashlights, walkie-talkies, and other implements. The quality of merchandise available in Teheran was considered by the underworld superior to that of any Asian city. And in Karachi, Charles engaged two associates. Both were French, both trailed substantial criminal records including participation in robbery and murder, and both were named Pierre. They became, in Charles' argot, Pierre le Premier and Pierre le Deuxième.

By late October, the scenario had been written, polished, and rehearsed, with but one last chore to accomplish. From a Delhi printer who did not question what certain customers requested him to accomplish, Charles obtained calling cards of the highest quality. They introduced in discreet raised script, "J. Lobo, Director, The Casino at Macao." On a late October night in 1971, Charles dropped one on the silver tray of a waiter in the Ashoka Hotel's Club Rouge et Noir. Next to it he placed a twenty-rupee note. And he directed that the card be delivered to the night club's struggling American dancer, performing tedious homage twice nightly to the gods of India.

After an hour of trying to force the drilling bit through the floor of Room 289 in the Ashoka Hotel, Charles swore and silenced the machine. Pierre le Premier had another drill in his sack, but it was too noisy for use at 2 A.M. The decision was made to wait until the morning, when construction work elsewhere in the building would absorb the noise.

On her bed, La Passionara summoned a shred of hope. Perhaps these dangerous men were going to leave and return at sunrise. She tried to keep her voice calm. "I think that is a good idea," she said, encouragingly. "I need some rest for my performances." Charles smiled and shook his head to stick a pin in *that* balloon. No. They would not be leaving. They would pass the rest of the night in the hotel room, one resting, the other spelling as guard, until dawn. "I think," said Charles, "that you realize now we are serious businessmen. I do not believe you will cry out for help or do anything foolish. Because if you make a single sound, we will tie you up." He stared at the dancer with such intensity that she felt not only terrified but naked.

At 7:30 A.M., La Passionara swam out of a half-sleep and saw Charles sitting beside her on the bed. He wished her a good morning and directed that she order tea and toast—for two—from room service. When the waiter knocked, Pierre le Premier hid in the bathroom and Charles sat casually on the sofa, as if a contented lover or an early visitor. Nonetheless, he watched his hostage with a force that convinced La Passionara she would be shot if she so much as arched an eyebrow.

Nourished by the light breakfast, the two men waited until 9 A.M. when the sounds of hammers and electric saws could be heard elsewhere in the hotel. Then they recommenced their own drilling, fighting the thick stubborn floor for twenty-minute bursts, waiting to let the machines cool and for Pierre to check the corridors outside to make sure the drilling noise had not aroused anyone's interest. From time to time Charles spoke into a walkie-talkie, informing the dancer that a second accomplice—Pierre le Deuxième—was stationed in the hotel as guard and lookout. At one point in the morning, Charles laughed. "The ceiling in the jewelry shop below is shaking like an earthquake," he said, as if delivering a news bulletin. "But nobody is paying attention to it." When a bearer came to clean the hotel room, La Passionara went to the door and delivered the lines that Charles had given her, that she was ill and did not want to be disturbed. As she spoke, Charles stood behind the door and held a gun a few inches from the dancer's liver.

For most of this second day, the two men drilled, cursed, and choked on dust, menacing the hostage occasionally with a gun, or a knife, or, at one point, the drill itself. And at each mealtime, they instructed her to order from room service, being careful to replace the carpet over the drilling site. "Do you have to pay for this?" asked Charles when lunch arrived. No. Meals were in her contract. Charles nodded approvingly, as if he did not want the young woman to bear the expense of his board.

But by dusk, as the purple haze of cooking fires fell over Delhi like a highwayman's cloak, and the sounds of militant rallies and marches to gather steam for the defeat of Pakistan swirled about the city, the first drilling bit snapped in two. Then a second. They simply could not penetrate the floor of Room 289. Frustrated, Charles pulled a building plan of the hotel from his briefcase and pored over it. He found a fallback position. An air-conditioning duct seemed to lead from the second floor to the ceiling just above the jewelry shop. Both men were slim enough to squeeze through the foot-wide passageway. Anticipating a chill, Charles demanded sweaters from La Passionara. Then he tied her to the bed, spread-eagled, strips of sheet fastening her arms and legs to the four corners. A gag was stuffed in her mouth to discourage screams. Tears streamed down her face, and for the first time in her life Esther Markowitz felt completely helpless, caught up in a situation over which she had no control and no options.

While Pierre le Premier stayed in the hotel room and watched La Passionara, Charles located the air-conditioning duct in the corridor. But after ten minutes of study he decreed that it was too narrow to accommodate even his slim frame. He reported this disappointing news to his accomplice, then sat down on the sofa, cupping his head in his hands.

Pierre offered the suggestion that a hand grenade could be dropped down the air-conditioning duct. There were two flaws in the idea, answered Charles sarcastically. Number One: they did not have a hand grenade. And Number Two: it would not only blow up the jewelry store and probably send gems raining all over this end of the hotel, it would also summon half the hotel staff. Suddenly Charles snapped his fingers. Acid! A powerful etching acid could eat its way through the marble floor in La Passionara's room, quietly, perfectly! He looked at his watch. It was a little past six in the early evening. Stores were closed. The blackout would be in effect again. It would be impossible to locate the right kind of acid until the next morning. "So," said Charles, once again regaining his control, "we will stay another night with the internationally acclaimed dance star."

La Passionara, now untied, cried out, surprised that her voice would contain such authority. "But I must dance tonight!" she said. "Two shows!" It was Saturday, and the dancer knew that a group of friends from a classical music study group were planning to attend. Afterwards there was to be a midnight supper at a cafe in Delhi where hundreds of thousands of glass beads dangled in pink and amber strings from the ceiling, and where the few cabaret performers in the city went to unwind after performance.

Charles gave a Gallic shrug and turned his palms upward. "Call the director and tell him you have the curse," he said. La Passionara shook her head anxiously. "That's not reason enough to cancel," she said. "The show must go on—that is the code of all performing artists."

"If you dance tonight," answered Charles with the hint of a tease, "it will be in this room—and only for me. Call the club director and cancel."

"He would never believe me," pleaded the dancer. If she did that, the hotel would send a doctor to the room to examine her. The only reason a dancer would cancel a performance would be a broken leg. At that, Pierre le Premier smiled. In his eyes, La Passionara saw the ability to accomplish just such an excuse. Now she began to negotiate. Had she not obeyed every dictum thus far? Had she not remained silent, not interfering with their varied labors? Her entire life was devoted to dance, and on this night many important people had booked tables to see her. "Please," she begged, "please let me dance." If the two men chose to, they could occupy the best seats adjoining the stage, and, if necessary, Charles could train his pistol on her as she danced.

For a few moments, Charles apparently toyed with the absurd suggestion. La Passionara sensed her captor's indecision, and it was enough to give her fantasies full rein. Even with Charles sitting at ringside, surely there would be an opportunity to escape. She raced through the act in her mind. At several moments, her choreography whirled her past a carved teakwood screen. Perhaps she could detour behind it and yell for help. Or, if all else failed, she could simply fly headlong into the arms of a patron and scream.

Charles shattered her scenarios. *If* he permitted the show to go on, then not only would he and Pierre occupy a prominent table, there would be several other accomplices scattered about the room. All of them would carry weapons. "If you made trouble," said Charles, "a lot of shooting might occur, and a lot of innocent people, particularly you, would get hurt." La Passionara chewed on this.

"Would you really shoot me?" she asked.

Charles nodded matter-of-factly. He hoped such tragedy would not happen, he went on, for he was opposed to violence, and he had come to like the American woman. Up to this point, she had caused no trouble.

"Where would you shoot me?" asked La Passionara, pushing him a little.

"There," said Charles, gesturing at her heart. "I would not disfigure your face, or your legs. I have respect for them." Pierre laughed. He heard a shade of gallantry in Charles' answer, and he wondered what his superior saw in this fluttery, silly, long-in-the-tooth dancer. If he were in command, he would have stabbed her long ago.

Charles ended the negotiations. No. He could not permit La Passionara to perform. He was tired, his nerves were taut, he could not tolerate a new risk. Moreover, it was not his choice to make. He was part of a "larger organization" that had conceived the undertaking. La Passionara gathered that he was speaking of something akin to the Mafia, although he did not use its name. All he would say was that the "organization" imposed a code of honor on its employees, and Charles' honor depended upon his successful completion of this robbery.

La Passionara made one last plea. If this man had a

code of honor, how could his conscience permit terrorizing
an innocent woman with threats of murder? Charles must
have liked the question, for he measured his reply and
spoke carefully. "All people are different," he said. "You
were born to be a dancer, I was born to be a gangster.
What we do, you see, is not in our hands, therefore conscience has no part of my psychology." He handed her the
telephone. His gun was at her breast. With very real pain
in her voice, La Passionara called the club director and
said she was too ill to dance.

Somehow Saturday night passed, the dancer drifting in
and out of tortured sleep, her arms once again lashed to
the bed because her captors were similarly needful of rest.
They had started to gag her again, but she had promised
not to make a sound, pointing out that if the noise from
the pneumatic drills had not summoned the hotel management, then it was unlikely that one female cry would bring
the police. Besides, every officer in Delhi was concerned
with keeping the peace under the blackout.

During the long night, the dancer saw and heard and
felt an array of events, disparate but indelible in her
memory. Sometime after midnight, an elephant trumpeted
in the distance, probably the enormous beast who spent
daylight hours patiently bearing hotel guests around the
gardens, dressed in red and gold blankets and wearing a
headdress of fake glitter. Never had she paid much attention to the animal, but now she realized that he was
chained every night—between performances so to speak—
and she felt empathy. And once, just before dawn, she
felt a hand gently touching her brow, fingering her long
hair. But when she opened her eyes, she saw Charles
moving away. Pierre passed the night curled up beside
the door, his body against the crack, like a faithful guard
dog.

On Sunday morning—she had now been a prisoner for
almost thirty-six hours and still in her bathrobe, which
had begun to smell from spilled cosmetics and the perspiration of fear—La Passionara cracked. She screamed. Charles
bolted from the sofa and grabbed a pillow to press against
her face. She was on the cliff's edge of blacking out when

he released her. "I'm sorry," she said, when she regained her composure. "I can't take any more."

Charles dispatched Pierre le Premier in search of the necessary acid and ordered La Passionara to take a hot bath. It would soothe her disposition. She shook her head. She did not want a bath. If she did not take a bath and calm down, warned Charles, then he would prepare something to ensure her quiet. From his briefcase he withdrew a glass vial and within were pills of many colors, like an assortment of holiday candy. Persuaded, La Passionara rushed to the bathroom and began running hot water. "Leave the door open or I will break it down," said Charles. "I don't want to look at you, so you have no reason for modesty."

The bath lifted Esther's spirits a little, and she told herself that she was going to survive. If these men had not hurt her in what was now approaching two full days and nights, then—she reasoned—they would not do it now. If she was not fatally mistaken, Esther sensed a dichotomy within Lobo. On the one hand he was without doubt a dedicated thief and assailant, but conversely he was also *sympathique* and possessed of a certain tenderness. Each time he had tied Esther to the bed, Lobo had arranged the ropes so that they would not cut her flesh. If she winced, then Lobo shifted them about to cause her the least physical discomfort.

All she had to do was hang on a little longer and either the men would leave or someone at the hotel would surely start to wonder why she had not been out of her room since Friday midnight. She clung to these thoughts until midday, when Pierre le Premier returned with the news that he could not find acid on this autumn Sunday morning in New Delhi. His colleague, Pierre le Deuxième, had scoured other parts of the city, but neither of them had been able to find anything stronger than photographic developing fluid. Lobo cursed in a language that Esther did not understand. But she saw a frightening anger settle over his face, like a man betrayed. Prudently, La Passionara went to her bed and assumed her role as the most docile of captives, not daring to utter a sound.

Lobo soaked in the gloom of the predicament for more than an hour, remarking now and then that perhaps the

project should be abandoned. But in his mind must have
been the wrath he would incur from Maurice, his patron
in this matter. Once before, in the planning stage, Charles
had mentioned that he might withdraw from the robbery.
Maurice had pointedly emphasized at that time how much
money Charles owed the casino in Macao, plus the $3,000
advance that he had been given. Maurice was not a man
who would be graceful with unpaid bills.

Unable to drill a hole through the hotel room floor, or
burn an entrance with acid, Charles decided to take a
more direct approach. He conceived a new plan, in which
La Passionara would star. As it was explained, hers would
be a bravura performance.

Shortly after 5 P.M., the Rajasthan Emporium, purvey-
ors of fine gemstones, received an imperious telephone
summons from La Passionara, the dancer who was currently a guest in the Ashoka Hotel. She asked the salesman
who answered the phone, a man named Ralayan, to bring
a sample of his best wares to her suite. She was indisposed
and unable to come personally to the shop. Her orders
were explicit: her mother was flying in from the United
States tomorrow, and she wished to welcome her with a
splendid gift. If the Rajasthan Emporium did not have the
most exceptional jewelry, then do not bother to come.
Ralayan gushed his assurances.

La Passionara hung up, her hand trembling. Lobo withdrew the gun he had placed at her neck, and bowed in
appreciation. She had recited her lines professionally. In
fact, Lobo was so pleased with her conduct that he wanted
to award her a share in the revenues to come. From his
pocket he withdrew a large wad of American currency
and pointedly dropped the bills in a box of tape cassettes.
The dancer made mild protest that she did not wish to
have financial collaboration with Lobo, but he insisted. It
did not matter, anyway, for later in the evening Lobo
would take back the dollars and substitute a stack of Indian
rupees worth about eighty dollars.

When the salesman Ralayan knocked at the door, La
Passionara steeled herself. Lobo was in the bathroom,
Pierre le Premier positioned on the sofa, a gun in easy
reach behind the pillows. His role was to pose as the
dancer's social secretary. She swept to the door and opened

it grandly. Lobo had permitted her to dress in a brilliant red velvet dressing gown and to wear her own jewelry. Her dark hair tumbled loose about her shoulders and the effect was not only dramatic but quite beautiful.

Ralayan made obeisance with prayerful hands and opened a case of rings, bracelets, and necklaces. They were the finest creations in Delhi, murmured the salesman, fitting to welcome the great star's mother upon her arrival. "Perhaps," said La Passionara, affixing what seemed to be a highly trained eye on the dazzle spread before her. She picked up a few stones, held them to the light, dropped them as if they were the paste imitations found in Cracker Jack boxes. Surely Ralayan did not present these inferior pieces as the kind of quality jewelry that a person in La Passionara's orbit would appreciate. She fingered her own antique necklace, knowing that any jeweler would appreciate its extravagance. The salesman poured forth apologies. He had not understood that his client wished to purchase something more substantial than a simple ruby or sapphire ring. Could he return to his shop and locate the most choice gems, those held back for only the most demanding clientele? La Passionara nodded brusquely and dismissed him, in the manner of a great Maharani who was probably wasting her time.

When the salesman was gone, Lobo emerged from the bathroom grinning. He applauded her performance. He knew that the shop would not send up its best merchandise on the first summons. But *now* they would open their vaults. Lobo clapped his hands. The drama was approaching the final scene. Esther was made to sit in a prominent chair, her feet bound with ropes. Over her lap, Lobo carefully placed a blanket. He apologized as he worked for having to bind the dancer one last time. But he promised to lift the blanket at the moment of revelation and reveal that La Passionara was a captive and not part of the plot to rob the salesman. This would be her insurance policy should the police wrongly assume that she and Lobo were connected. Lobo surveyed the room like a choreographer. Everyone was in place. Pierre le Premier, posing still as the dancer's secretary, would open the door. Lobo took his position in the bathroom. It was 7:30 P.M. Despite her fear, La Passionara also felt the tingle of apprehension that any performer knows while waiting for the curtain to rise.

The owner of the shop, Mr. Pradash, came personally to Room 289 and knocked respectfully. He had not realized the importance of this customer, and he would now present his wares himself. He was shown into the room by a thin blond man who gestured toward La Passionara, sitting almost regally in her chair, the blanket across her lap. She bade the merchant to approach. With ceremony, Pradash opened his case, and this time the dancer could not feign displeasure. Before her was spread a breathtaking array of jewels—a necklace of gold and rubies with matching earrings that would cascade to the shoulders, an elephant brooch of exquisite jade with emeralds, rings with sunbursts of sapphires. There were but a few pieces nestled in the forest green velvet, but each was magnificent. As she examined them, attempting the tiniest frown now and then (as if she were in the bazaar, haggling), the bathroom door swung open. Lobo stepped into the room, a towel at his hands. He would have Pradash believe that he had been drying his hands, but La Passionara knew that under the towel was a gun. With studied casualness, Lobo glanced at the stones, then began a conversation with the merchant. It was as if two old friends had suddenly encountered one another on a street corner. Lobo chatted about the weather, the current films, the likelihood of war with Pakistan. They sat on a sofa together, one with a towel at his hands concealing a gun, the other with a case of jewelry on his lap. La Passionara began to tremble. In a moment she would scream again. The pressures of the maniacal weekend were ready to blow. Lobo sensed this and with great calm he let the towel slide from his hands. He lifted the gun and placed it at the jeweler's heart. With his other hand, he reached over and tugged at the blanket that draped the dancer. It fell to the floor, revealing the ropes that bound her feet. At that, La Passionara broke and sobbed until Pierre rushed over to stuff the fallen towel in her mouth as a silencer.

Now Lobo revealed the truth of Room 289. And he was hugely annoyed that Pradash had only brought these few pieces, not a more substantial representation of his treasures. He gestured at Pierre, who frisked the jeweler

and found the keys to the emporium. Lobo explained that
he had no choice but to wait until past 10 P.M., when all
the shops in the hotel arcade would be closed and the
corridor free of people. Then he would feel more comfortable in entering the shop and cleaning out the shelves.
"We will wait," said Lobo, putting a music cassette on
La Passionara's tape recorder. Pierre tied the jeweler by
his hands and legs and dragged him into the bathroom,
where Charles stuffed a cloth into his mouth. When he
was content that Pradash could not disgorge the gag and
was effectively silenced, Charles instructed La Passionara
to order dinner from room service. He even permitted a
chambermaid to enter the room and draw the drapes for
the evening's blackout. It occurred to La Passionara that
this man somehow enjoyed these flirtations with danger.
They were a test of his strength and cunning against
others' weakness. When the waiter arrived with a serving
cart, Charles was polite, talkative, and exhilarated. He did
not show a glimmer of concern that a bound and gagged
hostage was lying on the floor of the bathroom and
another was trembling as she signed the bill. If either of
them had cried out, the tightrope on which Lobo walked
would have been snapped. But he was in control of the
moment and La Passionara envied him that.

Around 11 P.M., Charles excused himself and left the
room, ordering Pierre le Premier to guard the two hostages. When he returned a half hour later, he carried a
BOAC flight bag that bulged like an overstuffed turkey.
He carried it to La Passionara and told her to look inside.
The excitement on his face was that of a child bearing a
gift to his mother. The flight bag contained major treasures
of the Rajasthan Emporium, and their combined brilliance
was like staring at a greedy fire. His hand snaked into the
bag and he seized a fistful of gems, dropping them onto
the dancer's lap. "Choose one," he whispered. La Passionara was tempted—she could not deny that—but she was
still smart enough to decline. Charles shrugged. There was
no time to argue. While he had been inside the shop raiding the strongboxes—he had gained easy admittance with
the owner's keys—he had seen a hotel guest stroll down
the corridor. The man had glanced idly into the shopwindows where Charles pressed his body against a wall.

He walked on, but Charles was nonetheless worried that he might have had second thoughts.

The two men lifted La Passionara from her chair and carried her into the bathroom, where she was dumped on the floor beside the merchant. One last moment of unpleasantness would be necessary, said Charles, almost apologetically. He would have to put the two hostages to sleep. La Passionara whimpered protest, but it was not successful. Forcibly stuffing sedative pills into Pradash's mouth, he worked the jeweler's jaws like one does for a puppy who must take unwanted medicine. Then he turned to the dancer.

Charles took a table napkin from the room service cart and gagged her. Then he bent down and looked at her with brusque respect. Since Friday midnight a strange bond had been forged between them. At one point Charles had even spoken of his wife and daughter and had shown La Passionara their photographs. Now he made an offer. "If you promise to be a good girl, I won't give you medicine for sleep," he said. La Passionara nodded vigorously. "And don't try to raise an alarm until 5 A.M.," he warned. There were other men in the hotel who were part of the plan and who would not be as "easy" as Charles. "Just rest there. You've earned it." La Passionara pointed to her gag; she wanted to answer. Charles pulled it away long enough for her to speak. She promised not to stir until the sun rose. And she thanked him for sparing her life.

On his way to the door, Charles remembered one last thing. He paused and looked toward the bathroom and called out softly. "Someday I hope to see you dance," he said in parting. "You are beautiful. I am sure that your dancing is beautiful, too." When the door shut, La Passionara was crying—but not altogether out of fear.

CHAPTER FIFTEEN

Palam International Airport in Delhi is at its busiest between midnight and dawn. Most international flights take off or land in the capital of India during the dark hours because Delhi is midway on the global sweep between Europe and the Far East. In the early moments of November 1, 1971, the airport was in a state of unusual tension. Its corridors and waiting rooms had their normal complement of beggar children striking poses calculated to earn sympathetic coins, and tea sellers, and veiled Moslem women munching spicy meat patties behind their masks, and holy men sitting cross-legged on plastic chairs meditating and writing their thoughts on scraps of brown wrapping paper, and Western travelers wandering dazed or angry through the maze of red tape that is bureaucratic India (every document seems to be written in triplicate, even the receipt for purchasing a postage stamp). But overlying all were squads of fierce-faced soldiers toting carbine rifles and scrutinizing everyone.

Knowing this in advance, Charles timed his arrival at Palam so that he would have just enough time to purchase a ticket to Teheran, zip through customs, and spend but a moment or two in the departure lounge. It was not his desire to endure dangerous waiting time in a swarm of police and soldiers, particularly as he was carrying a fortune in stolen gems and $10,000 cash in a flight bag. An hour had passed since he slipped quietly out of the Ashoka Hotel by a side entrance. The prearranged scheme was for the two Pierres to take a train to Bombay, thence by plane to Teheran, where the proceeds of the robbery would be divided. But as the courier, Charles had been instructed to leave Delhi on the first available plane.

Well-dressed travelers often merit deferential treatment in Asia, and Charles had been careful to change clothing after his long weekend in La Passionara's hotel room. He also knew that customs agents in India are capricious, more often than not waving affluent-looking Westerners through without opening luggage.

Charles purchased his ticket with a wad of the Indian rupees he had recently obtained from the jeweler's safe box, passed through passport control without incident using a counterfeit document bearing the name "Gillian," and was approaching the long tables where customs agents examine luggage and mark clearances with brusque chalk strokes. Beyond this last hurdle was the transit lounge, where passengers were already filing wearily onto a shuttle bus for delivery to the airplane. Then the cards once again turned sour.

"Mr. Gillian!" Someone was calling his name. And no one knew it, for this was the first occasion Charles had used it. He fought off his instinct to turn around and respond. He did not flinch even as the name came at him again, closer this time. Then there was a polite but firm hand on his shoulder. An agent for Air India was telling him that there was a problem with the ticket.

"What problem?" growled Charles impatiently. He tapped at his expensive watch. The flight was already called.

It seemed Charles had paid for his ticket in Indian currency, and that was not allowed except for citizens of that country. Foreigners must pay in hard currency—dollars, pounds sterling, francs, the like. Charles huffed and sputtered like a very important lion caught in a very impudent trap, knowing that growls sometimes frighten away ribbon clerks. But this time they did not work; the agent insisted that Mr. Gillian return to the ticket desk and refinance his journey. The plane would not leave without him, assured the agent. Only five minutes passed while the hugely out-of-sorts Charles satisfied the airline with substituted currency, but the brief loss of time was incalculably expensive.

When he returned to the baggage examination table, the inspectors were pawing thoroughly through all hand luggage. War fever was in the air And even though Charles had packed the stolen gems beneath a false bottom and had stuffed the rest of the bag with odd sweaters, papers, and tourist paraphernalia, a new anxiety swept over his escape. While he mentally debated an alternate plan, a commotion broke out behind him. Sweeping through the crowds of travelers, carving a path like a bowling ball knocking down pins, a wedge of police was escorting an out-of-breath Pradash, the ravaged jeweler of the Ashoka Hotel. They were canvassing every departing traveler. La Passionara obviously had broken her vow and had screamed for help the moment Charles left her hotel room.

Caught in a vise—a customs agent at one end and onrushing police at the other—Charles smiled, appreciating the insanity of the moment. And he did what any prudent man would do in a quandary like that. "I'll be right back," he told the baggage inspector. "I have to go to the toilet." With that, Charles nimbly leaped across one long table, found a promising hallway, ducked through an empty office, and threaded his way into the brisk midnight air that contained enough fog to mask his long and successful race to sanctuary.

Behind, on the customs table, was left the flight bag. One ripe fragment of irony remained. The inspector had glanced routinely inside, saw nothing, zipped up the bag, chalked his mark of approval, and was waiting for the passenger to return from the toilet when Pradash arrived with the police, falling on his stolen jewels with tears and laughter.

The next morning Charles slipped quietly onto the first train for Bombay. The humiliation of losing the gems still stung, but there remained a sense of excitement that had possessed him throughout the long weekend in La Passionara's hotel room. He would later tell a friend, "I would have happily gone through the entire experience again. I felt alive every moment—and dead when it was

over." Delhi's newspapers were full of the audacious enterprise. La Passionara's photograph had captured her in a
bad moment; she looked like a woman just rescued from
a capsizing ship with her hair in wild disarray, her face
wrinkled and worn. She told a vivid tale of her captivity.
Pradash told police that the mysterious "Mr. Lobo" was
probably a professional killer because his eyes had gleamed
homicidal. Charles kept the newspapers, for they would
verify that the gems had been reclaimed at the airport. He
did not want Maurice, his patron, to suspect that he had
not been honest in losing them.

From Bombay, Charles flew to Teheran, encountering
no difficulty in leaving India—word does take a while to
get around the enormous subcontinent. He was also traveling on a new stolen passport, an item as easy to purchase in Bombay as a sweetmeat on a street corner. In
Teheran, Maurice was surprisingly docile, although he did
lash his bumbling apprentice with questions and criticism.
Charles had anticipated more, indeed the blade in his
pocket was well honed. But there was no need for violence.
Maurice had another proposal. As Charles was now in
debt to the Englishman for the $3,000 advance against
his Macao gambling losses, and the substantial sum required to prepare the aborted jewel robbery, perhaps the
young man would like to undertake a robbery in Bombay.
The object was a small neighborhood bank which normally
had insufficient moneys to draw Maurice's attention. But
on a certain afternoon it would contain substantial funds
from a lottery. One man could easily handle it. Charles
agreed. He was given a pair of tear gas pistols which
could be used solely as bluff, but if required they would
cover most any difficulty. The two men parted once more,
planning to meet several days hence at the Taj Mahal
Hotel in Bombay. Maurice murmured his good wishes
for successful endeavor, adding that it was in Charles'
best interests to accomplish this work quickly and efficiently.

Charles was reunited with his near hysterical wife at a
hotel room in Bombay, but he had no time for Hélène's
rantings about her loneliness and bewilderment. He made

cursory apology for having been away for so long, but
blamed it on "business." The child, Shubra, was one year
old and a vivacious pixie with dark curly hair and deep-
set brown eyes. From his pocket Charles pulled a gold
ring with a modest ruby stone, one that he had somehow
failed to put in the flight bag. Hélène thought it was a love
token for her, but instead Charles put it on the tiny finger
of his child, frowning that it was far too large for the
baby. "We'll have it cut to size," he announced.

A few days later, on November 12, 1971, Charles was
walking briskly through side streets near the wonderful
old Taj Mahal Hotel, a spreading jumble of Gothic and
Indo-Saracenic splendor, when he stopped at a cafe frequented by an occasional film star, and by scores of those
who pretended to be connected to the fantasy world of
inane music, pageantry, and discreet sex that is cinema
in India. Once Charles had been asked by a director to be
an extra in a crowd scene that required foreign faces, and
although he did not have time at that moment, the notion
of becoming a film star someday was tucked in one
corner of his head.

While he stood at the cafe entrance and looked around
for a friend's face, two policemen observed him, walked
up, and, of all things, arrested him on charges of car theft
and fraud. One of his long ago customers, a lawyer to
whom he had sold one of the "imported" European automobiles, had recently been ensnared by authorities for
illegal paperwork, and he had revealed that the seller of
the Mercedes car he was driving had been one Charles
Sobhraj. The lawyer had given police a detailed and
accurate description of the man in question—late twenties,
slim, Oriental caste to his face, horn-rimmed glasses,
powerful hands, well dressed, well spoken, very very
smooth.

Charles exploded with wrath over this outrageous case
of "mistaken identity" and he reached for his identification papers. In his breast pocket he normally carried a
false passport to smooth over uncomfortable encounters
like this. But he inadvertently withdrew as well one of the
calling cards that announced "J. Lobo, Director, The
Casino at Macao." As every newspaper in India had for

the past week carried breathless details on the Ashoka Hotel robbery, it did not take long for police to realize that a major fish had swum into their net.

When someone called Hélène to inform her that Charles was in the embrace of India's police and being transported to Delhi to be held without bail, she wrote in her diary, "Nov. 14, 1971. *My life ends.*" Then she thought awhile, took the ring that Charles had planned to cut down to fit Shubra's tiny finger, sold it, and purchased a plane ticket to Delhi.

Almost enthusiastically, Charles made elaborate confession. Throughout his career, he generally made an immediate statement to police, for he well knew that such could not be used against him in most courts. Moreover, he chose to speak in French, realizing that much would be lost or garbled in translation—a point he could capitalize on in his defense. And he knew that by confessing he would avoid being roughed up by police, whose reputation for pounding admissions out of suspects was a fact of life on Charles' side of the street.

The statement was not only breathtaking in its lack of veracity, but a revealing self-portrait of how Charles wanted the authorities—and anyone else who read it—to view him. Much of it was purest fantasy, what he felt his life *should* have been:

> I was brought up by my father in Saigon. He is a very important businessman who owns four tailor shops and a hotel. I had schooling in Saigon and France. There I went to the Sorbonne, where I completed my university education 1963–64. I then studied law for three years, and thereafter I went to a scientific academy where I studied for two more years. I met my wife at the University where she was taking her master's degree in Spanish. I fell in love with her and we got married in 1969. After my marriage, I took a job with a fire extinguisher company, where I got 20 per cent commission on sales, earned from $1,000 to $1,500 a month, and had 20 persons working under me. I also studied an IBM programming course. I left this company after one

year and then started my own business. I would
purchase goods from manufacturers and supply them
to shopkeepers. From time to time I engaged in
foreign travel. I left this business in 1970 to begin
an export business with my father in Saigon . . .

That Charles took the dirt of his life and by alchemy
transformed it into gold was less remarkable than his
accusation that Esther Markowitz, alias La Passionara,
was part of the plot to rob the Ashoka Hotel jewelry store.
Cruelly and ungallantly, Charles swore in his statement—
apparently in punishment for the preliminary alarm the
dancer had sounded—that La Passionara had been in on
the scheme from the beginning, that she had purposely
booked Room 289 of the hotel, and that she had lured
the robbers into her confidence. He made it sound so
convincing that police arrested the *artiste*, now a major
celebrity in Delhi and drawing packed houses, and flung
her into Tihar Prison on the outskirts of Delhi, where her
screams impressed no one.

Several days after his arrest, while waiting in a police
lockup outside a magistrate court for an appearance,
Charles suddenly doubled over in what seemed excruciating and genuine pain. His face blanched white, his body
convulsed with spasms. His pain seemed so genuine that
the officer in charge ordered the prisoner taken to a
hospital for examination. There, when a young doctor
pressed his fingers against Charles' lower right abdomen,
the confessed jewel thief screamed. "It's an old ulcer,"
he gasped. The decision was made to perform an appen-
dectomy, and at this Charles got more than he had bargained for. It was his intention only to gain admittance to
the hospital for a day or two, during which he could
perhaps find a way to escape. During his years in prison,
his confreres always said the best place to spring out of
confinement was a hospital. When the diagnosis was made,
Charles tried desperately to back-pedal, but it was too
late. Very well, he must have thought, we'll see what we
can do with a missing appendix.

A few days later Charles was recuperating in a private
room guarded twenty-four hours a day. He was not per-

mitted to go to the toilet without a policeman to whom
he was handcuffed. But he was permitted to have visitors,
and on the night of December 4, 1971, his wife Hélène
brought him a bouquet of marigolds and a tin box of
macaroons. The guard pawed through both flowers and
cookies and was satisfied they contained nothing inappropriate. This was the young woman's third or fourth visit,
and by now the guards were accustomed to her.

The hospital room was dark and stuffy, the blackout
still in effect throughout Delhi. The guard would not permit even a candle. Charles was handcuffed to the railing.
Hélène's nostrils were assaulted every time she sat beside
her recuperating husband. The marigolds she brought could
not overcome the odors from decades of sick and unwashed who had slept in this room.

The young couple spoke softly in French, even though
the guard had forbidden the foreign language. Whenever
he clapped his hands and ordered, "English!" they would
obey, making mundane remarks, then slip gently back into
French whispers. An hour passed. The guard said it was
time for Hélène to leave. Could she not have but a few
more minutes? she begged. The guard agreed. Another
hour crept by. There was silence in the room. The guard,
sitting in a straight-backed chair, tilted his head against
the wall. A few more moments of breathless suspense.
Then gently, just as Charles had predicted, the guard
began to snore, rattles building like a drum.

At that, Charles gently touched his wife's hand. She
nodded. They had rehearsed the scene many times. Hélène
knew what she was supposed to do. Trembling, she sent
feathery fingers dancing into the pocket where the guard's
keys clearly protruded, tightening her grip, slowly extricated
the ring. Quickly she unlocked the handcuffs that imprisoned her husband. Charles rose silently from the bed,
kissed his wife, murmured "*Je t'aime*," and slipped out
into the darkened hospital corridor. Hélène took his place
in the bed, pulled the covers over her head, and tried not
to cry out from the fright over what she had done.

With studied calm, Charles strolled out the front door
of the hospital in his pajamas, hardly an unusual costume
in India, where millions of men wear the same. He hailed
a taxi and ordered the driver to cruise around an upper-

class residential neighborhood near the embassy district. Police later theorized he was looking for a suitable house to burglarize. But, apparently unable to find a score, Charles directed the taxi driver to take him into a swarming district near the old Delhi train station. There he found a cheap hotel and slept fitfully. His incision had broken open, and he tore the sheets to bind it anew. At dawn he wrapped a blanket about his body, swirled the remaining strips of sheeting about his head, and, thus resembling a peasant of the lowest caste—staggered to the station and bought a ticket for the next train to Bombay. As he spoke to the clerk, a policeman noticed him, suspiciously wondered why a vigorous-looking young man with a European aura was masquerading as an untouchable, and started over to ask questions. Foolishly Charles bolted, trying to run, but there was no strength in his legs, and he surrendered readily when a cordon of police delightedly made capture.

Of course Hélène was now under arrest as well, fortunate that hair was still on her head when the duped guard seized her and yanked her from her husband's sickbed. She pretended complete innocence and spoke with a thick tongue, as Charles had instructed her. The drama called for her to suggest that somehow Charles had drugged her—a remarkable feat for a handcuffed man— and had tossed her unconscious body onto the bed. Nobody believed a word of it, nobody was affected by Hélène's copious Gallic tears. And as she passed her first long night in a Delhi jail, she wondered how she had let Charles talk her into the dangerous charade. He had been so convincing. He had sworn in their first visit together after his arrest for the jewel theft that he had been *forced* to take part. The gamblers who held his IOUs from Macao had threatened his life, and Hélène's and the baby's as well. He was only trying to protect his adored wife and daughter from the flashing knives of Oriental killers. Now he needed Hélène to help him escape from the Indian authorities. As soon as he was safely out of the country, he would write the judge and swear that Hélène was innocent. "They wouldn't keep a French citizen with a baby in custody," insisted Charles. The French Ambassador would cause a lot of trouble. Hélène made mild protest that she was not theatrically capable for such a performance, but Charles propped her up with silky whispers and promises of an immediate return to Paris. All of this she replayed in her throbbing head as she sat huddled against a mustard wall in the police lockup and watched an old woman with no teeth and a face darker than a mahogany table importune her to sip milky tea from a glass that had, in Hélène's estimation, probably been used by lepers.

Presently she was released on $300 bail put up by a friend with connections at the French Embassy. And promptly Hélène made plans for a return to France with Shubra, even though when her handbag was returned to her from police custody it no longer contained her legitimate passport, $200, and an air ticket from Hong Kong to Delhi. The loss hurt, but she would have forfeited a decade of her young life to be out of jail. One of the policemen taunted her that she now had a substantial dossier with Interpol, and though she was not certain how this could be true, Hélène feared that just from being Charles Sobhraj's legal wife she was guilty by association. To a friend in Paris she wrote: "All I want to do is leave this pagan part of the world and come back to civilization —France! And I never want to see Charles again."

But one midnight in late December, as Hélène waited for word from her parents, or Félix d'Escogne, to whom she had sent an urgent cable beseeching money, a rap came urgently at the door of her hotel room. When she answered, no one was there. But a note fluttered at her feet in the chill breeze of the open-air hallway. She read it quickly. "Charles is dying. He took his life to save yours."

CHAPTER SIXTEEN

Ten miles from the heart of Delhi, in the core of an enormous military reservation, squats the hideous prison known as Tihar, which, by Indian standards, is not such a bad place. When a Western attorney once visited the forbidding fortress where ravens perch in symmetrical intervals like carved gargoyles along the mustard walls, where old women using prehistoric tools hammer at granite rocks, smashing them into pebbles for road repair and earning five rupees a day, he shuddered. The lawyer wondered out loud how human beings could be confined in a place that was barely fit to contain American zoo creatures. "India is a poor country," the guard said. "We have six hundred million people and many of them are hungry and many of them have no place to sleep except the streets. Why should we provide better accommodations *inside* the prison than out?"

Hélène flew in heavy grief to the prison, screaming at the taxi driver to hurry. But the cabs of Delhi are fatigued contraptions, long since bereft of springs to shield passengers from potholes. And rare is the driver who puts more than two pints of shockingly expensive gasoline into his tank, just enough to go a few miles until the next fare provides coins for a bit more. The road to Tihar is eternal, the last few miles through villages choked with children playing in the red clay ruts, families washing at a pipe that dribbles occasional water, oxen occupying the right of way and oblivious to horns and cries. Anyone who takes a taxi to Tihar begins to wonder if the destination will ever be reached, particularly since the last few miles are usually punctuated by the disturbing boom of cannons firing at target practice.

Her prayer was that she would reach Charles before he drew his last breath, for she knew now that she still loved him. Whether the love was genuine at this point, or the acknowledgment that Charles was the only person on this side of the world who cared for her and could probably get her out of India was not a matter for internal debate.

At Tihar, Hélène had to stand outside the front gate for sweltering hours, in confused mingling with the other women who had brought their men containers of thick curried soup and dried fruits. No one seemed to know anything. The guards spoke but few words of English, and Hindi was as incomprehensible to Hélène as French was to them. She attempted tears and cries, but they served only to make the guards withdraw; smiles and flirtations accomplished even less. Finally a man who seemed to possess authority as well as a kind face and a command of English told Hélène that she could not be admitted inside the walls without written permission from a magistrate, or in the company of an advocate. At that, Hélène's patience snapped. She sank to the earth howling. These barbarians had somehow killed her husband, and now she was going to reveal to the world how foreign nationals were treated in this hellhole of a country! The man looked stunned, excusing himself. When he returned, he brought startling news that Charles Sobhraj was not dead at all, only a little weak from refusing to eat. Some sort of hunger strike to protest his treatment. The official led Hélène to a room where polychrome photos of Nehru and Indira Gandhi smiled benevolently on her, as did two guards. Eventually her husband appeared, wan, subdued, and chained—but very much alive.

They spoke in French, Charles whispering that he had bribed one of the guards with a few rupees to turn a deaf ear. Most important, he had just engaged a lawyer who was even now flying to Saigon to obtain money from Sobhraj the Tailor. When his father learned of the son's desperate position, surely he would advance sufficient moneys to post bond. Once that was accomplished, assured

Charles, they could leave Delhi on the next flight. For France! It was a promise. Charles made it sound less like a farfetched possibility than a guaranteed law of nature. Later, years later, Hélène would continue to wonder why she let herself be convinced by this man to stay at his side. But she was not the only one. The trail of those conned by his tender promises would by that time stretch farther than Marco Polo's peregrinations.

Rupinder Singh was born in 1948, the year of India's rebirth. He considered it symbolic. His would be a brilliant career in the law, following in the footsteps of his well-respected father, a leading Delhi advocate. Rupi, as everyone knew him, was rail-thin, black-bearded, and had weak eyes always hidden behind blue-tinted glasses. Unusually tall and thin for an Indian when he put on his ever-present dusty black blazer and one of the many bright-colored turbans for each day of the week, Rupi could have been a casting director's dream to play a night club mind reader. It was Rupi's good fortune to be in one of Delhi's central jails on the day when Charles was booked for the Ashoka Hotel robbery. At the time he was attending to paper work necessary to post bail for another accused thief when he heard his name being called. Even though this was his first year as an advocate, and even though he was but twenty-three years old, Rupi's ego and professional opinion of himself were substantial. His name, Singh, means "Lion," after all, and though he more resembled a secretary bird, he was ever ready for combat. This is how he remembers his first encounter with Charles Sobhraj:

I turned around me and beheld a very youthful man whose face was neither East nor West, but who had a commanding personality. I was not surprised to be engaged because I was very popular due to my handling of various murder and smuggling cases, and because of the honored reputation of my father. In that jail, people knew my name. Charles told me that he was the son of a millionaire in Saigon who would willingly post bond and pay all my fees. He was very convincing. He also asked me to look after his wife and daughter, whom he loved very much.

Somehow Charles managed to obtain a prepaid round-
trip air ticket for Rupi, and a modest cash advance, and
off the young lawyer flew to Saigon, a city approaching the
tragedy of war's end. The address which Charles had given
him, the Hong Kong Tailor Company, Ltd., no longer
housed Mr. Sobhraj. The tailor sold his business three
years earlier and was in retirement. No one knew where.
Rupi went from door to door, imploring blank Vietnamese
faces to help him, finally learning that the old tailor was
living in a villa on the outskirts of town. There he found
Mr. Sobhraj, aged, heavy, dying, jewels sparkling on thick
fingers, attended by one Vietnamese wife and one French
mistress, demanding that Indian food be served him at
lunch, French cuisine at dinner. Rupi went directly to the
point; his son was in prison, his son needed 40,000 rupees
for bail; his son promised to pay it back; his son loved
him. The old man sat silently on a brilliantly cushioned
chair for several moments, staring at Rupi with what
seemed to be simmering anger. Then the tailor sighed.
"Ah, that boy," he said, "he always had brains—but they
are on the wrong side of his head." He padded to a safe
and found a brass box and withdrew the requested money.
"What does it matter?" he said, dropping the bills into
Rupi's hands. "My life is over. This city is over. The sum
of everything is nothing."

Hélène dispatched her daughter back to France in the
care of a friend who promised to deposit Shubra with her
grandparents in the Paris suburbs. With the baby went a
note that did not fully explain the crisis that Charles and
Hélène faced, only that they were ensnarled in difficulties
of a red tape nature and that as soon as the bindings were
cut then they would speed to France and collect the child.
For the first few months of 1972, Hélène's life style
drastically declined from suites and room services. She
lived in various cheap hotels, existing on the few hundred
rupees that Charles managed to smuggle out of prison or
pass from his lips to hers on visiting day. She never knew
how Charles obtained money, but there was no doubting
his resourcefulness. She gathered he always collected due
bills and cashed them in emergencies.
Remarkable also was his ability for long distance sur-

veillance. When on a February night she attended a dance given by the French community in Delhi and spent a rare evening of laughter, Charles bitterly condemned his wife on their next meeting. How could she dance the night away and smile at men with her husband in prison? His mood was foul. "How did you know I went to the party?" asked Hélène.

"I know every breath you take," answered Charles. He had many people "working" for him on the outside.

La Passionara spent several weeks of additional terror while she was caught up in India's snail tracks of justice. No amount of indignant denunciation of Charles' accusation that she shared guilt in the Ashoka jewelry caper moved the authorities to dismiss charges that she was an accomplice. An official First Information Report, the Indian equivalent of an investigation and police complaint, was lodged against the American dancer, replete with ripe and vivid language. Her participation was "a malicious and nefarious plan as a result of which the accused persons succeeded in their designs . . . She is an active member of the International Gang of burglars and has played an important part in commissions of crime . . . Keeping in view the intensity of crime she has done, it is strongly recommended that bail be denied and she be sent to judicial lockup . . . as she is likely to escape and leave India by one way or the other . . . perhaps by forged passports as is the custom of this gang . . .

From their retirement in Arizona, Esther's parents sent $2,500 to engage an advocate and pay for bail, which was eventually granted. The advocate asked the dancer if there were any way she could prove (1) that she had never met Charles & Company before the robbery, and (2) that she was indeed a serious *artiste* and not a jewel thief. Helpfully, La Passionara remembered writing her guitarist boy friend in Japan the very night that "Mr. Lobo" first proposed that she dance at the casino in Macao. The letter was located, its postmark verified, and its contents clearly those written by a breathlessly excited performer who had just been offered a potential leap to stardom by a mysterious "Chinese" businessman. *That* helped. But the knight who rode to La Passionara's rescue was an eccentric ma-

haraja named Gajapati Kaju. He was an old man in his
sixties with a long and ill-tended gray beard, a wife and
three large daughters, and the remnants of a family fortune that once included most of the elephants in Madras.
Gajapati Kaju also jogged three miles each morning around
the streets of Madras and ate only one meal a day, though
hostesses in Delhi often remarked that he consumed more
in "one meal" than most men did in a week. He was a
patron of the arts who had taken an interest in La Passionara when she was studying dance in his city. On the
crested stationery of his ancient family, he wrote an eloquent letter to the courts on her behalf.

In it he raised numerous points with Sherlockian de-
duction:

—La Passionara had not *asked* for Room 289, it was
assigned to her arbitrarily by the management. In fact,
she had not even liked the room and had requested a substitution because she disliked the long walk to the elevator
in full makeup and costume.

—Why didn't she yell for help? Easily explained, reasoned Gajapati Kaju; she was terrified. She did not inform
the various waiters and cleaning people who visited the
room over the weekend siege because (1) Charles had a
gun aimed at her liver, and (2) she was in a state of shock.

—She telephoned the front desk immediately for help as
soon as the robbery was completed and Charles was gone.
If she was an accomplice, surely she would have waited
until dawn, until Charles and "the booty" were safely out
of Delhi.

—If La Passionara had not acted with such dispatch,
then the stolen jewels could not have been recovered as
they had been at Palam Airport.

"It is my fervent prayer that all charges against this
unhappy young woman be dropped as early as possible,"
wrote Gajapati Kaju. "She has suffered very greatly."

Whether the letter was sufficient to melt the hearts of
Delhi's police and prosecutors, or whether its signature
carried the clout of an imperial but not forgotten past, is
not known. Whatever, the charges against Esther Markowitz were dropped "for lack of evidence" and La Passionara fled India without looking back. She did stop long
enough to respectfully and gratefully kiss Gajapati Kaju,

who, sometime later, went for his regular morning swim in the Indian Ocean near Madras and drowned. Only his spectacles were washed onto the shore.

Rupinder Singh, using the tailor's money, posted bond for Charles Sobhraj and was not very surprised when his client disappeared from India. Although authorities in Eastern nations usually seethe and cluck their anger at Western criminals who pay for the benevolence of the law and then abuse it by skipping out, the truth is that often this is a much desired solution. Thus are the courts relieved of further prosecutional responsibility and thus is a government spared the housing and feeding of an unwanted felon.

Charles and Hélène began the journey home to France, where they would fetch the baby and begin a new life. But their route was hardly non-stop. Leaving Delhi for Bombay, where Charles purchased two crudely forged passports on the street, they proceeded to Pakistan, where more-genuine-looking passports were for sale, then to Kabul, capital of Afghanistan and ancient crossroad of trade routes from East to West for a thousand years. Charles promised his wife that they would pause but briefly while he attended to "business." Here Ghenghis Khan in the thirteenth century slaughtered so many people that the earth turned red and the rocks glistened with blood. And here, seven centuries later, 90 per cent of the populace lived in the most primitive conditions, the average resident earning less than seventy-five dollars a year and drawing more sustenance from kinship in tribes than to an erratic government structure that wobbled from monarchy to militaristic dictatorship with scant betterment in the way of life. Kabul held no interest at all for Charles as a sightseer, but it did contain a substantial number of smugglers coming or going from Europe to the East, plus a large colony of "hippies"—the word refused to go away—who relished the hashish of the region, despite the very real possibility that a hand might be sliced off by the police in a public square should a dealer be captured. It would become the pattern of Charles' criminal activities that while he generally angled for worthy trophies—i.e., a foolish dowager with rings on her fingers, cash in her purse, and an eye for young men wearing tight pants—he often had to settle for a near comatose youth whose back-pack contained but a few dollars in traveler's checks and an air ticket and a passport.

For two months, Charles and his wife rested in Kabul, enjoying the comforts of a modern hotel. Somehow Charles had come into money again—Hélène never knew its source—and the long stay was a period of relative tranquillity for the couple. As much as Hélène yearned for the boulevards of Paris, it was comforting to have her husband beside her each night.

In mid-1972, Charles announced it was time to leave and he booked air passage to Paris, with an intermediate stop in Istanbul. But they got no further than the Kabul Airport, where police rushed up, surrounded the couple, and arrested them both. It seemed Charles had neglected to pay the hotel bill for two months in residence. At the moment they were intercepted, Charles whispered urgently to Hélène in French, "Deny that you are my wife. Deny that you know me. Don't tell them anything." Hélène did as she was told and had to endure but one night in police custody before she was released. Her passport, unfortunately, was retained pending outcome of the investigation, and once again the young Frenchwoman found herself alone, broke, void of identity papers, and condemned to fending for herself in an exotic city where she spoke not a word of the language. That night she slept underneath a thorn tree amid a colony of Western youth and politely declined the hashish pipe offered her. A few days later, two men found her on the street and gave her a note, a false passport, and some money. It was from Charles, and in the note he apologized for the "small spot of trouble." He was taking care of it, the note said, and she should wait for him in a hotel.

Red Eye was his name, an appropriate description for orbs usually streaked with crimson irritation from the smoke of Afghan hash. Once Red Eye was the most clean cut of American youth. His name was Peter Tovale. On the day that John F. Kennedy was assassinated in Dallas, Pete was a freshman at a West Coast university. Polite, intelligent, and ambitious, he was surely directed toward membership in the community of buttoned-down young men who were so gracefully changing the country. A year after his president was killed, Peter's hair was as long as Ringo Starr's, and two years after that he was part of the belligerent occupation of the dean's office at his university, protesting both the Vietnamese War and the school trustees' refusal to divest its endowment funds of shares in businesses that operated in South Africa. Then a series of personal tragedies—the loss of a parent, the breaking up of a love affair with a girl who carried his baby and in anger aborted it—caused Pete to accept his draft notice and enter the fellowship of the U. S. Army. In the back of his head was the vague idea that if he were sent to Vietnam perhaps he could undermine the U.S. involvement there. But the fates instead dispatched him to Europe, where he found himself performing a most astonishing job in defense of his country. He was engaged as an Army censor, his franchise being advance viewing of Hollywood movies before they could be shown to the troops. His was not the only voice; he served on a committee which determined what films properly upheld the traditions and morality of the Stars and Stripes. *The Green Berets*, John Wayne's strident trumpet blast of endorsement for America's role in Vietnam, won enthusiastic approval, Pete's vote of negation withstanding. But *Easy Rider*, the landmark film which presented Peter Fonda and Dennis Hopper as two counterculture drifters who were brutally murdered by Dixie rednecks, was deemed too radical and of moral danger to America's soldiers.

During his years with the military in Europe, Pete fell in love with a German girl and intended to marry her, saving $5,000 for their beginning. But the girl canceled the affair, throwing Pete into foul depression, and when his service was done, rather than return to the U.S., he elected to wander. Using the $5,000 to purchase an old camper, Pete pointed it East and drove through Europe, across the Bosphorus, and into Asia. By late 1971, he was broke, but rich with memories of girls he had found on the road and exotic grasses smoked in Turkey and Iran. He lost thirty pounds; he was gaunt, ill-nourished, and usually deeply stoned by each midmorning. Christmas found him sitting in a Kabul cafe frequented by young people and trying to determine if the Bangladesh War made it inappropriate for him to drive the camper through Pakistan into India, his next major destination. Another American man, named Dennis, was king of the cafe this night, the maypole around which all the disenchanted wanderers danced. He was from Oklahoma, a former star football player, now wearing a dirty Afghan coat whose fur blended with his beard. Dennis invited Pete, now known as Red Eye, to share a room where one corner was available to spread a bedroll. A couple of girls went along with the offer; Pete enthusiastically accepted.

Two days later, Dennis was arrested at the Kabul Airport for hashish possession, and when police searched his room, they found sufficient crumbs of the illegal substance to seize Red Eye as well. The irony was that the hashish was not his; indeed he had not used the drug for several days, having grown concerned over the deterioration clearly taking place in his grotesquely thin body.

Red Eye was put in a room behind the fire station, where foreigners were held, protesting his innocence and weeping on Christmas Day for lost dreams and a faraway home. A lawyer suggested that for $1,000, presumably to be spread around various official palms, Red Eye could gain freedom. By selling the camper and all his possessions, he accumulated the needed sum. Then Dennis and another Western drug user managed to escape from the fire station, and hell rained on Red Eye. He was sentenced to a minimum of six months with an open end, then transferred by furious police to the central Kabul prison, Damazan, a fearsome place the color of mud. Huge, thick medieval doors with leather seams and studs swung open to receive Red Eye. His body went limp. He was half dragged to the "Western section," which consisted of a row of one-room mud huts, adjacent to the main prison wall. Armed guards walked across the roofs of the huts, their footsteps pounding in each prisoner's ears day and night.

"As prisons go," Red Eye would one day say, "Damazan was rock bottom. The depths." Nothing was provided for prisoners save a cell to confine them. No food was served, and unless an inmate had funds to purchase sustenance, then he could wither and die from malnutrition. Nor were blankets available, nor medicine, nor protection from the rats that scampered through the huts in search of nourishment, nor the occasional adder that slithered in and had to be chased away with clumps of the earthen floor.

By spring 1972, Red Eye had grown accustomed to his bleak world, having learned the way of life inside Damazan. If a prisoner had money, he could hire a *bacha*, an errand boy, who could be dispatched to the bazaar just outside the fifteen-foot prison walls. There food or clothes or drugs could be purchased, the last highly coveted, for there was little else to do in the Kabul prison save smoke enough hash or inject enough morphine to induce a blessed unconsciousness. Thus were nights gotten through.

One broiling April noon, when the earth was parched and prayers were being offered in the mosques for an early monsoon, Red Eye saw an unusual parade approaching the huts of Western prisoners. A large squad of police and soldiers was escorting a young man who was wearing the latest style in French suits, with tinted glasses shielding his eyes, with expensive shoes gleaming from recent polishing. The elegant man carried a leather attaché case and walked with grace and authority. For a moment, Red Eye thought the approaching newcomer was a high-ranking government minister, perhaps the Prime Minister's son. But he was rudely deposited in the mud hut, just like the other prisoners. The new man looked around, grimaced, and introduced himself. His name was Charles Sobhraj, and as soon as the guards left him alone, he announced immediate plans to escape. "Lots of luck," said Red Eye. The prison had more guards than inmates. If anybody ever drifted near the wall, he was shot.

Red Eye studied the new man with interest. On his wrist was a Patek Philippe watch that had to sell for $2,000. How had he managed to keep that? And the attaché case? And what had brought him to this dead end? To a mud hut prison? "They're fools," said Charles. "Somebody told lies about my passport. Fortunately my wife managed to get out. She's in Teheran waiting for me."

"How long are you in for?" asked Red Eye.

Charles shrugged. "That's isn't relevant," he said. "What's important is how long it will take to get out." Quickly Charles dropped a few weighty biographical facts about himself, in the bragging manner of a new kid in the neighborhood who is contending for team leadership. He said he had to reach Teheran *posthaste*, as there were, in addition to his wife, jewels waiting to be sold. His business, he told Red Eye, was the exporting of gems from India and their sale in other countries to wealthy Arabs and Europeans. In the first ten minutes of their association, Charles offered Red Eye a job as courier and said he could make $5,000 a month to start. Red Eye hadn't encountered a hustler like this since he had sold encyclopedias door to door at the age of seventeen in Oregon.

Immediately Charles began pacing around the hut, studying its dimensions, making sketches on the dirt floor with a stick. The room was approximately nine feet wide by twelve feet long and contained six prisoners. The "Western section" was considered minimum security, and aside from the eternal footsteps that sounded on the roof, the guards paid these men little attention, save a cursory check once or twice a day, sometimes not at all. The huts were directly adjacent to the main prison wall, beyond which was the bazaar. The cries of merchants and shoppers haggling could clearly be heard. The bazaar was enormous, an easy place to disappear if only the wall could be transgressed.

After half an hour of earnest study and calculation, Charles determined that a tunnel could be dug from the floor of the mud hut, underneath the wall, and surface once again at the edge of the bazaar. He opened his briefcase and produced a metal spoon, stolen from a hotel in Delhi. "Who wants to go with me?" he asked, holding up the spoon.

"What are you going to do with that spoon?" asked Red Eye.

"Dig the tunnel," said Charles, whereupon Red Eye, modestly stoned at the moment, broke into laughter and rolled into the corner of the hut in a merry ball.

"I'm quite serious," said Charles. "It can be done. But I need help."

"Not a chance," sneered Red Eye, who theoretically had but two months left to serve. He did not wish to risk an extension.

Two other prisoners in the hut, an Englishman and a Canadian both refused as well. But a Frenchman in his fifties, a distinguished-looking gray-haired man who brought

to mind the actor Jean Gabin, spoke up softly. His voice
trembled. "I should refuse, too," he said, "but I want to
get out. I am going to kill a woman." Red Eye knew of
whom the Frenchman spoke. He had heard the story many
times. The woman in question, after quarreling with
Frenchie over something trivial, had been expelled from
his hotel room and out of spite she informed the police
that his luggage contained several passports. A search by
authorities turned up six, including false identity papers
and a few gems, the ownership of which was unprovable.
Frenchie was given two years as a smuggler, and he had
served more than half. Every day of his confinement he
cursed the betraying woman with the rawest of hatred.

"Good," said Charles sympathetically, "we begin." He
bent the teaspoon, crouched down, and made a modest
scratch in the rock-hard earth. Red Eye watched in fascination. He predicted silently that the elegantly dressed newcomer would abandon the idea within the hour. But by
nightfall, Charles had reached a depth of three feet, having
already excavated rocks as large as melons. At this point,
Red Eye grew nervous, for if the tunnel were discovered
by guards, then every man in the hut would receive punishment. To ensure his nonalignment, Red Eye moved to
the hut next door, an easy enough thing to do. Though he
declined to join the diggers, Red Eye made an important
contribution to their security. He had previously obtained
a set of bongo drums at the bazaar and now he sat in the
doorway of his hut, beating them all day long, until his
hands were weary, camouflaging the noise of the excava-
tion. And if the guards seemed headed toward the hut
that contained Charles and the Frenchman, Red Eye would
find a way to divert them with conversation, at least long
enough for the tunnel to be covered with a blanket.

On the second day, Charles faced the problem of what
to do with the dirt he was excavating. Some of it could
be emptied into the outhouse toilet, concealed in the men's
shirts when they went there for relief. But as the toilet
was cleaned once a week, the diggers could not risk putting too much earth into it. Charles directed that the debris
be spread evenly on the floor of the cell underneath the
bamboo mats on which the prisoners slept. Every day the
floor grew in height, and after four days of digging the

guards had to actually step up to enter the cell. But still
they did not seem suspicious. Whenever a guard approached, Red Eye signaled, and Charles extinguished the
faint twenty-watt light bulb, lighting a candle instead that
gave the scantest illumination. When one senior guard,
proud of the prison's electricity, wondered why the stupid
foreigners preferred candlelight, he was told by Charles
that it attracted fewer insects.

On the fifth day, concluding an incredible marathon of
more than a hundred hours during which Charles hardly
slept or ate but still retained his mental and physical
powers, the tunnel was nine feet deep, whereupon it curved
and continued straight ahead for another fifteen feet, then
back up again to within a few inches of an exit just on the
other side of the prison wall. Charles and Frenchie crawled
its distance three times to check its safety and accuracy.
Then he summoned Red Eye. "We're going. Tonight. Do
you want to come along?" Tempted as he was, Red Eye
refused. But he did promise to meet Charles one day again,
somewhere, someplace along the trail of the wanderers.

Red Eye asked one favor. Inside Charles' attaché case,
which the guards had still not confiscated, was a small vial
of chloroform. Charles had shown it to the American one
day. Red Eye knew that the moment the escape was discovered a volcano of recrimination would erupt. "I want
to be totally out of it," said Red Eye. "If I'm really
zonked, maybe they'll leave me alone." He asked Charles
for enough chloroform to ensure a heavy sleep. "I want
to be convincingly dead to the world when the guards
start hitting people."

Charles agreed readily, grateful for the interference
Red Eye had run with his bongo drums. He poured out an
inch of clear liquid into a small cup and gave it to Red
Eye, who wondered if he would ever wake up once it was
consumed. He realized his options were slim. Either drink
the chloroform or get the hide stripped off his back.

On the night of the escape, Red Eye was lying on his
blanket reading by a candle stub, when the prison was
shattered by a cacophony—sirens, shouts, whistles, the
barking of dogs. He sat up quickly, saw Charles running
into the hut. "We're busted," cried Charles, his eyes wild,
his body covered with dirt.

"Sorry," said Red Eye, prudently reaching for the glass of chloroform. Without hesitation he drained it and waited for unconsciousness to shield him from the wrath of the guards. He would later learn what had happened to Charles and Frenchie—an exceptional stroke of rotten luck—or fate. The two men, Charles leading, had crept safely through their tunnel, under the main prison wall, and up again on the side of freedom. Charles removed the last remaining chunk of dirt and saw the stars of a hot night brilliantly welcoming him. With caution he raised his head into the open air and checked to see if anyone was watching. How unkind was this moment! An off-duty prison guard happened to be strolling toward the bazaar and had stopped to light a cigarette. At that instant, he saw a human head rising from the earth, like a miraculous cabbage, or a rabbit sniffing out danger. The guard drew his gun and fired a quick shot, whereupon Charles prudently withdrew and hissed at Frenchie to retreat back to the prison hut. The guard meanwhile discovered the tunnel and attacked it with a stick, forcing a cave-in. Then he raced to the main building and reported an attempted escape. The major in charge, a stout man with a beautifully tended mustache, reacted violently. As if charging an enemy encampment he raced to the line of huts that housed foreign prisoners and ordered each of them into the common yard. There were ten, including Red Eye, who was yanked from his drugged sleep and dragged to the lineup. Two guards had to prop up his body. The major surveyed the motley group for a few moments in silent suspense. Then he grabbed the rifle of an aide and pointed its bayonet at Red Eye's throat. "No one escapes from my prison," he said in thickly accented English. He drew the bayonet back, and Red Eye feared that it was the moment of his execution. The major's eyes bulged and the veins on his temples pounded in angry red streams. One of the sergeants boldly grabbed the rifle and whispered something at the major, presumably the suggestion that it would be troublesome to kill an American in front of so many witnesses.

His face now as red as the morning sun, the major ordered the ten prisoners to his office, where they were told to stand in a circle, hands held, facing outward. The guards now played a torturing game, circling slowly, de-

manding information as to the name of the ringleader,
slapping faces, punching stomachs. Charles readily confessed that it was he, and he alone, who dug the tunnel,
but the major refused to believe him. Red Eye noted that
the major seemed to treat Charles with a certain deference,
as if a man who wore French clothes, a $2,000 watch, and
who stayed in luxury hotels did not have the capacity nor
the deviousness required to soil his hands in digging. The
men began to bleed and faint. Red Eye tried to slip back
into unconsciousness, but even the chloroform failed him.
Charles cried many times, "Please believe me. It was me,
only me!" But the major would not accept the *mea culpa*.

The beatings lasted until dawn. The Frenchman passed
out sometime after midnight, and Red Eye later learned
that he had gone into severe shock. Finally the major
grew weary of the interrogation and ordered the prisoners
taken back to their cells—in handcuffs that could not be
removed. Guards tore apart the huts, confiscating spoons,
anything that might be used as a digging tool. But they
did not take Charles' briefcase. Red Eye assumed that
somewhere along the way money passed hands. But at this
point he did not care. His eyes were so swollen from the
beatings that the world was two narrow slits. Mercifully he
fell asleep.

After a while he awoke. Charles was standing over him.
His handcuffs were unlocked and dangling from one arm.
"I'm sorry for so much trouble," said Charles. He knelt
and with a key easily unlocked Red Eye's handcuffs. "Don't
take them off," cautioned Charles. "If the guard comes
around, make it look like they are still locked." Red Eye
was astonished to learn that in one hidden compartment
in Charles' briefcase were nine different keys, all supposedly masters to the handcuffs of nine separate Asian countries. Charles confided that he had bought them in Hong
Kong and was thus able to foil the police wherever he
went. "I paid enough for them to buy a Rolls-Royce," he
told Red Eye. "There are times when they are more
valuable."

Late that afternoon, the guards appeared and moved the
ten Western prisoners into maximum security, that being
little more than a dirt box three feet wide and five feet
long, high enough for a man to crouch. Two prisoners

were put into each box, stripped nearly naked, and left
to cope with the spiders, the dark, the cold. Red Eye drew
Charles as his roommate, and he still possessed his briefcase. The one privilege that remained for the men in solitary was to send the errand boy, the *bacha,* to the bazaar
for rice, beans, or tea. When the youngster came around
to take orders, Red Eye's shopping list was brief: some
hard candy that would linger in the mouth for hours, and
Mandrax, a powerful sleeping powder. Charles asked the
bacha to go to the pharmacy and purchase a large syringe
—not an unusual request as the prisoners frequently
bought paraphernalia to use in their drug ventures—and a
drinking glass.

"What the hell are you up to?" asked Red Eye. Charles
shrugged, but in his eyes were the makings of another
escape plan. Red Eye marveled at his capacity. Clearly
Charles would hatch scheme after scheme until something
worked.

When the boy returned with the requested purchases,
Charles seized the large syringe, big enough to draw blood
from a horse's limbs, and studied it carefully. Then he
called to Red Eye, waking him from a Mandrax-induced
sleep. Red Eye could barely focus, but when he collected
his senses, he realized what Charles was planning. He
shuddered, with a large measure of horror. Charles was
plunging the syringe into his own arm, then filling it with
his own blood. "Empty this into the glass," he directed
Red Eye, who obeyed, but turned his head away as he
expelled the dark fluid from the syringe. "Now give it
back to me," ordered Charles, taking the syringe again.
The water glass was a quarter full. Twice more Charles
filled the syringe and twice again Red Eye emptied his
cellmate's own blood into the glass. Now it was almost full.

"Thank you," murmured Charles weakly. "I will see
you again someday. Don't forget you can always work for
me." Whereupon he threw his head back and drank in
his own blood, forcing himself to cough and spilling it on
his chin and shoulders and staining his shirt red. He looked
now as he had schemed to look—like a man with critical
internal hemorrhaging. Red Eye screamed for a guard.
When the guard came, he was stunned—Charles seemed
to be on the threshold of death. A stretcher was brought

to take the bleeding prisoner to Vazir Akbar Khan Hospital, his feet and arms handcuffed. Red Eye sat down on the earth and pondered the exceptional lengths that this man would go in pursuit of freedom. But they were beyond his comprehension.

At the hospital it was determined that Charles had a bleeding ulcer and would be treated for several days. He was placed in a private room under twenty-four-hour police guard. Someone started to take away his attaché case, but Charles pleaded that it contained photographs of his wife and daughter—and as he was probably going to die, could he not keep these precious icons in his reach? Permission was granted.

A day or two later, when Charles seemed to be mending, the handcuffs were removed and only his feet remained locked to the bed. He asked the guard for a cup of tea. The guard agreed, ordering one for himself as well. When the tea arrived, the guard accepted the tray, put it down, and went to shut the door. In that fraction of a moment when his eyes were off the prisoner, Charles poured a splash of chloroform into the guard's teacup. Five minutes later, the guard was in the embrace of Morpheus. Calmly, just as he had planned, Charles found a key in his briefcase that opened the cuffs on his feet. He walked quietly out the front door, two weeks to the day from when he was first thrown into Damazan Prison.

Sometime later Red Eye got a postcard from Teheran. On the front was a photograph of the crown jewels, and on the rear was scrawled: "Safe trip out. No problems. Thanks for everything. Hello to friends. Love C." Red Eye stared at it for a long time and then he began to laugh, so raucously that the guard pounded a rifle butt on the mud hut roof as a warning to shut up.

CHAPTER SEVENTEEN

In Charles' own words, dictated patiently to a police stenographer a few years later, his travels during 1972 were astonishing. The stenographer tried to follow the routes by marking red lines on a map of Europe and Asia but after a time gave up. The map was starting to resemble a demented spider's web.

Having escaped from police custody in India and Afghanistan, Charles spun around half the globe like an overwound top. Some of his story was surely fancy, but again much of it was true—as police would one day satisfy themselves. The stenographer wrote an appropriate addendum at the bottom of Charles' statement: "This man lies on every point." But she nonetheless typed out a report that would become part of a burgeoning dossier:

"After I left Kabul," said Charles, "I left my wife there to look after the charges against me. I went first to Pakistan and bought a forged passport. Then I went to Karachi and Teheran, where I stole the passport of an American businessman. I flew to Rome in mid-1972 using this American's passport. In Rome I remained only a few hours and then flew to Paris to visit with my mother-in-law and to pick up my daughter, Shubra, who was very glad to see her father. We telephoned Hélène in Kabul and sang a song to her on the telephone. We then flew to Rome, Copenhagen, and stayed about two days. There I hired a big Fiat and paid about $150 advance deposit. I drove with Shubra to Yugoslavia and was headed for

Bulgaria. I had purchased about twenty passports from hippies in Rome near the Spanish Steps. These were professional hippies, so I was fully satisfied that the passports were clean. When I got to the border crossing between Yugoslavia and Bulgaria, everything was fine until my daughter made water on the car seat where my passport was resting. It got wet, and the customs authorities were suspicious. They told me to pull my car over to the side, and when they opened the luggage trunk, they found the twenty passports I had purchased in Rome. There was no important official at the border at this hour of the night—about 11 P.M.—so they took me to a village about eleven kilometers from the border. The car was detained by customs authorities. They told me to report the next day at 9 A.M. to see the chief. My daughter and I had a late supper, then we decided to leave. We took a taxi all the way across Yugoslavia to Italy. Oh, I forgot to say that along the way I managed to buy two new passports, one for me and one for my baby girl. We put our pictures on them and changed the names. It was thus easy to cross the border back into Italy . . . We flew to Rome. There I was able to buy ten new passports, all good ones, and I flew next to Beirut—not a good city for my line of work. Then we went to Pakistan and finally back to Teheran, where my wife Hélène was supposed to join us. We stayed at the Hilton Hotel. I met an Italian girl at the Hilton whom I had known earlier in my career. She managed to get one passport for me from a businessman, and when this man reported the theft, the Italian girl was arrested. She informed the police about me, and I was picked up. My daughter was put in the care of the French Embassy. Shubra was sent home to Paris to live with her grandparents, and I was convicted on passport fraud and given six months' imprisonment. My wife Hélène flew to Teheran from Kabul and came to see me in prison. Then, on my advice, she left for France . . ."

There was a certain amount of truth in the odyssey—the day would come when police of a dozen nations would attempt to trace every step that Charles took. But there was considerably more to the tale from the point that Charles poured chloroform into the Afghanistanian guard's

evening tea up to the day that Hélène "on my advice" left
for France.

For one thing, he used so many different false names
that the wonder was how he could keep track of just who
he was supposed to be at any given moment. The report
that Iranian police compiled on Charles' activities in 1972
alone showed that he called himself Dr. Jalian Clair,
Charles Sounder, Adolph Nomer, Dr. Marshall Golian,
and Salim Harady. He represented himself to be everything from a professor of classical literature at the Sorbonne to an Arabian oil sheikh. His principal endeavor
during this period seemed to be traffic in gems and stolen
passports, small potatoes crime.

But it would one day come to light—and an official
accusation be made—that Charles participated in a far
more serious matter during his 1972 crisscrossing of Europe and Asia. He was believed to have killed a man, presumably his first. By the time that the Interpol office in
Pakistan tied the murder to his coattails, it would be almost insignificant considering the rivers of spilled blood
attributed to the violent young nomad. The victim, said
the Pakistani authorities, was a fat tour guide and chauffeur named Habib, who lived in Rawalpindi, the ancient
city once the interim capital of Pakistan. Habib was engaged in September 1972 by a handsome young French
couple who called themselves "Mr. and Mrs. Damon Sea-
men." He was commissioned to drive his customers to
Peshawar, a city fabled for its Street of Storytellers, where
for centuries traders from all corners of the East have
gathered to tell tales, barter lambskins for dried fruits, and
haggle over the price of knives. But Habib never returned.

A year later, Pakistani police arrested a woman named
Maria Nunez, who told a horrifying story of what had
happened to Habib the guide:

> I was with Charles on the trip to Peshawar . . .
> Along the way he gave the driver, Habib, an injection
> of something to make him sleep . . . Pretty soon he
> died . . . So Charles put the man in the car trunk be-
> cause he was dead . . . A kilometer or so down the
> road, Charles threw the corpse into the river in a
> forest . . .

A charge of murder was thus filed against "Damon Sea-men," later discovered to be an alias for Charles Sobhraj, and the news telexed to every border station in Pakistan. But arresting the suspect would be something else, and peeling the artichoke down to the core where lived Charles Sobhraj would take years. From this point on, Charles rarely used his real name. He was a different man every week, with a different identity, personality, language, and passport. He was on his way to becoming one of the most brazen and ingenious—but not necessarily successful—operators of modern Asian history.

In late 1972, Charles appeared in Teheran under one of his assumed names and checked into the Hotel Napoleon. From there he cabled money to Hélène in Afghanistan and she hurried gratefully, if angrily, to his side. Almost a year had passed since Hélène had slipped into her husband's bed in Delhi and allowed him to escape, and still they had not made the promised return to Paris. But her temper was softened by a reunion with the little girl, Shubra, now almost two. Charles had stopped off in Paris during his journeys and fetched his daughter. The child looked tired but otherwise adorable and full of chatter about all the interesting places where her daddy had taken her. The young family—father, mother, child—spent a tranquil week in Teheran dining at the best restaurants, watching a royal parade, feeding elephants at the zoo. Charles had expensive bracelets and earrings to adorn his women, and to any passerby the family must have seemed rich and sophisticated and loving.

Late one evening in their hotel suite, however, Hélène lost the thin edge of composure she had so desperately tried to maintain. Tears became screams. Anger filled the room. Charles slapped her. Hard. She threw a chair at him, nicking his cheek and causing a trickle of blood. He wiped it off and flung it onto *her* face. Falling to her knees like a supplicant, Hélène begged to know what was happening. What was their life? What was to be their future? If Charles put as much energy into some legal business as he did into illegal work, she accused, then he would be a millionaire, and his family would be secure.

When Charles responded with a mocking smile—and

silence—Hélène rushed into the bedroom, snatched her sleeping child, and began throwing clothes into a bag. She was going to the French Embassy and if it was closed she would sleep on the steps for the night. The next morning, she was going to find passage back to Paris. If it were necessary to stand on the street and sell her sex, she would do it. The boil was lanced. For three years of marriage she had waited in hotel rooms or prison lobbies. "I even have a police record thanks to you," she cried. "And for all I know, so does my baby daughter."

Quickly Charles sought to pacify his distraught wife. He took her in his arms. He crooned his old song, that he was only trying to save enough money for the good life —for her, for the baby. They would leave tomorrow for France if she was all that insistent, but it would be more convenient if he could wait just a few more days in Teheran for a courier who was on the way from Rome. Charles was setting up some sort of international "network" for his "export business." Once again, wearily, Hélène agreed. During the night she wrote a letter to her parents in France. "We have had trouble," she wrote, "but Charles is changing for the better, and he still loves me. Shubra is precious."

A few days later, Charles was arrested while standing in the lobby of the Teheran Hilton. Someone had informed on him. In his briefcase police found several passports that were not his, plus assorted foreign currencies and gem-stones that aroused their suspicion. Iran's fearsome secret police, SAVAK, began questioning Charles to determine if he was part of a ring that provided passports to terrorists who slipped in and out of Teheran and plotted against the Shah. For several lonely but familiar days, Hélène was once again in the dark as to her husband's whereabouts; he had left their suite one morning saying he would be back by lunch. Then the French Embassy rang to inform her that Charles was once again in jail—and in serious trouble. An official told her that Charles' situation was grave. The Iranians did not deal lightly with those who were in opposition to the Shah. Actually Charles did not have a political thought in his head; his reasoning stopped at the daily money exchange.

Could she at least see her husband? asked Hélène. The French diplomat shrugged. He would try. In December, Hélène played the scene again, wife visiting husband in prison, this time with one variation. She was resolute. "I can't live anymore like this," she told Charles, who for the first time since their marriage was pale and frightened. Bruises colored his arms and neck. He said he had been beaten. "I think I'll always love you," she went on, "but I have to think of our daughter." The French Embassy was advancing her the plane fare back to Paris. There she would file for divorce. There she would change her name. There she would hide. If Charles ever tried to find her, she would hire a bodyguard. Charles listened to her well-rehearsed farewell, but he could not even raise his voice. Three guards with machine guns watched him, at arm's length. He spoke urgently in rapid French. His plight was minor, he insisted. It was a mixup, a case of mistaken identity. He would be out "in a day or two."

Hélène held fast. She fought back tears. "The French Embassy says you will *never* get out of Iran," she said. "And my darling, I somehow hope they are right." Hélène rose and did not kiss her husband goodbye. All she said as she left the room was, "Adieu, Charles." Her husband's cries echoed after her, tormenting her as she boarded the plane for the return to Paris. She could not sleep, not on the long journey, not in the taxi to her mother's home, not until she fell into her parents' embrace and fainted. It was Christmas Eve, 1972. The next morning she went to mass and lit a candle and prayed to God that she would never see Charles Sobhraj again.

In France, Charles' family knew little or nothing of the errant son. Not since he had disappeared years earlier with a pregnant bride had Song seen or spoken with her firstborn, the only news being an occasional postcard drifting in from some elegant hotel in the Far East. The message was always more or less: "Am in Hong Kong seeing the sights, doing business. Hélène and the baby are beautiful. Love, your son Charles."

Félix d'Escogne, however, knew more. Twice he had received urgent cables from Charles or Hélène in the East, beseeching money for bail, and once his suspicions were

confirmed when he visited Bombay on business and was
welcomed by Charles in his best maharaja mood. Not even
Sobhraj the Tailor had received this kind of joyous embrace when he visited Paris. Charles leased a suite at the
Taj Mahal Hotel, filled it with roses and vintage wine,
escorted his patron to the most favored clubs and restaurants of the city—a remarkably bold undertaking, as
Charles was wanted by Delhi police for the Ashoka Hotel
robbery. But Félix was not fooled. He saw the unmasked
pain and worry in Hélène's eyes, and even as he bounced
his goddaughter Shubra on his knee, he knew that Charles
was engaged in some unspeakable enterprise. Often Félix
tried to draw his troublesome friend into private conversation, but whenever the touchy subject of Charles' real
private life was approached, some excuse was found to
cease talking. All Charles would tell Félix was that he was
a successful businessman, planning to open discos and
drugstores in Asia, involved in something vague which
seemed to be buying old slot machines in Beirut and im-
porting them to Asian casinos. Fortune, if Charles was to
be believed, rained blessings each day on his family.

Over the years, Charles continued to write voluminously
to Félix, telling of a $5,000 Rolex watch he was buying,
of a trip to the United States that never came off, of
losing $50,000 in various casinos, of being asked to star
in an Indian movie, finally of the break with Hélène. But
as Charles told it, he caught his wife having an affair and
threw her out.

"With deep sadness I write this letter," he told Félix.
"I have decided to divorce Hélène . . . I am going to give
her 5,000 francs. It's a very very long, very very tragic
story. Little clues and indications and putting things together have finally spelled the truth. I got the proof two
days ago . . . It is such an incredible sadness, even though
I know it is the truth. She wanted me to open a private
bank account for her, and when there was enough money,
she would leave for Hong Kong with her new man. So
I refused! Finally I have come to believe that in life you
can be confident in friendship only from man to man,
like you and me . . ."

And while Hélène waited miserably in Kabul, after
Charles' great chloroform escape trick, she had written

Félix a letter ripe with pain and worry. "I won't go into the details of these last months," she wrote, "but I will say that Charles' situation with Interpol is not very good. Neither is mine after what recently happened. My name has a dossier now, for the first time. My father would die if he knew it.

"On July 2, Charles and I were put in prison in Kabul, and on the evening of July 29 he escaped from the hospital. Three weeks have gone by and I haven't heard from him. The only thing I know is that he hasn't been caught. Maybe it's better that he left Afghanistan. I hope he won't set foot here again. I'm worried sick, but I must stay strong to fight all the new problems. Charles really must stay 'quiet' for a few years after all his trouble. He has been 'noticed' too much these last months. He has so many other problems—material and psychological . . . Marriage to him has not been the happiness that I wanted it to be . . . Tell Charles never to come back to this country or to France. It's too dangerous for him . . . My fear is that he will run out of places to go."

Félix did not pass along the disturbing news to Charles' family. He was particularly careful not to tell André Darreau, the one member of the family who beseeched him regularly for news of Charles, and the one member of the family who seemed most like his half-brother in every disturbing way. In manhood, André had become a twin of Charles, the same slim, powerful body with roughened hands honed by karate, the same piercing brown eyes, the same mélange of East and West in his facial caste, the same grace and power in his step. André had come to Paris in the early 1970s, had knocked on Félix's door, and when it was opened the older man gasped. He thought Charles was on his hearth. But as the two men became friends, Félix was relieved to discover that André was unscarred from growing up in a household that contained a capricious Vietnamese mother and an invalid French father and a half-brother who stirred tempests by stowing away on boats to Africa. But clearly André still worshiped Charles, and Félix feared that the most muted siren call from the East could lure the youngster there.

Because André was well educated, bright, and full of

promise, Félix helped him find a small flat, loaned him a few sticks of furniture, steered him into a job as apprentice clerk in an insurance office. The incessant questions about Charles' whereabouts soon thinned, then after a time they stopped. Figuratively holding his breath, Félix watched with tenuous pride as the twenty-year-old youth worked responsibly and began a routine life in the most beautiful city on earth.

One summer night in 1973, the telephone rang in André's apartment, and when he answered it, the crackle and static of a faraway call waited for him. "André?" finally came the voice that was instantly recognizable. *"C'est Charlot."*

The receiver trembled at his ear. André could feel the power of his half-brother, Out There, from whatever romantic and mysterious place he was calling from. "Just hearing his voice sent chills across my body," André would recall years later.

Once before, when André was seventeen, Charles had called when the boy was a student in Marseilles. He had offered André a job "in my organization," and with reluctance André refused. But he could recall the conversation word for word:

Charles: "You are older now. You must be tall."

André: "One meter seventy."

Charles: "Almost as tall as your big brother. It's time for you to join me. Come to India. I'll send the ticket. Meet me at the Taj Mahal Hotel in Bombay."

The temptation had been enormous, but André could not put down a coincidental wave of fear. He rejected his brother's overture. Now, as he heard Charles warming up with family inquiries over the crackling long distance line, he suspected a second invitation was forthcoming.

"Do you remember the last time we talked?" suddenly asked Charles.

André held his breath. "Yes, of course. It's been sleeping in my mind."

"Then it's time for you to become a man. I'm in Istanbul. I need someone I can trust. I'm sending you a plane ticket."

André could not answer. He began to stammer.

"There are two kinds of people in this world," said

Charles. "Those who take risks, and those who don't. I'll meet you at the Istanbul airport. You'll recognize me, won't you?"

"Yes," whispered André. "Oh yes."

CHAPTER EIGHTEEN

Even as the Air France jet taxied toward the Istanbul terminal, André Darreau saw his half-brother through the window. There was no mistaking Charles, dressed as he was in sleekest navy blazer, a celebrity's dark glasses masking his eyes, two aides hovering in discreet attendance. He looked like a Greek tycoon, or the son of one, and André felt threadbare in his slacks and turtleneck sweater. When André pushed his way through customs, apprehensive over reunion with a brother he had not seen for almost a decade, he heard his name paged. On the courtesy phone, Charles spoke brusquely. "Welcome," he said. "When we meet outside, my name is Alain. *Comprends*? Alain Gauthier. I will explain later."

André found his luggage, cursed its cheap plastic exterior, and walked slowly toward Charles/Alain, waiting for him with a broad smile. The two men fell into one another's arms and kissed on the mouth. Charles introduced his two aides, a *garde du corps* and his *homme à tout faire*, explaining that his business interests were such that he required both a bodyguard and a Man Friday to serve him. Several days would pass before André learned that the bodyguard, whose shoulders were a yard wide, was a Dutch killer, and the secretary none other than Pierre le Premier, who had bribed his way out of India, just as Charles had taught him.

Charles had summoned his two henchmen to Istanbul after one of his less spectacular escapes from custody in

Teheran. The Iranians had granted Charles bail while an
investigation was made of the stolen passports found in
his briefcase. Giving Charles bail was like telling a cat
not to prowl at night. Immediately Charles made his way
to the Iraqi border by stolen car, thence overland to
Turkey, where, in Ankara, he romanced a wealthy young
woman and "borrowed" enough money from her to set
up shop in Istanbul.

A chauffeured limousine bore the men to a hotel, Charles
and André speaking of trivialities—the weather in Paris,
the new fashions, the agonies of airplane food, the sights
to see in Turkey. But the moment they were alone, in
Charles' suite, the conversation turned intimate. Obviously
Charles was hungry for the embrace of his own blood. He
peppered André with questions: How was Song, their
mother? Was the French lieutenant still suffering from
headaches? What were the other children doing? Was
Leyou still angry over the 6,000 francs that Charles had
"borrowed" and lost at baccarat?

André answered as best he could, then ventured a
question of his own. Why was Charles using another name?
The answer was vague and rambling, something about an
unresolved problem with police somewhere, long ago. As
Charles was now in Istanbul on a major business venture,
he did not want some old sore to erupt. It seemed more
appropriate to use a fictitious name for the time being.
"Everyone does it in the East," said Charles. "I know
men who change their names like they change their underwear." André laughed; if Charles said something was true,
then it must be true.

André had one other question. What of Hélène? And
the baby? Charles' face turned dark and anguish filled his
eyes. He cursed his estranged wife. She had turned out to
be a cheat, a deceitful woman who played around and
did not take proper care of the child, said Charles. He
had banished her from his life until "she gets her values
in order." It was in Charles' plans to someday take custody
of Shubra away from her mother. André murmured sympathies and support, thinking briefly that this must be the
reason why Charles had summoned him to Istanbul. But
he dared not venture the question. The moments in Charles'

presence were full of an eerie power. André was in the grip of a force he did not understand. The best he could do was to sit rapt and try to meet the gaze of his half-brother's seductive eyes, worried all the while that he appeared like a clumsy, ill-prepared student at the feet of a master.

About the suite were scattered the latest newspapers in French and English. Abruptly, as if he were a newscaster, Charles began delivering a commentary of the world's current events—Watergate, the Socialist surge in France, the new war winds in the Middle East, the fluctuations of gold on the Swiss exchange. He rattled off the latest valuations of a dozen hard currencies. André listened open-mouthed; he had no idea that Charles was so well informed. He noticed grammar books in Russian and Chinese on a coffee table. "I'm learning those languages," said Charles. "By the way, can you speak anything besides French?" André shook his head. A little English, a few phrases in Italian.

"In my business, languages are money," said Charles. He spoke French, English, German, Spanish, Italian, Vietnamese, and enough Greek and Hindi to get by. "They're easy for me," he went on. "It simply takes concentration. Like everything else I do." On the floor was a large satchel from which spilled paperback books, mostly mysteries and spy yarns, with a few classics. "I read them for entertainment—and homework," explained Charles. "Joseph Conrad, Graham Greene, and Somerset Maugham have been there before me."

A chess set of finely carved ivory rested on a dresser, causing André to comment that he enjoyed the game. Charles quickly set up the board, destroying his half-brother in a few moves. "Do you know karate?" then asked Charles. André nodded cautiously, wondering why his brother was rummaging in all the compartments of his life. "How good are you?" asked Charles. A shrug. André said he usually went to a karate club in Paris three times a week. Charles frowned. That was not what he meant. Could André "put somebody out"? André nodded, unenthusiastically. He supposed so. But karate was just a sport to him, not a weapon.

"Show me how good you are," commanded Charles.

They squared off, André feeling fear—there was no other word, Charles with a look of unbrotherly menace on his face, testing, measuring, criticizing, at last complimenting. Then he stretched out on the floor and ordered André to leap on his stomach and jump up and down. André declined. Charles insisted. André did as he was told, discovering that Charles' stomach was flat, hard, muscled, impervious to hurt. "I will be doing that to *your* stomach in a few weeks," said Charles.

André went to the bathroom and washed his face with cold water. He was confused. Since the plane had landed in Istanbul, things had been out of focus. He had not seen Charles for years; now he was discovering that the brother he idolized was obviously rich, certainly well informed, estranged bitterly from his wife, using a false name, and either eccentric or well on the way to crazy. He summoned courage and bore directly to the point. What *was* Charles' business. What did Charles want with him?

"We will get to that soon," said Charles briskly. "Come, let's walk. I will show you Istanbul."

They toured the Hilton public rooms where André heard all the languages that Charles could speak. The lobby swirled with color, with wealthy women and men promenading across carpets of lime and violet. Shops offered jewels and antique statuary and carved ivory pipes and brilliantly woven carpets—a bazaar, but a sterile one, with no dirt, or odor, or necessity to haggle. On a terrace off the lobby, Charles gestured at the city, to the Bosporous, to the minarets and looming domes of the great mosques that reared up like ghosts from gray mists and smoky dusk. "They think they are Europeans here," said Charles, "but they are really Asian. Rather like me." Charles led André through an English pub in the hotel basement, into a scarlet-walled cocktail lounge where an American girl sang listless pop, finally to a casino operated by Italians and crowded with tanned men in dark glasses and lovely women with restless eyes. "Recently I won so much money at baccarat here," whispered Charles, "that the house got worried and sent in a beautiful girl to sit beside me and distract me. It did not work." While they spoke, André noticed two casino officials looking at

Charles and murmuring to one another. Obviously his
brother caused a stir in this moneyed chamber.

Now it was dark; a full day had spun by. But André
was not weary. Just being with his brother charged him
with energy. He found himself walking obediently down
a cobblestone lane, heavy with darkness and forbidding
shadows, toward a dimly lit building. Charles was taking
him to Istanbul's leading *hamami*, Turkish bath. In cavern-
ous rooms whose marble walls and vaulted ceilings glistened with moisture like the bodies of the men who lay
on slabs beneath them, Charles and André underwent the
rite of cleansing. First was a massage that veered on sad-
ism; the masseurs pummeling their bodies to the threshold
of pain, twisting and bending limbs like pretzels, kneading
muscles so tightly that André feared he would cry out in
pain. But beside him Charles lay immobile, no expression
save that of an *observateur*, watching for a flicker of weakness in André. The masseurs took them to another room,
made them sit on the floor beside large marble basins,
attacked their lean, nude, muscled bodies with stiff brushes
and rough cloths and strong soaps, drenching them a
dozen times until their skins glowed pink and new. A
giant wandered past, one of the masseurs, with a mustache
like raven wings and shoulders broad enough to prohibit
entry through most doorways. Charles nudged André.
Could he put *that* man out? "I don't think so," said André
truthfully. Charles smiled. "Neither could I," he said. "Not
with karate. But there are other ways."

Later, when the night was old, Charles and André
walked through a covered flower market hidden in a maze
of tiny streets, merchants offering spectacular arrays of
tulips more rich in color and texture than any in Holland,
roses with petals more creamy than from any English
garden. Down an alley was a jumble of open air cafes
where thousands of men were gathered, smoking strong
cigarettes, drinking liters of dark, bitter beer, dipping tiny
crayfish into bowls of spiced yoghurt, summoning vendors
to buy pistachio nuts and toasted almonds and potato
chips just lifted from vats of grease and fried oysters on
a stick. Counters bent under heavy bowls of figs and
sugared dates and rich pastries drowned in honey and

toasted coconut. The air was rich with men laughing. A
bear danced for coins. Blackbirds perched under ancient
gables and swooped down to steal food from unattentive
diners. Music from a score of cafes dueled to be heard.

Charles found a table and ordered two teas. He did not
drink liquor or wine, nor did he smoke. He could not
afford vices, he informed André. The younger man was
struck by the total absence of women. The swirling street
of cafes was a club for men. Why? "Turks leave their
women at home," explained Charles. "Turkish men only
trust Turkish men. It's not a bad idea. Women are be-
trayers." As they sipped their tea, Charles studied the
men around him, remarking now and then on personalities,
seemingly speculating on whether this man was a failure,
or this man destined for success, or why this man looked
so desperately unhappy. André was spellbound. What he
was hearing was not idle cocktail party talk, but what he
took to be a precise psychological capsule of complete
strangers.

"Psychology is very important to me," said Charles. "It
is the principal weapon in my business. I use psychology
like stupid people use guns."

Throughout the longest night of his life, André listened
while his brother spoke of psychology. Charles said his
education had not really begun until he entered Poissy
Prison. Had André heard of his incarceration? The younger
man nodded discreetly. He had been present the night
Félix first came to the house in Marseilles and a detective
had taken the place of his father in bed. At that, Charles
smiled.

He had come to believe, said Charles, that into each
life is placed a series of tests. They are shocks, they are
crises, they are turning points. And if a man is weak, and
succumbs to these tests, then he is crippled for life, imprisoned by stupidity and lack of understanding. "I have
had many shocks," said Charles, "and from each of them
I have learned." Destiny had teased him unmercifully,
said Charles, but he was no longer afraid of it.

His study of many psychologists, particularly Jung and
Nietzsche, had taught him to discern easily, usually at first
meeting, the kind of personality a person possessed. He

had spent all of this day and night studying his half-brother, said Charles, and he was pleased. He found André to be "Non-Emotive, Active Secondary." André's face showed blankness. That meant, instructed Charles, that his little brother was reasonably independent, open to challenge, probably a bit of an egotist. Correct? André nodded dumbly.

"As for me," said Charles, "I am Emotive and Active Secondary. That type of personality usually obtains 'the highest place' in society—bank directors, presidents, world leaders. This is not conceit," said Charles, and André would always remember the words. "I know who I am. I know my limits, my talents. I never fool myself. I may cheat others, but I never cheat myself."

He delivered a parenthetical sermon on how André must never be submissive. He must never be a "follower" in life. There are inferior beings and superior beings, instructed Charles, and it does not necessarily come with birth and conditioning. For a long time he blamed his troubles on parents and early life. Then he realized that these experiences could strengthen, not weaken, that he could *use* everything that ever happened to him.

Charles instructed his half-brother to read a good biography of Adolf Hitler, "not for approval of the man, but to understand how one person achieved such power. He was a little man, ugly, but he almost captured the world . . ."

Some people are unlucky from the moment of conception, reasoned Charles. They are condemned from the moment they come into the world. They are told this, and they begin to believe it, then they accept it, then they die. And no one cares. No one remembers. "The inferior being cannot overcome the feeling that life has cheated him. This does not have to be true. You *can* change your destiny. You *can* wrestle with fate. Trust me. I will prove it to you."

At that, André felt a chill. He knew that the moment of revelation was near. Now he was feeling the clamp of fatigue, but Charles rattled on, as fresh as the approaching morn. Walking to the window and looking out at the mauve glow that would soon push away the night, a new sun coming out of Asia with its gift of light and warmth for Europe, Charles waited until the sky was red, until his face glowed scarlet. "You probably think I'm egocentric," he said softly. "Of course I am. It's not an attractive quality perhaps, but I accept it and live with it . . . I am also an adventurer. How many people lie down in their graves without having felt one drop of excitement in their blood?"

Charles turned and beckoned André to join him at the window. Together they looked out at the crossroads of two continents. "I need you, little brother," whispered Charles. "I need my own blood beside me. Will you join me?"

There was not a moment's hesitation. André would look back and remember that he did not wait a microsecond before nodding his assent.

"Good," said Charles. "Tomorrow we begin."

"Begin *what*?" asked André.

"My business is quite simple," answered Charles. "I am a thief."

André plunged into a quick but thorough training program. First there was the basic matter of appearance. Charles took him to a tailor and ordered suits cut elegantly, in dark blue or anonymous gray, conforming to his dictum that for this line of work André should be well dressed but not conspicuous. Next he dictated a list of newspapers, magazines, and travel books to devour, so as to enrich his conversational capacity. Within two days, André could pass a test on the splendors of Istanbul, from the emeralds in the Topkapi Museum to the hours open to a non-Muslim for visiting the Blue Mosque. And, over and over again, Charles defined the demands of the work: André's job was to meet prospective victims. It was absurdly easy. These people are usually on holiday. They are keyed up, far away from home, grateful for any kindness, thrilled when they meet someone who speaks their language. French people are especially happy to find someone who speaks French, as they consider non-French-speaking people to be barbarians. You meet people by asking for a light for your cigarette, or striking up a casual conversation in a bar, or making some idle comment about the weather or something interesting you have seen or someplace you plan to go. Once the connection is made, then you find out the person's interest in life. First the line of work, then his or her weakness. And this must be accomplished in the first few minutes of conversation. The trick is to hook the person into spending an evening with you. If it's a man and he wants girls, okay. You know where to find girls. The best girls. If it's a woman and she wants to pat you on the leg, surrender slowly before purring like a lapdog. If it's jewelry, fine. You know the most attractive bargains in Istanbul, at least 50 per cent cheaper than anywhere else. Hashish? Certainly. You know where to buy the best—discreetly. Queers? Sure, you play the game—up to a certain point. It all comes down, taught Charles, to discovering the vice —the French word is *défaut*—as quickly as possible, and in normal conversation without going out of bounds. One never just comes out and asks, "Do you want girls?" Or "Do you want to buy hashish?" That is the territory of a cheap hustler. André was to appear as a respectable, responsible tourist, as a businessman with sophistication and connections. Once confidence was established, then an evening of dinner and entertainment could be undertaken.

And with the forbidden fruit dangling in temptation before the victim, the night traditionally concluded with the administering of enough sedatives—usually Valium or Mogadon, a colorless and tasteless potion to induce sleep —so the money, valuables, and travel documents could be appropriated in return for all this splendid care and attention. In the vernacular of Interpol, Charles was a "drug and rob" man, whose ancestors went back to antiquity.

Charles had one hard and fast rule, inviolate: he would not use anything that could later be used in evidence. That meant no weapons. No guns. No knives. And, paramount, no drugs. "Do not use them or deal in them," insisted Charles. Promise them, but never fulfill the promise. Horror stories rained on André's ears concerning Western youths who were rotting in jails from Istanbul to Singapore for stupid traffic in drugs.

Each morning the brothers arose early and took an hour's karate practice before breakfast, concluding by jumping on one another's stomachs and kicking hard into

crotches shielded by pillows. Within a few days, André
felt equal to Charles in both prowess and strength and
looked forward to proving to his older brother that his
muscles were well toned.

Next, a light meal of fresh juice and fruit, a lean sliver
of meat, a handful of vitamins. Then a drill on current
events. Who was H. R. Haldeman? What was Richard
Nixon's defense posture on Watergate? What was the
Swiss franc worth? What was Saigon now called? Who
was Atatürk? How does one fly from Cyprus to Athens?
What *is* the dispute over Cyprus, anyway? What is the
standard price of a four-by-six Moroccan carpet? How
does one deal with a traveler's stomach? What are top
American television shows? Who is Al Pacino? Where
does the Shah of Iran ski each winter? André read deep
into each night—*Time* and *Newsweek* and the *Times* of
London and the Paris *Herald Tribune*, laboriously con-
sulting his French-English dictionary, dreading the quiz
that Charles would put him through. They spoke now
only in English, total immersion, and within two weeks
André was reasonably conversant.

André also learned that in addition to the Dutch bodyguard and Pierre le Premier, who were in another hotel
and lounging around waiting to be called, Charles had
others on his payroll. They included sumptuous young
women who were willing to drape themselves over the
arms of prospective victims and withdraw discreetly at the
moment that Charles laced a cocktail with five Valiums.
Usually the girls were French or American, and André
found them to be attractive, chic, and intelligent. Years
later, André would recall how easily Charles recruited the
bait:

"He had extraordinary power over women. Give Charles
a few hours around a girl and even if she were convent
educated and the daughter of a police inspector, she would
usually do what Charles asked her to do. He represented
mystery, intrigue, romance. He was a woman's fantasy of
one moment of adventure—and danger."

Not long into his education, André saw how it worked.
Charles noticed a striking young American girl around
Istanbul. In her early twenties, she was blessed with a
bountiful figure and a merry laugh; men turned to stare

when she passed. The only trouble was—she had a boy friend in tow and planned to marry him. Charles was determined to steal the girl, if he could sunder the relationship.

He began with the boy, having sized him up as "weak" and "passive." The youth, Tom, twenty years old and from a Chicago suburb, had no discernible goal in life and seemed content to drift and wander and squeeze his girl friend's hand. Charles bought him dinner, stroked his ego, praised his potential, gave him "respect." Dreams were floated. What was Tom's secret desire? A Mercedes? A castle? A mountaintop? A poem? As it turned out, Tom had vague thoughts of opening a store in a college town, one that would sell jeans and have a small restaurant attached, with folk singers. Charles thought that was the most wonderful dream in the world. He sympathized, he understood, he offered ways to realize the dream. But he warned Tom not to burden himself with the demands of marriage. By dawn, Tom was putty to be shaped by the sculptor that was Charles. He was dispatched on an imaginary errand into the Turkish countryside, a trip that would take days, his order being to search for a place that sold exquisite antiques.

When he was gone, and out of the way, Charles moved in on the girl, Sherry. Now his tactic changed. He tore the absent fiancé to shreds. He characterized Tom as a loser, a failure condemned to life's slag pile. André, present, listened to the conversation with fascination and dared not intrude.

Sherry disagreed. She said Tom had always been good to her and good for her. "Goodness and weakness are often a synonym," shot back Charles. He ordered the girl to wake up and face reality. How could she commit to a man with no direction to his life? Soon Sherry began to waver, and Charles pressed, circling like a picador, thrusting darts of doubt and worry. Then she chimed in with minor flaws in Tom's character, each of which Charles agreed with, seized, and magnified to grave disorders.

When Tom returned empty-handed from his foray into the countryside, he discovered that Sherry was cool to him. She announced newly found intentions of "waiting" before any marriage, of "needing time to think." Surprisingly, Tom did not receive the news with noticeable discomfort. It was fine with him, he said. Charles promptly gave Tom another assignment, to visit hippie hangouts near the Blue Mosque and determine if there were any prospective "clients" who might be relieved of their passports and traveler's checks. His commission would be 50 per cent of any proceeds. Nodding as if the assignment were the most routine of jobs, Tom left immediately.

Sherry went to work as well, becoming, in effect, a prostitute. "She had never been one before and she would never be one again," recalled André. But for Charles she would entertain a client, lead him on, go to his room, partially disrobe, and wait for him to pass out. Then she would call Charles and watch while the man's pockets were stripped.

Often André tried to analyze the phenomenon of why men and women with no previous frame of reference for this kind of work would tumble so quickly to the exhortations of his half-brother.

"They did it because they fell in love with him," he told a friend. "The men saw in Charles everything they could never be. And the women wanted him for a lover, although few ever got him. And they also did it because they were rewarded well. Sherry left Istanbul with $3,000 cash and a $2,000 wristwatch on her arm. Her boy friend was last heard from in jail, where he had been arrested on a dope charge. Charles was right, of course. Tom *was* weak. Tom *was* doomed to failure."

Over several months in late 1973, Charles and André and their cohorts successfully robbed several tourists, though the proceeds were disappointing. One netted $6,000, but after commissions were deducted, and bills paid for dinners and hotel rooms and medicines, the profit was less than $1,500. By early November, André noticed that Charles was restless, fretting that his season in Istanbul was failing. He could not afford to stay too long for fear that police or hotel security would unmask him. In their later analysis of the case, Interpol theorized that specializing in tourist robberies gave Charles a certain advantage, for he usually selected victims who were in Istanbul for only a day or two. After a robbery, it was easy to withdraw and rest in a small hotel for several days, making sure the victims had left the country before returning to the forest for more hunting.

One autumn night, Charles nudged André and gestured toward a pair of potential victims who reeked with promise, an American couple, both past sixty, she wearing a full length mink with diamonds on her fingers and earlobes, he in a well-cut suit and shoes not run down at the heel. Their attitudes were those of people accustomed to money and power. Most important, they were old, and they clung to one another walking across the hotel lobby as if venturing into a maze of darkness. They seemed lonely. Their names were Phil and Ethel and they were on a round-the-world trip to mark their fortieth wedding anniversary.

The next day Phil and Ethel were under scrutiny. Charles watched their every public move, as André later put it, "like a hawk watching a mouse." When they spoke to the concierge, Charles was nearby, absorbed in a travel folder. When they took tea in the lobby, Charles was seated behind, on the adjoining sofa, listening, making mental notes. Then, at a moment when Phil and Ethel were waiting for an elevator on the floor where they were staying, a voice called out, "Wait, please!" and up hurried Charles, full of smiles and gratitude. By the time the elevator reached the lobby, Charles was well enough connected with the couple to invite them for a drink. Would they mind if a business associate from Paris joined them? Thus was André brought in. Charles and his brother used fake names and fake identities, posing as importers and speculators in currency. At first, the American couple seemed foolish and vacuous, but as a long evening crept by, they became appealing. Deeply devoted, still in love, they touched hands often, not out of nervousness or habit, but because they cared for one another. Phil spoke freely of his business—grain futures, of which Charles knew enough to speak intelligently. She was a retired high school counselor. They had no children, but they had each other, and a pair of basset hounds back home they fretted about. Charles swept everyone up and into a taxi and to a cafe beside the Bosporus, where raucous Turks sang and whirled Ethel about the dance floor. Phil's eyes glowed with delight. When it was time to settle the bill, Charles reached quickly, but Phil beat him, producing a folder of traveler's checks thick with hundreds. The two Frenchmen stared at the money and their eyes met fleetingly. But Charles did not seem as confident as André reasoned he should have. Something was worrying him.

Back at the Hilton, they all took a nightcap in the English pub, Ethel bubbling about the glorious, romantic evening she had spent with three handsome men. She kissed Phil giddily and he kissed her back, neither noticing when Charles moved his hand across their glasses, dropping Valiums into each. At the same moment, Charles checked his watch. André knew what he was doing. From practice and study, Charles knew the time it required to put someone to sleep with Valiums, relating the medication to weight, age, and amount of alcohol consumed. It was André's guess that on this night the elderly couple would collapse within twenty minutes, but by then Charles would have escorted them upstairs and into their bedroom.

André waited for the reaction. He had seen it before. It rarely varied. A victim first grows dizzy, feels a vague malaise, refuses to acknowledge it with the hope that it will pass. Then the eyelids grow heavy, speech becomes slurred, bones turn to jelly. Charles always waited for the precise moment when the victim was on edge of passing out but still able to enter an elevator and walk down a hotel corridor, sometimes sagging on the way.

But after fifteen minutes had come and gone, Phil and Ethel were still very much among the conscious, not wanting to end the party. André could see that the drugs had hit, had hit hard. On their faces were puzzled looks. But neither was willing to acknowledge that their old bodies were under assault. In defense, Ethel reached out and clasped her husband's hand as if it were the last branch on the cliff's edge, and he moved his head to her shoulder. They remained thus, looking both tender and silly, for several more minutes, long past the instant when they should have crashed onto the floor. Charles studied the couple carefully, while his mouth made inane conversation about investments in Asia. Then he spoke softly. "You seem a little under the weather," he murmured. "It's been a long night. May I help you to your room?" Ethel nodded gratefully; she could no longer make words. Phil's eyes were glazed and he shuffled slowly, like an old man just released from a hospital bed.

Charles and André helped them across the lobby, into an elevator, propping them up until the room was reached. Without being asked, Phil handed Charles the key. Charles guided them to the bed as lovingly as a parent to a child, and he whispered good night. Ethel tried to smile and her lips formed a deeply felt "Thank you."

With that, Charles left. He did not even look about the room. On the ride back down, André wanted to ask why Charles had left the old couple without taking anything. But he lacked the courage. Instead Charles spoke without prompting. "Those people are superior. I respect them."

The next morning, Charles telephoned to make sure Phil and Ethel had survived the night, then took them to lunch, even provided a chauffeured car and a camera to use for their remaining day in Istanbul. The Americans left Turkey happy, enriched with stories to tell of dashing Frenchmen encountered in romantic, dangerous Istanbul. They would never know that they stood on the precipice —and due to the strength of their love, a love that Charles had never experienced—they were permitted to keep their money. And their lives.

CHAPTER NINETEEN

November 10 is the anniversary of Kemal Atatürk's death, when Istanbul mourns each year for the father of modern Turkey. The bars close, movie houses still their projectors, mosques are crowded, old women weep on street corners. On this day in 1973, an interesting middle-aged couple from Paris checked into the Istanbul Hilton and were disappointed to discover that the city was shrouded. Both actually should have remembered, since the man and the woman had been reared in Turkey and made annual return visits to Istanbul to visit families and to show off their French trappings.

Anton Kecvic and his wife Krista had been born to poor Armenian farmers, had made their separate ways to Istanbul, had become associated in menial work for the garment industry. They met and married young, forming a strong and successful partnership. Krista had an adventurous sewing needle and a flair for design; Anton possessed the ability to merchandise her clothing, first from pushcarts, then from a tiny stall buried in the bowels of the spice market, finally into export. They moved to Paris when both were nearing forty, began a dress and lingerie business, and lived elaborately on a side street near the Avenue Wagram.

Each autumn they returned to Istanbul and, rather than favor one relative over another with their glamorous presence, always stayed instead at the Hilton, where, in the best sense of the word, they could go home again.

Krista swaddled her thickening body in black mink, and on Anton's finger sparkled a major diamond. She was growing heavy, hair bleached platinum on the Faubourg Saint-Honoré, troubled by migraines. He was thin, aquiline, balding, dour. But each felt rejuvenation at the homecoming, the ego lift that comes when money is displayed to those of the same blood who never realized the dream to seek and find success.

Signing the hotel registration card, Anton told the clerk how disappointed he was to arrive on Atatürk's memorial day. He had planned an evening of gambling in the hotel casino. He also remarked that perhaps it was a blessing as well, for Krista would be delayed at least one day from her assault on the city's jewelry shops. As Anton talked, he did not notice the thin and well-dressed Oriental-looking man who hovered nearby, browsing through a folder.

For the next two days, shadows trailed the Kecvics. When Anton met an old grizzled friend from the Istanbul garment district, and spoke of his long-unrealized plans to someday crack the Japanese market with his line of lingerie, Charles, sitting nearby and sipping a cocktail with a young woman, overheard every word. And when Krista made mock complaint to a cousin over a cottage cheese lunch in the hotel's coffee shop, carping that Anton was an overly enthusiastic gambler who brought several thousand francs to Istanbul to finance his passion, André was two tables away and absorbing all.

On the third day of the Kecvics' stay in Istanbul, Charles made his move. He booked Room 410 in the Hilton under an assumed name and called a meeting of his associates. Present were André, the Dutch bodyguard, whose name was Van Dam, and Pierre le Premier. No women would be needed for this project. As was his custom, Charles began the meeting with a karate exercise, demonstrating with André that their extremities were potentially lethal weapons. Charles did this regularly, as if to remind his associates that any betrayal or misdeed would be punished accordingly. Then, invigorated by the flying kicks and menacing postures, Charles clapped his hands together. He had good news for his group. He had chosen one last business venture for the season in Istanbul. If it were successful, and he had every reason to believe it would be, then they would leave Turkey immediately and take a long holiday. The potential for this finale in Istanbul was substantial, ample to finance at least six months of indolence for all involved. He outlined the plan, made everyone repeat his respective responsibilities, then dispatched each on various errands. André was sent to the central bazaar to purchase toy pistols. Van Dam had to find a printer who could make up a calling card instantly—and in Japanese characters. Pierre was sent to find a book on the Far East textile market. And everything had to be done by sundown—when the casino opened.

That night, the cards were kind to Anton Kecvic. At the baccarat table, he won more than 25,000 Turkish lira (about $5,000) and was in an ebullient mood. Two chairs away, an Oriental man was less fortunate. He had lost steadily all evening, although the sums were minor. When Kecvic rose to take a break and took a light whisky and soda at the bar, he noticed the Oriental man had done the same and was depressed at his losses. Kecvic consoled him in English, and the loser responded in French. "You speak French!" exclaimed Kecvic, happy as any Frenchman is to encounter a man with the same tongue in a place far from Paris. "I am Japanese," said Charles, who introduced himself as Mr. Okada, "but I have spent much time in Paris." Mr. Okada presented his business card, its ink barely dry, and he received one in kind from Anton Kecvic. The two men made small talk—of Paris, of baccarat, finally of business. Mr. Okada revealed he was an investment counselor who was interested in marrying Paris couture with Japanese labor and money. He was on his way to France for discussions with clothing manufacturers. How extraordinary! exclaimed Anton Kecvic. That was precisely what *he* had in mind.

Mr. Okada spoke extensively of the Eastern potential for fine clothing, how Japanese women were ready to buy French design, throwing out impressive statistics as to labor costs, share of the market, the possibility of using cheap Indian seamstresses in Delhi and of exporting by sea to Japan and, potentially, Los Angeles. He held Anton Kecvic spellbound. And, as icing on this tempting *gâteau*, it so happened that there was *another* Japanese business-

man in this very hotel who was interested in financing such
a venture, having made a fortune in electronics and now
wanting to diversify. This man was named Saito and he
was eccentric, rarely leaving his hotel room, preferring to
have visitors call on him. He was extravagantly wealthy
and difficult to meet, but Mr. Okada felt certain he could
arrange a rendezvous, perhaps for tomorrow night in the
casino. Anton Kecvic went to bed happy, twice blessed,
by the cards and by the "coincidence" that had seated the
intriguing Mr. Okada two seats away at baccarat.

The next night, Kecvic waited in his room, as per
directions, and around ten came the expected telephone
call from Mr. Okada. Great news! The mysterious Mr.
Saito had agreed to meet with the French lingerie manu-
facturer. Come quickly! Excited, Kecvic rushed to the
rendezvous, dressed in his best, leaving Krista grumblingly
alone to dine from room service.

But in the casino, Mr. Okada was glum, checking his
watch and glancing at the entrance. He sighed and apologized to Kecvic. It seemed that Mr. Saito had stood them
up. Hugely annoyed, but knowing a little of Japanese
protocol, Kecvic contained his feelings and said he would
be glad to wait. Half an hour dragged by. Mr. Okada
went to the house phone, spoke expansively, returned to
inform Kecvic that the object of their attentions was feeling a little under the weather and that he wished to receive
them in his hotel room. That was fine with Kecvic; the
casino was crowded and noisy.

Room 410 was empty and bereft of signs that anyone
was in residence. It was a simple room, hardly the kind
of accommodation that a wealthy Japanese would occupy.
Quickly Mr. Okada had an explanation: Mr. Saito engaged this chamber solely for business meetings, not
wishing to sully his personal suite with talk of finance.
Ordering coffee from room service, Mr. Okada bade his
friend to sit down and speak once more of beautiful Paris.

When coffee came, Kecvic sipped at his impatiently,
then sprang to the window and looked out at the great
city. While he enjoyed the view, Charles poured a substantial jolt of sedatives into his cup, knowing that his
intended victim had put so much sugar into the coffee
that he would never taste anything else. Indeed Kecvic

did drain his cup without comment, after which he rose to leave. Mr. Okada begged him to wait a few more minutes. With a sigh, Kecvic sat down and stared grimly at the door. As Mr. Okada watched, Kecvic did nothing but drum his fingers against his chair. He did not even rub his eyes. The drug did not seem to be working, even though enough sleeping potion was now swimming in his stomach to put out a man twice the size.

"Enough," decided Kecvic. He was tired of waiting for the undependable Japanese industrialist. He would be in the casino and available immediately should the old boy turn up. Mr. Okada stammered, thinking hurriedly. Yes, of course, it *was* rude of Mr. Saito to keep the important Frenchman waiting. Perhaps he was delayed on a long distance call. Probably he was trying to conclude some major stock transfer. Excuses poured out of Mr. Okada, but they did not work. Kecvic had his hand on the door-knob.

"Wait, please," said Mr. Okada urgently. "I'll go down with you. I just want to use the toilet quickly." Into the bathroom disappeared Mr. Okada and a moment later out burst two men with pillow cases over their heads. They were André and Van Dam. Before Kecvic could cry out, he was slammed to the floor and a strip of adhesive tape slapped over his mouth. Then Charles stepped out, no longer bothering to disguise himself as Mr. Okada. The Istanbul police report would describe Charles' demeanor at this moment as "being like a Palestinian guerrilla out to kill a Jew." Angry that the drug had not stilled his victim, Charles took a syringe and, holding it over Kecvic like a dagger, plunged it three times into the dressmaker's arm. When Kecvic's eyes finally closed, Charles stripped away his wristwatch, his wallet, and the cash in his pocket, irritated that he was not wearing the diamond ring. Prudently, Kecvic had placed it in a safety deposit box at the front desk. Charles surveyed the take hurriedly; the proceeds were not anywhere near what he had expected. He improvised a sudden second act.

Leaving André and Van Dam to watch over the slumbering Kecvic, Charles rushed to the lobby and telephoned Krista. When she answered, Charles put on his Mr. Okada act again. Would it be possible for Madame Kecvic to

honor the men with her presence in the lobby? Her husband and Mr. Saito had just concluded a remarkable
business deal, and they wished to celebrate with champagne and late supper. A beautiful woman's presence was
necessary to seal the bargain. Succumbing instantly to the
flattery and the good news, Krista promised to be down
in ten minutes.

When she appeared in the lobby, Mr. Okada rushed
forward with a smile, a bow, and a slight change of plans.
The other men had gone to Mr. Saito's room to sign important documents. They wanted Krista and Mr. Okada
to join them there. When the door to Room 410 opened
in response to Mr. Okada's soft knock, Krista saw her husband lying on the floor, his eyes and mouth taped. Before
she could scream and rush to him, rough hands tore the
fur coat from her shoulders, pushed her onto the floor, and
slapped tape across her mouth. Charles ordered her to
kneel before him, and he ceremoniously tore enough of
her gown to reveal a bare shoulder. The last thing she felt
was a needle plunging into her arm, then she fell, beside
her husband. Charles pulled the rings from her fingers,
rifled her purse, found her room key. He left the others
to watch over the drugged couple, rushing to the Kecvics'
room and taking their passports, traveler's checks, and a
watch.

Just before dawn, Charles, André, and two other henchmen quietly left Room 410, where within Anton and Krista
Kecvic were sleeping deeply. A "Do Not Disturb" sign
was placed on the door and the gang left the hotel unnoticed, having several chores to accomplish before all
could leave Istanbul on a midmorning plane. André was
sent to a smouldering garbage dump to dispose of the pil-
lowcase hoods and the toy pistols and the syringes and
the freshly printed calling cards and the book on Eastern
mercantile commerce that Pierre le Premier had fortuitously found at the USIA library.

Charles made a snap assessment of the long night's proceeds and decided that their efforts had netted between
$15,000 and $20,000—about half as much as he had anticipated, but still in all—not bad. The Dutchman and
Pierre le Premier were given their salaries, they having
committed to the project for flat fees, and Charles asked

them to be available several months hence when he would reassemble his group for more work, perhaps in Rome.

On the taxi ride to the airport, Charles cursed the driver, accusing him of taking a roundabout route and bilking him. "You are a thief!" cried Charles, preparing to do battle over perhaps one dollar until André soothed him. On the flight to Athens, Charles nudged his half-brother and handed him 5,000 French francs. The night before they had been in Anton Kecvic's wallet. "Now do you see how easy it is to pluck the fruit from these trees?" asked Charles. André nodded, but he could not resist looking at every face on the airliner throughout the flight, fearful that a policeman would stare back at him. But such worry did not intrude on Charles, for he rattled on and on, talking of his need for a long rest, throwing up grandiose plans of sending André to college in Hong Kong to obtain a degree in business, of using André as a front man because he had no police record and could thus obtain liquor permits for a string of restaurants and discos in Asia and Europe, touching his younger brother's arm affectionately and murmuring his vast contentment in having his own blood beside him in enterprise. Someday, vowed Charles, he would bring other members of his family into the business. It was his dream to employ them all—half-brothers, half-sisters, cousins in India, even Song in Marseilles if she could extricate herself from the French lieutenant's headaches.

"They will love me," said Charles. "Don't you think they will love me?"

André nodded. At this moment he was not certain that love tied him to his half-brother. But he was nonetheless bound.

The sister of Krista Kecvic went to the Hilton Hotel on this day for a prearranged lunch. When she knocked on Krista's door, there was no answer, nor was there response to the telephone. She waited most of the afternoon, her concern mounting. She convinced the hotel management to open the door, and the room was empty. Police were notified; a search of Istanbul ordered.

But not until thirty-six hours later did a chambermaid report that a "Do Not Disturb" sign had been hanging on

the doorknob of Room 410 for almost two days. When
the room was opened, the bodies of Anton and Krista
Kecvic were discovered, barely alive, still unconscious.
Rushed to the hospital where they made a difficult re-
covery, the couple told fearful stories of having been
drugged and assaulted by a brutal Japanese businessman
named Mr. Okada.

Mr. Okada by this time had changed identities. Charles
put his own photograph on Anton Kecvic's French passport and used it successfully, with no problem, to enter
Greece. It was either a brazen epilogue to the dramatic
crime or a blunder that an amateur pickpocket would not
have made.

Charles and André checked into a small hotel in Athens
where the intention was to rest and plan their future. For a
day Charles read philosophy books, sitting in a hot tub
and sipping tea. The exhilaration of the caper in Istanbul
had worn away quickly, and André noticed a conspicuous
melancholy wrapping his half-brother. He dared not ask
Charles during one of his reflective periods, for he had
learned that no intrusion was permitted when Charles was
thinking. Instead he wisely left him alone, electing to prowl
the streets of Athens, his pockets full of money, in search
of taverns and women with large breasts. After two days,
sated, his stomach filled with ouzo and his heart mildly
stirred by the passions of a Greek waitress who knew
sexual tempos beyond his capacities. André returned to
the hotel room and discovered Charles morose and snap-
pish. The reasons came immediately. "There's simply not
enough money," said Charles. He had less than $10,000—
not enough to take off half a year or more and hire a
lawyer to fight Hélène in Paris for custody of their daughter (or, failing that, to impress Hélène with a documented
fortune and *buy* her back). A map of the world was spread
on a table, and several countries had angry red X's slashed
across them, these being those territories where Charles
Sobhraj was wanted by the police. Hong Kong, India, Pakistan, Afghanistan, Iran, Istanbul—he had worked his way
across Asia, and his wake was a storm of warrants and
furious police itching to clamp their hands and their chains
about his neck. He told André that he dared not even re-

turn to France; his criminal record there and his clouded
citizenship would probably result in his being arrested the
moment he set foot on French soil. "Europe's a big place,"
ventured André. It was the wrong thing to say. Charles
grabbed the map and crunched it into a ball and threw
it into a corner. He was afraid of Europe. In the East he
could operate. In the East, he could disappear in the awesome stretches of land and the crowds of the major cities.
In the East he was a chameleon, able to resemble whatever nationality he chose to resemble. But Europe was
different. Police had more sophisticated ways—computers,
communication networks, telephones that connected callers
in minutes rather than hours or days. And bribes, the
"Asian way," as Charles called such palm greasing, were
not so blatantly negotiated. His destiny was clearly in the
East—and yet he could not risk going there again. The
next day he bought a map of South America and began
studying it.

    That night Charles dressed and left the hotel. He told
André he was going to look around. At the Athens Hilton
bar he met an elderly Japanese professor of classical literature who was in Greece to worship the ground where
Sophocles and Euripides had walked. Easily Charles slipped
into a new role. He was, at all times, a brilliant actor and,
once immersed in a new identity, felt whole again. What
a coincidence, said Charles. He, too, was a classicist, teaching now and then at the Sorbonne, but now on long sabbatical, writing a novel based on the tragedy of Medea.
The old professor, whose name was Negishi, smiled and
bowed his head in respect to a colleague in the groves of
academe. They drank a toast to the glory of Greece; they
spoke in a curious but workable lingual meeting ground
of Japanese, English, and French. Within an hour the men
were devoted friends. Charles proposed a day of sightseeing, knowing as he did an excellent guide who could show
them portions of the national library that were normally
impossible to enter. Professor Negishi glowed in the fortune that had brought him to a hotel bar—when indeed
he had planned to stay in his room and retire early—and
positioned him next to a colleague of scholarship and
goodwill. Then Charles proposed a night on the town. Had
his new friend from Japan visited Pláka, the fascinating

district of tavernas and cobbled streets, nestled in the lap of the Acropolis, a festival of joyous celebration each night?

They made their way up steep steps, past cafes whose innards swam with *bouzouki* music and the laughter of wine, pushing through crowds of tourists that danced under grape arbors, looking up now and then at the soft golden lights that illumined the Parthenon and made the ancient hilltop a crown for the revels. They dined on lamb smothered in garlic and pepper, on rich meat pies, on platters of black grapes and chunks of melons. They sang, they clapped when the strong young Greek men and women locked their arms and danced past their tables, and they drank. Professor Negishi was so overcome by the bacchanal that when his eyes suddenly became heavy he grew apologetic. He was old, and he wore out quickly, and he was sorry to feel fatigue so early in the evening. Charles was tender and understanding. Jet travel is wearying. A new country assaults the body's habits. All the professor needed was a good night's sleep. Tomorrow they would be ready for scholarship. Professor Negishi, barely able to nod his assent, fell asleep in the taxi going home. Charles helped him into the Hilton lobby, grateful that it was still crowded at midnight, suspecting that anyone who saw them would guess the young man was helping his inebriated father to bed.

The next midday, when the elderly professor awoke with a heavy head, he had the faintest memory of his new young friend tucking him in and whispering, "Sleep well." Then Negishi discovered that his passport, his Nikon camera, his wallet, his watch, his return plane ticket to Tokyo, 10,000 yen and $820 in traveler's checks were gone.

And so was Charles' depression. André saw the gloom lift from Charles, and he knew now that his brother was a hunter. Unless all of his senses were engaged, unless a target was in his sights, he was an empty man. The robbery of the Japanese professor was classic. Quick. Neat. No violence. From start to finish, done wthin four hours.

After Charles determined that Professor Negishi had returned to Japan and was no longer around to identify the young "scholar" who had shattered his trust, he ventured boldly again into the Hilton lobby. Touring the public

rooms and watching the guests with a casual but piercing
study, Charles zeroed in on an Egyptian, Khymal by name,
a huge man with a florid face, a damp collar, and a furtive
air that suggested to Charles that here was a royalist whose
socks were stuffed with gold. After several hours of sur-
reptitious examination, Charles decreed that extra hands
would be needed to handle Khymal. The potential victim
weighed at least 250 pounds; André was willing to help
drag the fat carcass to his hotel, if necessary. And as
Khymal spent most of his time sitting on a well-positioned
divan in the Hilton lobby, watching the Western women
clatter across gleaming marble floors, their legs under terry
cloth robes still dripping from the swimming pool, Charles
reasoned that he must provide a provocative bit of bait
for this whale. Fortunately, Charles had encountered an
old friend in Athens the day before, a ripe, post-hippie
American whose name was Mary Claire and whose principal charms were a body six feet in length and a bosom
that had once appeared in a girlie magazine extending
over two pages.

Mary Claire had once assisted Charles on an unsuccessful job in Singapore, and now she had fallen on hard
times. She was dressed poorly and in need of a hair styling
—and money. Charles promised her $250 for a few hours'
work, bought her an inexpensive but well-cut dress that
showcased her breasts, cut and combed her hair himself,
and sent her forth to perch on the rocks and sing. Khymal
discovered her and André in the hotel's taverna. She
smiled provocatively; he moved like a truck getting a
green light as a tricky intersection, and within two hours
was sprawled unconscious beside the bed in a cheap hotel
where Mary Claire had lured him. He would not awake
until dawn. But as he slumbered, Charles took the hotel
key from his pocket, located his room at the Hilton, and
stripped it of 3,000 French francs, $250, an Egyptian
passport, and a few German marks. While he looked
around the room for anything else worth taking, André's
eyes fell on a doll that Khymal had probably purchased
in a souvenir shop. It wore Greek national costume and
when pinched on the buttocks made a piercing laugh, like
a whore full of ouzo. André laughed and put it in his
pocket. Charles thought that such was a waste of effort,

but if his younger brother wanted to play with dolls, then so be it.

With two successful scores accomplished back-to-back in Athens, André assumed that Charles would want to stay in the city for several weeks, it being always crowded with tourists and having many first-class hotels should the Hilton grow too hot for their activities. But in deep November, a stormy day in Athens with dark sheets of rain sweeping over the chalky hills and turning the Aegean churning black, Charles abruptly announced leavetaking. Two policemen had looked at him sternly in Constitution Square this day when he met with Mary Claire to settle her fee. And the political climate of Greece troubled him. Though George Papadopoulos had fallen, and the dictatorship of the colonels shattered, Athens was still heavy with soldiers and police, not a comfortable environment. His eyes were now aimed at Beirut, a pleasant city to pass the winter, more Asian than European, and brimming, rumor had it, with reckless Arabs enriched by oil and eager for hedonistic delights.

With one of the several stolen credit cards that nested in the false bottom of his attaché case, Charles purchased air tickets for himself and André. Routinely they passed through passport check at the airport, cleared customs, and squeezed onto one of those jammed shuttle buses that would deliver them to the runway where their jet waited. André was also relieved to leave Greece. He was not yet sophisticated enough to overcome the apprehension that he felt every time he presented a false passport to an official. He envied Charles' ability to drum his fingers impatiently at the counter, feigning annoyance, as if he were a diplomat forced to deal with a bothersome functionary.

But now, on the shuttle bus, his fear was sliding away and he saw a little girl, three or four years old, standing in front of his seat and swaying. He smiled at the pretty child, she responded with a diffident look. Impulsively, André reached into his flight bag, which contained magazines and a few souvenirs. He found the doll that he had stolen from the Egyptian. Holding it before the little girl, he pinched the doll's bottom and out burst a cry of raucous laughter. The child was enchanted, begging to try. André showed her where to pinch, and for several moments, the

doll and the child and the apprentice thief laughed together.

But fate was eavesdropping and elected to play an ironic
prank. Over the laughter of the doll roared an outraged
scream, and through the crowd on the bus lunged the
enormous body of an Egyptian with a florid face and a
sweating collar. "It's *him!*" cried Khymal. "The one who
robbed me!" The shuttle buses at Athens Airport make
more than five hundred trips a day from terminal to runway, and transport tens of thousands of passengers, but a
force more powerful than coincidence placed victim and
assailants on the same one. As Khymal tried to wrap his
thick fingers around André's neck, the younger brother
sputtered innocence. But a ring of police with rifles were
called to surround the bus. And by nightfall, both Charles
and André were in jail, even as Khymal the Egyptian knelt
toward Mecca and thanked Allah for the blessings of
destiny.

CHAPTER TWENTY

There was no room for maneuvering. In Charles' luggage, Athens police discovered four walkie-talkies, several expensive gold watches, one of which had recently graced the arm of Khymal the Egyptian, a gold Dunhill lighter, a radio, two gold Parker pens, assorted currencies, stolen credit cards, and half a dozen passports, the most intriguing two of which were Khymal's, and a French document belonging to Anton Kecvic but bearing the newly pasted photograph of Charles Sobhraj, looking reasonably like a Turk who had found prosperity in Paris.

As the news of the Istanbul robbery of the lingerie maker and his wife had received widespread notoriety in the tabloid press of Greece, it was not difficult to connect Charles with the sensational crime. Istanbul promptly began asking the Greeks to turn over the two prisoners so examples could be made of—to use the exact language of a high-ranking Turkish policeman—"these depraved bandits who violate the peace of Turkey by assaulting our tourist guests."

Reposing under heavy guard in an Athens police lock-up, Charles sifted through his options. One thing he could not tolerate was extradition to Turkey. He suspected the minimum sentence he would receive there was twenty years, provided he survived the beating he would surely receive from enthusiastic interrogators. Better that he remain in Athens, dally with Greek law, and search for some way to elude long-term punishment. He found himself

alone with André for a few minutes in a corridor outside
a police captain's office and he whispered urgently, "Don't
admit anything. Say nothing. Let me handle it. I know the
Greek law."

Charles knew one interesting fact in the Greek code of
justice; a prisoner could be kept in jail for a year and a day
without going to trial. But then, if a trial had not begun,
the prisoner had to be released. He elected to gamble and
play with the year and a day. Who knew what might
happen in that length of time? Charles refused to make
a confession. He denied robbing the Egyptian. He denied
using Anton Kecvic's passport and insisted he had no
idea how it got in his briefcase. Perhaps the police had
planted it and the other incriminating items. He refused
to plead one way or another to a charge of robbery and
assault. All of this was designed to make it harder for the
Greek prosecutor to assemble a case, and Charles further
intended to file a flurry of delaying motions.

He had squeezed out of precarious positions before,
but one thing nagged at him. He prayed that the Greeks
would not uncover his long ago conviction *in absentia*
for the drugging and robbing of the Englishman, Converse,
on the island of Rhodes. That meant thirteen months in
prison, possibly more, as he had fled to avoid prosecution.
Charles doubted that the Greeks would make the connection. One government had fallen since then, the new one
seemed shaky. Records often disappear when governments
collapse. At least Charles hoped they did.

An Athens magistrate directed that Charles Sobhraj
and André Darreau be confined in the prison called Korydallos while the case went through the legal process. Upon
hearing this, Charles felt modest elation. In the grapevine
of the underworld, Korydallos was, as prisons went, not
a bad place. Compared to the dungeon of, say, Kabul, it
was almost luxurious. Charles could "operate" in Korydallos, and, to confound his captors even further, he conceived a bizarre—if self-serving—trick.

En route to the prison, in a police van, Charles was able
to speak to André, who was lashed to his half-brother by
chains at hand and foot. "The moment that the police
turn us over to the prison authorities," said Charles, "the
jurisdiction changes. The police know who we are, but

the prison officials do not." André nodded, but he was unable to follow this riddle. Charles continued. The prison authorities did not even know they were brothers, only two Oriental men who looked a little alike. But Europeans think *all* Orientals look alike. So, proposed Charles, the moment they stepped across the prison threshold, they would switch identities.

Not unrealistically, André wanted to know what this would accomplish. Why would Charles want to become André Darreau, and vice versa? At this point, André was probably thinking he had put quite enough trust in his seductive brother. A few months before, André had been living quietly in Paris, gainfully employed, living modestly but reasonably well, enjoying the delights of girls in short skirts and boulevards to follow them on—and now he was riding in a police wagon toward an unknown sentence in a Greek prison. Not to mention Turkish police who were practically standing at their border begging the Greeks for extradition. Sensibly, André shook his head and refused to assume the name and identity of a man wanted in six countries and two continents.

But Charles persisted. He had thought this one out carefully. It gleamed with Machiavellian luster. After a few weeks inside, the authorities would discover that André Darreau had no previous criminal record in Greece, that the case against him was weak, and that he should be released with a scolding—and expulsion from Greece. A light began to dawn on André. If Charles were to become André Darreau, then *he* would be the one to gain freedom. "What about me?" André said coolly.

Charles shushed him. Once he was safely out of the country, he would send a coded telegram to André in Korydallos Prison. Then all André had to do was step forward, ask to see the warden, reveal that he was the real André Darreau, that the stupid authorities had released the wrong man.

André chewed on this for a minute. They would be at the prison gates in another few moments. There was little time to argue. He found one more question. But wouldn't the warden be furious and take it out on him, he asked? Charles shook his head. André would then threaten to telephone the French Embassy. Greece has a new govern-

ment, they cannot afford the embarrassment of keeping a
French national in prison, particularly when he is the
wrong man. André had no time to mull the scheme, for
Korydallos was coming into view. Only twenty minutes
from the heart of Athens, it sat on a sun-baked hill near
the port of Piraeus, almost washed out by the intense
white light of noon. Set down in the heart of an industrial
district, the prison, with its gray and cream walls, could
be taken for a factory, save for the Greek women, some
ancient grandmothers, others vividly painted birds of the
street, who stand outside and call endearments to their
men within.

The two men were escorted through a cool and airy
entrance, into a pleasant garden with carefully tended
beds of marigolds and daisies, and orchards of figs and
olives, into a building called Section 4, where prisoners
were kept while awaiting trial. The floors were green
speckled marble, the walls washed frequently with soap,
the recreation room containing television and a radio.
And when a prison official came to count heads and take
identities, he called out from his clipboard, "Charles
Sobhraj?" After a moment of hesitation, André Darreau
stepped forward. And when the subwarden said, "André
Darreau?" Charles Sobhraj stepped forward promptly,
bowing obediently. From that moment on, the two brothers
had traded places.

A few weeks passed. The days became routine. Charles
and André were fortunate to have been placed in the same
cell, on the second floor of a wing devoted largely to
foreign prisoners. Morning wake-up was not even until
seven-fifteen. "I've been in jails where they throw you out
of bed at five," said Charles. And the food was, all in all,
good. Milk tea and toast for breakfast; fish, vegetables,
and fruit for lunch and dinner. No work was required,
thus the days were free for reading, writing letters, or
milling about in a recreational area. They passed themselves off to the other prisoners as Vietnamese, Charles
not wanting to become friendly with anyone he did not
feel could benefit his cause. The Number One rule in
prison, he cautioned André, is to pick your friends carefully. One never knows who is squealing to guards. Because nobody could speak Vietnamese, Charles and André

were left alone. They further ensured this by staging
karate exhibitions replete with ominous grunts and cries.
The first week in prison, André was cornered by a three-
hundred-pound Greek who approached with a gleam in
his eye and arms prepared for a bear hug. When André
demurred, the Greek was outraged and lunged at his
rejector. André waited calmly until the giant was but a
garlic breath away before sending out a vicious kick to
his kidneys, followed by a chop that almost sliced open
his neck.

Charles used his free hours to study Greek law, writing
an eloquent letter to the court pleading for his release
(he being at this point André Darreau). Quoting from
sources as varied as Plato and modern as novelist Nikos
Kazantzakis, shuddering at the loss of personal liberties
under the shameful half decade of the colonels (Papadopoulos was in another wing of the prison), reminding
the bench that Greece was the cradle of democracy,
Charles concluded his petition by pointing out that he had
fallen under the influence of evil associates. If the court
in its compassion would release him from bondage, then
he would leave the country and never return. Signing
André's name with a flourish, Charles mailed the letter
and predicted that both would be free in a fortnight.

Two months passed. No response from the letter. Bleakness settled over André, anger over Charles. Each day the
men waited and each day they were disappointed. André
asked why Charles did not reveal the switched identity
plot. The response was that Charles felt it was not "fool-
proof," and besides, he had to be out of prison in order
to make it work. For several more days he brooded. "I
think," he at last told André, "we can escape." He asked
his half-brother for patience.

For the rest of the day Charles was absent from his cell,
wandering around the communal room, talking in whispers to both prisoners and guards. That night he astonished
André by unbuttoning his shirt and pulling out a map of
Korydallos, plus a set of architectural plans. "Where did
you get them?" exclaimed André. Charles smiled and
shook his head. "One learns when one has to," he answered.

The two men studied by candlelight. Charles was stimulated to discover that a large water canal ran underneath

Section 4 of the prison to accommodate the runoff from 120 cells. This canal emptied into a major water main outside the walls to join the Athens sewer system, presumably flowing thereafter into the harbor at nearby Piraeus. Most Greek prisons had very small water pipes, impossible for a man to crawl through. But the pipes beneath Korydallos seemed large enough, particularly if a man was small, compact, and strong—"like us." A little digging down to the pipes would connect the men to freedom.

They faced an immediate problem before any tunnel digging could begin. Charles and André occupied a cell on the second floor and would have to finagle a transfer to the ground floor. Therefore they turned testy, fighting, yelling at one another, causing such commotion that the other prisoners complained. One morning the guards marched in and announced that the two Vietnamese were being moved to the first floor where they would be watched more carefully. The guards were tired of running upstairs to quell disturbances. If the two men did not stop quarreling, they would be separated and thrown into solitary. Understood? Charles made theatrical protest in Vietnamese, but on the way downstairs he winked at André. So far, so good.

Now they became model prisoners, as quiet and as obedient as lambs, and the guards soon withdrew their heavy attention. The next problem, said Charles, was finding two more men to help. The floor was a foot thick, composed of cement with a marble overlay. And it would be safer if the tunnel were dug in another cell, for his estimate was that the work might take six weeks. The possibility of the guards discovering the work-in-progress had to be faced. If that unfortunate event occurred, then it would be better for Charles and André if the hole were found in somebody else's cell floor.

"We must study this carefully," said Charles. The one hundred or so prisoners in Section 4 were, for the next few days, scrutinized by Charles as carefully as tourists in a Hilton lobby. He was disappointed not to find any Frenchmen, except for one rag-and-bones morphine addict from Normandy who insisted he was once Edith Piaf's lover and who sang obscene songs about George Pompidou. Attention settled on a pair of young American boys nailed on a minor hashish charge. Their names were Pete and Snapper, their misfortune having been caught with a few grams of hash in their knapsacks. Both were terrified by their confinement and were happy to receive a visit from Charles and André, who seemed wise in the ways of prison and Greek protocol. As a fillip, the Americans had been militantly opposed to the U.S. involvement in Vietnam and they were pleased to meet two actual Vietnamese victims of the war—or so Charles had them believe. Long discussions on the fate of that ravaged country were held, with Charles paying them lavish compliments for their opposition. He was more interested in the fact that both Americans had been college athletes and still had strong bodies with heavily muscled arms and shoulders.

The four prisoners became friends, a convenient arrangement since their cells were directly opposite one another on the central corridor. During the daylight hours, prisoners were allowed to have their cell doors open, and visiting went on routinely if there was no noise or trouble. Nothing was mentioned about an escape for several days. One night André asked Charles why he had not broached the subject. The answer was that he had to be convinced of their dependability—and their hunger to escape. It was Charles' intention for *them* to conceive the idea of breaking out. *They* would recruit Charles and André. "I'll never understand you," said André truthfully. "A day with you is like a month with anyone else."

When next the four met, Charles deftly turned conversation into a discussion of what penalties they might face. How much hashish were they accused of possessing? Twelve grams, said Snapper. He was a tall, gangling boy from Texas with sandy hair and a freckled face, appealing despite a scraggly beard and a rarely washed body. Not even half an ounce, chimed in Pete, who was from Oklahoma and had fled first to Canada to avoid the draft, thence to Europe, where he married an English girl only to find out that she had another husband, who sold computers in Malta.

Charles whistled sympathetically. Twelve grams did not seem substantial, but he knew a previous prisoner in Korydallos who had been caught with only one gram—and

received a six-year sentence. The two Americans were
stunned. They had been led to believe by a lawyer that
they would get less than a year, probably suspended at
that. Charles shook his head in disagreement. The Greeks
were fanatic about punishing drug pushers. Under the
dictatorship of the colonels, judges meted out death in
certain drug cases.

Gloom settled óver the Americans' cell like a final curtain. Calculatedly, Charles moved the talk to *his* case;
he and his "friend"—they were still concealing the fact
that they were brothers and using switched identities—
probably faced staggering prison terms, perhaps life on
charges of armed robbery and assault.

"Life!" echoed Snapper in disbelief.

Charles nodded sadly. The blame should be placed, he
felt, on the Vietnam War. He and André had been forced
to flee their country, winding up in Greece alone and
broke, pressured to commit robbery just to buy food. The
Americans were all consolation.

Charles sighed. If he only knew how, he would attempt
to break out of this prison. Someone had given him a map
of the underground beneath the cells, and it seemed there
was a water pipe big enough to crawl through. But he had
no idea how to accomplish a tunnel. Slowly, brilliantly,
Charles made the American boys feel it was not only their
idea but their *duty* to help the Vietnamese escape. And
they could make it, too! They would commence digging
immediately, in their own cell. Would Charles and André
consider helping?

Later André congratulated his brother. The tactic had
been daring. He had taken his own idea and grafted it
on two strangers. "You see what I mean about using
psychology?" said Charles. He yawned and commanded
silence. They needed sleep. Tomorrow they would dig to
freedom.

Their tools were a handful of rusted nails, a fork, and
a spoon. With these, the four men intended to cut through
a foot-thick floor, burrow into the earth for almost six
feet, and then—who knew what or where? To reach this
point would take, Charles estimated, eight solid weeks of
work, work every day, work seven days a week, work

from sunrise to lights out—with a guard station only twenty feet away. The feat was breathtaking in its ambition and danger. After two weeks, a hole was cut through the foot-thick floor, then, once the earth was reached, Charles and André spent all of the time actually inside the tunnel. It was wide enough only to accommodate their slim bodies, not the broad-shouldered Americans, a fact that Pete and Snapper did not fully understand. Charles made an occasional vague remark that "when it was time" the hole would be widened. In the Americans' naïveté they believed him.

Only one man could work inside the hole; the three others passed the time in distracting conversation, card playing, karate, anything to make the scene appear normal when the guards strolled by. At the very beginning of the labor, Charles devised a clever way to conceal the hole. He found a piece of paper and drew a marbleized design that matched the floor exactly. The custom in Korydallos was that prisoners could clean their cells if they wanted to—or, failing that, they could live like pigs. The American boys had been known as poor housekeepers even before they met Charles, so the guards never remarked or grew suspicious of the layer of dirt that covered the piece of paper that covered the hole.

The most demanding problem was how to dispose of the dirt and rocks. Charles solved this by teaching each man to stuff dirt into his shirt, walking like a pregnant woman into the recreation yard, and discreetly emptying the soil into a corner, several times a day. As the weeks passed, the men experienced exhilaration, fear, hope, and —inside the hole—terror that clawed at the heart. "There's no air, there's no light, you realize you are nothing," gasped André when he emerged after an hour below. He was carrying a rock as big as a watermelon. Charles made light of the discomfort, even the muscle tears and stabbing pain, for he had to be the cheerleader, keeping spirits up and determination alive when a bent spoon encountered a stone eighteen inches in circumference.

When the hole reached six feet, Charles directed that the digging flatten out and turn in a direction toward what he believed to be the large water pipe. But in the ninth week of endeavor, when André was digging, he encoun-

tered an unexpected brick wall. Charles shook his head.
There was no wall on the plans. "Perhaps it's some old
ruin," suggested Snapper, who was interested in archaeol-
ogy. He had, in fact, gone abroad to join a dig in Egypt,
but was refused employment and discovered instead the
joys of non-committal drifting and smoking hashish. Charles
doubted the wall was ancient. He went down, looked, and
then told André it would have to be cut through. There
was no alternative. Aching, caked with dirt, André dropped
back into the hole and began chipping away at the mortar
between the bricks. Hours passed. Charles relieved him.
More hours. André returned. A hole was almost accomplished.

Suddenly, with a cracking noise, the wall broke and a
flood of water rushed out, sweeping over the terrified
prisoner and quickly starting to fill the hole. André
screamed, but water filled his mouth. He was going to
drown! Desperately he clawed at the now slippery passage,
tearing chunks of mud, fighting his way up the longest
six feet of his life. Charles heard the water and plunged
the top half of his body into the hole to rescue his half-
brother. He pulled André out and laid him down, hurriedly
wiping the water from his face and arms. At the same
time he directed Snapper and Pete, nearly paralyzed with
fear, to throw rocks into the hole and dam it up. As it
happened, the afternoon's dirt and stones had not yet
been dumped in the recreation yard. The four men watched
in suspense as water gurgled almost to the level of the
cell floor, then, blessedly, receded. Not a drop splashed
over into the cell to incriminate them. Charles would not
permit despair. "We'll start again tomorrow," he said.
"The earth will be softer now."

But during the night, water backed up in a drain two
cells away and a Lebanese prisoner yelled for a guard.
The next morning, authorities searched every cell to determine if some prisoner had been messing with the plumbing.
A squad of guards appeared in Pete and Snapper's dim
and dirty cell, looked about, but, incredibly, did not spot
the piece of paper and the hole underneath.

Finally it was decided that no prisoner had anything to
do with the minor flood, and after a day or two prison
routine resumed. With one irksome change. A more or

less permanent guard now stood outside Pete and Snapper's cell because from that vantage point he could eye several others. It was impossible to resume digging.

This did not turn out to be a problem for Pete and Snapper because within a few weeks their lawyer won their release, using money sent by Snapper's parents. The Americans came around and shook hands with Charles and André and kissed them comradely and promised to meet again someday. Charles waited a decent amount of time for them to get out of Greece—a day or two—then he called the warden and tattled on them. He pulled off the piece of paper in their cell and revealed the hole. He would have informed sooner, he said, but the Americans had threatened him, and they were big and strong, and he was slight and afraid. The reward was less than Charles had hoped—double milk rations for a week. He had anticipated a job as orderly in the hospital, from where he could have taken flight.

But Charles did not stay in favor very long with the prison administration. Somebody squealed on *him*. He never learned who spilled the tale of the tunnel; it could have been some prisoner with a grudge, perhaps some spurned homosexual with a grievance. Whatever, guards marched into Charles' cell one April morning in 1974 and accused him of masterminding an attempted jailbreak. Hauled before a magistrate and—still known as André Darreau—Charles was given an eight-month sentence on the usual charge of "disobedience to the Greek government." With it came a chilling punishment—transferral to the island prison of Aegina, a place of utter dread. The Greek version of Devil's Island, Aegina was considered escapeproof, perched on savage volcanic cliffs with a sheer drop of several hundred feet to the choppy sea. The prison site was rich in history, having been a fortress in modern centuries, but before that a lookout for great sea battles. Only sixteen miles from Athens, the island had changed hands more often than a bone of the crucified Christ, occupied at one time or another by Mycenaeans, Dorians, Spartans, Athenians, Romans, Venetians, Turks, and pirates. Briefly it was even the capital of Greece. After World War II, Aegina became a popular day trip for tourists who wandered about the well-preserved temple

of Aphaea and sunned on beaches or admired the yachts
that bobbed like toys at rest in the harbor. Within a few
days, Charles had learned all of this, and the dimensions
of the island, and the precise distance to Athens, and even
the number of police who lived and worked there. But it
did him no good. The prison of Aegina was built before
"rehabilitation" became voguish. Prisoners were locked
in tiny, barren cells that opened onto dark and narrow
corridors. There was no recreation area. Life began and
ended in the cell. And if Charles had any notion of digging here, his tunnel would need to bore through five
hundred feet of rock, then open onto a sea whose waves
smashed angrily against rocks that had even turned away
Odysseus. They looked like the jaws of a sea monster. He
tore his brain searching for a way to escape. There was
none. The walls of the prison echoed with terrible stories
of men who had tried, whose broken bodies were found
on the rocks, who were shot dead before they could reach
a nearby grove of olive and pistachio. Medical complaints
were dealt with by a local doctor who dropped by on
request. There was no hospital ward. Mail was heavily
censored. Scant news of the outside world filtered through
the thick stone walls. Around him, men were going mad.
He could hear their babblings in the night.

Charles endured almost a year in Aegina. One day he
fell ill, to his advantage, he reasoned. It was a touch of
dysentery, but Charles decided to turn his complaint into
a matter of the gravest medical import. He started to fast,
not so the guards would notice him, but by burying his
food. Within a week he was thin and pale and feverish.
He found a stone and stripped off his clothes and pounded
his stomach until he raised bruises. He prayed they would
be taken for internal hemorrhaging. Then, barely able to
stand, he pleaded for a doctor.

The decision was made that Charles should receive an
examination and tests in an Athens hospital with better
diagnostic equipment. Once a week, a boat from Aegina
went to Piraeus delivering the seriously ill men, then
brought them back again. On the morning that Charles
left Aegina, he was almost carried out of the prison, but
though his body was weak, his mind was clear. He turned

to look at the terrible place. He was getting out of hell; he swore that he would never return.

A young doctor at the Athens hospital examined the prisoner known as André Darreau, drew blood, collected urine, studied vital signs—and ordered that he be returned to Aegina pending the outcome of tests. The prisoner did not seem critically ill, only suffering probably from nothing more serious than stomach flu. Charles fought for a reason to stay. What about the bruises on his stomach, he cried? The doctor shrugged. Perhaps the prisoner had fallen down and did not remember it. The tests would show if there was internal bleeding; he would be only an hour away by ferryboat. Charles almost wept, begging with passion that seemed unlikely in a man as sick as he pretended to be. But the doctor denied his plea and went away to summon guards. Charles was left alone for less than two minutes. But in that fraction of time he was able to rifle a nurse's or patient's purse that had been carelessly left on the counter. And in the purse he found a possible means of freedom.

When the guards came, Charles allowed himself to be led away without complaint, praying that they would not search him. As insurance he put on his near-death act, looking so desperately sick that the guards did not want to touch him, or chain him. Charles was placed in the back of a small police van with four other prisoners. The human cargo was dispatched to the dock at Piraeus, where the prison boat would take the men back to the island.

There was an unexpected wait. The boat was overdue. Charles peered out the cage windows of the van. Outside were old women with mesh shopping bags crammed with items purchased in Athens, and young sailors in tight white pants, and whores both on duty and waiting to go home and visit Mama on an outer island. Charles was pleased to see the crowd building; more than two hundred people milled around the police van.

He had to move quickly. Softly he asked the prisoner on his right for a match. They were officially forbidden, but most prisoners usually had them tucked away, in the event a cigarette could be obtained. Charles was in luck. His seat mate handed over a full book. Suddenly Charles stood up, reached into his pocket, pulled out a large bottle of French perfume and, blessing the woman whose purse contained it, broke off the neck like christening a ship and splashed the perfume onto a pile of oily rags. Then he ignited the book of matches and flung it on his concoction. Fire burst out, spreading greedily. The prisoners began to scream, pounding on the walls of the locked van. One of the guards peered through the mesh curtains and rushed around to open the rear door. Men on fire came tumbling out, their screams infecting the crowd standing nearby. Pandemonium! Sirens pierced the air. Tourists snapped pictures. Burning men rolled off the dock into the water.

And Charles Sobhraj slipped quietly into the crowd, moving gently at first, then running with a speed he summoned from deep within his abused body. No policeman saw him get away, none of the people on the docks even tried to stop him. When embarrassed police returned empty-handed from a search of the immediate area, they asked some of the onlookers why no one had intercepted a dangerous criminal in his escape. One old woman spoke up, grinning: "I thought it was actors," she said. "I thought it was a movie."

A few days later the telephone rang in the apartment of Félix d'Escogne in Paris. Beirut was on the line. Charles, sounding fit, pretending to be in the embrace of success, spoke animatedly to his old friend. Then he wondered, by the way, had Félix seen Hélène lately? Félix tried to stall and change the subject, but Charles would not tolerate it. He demanded the truth.

Félix spoke bluntly. Hélène had met an American. She had divorced Charles. She had married the American. She had recently moved to America with her new husband and Shubra. "I don't think you could ever find her," said Félix sadly.

"I see," murmured Charles.

Félix pleaded with Charles not to interfere. "If it helps," said Félix, "I think she still loves you. But she can't live with you."

Charles hung up and spent several days in silence. He was not even stimulated by the crowds of free-spending

Arabs who filled Beirut's hotels and casinos. He entertained anger, self-pity, despair, and indecision. One afternoon, walking alone on the spectacular beach near a strip of high-rise condominiums, he distilled his situation to basics. He must regain his strength. He must fill his pockets. And he could do that only in the East. His destiny was clearly there, in the enormity of Asia. There were countries left where the police did not know him or want him. And even in those where he faced arrest, he was not overly apprehensive about entering. India was a subcontinent; what happened in Delhi was not known necessarily a thousand miles away in Bombay. He booked a plane reservation for Hong Kong, with the idea that he might get off somewhere along the way.

When word of Charles' spectacular escape reached André, still in Korydallos Prison in Athens, he promptly informed the warden that a grievous mistake had been made. The man who escaped from the burning van was Charles Sobhraj. He was the *real* André Darreau. Never was such salt rubbed in a wound. While André waited confidently for his release—hadn't Charles promised it would work?—the Greeks responded rather differently. Perversely, in fact. Instead of turning him loose, the Greeks delivered André into the eager arms of the Turks. In an Istanbul courtroom, before three judges in thick crimson robes, André Darreau, the *real* André Darreau, was sentenced to eighteen years at hard labor.

Just before he sagged limply in the arms of his attorney, André was heard to cry out, *"Charlot! Aides-moi!"*

Book Four

SERPENTINE

"Either we live by accident and die by accident—
or we live by plan and die by plan . . ."

—Thornton Wilder,
The Bridge of San Luis Rey

CHAPTER TWENTY-ONE

In her eighteenth year, Jennifer Maria Candace Bolliver fell deeply, joyously in love. "He is perfect," she wrote to her friend Carmen in Los Angeles. "He is forever." Jennie's choice was a lad named Christopher Ghant, who was fire-pole thin, and almost six and one half feet tall, with a trace of blond beard dribbling on his chin, and a countenance of such serenity and peace that women gathered in small groups to remark on his beauty as he passed. He strode through life on stilt-like legs, finding his way through haunting blue eyes, and he was gentle. No one ever saw him flare in anger or even raise his voice much beyond the softness of a muted cello. When Jennie slow-danced with Christopher, she came only as high as his breastbone, and he could almost wrap his arms around her twice. It was the merging of a firecracker and a taper, but so quickly did they become lovers that both believed forces deeper than they could understand had willed their union.

Christopher possessed a restless mind that leaned toward the slightly weird, having studied the Rosicrucians, white magic, yoga, and assorted oddities. He was also an excellent mime and adept at T'ai Chi, the Oriental marriage of mental and physical disciplines. These he taught on an informal basis at the Nova School in Seattle, where teachers were called "co-ordinators" and often were not much older than their students. The school was interesting, the ultimate result of an era when the avant-garde—some

critics say foolishness—was in educational vogue. Nova
was a school without rules or structure, where fifty spe-
cially chosen youngsters were in attendance, the criteria
being intelligence and a leaning to the off beat. Anybody
could do or not do whatever came to mind. Students decided what the curriculum was to be, hired and fired co-
ordinators, attended class or played hooky, according to
the juices flowing on any particular day. They could bake
bread for six hours, or weave blankets, or study Euclidean
geometry, or gestalt therapy, or skip rope from nine to
three. Classrooms were in an old office building in the
core of the city, and when Jennie applied and was accepted,
she felt it was the most important accomplishment of her
life. Her past would not have seemed conducive to awarding a girl like Jennie complete freedom. She would not
have seemed to be the kind of young woman who could
walk on a path without directions, but she found Christopher, and he was the guide that she had sought.

Changes, remarkable changes, washed over Jennie. Banished suddenly were the eccentric coiffures, and she took
to wearing her hair long, naturally brown, and soft. She
washed and brushed it so religiously that each strand
gleamed. Her peacock feathers and fringes were bestowed
on a friend, and in their place Jennie chose simple long
skirts and blouses. One necklace was sufficient instead of
ten, and her earlobes bore only modest gold circles instead
of bangles that tumbled to her shoulders and jangled when
she danced. Drugs were still around—after the abortion
of her baby Jennie had spent two solid weeks in an LSD
haze—but upon entwining her life with Christopher, she
seldom used them other than to attempt "mystical experience." She wrote to Carmen "I haven't smoked grass in
a month. My boy friend and I get high on yoga and meditation and each other!"

Christopher was equally smitten. He told a friend about
Jennie: "I liked her on first sight, I fell in love with her
after a week. She has long curly hair, big romantic eyes,
quick wit, a very sharp mind, a little lazy, but adorable to
look at and be next to." A thread that bound the young
couple was their need for someone to cling to, neither
having a stable home life. Christopher's parents had been
killed in a plane crash, and he, the only child, inherited

enough money to fend off state agencies that sought to declare him a ward of the court. Somehow he managed to live on his own, and rather well, and invited Jennie to join five or six other similarly socially disenchanted youth in a communal house located in the Queen Anne district. As Jennie decorated her "space"—putting up paper lanterns over bare bulbs, tacking fabric remnants from Woolworth's onto walls, painting floors lacquer red, and constructing perfectly appropriate furniture from orange crates, she began to cry, and Christopher went to her in concern. "I'm not sad," she sobbed. "I've just never been so *happy*."

Sex for them was not the urgent coupling of teen-agers, but that of experienced lovers, touching slowly, caringly, softly, with quiet guitar on the stereo and a fire dancing to expel the fog from Lake Washington that shrouded windows in the old, old house. One night Jennie told Christopher, "This was meant to be. We had nothing to do with it. All we can do is pray it will last."

The Queen Anne district also contained a large colony of old people, mostly struggling to get by on pensions, frightened of crime, wanting little more than a dignified ride down life's last hill. They envied the youth and beauty of all the Jennies and Christophers, strolling with arms locked, oblivious to trash in the gutter and shadows behind the trees. Jennie became friendly with many of the old people in her neighborhood, in particular a dramatic woman with majestic though fallen bosom and purple hair. She called herself Madame Crystal and was probably eighty, although she admitted only to fifty-five. She also claimed to have danced with the Paris Opéra Ballet, on legs now thick and varicosed. She recalled extraordinary suppers at Maxim's in Paris and the Savoy Grill in London, but she was so poor near her own last midnight that all she could offer Jennie was a mock Italian supper from time to time. Madame Crystal once set *pasta à la Caruso* on her table, and Jennie recognized it as Kraft's macaroni, twenty-five cents a box, with extras tossed in. But she ate it with gusto. Madame Crystal sang arias from *Tosca* for Jennie, sometimes switching in mid-song to *Traviata* if memory failed her, and she served jug wine in jelly glasses as grandly as if they were Waterford. She spoke of con-

tinuing beaus who pestered her solitude, but Jennie never
saw one, discounting the "maintenance engineer" from
down the street who was really a janitor and who took
Madame Crystal to a bingo game and gave her the West-
clox alarm that he won.

Often Jennie accompanied Madame Crystal on errands,
or lunches at the senior citizens' center, where for fifty
cents a plate of hot food warmed old bones, even to the
county hospital where the old people had to wait, often
for three quarters of a day. Through Madame Crystal,
Jennie met Sadie, who was soon to die of a stroke, and
William, a retired civil engineer with six grown children
who telephoned him faithfully once a year—on Christmas
morning—but not otherwise, and The Dealer, a former
Broadway stagehand who would be playing gin rummy—
prophesied Madame Crystal—on the day they lowered
him into a pauper's grave. Jennie loved them all. Not only
were they full of *life*, they were funny and dear and
almost pathetically grateful when children as callow as
Jennie called on them and sat next to them and touched
their arms and *listened*. Jennie called Maggie in Southern
California and said, "Grandma, I've been thinking of you
all day. I love you and Cap so much." Maggie murmured
her appreciation. But Jennie was not done. "I want you
to forgive me for putting you and Cap through all that
hell." Maggie dispensed immediate forgiveness. She still
loved her tempestuous granddaughter; she had never
stopped, even in the hours of crisis. "My life is changing,
Grandma," Jennie went on. "I'm discovering new values.
I've become very interested in the problems of being old
in this country." After graduation from high school,
Jennie planned to study the new field of geriatrics. After
the frenetic years of rebellion and meddling with her head,
Jennie was content; she had purpose, and a man to love.

Conversely, Christopher was at loose ends. He had not
yet located any goals within himself. He looked about him
and his generation was quiet. The decade of social protest
was over, the Sixties were dead. Youth were following the
old rules—college, labor, marriage, children, the American cycle. Christopher told Jennie that he was not yet
ready to settle into a nest, he had to confront a lingering
discontent. He asked for her patience, and Jennie, of

course, agreed. Whatever Christopher wanted, be it in work or love, she would accept.

After a time of meditation, Christopher announced to Jennie that he wanted to take an open-ended trip around the world, in the classic tradition of seekers, not knowing what he was looking for, stimulated by the act of wandering, of exploring both himself and new landscapes. Did Jennie want to accompany him? Or wait for him? "If you think I'm going to let you wander around the world without me," she said, "then you have found some new kind of drug."

The two plunged into an exhausting campaign for funds, Jennie working eighty hours a week as a waitress, Christopher steaming up his hobby of painting weird canvases of twisting, turning abstract figures with sand tossed at random and then set in place by shellac. They were at every flea market, every sidewalk art sale, Jennie hawking the pictures like a carnival barker, Christopher cross-legged on the ground making instant new ones. Within three months they had accumulated $2,000 each—enough.

Madame Crystal gave a dinner party to wish Jennie bon voyage. A dozen old people came, in their finest, carrying lavishly iced cakes and fruit cobblers and travel advice accumulated over long lifetimes. Their going-away gift was a leather passport case, and at midnight, Madame Crystal emotionally sang "I love Paris" and "Home, Sweet Home." Everyone kissed, and Jennie had tears in her eyes.

Spilling travel folders and guidebooks, their young faces flushed with excitement, the lovers hurried to California, where Jennie wanted to say goodbye to friends and family. Carmen, her onetime best friend and co-adventurer in matters of sex, drugs, and mystical exploration, was astonished. "I couldn't believe my eyes," she said. "This wild little girl went off to Seattle and then this Earth Mother came back home to the beach. Jennie was into ecology and Earth Shoes and she didn't shave her legs or under her arms, and her hair was uncut and unstyled, and she spoke of all the starving people in the world, and how our society dumps on the senior citizens. I sat there and watched this strange girl bend her body like a pretzel into weird yoga positions, and I realized I didn't know her

anymore. She told me that everything we had done together was a waste of time. How can you cancel out your
youth?"

Maggie and Cap also stared at their granddaughter in
her latest transformation. Maggie wondered, "Where are
all your clothes?" Jennie smiled. "I gave them to the poor
people in Seattle who never had anything beautiful in their
whole life," she answered. All she now owned were faded
blue jeans, a sweater, and a bedroll. The young couple
stayed a few days at Maggie's home—in the same bedroom
—and Jennie fretted over what her very Catholic grandmother would think of the new intimacy. On the first
morning, Maggie prepared breakfast and knocked at Jennie's door and heard scramblings within. When the door
was opened, Christopher was curled in a blanket on the
floor, Jennie pretending that she had slept alone in her
bed. Maggie set down the breakfast tray and asked Jennie
to help her bring in something forgotten. In the kitchen,
Maggie smiled and tried to be modern. She did not want
the children to be ill at ease in her home, however much
an unmarried couple sharing the same bed shocked her.
"You know, Jennie," said the grandmother, "I'm not
stupid."

Jennie giggled. "I know you're not."

"I just want you to know that you and Christopher are
. . . are *welcome*," said Maggie, trying not to falter.

Jennie kissed her warmly. "Christopher and I said our
own vows, in a beautiful forest, and we're as much married
as if we'd hired all the preachers in California." Nodding,
Maggie accepted that. It was new and different, but it was
not the time for a sermon on morality.

On the day they left, Maggie took Christopher aside.
She was concerned. "I practically raised that beautiful
girl in there," she told him, "and I love her more than I
can tell you." Christopher nodded. He knew the depths of
that love. Maggie hurried on. "Then you'll understand
what it's like to permit a nineteen-year-old girl to go off
running around the world with no schedule and not much
emergency money . . . You're very tall and perhaps strong,
but you look frail to me, and I'm worried that you can't
take care of Jennie if something happened."

Christopher put his arms around the old woman and

she felt strength in them. "However much you love Jennie," he said, "I love her more, in a different way. We are one, and I promise that nothing will happen to her."

Then a baker's van honked outside, and the travelers were gone in a flurry of kisses and waves and great expectations.

They were away almost a year, flying first to Luxembourg on Icelandic Airlines, at that time the least expensive wings to Europe, thence meandering about Europe, settling in Greece for a few months, where both worked in a hothouse and tended vegetables. When the job ended, they took the ferryboat to Crete, intending to rest at the ancient Roman caves of Matala, which have for years housed colonies of the young and disenchanted. Playing one day on a beach, Jennie found a pebble whose shape interested her. It seemed to resemble a little potbellied god. Christopher examined it and pronounced that Jennie had discovered a perfect replica of Lord Buddha. With that, the stone fell from Jennie's hand, almost as if bidden, and disappeared into the sea—like a drowning man. Perhaps, Christopher would later reason, this was the first omen. It disturbed him and they moved on to Istanbul.

By bus and train and thumb they worked slowly across the world. In Iran they waited for the winter snows to melt further so they could drive through the Khyber Pass with a friend in an old truck. In Afghanistan a trader told Jennie she would be worth six white horses, perhaps seven if it was necessary to bargain. Finally, India, and a sense of awe. She wrote to Madame Crystal: "India assaults me. It is a country of color, hot colors. Reds, pinks, oranges, gold. Everywhere you look, there is something brilliant to see, or hear, or smell. The poverty is overwhelming at first, but after a while you realize that it was here before you came and will be here after you leave. There is nothing you can do about it, except try to see things beyond it . . . Never again will I take sit-down toilets and showers for granted!"

Their path wound down the subcontinent to Goa, the former Portuguese settlement that pooches out like a belly button on the western edge of India. Goa became lustrous to the young during the 1960s when the Beatles and Mia

Farrow went there to meditate and dance on the clean
and then empty sands. In the decade after, tens of thousands of young travelers stopped in Goa, some living for
years in thatched huts that rented for ten dollars a month.
When Christopher and Jennie arrived, it was hardly the
idyllic place of their imaginations. The sun was relentless,
Jennie could not walk more than a dozen paces on the
beach without burning her feet. The colony of a hundred
youths lay soaked in sweat, many of them so deeply
stoned that they did not even feel the heat. One night, at
an outdoor cafe where a few kids were dancing listlessly
to music from an English boy's cassettes, Jennie and Christopher began to speak with a thin and pale but serene
American who was older, perhaps thirty, and who seemed
to be at total peace with the world. He told them of a
month spent in Katmandu, Nepal, studying at a Buddhist
monastery that welcomed Westerners. The experience had
been the most important event of his life, and though he
was forced by financial problems to return to America,
someday he would go back to the Himalayas and devote
his life to meditation.

Jennie found the man to be moderately interesting, but
Christopher stayed up until dawn, fascinated. He was
actively searching for something new to sink his metaphysical teeth into, and this form of Buddhism—the Maha-
yana tradition—seemed challenging. "Someday we should
go to Katmandu," said Christopher, and Jennie agreed,
not so much as an endorsement of the plan but to acknowledge the hope that her lover would soon find an anchor.
Clearly he was drifting away from her.

Somewhere along the road, a tiny wedge had developed
between Jennie and Christopher, and by the time they
reached the steaming sands of Goa, it was widening. "I'll
never know why Christopher is suddenly distant," wrote
Jennie in her journal. "He says he still loves me, but what
he says and does are two different things." For the first
time since their relationship began, Christopher had become sexually disinterested. More often that not, the night
would end with a dutiful kiss on Jennie's cheek, then
something muttered about the need for abstinence so as
not to muddle his fermenting mind. Sometimes Christopher climbed out of his sleeping bag and crept away, find-

ing a place to sit and think and be completely alone. Never before had Jennie felt left out, even for a moment. She tried to be interested when Christopher spoke of the wheel of reincarnation and of the teachings of various lamas from Tibet, but what she really wanted was for her lover to hold her and need her—and mean it.

One night at a party held under the palms on the beach, Jennie puffed happily on the hash pipe every time it circled, sang loudly, danced with anyone who asked, and if no one asked, then all by herself. After midnight, when Christopher was sitting with a small group of youths discussing nirvana and how to obtain it, Jennie stripped off her clothes and ran to the sea and swam naked, her laughter drawing others. She passed out and spent the night in someone else's hut, and the next morning, embarrassed and fuzzy, hurried to Christopher with an apology. He looked at her with sadness, but understanding. "Until you understand the meaning of karma," he said, "there will be more nights like that."

They splurged and flew from Delhi to Katmandu, only an hour's journey but a step back through the curtains of time, to centuries lost. Out the window of their plane, the two youngsters looked in awe at the Himalayas, white-haired giants patrolling the roof of the world, then thrilled as they plunged through frothy clouds into the eerie green valley of Katmandu. Hardly were they through customs when Christopher was asking directions to the Kopan Monastery.

It was a place of primitive comfort and surpassing beauty. Founded in the 1960s by a white Russian princess named Zina who wanted a place for Westerners to study Buddhism (Princess Zina would later die of peritonitis while in residence at another monastery several thousand feet higher in the mountains), Kopan demanded an arduous walk before its gates could be reached, a metaphor, perhaps, for the enlightenment offered within.

The path began for Jennie and Christopher at one of the great Buddhist stupas, or temples, on the outskirts of Katmandu, an exotic, soaring structure whose tower is celebrated for the enormous painted eyes that stare omi-

nously in the four directions, eyes that bore into the soul
of anyone who dares look back at them. From there, the
couple found a goat path road winding up through terraced
rice fields of hot green stretching as far as the human eye
could see. Water buffalo also claim the path, and travelers
must scurry to give them room. Little temple dogs dart
out to yap disapproval, and women with yokes on their
shoulders and baskets heavily loaded with vegetables climb
surely to their stucco farmhouses, often hidden behind
rows of corn twelve feet high.

The monastery sits atop a graceful hill; often fog so
blankets the valley that Kopan seems to hang suspended
in the clouds. Students are told of farmhouses nearby that
can be rented for less than ten cents a day, but Christopher and Jennie were running low on funds. They decided
instead to pitch their tent on a second hill, just above the
monastery, between two great firs. A green banner was
stretched between the trees to wish happy birthday to His
Holiness the Dalai Lama.

"I can't believe I'm here," wrote Jennie to Madame
Crystal in Seattle. "We are literally on top of the world,
and we will stay for 30 days, studying Buddhism and
meditating. The first day it was hard to concentrate on the
lectures, because I was picking lice out of my hair. We
bathe (hah!) in ice cold water from a spring. Christopher
and I are fine, a few problems along the way, some
pressure and minor traumas, but I think this place will
strengthen our love."

Writing letters, as Jennie would soon learn, was frowned
upon, as were any worldly diversions, particularly drugs,
alcohol, tobacco, and sex. For thirty days, the youngsters
were put into a metaphysical pressure cooker, the point
being to remove distractions, to stop "extraneous input to
the mind," to turn off all the sensory stimuli that continually bombard people before the hill in Kopan is
climbed. They rose before dawn and spent an hour meditating, chanting mantras, trying to visualize Lord Buddha
by first concentrating on a tiny speck of light and allowing
it to grow into a figure with moving hands and surrounded
by translucent light. Breakfast was barley cereal and
yoghurt, then came a long morning of "discourses" by
Lamo Yeshe or Lama Thubten Zopa Rinpoche, who at

the age of three, in Tibet, was declared to be a reincarnation of a dead lama. The lamas sat enthroned in the main hall of the monastery, in front of a glass case with dolls representing important Buddhist figures. With their china faces and ornate gold robes, they looked like the toys of a rich little girl.

There was little fun, rare laughter. The teachings of the lamas dwelled upon suffering, of preparing for death. "All is suffering, all is emptiness, all is *dukkha*," said the lamas, quoting Lord Buddha. And one is condemned to endless reincarnations until the spirit is cleansed by meditation and thus permitted to leave the wheel of dying and returning—and dying again. The goal is to reach nirvana, the state of bliss. "The first step toward becoming free of suffering is to recognize the cause of suffering," wrote Jennie in her journal, "and you can be rid of it—only through meditation." She then wrote: *"That makes sense."* Karma was not difficult to grasp. Jennie understood within a few days that it simply meant that a person brings on inevitable results, be they good or bad, due to the way a life is lived, or, importantly, the way a previous life was lived.

"Is karma destiny?" asked Jennie of one of the monks. He smiled and answered, "Perhaps destiny is karma."

Something curious happened.

Before the end of the month's stay at the monastery, Jennie and Christopher switched roles. She became the devoted, dedicated student; he found the study course interesting intellectually, but not one that he could accept fully as a life style. One late afternoon they sat on their hilltop sipping tea and watching the sun die behind the great mountains, a ravishing symbol of the Buddhist belief that all is cyclical. Far away they could hear strange music of drums and horns from the valley, and the subdued giggling of the seventy young boys who were enrolled as monks-to-be in the monastery, some as young as four, all wearing brilliant purple and saffron robes and cognizant that most would never leave this mountaintop.

At Kopan were several Westerners, including a dozen Americans, who had taken the vows of monks and nuns. Their lives were ones of enormous sacrifice, celibacy, and

withdrawal from the world, even to the point of taking
new names, never again using the ones on their birth
certificates. Christopher remarked that he could never
make such a commitment; he did not see the value of
retreating from the world rather than challenging and
perhaps changing it. Jennie listened and was silent. Then
she said, "I could. I think I could find peace here."

Christopher did not intrude on her comment, for he
doubted if she would feel the same once they returned
to Seattle. "Jennie was going through changes," he would
one day remember. "Our directions were not toward each
other anymore, but to our inner selves. Jennie began to
perceive things differently at Kopan. Up to that point she
had been a creature of her environment. Now she realized
that she was an individual—incarnate!—and she got in
touch with those personal energies that are not forced on
you from parents or friends or home town. Jennie began
to know that she was much, much more than what she
was programmed to think of herself. And she no longer
felt guilt over some of the dark moments in her past."

Before they left Nepal, Jennie and Christopher decided
to climb to a place almost fifteen thousand feet in the
Himalayas, to the monastery called Lawuda, built on the
site of a cave where one of the lamas had lived "in a
previous life." He had vowed to return and build a school
for Sherpa children. For Jennie and Christopher it was
the supreme experience of their young lives.

They began at Lamosangu, traditional starting point for
the Everest expeditions, the easternmost point on the road
to China. For several days, the couple climbed through
terraced wheat fields and jungles of rhododendrons afire
with pink and scarlet blossoms, passing through several
villages a day and besieged by children who importuned
for coins or sweets.

The climb was hard, the red clay dust difficult to wash
away, the centuries-old path often so worn by the feet of
the ancients that the sides were shoulder high. Each night
they stopped at a Sherpa house for shelter, eating rice
and *dal* (a lentil curry) and paying only twenty cents for
bed and board. They slept in their bedrolls, thrown down
on earthen floors with beds of leaves, next to the farmer's

animals. Up and up they climbed, across narrow ridges, over six major rivers including one so full of minerals, so boiling with its rush from an Everest glacier to tumble down the mountain, that it gleamed white and was called, appropriately, Milk River.

They stopped briefly at the Namche Bazaar, a trading post in the mountains for Sherpas. These hardy mountain men go in and out of what was once Tibet, now China and officially forbidden to enter, and they return to Nepal with wares for sale—tea, sugar, wool, cups, thermos bottles from Shanghai, cooking oil, kerosene lamps. Jennie was enchanted by the Sherpas, they being scarcely taller than she. Christopher laughed when one of the Sherpas offered her a bite of cold boiled potato from his pocket; the strong little men eat them constantly on treks. As Jennie munched the mushy vegetable with distinct lack of enthusiasm, the Sherpa stared at her with what appeared to be moonstruck infatuation. He began to speak passionately, but Christopher pulled his lady away gracefully.

From the bazaar, the travelers turned west, leaving the Everest route, pushing higher and higher into the clouds and fog. One false step and they would plunge ten thousand feet. Then, startlingly, as if the curtains opened on a great stage, the grayness vanished and the monastery was in view. Sherpa children ran out laughing to greet the tall boy and his little companion, both puffing, both ecstatic. Bells rang to shatter the icy silence.

It was a moment of clarity, denied to all but a very few. They stood on the edge, thousands of feet above the clouds, with crystal beads of ice hanging suspended from their hair. Winds whistled through holes in the mountains, and above stretched a sky so blue that it could never be imagined. From far away came the occasional tinkle of a yak bell. The view of the Himalayas was so staggering that it seemed wrong for human eyes to look upon it. The wisdom of Buddha, if one believes, is powerful here. Jennie felt removed, severed, alien to the earth plane.

They held one another until the light was gone and darkness wrapped the summit of the world and stars came out close enough to touch. And both of them knew that it would never be the same between them again.

CHAPTER TWENTY-TWO

Each night, Pan American's Flight 2 roars off the runway at John F. Kennedy International Airport, turns sharply to glide briefly over the lights of Manhattan, then noses east across the Atlantic, circling the world in little more than forty hours, making oceans, continents, wars, mountains, and men seem insignificant and characterless.

On May 4, 1975, the 747 landed in the steamy early evening at Teheran, and, as the flight had lost time earlier in Europe, transit passengers were requested to stay on board. Two weary young French passengers were annoyed, as they had wanted to stretch their legs. But as they both worked for another airline, they grumbled only to themselves and settled for standing at the open door and taking the sticky night air and gossiping with the stewardess. One of the travelers was Jeanne Paumier, a reservations clerk who was the classic French girl—a tiny gamine from the Rive Gauche with hair cropped like Piaf's and with an inherent sense of flair and chic. Her companion was a friend—and only that—named Christian Rucher, also a reservations agent. They were traveling to India for a ten-day vacation, most of which was to be spent in Kashmir, whose lakes at the top of the subcontinent near the Pakistan border have enchanted sultans and romantics for centuries.

Abruptly a surly voice whiplashed behind them. They turned and beheld an angry young man in dungarees. He appeared to be a hippie of Oriental blood, for his hair was long and unshaped, stuffed under a leather cap. A new black beard dribbled unappealing from his chin, and his eyes were concealed behind dark glasses. He spoke in hot and accented English, informing the stewardess that he wished to disembark and purchase caviar and that he was going to do just that, rules be damned! He seemed used to ordering people around. Jeanne speculated that he was a rich man's son who grew up kicking servants and torturing cats. The stewardess, not wanting a scene, told the pushy traveler he could have ten minutes inside the terminal. No more. At that, Christian Rucher asked permission to get off for a smoke—and that, too, was granted. Inside the terminal, the two men introduced themselves. Christian shook hands with the hippie, who gave his name as "Alain Gauthier." He was, of course, Charles Sobhraj. His profession, he said, was photography, and at that revelation, Christian understood better both the man's wardrobe and his abrasiveness. Photographers in Paris are known for wearing blue jeans and bullying people. Alain said he was traveling to New Delhi on assignment for *Paris-Match* to do a *reportage* on India, that country being a growing favorite of French travelers.

When the jumbo jet flew off on the Teheran-Delhi leg, Gauthier wandered down the aisle until he found the seats of Christian and Jeanne. Without being invited, he perched on the arm, filling their ears with tales of the wonders and perils of India. When he learned their vacation destination, he shook his head as if he could not believe the coincidence. He, *too*, was going to Kashmir, had in fact been there many times, and could assist them in negotiating for a houseboat, the most desirable accommodation. How lucky they were to encounter him, rattled Alain, for the houseboat agents were notorious sharks whose quoted prices usually began at thrice the real value.

Later, when the plane landed at Delhi, Jeanne agreed that Alain Gauthier was a lucky find, leading them with assurance through the confusing maze of Indian immigration. The moment a newcomer steps inside the terminal, an ominous knot forms in the stomach. Above, in the glass-walled balcony where people wait for family reunions, bodies are packed together tightly, staring down at the serpentine lines of passengers. The men are in cotton pajamas and turbans, their women in saris with jewels in their nostrils, children huddled against parental bodies like knots on a tree branch. Their faces are copper dark and forbidding, and at that moment the revelation clutches everyone who experiences it for the first time. India!

Due to Alain's expert interference, the young French couple cleared customs quickly and found themselves in a taxi with their new friend, hurtling through the sleeping boulevards of the city. Alain seemed to know everything, pointing out embassies, hotels, important villas, and at the same time cursing the driver for going too fast, too slow, or on roundabout routes that increased the fare unnecessarily. "Everyone in this country is a thief," said Alain. "You must be constantly alert . . . If this driver takes one more false turn, I will report him to the Minister of Tourism."

After a few hours sleep, Alain rang Jeanne's hotel room, and, greeting her and Christian in the lobby like long-separated friends, presented gifts. For Jeanne, he had purchased a gold and amethyst ring. For Christian, a dagger encrusted with fake stones. Outside was a car engaged to whisk the newcomers about the city, the Red Fort, the Jama Masjid and Humayun's Tomb blurring before their eyes like a twenty-minute footrace about the Louvre with time only to see the Mona Lisa, Winged Victory, and Venus de Milo. Alain was truly incredible, a bulldozer clearing a path through the congested madness of Old Delhi, as familiar with the rabbit warren of streets in Chandni Chowk bazaar as the boulevards of Paris, threatening the beggar children with their broken bodies and directing the French visitors to have no pity for them as they were "professionals," forbidding them to eat tempting sugared apricots or sesame-crusted pralines from a street peddler, but taking them instead to an outdoor restaurant called Moti Mahal, which Jeanne's eyes merited no marks for hygiene, but from whose *tandoori* ovens emerged incredible chicken that had been marinated in yoghurt and spices and flash-broiled in a brick-walled pit to seal the juices beneath a peppery crust. While they ate, a troupe of musicians performed and a fat woman with several pounds of jewels around her huge bosom sang endless songs of enormous heartbreak and smoked hashish without an eyelash of emotion. At this moment, Jeanne fell in love with India, overwhelmed by the exotic pageant that played continuously about her. And she thought to herself: "What an incredible stroke of fate to have met Alain Gauthier on that plane. We would never have found a restaurant like this." Throughout the meal, she examined Gauthier surreptitiously. He held no sexual appeal for her, despite the muscles and authority. His visage was Oriental, and such men were of no interest to her. But there was an undeniable fascination, a lure, a force that made him the focus of every moment. If either of the French began a sentence and Alain interrupted, they fell into respectful silence and listened to what *he* had to say. Alain Gauthier, obnoxious as he could be, was a man to whom attention was given.

That night Jeanne wrote in her diary: "Today I met a very famous journalist and photographer. His name is Alain Gauthier and he knows everything about India. He seems to know everything about everything! He is taking us to Kashmir."

But before they left the capital, Alain begged a favor from Jeanne. His English was inadequate, confessed Alain, and he needed someone to translate a few telegrams from his French into English before sending them. The cables all seemed to deal with money and travel, with messages like "funds will be available soon" or "new venture planned for Bangkok," and they went to addresses in Paris, Marseilles, Athens, Istanbul, and Hong Kong. Some were signed "Alain" and others "Charles." When Jeanne questioned the disparity in signatures, Alain smiled. "You know we French all have several *prénoms*," he said. "Some people call me Alain. Others Charles. And most call me *chéri*." Jeanne laughed and let it go at that.

They flew to Srinagar, the most important city in the Kashmir region, an enormous valley larger than Great Britain, cuddling tranquilly in the lap of the Himalayas like a lamb protected by fierce mastiffs. Since the Emperor Akbar first came in the sixteenth century to escape the staggering pre-monsoon heat of Agra, Srinagar has been a fashionable vacation place for wealthy Indians. Here is not the India of one's imagination, rather a first cousin to

Switzerland. There are even yodelers and St. Bernards. The natives, mostly Moslem, are more loyal to neighboring Pakistan than to India, their region having been a major bone of contention since the two countries were sliced by the 1947 partition.

On the slopes of the great mountains, where frozen glaciers endure all of the year, where herds of cattle graze on buttercups, the armies of India and Pakistan patrol their respective sides on sleds and skis, shouting obscenities at the other. Forests of pointed rifles can be glimpsed. But the tourists who come to Kashmir are not overly concerned with military posturings. They want to smell the attar of blossoms that bloom in the meadows and orchards, hanging over the region like an eternal cloud of perfume, or laze on mirror lakes where kings once whispered adulterously into the ears of beautiful women and created the gardens called Shalimar to attest their love.

The airport at Srinagar is small, rural in fact, and the moment tourists are disgorged from the Delhi flight, seasoned importuners set upon them. Young girls in swirling pink and lime saris offer platters of shining mangoes and the sweetest oranges on earth. Others tempt with flowers, necklaces of marigold and palmyra and roses the color of sunsets. Men with great waxed mustaches and flirtatious manner drape and lock bracelets and pendants about a woman's neck before she can summon a refusal, and over it all, like an operatic tenor drowning out full orchestra and chorus, blares the beseechment of the houseboat agent, a salesman rivaled in pushiness only by the camel drivers at the Giza pyramids.

"Don't buy anything, don't say anything," commanded Alain to his wards, weaving through the high pressure sales force toward baggage claim. Never was Jeanne more grateful for this savior. Neither she nor Christian was adept at bullish maneuver and surely they would have been trapped into leasing an undesirable houseboat at an exorbitant price. Contentedly she sat on a bench and watched the confusion whirl about her. Her eyes suddenly caught those of another young woman, thirty maybe, whose face was profoundly weary. Stunned by the chaos and the heat, she pressed her hands to her ears to shut out the showering sales pitches. Jeanne imagined that here was

a lower-class English girl, probably from Manchester, a
filing clerk or shopgirl. She was decidedly plain, with a
pointed nose and spectacles that sagged on the slope. Her
blue jean cuffs were rolled up to reveal an unstylish glimpse
of white athletic socks and tennis shoes. But when she
looked back at Jeanne to smile shyly, obviously pleased to
locate a sympathetic face as bewildered as hers, there was
a modicum of appeal. Then an older, plumpish, balding
man with sweat drowning his beet-red forehead appeared
and put his arm around the girl, Jeanne nodded to herself.
They fit. Of course they are man and wife. They are made
for one another. Jeanne hoped that Kashmir would drench
them in romance.

Then she heard her name called. Alain was beckoning,
Christian beside him. It seemed the Class A houseboats
had leaped in price and the best thing to do would be find
another couple with which to share. The houseboats are
conducive to sharing, containing private apartments and
enough decks for sunning to ensure privacy. In that case,
suggested Jeanne, she had just noticed a girl who seemed
to be English, and her man, and they were dazed by the
turmoil of negotiating. "Perfect," said Alain, and in a
moment, Jeanne had the couple in tow. She had addressed
the girl in English, but had received a reply in a heavy
accent. "Ah, you are French!" exclaimed Jeanne, as happy
as if she had stumbled onto a bistro in the desert.

The girl smiled and introduced herself. She was Marie-
Andrée Leclerc, from Quebec. And her friend was Bernard, also from Canada. Alain Gauthier leaned forward
and kissed Marie-Andrée's hand, startling her with his
gallantry. For a few heavy moments there was silence while
Alain scrutinzed the Canadian woman, like a jeweler examining a questionable stone. Then came the welcome intrusion of a houseboat agent who yelled that all the choice
accommodations were rapidly disappearing. "Forgive me,"
murmured Alain. He was taken aback for a moment.
Marie-Andrée, he said softly, was almost a double for his
ex-wife.

Then, like a child walking a fence to impress another,
Alain returned to the haggling with vigor. Furiously he
denounced the agent as a thief among thieves. Three times
he ordered his friends to pick up their luggage and stalk

theatrically from the terminal. And three times the agent
ran after them, lowering his price. Gripping the agent's
shoulder and squeezing it tightly, Alain said threateningly,
"All right, we accept. But if this houseboat is inferior, you
will hear from me."

The Sultan's Embrace was typical of the houseboats first
ordered built by British tourists in the nineteenth century
who were unable to purchase land from the crafty natives
of Kashmir. They were willing to lease only water rights.
Ninety feet long and only fifteen feet wide, built of teak
and mahogany with exquisitely carved filigrees and fur-
belows, it was permanently anchored on an inlet of Dal
Lake, choked by lotus blossoms of gold and pink. Her
neighbors were boats named Lotus Garden and Your Paradise and Super Duper Deluxe and Shalimar Nights. Each
couple took a private bedroom, and Alain moved into the
third—alone. But from the moment all stepped foot onto
the Sultan's Embrace, Alain was the dominant member,
captain of the ship and master of everyone's life.

On the first night, the resident cook prepared chicken
curry and set it proudly on a highly polished dining table.
Jeanne had not given her appearance much heed, thus she
was surprised to see that Marie-Andrée had combed her
hair becomingly and wore a soft, clingy summer dress. She
looked younger and far more attractive than she had
standing at the Srinagar Airport. Immediately Jeanne
caught onto the reason why: the Canadian girl was smitten by Alain Gauthier. Fantasies danced unhidden in her
eyes. But on this night, the object of her attention was not
receptive. Alain greeted the others, bade them to sit down,
took one bite of chicken curry, and yelled imperiously for
the cook. "This is garbage," he said. He picked up the
serving platter and threw the food into the quiet lake
where it sank in a bed of water lilies and was attacked
by a flurry of brilliantly colored fish. The cook was ordered
to go into town and purchase a roast chicken from a
restaurant.

Later that night, in the privacy of her room, Jeanne
commented to Christian. Throughout the awkward dinner,
Alain had bragged—yes, that was the best word, bragged—
about his accomplishments. If one could believe him,

Alain had been a French national champion in karate, a decorated military hero, and the possessor of a law degree from the Sorbonne. He had photographed leopards in Kenya and had been in the front lines during the Vietnam War. Christian was not impressed. "I don't think he's real," she said. "I'm suspicious of everything he says."

Jeanne fell asleep while thinking about the potential for tension in the week ahead. Marie-Andrée had set her cap for Alain Gauthier, and her boy friend, Bernard, would soon catch on.

Cries from peddler boats circling the Sultan's Embrace broke sleep. Jeanne looked out her window and was enchanted. The lake was pearl gray silk, with fingers of mauve from a drowsy sun not yet over the mountaintops, and already the waters contained a floating market. One canoe was so laden with fresh flowers that the old woman's head barely stuck out from the blankets of lotus shaded in salmons with spidery innards of gold. Another offered fresh-baked breads, with mint and cheese hidden inside, and French style rolls. There were laundry boats and pharmacy boats with aspirin and diarrhea potions, boats that offered fur jackets and blankets, those that had candies and fruits, others that tempted with just-caught and still-wriggling fish for breakfast. While Jeanne watched the pageant with fascination, the door of her bedroom opened and Alain appeared, nearly nude, wearing only underwear, his muscled chest and legs on calculated display. His bathroom was not working. Could he use hers? Use it he did—for two hours, dipping into Jeanne's toilet kit for shampoos and skin moisturizers and into Christian's for after-shave. He emerged with glowing skin and carefully groomed hair, a considerable change from the hippie of yesterday. Changing into a bikini, he led his charges to the top deck and stretched out like a well-mannered ocelot at the feet of the two women. Marie-Andrée pretended to read, but Jeanne noticed that her eyes kept darting nervously over her *policier* to admire the oiled body that turned before her as if a peacock on a rotisserie. After a while, Jeanne bit her lip to keep from laughing. Not only was Alain conducting a blatant campaign for feminine attention, he was not even very good at it. Amateur, thought Jeanne. "But he is after *you*, chéri," whispered Christian maliciously as he dived into the quiet lake.

True. For the rest of the week, Alain flaunted his muscles and karate stances for Jeanne, to the point where she felt like telling him not to waste his time. And he ignored Marie-Andrée, who watched him with barely disguised hunger. Bernard the Boyfriend watched everybody. "This is really a farce," Jeanne told Christian. "Alain is after me, Marie-Andrée is after Alain, and Bernard is out in the cold."

Each day contained new splendor, realized on a stage of impossible beauty. They hired *shikaras*, gondolas painted in hot colors, with cushions covered in brilliant fabrics, with matching curtains to pull for privacy like lovers do in a Paris restaurant. Behind the curtains stood the boatman, usually a strapping fellow of handsome mien and wide, strong shoulders, singing exotic melodies as he dipped heartshaped paddles into the quiet waters, guiding his customers through the canals and water farms to the fabled gardens of the sultans, where waterfalls tumble down terraces, where groves of *chenar* trees from ancient Persia shade secluded pools.

They drove an hour away from Srinagar to the village of Gulmarg where the world's highest golf course spreads out at 8,700 feet above sea level. Here Alain staged his notorious haggling performance and after several moments of fury engaged the small but sturdy Himalayan ponies for all to ride up rocky trails, through thick forests where high noon is like twilight, across rushing cold streams from melted snow, stopping only at tent camps for tea and stale biscuits. At the summit, Marie-Andrée dismounted and looked out at a staggering panorama, the Himalayas above, the gentle valley of Kashmir below. Cold winds blew against her face and turned her cheeks rosy, and she went to Alain and said, with great emotion, "This is the most beautiful thing I have ever seen. I will never forget this moment."

There were also odd moments, puzzles. Alain took to disappearing from the houseboat for several hours, instructing the group to join him at a restaurant. One night everybody went to the designated place and Alain was discovered deep in conversation with three young women—two English, one Chinese, all vaguely hippie-ish. Jeanne called out his name, and Alain turned with quick annoyance that melted into what appeared to be embarrassment. It was noted that Marie-Andrée was the most upset upon encountering Alain surrounded by three vivacious women.

And there was the matter of photographs. Or lack thereof. Throughout the week in Kashmir, Jeanne sought to take a picture of the entire group, either on the houseboat or shopping for lacquered papier-mâché boxes at two favored stores—Subhana the Best and Subhana the Worst. Or lazing on the soft grass of Shalimar gardens. But each time she raised her camera, Alain ducked, or insisted that he, being a professional photographer, could better take the shot. Later, when she returned to Paris and had her film developed, not a single image of the man who dominated the week had been caught. Eerily, the two or three exposures that Jeanne clearly remembered as having included at least a partial piece of Alain's face, were completely blank—as if he had forbidden the film to capture his features.

On another day, when the two women were sunbathing privately on the Sultan's Embrace, Jeanne drank in the beauty of the morning and sighed. She looked at Marie-Andrée, lying face down and tanning her back. "You are lucky," said Jeanne, "being in a place like this with your boy friend." Marie-Andrée raised her head and shook it in disagreement. Bernard, she said, was a very nice man. But she did not love him. Then, hastily, Marie-Andrée said that she had a secret lover back in Canada whom no one knew about. She was sending him daily postcards from Kashmir. "What's he like?" idly asked Jeanne. This caused Marie-Andrée to stammer, and Jeanne tactfully changed the subject. She did not believe Marie-Andrée had a secret lover, or *any* lover for that matter. She did not think Marie-Andrée knew a damn thing about men.

On the last night on the Sultan's Embrace, Alain appeared for dinner in tight jeans and nothing else, his bare chest rubbed with oil. He produced a bottle of imported scotch, a rare and expensive indulgence in India. Its purpose was to seal the fellowship of a perfect week, he an-

nounced. Everyone sipped casually, everyone save Marie-
Andrée. She drank heavily—and quickly was drunk. She
took off her blouse and underneath was her bikini top.
The night was torrid. Sex hung in the air. The girl from the
village in Canada began vamping Alain as if she were an
inexperienced hooker on the street for the first time. Dancing alone on the deck, clutching her body, she brushed
past the man she wanted. Bernard tolerated her behavior
for a little while, then angrily said good night and went
to his room. Trouble was brewing, as surely as first thunder
heralds an approaching storm. Jeanne whispered in Christian's ear that it was best to take cover. She was French
enough to hope that Marie-Andrée would get what she
wanted, but she further hoped that the sun would rise
without blood on the Sultan's Embrace.

Nothing happened. Alain and Marie-Andrée were left
alone on the deck and he watched her dance for a few
moments, then abruptly left and went ashore. Marie-
Andrée was abandoned, and humiliated. She began to cry
and she stayed alone until past midnight. The next morning she hid behind dark glasses and did not speak beyond
necessities on the trip back to Delhi. "Alain's a real bastard," said Christian in dissection of the week. It was his
accurate opinion that Alain was about to drive Marie-
Andrée crazy.

They all left for Agra on the Taj Mahal Express, a
crack train that departs Delhi each morning at seven,
reaches the city that contains the monument to love by
late morning, then brings tourists back by dusk. Alain
arranged everything and, en route, spun gauzy tales of the
Taj. He told his stories well, how the great tomb was built
by Shah Jahan, fifth Moghul emperor, to assuage epic
grief over the death of his wife, a young woman who not
surprisingly died while delivering her *fourteenth* child.
Jeanne found the account diverting, but Marie-Andrée was
spellbound, hanging on every word. The pain of the last
night on the houseboat was either gone or hidden carefully. She looked exactly like a lovestruck teen-ager,
thought Jeanne, and she would no doubt forgive Alain for
any wound.

The Taj Mahal usually dazzles visitors, for it is one of

the few monuments in the world that is even more beautiful than photographs. Marie-Andrée was transfixed, freed
from a life that had ranged from the land of dull to the
shores of bleak. At this moment, she was standing before
the most beautiful building ever erected as tribute to love,
and her guide was a man whose life was everything hers
was not. Her face showed that nothing else mattered. She
had this one moment, precious, precious enough to keep.
Alain Gauthier was a son of a bitch, thought Jeanne. A
transparent son of a bitch. But give him this: he made a
frustrated woman's life a little more bearable.

On her last night in India, once again in Delhi, Jeanne
surrendered to Alain's wheedling and agreed to meet him
for a private drink. He had been suggesting it for days,
wanting to talk "business," and, having considerable gratitude for the labor he had performed both in Kashmir and
Agra as unpaid tour director, Jeanne consented. Christian
warned her to be careful, and Jeanne laughed, assuring
her friend that she had discouraged men more persistent
than Alain on the Métros of Paris.

Their rendezvous was the Cellar, a gloomy night club
on Connaught Circle, the hub of Delhi, with walls dark
as midnight, with reasonable facsimiles of American-style
hamburgers to capture Western tourists, with secluded
booths occupied—it is not difficult to imagine—by men
who would not welcome a police knock at the door. When
she entered, Jeanne saw Alain immediately, commanding
a corner table and talking with two long-haired French
boys who looked like junkies. As she approached, she
noticed that one of them had a grimy hand outstretched,
in which nestled a few tiny red stones. Alain was lecturing,
frowning. Jeanne interrupted.

"*Ah, bonsoir, chérie,*" said Alain, rising to kiss Jeanne's
cheeks perfunctorily and dismissing the French boys with
a commanding wave. She started to sit down, but Alain
wanted a change of locale. "It's too noisy to talk here,"
he said. The evening was new, but the rock music was
already shattering. They found a taxi and Alain snapped,
"Oberoi Hotel." Jeanne was impressed by his choice, the
Oberoi-Intercontinental being Delhi's flossiest, direct from
the Miami Beach school of architecture, but gathering

place nonetheless for the rich and powerful. It was only
a few minutes away from the Cellar, but on this night the
driver elected to take a more circuitous route and increase
the fare. Absorbed in an anecdote, Alain at first paid no
heed to the driver. Then he glanced out the window and
saw an unfamiliar street. Exploding with curses, Alain
rocketed forward in his seat and put his hand on the
driver's neck and squeezed—hard—threatening even more
unless the man shut off his meter then and there and made
the rest of the ride free. "You must act this way with
thieves," said Alain, returning to his story unruffled. But
Jeanne was troubled, not only by the fearful way that
Alain burst into violence, but because he always selected
the weak and the subservient for his wrath.

They drank a sweetish white wine in the bar and ate
fresh oysters from the Arabian Gulf and looked down on
the Oberoi's huge swimming pool where clusters of people
were content just to stand in the shallow end of the tepid
water, sipping tonic, trying to find relief from the night
heat. In the distance, beyond Humayun's Tomb, lightning
crackled in the sky, but it was not yet time for the monsoon. This was May and only an overture. Jeanne was preparing a quick leavetaking when Alain reached across the
table and took her hand.

"I believe very strongly in destiny," he said. Everything
in life had a purpose.

"For example?" questioned Jeanne.

The way they met, answered Alain. He had not intended
to take the Pan Am flight that introduced them. He was,
in fact, booked on another. But at the last minute he
changed reservations. Some force put him on that plane,
that same force that collided his life with Jeanne and
Christian—out of three hundred other people on board.

But, pointed out Jeanne, that might also be called "coincidence."

Alain shook his head. "Nothing is coincidence," he said.
There are no "accidents." If, for example, Jeanne left the
Oberoi this night and had a choice of walking either to
the right or the left, perhaps one destination would lead
safely to her hotel, the other into the arms of a robber.
"You make the choice," he said. "You are responsible for
every step you take."

Jeanne nodded in agreement. The only step she wanted to take was out. She began fumbling for a tactful farewell. Alain was not yet done, not nearly done. "You and I," he said, "we are like brother and sister after one week." That could hardly be the product of coincidence. It was *destiny*.

At that, Jeanne relaxed. No longer did she worry about fending off amorous lunges from Alain, particularly since he considered their friendship to be "brother and sister."

"I want to talk business," he reminded her.

And what was his "business"?

He did not hesitate. "The illegal business," he answered, as routinely—and as pridefully—as a surgeon might speak of open-heart operations. Black market currency exchanges, buying precious stones in India and smuggling them into Europe and Hong Kong, stolen cars, fraudulent passports, all of it absurdly easy. "My customers are so trusting and so stupid," he told Jeanne, listening openmouthed, astonished not only at the catalogue of horrors but at the brazenness with which he delivered his account—and to a person he had known only one week. At the conclusion of his tale, as if to prove something, he invited her to peek inside his jacket and glimpse three stolen passports. She nodded appropriately, for she felt it was important that she show respect. Then leave. Fast. She rose and mumbled an apology of fatigue, an early flight to Hong Kong and all that.

"Wait," ordered Charles. "Sit down. I want you to work for me."

Jeanne almost laughed. "Me?" she echoed.

Many respectable people did, insisted Gauthier. *Many*. Did Jeanne remember the three girls in the restaurant at Srinagar, the two English and the Chinese? She nodded. *They* were employees of his, couriers of money, gems, passports, whatever, to countries that he designated. They were also commissioned to find men whose assets might be taken while in the pursuit of romance. And the two French boys earlier this night at the Cellar? Jeanne nodded again, dumbly. *They* worked for Alain Gauthier; the stones they were discussing would tomorrow be smuggled through customs in Rome and sold at a jewelry store near the Spanish Steps.

Now his desire, what he had devoted this entire week

to, was the hiring of Jeanne as his very special courier.
Her credentials were appealing. Working for an airline,
she traveled extensively, she was usually waved through
customs with little or no baggage inspection, she looked
respectable and ordinary. She could anticipate earning an
easy $50,000 the first year. So could Christian, if she
could enlist him.

Indignant, Jeanne refused. The idea was absurd. She
started to say more, but Alain smiled and shrugged. He
had made his pitch. He had not been successful. It seemed
of no more importance than losing a hundred francs at
roulette. He would win it back on the next spin. What did
seem important was the revelation itself. It's crazy, thought
Jeanne, but this little man *wanted* her to know he was a
crook. She wondered if she was but one of a score of
women whom Alain was importuning. One other thing
struck her: Alain seemed pathetically anxious to collect
people, make them dependent on him, like a lonely old
woman Jeanne knew in Paris who took in stray animals
and gave them names belonging to absent family members.

Alain was scribbling something. He handed it to Jeanne.
If she was ever in Hong Kong and needed money, all she
had to do was call this number. As they walked out together, abruptly Alain turned the conversation to Marie-
Andrée. Had Jeanne noticed the way she behaved all week?
he wondered. "She has been after me," said Alain. But, he
rattled on, oblivious to the shock on Jeanne's face from
being asked to become a criminal, he was not interested in
Marie-Andrée. "She is boring," he said.

At that, Jeanne rose to her friend's defense. "Being shy
and being boring are two different things," she said testily.
"And, truthfully, *chéri*, she's too good for you. *Au revoir,*
Alain."

"Perhaps," said Alain, smiling, his eyes hidden behind
dark glasses. But Jeanne drew no warmth from the smile.
She hurried out, not daring to risk even a farewell glance.
The next morning, she and Christian flew gratefully out of
Delhi, troubled and confused by the week, both wondering
what would happen next—and to whom.

Alain took dictatorial charge of Marie-Andrée and Bernard's remaining days in the Far East. They must see

Katmandu, he ordered, and quickly they were in the kingdom of Nepal—as guests of a man whose largesse seemed boundless. First-class hotels. Three-star meals. Gambling at the Hotel Soaltee casino. Abruptly he gathered the Canadians up and transferred them next to Bangkok. It was a new Alain Gauthier. No sexual posturings. No temper tantrums. Only gallant flattery for Marie-Andrée, respect for Bernard. He made their vacation perfect.

But after a day or two in Bangkok, a city whose air is fouled by awesome traffic jams and whose restaurants offer dishes enhanced by spices alien to the Western stomach, Bernard felt his innards bedeviled. He took to his bed and was smote with severe nausea and stomach cramps. Alain was all consolation, delivering a lecture on the perils of food and drink in the East, producing a spoonful of some private medication. Bernard took it gratefully and soon fell asleep. Passed out is a better phrase, for he slept almost twenty-four hours.

Just before he surrendered, however, Bernard weakly insisted that Marie-Andrée continue with her sightseeing. After all, she would never be in Bangkok again. He would be angry if she wasted a day at his bedside. Marie-Andrée agreed, reluctantly, but as soon as she completed a scheduled trip to the royal palace, she promised to hurry back and minister to her stricken friend.

Viewing an old palace was not her intention. As Bernard slept, Marie-Andrée slipped quietly out of the hotel, found a bicycle rickshaw, and gave the driver her destination. He delivered her to a small hotel near the river, on a side street, beside an open air market where live eels were thrust at customers and where children played while wearing demon masks.

At a designated room in the small hotel, Marie-Andrée knocked and waited nervously. She was preparing to run away when the door opened. Alain Gauthier smiled in welcome. He was a different man. His beard was gone, his hair was styled, his clothes were new. He smelled of French cologne. He took her in his arms and murmured that he had been waiting impatiently for this moment since the morning they first met at Srinagar Airport.

Tenderly, capably, he put a thin gold chain about her neck and undressed her. He marveled at her body. She went willingly to his bed, grateful for the bamboo shutters that threw shadows across the linens and hid the scars on her leg. If only the shadows would hide the secret that she was thirty years old. And this was the first time that counted. And she was frightened.

CHAPTER TWENTY-THREE

Homecoming!

Her family was waiting at the airport when Marie-Andrée flew back from her great adventure, bags overflowing with brass candlesticks, embroidered purses, sandals, silks, treasures for her mother, her father, her brothers and sisters, her employees, her priest. She was radiant as she flew into her family's arms. A new vivacity emanated from her. Denise, her younger sister who bore a remarkable resemblance but who was far more aggressive and ambitious for accomplishment, noted something more. A woman's intuition told her that it was finished between Marie-Andrée and Bernard. They were polite toward one another, but theirs was not the bond of lovers. And if Marie-Andrée was this ebullient in the wake of breaking off a prospective marriage—the *only* prospect that Denise knew about—then her sister must have found solace in the Far East beyond temple gazing. As soon as the two sisters could steal away for a private moment, Denise's hunch was confirmed. "I met a man," confessed Marie-Andrée, her eyes dancing. "He is very intelligent, nice, and cute. And *rich!*" Ecstatic memories poured from her —gondolas with heart-shaped paddles, sunsets over the Himalalyas, the Taj Mahal on a blistering noon, a temple in Katmandu whose god was a golden monkey holding a parasol. And always Alain. Each sentence seemed to contain his name. Or sometimes it was Charles. Denise was confused. What *was* this man's name? Alain? Or Charles?

Marie-Andrée shrugged. "Both," she answered. "He is a very important businessman and people call him by different names."

There was more to tell. Intimate details. On their last night together, Charles—and that was the name only his *closest* friends called him—had stolen her away from Bernard for a few moments and had whispered that he was in love. "He wants me to come back to Bangkok and visit him," blurted out Marie-Andrée.

"Well, are you going?" asked Denise, who was not shocked, only happy over her sister's uncharacteristic fling into romantic madness. Marie-Andrée hesitated, and Denise saw in her eyes a sense of loss. Then she shook her head. The old demeanor settled over Marie-Andrée's shoulders like a spinster's shawl. No. Of course not. Enough money had been spent on impulsive adventure. Now it was time to return to the Clinique d'Orthopédie, to resume *la vie normale.*

"Perhaps someday . . ." began Denise.

Marie-Andrée shook her head. She was resolute. She would never see Charles again. Besides, it was silly and something she should not have done. "But at least you have the memory," said Denise. "That's more than most people have."

Marie-Andrée agreed and held her sister tightly and blessed her for understanding.

The first letter to arrive was a poem. Noting its Bangkok postmark, Marie-Andrée opened it carefully. And then she read:

> Eternal woman,
> Eternal love,
> Eternal petite Andrée,
> I love you,
> I adore you,
> Come back to me.
> —Charles

She had been home less than a week.

Then, while these words burned Marie-Andrée's heart, quickly came more:

"*Petite femme adorée*, I love you, and I want you to become my wife. I need you, your presence, your love . . . I want you to believe in our love, *chérie*. True, we must not make decisions quickly. But these opportunities do not repeat themselves every day. It is necessary to know in life *chérie*, when to seize the opportunity. When you want it, my love, you can become my wife . . . I kiss you tenderly, my love . . . I adore your body, my darling . . ."

Fourteen postcards arrived in *one day*, each embarrassingly encrusted with love from Charles. And telephone calls, from the far side of the world, catching her at work, at home, a sensuous voice reaching out from India or Sri Lanka or Thailand, exposing her in the mundane spaces that marked her life. Each night after work she raced home to search her mailbox and sit beside the telephone. She wrote back to him noncommittally, addressing her messages to *poste restante*, spare letters of ordinary news —the weather, her family, her Pinto, a veiled and painfully constructed sentence or two at the close thanking him for his attention. His letters intensified, in number and in passion:

My adored Marie-Andrée:
   If you come back, *when* you come back, I will have much more time to devote to you . . . I want us to take ten days rest on an island in the Philippines in a little villa on the beach. There you don't see anyone, there we can make love, there we can explore our bodies, talk intimately one to the other and plan our march toward the future . . . Until we meet again, I squeeze you very strongly against my body and I kiss you, my love . . .

A few days later, his love came wrapped in promises of gold:

My little adored girl:
   I cannot stop thinking of you and I feel very alone. One thing is certain—I am sure of my love for you, and my love is deep. Oh, *petite fille*, I want

to squeeze you and murmur in your ear, *"Je t'aime."*
. . . I have just ordered a beautiful evening gown for
you in red Thai silk—and another in turquoise . . .
In two days, I will meet one of my clients, a jeweler,
and I will buy from him a complete set of gems for
you (*precious* stones, of course)—a necklace, earrings, bracelets, and a ring—made from rubies, diamonds, and gold—to go with your silk robes . . .
Good night, *chérie,* sleep well. I am beside you.
Reach out and you can touch me . . .

Marie-Andrée *tried* to think logically and reason things
out. For hours she sat beside the St. Lawrence, not interested any longer in the promise across the river. Quebec
City, in fact, loomed provincial to a woman who had just
returned from the far side of the world and who now had
enough personal drama in her life to negate the need for
fantasy. She read Charles' letters, and reread them, throwing up a thousand barriers to his exhortations. During the
first week on the houseboat, she indelibly remembered,
Charles had scarcely looked at her. His eyes were trained
mainly on Jeanne, on those three hippie girls in the cafe
at Srinagar. And when Charles at last warmed to *her,* it
was not until Jeanne had left. Their moments together were
stolen, hidden from stolid old Bernard; an affectionate
whisper here, a touch of his arm on her elbow while
entering a taxi. And their one *intimate* afternoon together
had been, at best, clumsy. She had been so embarrassed
both at the ease of her capitulation and over the possibility
of being found out that their lovemaking had hardly been
the stuff of epic poetry. Had Charles even mentioned *love*
when they lay in the bamboo shadows that afternoon? She
could not remember.

Suddenly a telegram arrived, offering a round-trip
ticket to Bangkok, followed by another telephone call.
Marie-Andrée chastised Charles mildly for spending so
much money on long distance. "What is money?" he
answered. "We are talking about love."

The decision was too weighty for her to make alone.
Marie-Andrée summoned Denise to the apartment down
the street from Mama, and showed her the letters. Denise
read with raised eyebrows, swallowing the private thought

that they sounded like love-sick letters passed between teen-agers at school. To her sister, these were obviously waves crashing against a deserted beach at midnight under the full moon. "It would be hard for a woman to resist such words," Denise said tactfully. "What are you going to do?"

Marie-Andrée burst into tears. "I don't know," she said. "I simply don't know." She was the prisoner of enormous torment.

The counsel of a friend was sought, a lawyer in Lévis with whom Marie-Andrée had dealt professionally for years in business matters regarding insurance claims and medical reports. His name was Bouvin, and they respected one another. They met for drinks at the Tahiti Lounge, adjoining the restaurant where Marie-Andrée had moonlighted as a waitress to buy her Pinto. Now, over tall rum drinks, they reminisced about their years of friendship. Bouvin knew something else was on the girl's mind, but he would let her get to it in her own good time. Always he had found Marie-Andrée to be diligent, a leader in her office, and a thorough professional. She was dependable. When she promised to produce a document, she did. On time. She was not a gadfly like the younger girls of Lévis. Hers were old-fashioned Catholic values—devotion to family, church, hard work. The only shadow on her life, Bouvin reasoned, was the lack of a husband. She was thirty and on her way to becoming an old maid.

Marie-Andrée danced around the subject for a time, speaking animatedly about her trip to the East, then paused and blurted everything out. She showed him one of the letters. What would Bouvin think if she elected to accept Charles' offer of a round-trip air ticket to Bangkok? "What can I lose?" she asked the lawyer, pleading for his favor. She answered it herself, "Only my job—and I can always get another one." She had $2,000 remaining in her savings account from the knee injury settlement, and with that in her purse, a safe return home would be ensured. Just in case.

Bouvin listened and pondered. He did not want to speak hastily. Of course he had already heard the delicious news, it having spread like brush fire through the small town. "Marie-Andrée's caught herself a millionaire," people were saying. Her lover had become, in random accounts as the gossip circulated, a wealthy businessman, or an important politician, even a fabulously rich maharaja who made love to her on a bed of tiger skins and poured emeralds into her ears.

Bouvin knew Marie-Andrée well enough to realize that she was not an impulsive creature, that she had obviously been wrestling with this decision for weeks. Probably nothing he could say—or not say—would likely change her mind. All she wanted from him was a trusted voice of authority to say: No, You're Not Crazy, and: Yes, Follow Your Heart. Still, a shard of worry nagged at him. Facts did not square. The girl on the other side of the cocktail table was *not* the most gorgeous, or desirable, or even intelligent woman in the world. If this "Charles" were all that much of a catch, why would his love be so quickly ensnared by what was—awful truth—a plain and quiet and dull girl from the Canadian boondocks? But Bouvin could not tell her this. He looked at his old friend and he saw the hunger of anticipation on her face. It shared a place with naïveté. Finally he smiled. And nodded. "What can you lose?" he agreed. Just one thing, he cautioned. If, upon arrival in Bangkok, there is any hint that this Charles is somehow involved in drugs, or in any endeavor that might solicit the attention of police, then get out fast. Come home. Thailand has a military government. Civil liberties are not what people take for granted in Canada. Lawyers cannot protect people the way lawyers can in the West. Marie-Andrée listened and nodded her appreciation for this information. "But Charles is not mixed up in anything wrong," she said. "He's a very rich man. He's in the import-export business. He's a *multimillionaire*."

If he *is*, mused Bouvin to himself, summoning the most charitable thoughts, then perhaps he can afford such folly. Maybe there *is* a dashing young millionaire over there who, for reasons known only to the heart, has fallen madly in love with an unfrilled secretary with a slight limp.

For a few more weeks, Marie-Andrée suffered at this crossroads of her life, one path the familiar rut of thirty

years, the other a new and untraveled avenue to . . . what?
Where?

The letters kept coming, and now they were written on
hotel stationery whose imprints would make anyone's
imagination dance on the far side of reason. Charles
wrote to her from the Taj Mahal Hotel in Bombay, the
Oriental in Bangkok, the Peninsula in Hong Kong. And
his messages began to emphasize the baby they might have
together, Charles having no doubt shrewdly calculated
that this desire was the most potent card he could play.
Two letters dated June 29, 1975, touched the maternal
longings in Marie-Andrée:

> My darling . . . I love you more and more and
> desire strongly that you have my child . . . I would
> love for you to be my wife and the mother of my
> children . . .

And, a second:

> During the past couple of days in Colombo [Sri
> Lanka, formerly Ceylon], I met three Swiss couples
> from Geneva. They had come to adopt a Ceylonese
> baby. This meeting made me desire more strongly
> for us to have our own child. We would be able to
> have our baby by the end of 1976. What do you
> think, darling? Because by then, we will be stable.
> I have so many places and so many things to show.
> I desire your body and your caresses, my *chérie
> adorée* . . .

At a family dinner in late July, a few days after her
thirtieth birthday, Marie-Andrée ate quietly as was her
custom, complimented her mother on the meal, helped
clear the table, and then, over coffee, made an announcement that was as startling as if a nun in the family had
revealed plans to leap over the convent wall. She was (1)
quitting her job, and (2) accepting Charles' offer to join
him in Bangkok. Marie-Andrée had her case all prepared.
She presented it quickly, before the words stuck in her
mouth. This was too good an opportunity to pass up. It
was a "fling," nothing serious. She would be back in Lévis
in a few weeks. Her mother, Marie-Paule, burst into

tears, and Augustin, her father, shook his head in stunned
silence. His face was gray, and Denise, having learned
the decision earlier that day but keeping a vow of secrecy,
worried now that their father's rusting heart would break.
Everyone at the table, save Denise, began presenting
reasons why Marie-Andrée should not do this. It was
rash. She did not know this man well enough to accept
such an expensive trip. Strings surely were attached. It
was simply unlike this careful, cautious daughter to dance
past midnight when good girls were at home alone. And
safe.

Marie-Andrée knew what was coming, and she clamped
figurative hands over her ears to shut out her family's
protests. She had dreaded this scene and wanted only to
end it. She loved her family, but she was weary of being
dutiful and obedient and predictable. "I've done nothing
but work, work, work," she told them. Didn't she deserve
one tiny flash of erraticism? She was thirty years old, she
reminded the family. "And you can't stop me."

It is fair to consider, at this point of the tale, exactly
what Charles Sobhraj was up to, streaking about the Far
East's toniest hotels and conducting an extraordinary overseas love affair that was scandalizing a remote Canadian
town halfway around the world, devastating the heart of a
neurotic woman who was an unlikely candidate for his
ardor. What did Marie-Andrée have to offer him? Perhaps
he was legitimately smitten. Perhaps she did indeed remind him of Hélène, both being French, subservient, quiet,
the daughters of solid bourgeois families, women who
inherently bore the respect for which he yearned. Then
again, Marie-Andrée might have seemed the perfect
woman to smuggle his jewels from place to place, she
being the kind of anonymous person to whom little or no
attention was paid. A psychologist might suggest that
Charles was still looking for a mother, for a woman noble
enough to be put on a pedestal and worshiped. But most
likely was Félix d'Escogne's analysis when, much later,
he learned of the strange liaison between the boy he had
met in Poissy Prison and the girl who had sat in loneliness
on a riverbank.

"Charles is a collector," Félix told a friend. "And a

destructor. For some reason he decided he wanted this girl. She was, for a few moments, as desirable in his eyes as an antique diamond. But was she someone he wanted to love? Or was she some*thing* he wanted to own?"

After a cheerless farewell to family, Marie-Andrée flew alone to Bangkok at the beginning of August 1975. This time the journey was long and uncomfortable, with substantially less of the joyous excitement that had consumed her just four months earlier when she left on the same trip with Bernard. He had not chastised her when the decision was made known; he had wished Marie-Andrée well and had told her that he would always be there—in Lévis—should she need him. But behind his small smile was the grip of pain. She saw it in his face. It was something she understood all too well.

En route to Bangkok—and Charles—Marie-Andrée wrote the first entry in what would become a poignant journal, and one day of interest to police in a dozen countries. "I am arriving in Bangkok," she wrote with trembling hand. "I feel like a just married girl coming for the first time to the bed of her husband, nervous but happy by the thought of a journey to be taken and *possessed* by the man she loves."

She shut the diary and looked out the window, watching the land come into focus, masses of green and gray blurs turning into brilliant verdant rice paddies threaded by the muddy Chao Phraya River, a serpent guarding the city in its coils. Flashes of gold in the sunlight became the brilliant spires of Buddhist temples, like fantasy candles on a cake—and over the booming modern city a blanket of hazy smoke rising from the most infernal traffic jams in the world. Now apprehension gnawed at her. She wished for a few days alone in Bangkok, time to rest and smooth the travel wrinkles from her face and accustom herself to the exotic rhythms. She began to hope that Charles would not be at the airport, that a telegram would be his stand-in informing her that he had unexpectedly been called to Hong Kong and would join her in three days. But such worry was put aside when the plane landed and she searched urgently through the misted window for a glimpse of *him.*

* * *

Indeed Charles was waiting for her at Don Muang Airport, but he barely made it on time. The day had been busy. It had included a lengthy visit to a jewelry store in a large, American-style shopping center next to a deluxe hotel in the swarming heart of Bangkok. The romantic might surmise that Charles went there to pick up a trinket of welcome to honor the arrival of the woman he supposedly loved and had seduced with written declarations of passion and palaces. But this was not exactly the purpose of his business. Or even close to it.

It is necessary here to back up a few months to the very week that Marie-Andrée first made love to Charles in a cheap Bangkok hotel and returned to Canada with radically altered emotions. While the medical secretary mooned over the summer snowstorm of letters that soon fell on her, Charles was busy trying to make a few bucks. He set up temporary "headquarters" in Bangkok, not because he liked the city. In truth he found it noxious, devious, and twice as expensive as India. But Bangkok contained several elements that were valuable to his line of work—an enormous tourist trade (and those who traveled so far were generally affluent), good airline connections, a jewel industry, and an air of hedonism that was as tangible as a whore's perfume. Further, it did not escape Charles' attention that the police of Thailand were notoriously corrupt and manipulatable in "the Asian way," i.e., bribes. Paramount must have been the fact that Thailand was one of the precious few countries left in Asia which did not possess a dossier as thick as a travel guide on his criminal past. Charles knew that in some file somewhere rested an Interpol rap sheet, but he did not intend to use his real name here anyway. He was Alain Gauthier, and if that name caused trouble, he would change it again —and again—and again.

During a day of casing the favored shopping areas for Western tourists, Charles had wandered into a hotel arcade, entered a plush store, and immediately saw a strikingly beautiful Thai girl glide toward him gracefully. She was dressed in an American-cut dungaree suit. Her name, he soon learned, was so unpronounceable to Westerners that she answered simply to "May."

At first sight, May mistook Charles to be a Thai, for his skin had the almond hue of her people, and his face bore the caste of Asia. But when she welcomed him in Thai, he could not reply. As she spoke poor French, they settled on English, the tongue of Western commerce in the city. On this first meeting, Charles did not purchase any jewels from the shop where May was a most decorative saleswoman. But he did seize an hour of her time, speaking rapidly about the gem business, revealing his plan to set up a business that would purchase stones direct from the mines at fabled Chanthaburi near the Cambodian border, then sell them directly to tourists at substantial markups. He said he held a degree in gemology from some European institute whose name May did not catch. And as he chattered, Charles sent his eyes roaming around the store, but now and then they settled briefly on May and she found herself ill at ease under his intense scrutiny.

When he left, abruptly, without buying, one of her colleagues asked who that strange customer was. May shrugged. "Some hustler," she said. Bangkok had more of them than Hong Kong.

She thought no more of him until several weeks later when Charles popped back into the store, looking prosperous and dressed in a custom-tailored safari suit. This time he purchased four rings, worth about $250 each, of middling quality—infinitesimal diamonds and sapphire chips. "I will sell these tonight," he confided. "And I will triple my money." Presently he took her to dinner, where May became privy to a bit more. Charles held the belief that tourists come to Bangkok with the desire to purchase good jewelry, but that they are overwhelmed by the hundreds of stores that congest the city—in addition to their ignorance of quality and value. He looked about the dining room of the Sheraton Hotel and he gestured toward a bar. "I can go over to that bar and sit down and within five minutes strike up a friendship with a tourist," he said. Then, a day or two of helpful courtesies, perhaps a dinner, a personally guided tour of the floating market or the Temple of Dawn, and—Charles snapped his fingers—that person is willing, *eager* to buy his gems. He was building his business on "trust" and "confidence"—and natural human greed for a bargain. That he was selling his wares for thrice what they cost in reputable shops was not the point. Since he had seen May last, Charles had been to Hong Kong, Tokyo, and Teheran selling stones. And if May was not impressed by all of this heady talk, Charles let her know that he was also in the "oil business" in Teheran. By the time dessert came to the table, May was reasonably certain that a major millionaire was sitting next to her, his knee suggestively dancing against hers. From his pocket he withdrew a few jade and sapphire rings, all of good quality, and he invited May to select one to mark their first date. She chose a modest jade band. "The next one I give you will be all diamonds," he promised.

Even as he was writing his love letters to Canada, Charles took May for a lover, or reasonable facsimile thereof. He liked to go to discos, but Charles was a terrible dancer and May was embarrassed to be seen on the floor with him. He liked bowling, but he was poor at that, too; May regularly beat him. Each night when they dined, usually at Chinese restaurants, there was little conversation save incessant questions about the jewelry business, so many that May began to feel she was teaching a class in gemology. And in bed, at the various second-class hotels where Charles stayed, moving around the city like a desert emir and rarely staying more than one night in any inn, explaining to May that he was looking for a luxurious penthouse to buy, he was a clumsy and inattentive lover. His forte was stripping the clothes from his body and parading about the room, striking provocative poses and displaying his powerful body. But once between the sheets, excuses and sudden fatigue were usually pleaded, and quickly Charles was asleep, leaving May frustrated and bewildered.

On the morning of August 2, 1975, Charles ran puffing into May's jewelry store to reveal he was on the way to the airport. He had to meet a "friend from Canada" who was arriving to join his business. That was good news to May. Charles needed an aide, someone to help him keep appointments and thus avoid standing up people, which he had done to her more than once.

* * *

Marie-Andrée cleared customs easily, Bangkok being a city that does not overly scrutinize Western travelers, and saw Charles waiting, smiling, happy to see her. She ran into his arms, but all she received was a hug that would have been suitable for reunited elderly sisters. And then she was stuffed into a hot taxi where sweat poured down her face on the long drive to the city, inching along canals and processions of monks with gleaming bald heads, stalling in traffic, Charles rattling away about this and that, but never about *them*.

When the taxi pulled up in front of a deluxe hotel, where Marie-Andrée erroneously assumed the honeymoon suite was waiting, Charles instead led her like an unwilling mare to the shopping arcade, insisting that she meet his "special friend." Marie-Andrée protested. She was exhausted, her body clock damaged by crossing too many time zones. She was hot, too disheveled to meet anyone. Her hair was plastered wet to her face; dark patches of perspiration blotched her clothes. What she wanted was a cold bath, a dark room—and Charles.

Before she could make further protest, Marie-Andrée was pulled into the refrigerated cool of an elegant shop that offered bolts of brilliant silk and showcases of rings and necklaces that bespoke Oriental grandeur. A stunning young woman scarcely more than twenty approached, her feet barely touching the carpet. Her complexion was cream, her hair richly dark and cut as if by a Paris coiffeur, her eyes showed happiness at the sight of Charles. They embraced, gently, but more tenderly than what Marie-Andrée had received in welcome. Then Charles turned to Marie-Andrée and did something impossibly cruel.

He put his hand around May's slim waist and he said, "This is May, my girl friend." Then he gestured to the disheveled, perspiring girl from Canada and said, "And this is Marie-Andrée, who has come from Canada to be my secretary."

May fumbled for a word of greeting, but the moment was more than awkward. It was heavy with pain for both women. Immediately May realized that Marie-Andrée considered herself to be more, far more, than Charles' "secretary." And though Marie-Andrée tried to smile and express friendliness, her eyes were suddenly red and moist, and she turned away hurriedly to feign interest in a tray of gems. If Charles discerned the anguish in both women, he did nothing to assuage it.

That night they dined, *à trois*, and neither woman could manage more than a bite or two of food. Swallowing was difficult. Conversation impossible. And, incredibly, on her first night in Bangkok with the man who had written of a love so intense that it would rival that of the gods, of his minute-by-minute desire to worship her body, Marie-Andrée found herself in bed not only with him, but with *another woman*. The three of them—Charles, Marie-Andrée, and May—passed the night in a cheap hotel, neither woman able to sleep, both unwilling players in an absurd farce that was void of laughter. Nothing happened, nothing at all, nothing save an occasional muffled sob that was masked by Charles' snoring. He was in the middle, content, an arm around each girl, surrounded by people that he assumed loved him. And would be grateful to share him.

During the most terrible night of her life, Marie-Andrée almost summoned enough gumption and courage to get up and get out—on the next plane back to Canada. But that would be humiliating. She would face ridicule the rest of her life in Lévis. And every time she felt the curve of Charles' naked body against hers, resolve weakened. And a little surge of competition was born. She had thrown away her life in Canada to come to this man's bed—and if she was any kind of a woman at all, she could get rid of the bitch on the other side.

CHAPTER TWENTY-FOUR

Annabella, stuffed with sedatives and tranquilizers, could not bring herself to return to the cabin in the thick woods of central California where Jimmy killed himself. As spring awakened the forest, she moved back in with her parents, into the room where she had spent her teens, a womb of chintz and lace and stuffed animals, coexisting with memoirs of her long stay in Europe. She found an old framed quotation in the closet and put it on the wall beside her bed, finding, perhaps, a certain irony in its message:

> *There is no difficulty that enough love will not conquer; no disease that enough love will not heal; no door that enough love will not open; no gulf that enough love will not bridge; no sin that enough love will not redeem. It makes no difference how deeply seated may be the trouble, how hopeless the outlook, how muddled the tangle, how great the mistake. A sufficient realization of love will dissolve it all. If only you could love enough, you would be the happiest and most powerful human being on earth.*

For a long time, Annabella stared blankly at this quotation, or at the inanities on the television set, or at novels that she held in her hands but did not really read. She went irregularly to a therapist who counseled her after her husband's death. He suggested a long period of treatment and a quick return to as much activity as she could stand. But Annabella was never very confident in the value of psychiatry. What she had to deal with was guilt, and it was the one emotion that was her constant companion. "If only I had taken Jimmy back," she said so often. Or, "If only I had gone after him when he jumped out of the car." Or, "If only I had recognized his pain and gotten him some help."

Nonsense, said her mother Jane, who was busy arranging shopping trips, discreetly telephoning her daughter's friends and beseeching them to offer invitations. With quiet desperation, Jane was trying to crowd her daughter's life so that the inevitable would not occur. But in her heart Jane felt the futility of her endeavor. She saw flight coming as clearly as a train on a Kansas prairie. Forestall it, perhaps. But not stop it.

In early summer, 1975, as Marie-Andrée was tormented in Canada by the deluge of love letters from Charles, and as Jennie Bolliver was trying to assemble a life in Seattle after her journey around the world with a now distant Christopher, Annabella went to San Francisco for a weekend with some old friends from Stanford. She tried very hard to make the weekend pleasant and not let any of the dark shadows within her fall on the others. But for the most part she was gloomy and silent. A friend named Marcia, who was a post-graduate student in psychology, watched the unconcealed anguish festering in Annabella and took her aside. The group was going to Sausalito for the afternoon. Marcia had a better idea. She knew where the world's greatest omelet was served, and where they could have a heart-to-heart talk. Gratefully Annabella agreed. She was tired of putting on a counterfeit face. The two women, both in their late twenties, went to a San Francisco restaurant called Mama's, where spectacular omelets stuffed with sour cream, avocado, tomato, and crab meat are the specialty. They gorged themselves and drank herb tea until the afternoon was almost gone. Marcia turned blunt. It was a time for direct talk even if it stung. She suggested that Annabella was hanging onto the guilt over Jimmy's death, long past its nuisance value. What good was it doing her?

Annabella shook her head. It was not a question of

"good." She simply could not escape the emotional con-
demnation that when her husband held out his hand for
help, she refused to take it. And now he was dead. She
did not enjoy the feelings that ate at her like acid, but she
could not expel them.

Marcia reached into her repertoire of case histories.
For a time she had worked at a crisis clinic in the psychiatric ward of a Los Angeles area hospital. People walked
in off the streets and obtained immediate therapy. Analysts
were trained to deal with a problem in the first few minutes.
Once, when Marcia was on duty, a thirty-nine-year-old
middle-class housewife had come fearfully in what seemed
to be emotional disintegration. Her marriage was ghastly,
to an icy man who refused to leave their home for any
social affair, who rejected intimate talk, who had not
made love to her in a decade, who threatened suicide each
time the woman spoke of leaving him. Annabella listened
to the story attentively. What was the point?

The point, said Marcia, was that this unfortunate woman
had dug her own pit, sprung her own trap, attached her
own chains. She blamed her husband for all of her pain,
when indeed she *fed* on it. She had written her life script
so that she wanted to feel guilty and abused. She was a
coward, said Marcia. "Guilt," she continued, "is the least
valuable and most destructive human emotion. You've paid
your penance to Jimmy, but you didn't put those sleeping
pills in his mouth. *He* did. He was sick but it was *his*
responsibility. He was trying to make you feel guilty—
and God in heaven how he succeeded!"

Not long thereafter Annabella told her mother that she
was cashing in her life in California and returning abroad.
The news was not a surprise. Jane remembered a twenty-
year-old returning from two years in Europe and saying,
"Right now I am in this country, but I am not a part of
it." And Jane made no protest. As she drove her daughter
to San Francisco and put her on a plane that would
eventually set down in Europe, Jane accepted the terms
of this leave-taking. Annabella would not be returning
except as a rare visitor to the storybook valley in this
softly beautiful part of California.

In their last moments together mother and daughter

avoided the emotional issues and dealt with logistics and maternal advice. Annabella's travel plans were vague and open-ended. She intended to visit friends·in Europe, then thread her way across the Middle East into India, where she wanted to meet Sanjoy's parents in Bombay. It seemed important as part of her recuperation to face the family of the boy whose destiny had brought him to California, to the promise of a rich new life, to the back seat of a stupid airplane that crashed and burned on a foggy night in San Luis Obispo. It was an appointment she had to keep, one last burden to lift from her shoulders.

"If you run out of money, or feel you're going to, call us. Promise!" ordered Jane. Annabella hugged her mother. She doubted if it would be necessary. In her purse was an around-the-world airplane ticket and $3,000 in traveler's checks. And if the cupboard grew bare, she could find a job. She had done it before.

"Call us anyway," pleaded Jane. "It's good for both of us when you connect with home." She tried not to sound demanding, for Jane respected her daughter's maturity and independence. She still considered Annabella to be her best friend.

Annabella nodded assurance, and on her face was one of the first genuine smiles since the tragedy of Jimmy. At that moment, she was exceptionally lovely, thinner, her eyes huge and luminous from the long season of grief. Finally a spark was in them that might burn away their deadness.

In Seattle, Jennie told herself she was sated with world travel and it was time to make a new life. She rented a tiny coach house in a college district and filled the two rooms with plants, pillows, straw mats, miniature figurines of Buddha and Hindu gods. These were pieces of Jennie, and they were as precious to her as a rich man's gold. Incense burned continuously. A quotation from Buddha about the necessity of suffering was tacked to the front door beside which slept an eccentric cat named Doloma, to whom Jennie spoke in Tibetan. When one of her girl friends exclaimed over the little house, Jennie said, "It's all I ever want. I can stay in here a week and lose all track of time."

With a nest well feathered, Jennie enrolled in a junior college to study biology and holistic medicine, nursing the intention to set up a lay practice someday in Seattle and convince people, particularly the elderly, to foreswear meat and pills that doctors prescribed. A disciple of fasting, Jennie went without food or beverage for forty-eight hours at least once every month, convinced that urban poisons were being expelled from her body. Around her neck she wore a Buddhist token, several red wool strings braided together and tied in a tassel. Jennie never took it off, for she believed it protected her from all harm.

On her twenty-first birthday, Jennie celebrated with old friends, mostly graduates from the Nova experimental high school. None of these youngsters to whom complete academic freedom was granted had progressed very far, either professionally or emotionally. They were remnants of the counterculture, leftovers, still speaking the vernacular of the disenchanted, but quietly slipping back into the mainstream of American life. Cassie, a quiet, pioneer-looking young woman who made beautiful tapestries on a loom, was trying to establish business relations with major department stores. At twenty, she counted one broken marriage, and a second one in jeopardy. Margret, an erotically beautiful girl who had spoken fire half a dozen years earlier and intended to stir the blacks of Seattle into rebellion, now worked as a widower's housekeeper. Her reading pattern had shifted from Karl Marx to Tolkien. And there was Cybilla, who, after dalliances with the most desirable boys in her orbit, was now living openly with a woman and committed to the militant lesbian wing of the women's liberation movement. Carmen, Jennie's long ago friend from the beach years in Southern California, was now lost to domestic anonymity as the wife of a dentist.

But the major trauma was Christopher.

They returned from the Far East as the best of friends, nothing more. Jennie tried a hundred times to analyze the reasons for the disintegration of what had been to her a love of epic proportions. "I don't know," answered Christopher. "It's nothing I can put my finger on. It's nothing you've done, or I've done. It's simply that we've grown apart. We need some time away from one another."

Jennie agreed, trying not to show her wounds, but there were times when she would stay inside the coach house for days, weeping, angry, frustrated, at a loss. She tried to convince herself that Christopher was not any longer the man she had loved, certainly not the free spirit who had climbed mountains and whose mind was a restless probe of all established values. Now he was planning to open a health food store and was caught up in talk of bank loans and accountants and even *franchises*. "I was the number one flake in my crowd," she told Margret. "Now I think I'm the only one with any sense left."

Other wars, "negative forces," as she called them, were festering in Jennie's head. Although she professed contentment at the order of her new life—home, college, part-time work as a bookstore clerk—she found it difficult to obey the vows she had made at Kopan Monastery in Nepal. There she had promised not to drink, smoke, swear, kill, lie, or engage in carnal activity. To one of her Buddhist friends in Seattle, a woman named Olga, Jennie made a tearful confession. "I can go two or three weeks without even thinking about sex. Then I say to myself, 'Jennie, you're twenty-one years old, in the prime of your life, you're healthy, reasonably attractive, and everybody you know is out dancing.' So I go. And then I come home and suffer for a week."

Olga told her not to worry, that when her priorities were in order, the "negative forces" would no longer be a problem.

Jennie liked to join Margret and Cybilla at a Seattle discotheque called Shelly's Leg, owned by a young woman who had lost a leg in a cannon-firing accident and used the money obtained in a lawsuit settlement to open a night club. The disco had a large homosexual clientele, but Jennie was nonetheless welcomed for her passionate and uninhibited dancing. Once on the floor, she boogied with abandon, her rationale being that it was a good way to lose weight. She liked going to gay discos because "you don't get hassled." Now and then Jennie encountered a lesbian looking at her for a beat too long, but no overtures were made that she could not handle. More troubling to Jennie was the realization that when she was dancing she was the center of attraction, and she liked it. In fact, she cherished the spotlight. This probably violated some Buddhist tenet, she told Olga, but surely it would not destroy her soul.

And there were special nights when Christopher was there, when they danced together for old times' sake. Jennie pretended to be disinterested in her former lover, but from their vantage point, Margret and Cybilla could witness the longing in her eyes. It grew worse when Christopher appeared one evening with a girl friend, a thin young woman named Francine, who seemed vacant and boring to Jennie. Francine was not a good dancer, and Jennie seized upon this shortcoming to remind Christopher what it was like to partner a woman whose movements were sensual and exciting.

But always Jennie went home alone, where she would first try to handle the anger that swelled over Christopher's companion, then read from her Buddhist literature before falling wearily into bed and fighting back tears. All of this she tried to conceal from her friends, but rejection is the cancer of love. And heartbreak is impossible to hide.

Jennie saw Madame Crystal less frequently, as she now lived farther away from the old woman's neighborhood. But they stayed in telephone contact. One afternoon Jennie called her friend and was mildly disturbed when no one answered. Madame Crystal was deep into her eighties, infirm, and rarely went out anymore. When the phone rang unanswered again that night, and the next morning, Jennie called The Dealer, whose daily gin rummy games were no longer held because he could not see the spots on the cards. Where was Madame Crystal?

"Well," said The Dealer, "I believe she's dead."

"Dead?" Jennie was shocked. How? When? Was he sure? The Dealer's voice was old and cracked but he was able to tell the story. Madame Crystal had come down with the flu and seemed to be getting better. Then a turn for the worse; she would not let anybody enter the house to nurse her, for she lacked the strength to get dressed or put on makeup. Her sister was coming from Long Island, so the old people were not too worried. Then, when nobody answered the phone and when none of the old people heard from Madame Crystal for two or three days, a delegation went to visit. The front door was locked; inside, no sign of life. The plants were dying. A policeman came to break down the door. Madame Crystal was dead on the bathroom floor, dead for at least three days, so dead that she had sort of melted on the tiles.

"Why didn't someone call me?" cried Jennie.

"I guess nobody thought of it," answered The Dealer. "Out of sight, out of mind."

Jennie asked where Madame Crystal was buried. She wanted to visit her grave. "Then you'll have to go to her sister's house on Long Island. Crystal was cremated and they took her away in a tin box."

"I am so guilty," Jennie told her friend Olga. "I loved Madame Crystal, but I didn't show it when she needed me the most. Is there anything more cruel than to die alone? I hope she knows I loved her." For three days Jennie secluded herself and meditated before a table filled with burning candles, hoping to speed Madame Crystal's journey through reincarnation. She was certain the old woman would be reborn, that her "life force" would be renewed quickly. Christopher had once told Jennie of the Rosicrucian belief that reincarnation occurs forty-three days after death. Jennie prayed that she would become aware of her friend's incarnation. It would assuage a part of her grief and guilt.

Loneliness was now intolerable. Jennie dated frequently. She took a series of boy friends, none of whom lasted very long, none of whom was permitted intimacy. They were kept at arm's length, Jennie explaining, if all else failed, that she had taken a vow of celibacy. It was true, in part, for Jennie was engaging in an informal sexual fast, trying to cleanse her spirit of "impure thought." It was not her intention to stay celibate forever, she told Cybilla, "only until I decide who I am." The girls sensed that Jennie was wrestling with a difficult decision, but one which she would not share. She seemed to be trying on several different hats. One night she accepted the invitation of a gay woman to go home, but once there they talked until almost dawn and then fell asleep in the same bed without touching one

"Psychology is very important to me. It is the principal weapon in my business. I use psychology like stupid people use guns."

(Sipa Press from Black Star)

Charles Sobhraj. A mélange of East and West, he emitted messages of raw sexuality.

(Sipa Press from Black Star)

"I know who I am. I know my limits, my talents. I never fool myself. I may cheat others, but I never cheat myself."

Marie-Andrée Leclerc—thirty years old when she first traveled away from her small Ontario hometown. The romance of traveling through India quickly gave way to Sobhraj's charm. Within a year she would be his chief accomplice in a series of brutal crimes.

Sobhraj "always paraded his masculinity as if he were afraid it might go away."

(Sipa Press from Black Star)

Henricus Bintanja. The discovery of his murder by the Dutch Embassy in Thailand triggered an Interpol investigation that led to the arrest of Sobhraj and Leclerc.

Sobhraj in chains en route to his trial. Marie-Andrée is to the left. Of her Sobhraj would say to the judge, "She is a victim of love. She should not be accused of anything else."

(Sipa Press from Black Star)

another. "I just wanted to see what it was like," explained Jennie to Margret and Cybilla. "And I don't think it's for me."

The core of Jennie's discontent was Christopher. She still loved him, no matter how many nights she lay alone and tried to deny him. The boys that Jennie dated did not know that she was using them as actors in a charade. But she often plotted to learn where Christopher was going on a particular night, then managed to show up with a new beau on her arm, seemingly happy, carefree, and glad to be purged of a childhood romance.

Matters came to a head one evening in early 1975 at Margret's house, where some of the girls were piercing their ears. Christopher was present with Francine, who was waiting her turn. Jennie appeared and watched, then turned abusive, making catty remarks about how a ring through Francine's nose might be appropriate, so that Christopher could lead her around. Someone was smoking marijuana, and Jennie seized the joint, dragging on it deeply, turning up the record player to ear-shattering volume, dancing by herself provocatively, taking every opportunity to bump against Christopher. The others watched for a while with amusement, then everyone began to wish Jennie would clear out. Tonight she was a pain in the ass. Christopher asked Jennie to step outside for a breath of air.

On the porch, Jennie fell straightaway into his arms and clutched him like a woman in jeopardy. The dam had broken, her emotions rushed out nakedly. She *wanted* him, she *needed* him, she *loved* him. Christopher was touched by the confession, but it was hardly news. Like everyone else he had seen through the flimsiness of Jennie's behavior in recent months. He cradled her face in his slender hands and begged her to understand. It was simply not possible to give up Francine, for he loved her. "You and I agreed that we needed different experiences," he reminded her. "We said we just couldn't occupy the same space for a while. That's still true."

Jennie's tears kept falling. She began an angry assault against Francine—how could Christopher choose such a loser? He shushed her. "That's beneath you," he said.

"These are negative forces of pride and hate coming out. You know how to deal with them. You know better than I do."

They embraced one last time, but it was fraternal. Once, while resting on their trek up the Himalayas, they had decided that their relationship was so warm and close that they must have been brother and sister in some long ago incarnation. Christopher searched now for a graceful way to end this painful confrontation. "Francine and I are going to Hawaii for a while," he said. Jennie jerked her head up in shock. Was Christopher actually going on a trip with this girl? It seemed a desecration of everything *they* had done together. Christopher nodded. "When I get back, maybe we can . . ." His voice trailed off. He did not want to even hint at a reconciliation. But Jennie took it that way. A flicker of hope caught fire within her. She began to speak hurriedly of the coming summer; perhaps they could go camping, or even return to the Far East after Christopher was rid of Francine.

With sadness, the gentle tall man stared down at the agonizing little girl below him. Jennie refused to understand that whatever they once had was indeed wondrous, but now it was gone. What remained was—on his part— only a special friendship. With that, he left her, unable to say more. Several days later, Christopher commented to one of the girls in the crowd that Jennie had behaved "childishly." Naturally the remark sped its way to Jennie, who said, sweetly and tartly, "Childish? He should know."

In the spring of 1975, Jennie went to Southern California for a meditation retreat sponsored by the Kopan Monastery. She was joyful in anticipation of a reunion with the two lamas from Nepal, Zopa Rinpoche and Yeshe, and for a week she sat at their feet drinking in wisdom and challenge. Then she requested a private moment with Lama Yeshe, a solemn, round little man with a face of both cheer and sorrow, as if the masks of comedy and tragedy had been joined. The lama was pleased to speak with Jennie, for he well remembered her stay in Katmandu. Then he asked what was on her mind; he could tell that she was troubled.

Since her return to Seattle from the Far East, began Jennie, she had been struggling with "negative forces."

Often they overwhelmed her. She spoke candidly of her unfulfilled love for Christopher and his rejection of her, of moments when she had been tempted by dancing and drugs and homosexuality. In fact, she said, most of her twenty-one years had been pretty much of a disaster. Only in those precious days she had passed in meditation at the monastery, in the bosom of Mount Everest, only there did she feel contentment. The lama nodded. He understood the worth of her problem, the pain she was suffering, and the peace she had found at Kopan.

"I have been thinking seriously about returning to the monastery and taking the vows of a nun," she said.

The lama was not surprised; hers was not a unique revelation. Often he encountered young people whose lives were not proceeding well and who felt miracles would occur in the romantic, once forbidden land of the Himalayas. A word of caution was always in order. "A change of locale may produce a new flower," he counseled, "but the roots will have the same disease." Rather than take the vows of a nun at this troubled moment of her life, the lama countersuggested that Jennie remain in the United States, continue her study and meditation, perform missionary work for the monastery, and, with diligence, reach the same enlightenment at home. No need for flight to Asia.

Jennie wrestled with her soul when she returned to Seattle. Refusing to see friends, she turned them away on the pretense of study, or minor illness. Nor would she speak on the telephone. She did call Christopher and was annoyed to learn that he was still in Hawaii with Francine. During several weeks of contemplation, Jennie roamed about Seattle like a phantom, sitting for blank hours on a pier and gazing at the murky waters of Lake Washington, walking the streets with her head bent like an old worried woman, climbing a tree in her favorite park and perching in its branches. Then she made her decision.

She would return to Katmandu. It was the only place on earth where she knew total peace. And there, despite what the lama had cautioned, she would probably take the vows of a nun.

* * *

None of her friends knew the depth of Jennie's reasons for her return to the East. All she told them was that she felt the need for further study at the monastery. No one suspected that it was in her mind to put on the robes and stay forever. She fantasized what they would all think, Margret and Cybilla and Olga and even Christopher, *especially* Christopher when and if he returned from his tryst with the hated Francine. She wanted them all to picture her on the day of ordination, after Lama Yeshe had become convinced that her motives were genuine and that she had taken the necessary "refuge" in Buddha, his doctrine, and in Sangha, a monastic community of at least five fully ordained monks. Then she would go to a barber in the city of Katmandu to have her hair shorn, save one last lock. After a lifetime of bleaching, tinting, dyeing, teasing, cutting, spraying, and styling, how wonderful it would be to rise each morning and having nothing but a fuzzy scalp! Then, on the special day of days, Jennie would go to the tailor and pick up her newly sewn robes of burgundy wool and saffron trim. Her sisters would accompany her on the long walk back to the monastery, singing their love all the way, through the terraced fields of rice, past the obedient yoked water buffalo, laughing at the temple dogs that darted out to pester passersby. And in the distance—the fog-shrouded crown of the Himalayas. Perhaps, on Jennie's special morning, the clouds would move away and bless the newest nun with a clear view of the greatest panorama. An omen!

Then, clad in her robes, her face shining, she would swear to thirty-six ancient vows in the presence of five fully ordained monks, including, perhaps, one of the tutors of His Holiness the Dalai Lama himself. Jennie would promise not to handle gold or silver, not to sleep in a high or wide bed, not to engage in worldly entertainments, not to engage in any sexual activity, not to sit in a chair that had been occupied by a person who had taken more vows. Finally, she would be blessed by the lama, who would cut off the last remaining lock of hair and pronounce her new name. Part of it would be taken from the name of the lama who ordained her, another part from *his* guru, thus continuing the lineage.

And thus would a past be wiped away. Jennie knew

from conversation with another Western nun that it took months, perhaps a year or two before thoughts of a previous life in America were first blurred, then abandoned. But she was ready for a life similar to that of the Carmelites, one of contemplation and prayer, study and meditation. On her ordination day she would reach *sramanerika*, the beginning plateau for a Buddhist nun. After more meditation and study, she could progress to the highest level— *bhikku*. The word means "beggar."

But all of these thoughts Jennie kept to herself. She could not trust the girls in Seattie to understand. Nor would Christopher appreciate the clarity of her purpose. There was also the consideration that she might change her mind. Jennie well knew that each year a few men and women "took off their robes" and left the monastery in failure and disgrace, unable to cope with the severity of the life, and condemned to the anguish of having reneged on a paramount commitment. Should that unlikely tragedy befall Jennie, she would not want anyone else to know it.

"I think I was meant to go!" exclaimed Jennie a few weeks later. The money was pouring into her secret treasure box that once contained a prom invitation and a crushed corsage. Now it housed a tiny statue of Buddha blessed by the Dalai Lama, a photograph of Christopher standing beside a great temple in Katmandu, and a growing pile of currency to finance her return to Nepal.

She sold her VW the first day she taped a "For Sale" sign on its cracked back window. A garage sale cleared out furniture and clothes. A long-forgotten hundred-dollar loan made to a friend in California years earlier suddenly arrived in the mail with a note of apology. Within six weeks, Jennie had enough to buy a one-way air ticket to Katmandu, and an addition $1,500. As the monastery only requested thirty dollars a month for room and board— and even that was not obligatory—she was assured now that the trip was possible. She set an early date in October 1975 for departure.

With time running out, Jennie needed to take care of the loose threads that dangled from her life. She visited each of her friends, apologizing for forgotten and trivial social misdemeanors that somehow seemed important to her. Only Christopher remained, and though he was back in town from Hawaii and now openly living with Francine, she could not push herself to call him.

Instead she hurried to California to say goodbye to Maggie and Cap. They were pleased with the manner in which their granddaughter had matured. Many of Jennie's girlhood friends were either divorced, in jail, caught up in heavy drug tragedies, or condemned to lives of boredom in dead-end jobs and marriages. But Jennie walked with serenity, and seemed to have purpose, and was spunky enough to go after what she wanted. Still a devout Catholic, Maggie was not overjoyed that her granddaughter prayed to Buddha, but Cap reminded her that since hundreds of millions of people in the world worshiped the potbellied gentleman with the benevolent smile—many more than those who prayed to Jesus Christ—there must be something to it.

Only one incident marred the last days at her grandparents' home. Maggie passed by Jennie's old room and heard her weeping softly. "What's the matter, honey?" asked Maggie, unable to resist entering and sitting beside her on the bed.

"Oh, Grandma, if I have to come home, will you send the money?" said Jennie, with urgency in her voice.

"Come home? But you haven't even gotten there yet. How much money are you talking about?"

"Maybe two thousand dollars."

"If I have two thousand dollars when you need it, it's yours. You know that." Jennie nodded and hugged her grandmother, who started at that moment to worry. She wondered if Jennie had some kind of premonition she would not share.

Later that day, Jennie was poring over a map with Cap, who as an old sailor envied the young woman's journeys over the seas of his salad years. Jennie intended to fly from Seattle to Hong Kong, and thence, if time and money permitted, on to Bangkok for a day or two, there being an important Buddhist temple in the city which she wanted to visit. She would reach Katmandu in the latter part of October. She promised to write at least three times a week.

"Bangkok?" echoed Maggie. She frowned. "Don't go to Bangkok."

"Why not?" asked Jennie.

"I don't know," said Maggie. "It's just a funny feeling I just got when you said the word. You're so friendly and outgoing and naïve that someone might take advantage of you."

Jennie smiled and looked conspiratorially at Cap. They shared a love of adventure that Maggie did not have. "Oh, Grandma," she sighed. "I'm a Buddhist. Nobody would harm me."

On her last afternoon at Maggie's, Jennie rang up Carmen, her friend from the beach years. The two young women spent a happy afternoon of reunion together. Several other girls from the old days dropped by and the afternoon was magic. Carmen remembered it well: "We were like teen-agers again at a slumber party—gossiping, discussing boys, evil teachers, drug trips, séances, mystical experiences—the whole grab bag. All of us drank wine and got tight as a drum—except Jennie. She didn't drink a drop and she was the happiest girl in the room. Bubbly!" The others envied Jennie, for her eyes were clear, and her face, naked of makeup, glowed with health and vision.

Late in the day, when there was no more wine in the jug, Carmen and Jennie shared a private moment. The day had been devoted to memories, and nobody suspected that Jennie was leaving on a spiritual quest from which she intended not to return. But Carmen, warmed by the wine, studied the friend she had known so long and sensed there was more to the journey than simply "further study" and "meditation." She spoke carefully. "It looks like you've finally found the answer," ventured Carmen.

Jennie smiled. "You remember all those years when we acted crazy, looking for something? I didn't even know what it was. I didn't know the question—much less the answer." Carmen nodded, memories of yoga, TM, hypnotism, séances washing over her in flashback. How well she remembered Jennie's frequent observation that she was a person trying to find water, digging one well, coming up dry, digging another, and another, her thirst never slaked.

"You see," said Jennie, "I've stopped digging wells. Going back to Katmandu may not be the final answer to my life, but right now it's a solution."

They went out on the town for a going-away party—Jennie, Carmen, and two other girls—touring the old haunts, driving along the beach where a new generation was ensconsed but as purposeless as the ones who had danced on the sands before, winding up at Big Daddy's, a disco in Santa Monica. The crowd was sparse, and the girls were forced to get on the floor alone. Then a handsome black man appeared and gravitated toward Jennie, as if obeying a force. Other dancers cleared a circle for Jennie and the black man. They danced for an hour, until perspiration soaked their bodies, doing the "bump" and melding their limbs in raw primeval sexuality. Carmen thought to herself, "Jennie's caught herself a humpy dude for her last night in the old home town." Then, abruptly, Jennie kissed the black man politely on his cheek and returned hurriedly to her table. Whatever fire had been lit was now doused. Carmen would recall the moment: "It was as if Jennie walked to the very edge of the cliff, with the valley of temptation below. But she refused to jump."

On the drive home Jennie was strangely silent, embarrassed for letting herself surrender to an hour of dancing.

On the night before her departure, in Seattle, Jennie was rushing to one last going-away party given by her girl friends. But she had a final piece of business to attend. Summoning her courage, she telephoned *his* number and kept her voice steady when Francine answered. When Christopher took the phone, Jennie said, "I'm leaving tomorrow for Katmandu. I'm going back to Kopan. I may be gone for a while." Of course Christopher knew. He had heard the news from all of their mutual friends. But he felt the decision was so powerful that it was not a subject he could initiate. He was waiting for Jennie to tell him.

"I hope you've thought it out carefully," said Christopher.

"I have. It's something I must do."

They spoke trivially for a few moments, then Jennie cut through with the worth of her call. Was there any possibility that Christopher might join her at the monastery some distant day? In her voice could be heard the memory of nights together in a tent on a wind-whipped hill above a monastery. Obviously Jennie held the smoldering hope that somehow this flight to the Himalayas could effect a reconciliation. Christopher was stunned. He had assumed, incorrectly, that Jennie was over their breakup. He had to move quickly to send her away with grace and affection, and acceptance of the truth. "Francine and I are thinking about traveling East someday," he said. "Maybe we could meet at Kopan. Maybe. I'd write you first."

Jennie was silent. It took a long while for her to answer. "I'd like that," she finally said, her voice sliding in all directions. She was close to tears; Christopher could feel her pain as well as hear it.

"I want you to know," he said, "that in my heart you are my constant companion."

"And in mine, too." Jennie hung up quickly.

Jennie and her girl friends played charades until well past midnight, then fell into dark and varied conversation. Sex was covered thoroughly, Margret wondering how Jennie handled a long stay in a monastery. "I don't know of any way to put this tactfully," she said, "but don't you get horny? Or do they put something in the gruel?"

Jennie laughed. "The first time was terrible," she said. "Christopher and I slept together, in a tent, but we weren't supposed to touch. During the night I'd find myself snuggled up against him, then the realization hit that I wasn't supposed to be even close. So I'd scrooch over . . . After a while, your head gets so busy that the rest of you shuts up." For the past several months, Jennie had been celibate, although the others did not know. They realized that she had suffered from her membership in the new sexual liberation. On her scorecard were two abortions, a string of one-night stands, a flirtation with homosexuality, the sorrowful and still unrequited affair with Christopher. Each of the other girls had similar misadventures of the heart, and they almost envied Jennie going to a place where sex was not allowed to be a nuisance.

And, finally, just before it was dawn and time to leave for the early morning flight, they spoke of death, a curious subject for a going-away party, but one which Jennie herself initiated. She raised the possibility that she might perish on the far side of the setting sun.

"Don't talk that way," said Cassie, the pioneer-looking friend with thick rimless glasses and a long gingham skirt. "You're just worried about the plane falling down."

Jennie shook her head. "Maybe. But I also recognize the fact that I am entering a new stage of life . . . There may be dangers. But they don't really bother me. If I die, I die. It's not *my* decision to make anyway."

Margret wanted an amplification of that murky comment.

"I'm not in control of my life, nor is anyone. Karma is. The best we can do is lead a good life in preparation for death."

The girls fell silent, chewing on destiny and its puzzles. Someone began speculating on the "best way" to die. At this, Jennie said something eerie. This girl who had been afraid of water all her life, who would not even stand in the shallow end of a swimming pool, Jennie suggested that drowning was best. There would be the initial fright, she said. Then a euphoria takes over as the lungs fill with water. "I've known for a long time that I have a water karma," she said.

Margret shuddered. Enough talk of death. The faint shimmer of dawn was coming through her living room window. But Jennie would not let the subject go. "Death is just another form of life, anyway . . . Can't you see the beauty?"

Before leaving, Jennie asked to make a pact with her friends. If she died, if any one of them died, then there must be cremation. The others nodded in agreement. They put their fists together and swore. No burial! "The body isn't important," said Jennie. "I don't want to be bound by any of my remains left on earth. I want to get on with the next phase—whatever it is."

"You mean," said Cybilla, "that you don't want part of you staying under the ground down here . . . while the rest is somewhere else?"

"Exactly," said Jennie.

The girls watched their friend struggle through airport security, laden down as she was with items for the monastery—a garden hose, a typewriter, a bedroll for one of the Tibetan children she had made her favorite. They watched as Jennie walked out to the waiting jet, which, on this day, was being boarded by one of the old-fashioned staircases. When Jennie reached the top step, she turned and looked toward the terminal, knowing her friends were peering through the wall of glass.

A broad smile cracked her face. Then she did something typically Jennie: she jumped into the air and clicked her heels together! With that, Jennie was swallowed up by the plane that would rush her across the earth to a quiet place on a hill outside Katmandu where, perhaps, she would become a nun; or where, perhaps, Christopher, after studying his heart, would come once again to love her.

CHAPTER TWENTY-FIVE

For several listless days, Marie-Andrée moped around the Rajah Hotel in Bangkok, her physical being assaulted by jet lag and her emotions torn by the puzzling and painful burlesque that was Charles' welcome. "I find my love rather distant," she wrote in her journal, employing remarkable understatement, "giving me the impression of not wanting us to be intimate. I am disappointed. After the second day, the only word is disappointed. Disappointed by his behavior toward me! I have the feeling of not being able to please him. I have the feeling that his love for me is not that deep, and the worst of it is that I shall have to play the role of a secretary toward a woman he wants to conquest . . ."

Before the first week was over, Charles pried out of Marie-Andrée the information that her purse contained $2,000 in traveler's checks. His attitude softened and his affection increased in direct proportion to this revelation. Suddenly May disappeared from the other side of the bed. He banished her, Charles confided, because he wanted Marie-Andrée to understand fully the scope and horizons of his "business." From his pocket he pulled a handful of tiny stones and dropped them on Marie-Andrée's pillow. These were worth several thousand *bahts*. It was his intention to find tourist customers who would pay twice or thrice what he purchased them for. And it was necessary that he remain friendly with May, for she was extremely knowledgeable in the gem business and could spot a flawed ruby without a magnifying glass. Moreover, she could steer clients to him, and tip him off to possibilities of major sales. "Thai girls are very proper," Charles said. "May would not help me with my business unless she thought I loved her." *That* was the reason for his charade, and *that* was the reason why Marie-Andrée would have to tolerate the role of secretary. Only for a short while. Only until his jewelry business grew successful. Then he came directly to the point. He wanted Marie-Andrée's $2,000 to invest in his endeavors. His absolute guarantee was that she would double her money if not increase it tenfold or more.

Prudently, the Canadian girl refused. This was her insurance money, her return to Canada if this fling did not work out, as indeed it seemed unlikely to do. But Charles wheedled and cajoled, and kissed and held her, and whispered the words that she wanted to hear. She cashed $1,000 of her checks and the money disappeared into Charles' pocket. True, she extracted a *quid pro quo* for her investment, that being the permanent expulsion of May from Charles' schedule. But this promise lasted about as long as the ice cubes in a Bangkok gin and tonic.

On a Sunday morning not long after Marie-Andrée's return to Bangkok, Charles slipped out while she was still sleeping under a listless ceiling fan in the thick August heat of their hotel room. He picked up May and went to the Thieves' Market, a carnival of vendors under crimson and orange tents. In one section, an explosion of tropical flowers blinded the eye—shiny, waxy anthuriums, tapioca trees in dragon pots, pink lilies with milky poison in their stems, monkey tails seemingly sewn from chenille, white bleeding hearts whose sorrowful petals, the legend goes, mark the tears of a girl whose lover abandoned her. Huge straw baskets of fruits and vegetables consumed acres in the market, with toothless old women chanting and cackling as they offered up rose apples and jackfruit and clusters of dreary-looking brown sapodillas that, when peeled, transform into creamy yellow flesh, translucent and sweet.

But Charles was not interested in flora or fauna, hustling May through the market that offered serpents and fighting cocks and monkeys that screamed displeasure. Nor did he stop to wander through the rabbit warren where antiques were sold and where the sharp eye might discover a Ming vase or a brass chest from Peking. His destination was an area of hustlers who hawked raw gemstones freshly dug from the red clay near the Cambodian border.

May was in a foul mood, angry over a myriad of misdemeanors that Charles had committed against her, uncertain as to Marie-Andrée's role in this triangle, tired and sweating after being led like a donkey through the crowds. They finally stopped at a stall where blackish-red rubies were for sale, and Charles picked out one and presented it to May as a peace offering. He was sorry for the confusion over Marie-Andrée. The Canadian was *only* his secretary. She would never be anything else. "I want to marry you," said Charles, "but I can't do it for four years." May didn't believe any of it, but she was intrigued enough to ask how he hit upon the unusual waiting period of four years. "Because my life is very complicated," he answered, and May believed *that*.

Nearby a pen of white spitz puppies barked exuberantly and caught May's attention. She knelt and picked up a small ball of wriggling white fluff. Noting her interest, and hoping to pacify her, Charles made a proposal—the ruby or the dog. May was spoiling for a fight anyway and she scowled. "Why don't you buy the dog for Marie-Andrée?" she suggested sarcastically. "Then she'd have someone to keep her company."

Marie-Andrée loved the dog. She named it Frankie and she cradled it as people do who need love and are not getting it anyplace else. But Charles lacked even the grace to allow her an unclouded moment of happiness. "We can sell the dog in Europe someday for three times what we paid for it here," he said.

For almost a month, Charles juggled the two women, not very deftly. He moved from hotel to hotel, Marie-Andrée and her dog in weary tow, making it a point to have breakfast with the Canadian girl, usually at a Chinese restaurant, then disappearing until midnight or later. In those hours, Charles was usually at loose in the city, haunting tourist gathering places, then dining and dancing at discos with May. If either girl complained, he made her seem ungrateful for not appreciating the time he allotted. And by the end of August 1975, Charles had managed to extricate another $800 from Marie-Andrée's purse, leaving her with very little as get-back-to-Canada funds. Then her tourist visa for Thailand, good for twenty-one days, neared expiration. Marie-Andrée pestered Charles what to do. No problem, he answered. Visa extensions are easy to obtain, particularly for someone like Charles, who had "influence" with the police. He reminded her that Bangkok was a city oiled by corruption; a few *bahts* placed in the right bureaucratic palm could accomplish whatever was needed. But the expiration date came and went, and each time that Marie-Andrée brought the subject up, he accused her of being a scold and a nag and that it was impossible to get business accomplished with feminine whinings buzzing in his ears. Thus was she now illegally in Thailand.

Marie-Andrée had other grievances. What of those trips to exotic places that Charles had promised in his letters? Where were the villas in Sri Lanka and the beach cottages in the Philippines? Where were the gowns of red silk, and the necklaces and earrings of rubies and turquoise? Thus far, all Marie-Andrée had seen was the inside of various second-rate Bangkok hotels, and her only gift was a white fluffy dog that Charles intended to sell. But she must have gotten through to the man, for he found a little time to pay ardent attention to the frustrated visitor from Canada. So much so that she was able to write in her journal:

"Life is going on . . . I have had two weeks of physical relations with Charles that finally gave me a sense of communication both physical and spiritual . . . and some tenderness that is essential to me. I did, after all, give up my family and my country to be with my beloved . . ."

Pattaya is the Waikiki of Thailand, two hours by car south of Bangkok, a once slumbering fishing village pumped up and painted by Western commerce into a vulgar parade of high-rise hotels and infernal motorboats that assault the placid sea like mosquitoes on a sunbather. But the weather is benevolent year round, and elephants can be rented as taxis, and the main drag is a mélange of German sauerkraut and French crepes and Japanese noodles and American disco. Tourists usually love it, particularly those smart enough to hire a boat and find the remote peace of a coral reef isle where the snorkeler can

delight over sea creatures as brilliantly colored as the
flowers in the Thieves' Market.

On the very first day of September 1975, a young Australian PhD candidate and his Indonesian bride sat on the
sands of Pattaya beach and sipped coconut milk from
shells. It was the intention of Russell Lapthorne and his
wife, Vera, to spend but this one day at Pattaya, for their
schedule was crowded. In the days to come, they would
thread through the fringe of Asia, stopping at the ro-
mantic-sounding places called Hua Hin, Hat Yai, Penang,
and Kuala Lumpur, final destination Singapore before flying home to Melbourne, where he was a graduate student
majoring in politics and sociology. The Lapthornes were
very much in love and they entwined their arms to drink
from the coconut shells, ignoring a gaggle of Thai boys
who were laughing and pointing from behind palm trees.

Another couple suddenly rode up on bicycles. The man
was dressed in swimming trunks and a polo shirt. He was
at first glance, thought Lapthorne, an Oriental, for the
face was tinged burnt gold and the hair, though styled
European, was thick, black, and coarse. But when the
man waved and spoke a cheery "Hello," then launched
into a rapid inquiry about where to buy such coconut milk,
Lapthorne heard French-accented English. The woman,
who hung back shyly, spoke little, for she was not comfortable in English. Their names, they said in introduction,
were Jean Belmont, of Paris, and his wife, Monique, once
of Canada.

Without being asked, Jean Belmont and his quiet wife,
whose face was angry pink from the tropical sun, joined
the Australian couple and within moments a friendship
was struck, the easy kind that people fall into when on
vacation. Monsieur and Madame Belmont revealed very
little about themselves, save that they had been in the
resort city for four days and were in the middle of a trip
that had taken them from France to Beirut. Later they
would travel to Bali and the Philippines before a regretful
farewell to the East and a return to Paris, where Belmont
was a "manufacturers' representative" and where his wife,
Monique, was in "fashion."

Presently, Belmont stripped off his polo shirt, paused in
calculation to display his strong body, and plunged into

the warm sea. But he returned quickly, complaining that the water was dirty and that civilization was destroying one of nature's most idyllic treasures. It is true, agreed Lapthorne. For that very reason, he and his bride were going to Hua Hin, a remote and little-known beach on the other side of Thailand, where lovers could find a less commercial paradise.

How remarkable! exclaimed Belmont. He and his wife were considering the very same trip, but they were apprehensive about going there alone. How would it be if all four journeyed together? Oh, five really, if one included Monique's white puppy. Its name was Frankie, and Monique rarely let the yapping creature out of her embrace. The Lapthornes noted right away that Madame Belmont was fantically devoted to the dog.

The two couples returned to Bangkok separately and rendezvoused at the train station for a half-day ride to Hua Hin. There they took adjoining rooms at the ramshackle Railway Hotel, with a common veranda overlooking the Gulf of Thailand. The beach was spectacular, empty for miles and lined with bending palms, like a boulevard void of traffic. Monique and Belmont went for a stroll alone, until the skies turned dark. They returned drenched in a summer rain. They had been quarreling. Monique seemed nervous. She hated Hua Hin. The hotel displeased her. Belmont shot her several fierce shushing looks. All of this would be one day remembered.

The four young people sat on the common veranda of their rooms and watched the storm pester the sea. Belmont was playing the role of host, making sure everyone was comfortable, promising that the rain would end soon. He called room service and ordered four chocolate milk shakes. The drinks did not come for some time, not until the two couples had gone to their separate rooms to take a nap. The Lapthornes were aroused by Monique knocking at their door, bringing two glasses of chocolate milk shake. She watched while the Australian and his wife emptied the glasses, then mumbled a broken English invitation to dinner at a restaurant in town.

During the night, the Lapthornes were both racked by nausea and diarrhea. They put the blame on the restaurant

meal or snacks they had on the train from Bangkok. Belmont was tender in his sympathies. "I heard you getting
up and down all night, and the toilet flushing," he said the
next morning, being as he was on the other side of a thin
partition. "I will buy some canned milk. It's the only thing
to take for the Asian stomach."

The Lapthornes groaned. Their stomachs could not tolerate even the thought of nourishment. But at least the
sun had appeared and they could lie on the sands and try
to ignore their bellies.

For most of the morning, the Lapthornes drowsed under
the intense tropical sun and listened dimly while Belmont
rattled on. He was remarkably adept at squeezing information from the couple. Before noon, Lapthorne had revealed how much he earned at the university where he
taught, how much money he had received in travel grants
from a foundation that endowed him to write a textbook
on the politics of Southeast Asia, and, most fundamentally,
how much he carried in traveler's checks.

That afternoon, while the Lapthornes sought an unin-
terrupted nap, Monique appeared without being asked,
carrying two more glasses of chocolate milk. The Lapthornes both noted she looked nervous, standing there and
waiting for the treats to be drunk—as if ordered to do so.
Vera sipped part of her glass, but Lapthorne was absorbed
in a book called *Oil Politics* and promised to drink his
later. Within ten minutes, Vera Lapthorne felt a new
surge of nausea, this time accompanied by dizziness. Her
husband advised her to rest while he continued reading.
Russell drank his chocolate milk and it tasted good. "I
think I'm getting better," he told himself, even as a profound dizziness swept across him. As he tried to stagger
to the bedroom, stumbling like a fly caught in aspic, he
would remember casting one final glance back at the common veranda. Jean Belmont and Monique were standing
there, curious, like dream figures, blurred around the edges.
They made no attempt to help, even as he crashed to the
floor and blackness enveloped him. It was early afternoon,
September 4, 1975.

Not until almost forty hours later did Russell Lapthorne
regain consciousness in a hospital room. Vera smiled
feebly at him, her face ghastly pale. She knew little more

than he. Both had been found unconscious on the floor of their hotel room and had been rushed to this hospital, where their stomachs were pumped.

Where were Jean Belmont and Monique? wondered Lapthorne. Vera raised her shoulders. She did not know. When the couple was strong enough later in the day to return to the Railway Hotel, they found the door to the adjoining room locked. Angrily Russell Lapthorne tried to force it. Then he ran to the reception desk and demanded to know what had happened to the Frenchman and his nervous wife. The Belmonts checked out shortly before the Lapthornes were found ill, said the desk clerk. No forwarding address.

Not only were the Belmonts gone, so were the Lapthornes' passports, marriage license, driving permit, wedding ring, gold chain, movie camera, wristwatch, and moneys and checks totaling $1,100. Plus their unused air tickets for Australia.

The Australian couple tried to make a complaint against the Belmonts, but the language barrier was impossible. "No one was interested in what had happened to us," Lapthorne would say. "I told the police that I wanted to press charges—but the statement they took from me in no way resembled what I said."

Six months later, an Interpol detective would fly to Melbourne and obtain complete statements of the incident. The detective would also show photographs of a couple suspected in this drugging-robbery. No doubt about it, said Lapthorne, whose opinion was immediately endorsed by his wife. "I would recognize them anywhere." The photographs were of Charles Sobhraj and Marie-Andrée Leclerc.

Worth emphasizing here is the fact that Marie-Andrée had been in Thailand for only a month when the Lapthornes were robbed. Yet already she was using a fictitious name—Monique—a fictitious address—Paris—a fictitious identity—wife of Jean Belmont, and—the accusation was made—she was serving poisoned chocolate milk as efficiently as she had once served coffee at Marie-Antoinette's restaurant in a small town in Canada. The charms and powers of Charles Sobhraj worked quickly on the woman whose life had almost smothered from boredom.

CHAPTER TWENTY-SIX

A surprise awaited Marie-Andrée when she returned to Bangkok wilted from an eight-hour train journey up the Gulf of Siam. She needed one. From the moment they had left the Lapthornes at the Railway Hotel, the Canadian girl had been jumpy and nervous. Her stomach danced and pitched, her body trembled.

On the train she held her dog tightly to her bosom, clutching Frankie like a dowager's toy, and once, during a brief stop at a remote station, the puppy squirmed out of her arms and into a crowd of peasants carrying bags of yams. Screaming, Marie-Andrée leaped off the train and retrieved the animal, sobbing for the next hundred miles while Charles soothed her. There was no need for anguish, he insisted. He *loved* her. He *needed* her. He wanted to *marry* her. Soon they would have their own baby. He made eloquent apologies for the strain of Marie-Andrée's first few weeks in Bangkok, the continual moving around from hotel to hotel, his attention paid to May. All of this was part of his master plan. And now, it was coming together.

"Do you really love me?" asked Marie-Andrée, for that was her principal consideration.

"Of course, *chérie*," answered Charles cheerfully. "You will see."

In Bangkok, a taxi bore the young couple into the heart of the city, to a district near a major canal where embassies nest discreetly behind forests of banana trees and lavishly groomed gardens of lemon and bougainvillaea, with parrots screaming and monkeys scampering about the branches like landlords. It was a very good part of town, near major hotels and only a short stroll from Patpong, the tenderloin of Bangkok, a strip of massage parlors and clip joints redolent of sex and known to the tens of thousands of American soldiers who retreated there for R & R during Vietnam.

The taxi stopped in front of Kanit House, a five-story stucco mock-modern apartment building that could have been set down on any side street of Hollywood. Built around a kidney-shaped pool, the structure had an open-air elevator connecting each floor, with breezy corridors open to the weather. The tenants, very transient, were mostly young—lower level embassy personnel, airline flight crews, students. The garage was crowded with dusty MG's and Renaults.

With the pride of a knight showing his lady the new castle, Charles led Marie-Andrée into the lift which wheezed and groaned its way to the fifth floor. There the surprise was waiting. Charles had rented the penthouse, especially for Marie-Andrée! He opened the door to Apartment 503, a cheerless and dark two bedroom flat with linoleum floors long bereft of gloss, and plaster walls caked with dirt, bits and pieces of ancient food swept into corners. But there were sliding glass doors opening onto a breezeway where one could look down at the pool, or across the city to see a Buddhist temple spire flashing on the horizon. The furniture was wretched—motel chrome, impersonal and uncomfortable.

For Charles it was a summit to which he had somehow climbed—a tangible statement of his position on earth—and he wanted Marie-Andrée to share his excitement. She summoned modest enthusiasm; anything would be better than nomadic prowls through the cheap hotels of Bangkok where the towels were as thin as cheesecloth. Charles fairly glowed as he dramatized the possibilities of the "penthouse." A little paint here, some imagination there, and presto!—they would not only have a splendid place in which to live, but one to which he could bring customers and friends. The second bedroom, need it be pointed out, would be perfect for a nursery. Already Charles had commissioned new business cards bearing his pseudonym: "A. Gauthier, Gem Dealer, Kanit House, Suite 503, Bangkok, Thailand." He tossed a handful at Marie-Andrée and they rained about her shoulders like rice falling on a bride.

By nightfall they were in residence, in each other's embrace on an old iron bed, and for the moment Marie-Andrée was content. She would write in her diary: "I am very happy . . . At last we have found a new home. I think this is the real beginning for us. I am filled with hope."

She set about attacking the flat, washing the walls with lye, painting cool greens and blue trim, tacking up cheap but vivid fabrics over chairs and pillows, crowding corners with temple rubbings and teak elephants and dragons painted on parchment papers. Candles and incense sweetened the air. When she was almost done, Charles brought home a punching bag and affixed it to the living room ceiling, a shockingly ugly center of attention. It was for his karate, he told her, ignoring her pleas that it disgraced the aesthetics she had so labored to achieve.

From the Thieves' Market, Marie-Andrée purchased pots and pans to establish a kitchen, and within a few weeks the dreary flat was colorful and bustling. She had made a home! From the stove rose the temptations of *boeuf bourguignonne* and *tartes*. Frankie slept contentedly on a pillow when he was not yapping at an occasional mouse. And to complete the little family, Charles brought home a baby monkey who grew so quickly and who refused toilet training so absolutely that Marie-Andrée sewed diapers to dress the creature. He was christened Napoleon and spent much of his time clinging to the chain that suspended the punching bag, glowering at all, particularly the little dog, for whom he held unconcealed hostility.

The weeks of happiness did not last long.

One morning Marie-Andrée went to the market to purchase fresh food for lunch in the tradition of French housewives who buy provisions for each meal, and when she returned, Charles was sitting in the living room with May. Both were awkward and embarrassed. Charles leaped up like a man caught with his fingers in the cashbox and rushed out, mumbling something about an appointment. But May stayed behind, insolently, making hypocritical conversation about how "charmingly" Marie-Andrée had decorated the apartment. Marie-Andrée had not seen the beautiful Thai girl for weeks, Charles having promised that he was no longer interested in her. But at this moment, the cream on his whiskers showed that May was clearly back in favor.

How was Marie-Andrée enjoying the new apartment? wondered May. The Canadian girl nodded cautiously, indicating her pleasure. How nice, purred May. She *knew* the flat would be perfect; that was why she had chosen it and put down the deposit.

"*You* found this apartment?" gasped Marie-Andrée. May nodded a little perversely. Charles had given her the assignment and she had looked at dozens before finding this one, in such a good location. He had even paid May a "finder's fee." There was no need to elaborate on *that* —Marie-Andrée got the point immediately—but May was anxious to sing hymns to Charles' sexual capacities and proportions, hoping that he had demonstrated his full talents to the Canadian visitor.

The next entry in Marie-Andrée's diary was etched in bitter pain.

"Charles is seeing May again. My heart breaks at the news . . . I feel frustrated, nervous, aggressive. Everybody can read the sadness in my eyes . . . I am not understood, not loved, not wanted, not satisfied. I have no more personal money, my visa has expired, my passport cannot be used. I have the feeling of being a prisoner . . . But I still love him. Oh, God, I want him . . ."

Dominique Veylau sat in a cafe on a warm late September night and drowsed in the intoxication of Chiang Mai, Thailand's "Rose of the North," a city of such pale gold beauty that both the eye and the soul are ravished. He was almost done with the East, and here was an appropriate place to say *au revoir* and return to France. For two years, Dominique had roamed about this corner of the world, working for a time in Australia as a clerk, then taking his carefully hoarded money and splurging on a glorious spin about Asia. Now he was almost twenty-five, and he had only $1,500 left, and it was time for a dutiful French son to quell his appetite for the exotic and accept the dictates of his heritage—work and wife and child and church.

He had allotted himself only one day for Chiang Mai, but that was an error. The city of wild orchids and of women celebrated for shyness and beauty, of districts where thousands of paper umbrellas sat drying in the sun like butterflies at rest, where the ear seldom failed to hear the tinkling of ivory chimes in the soft winds—here was a place that needed a week if not a lifetime. On this afternoon, Dominique had paused at the foot of the Dragon Staircase, carved long ago in dark centuries, and as his eyes traveled in wonder up the twin serpents whose rippling humped backs framed the gigantic steps leading to the Doi Suthep Temple, he realized how unfortunate it was to behold such awesome spectacle without a companion. He was lonely, and each time he wandered into a temple courtyard and felt the serenity and peace contained therein, he wished for someone to share his feelings. Someone was.

"I think you must be French," intruded the stranger, breaking into Dominique's solitude on the veranda of the restaurant.

"Oui, monsieur," answered Dominique, looking up to encounter an Oriental-looking young man wearing horn-rimmed glasses. Beside him was a thin and sunburned woman about thirty whose nose was as red as a cherry. Introductions came quickly. The man said he was "Alain Gauthier." The woman was his wife, "Monique," probably Canadian, for Dominique heard the accent in her voice. They were pleasant, smiling, and charming.

Immediately, Alain Gauthier seized command of the evening. As he lived in Bangkok, he knew the most succulent dishes on a Thai menu. A dozen small bowls of fiery food appeared on the table—bites of beef and pork and chicken cooked in mint and peppers, with quarts of heavy dark beer to cool abused throats. And within an hour, Dominique, normally a reticent man, had spun his life story for the friendly couple. Of particular interest to Alain was Dominique's revelation that he had recently worked in Australia as private secretary to a large firm's managing

director. Moreover, he spoke good English and seemed
capable of handling complex business matters with panache.
He had some experience with banking and knew a fair
amount about international currency transactions.

But what of Alain? inquired Dominique. What was his
occupation?

The gem business, answered his new friend—like everybody else in Bangkok.

Did he do well?

Alain shrugged ambivalently. The problem was in finding competent people to work as his associates. But enough
of business! Alain clapped his hands for the bill. The
evening was young, with the scent of blossoms in the air
and music floating on the breeze. He knew a place where
beautiful women danced in swirling silks and masks, to
the music of gongs and drums written a thousand years
ago. If that did not catch Dominique's fancy, then Alain
knew another place where Thai girls boxed one another.
It was a memorable experience, he rattled on, seeing a pair
of slim and petite young women walk into the ring, bow
ceremonially, then proceed to kick the devil out of one
another, their feet drawing blood.

But as Alain spoke, leading Monique and the new friend
out of the restaurant and toward his rented automobile,
Dominique felt his head swim. He staggered. He tried to
keep walking, but a profound weakness had taken over
his steps. All he would remember was trying to keep from
fainting, and Alain and Monique murmuring tender solici-
tudes as they drove him to his hotel.

The next morning, Dominique awoke and was startled
to see the new faces from the night before standing over
his bed. *"Bonjour,"* said Alain Gauthier. "How do you
feel?" Dominique moaned and tried to remember the
evening. But the agonies gnawing at his belly were not
sired by alcohol. This was not a hangover. He felt deathly
ill.

"You have dysentery," diagnosed Alain Gauthier. This
damn country! It had surely been picked up somewhere
on his journey. As he spoke, Monique knelt beside the
bed and wiped the French youth's brow with a handkerchief that smelled of French perfume. It was cool and her
touch was gentle. Alain talked on and on. He was an

expert at tropical disease, having lived so long in the East. He feared that Dominique was so ill that it was dangerous to stay alone in a remote city like Chiang Mai, where medicine was not far removed from the jungle. Better that Dominique accept a free car ride to Bangkok, where he could recuperate in Alain and Monique's apartment.

"You must trust me," said Alain. "You must give yourself completely over to me."

Dominique was too sick for anything but a feeble nod. At that moment he was enormously grateful for the attention and care being offered him. It would be a while before questions begin to haunt him. Why had he fallen ill so abruptly? Why did he awake with two strangers inside his locked hotel room?

Dominique was installed in the second bedroom of Apartment 503 and spent his first two weeks drifting in and out of consciousness. He could barely remember nodding assent when Gauthier suggested that his passport and traveler's checks should be put in a place for "safekeeping" until he was fully recovered. And he was faintly aware that Gauthier appeared once or twice a day with a spoonful of "medicine" which, upon consumption, seemed to speed him to the bathroom, where his aching innards voided what little was left within them. Monique was his blessing, for she spent hours sitting beside his bed, her face showing concern over his torment. He begged now and then for a doctor, but Monique disagreed. Doctors were expensive. Doctors were unreliable. Better that he trust Alain, and her. They knew how to treat tropical illnesses. "Trust Alain," she murmured. "Alain knows best."

Other fragile lives clung to Alain Gauthier, A.K.A. Charles Sobhraj, alias half a hundred other names, affixing weak vines to what seemed to be the sturdiest of tree trunks. For several weeks in the bizarre autumn of 1975 in Bangkok, a willowy and theatrical Italian woman known as Miss Simonetta became part of the entourage, moving into the apartment and sleeping on a sofa until Marie-Andrée decided that she was not a customer, but more likely the latest romantic interest for the lord of this curious manor. Thus did "Monique," as everyone knew Marie-

Andrée, angrily throw the Italian girl out one morning
while Charles was prowling about Bangkok looking for
customers. When she informed Charles of her action, he
seemed less interested than if she had stepped on a taran-
tula and dropped it in the garbage.

But later May dropped by on some pretense of business
and congratulated Monique for the forcefulness with which
she had dealt with Simonetta. By the by, murmured May,
did Monique know that Simonetta was pregnant? Monique
was startled. By whom? May smiled maliciously. "I don't
know," she replied. But Alain had been asked by Simonetta
to pay for an abortion. That more or less answered the
question, didn't it? "Alain told her 'no,' " continued May.
"He told me an abortion can be big trouble. It might
bring the police. He gave Simonetta some money, I know
that."

That very night Marie-Andrée demanded to know from
Charles just how involved he had been with the Italian
girl. Charles sighed and said nothing. Marie-Andrée let
it go for the nonce, but months later she discovered Simonetta's passport in a box of Charles' personal papers.

In early October, shortly after Charles and Marie-Andrée
returned from Chiang Mai with the ailing Dominique in
tow, an interesting new couple appeared at Kanit House
and leased an apartment. They were both French, the
husband, Raoul, being a short, sturdy fellow who was
newly arrived in Bangkok to become a *sous-chef* at a leading restaurant, his auburn-haired wife, Belle, a half head
taller, with a manner that blended both salt-of-the-earth
practicality and Parisian chic. In their late twenties, both
possessed a spirit of adventure. Their marriage was rich
with love and exploration. Raoul had learned his trade in
some of Paris's best kitchens, but he became afflicted with
a severe case of wanderlust and tried to obtain a visa for
the United States. Disappointed to learn that it would
take months if not years, Raoul looked about the map. A
friend knew of a tempting job possibility in Bangkok,
which certainly seemed far enough away, and romantic.
"What would you say to living in Bangkok for a couple
of years?" Raoul asked Belle, who would have set forth
in a raft for Tahiti on an hour's notice if the idea had

been attractive. "Sure," she said. "But where the hell is it?" Raoul scratched his head. "Don't know for sure," he said. "China, I think." And within a few days they were off, arriving in what turned out to be Thailand. There they discovered a small French-speaking community, a few hundred at best, but tightly knit as is Gallic custom. Quickly they became popular members. On evenings at home, Raoul prepared steaming kettles of *cassoulet*, or, if the sea's catch was bountiful, a *bouillabaisse*. Their apartment smelled like a fine French bistro, and there was even new Beaujolais, almost as quickly as it appeared in Paris's cafes. *Chez* Raoul and Belle meant hearty food, the latest jokes from home, and hot music from New Jimmy's or Régine's.

During the steaming days while she waited for Raoul, Belle often sunned beside the pool in a bikini from St. Tropez. Occasionally she looked up and espied a lonely-looking young woman peering down from the fifth floor. Belle inquired at the manager's office and learned that the woman was the wife of a local gem dealer. Quiet people. No trouble. Nothing much to tell.

One dusk the French chef and his wife were walking up the apartment stairs—the lift had collapsed—and voices were heard behind them. "Ah, you are French," happily exclaimed the man, who introduced himself as Alain Gauthier. "So are we!" Monique nodded shyly at Belle, who smiled back warmly to indicate that she recognized the woman who stood on the fifth-floor railing and looked down at the pool. The two women became immediate friends, both having long days to spend while their husbands worked in the city. Alain usually began his day stalking big game at the major hotels, the Dusit Thani, a favorite for Asian businessmen, or the Indra, whose shopping arcade was always crowded with Westerners, or the Siam-Intercontinental, built on lands leased by a royal princess and favored by Americans and Italians. Sometimes, if he hooked a customer, often Charles brought the potential score home for lunch, having notified Marie-Andrée to prepare a *quiche* or a *salade niçoise*. Often Belle flew into action to help set a suitable table to impress Charles' customers, and sometimes she stayed to eat, being a handsome adornment for the little apartment.

Alain fascinated Belle, even though she found him puzzling. His shirts for one intrigued her. They were always clean and freshly ironed—thanks to Monique—and they were always monogrammed on the front pocket. But the monograms differed; one day the letters read AG, another CS, still others later in the week. She could not resist asking why one night when they all sat around the pool sipping wine. "It's for my business," he said in a tone that cut off further inquiry. His manners were another thing. Though he presented himself as a man of uncommon sophistication, his table etiquette was almost primitive. His mouth was usually crammed with food as he delivered an anecdote, and if sauces dropped on his shirt front, he seemed not to notice them.

"Does he ever shut up and let you talk?" asked Belle one morning after a lengthy night-before session with Alain, who had chattered throughout dinner of his plan to open a great chain of jewelry stores across Asia, with headquarters in Bangkok. He was thinking of calling them Goldfinger's.

Monique shrugged in Gallic fashion and stuck out her lower lip, "Believe half of what he tells you," she said, testily.

Raoul believed less than that. From their first meeting, he had been suspicious of the energetic gem dealer. There were too many disparities in the autobiography. "At various moments," pointed out Raoul, "Alain has told us he studied psychology at the Sorbonne, on another night it was the law, then it was engineering somewhere else."

"Perhaps he studied all of them," suggested Belle.

"He's a hustler," pronounced Raoul.

The one fact that could not be disputed was that Monique was the most attentive of wives. When coffee was served, she watched Alain's cup like an overeager waitress, anxious to fill it without being asked, hovering nearby with the correct amounts of sugar and milk. She was bent on anticipating his every wish, often calling down to Belle in despair when Alain's favorite dish emerged from her kitchen less than perfect. Belle had learned from Raoul how to salvage anything, even burned soufflés.

Belle further noticed that Alain paid less attention to his wife than he did the dog, or the monkey. During

evenings *chez* Gauthier, Monique was scant more than a
serving girl, condemned to a corner of the room and
silence, rarely intruding into her master's conversation
unless bidden. Her role was clearly defined: housekeeper,
cook, laundress, and nurse—Dominique was still resident
in the guest bedroom and on occasion staggered gray-faced
and wraith-thin into the living room to find a bit of company. Alain always welcomed the young French boy,
explaining that as soon as he regained his health Dominique
was going to join his gem business.

When the two women grew close enough to share intimate secrets, Monique revealed more about herself. She
told Belle that her life in Canada had been boring and
unfulfilling. She would have perished in Lévis had she not
accepted Alain's invitation to join him in the East. Belle
was not certain that Monique and Alain were really
married; the subject was evaded whenever she raised it.
But clearly Monique wished to present herself as the gem
dealer's authentic spouse, and Belle was not one to tear
down an emotional façade. One thing she suspected was
soon confirmed—a lack of sex in the "marriage." Once
while the two women lolled beside the apartment house
pool, Monique seemed distraught, and when Belle cautiously asked why, the answer was painful. "Alain is so
busy with his work, he isn't interested in sex," she said.
"It's been almost a month."

That night, when Raoul came home, Belle could not
resist revealing the discord between the couple upstairs.
"I don't blame her for being *triste*," said Raoul. "She came
all the way here from Canada to be his lover, and when
she arrives, she finds out she's supposed to be the *bonne*."
Raoul believed that Alain kept Monique around as a
symbol of respectability, to go with the dog and the aura
of wholesome family life. "It's to impress his customers,"
observed Raoul. "I don't think he gives a damn about
Monique."

Belle felt the judgment was harsh. If Alain was all that
heartless, why was he taking such good care of Dominique,
a French boy he had only known for one night before he
brought him home and gave him the spare bedroom for
recuperation? "I think that's bizarre, too," answered Raoul.
"A strong young boy shouldn't be sick that long with

dysentery. It comes and goes—normally. He's looked like
the living dead ever since we first met him—and it's been
several weeks . . . Why doesn't he see a doctor?"

Belle nodded. The plight of Dominique had worried her,
too. In fact she had asked Monique why the sick man had
not gone to a hospital. "Alain knows how to care for him,"
was the answer. Besides, Alain had an "investment" in
Dominique by now. He expected the French youth to work
for him when he regained his health. If Dominique chose
to leave Alain's home, then he would have to pay twenty
dollars for each day he had been there.

"See what I mean?" said Raoul. "So much for his
humanity."

"It's cheaper than a hospital," said Belle in defense of
her friends.

"He might get *well* at a hospital," said Raoul. "I think
Alain just wants him around—for some strange reason.
I think Alain just collects people and makes them depen-
dent on him."

If a day's hunting was unsuccessful at the major hotels
in Bangkok, then Alain/Charles lowered his expectations
and often dropped by the Malaysia Hotel, an establishment
unlikely to be listed in any travel guide save those that
catered to youth with bedrolls on their backs, and very
little money hidden inside belts or pinned to Afghan vests.
The Malaysia was a well-known stop on the wanderers'
trail that began in Europe and snaked its way across the
mass of Asia. If one wrote ahead for a brochure, the
Malaysia would arrive in the mail looking like a first cousin
to the Hilton, rising modern, clean, and invitingly with
terraces and palm trees erupting from a tropical garden.
When the youthful traveler arrived, the hotel turned out
to be faded, shabby, but not without an economical charm.
The lobby was always teeming with youngsters and their
backpacks, their costumes patched together from the international roads—Indian silks, Pakistani blouses, shorts, sandals, beads and bracelets that clanked melodiously when
the girls strolled about.

It was here one October afternoon in 1975 that Charles
added two more to his entourage, a pair of French youngsters who by all rights would have worried a man in the
kind of business that Alain Gauthier undertook. They

were both young *ex-cops* from the French provinces, both in their early twenties. One, plump, was called Yannick, the other, tall and thin, Jacques. Though they had traveled for more than a year over half the world, they remained bucolic, trusting, and naïve. Charles hooked them in a quarter of an hour. That was all the time it took for him to learn that they were (1) trying unsuccessfully to find jobs as cooks and having no luck as they lacked Thai work papers, and (2) thinking about going to Pattaya beach for a few days.

In Pattaya, suggested Alain/Charles, there were plentiful work opportunities, as the resort contained scores of restaurants. The bureaucracy of Bangkok was not as evident, and temporary work could surely be found. Besides, Alain knew several important people in the restaurant business.

The next day, Alain filled his rented Toyota with an odd assortment—himself, Marie-Andrée, Frankie the dog, Napoleon the monkey, Dominique the sick Frenchman, and Yannick and Jacques, the newcomers and former *flics*. The drive was festive, French voices laughing and cheering on Alain as he threaded the small car through the terrifying—no other word will do—ordeal of Thai highway travel. The road from Bangkok to Pattaya is wide and excellent, but it is heavily used by trucks—each vividly painted in Day-glo colors and occupied by drivers who operate the behemoths like kamikaze pilots (sitting on only a small corner of the driver's seat and leaving the remainder of the cushion for Buddha, their constant and invisible companion). The custom is for overloaded trucks and overcrowded buses to play king of the road, straddling the center stripe, horns blaring, apparently condemned to eternal damnation if some other vehicle manages to pass. Corpses of dead animals—dogs, wild hogs, ravens—litter the route. Men with innards sogged by heavy beer lurch from roadside cafes and stumble onto the highway, risking a terminal squash, or causing a bus to plow into a soft shoulder and spill peasants from windows. And if this were not enough, hundreds of jitneys scurry up and down the road, picking up rural people and dropping them off a few miles later, like ants stepping lively around fallen trees. There is no more fearsome drive in the world for the unprepared, and each Monday morning Bangkok's newspapers are filled with accounts of weekend highway carnage.

They reached Pattaya safely, and Alain leased a second-class bungalow across the boulevard from the sea. Immediately Jacques and Yannick went out job hunting, while Marie-Andrée, ten pounds thinner, slipped into a bikini and took her dog to the beach. Dominique fell gratefully into a cot but could not sleep because the monkey kept dancing on his bedcovers.

En famille they dined that night at a German restaurant and then strolled along the soft and lovely sands. Lovers were entwined, and moans in the moonlight could be heard. Some made love in the shells of abandoned, rotting canoes. The music of guitars and drums filtered through the forests of palms, and from above monkeys threw down overripe bananas. Thin, ugly dogs wandered about, looking for fights with enormous crabs that claimed premiere residence on the sand.

Everyone was tired, but Alain would not permit the night to die so soon. He suggested a stop at a disco, and Monique, as if bidden, enthusiastically agreed. The two new Frenchmen were game, even Dominique, and for an hour or two the young people danced on the terrace of a hotel which featured young Thai boys trying to sound like the Rolling Stones. No one paid attention when Alain excused himself to make a telephone call and was gone for more than half an hour.

When they returned to the bungalow, cries of anguish immediately arose from the room where Jacques and Yannick were to sleep. Thieves had entered the bungalow in their absence; their passports, travel papers, and every centime were gone! While they tore apart the room looking for their net worth on earth, Alain Gauthier entered and was at first angered, then the most tender of consolers. He held out hope. New passports could be obtained from the French Embassy in Bangkok. It would take a while; they check these matters out carefully. But in the meantime, the boys could live in Alain's penthouse, help out with chores, and make the best of an unfortunate happening.

Jacques and Yannick had no choice. They accepted. The next day, when everyone returned to Bangkok, the apartment was impossibly crowded. But Alain found a solution. He rented the apartment adjoining his—504— and installed the two new Frenchmen along with Dominique.

How happy he was! His face glowed on the first night that all assembled in his living room. Charles looked about, almost in wonder, his eyes meeting the eyes of those who needed him, circling the room as if at a reunion, stopping to touch shoulders and speak in private murmurs. Was there ever a more apparent reason for happiness, neurotic and twisted, but nonetheless, happiness? At the age of thirty-one, Charles Sobhraj at long last had assembled the components of what he mistook to be permanence and worth—a lover, children, people who would defer and obey and love him. He had one, two, three, four people —and two animals—whose lives were welded to his. He was *pater familias*. He was head of a family. His family!

But what would become of them?

CHAPTER TWENTY-SEVEN

"Have spent a wonderful few days in Hong Kong," wrote Jennie to her friends in Seattle. "Went to a monastery on an island, felt wonderful peace and good vibes, then ate lots of strange food at a restaurant. Probably fried spiders! Realize now my decision to return to the East is the right one. On to Katmandu. Maybe a stop overnight in Bangkok. More later. Love to everybody, Jennie."

Jennie went to an airline ticket office in Hong Kong and inquired as to whether she could stop over in Bangkok without paying more money. As the woman reservations agent studied the flight book, Jennie spoke pleadingly. There were Buddhist shrines and temples that she wanted to visit before going to Katmandu. The agent nodded and smiled. It could be done. Jennie could not only travel to Bangkok without extra payment; she could spend a few days there. The young American's face reflected her joy.

On the four-hour flight, longer since the end of the Vietnam War because Western planes are forced to detour around the Communist country or else pay hugely inflated air rights to the Hanoi government, Jennie studied a Buddhist meditation book. She wrote her name on the flyleaf of the slim red volume, for she did not want to lose track of it when she arrived at Kopan Monastery. Her friends in Seattle had given it as a going-away present, and it was special. She planned to keep it, hiding it if necessary. Was this a sin? wondered Jennie. Probably. But a minor one. She wrote in her journal: "Karma has given me a beautiful trip and a beautiful destiny. How happy I am! I am worried about surrendering all my possessions when I reach the monastery—I have so few! But I believe I can keep the vows."

Annabella journeyed through Europe and discovered one of life's harshest truisms—nothing remains the same. Weeds take over the garden. She had hoped to slip back into those happy years when she was young, and single, when commitments were for another, faraway day. But now, as she wound her way through France and Italy and into Greece, at each place that held a memory she found only disappointment. Long ago friends, from almost a decade earlier, who had been fragilely bound through letters, were no longer what she remembered. Everyone was older, most were married, lives were filled with work and children—and there was no room to admit an American girl who had brushed against them so many years before.

Annabella was on the threshold of thirty and slowly she realized that most lives have fences built about them by that milestone. There was nothing for her to do but say hello, say goodbye, and move on, following the trails worn by the young. True to her word, she kept her anxious parents continually informed of her odyssey. From Afghanistan she wrote: "A man told me I would be worth 30 camels as a bride!" It seems that every American girl who visits Kabul is advised of her matrimonial worth in livestock. And from Pakistan, "Bit of a rough time here. Few hassles. Not to worry, though—am on to India." An occasional phone call ruptured the quiet nights of Northern California, and Jane's heart churned until she heard her daughter's voice, always with the assurance, "Don't worry about me. I'm doing fine. The money is holding out, and I've got it sewn inside my blouse."

Annabella felt the same apprehension about India that most travelers do, but she selected the most comfortable port of entry—Bombay, a city whose Western glitter can almost conceal the fact that 200,000 people sleep nightly on the sidewalks and gutters and bathe at public water pipes. The warmest of welcomes awaited Annabella at Sanjoy's home. His mother, Mrs. Fatima, presided over an upper-class villa with a wall around to shut out the harsh realities, and an armed guard to protect those inside from molestation. She was a heavy woman with a sweet face and an enormous ring of keys about her girth that opened and locked each door and cabinet in the house. Mrs. Fatima was flattered that Annabella would journey around the world to bring news of her son's brief and tragic life in California. She treated Annabella like a royal visitor and immediately pronounced her to be "my adopted American daughter." Later she wrote Jane a letter about Annabella's stay in Bombay:

> When Annabella was here, she was a joy to have in our home, and we all shared her love. I only wear white saris because I am still in mourning so I gave my colored ones to Annabella. . . . She draped them so beautifully. I massaged her hair with Indian oil and combed it in the Indian way . . . She could have become a motion picture star immediately! One day she combed out daughter Sushi's hair into eight braids . . . Annabella loved to stay in our home in a quiet way. Many times she asked me about my philosophy of life. I told her I believe there is no such thing as total death. She agreed with me that there must be a God, no matter what the religion. How else could we have met? What other force could have joined our lives from worlds apart? . . . She mentioned a "tough time" going through Pakistan. I told her over and over again that she should not travel alone, but she laughed and assured me she always found the company of foreigners and that she had faith in herself . . . What a beautiful girl! She loves mango ice cream and orange juice. She's learning Hindi and Gujarati . . .

When Annabella expressed interest in staying in Bombay and perhaps working at a hospital, as she had in California, an appointment was arranged at one of the city's better institutions. Annabella went to the hospital with great anticipation, having conjured visions of dedicated service and penance for whatever ill she might have done in her life. But once there, her illusions crumbled in the mass of suffering that began on the steps, continued through the

thronged foyer, and spilled into every corridor. The twin
devils of bureaucracy (of which India has more than
Washington and Whitehall put together), and lack of personnel and equipment made the hospital a well-meaning
but grotesque house of tragedy. A representative of the
hospital administration came to lead Annabella on a tour,
when from the emergency-room waiting room arose a
wailing. A woman had been crouched against a wall and
upon seeing Annabella rushed forward and clutched at her
clothes, holding on as if the American girl was the rope
of salvation. The hospital officer frowned and spoke
sharply in Hindi. Then he listened impatiently while the
woman—she could have been thirty or seventy, her face
was thin leather stretched over a frame of taut bones—
flung her chicken bone arm at an ancient man lying in the
corner.

The hospital worker glanced at him cursorily. The old
man wore street pajamas and weighed perhaps seventy-five
pounds, curled into a yoga knot. Then the official muttered
something brusque to the woman and with apologies
escorted Annabella out of the madhouse where a thousand
hurting people were squeezed into a room meant for fifty.

"What was that about?" asked Annabella.

Oh, *that*. The poor man in the corner was dead. But his
daughter refused to believe it. Someone would come soon
and take care of the matter.

"What did he die of?" asked Annabella.

"India," said the official.

She pushed on to Delhi, lured to the core of the city—
Connaught Circle—and found a hotel infested by a colony
of Western youth. Each day they spread blankets in the
circular green park and ate mango ice and complained of
"Delhi belly" and watched a dancing bear. One day a
hustler brought around an elderly but still surly cobra to
rise from a basket, the first serpent that Annabella had
seen in India. Talk among the youth on the grass was
usually threefold: (1) drugs and where to buy them safely,
(2) gemstones and which to buy and how to avoid glass
imitations, and (3) ways to reach and survive in Katmandu,
Shangri-La to those who had come this far in search of
something.

But most of her acquaintances in the park were too young, or paired, or stoned, so Annabella struck out alone to sweep up the sights of Delhi. One night she went to the Red Fort for the *son et lumière* presentation. The setting was spectacular, with colored lights rising and falling against the walls of marble palaces where for three centuries the history of India played out. The sounds of mounted warriors clattered against cobblestones as they came in the viewer's imagination from Persia to steal the Peacock Throne; harem women preened and giggled, fountains splashed, the pomp of dynasties thrilled the senses. Here Nehru spoke to proclaim India's new independence in 1948, and here a poet once wrote, the words carved into enduring marble, "If paradise be on the face of the earth, it is here, it is here, it is here!"

The night was sweet and smelled of jasmine and orange. During the spectacle, a man slipped into one of the bleacher seats beside Annabella and made an apology in English. Later, Annabella glanced discreetly at the new arrival, noting he was Western, dressed casually but well, and alone. When the show concluded with the Indian national anthem, and the harsh lights of utility glared on to wash away the magic, the man nodded warmly. He was American. One word led to another and Annabella found herself stopping for a soft drink at one of the refreshment stands that congest an entrance corridor where once elephants lumbered bearing princes on their panoplied backs.

His name was Mark, he said, and he was a textile buyer from New York who came to India three times a year, his mission to purchase the inexpensive cloth that could be fashioned into kaftans and sold at American department stores for twenty times the price in Delhi. His manner was easy and polite; he was not particularly handsome but nice enough to look upon. Annabella guessed his age to be nearer forty than the thirty-five he announced, but it did not matter. She warmed to him quickly and gratefully. In her months on the road, she had met many men, none worth remembering past sunrise. One Swedish youth in Athens had been remarkably attentive and romantic, with a body strong and golden, but when he asked to "borrow" fifty dollars, Annabella felt humiliated. In Istanbul, a Turk who claimed to have lived in Dallas for three years, but who spoke English as if reading it phonetically, entertained Annabella for a memorable day but then she caught his hand in her shoulder bag and sent him away with a rain of curses. "My advice is to either bring a built-in lover to Asia," she wrote to a friend in California, "or else take a vow of celibacy. The men are not too attractive, they all use too much hair oil, and as soon as they hear the word 'American' they think you're a Rockefeller."

But on this night in Delhi, Annabella needed someone to hold onto, and she gambled one more time. Mark was a take-charge person, packing her into a taxi and on the way to his hotel for late supper before she could demur, even had she wanted to. When the taxi arrived at the Akbar Hotel, Annabella sensed immediately that she was improperly dressed. Her jeans and an embroidered cotton blouse from Pakistan were suitable for her budget class of travel. But the Akbar was new and arrogantly expensive and listed in the *India on $5 and $10 a Day* guidebook under the category of "Break the Bank." Men who looked like diplomats or company directors stepped in and out of limousines, and the doorman, in a costume from the Raj, scrutinized each arrival almost rudely.

Mark saw her discomfort and made a quick suggestion. If Annabella would come to his room, he could find her a long skirt to wear to the restaurant, and perhaps a bit of glitter. Nothing more was meant by the suggestion, he said gently.

In his room, Mark found a bundle of cloth samples, rummaged hurriedly through it like a man doing card tricks, pulled out a gorgeous length of crimson and violet swirls, and bade a still-suspicious Annabella to slip out of her jeans. He spun the cloth about her waist, fastened it here and there with pins, and in less than two minutes had the young woman exclaiming with delight. She stood in front of a mirror and was as lovely as the new floor-length skirt. Mark slipped up behind her and fastened on earrings that tumbled in cascades almost to her shoulders.

They dined in the Sheesh Mahal, the hotel's supper club, an opulent homage to India's imperial past. Overhead, dangling like the earrings that Annabella wore, millions—literally millions—of red and green glass beads quivered, and mirrors ingeniously placed caught their reflections and made it seem that the room was an exploding galaxy of jewels. Never was a place so designed for lovers, and before Annabella had finished her appetizer, she knew that the night had just begun.

They spent a few days together, broken only when Mark had to go to the textile district for long hours of purchases and negotiations. During those barren periods, Annabella waited impatiently in her cheap hotel for Mark's return, having drunk her fill of Delhi's palaces and shrines. Something was happening to her that she had thought would not occur again. Less than a year after the suicide of her husband, she was interested in a new man, and although she dared not acknowledge the word, the notion of love hovered stubbornly over her thoughts. It was rash, she knew that, and foolish, she knew that, too. But she dared not examine these feelings too closely. For the moment she was happy.

She knew little of Mark, save that he was decent, well spoken, not addicted to either drugs or drink, divorced, and living in a house somewhere outside New York City. Once she had asked him for the address, but he could not find a pen and promised to give it to her later. He never did.

She was not sure where all this was leading, or even how long they could be together, for Mark seemed indefinite as to the duration of his stay in Delhi. Some questions he answered, others he brushed away, but always gracefully. One night Annabella was dressing to join Mark for dinner at Moti Mahal, when a bearer rapped at the door and said a phone call was waiting. Annabella flew down five flights of stairs and seized the telephone. She had never been called before at this hotel, and the only one who knew where she was staying was Mark.

"Hello?"

Silence.

"Hello? Mark? Hello?" No answer. The line echoed dully in her ear, her own voice sounding tinny and small. She jammed her finger against the button, trying to revive the connection. She thrust the receiver to the desk clerk, who shouted his own "hello" then shrugged and handed it back. Disconnected.

"Who was calling?" demanded Annabella of the hotel clerk. The man shrugged. He had no idea.

With a vague feeling of unease, Annabella went to the old restaurant where their rendezvous was set and waited for Mark. She waited almost two hours, sipping hot tea, before she finally telephoned the Akbar—only to learn that nobody was registered under the last name she knew Mark by. Nor had there been anyone there that week, nor did anyone hold advance reservations. Obviously Mark had given her a false name. Only at that moment did it occur to Annabella that she had never actually called the Akbar in search of Mark. Their meetings had always been arranged in person; he had always gotten in touch with her. A day or two later, black days of tears and anger, Annabella realized that she had been duped—and so pettily! It would be a long time, she decided, before she would make an emotional investment again.

Mark's cheap betrayal so soured Annabella that she made plans to return to the United States. She had been gone for almost five months, and she realized now that aimless drifting around the world was a game for the young. Annabella no longer had the resilience of youth. Certainly there were many places left in the world that she wanted to visit, but they would have to wait their turn, and be accomplished on normal vacations. "I'm on my way home," she wrote to a friend in November. "I'll come back to India some day, but I could never live here permanently."

She did not want to leave before purchasing some of the gemstones for which the country is known. After shopping around the better part of a day and obtaining prices on topazes, opals, amethysts, and green sapphires, Annabella telephoned home to California and spoke with Jane. She asked her mother to obtain comparative prices of the stones at retail prices in the United States. She was thinking of making a major purchase with the balance of her travel money, about $1,600, and she wanted to know if the profit potential was there for resale.

Pleased to hear her daughter's voice after several days of no contact, Jane peppered her with maternal questions. Her health was fine, answered Annabella. No trouble. Money holding out. "How do you like New Delhi?" asked Jane.

"Lots of temples," answered Annabella. "But all in all —a hell-hole."

And what was the next stop? California?

Bangkok, probably. But she might make a quick side trip to Katmandu. She had met a pair of Australian girls who were headed for Nepal on a bus, and it would be inappropriate to be this close and not take a look at the once forbidden country in the bosom of Mount Everest.

"Then be careful," urged Jane. "And have fun. And hurry home!"

"I'm on my way, Mama," answered Annabella. "Love to everybody."

When she hung up, contented by the call, Jane found her atlas and searched for Katmandu. She found Nepal just above India, tucked between the subcontinent and China, rather like a wedge driven between two great boulders to keep them from colliding. She touched the page. She both envied Annabella's great adventure—and felt a cold finger of fear brush against her cheek.

CHAPTER TWENTY-EIGHT

The town of Chanthaburi is completely off the tourist path in Thailand, secreted near the border of Cambodia with a surprising air of the American colonial South hanging over it like a mistake of geography. Old wooden houses with curlicues and carved lacy porches are whitewashed, with verandas fitting for the late afternoon and tall drinks. Rubber plantations and orchards of tropical fruits are foundations of the economy, and the women of the area are exceptionally beautiful, with a pinkish tinge to their almond skin.

But the lure for Charles Sobhraj in the autumn of 1975 was to be found in a lush and steamy primeval jungle just outside the city, where the blur of a brilliantly colored macaw and the screams of feuding gibbons in groves of bamboo and mango arrest the eye and ear. Here are the ancient jewel mines of Chanthaburi, scarcely changed by technology since time began. Half-naked men dig pits about six feet deep and ten feet across in gummy red clay soil, after first clearing a thicket of flaming rhododendron, tea trees, tapioca bushes, and wild orchids. The pits are filled with a foot or two of water, and the men—their skins as red as the clay—leap inside, kneeling in the gumbo and patiently scooping up basketfuls of rocks and earth. The contents are strained through bamboo sieves and the trained eye can discover among the dirty pebbles an occasional stone that, when cut and polished, becomes a ruby, or a sapphire, or garnets the color of blood. While the men and their sons work, the women—mostly fat, mostly wrapped in bright silk shirts—sit under the trees singing, gossiping, and polishing the stones. The fortunate tourist who can find the mines is instantly set upon by the women the moment he leaves his car, exhorted to purchase small boxes filled with remarkable bargains. A two-carat green sapphire can be bought for ten dollars, a good ruby of at least one carat for as little as three hundred.

Charles often left Bangkok after midnight and drove the six hours by darkness, both to avoid the frightening daytime traffic, and to be on hand for the first gem sales of the day. If he found little of interest at the mines themselves, or felt the fat women were in an exorbitant mood, he drove into the city of Chanthaburi, to a crowded strip of jewelry stores not unlike an exotic version of New York City's diamond district. Here the stakes were higher, for the stones had been cleaned and transformed into rings and necklaces at this stage. But even so, prices were considerably less than in Bangkok, and Charles usually returned to the capital with a tempting array of glitter. He told Marie-Andrée that if he could amass between $25,000 and $40,000 in capital, he could build an empire with the cornerstone at the primitive mines of Chanthaburi. He would guarantee the independent miners to purchase a fixed percentage of the stones pulled raw from the red clay, then establish a courier service to Bangkok, where his central office would be located. There, craftsmen would cut and polish and fashion the stones into jewelry to tempt women all over Europe, then the United States. As she heard this tale, Marie-Andrée nodded with barest interest. She had heard these schemes and pipe dreams before. And despite their grandiosity, the only reality Marie-Andrée knew was that she often had to prepare dinner for as many as fourteen people, then clean up, then fall wearily into bed—alone. Charles rarely slept with her, if indeed he slept anywhere. He kept his own hours, his own secrets, permitted no one entry, entertained no questions as to his whereabouts.

Often Marie-Andrée pressed to learn if he was still seeing May, and the answer was always a sharp "No." But one afternoon following lunch at the apartment, Marie-Andrée followed him, and Charles proceeded directly to the shopping arcade where May was employed. As she watched them embrace, two possibilities occurred. One was to get the hell out of Bangkok, somehow, and back to Canada. The other was to stumble into a movie palace across the street and sit in the cold darkness and weep. Which she did.

A new face appeared for dinner one night and Marie-Andrée at first mistook him to be a customer. He was an Indian from New Delhi named Ajay Chowdhury. He was polite, quiet, sexy, and devilishly handsome. Charles introduced him as "an old friend" but was not specific as to when and where they had met. Perhaps it had been an hour ago, perhaps five years. One never knew. Over the next few days, Ajay quickly moved in and became second-in-command and permanent shadow to Charles. Marie-Andrée gleaned a few bits of biographical detail. Ajay said he was the son of a Delhi foreign car importer whose life veered toward the upper class. Well educated, Ajay was an apparent ne'er-do-well who had dabbled in a dozen Delhi schemes—modeling, movie work, fashion, a hint of gigolo service when funds were low—but had failed in all. Now he was going into "partnership" with Charles, or Alain Gauthier, as he knew him, and the two men were inseparable. When they left the apartment together, Marie-Andrée's heart stirred, for the two were a striking pair, both with lean, lithe bodies in tight trousers, perfectly sculptured hair, Ajay taller and seemingly stronger, but Charles clearly the commander-in-chief, proud to have such an attractive adjutant.

And as the weeks crept by, Ajay was kind to Marie-Andrée. He sensed her despair and he always had a compliment for her food, or her appearance, or her looks, which the mirror told her were haggard and aging. If Charles noticed the attention Ajay paid to Marie-Andrée he did not remark on it. Probably he was glad to have another man pay court to the nagging Canadian woman. Or perhaps he had dispatched orders for Ajay to do so.

In Istanbul, most of the city's twenty thousand Jews live in a congested ghetto near the Galata Tower, known to tourists as the Fire Tower, a lighthouse of sorts that

dates at least as far back as the Genoese era of the fourteenth century, possibly as early as a Roman emperor in
the sixth century. For hundreds of years men were employed to stand watch twenty-four hours a day, looking
for fires, an important task since sixty major fires have
ravaged Istanbul to the point of total destruction in its
history. The Fire Tower has been a prison and an astro-
nomical observatory, and once, in the seventeenth century,
a man strapped on eagle's wings and, soaring hopefully
off the summit, tried unsuccessfully to fly across the Bosporus.

The Jews of Istanbul, clustered about the Fire Tower,
make up but a small fraction of the city's three million
residents, but they are traditionally hard workers, respectable citizens, and dominant in commerce, science and
engineering. Their existence up until the end of World
War II was a tenuous one, their history recounting perse-
cutions, fires set by arsonists that leveled their district, and
the threat during 1943 that the Germans were planning
to invade. At the last minute, Hitler changed plans and
moved his forces to Bulgaria for entry into Russia. During
the war, Jews were subject to a heavy tax levied specifically against them, and those who could not pay were
exiled to a village in Anatolia.

Today, Jews manage to live more or less unmolested in
Istanbul, though their forty-three synagogues do not com-
pare in grandeur to the 510 mosques, and their money is
usually hidden. But, then, few visible signs of great wealth
can be seen in Istanbul. The rich traditionally conceal
their gold, and some of the wealthiest families in the city
live on streets that also house beggars and toilet cleaners.

Leon and Rachel Hakim were typical of the Sephardic
Jews of Istanbul. Early in the twentieth century, Leon emigrated to the capital from a fishing village and at the age
of twenty found hard labor as a pushcart peddler in the
garment district. There he hawked his wares—cheap shirts,
ties, scarves—in the crowded cobblestone streets that make
the Sultan Hamam bazaar an impenetrable maze to the
tourist. Hundreds of thousands of shoppers each day
patronize the market, and within the air is ripe with the
odors of great wheels of white feta cheese a yard across,
of rich tobaccos and coffees, of newly slaughtered lambs

dripping blood and hanging from hooks. In the vaulted recesses of the ceiling, doves fly about, sometimes darting down for a nervy theft of rice from the huge burlap bags of the grocers.

Leon Hakim married a shopgirl named Rachel, who bore him two sons and a daughter. Life progressed orderly and well for the Hakims, Leon working his way from the pushcart to stock boy for a shirtmaker, to tailor, and, finally, to ownership of his own business. He opened a shop in the bowels of the market, down one flight of stairs, then another, then zigzagging half a dozen more, where he sewed inexpensive suits, often for Anatolian workers for marriage or burial. Leon raised his family in the shadow of the Galata Fire Tower, and he obeyed the customs and traditions of the Jewish society that had endured for a millennium. To Leon Hakim, the most valuable currency of all was respect, and he lectured Rachel and the three children on its imperative nature. "We are nothing if we do not have the respect of our neighbors," he often said. "If a man is president of Turkey and has not the respect of his people, then he is a failure." Respect was best obtained by following the traditions of the centuries, staying within the boundaries of behavior laid down by the elders of the ancient tribe. Leon expected his children to be quiet, obedient, thrifty, industrious, and—that word again—respectful. His expectation was not unusual among the Jews of Istanbul. Long ago they learned that prudence dictated keeping a low profile and becoming so accomplished in certain fields of endeavor that their *Jewishness* would be tolerated.

The first son, Israel, was of the mold and would one day become Mr. Solid Citizen, complete with pinstripe suit, a talent for business so blessed that one family shop would swell to five, and a tranquil home life with wife and many children. And Leon and Rachel's daughter, Rebecca, would walk on the same path of tradition and obeisance.

Only the second son tore Leon's heart and made him sit in shame among the elders and weep bitterly. The boy was Vitali—his name meant "life"—and not until he was twelve years old did he give off clues that he heard different melodies. Vitali was, in his formative years, normal, loving, obedient, in his place early for Friday night services and supper, and seemingly content even with the traditional stifling of Jewish youngsters in his community. He went to synagogue school for five years, earned good marks, and worked part-time at the family business. But on the precipice of manhood he stunned his parents by announcing, "I will not go to school anymore. I don't want to study." No amount of family persuasion, threats, and outrage could alter the boy's stand. Just when Leon was at the breaking point and preparing to banish the recalcitrant son to a remote family village, the elder son, Israel, stepped forward as peacemaker.

Israel had just opened his own tailor shop and proposed hiring his kid brother as errand boy. "He can learn the business, make a little money, and maybe the work will be so hard he would like to go back to school," suggested Israel to his father, who waved a weary hand in agreement. He would do anything to dry Rachel's tears, for she had been sobbing copiously since Vitali's bombshell. "I don't understand," she wailed. "This boy is good, he is ours, he is in the family, why won't he go to school and do like all good boys do?"

Vitali worked for three years in the tailor shop, running errands, darting through the market and "borrowing," as neatly as the doves an apple or a snitch of feta cheese from an otherwise busy merchant, pressing pants, learning to cut fabric. When Israel was inducted into the Turkish Army and was forced to turn his store over to a trusted friend to run in his absence, Vitali quit. He would not labor for a stranger. Now almost fifteen, he persuaded his father to send him to the mother country of Israel to live with distant relatives. That lasted for a time, then he returned to Istanbul. And back to Israel. And back and forth, coming and going, malcontent wherever he stopped during the middle teens of his life.

In retrospect, the Hakim family believes Vitali "turned bad" when he fell under the influence of a boyhood friend. They met at a summer resort on an island near Istanbul, where over a long season they let their hair grow long, were introduced to hashish, put on American blue jeans, and boogied to Western rock and roll. When Vitali appeared at his parents' home at the end of the summer in his new guise, Leon went straightaway to the temple to pray after helping his fainted wife to her bed.

At the age of seventeen, Vitali told his brother that he was leaving Turkey for good, bound for Paris. His head was full of fantasies, a cheap commodity at the fleabag hotels near the Blue Mosque, where the hippies slept on rooftops in clouds of thick hashish. Israel knew that his brother had been spending too much time there, and he tried to reason with Vitali. If the boy fled to Paris, he was forfeiting the right to what was turning into a substantial family fortune. Their father was doing well enough to move his family out of the tiny flat in the ghetto into a luxurious apartment building which he purchased near the heart of the city. It had green marble windowsills and hardwood floors and a gleaming marble staircase washed by servants who strapped sopping wet towels to their feet and walked slowly up and down.

"That doesn't interest me," said Vitali. "Istanbul is a dead end. Paris interests me. And maybe New York."

"But your life is in Istanbul," Israel would remember saying. "The family is here, so you *must* be here. You are part of something that is bigger than you. No one has ever broken the family apart."

Vitali shook his head. He refused to stay in Turkey. He rejected a life controlled by ancient laws. He could not spend another day worrying about what some ancient "graybeards said three thousand years ago."

"What are you looking for?" pleaded Israel.

"Freedom," said Vitali.

After that Vitali Hakim left Istanbul, mumbling words of love and apology to his mother, who was already dressed in black, and to his father, sitting dazed on the living-room sofa. When the door slammed, he called out in a voice that echoed after his second son, down the washed marble staircase, "Why are you disgracing yourself and your family? We are good people. We have *respect!*"

For a time, an occasional postcard drifted in from Paris, then London, finally New York, where Vitali played guitar at a night club in Greenwich Village and seemed to be living with a girl named Hannah, who studied white

magic and made shawls embroidered with ancient symbols.
Scant information was to be found on the postcards, rarely
more than "Am enjoying New York. Cold and snow coming. Love, your son." But Rachel treasured each card,
reading them, kissing them, keeping them locked in a box
that she kept at the back of her armoire. Leon feigned
disinterest, but Rachel knew he waited as eagerly as she
for the next meager dispatch. Six years slowly slipped
away.

One afternoon in the early 1970s, a surprise telephone
call ruptured the orderly routine of Leon and Rachel
Hakim's home. Their long absent son, Vitali, was at the
Istanbul airport. He faced a long layover between planes.
Would his parents receive him for a brief visit? Rachel
dropped the phone in tears, falling to her knees in grateful prayer. Leon grabbed the receiver and shouted welcome, then asked if Vitali could come to the apartment
after sunset so that neighbors would not see the prodigal
son. Vitali was not offended; he laughed and agreed. But
when, under the cover of darkness, he arrived, Vitali discovered both of his parents waiting at the curb, eager to
smother him with kisses and hugs. A feast was waiting
upstairs. Rachel proudly looked up at the windows of the
apartment building on the ancient street in Istanbul and
knew that the neighbors were looking down at the homecoming. "My son!" she cried. "My son is home."
Vitali stayed only for a few hours, explaining that he
had important business in Spain and could not dally in
Turkey no matter how much he enjoyed visiting with his
parents. They were gravely disappointed, but Leon had
spent much of the day warning his wife that the boy
would be different, that six years would have wrought considerable change in the thin teen-ager who left home so
long ago. Vitali now wore his hair long. It fell on his
shoulders. His mustache was not neatly trimmed in the
fashion of Turkish businessmen, but thick and sweeping
and fierce. He was a little overweight, with a potbelly,
but his chest and arms were thickly muscled. One earlobe
bore a gold ring, and around his neck hung necklaces.
His shirt was printed with astrological signs. He spoke of
the many things he had done—cabaret performer, magi-

cian (he made Turkish cigarettes appear from behind his mother's ears), poet, tour guide in Paris. He could speak English now, and French, and pretty fair Spanish. He was going into the "import-export" business and would stand to make millions within a few years if his plans were realized. He was funny and tender and loving, and when he was gone—as abruptly as he had come—Rachel felt as if she had been blown about by a storm, but one whose force she would gladly bear again. Leon sat at the window of the building he owned and watched the taxi take his son away. He sat there for a long time, before Rachel tenderly insisted that he take his soft tears to bed.

Several more years passed. Leon Hakim grew heavy and gray and even richer. His wife, conversely, grew frail and spent most of her time in religious activities. Grandchildren filled their lives. They were looked up to in the Jewish community of Istanbul and men made deference to the Hakims when they walked together on the streets. Rarely did anyone speak Vitali's name. The boy, wherever he was, was nearly thirty. Israel, the Hakims' older son, had received one sorrowful piece of information, but he did not share it with his parents. A police report came to his attention that indicated Vitali had been arrested in Spain on a drug charge. Apparently a substantial quantity of hashish and cocaine had been discovered in his possession. But as it was a first offense, Vitali was not sent to prison. Israel debated with himself for some time before deciding that the old people simply could not bear this news.

Ibiza, the sun-washed island in the western Mediterranean off the coast of Spain, counted among it's crops, in the early 1970s, dried apricots and figs, salt removed from seawater, magnificent fish for the kettles of Madrid and Barcelona, and "hippies." Few of the thousands of young people who flocked to the island were hippies in the classic sense, but any young person who arrived in Ibiza with longish hair, a backpack, and an air of non-commitment to anything save the sun and exotic cigarettes was immediately categorized and often hassled by the police. This is not to say there were no dark shadows on the

island. Ibiza was a magic center for the sale and purchase
of drugs. Historically, smugglers enjoyed its strategic position. Rumor often suggests that to this day white slavers
operate about the port, engaging down-and-out Western
women to serve as "*au pair* girls" in Arab countries. Not
until the contract is signed and the destination reached do
the girls supposedly discover they have been sold into
prostitution.

Among the young women of Ibiza in 1975 was a quiet
and talented French girl named Charmayne Carrou, who
had come to the island in search of the sun and who had
stayed to try and establish a dressmaking business. Charmayne was clever with her needle and sketches, and she
was enchanted by the bright Spanish cottons that could
be fashioned into billowing blouses and long hostess skirts,
with buttons made from bits of shells or fragments of
topaz. It was her intention to sell the creations at beach
boutiques, but after months of failing to establish a
merchandising outlet, Charmayne was not only unhappy
but broke.

Originally Charmayne had come to Ibiza at the invitation of a distant cousin, Zazi, who was the family scandal.
More or less disowned in Paris, Zazi was living unmarried
with a drug dealer in Ibiza and was celebrated for parties
that were considered failures if anyone went home before
dawn. Charmayne's parents were worried when their
daughter went away to visit Zazi, but they were reasonably sure that the values they had taught Charmayne
would help her resist the temptations of Zazi's hedonism.

In the larger sense, they were right. Charmayne had
little use for drugs, save an occasional puff at a marijuana
cigarette, and she had no interest at all in selling grass on
the beach—as Zazi once suggested. Charmayne believed
in the ethic of work, honest work, and she was not even
sexually promiscuous in a community where it was almost
de rigueur. One night, dining with Zazi and the drug
dealer, who was quickly falling out of favor, Charmayne
mentioned that her dress business was a flop—and that
she was bereft of funds. Sadly, she could see only one
road open—a return to Paris.

Dressing her face in best "I told you so" expression,
Zazi repeated her oft-remarked belief that Ibiza was a land

where the fruits of opportunity fairly fell from the trees. Yet Charmayne was so stupid she went hungry. Fortunes were waiting to be made on this island! As Zazi orated, she lolled on soft, plump cushions from where she conducted business, slept, and made love to a variety of partners. On her arms and about her neck were several pounds of gold jewelry. Recently she had taken to wearing clown-white makeup with rouge circles on her cheeks. The effect was weird, but then, so was Zazi. She also played, expertly, a small harp and liked to be encountered posing, as models did for the old masters' portraits of courtesans.

Charmayne demurred, as she always did, for she was powered by a substantial fuel called Catholic guilt. And though she no longer made confession or went to mass, it was impossible for her to become part of Zazi's crowd and schemes. Or so she believed. Just at the moment when Charmayne was about to be thrown out of her tiny flat for non-payment of rent, and was looking for any kind of legitimate work to sustain her presence in Ibiza, she went to dinner *chez* Zazi and by midnight had become enamored of the charms of a new man who had appeared in her cousin's entourage. His name was hard to remember, so much so that she surreptitiously wrote it down. Vitali Hakim. And he was less hippie than a full-blooded man with an enormous appetite for life. He spoke louder than anyone in the room; in a rich bass voice he sang the lyrics to every song that came on the record player, spoke in French and English and Spanish and cursed in Turkish. He delivered instant horoscopes to everyone in the room and warned Charmayne that Libras—her sign—were entering a period of dangerous passion. Later he made a live baby chick appear on the platter that had held a roasted chicken. Vitali Hakim was the most overwhelming, consuming—and entertaining—man that Charmayne Carrou had ever encountered. She was so smitten that she failed to recognize the traffic signals going on between the Turk and Zazi.

Within days they were living together. Charmayne sewed new shirts for Vitali which he wore while playing guitar at a joint on the beach that attracted young tourists and old fishermen. Each night Charmayne sat dream-like and listened to his songs, and those that were delivered in

French, and dealt with love, seemed to be performed with only her in mind.

In deep autumn, 1975, when the sun eased, and the winds blew colder, and few tourists save hearty Germans were left on the beaches, Vitali quit his job and spent the daylight hours helping Charmayne. She had sold two blouses to an Italian woman who had expressed an interest in representing Charmayne's creations, and now the French girl was hurriedly trying to finish a dozen more so that they could go to Milan. One afternoon Charmayne went to her workroom and was shocked to discover that her needles, fabrics, and works-in-progress were missing. She stared dumbfounded and started to search the room, when Vitali stepped up behind her laughing. "Enough of the sewing," he said. "Let's get married. And I intend to *buy* you a wedding gown."

Charmayne was flustered. She had known the impetuous Turk for only a few weeks. He seemed as dependable as the wind. How could she possibly even introduce this wild but gentle man to her parents in Paris, so conservative that France in effect ceased to exist with the death of Charles de Gaulle?

Choosing the first weapon of argument she could summon—searching for a way to delay rather than to refuse—Charmayne sensibly pointed out that neither of them had any money. Quite true, agreed Vitali. But he knew how to remedy that. In a few days he would leave on a business trip for the Far East. A "connection" was waiting. His voice turned serious. It would be beneficial if Charmayne would fly to Bangkok a bit later on and rendezvous with him there.

The Far East! Bangkok! It was coming too fast for Charmayne to absorb. She sat down and tried to think. At base, she was a simple girl, unsophisticated in the ways of the world of Zazi and Vitali. Finally she asked, *if* she went to Bangkok, what was she supposed to *do* there?

Once in Bangkok, answered Vitali, the two of them would meet, have a wonderful holiday, see the sights, then fly back home separately—either to Ibiza, or Madrid, or Paris, or possibly Rome. That was to be determined. Was that *all*? asked Charmayne. Vitali shook his head. The possibility existed that she might have to courier a small packet of gemstones that Vitali would be purchasing in Bangkok. He described the mission so glibly—refusing to fill in the holes—that it took a while for Charmayne to catch on that she was being asked to smuggle jewelry into Europe. And when the revelation dawned, she quickly refused.

Vitali turned on the salesmanship. The job was routine, he insisted. And it would be so lucrative that Charmayne could open her dress business *and* get married and never have to worry about money. This was a one-shot, he said. It was not to be repeated.

When Charmayne, in her confusion and worry over losing her man, finally agreed, Vitali kissed her enthusiastically and bolted out of the apartment to make plans. But his first stop was at Zazi's, where the Turk kissed *her* with considerably more passion, murmuring that the scheme was working, and that baby cousin Charmayne, with a face so innocent she could lead the celestial choir, was going to smuggle a few gemstones and several pounds of morphine powder in her luggage—if the connection from Burma were achieved.

Zazi, who was putting up seed money for this venture, smiled and assured Vitali that it would work. The planetary signs were in excellent order. Then she asked Vitali to lie beside her on the pillows while she played Nana Mouskouri melodies on her harp.

Jennie Bolliver landed safely in Bangkok and struggled through customs, explaining in sign language that the garden hose and other oddments in her baggage were meant for use at a monastery in Nepal. She crammed into a bus and at the central terminal bargained with a motor scooter taxi to take her to the Malaysia Hotel. In Hong Kong, an American girl had told her of the Bangkok hostelry that catered to the young and budget-minded. Once there, she paid six dollars for a single room and immediately found two new friends—a boy and girl from Atlanta who were studying Oriental poetry.

Quickly they set out to explore Bangkok, and quickly they became lost, trying to find the Wat Po, Bangkok's greatest temple and monastery. Suddenly the sounds of

music and laughter and celebration were heard nearby. It
sounded like a parade, and the three Americans ran to
see. A procession was in progress, a ceremonial pathway
to the monastery, led by a crowd of people in the throes
of a joyous party. A hundred Thais were snaking their
way down the street, prancing as if at a pre-Lenten carnival. A makeshift band was tooting inexpertly but robustly
on trumpets and flutes; others were banging riotously on
drums. And in the center of the merriment, a strange contradiction. An enormous umbrella, composed of brilliant
orange and red and lime silks, with golden fringe, was
held aloft to shield the blazing sun from the newly bald
and gleaming head of a young man, perhaps eighteen. He
was dressed in white robes and was borne on the shoulders
of his friends. Flowers and candies and fruits were being
thrown gently at him. The spectacle was rich with color
and happiness. But the young man's face was frozen, ex-
pressionless, in a trance. Immediately Jennie figured out
what was happening. "He's going to become a monk, and
he's on his way to the temple to take his vows," she told
her Georgia friends. When the monk-to-be passed, Jennie
bowed in respect and made the traditional Buddhist sign
of greeting. "He doesn't look too happy about it," said the
girl from Georgia.

Jennie disagreed. The young man was meditating and
his spirit was flowing over the crowd. Impulsively, Jennie
ran and joined the crowd, winding down the boulevard
until at last the great spires of Wat Po came into view.
Then Jennie dropped out, squeezing her way to a nearby
patch of grass. She sat down under a tree, and when her
friends found her, they thought she was ill. A curtain of
gloom had descended over the vibrant young woman.
Jennie declined an offer of aid, saying she was only tired
and needed to catch her breath.

The group proceeded into the temple grounds and
watched the novice monk disappear into a sea of saffron-
robed monks who welcomed him. And, with awe, they
gazed upon the Reclining Buddha, stretching one hundred
fifty feet in length, forty feet high, covered with a crust
of gold. Jennie remained somber for the rest of the afternoon. Her new friends from Georgia were disturbed; they

could not have known that Jennie was measuring her intended commitment against that which the young Thai boy had just made. The enormity of her decision must have been weighing heavily at that moment.

The next day, the two Georgians left for Calcutta. They exchanged addresses and mentioned looking up Jennie in Katmandu should their journey take them to the Himalayas. Jennie was alone, in a confusing and exotic land. She spent another day inspecting the various shrines, Bangkok being a city where Buddhism is more than a religion; it is an integral part of life. Each house, no matter how modest, has a miniature shrine in the front yard, some no bigger than a birdhouse, with tiny carved teak elephants attending Lord Buddha. Monks are everywhere, setting forth each morning with a begging bowl—although their religion forbids importuning. At one great temple, Jennie counted fifty-three images of Buddha in the courtyards, and at the Royal Grand Palace, she was stunned by the beauty of the Emerald Buddha, guarded by golden demons and monsters. And she wished that she could sell one of the bejeweled treasures to buy food and books for the youngsters at Kopan.

It was soon time to leave. On her last day, she packed and was sitting in her room when the air-conditioning sputtered and died. The October heat quickly turned her chamber into an oven. Since several hours remained before it would be time to board the airport bus, Jennie went downstairs to the lobby. There it was usually cool, with breezes drifting in, people lounging around, anxious to swap travel adventures. Jennie bought a lemonade from the coffee shop and sat down in a cracked plastic armchair. Presumably she did not notice the two men standing nearby and watching until they came up and took other chairs adjoining hers.

One of the men was East Indian, with a beautiful mustache and a sensuous air. The other, shorter, muscular, in horn-rimmed glasses, seemed Oriental or Eurasian. Both were sexy, the kind of dark-skinned men who had often tempted her. On the morrow, Jennie's intent was to cloister herself in a monastery clinging to the foothills of the Himalayas and renounce forever baser thoughts. But at

this moment, the two forces must have dueled within her
—the spiritual and the carnal. Eternal foes.

One of the two men gave Jennie a business card. She
read it and put it in her handbag. It said: "A. Gauthier,
Gem Dealer."

CHAPTER TWENTY-NINE

"Alain and Monique's apartment is like the Gare de Lyon," observed Belle to her husband Raoul, hearing music pour down from the fifth floor. "So many people coming and going!" Rare was the night when a party did not take place in the penthouse abode of "A. Gauthier, Gem Dealer." From experience, Marie-Andrée had learned to prepare casseroles and ragouts that could be stretched to feed whomever Charles brought home, as well as the permanent boarders who filled the adjoining flat.

On the night of October 15, 1975—as the events would one day be constructed—the unqualified hit of the party was an American girl whom Charles and Ajay, his shadow, had brought home. Her name was Jennie, from California, and she was young and tanned and vibrant. Her motor was racing on this night. She laughed louder than anyone in the room, drew from a repertoire of risqué jokes and wisecracks that even when translated into French made their impact, and turned the record player up to deafening volume. She dragged an unwilling Ajay onto the dance floor and taught him the "bump," which was, she announced, America's hottest new dance craze. Everyone laughed as Jennie aimed her hips at the slim Indian, then whopped her body against his. Later, Jennie tried in vain to get Charles or "Alain," as she knew him, onto the floor, but he declined, preferring to sit Buddha-like and scrutinize his guests. Of course Marie-Andrée did her scrutinizing as well when the two men turned up with a lively and very

young single American girl, but dismissed her soon thereafter as not a serious rival for Charles' affection. He did not
like hippies, he had told her that many times, and this
California newcomer in her ragged jeans and sweater did
not appear to be Charles' type at all. The main things
Jennie had going for her, it seemed, were her youth—she
could not have been much more than twenty—and a wild
abandon.

By late evening, the party was drenched in wine and
redolent of hashish smoke. The puppy, Frankie, yelped
enthusiastically and nipped at dancing heels. Napoleon
the monkey hung from a drapery rod, chattering. Dominique had risen from his eternal sickbed and was happily
on the sofa, probably grateful for a diversion from throwing up. His innards were still bedeviled; each morning
Charles appeared with a spoonful of whitish medicine
which he identified as Kaopectate. But the curious thing,
Dominique failed to notice, was that after taking the
medicine he grew worse. And weaker. The other two
French boys, ex-cops Yannick and Jacques, had fallen
similarly ill for several days after they moved into the
adjoining apartment. But one morning Charles pronounced
that they were well, and he discontinued their white medicine. Lo and behold, they felt better. Immediately Charles
dispatched orders, and the new men's duties ranged from
helping Marie-Andrée clean up, to shopping for food, to
going out in the city and looking for prospective gem
customers. On this night, they were as young and as
exuberant as Jennie, and they all danced as members of
the same tribe.

Others drifted in during the memorable evening. May
appeared and ignored the icy look on Marie-Andrée's face.
With her was a Thai nurse who had just been granted a
visa for immigration to be United States, where she would
go to work for a Southern hospital. That was cause for
celebration. With all the new women about, Marie-Andrée
sat on the arm of Charles' chair and put her hand firmly
on his shoulder, as if establishing territorial claim. "Don't
be silly, *chérie*," someone overheard Charles whispering,
picking up on the hostility Marie-Andrée felt for May,
"she's just working for me—like everybody else. Don't
be jealous. It's all business."

Loosening up, Charles quickly dominated his party like a floor show emcee. He read palms, taking a bit longer with Jennie and playing as if he did not notice her hand was moist and trembling as he analyzed her lines. Turning to Ajay, he did a little macho strutting, instructing the Indian to hit him in the stomach—full force!—to demonstrate the strength of his flat, karate-honed musculature. Ajay obliged, but he did not hit hard enough. "Again!" commanded Charles. And again. Fourteen times Ajay slammed his fist into Charles' stomach, and not once did the host show a flicker of pain or discontent. Everyone applauded and cheered—and perhaps feared, for that was the purpose. Refilling wineglasses and making sure everyone was having a good time, Charles was an attentive host, sipping only fruit juice himself, and always studying faces, reading them like maps to hidden treasure.

Toward midnight, Charles said—and several people heard him—"I like this American girl! She makes me laugh. It would be fun to take her to Pattaya." And where was Pattaya? someone asked. The tropical paradise on which dreams are floated, with the most beautiful beaches in the world. Perhaps the notion tempted Jennie, but on the morn she was to leave for Katmandu, headed for a life that no one in this sensuous apartment could have imagined.

· Patpong, the raw scar in Bangkok's midsection that sells sex and danger, crams into a few blocks wall-to-wall strip bars whose barkers stand in the doorway exhorting passersby to glimpse into the smoky darkness and espy nude female bodies undulating under blue spotlights, massage parlors of remarkable cleanliness and Miami Beach gilt and plush crimson décor where beautiful young women wear crisp, starched nurses' uniforms while sitting on tiers —like a church choir—behind one-way glass. These birds in a sterile coop watch television with bored expressions until a customer who has been peering at them through the glass makes a selection and a number is called.

The Thai military government periodically cracks down on Patpong and the strippers drape a little strategic gauze over the most merchandisable portions of their anatomies, but there always remain hidden places down dark alleys,

or behind warehouses where the shows continue uncensored—not only sexy, but cast in evil. It was at one of
these that Jennie was seen in attendance near midnight
on the night of October 15 in the company of two Asian
men.

At this club, a young Thai man with a perfectly sculptured body appeared and shucked his trousers to stand
completely nude before the audience. Already he was
sexually aroused, and when a young Thai girl of exquisite
beauty floated toward him in a diaphanous wrap, he tore
it from her body and began the act of love. The couple
performed public sex on a makeshift stage for more than
half an hour, the man disengaging from time to time to
demonstrate that his erection was genuine—and enduring.
And as a finale, he lifted the girl, facing him, her legs
wrapped about his waist, and carried her down into the
audience. There he stopped at each table and bent his
partner backwards so that she reclined among the customers' drink glasses. She invited each patron to stroke
her breasts or examine, as close up as desired, the penile
thrusts of the young man. In her mouth she carried bills
of currency placed there by approving customers.

Then the lights went out, and the presumption was that
the show had concluded. But there was to be more. Drums
from offstage began to throb and a deep blue pinspot
abruptly picked out a wicker basket that had been placed
onstage in the darkness. The basket quivered slightly; life
was within. Then the same girl returned, this time wearing
flashy sequins pasted to her breasts—nothing else—and
she removed the lid of the basket with the respect of a
religious celebrant. Kneeling before the basket, she beseeched it with her entwined arms. A cobra rose obediently from the container as gasps swept over the room.
The spotlight and the tempo changed to hot red. For a
moment, the snake seemed bewildered, its eyes glistening
like black opals in the theatrical lighting, its tongue fork-
ing out toward the girl. Then the serpent began to sway
in time with the melody of a flute that floated from the
darkness. The girl crept closer, still on her knees, thrusting her breasts out proudly so that they were but a few
inches from the great snake. It made an occasional move
toward the breasts, but always stopped short of a strike.

As if to dispel speculation that the snake was hypnotized by the sparkling sequins on her nipples, the girl cautiously stripped them away and offered her naked breasts— recently stroked by the customers—to the cobra. In that position she stayed for a time of paralyzing suspense, the audience not daring to breathe, then she slowly withdrew, pushing backwards cautiously on her knees until she was out of range. Without bowing, she disappeared into darkness.

Applause burst from the crowd, but the spectacle had still one more scene—an epilogue of horror. A wooden stake appeared on the stage and to it was lashed a live chicken, its feet tied together by rope and fastened to the stick. As the frightened creature squawked and tried to get away, the snake rose up once more from its basket, as if annoyed to be roused from a nap, and watched the chicken entangling itself in the rope. With mounting irritation, the serpent stared deadly at the noisy fowl, finally shot forward in a blur. Once! Twice! Three times the cobra buried its glistening snout into the screaming chicken. Floundering, the bird fell back and died; the cobra returned to its basket—and the proof was there that the snake had not been milked of venom.

"You have seen that beauty can charm the serpent," said the master of ceremonies in dullish patter that he used each night, "but when beauty is taken away, the serpent kills. Please show your appreciation for this performer as she passes among you. Thank you and good night."

From this point on, in or around the curfew of midnight, litttle else is known for the record. But speculation permits a myriad of possibilities. Perhaps Jennie was loser to the war of sensuality raging within her. Perhaps she had such grave doubts about being able to keep her commitment as a Buddhist nun that she abandoned her plan. Perhaps, as a Buddhist friend in Los Angeles would one day suggest, "She was unable to fight the negative forces and they overwhelmed her. She surrendered to them for one long 'Last Night on the Town.'" Perhaps, as authorities would believe, Jennie was given a drug that made her pliant to the wishes of Charles Sobhraj/Alain Gauthier.

Or, finally, this was where destiny had brought her.

At dawn, as a new, faint sun spread pale light and warmth over the serene Gulf of Thailand, an old man rode his bicycle along a remote beach near Pattaya. He was delivering eggs from his farm to customers. As he pedaled, he glimpsed a young Western woman lying on her back in the shallow water, hardly an inch or two deep, just at the edge of the sand, where the gentle morning tide was washing against her. The old man paused briefly to look, for the young woman wore a flowered bikini and her figure was full and beautiful in the mauve light of the new morning. She seemed to be resting, catching her breath after a vigorous swim. Ah, Western women are strange, he murmured to himself. He went on about his deliveries. His wife would screech at him if he were late getting home.

An hour later, the old man rode back on the same path and for the second time, under full sun, saw the same young woman. She had not moved, and now the stillness of her body was eerie. Waves were building, washing over her immobile face. Her eyes were open; she was staring at the sky. The old egg seller got off his bicycle and timidly approached the girl. When he was but a few feet away, he recognized what had happened and he began to shake as he cried out for help. Before him, almost covered now by the sea, was a young woman lying gracefully on her back, her face composed, her arms outstretched like a crucifix. Bits of shells, gleaming pink and pearl, dotted her body. She was dead.

Police came and made a primitive investigation, hoping that the death would not be serious enough to arouse the bureaucratic attention of Bangkok. Provincial police in Thailand prefer to be left to their own devices. Granted, they did check with Pattaya's major hotels to determine if a guest was missing. Nothing. When they were unable to identify the corpse, some official hurriedly proclaimed "death by accidental drowning" and ordered the remains to be placed in a huge plastic bag and sealed and hastily thrown into a paupers' cemetery. And forgotten.

Many months later, an investigation would finally be conducted, and the body exhumed for autopsy—with considerable problems. The gravediggers had forgotten exactly

where they buried the girl and had to dig several holes
before the right remains were found. In Bangkok, a
pathologist found salt water and sand in the lungs. He
called it "a terrible death." Jennie Bolliver's lifelong fear
of water was well founded. In her last moments of this
life, someone pushed her head beneath the sea and held
it there for a few moments of awful terror—until she
struggled no more, and euphoria took over, and karma
was fulfilled.

A day or two had passed. Marie-Andrée was sunning
beside the apartment house pool when Belle joined her.
The two women rubbed cocoa oil on their darkening limbs
and cooked in the blistering tropical sun. They spoke of
trivial matters, Marie-Andrée rousing on one elbow to
tell about an "amusing" American girl who had enlivened
one of her parties. The girl was a flirt and rather naughty,
gossiped Marie-Andrée. Her name was Jennie and she
had come on strong to every man in the room with her
sexuality.

"Is she still there?" asked Belle, tossing her head toward
the fifth floor.

No, answered Marie-Andrée. Charles said he took the
American girl with him on one of his midnight-to-dawn
Pattaya excursions, but once there she met some hippies
whom she knew and decided to stay. Nothing more was
said. The coming and going of Jennie Bolliver seemed but
a minor event in the frenetic days of apartments 503 and
504. Belle, in fact, paid little attention to Marie-Andrée's
tale. But she would clearly remember Marie-Andrée falling
silent for a long while after telling it and then murmuring,
with great emotion, "All I want to do is go home to
Canada . . . I should never have come here."

"Then why don't you?" wondered Belle.

"I can't," answered Marie-Andrée in a tone that cut
off any more inquiries.

Marie-Andrée wrote in her diary: "Work is setting in
so well that Charles and I must live our life with strangers.
But I accept it, for I swear to myself daily to try by all
means to make him love me. Because my love for him is
so intense. And it grows . . ."

* * *

More people came and went, so many that Belle marveled at the lavish hospitality. "How can Alain afford to wine and dine guests every night?" she asked Raoul. He had no idea, but a feeling persisted that more was going on upstairs than met the eye. "I'd rather you didn't spend so much time with those people," he told his wife. Raoul had heard that Gauthier was banned from entering at least one major Bangkok hotel because the security guards did not like him hustling guests in the lobby and public rooms.

Belle found her husband's remarks silly and ill-founded. Besides, her only interest was Marie-Andrée, or Monique, as she knew her, they both being French-speaking women trying to cope with life in a confusing Asian capital. Their relationship was confined to girl talk, anyway. The price of vegetables and coiffures didn't hurt anybody. But as October peeled into November, and as assorted minor events began to accumulate in Belle's head, she took pause. Unhappily, as a whole they did not set off an alarm bell. Not yet.

Once Belle noticed a pair of handcuffs, a spyglass, walkie-talkies, and binoculars resting on the dresser in Charles' bedroom. She could not resist asking him their use. "For my business," he said, clearly annoyed that Belle would pry. Later he hinted that he was somehow involved in espionage, with a vague reference to Vietnamese rebels who were working to bring about the downfall of the new Communist government. Belle hastened to inform her husband of this new angle of political intrigue, but Raoul scoffed. "He's about as political as that monkey in diapers," said Raoul, who once again warned his wife that she should not get involved with the curious upstairs tenants.

Then there were the passports. One morning Charles left the door of his portable safe open momentarily, and Belle glimpsed inside while Marie-Andrée was busy preparing coffee. She saw what appeared to be several passports, of different nationalities. There was also an open box of gemstones, most of them rubies.

Belle let it ride for a few days, then she ventured to ask Marie-Andrée why her boy friend's safe contained so many passports. A flicker of what Belle took to be either fear or

annoyance crossed her friend's face. "Ask him," said
Marie-Andrée. "He uses them for travel, I think."

And there were always the sick people. Dominique, who
had become part of the household two months earlier, was
a little better, though twenty-five pounds lighter than the
day he had met the couple at the resaurant in Chiang Mai.
He had finally stopped taking Charles' medicine, although
each morning he pretended to drink the small glass of
white liquid that his host brought to his room. Dominique
had managed to slip out of the apartment one day and
purchase his own Kaopectate. This he was taking instead
of Charles' doses. In early November he asked Charles to
return his passport, but the request was dismissed brusquely.
"You're not well enough to travel," said Charles. "You
can drop dead of tropical diseases if your body doesn't
have enough strength to fight them."

The two other Frenchmen, Yannick and Jacques, suffered tossing stomachs from time to time, but they were
not sick long enough to still their desire to work for Charles
and do his bidding, be it chauffeuring him about Bangkok
in a rented brown Toyota, or cooking when Marie-Andrée
was too weary to feed another pickup dozen on half an
hour's notice, or washing down both apartments regularly
with a strong lye cleanser to rid the odors of sickness.
Their goals were to amass $1,000 each to purchase air-
plane tickets for Paris and to repay Charles for his hospitality.

"Your friend Gauthier likes to play the Big Boss," observed Raoul one night after he went upstairs to extricate
Belle from a party. "He reminds me of a movie gangster.
Edward G. Robinson, maybe. He's got a nice wife—
Monique—to show the customers and prove how domestic
he is. He's got bodyguards, he's got pets, he's got mistresses,
he sits up there giving orders and acting mysterious. As
far as I'm concerned, he's phony. And I wish you'd stay
away from him."

Belle made a face of annoyance and went to bed—
pointedly—alone.

Later Belle chastised her diminutive husband for imagining dark scenarios. Alain and Monique seemed to her
like nothing more than a nice young couple trying to make
a go of it in a difficult place. True, their life was a bit

unorthodox. But what was "normal" anyway in the Far East?

In mid-November, two more young people became residents of the penthouse. They were Canadians and when they arrived, escorted by Charles, they both looked dreadfully ill. "What are you, a witch or something?" asked Belle flippantly of Charles when she noticed the new couple struggling to the toilet every few minutes.

"Why do you say that?" demanded Charles, trying to look amused but failing to cool the heat in his voice.

"Oh, I don't know," quickly backtracked Belle. "Just kidding around. Every time somebody comes to stay here, they get sick, that's all."

"Well, this is Bangkok," snapped Charles. "I can't help it if people get sick. I'm trying to help them."

Taking her friend aside, Marie-Andrée warned Belle not to tease Alain with words like "witch." He did not appreciate such remarks, and besides, it seemed cruel considering all he was doing for strangers in a strange land. "So sorry," said Belle, smiling, promising, but at the same time wondering why he was so upset.

The two Canadians were snared in Pattaya, the beach resort. Roger Klebar was a dentist in his late twenties, his wife Giselle, a lovely teacher and philosophy student. They were on an extended prowl of the Far East before settling down to the tedium of pulling teeth and grading term papers. Both were intelligent, seasoned travelers, usually cautious, but not sophisticated enough to avoid the charms of Alain Gauthier. Walking on the beach boulevard around November 15, 1975, they stopped to watch an elephant giving rides to tourists, when a French-speaking Asian man and his wife materialized beside them. The script was getting familiar, its actors growing experienced.

The couple introduced themselves as Alain Gauthier and his wife Monique, who was thrilled to meet fellow Canadians at such a remote place. She was hungry for news of her country; the dentist and his wife were happy to give it. That very night they dined at a lavish outdoor buffet at one of the big hotels; the Canadians often left the table and went to the dance floor, leaving their new friends alone with the plates of food. In retrospect, Roger Klebar would speculate that these were the moments when *someone* put *something* in their dinner. Later that night, after the Canadians had enthusiastically accepted their new friends' invitation to stay in their Bangkok apartment for a few days while Alain and Monique showed them the city, Roger and Giselle felt the first gnaws of dysentery. By dawn they were weak, and by the time they reached Bangkok, they could barely focus and nod to the numerous young people in the apartment before they fell gratefully into one of Gauthier's beds.

The next morning, the dentist and his wife woke to the sight of Monique standing over them with coffee. She was tender and comforting. She helped them drink, then drew back, watching. Quickly the Canadians fell unconscious and slept for more than twenty-four hours. When they awoke, they were frightened. The previous day and a half had been lost. They could not remember much beyond the dinner at Pattaya.

Alain appeared at their bedside and was all reassurances. Unfortunately, he explained, the Canadians had fallen ill with acute dysentery. One of the reactions was extended sleep while the body healed itself. He clapped his hands and in came Dominique to confirm that he had slept for long periods of time during the several weeks he had been ill.

"Perhaps we should call a doctor," said Roger, feebly. Alain disagreed. He was as experienced in treating dysentery as any Thai doctor. In fact, he had medications that Thai doctors did not even know about. "Trust me," said Alain soothingly. "You must trust me, and you will get well quickly."

Oh, and one more thing. So many people wander in and out of the apartment, suggested Alain to his sick guests, that it might be safer for them to give their host any valuables for safekeeping. Dutifully, the dentist handed over passports, airplane tickets, and traveler's checks, thinking at the time how lucky he was to be in the hands of a French-speaking host who really cared about people. Then he blacked out and slept for two days.

*   *   *

A week of terrible sickness. When she was conscious, Giselle staggered to the bathroom—twenty times on one day as best as she could remember. Roger swam in and out of lucidity, remembering only that either Alain or Monique appeared frequently at his bedside, exhorting the Canadian couple to take their medicine. It came in both pills and a tumbler of a foul liquid which Alain said was Kaopectate. Monique often spoke sharply, reminding the dentist and his wife that she had been a nurse in Quebec City and they had best follow her instructions.

"Are we dying?" gasped Giselle in the middle of one night as her husband tossed and moaned beside her. "No, *chérie*," he said. "We're just sick. We'll get over it." But in his heart, Roger must have wondered if his diagnosis was optimistic.

Then Alain went away for a few days. "Business," he said. Monique would look after the houseguests. One morning she brought in the regular glass of medicine and tablets and waited for the Canadians to swallow them. Roger asked her to leave it beside the bed. He could not force anything down his throat at this moment. Monique seemed annoyed, but she left the medicine on the table and promised to return shortly to see if it had been taken.

"I think this stuff is making us sick," whispered Roger. "Don't take yours." Giselle nodded, so weak that she would obey any dictum. Roger crept to the bathroom and threw the medicines down the toilet. Later that day he felt better—for the first time since he had fallen ill in Pattaya while dining with their new friends. But even now he did not make a connection; he only believed that Alain was giving him medicine that was not appropriate for his condition.

Surreptitiously, the Canadians continued to throw their medicine down the toilet each morning, and within a few days they felt well enough to leave. "Where are our passports and traveler's checks?" asked Roger routinely of Marie-Andrée. The request was a shock; she stammered that it would be best to await the return of Alain. He would be back anytime now. Besides, she did not know the combination to his safe.

As a compromise, or as delay, Marie-Andrée took the
dentist and his wife on a whirlwind tour of the city, then
to dinner at a good restaurant. A nervous hostess, her face
was pale, her hand trembling occasionally, so ill at ease
that Roger wondered if *she* was falling victim to the same
tropical bug. At this, Marie-Andrée smiled, a little sar-
donically. She changed the subject quickly, disgorging a
multitude of complaints against her absent "husband"—
how he kept mistresses on the side, how he refused to
communicate with her, how he denied her requests for a
return to Canada and a visit with her family.

Giselle waited for a tactful moment. Obviously, she
finally suggested, there are enormous pressures on a marriage in a country as difficult as Thailand. Marie-Andrée
stiffened. "Oh, I like my life very much," she said, now
defensive. "We travel. We see interesting places. We meet
people. It's just tiring, that's all."

"I think you're lucky," said Giselle. "You're living
everybody's dream."

Marie-Andrée pondered this and laughed.

"Yes, I'm lucky," she cried. "Oh God, am I lucky!"

In the last week of November 1975, Vitali Hakim flew
into Bangkok feeling fit and ready for success. The East
was one corner of the map where he had not walked, and
he was not only ready for a financial bonanza in Thailand
—provided the contracts from Burma materialized and
Charmayne showed up as directed to be the messenger
girl—he intended to explore what Bangkok had to offer,
from temples to flesh markets.

On his first night, Vitali gravitated immediately to Patpong and ate lobsters—small, spiny, but delicious—and
drank several quarts of the heavy Thai beer. He had
promised himself to do something about his girth, being
ten kilos overweight and having to strain to pull his astrological shirts over his swelling belly. But tonight was not
the occasion for diet. Stuffed and bleary-eyed, he found
an outdoor cafe where a boxing ring was the center of
attraction. There he watched two balletic but ferocious
bouts of Thai boxing before it dawned on him that the
combatants were curveless young women whose feet flew
off the canvas and against an opponent's cheekbone so

rapidly that they were blurs. Scattering a fistful of *bahts*
into the ring to display his pleasure, Vitali lurched out,
shopping around Patpong until he found a massage palace
with red velvet and gilt and nude statuary as décor. He
chose from the tiers of uniformed young women a masseuse
named Joi, and for what he calculated to be roughly seven
dollars experienced what he later referred to as forty-five
minutes of excellent but frustrating cock tease. Joi wanted
another twenty dollars before she would offer more ful-
filling massage, and at this Vitali roared with laughter. In
a decade of roaming around the world, never had he paid
a whore, never in his whole life, and he did not intend to
begin such commerce with a massage girl in Bangkok.

Now a midnight curfew was upon him and Vitali hurried
back to the Hotel Malaysia. He could not risk being
stopped by Bangkok police, for in his pocket were the
names of two contacts he was supposed to meet on the
morrow. One was a Scot, the other Chinese, and Zazi's
carefully organized plan was that they would come from
Burma with morphine and gems, which Charmayne was
to courier back to Paris.

The next day Vitali spent seven infuriating hours looking for the Burma contacts, but the address Zazi had given
him was no good. No amount of berating the taxi driver
could locate the designated apartment; Vitali returned to
the hotel in a grumpy mood. The thought occurred to
telephone Zazi in Ibiza, but jet lag and his long first night
in Bangkok overwhelmed him. He fell asleep. It was almost dusk the next day when Vitali roused and dressed
and went to the lobby to book a call for Ibiza. The operator said it would take several hours, but Vitali pressed
some *bahts* into her hand and pleaded that it be marked
"urgent." The Turk found a Bangkok *Post* and slumped
into a lobby chair. There he was, reading and dozing, when
two young men sat down near him. One seemed Oriental,
the other East Indian. They were friendly. Small talk
passed between them.

By midnight, the call still pending, Vitali Hakim checked
out of his hotel and moved with his luggage into the penthouse of Alain Gauthier and his friend Ajay. The last
thing Vitali did before he departed the Malaysia was to
leave a message at the desk for Charmayne. He put it in

a sealed envelope, marked it "urgent," and told the clerk that the designated person should be there in a few days. In Ibiza, he had given Charmayne the names of three hotels—one of which he would be occupying. He fretted over Charmayne. He could not risk missing her. She was so naïve at this sort of thing that she might panic and fly right back to Ibiza.

CHAPTER THIRTY

When Charles appeared with a rambunctious Turk in tow, Marie-Andrée was distressed. Another one! Where was he going to sleep? Every bed and sofa and cushion held a "guest," and the hours after midnight were ravaged by the sounds of people retching and toilets flushing. For the next day or two, Charles performed complicated choreography. From his actions, it seemed he wanted to get rid of the Canadians so that he could devote full time to Vitali Hakim. The Turk had mentioned wanting to make a "major" gem purchase. Moreover the Canadian dentist was growing irksome, demanding with increasing loudness that his passport and travel documents be returned. He also spoke constantly of wanting to visit Chiang Mai, the northern city of Thailand.

As had so many others, the Turk woke up presently in the grip of illness, the same malaise that seemed to strike most guests who accepted the hospitality of Charles Sobhraj/Alain Gauthier. The host appeared with comfort and a glass of medicine, after the taking of which Vitali passed out for two turns around the clock.

Then, miracle of coincidence, Charles informed the Canadian couple that he must leave for Chiang Mai as well and would be happy to give them free transport. The weakened dentist and his wife were grateful to leave their sickbed and quickly packed, pleased that the journey would take place during daylight so they could enjoy the scenery. Then Charles disappeared for what he said would be a few

minutes. He did not return until ten that night, clapping
his hands and ordering everyone to brace for an immediate
leave-taking for Chiang Mai. In a quarter of an hour, the
Toyota sped out of Bangkok, bearing Charles, the Canadians, Ajay, and Marie-Andrée, pouting and surly.

Just before they all left the apartment, Charles appeared
in the Canadians' bedroom with two large glasses of "medicine." It was imperative that his guests consume the doses,
he said, for the road was bumpy and their stomachs might
begin to dance. Roger faked taking his, and his wife,
Giselle, took a tiny sip. At that precipitous moment, Marie-
Andrée called out from the living room and Charles went
to see what she wanted. "Give me your glass," ordered
Roger of his wife. He dumped both glasses down the
toilet. When Charles returned, he was pleased to see that
his medicine had been drunk. "You'll feel better, I promise
you," he said.

Now, heading north, Charles drove expertly, dodging
wild dogs, making idle talk, turning his head now and
then to inspect the Canadians, asking how they felt, wondering how they could still be awake at such a late hour
after their long siege of illness. But after four hours and
more than two hundred miles, the Canadians were still
wide awake and oblivious to the annoyance their chauffeur
felt. Charles stopped the car at a garage and told Ajay to
come with him to check their directions. The two men
returned to the car looking grim. They had apparently been
quarreling. Ajay's manner was usually amiable, polite, the
perfect second-in-command, for he worshiped Alain/
Charles and hovered at his shoulder to do whatever was
bidden. Occasionally he played with a switchblade knife,
but there was no menace connected therein, more like a
youngster demonstrating his skill.

But as he got back into the car, Ajay was tight-lipped
and solemn. "We took the wrong turn someplace," snapped
Charles. He was lost. The roads were dangerous at this
time of night. It was almost 3 A.M. Signals changed. Back
to Bangkok. The Canadians were disappointed but they
did not protest. Nor did they realize it at this moment, but
by staying awake and alert they perhaps had saved their
lives. Later on, as more of the story became known, they
would be sure of it.

* * *

Charles sailed into the Canadians' bedroom with their morning medicine and asked courteously if they would mind being evicted—to a hotel, for only one night. An important "customer" was coming to discuss buying gems and there were too many sick people around. No privacy. Ajay and Monique would escort the dentist and his wife to a hotel and look after them.

Roger considered the proposal and said, "That won't be necessary. We're feeling better." He asked for his passport and traveler's checks.

These tropical diseases are tricky, warned Charles. Relapses can occur. Bodies grow dehydrated. Convulsions set in. On the living room sofa, Vitali Hakim could have confirmed the prophecies. After sleeping for almost thirty hours, he awoke to find his legs turned to gelatin and his stomach pitching. The Turk had arrived at the apartment full of his customary juices, stories, magic tricks, and astrological readings. Now he was desperately sick. "If I throw up one more time," he told one of the French youths, "I think I'd rather die."

The Canadians were taken to a cheap Bangkok hotel and installed in a room that Charles had prepaid. It filled up quickly. Monique and Ajay stood around awkwardly, like nervous guards, waiting for Charles to appear with instructions. Soon enough he arrived, with Vitali Hakim unsteadily beside him. The scenario had changed again. Now Charles had decided to go to the gem mines at Chanthanburi and the Turk was feeling well enough to go along. Vitali nodded trying to be pleasant despite his weakness. He was looking forward to the trip. Though he had been unable to find the two contacts from Burma, he obviously felt blessed that Alain Gauthier had dropped into his life. Not only was Alain solicitous concerning his health, he knew how to bargain for gems at the source. When Charmayne turned up, he would at least have a packet of precious stones for her to nurse back home to Ibiza.

Charles made a little nod at Ajay, and the Turk was helped out of the room, downstairs, where he would wait in the Toyota. Charles had one last chore to attend to before he could leave for the mines. He commented that the Canadians were once again pale and shaky. Another dose of his medicine should clear that up quickly. He poured two large glasses—more than he had ever offered before—and handed them to the dentist and his wife. They stared glumly at the tumblers. Marie-Andrée exhorted them to obey. "Take the medicine," she said. "He knows what's best for you."

"I hate the taste," said Giselle.

Charles sat beside the beautiful young woman and put his arm around her. "You're never going to get strong enough to leave Bangkok unless you take the medicine," he insisted. Giselle sipped a few drops.

But Roger refused. "It doesn't work for us," he said. "This stuff makes us even sicker."

Marie-Andrée took the bottle from Charles and poured herself a glass. She took a little herself now and then, she said, just as insurance. Do as I do, she was saying, reminding the Canadians that she had been a nurse in Quebec. She often passed herself off as a nurse, even though her credentials had not extended beyond clerical duties.

Giselle followed her lead and drank her medicine. Marie-Andrée took a large dose, then excused herself and went into the bathroom. Quickly the toilet flushed, but Roger thought he heard Marie-Andrée retching. At that, Roger put his glass down and refused to obey the doctor. Charles shrugged. He grew angry. If the dentist wanted to suffer a severe relapse and spend the winter in Bangkok throwing up, it was all right with him. Then he left, having more important fish to fry. The Turk was waiting downstairs in the car—two hours had passed—and they were going to the gem mines.

Inside the cheap hotel room, Marie-Andrée sat quietly with her two charges. Giselle was sleepy and trying not to succumb to her heavy eyelids. Roger held his wife against his shoulder. "What's happening to us?" he asked.

"You're sick," answered Marie-Andrée.

"But it shouldn't be lasting this long," said Roger. He and his wife had been suffering for almost three weeks, the length of time they had known Alain Gauthier and his wife. Just before she passed out, Giselle said to her husband, "I love you." And he kissed her tenderly. When she fell asleep, he continued to hold her.

Perhaps their devotion touched Marie-Andrée. Perhaps she was frightened. Perhaps she was not yet as sophisticated in these matters as Charles. Whatever, Marie-Andrée abruptly told the Canadians to come with her back to the apartment. The hotel room was a dismal place to spend the night. Roger agreed. He scooped up Giselle in his arms and carried her down the steps. In the taxi going back to the flat, Roger asked Marie-Andrée if *she* could return their passports and traveler's checks. As sick as they were, he wanted to leave on a flight, any flight, this very night.

That was impossible, said Marie-Andrée. In the morning, when Alain returned, everything would be given back to the Canadians. At that moment, the dentist noted that his hostess seemed torn beween conflicting forces. She was. Committed to Charles, she was nonetheless deeply touched by the depth of the love that bound two fellow Canadians in jeopardy.

Months later, an Interpol detective in Paris would study the case and wonder why in the name of God these poor people—all of them and those yet to come—didn't figure out what was going on? *Someone* should have entertained suspicion, particularly with sick people scattered around the two apartments like casualties of war. The detective's opinion was that the events occurred because of the innocence and naïveté of the victims, and the setting of the tragedies. Bangkok—strange, remote, exotic, a little frightening. "Those poor devils must have been grateful for any hand extended to them," speculated the Interpol man. "Had these druggings occurred in New York or London, then the victims would have been able to put two and two together." And there was an X factor—the power and persuasion of Charles Sobhraj.

It was almost dawn when Charles and Ajay returned to the penthouse from their planned trip to the gem mines at Chanthaburi. As the trip takes six hours each way, it would have been impossible for them to leave past 10 P.M. and return before 6. Vitali Hakim was not with them.

The dentist heard noises in the flat and went to the living room. Charles looked very tired. Ajay was disheveled, his hair uncombed for the first time that Roger could remember. Both men seemed to have been doing something physical—and wearying.

"Where's the Turk?" asked Roger pleasantly. "Did he buy out the place?" The dentist had liked Vitali and enjoyed his boisterous presence until illness felled him.

The Turk, answered Charles, met some friends in Pattaya. His voice was terse. He did not apparently wish to speak on this subject. But Roger pressed. Why didn't Vitali return to Bangkok? Charles shrugged. Apparently the Turk had decided on the spur of the moment to start traveling with these friends. He would not be coming back.

"That's strange," thought Roger, keeping a comment to himself that almost came flying out of his mouth impulsively. He had just seen Vitali Hakim's luggage and clothes. *They were still in the apartment.* That very minute. Why would he go away without them?

When his wife awoke, Roger informed her that it was time to leave. *Now.* Even if it caused an ugly scene. While she packed, Roger summoned his strength and found his host, who was sitting at a desk examining stones, holding them up to a light and peering into their facets. Quietly, but firmly, the dentist asked for his money and travel documents.

"I don't think you're recovered enough to leave," said Alain, hardly glancing up from his work.

"I think we are," said Roger, trying to put steel into a voice that was tissue paper.

"You must rest a few more days," said Alain. And take more medicine. It was imperative to take the medicine.

Suddenly, a voice interrupted. Marie-Andrée intruded, uncharacteristically. "Give them back to him," she said. "Let them go home." In her eyes were sadness and resolution.

The Canadians flew out of Bangkok that night, so grateful to leave that it would be a day or two before they discovered that several blank pages had been torn out of their passports, and about half their traveler's checks were missing as well. Later, they would count themselves lucky to have lost only paper—and a month of their lives.

On the morning of November 29, 1975, a group of laborers were walking along a road near the Siam Country

Club golf course a few miles outside the beach resort of Pattaya. A rising curl of smoke attracted their attention. It rose from a nearby field and seemed to have no purpose. One of the workers detoured into the field to have a look. Quickly he cried out. The others ran to see.

A human body was smoldering. Most of it was ashes. A scrap of shirt was the only bit of clothing left unburned. On it was an exploding galaxy and a bit of the sign for Scorpio. It would take many months before an identification was made and authorities determined that the victim was a Turk named Vitali Hakim. He had been slammed in the head with a heavy object, probably a piece of lumber. Then, stunned, but still alive, he was drenched in gasoline and set afire. The pathologist who sifted through the remains commented, "It must have been an excruciating death. And it took at least two people to do it."

The apartment at Kanit House was beginning to show the wear of three months' occupancy by "A. Gauthier, Gem Dealer," and his entourage. Marie-Andrée decided to redecorate and pried enough *bahts* out of Charles for paint and brushes. She and Dominique spent several days applying a tasteful and muted beige to the living room walls. When Charles returned from a two-day trip to the gem mines he scowled. He did not like the color. He ordered the walls to be painted again. This time he selected the color. Blood red.

Marie-Andrée found a demon mask in the Thieves' Market and hung it on the wall, appropriate to the décor.

CHAPTER THIRTY-ONE

December is the benevolent month in Southeast Asia. The monsoons are over, the earth green and new, the sun less cruel, the nights crisp enough for wool. But in Bangkok, in the apartment where Charles Sobhraj conducted a *danse macabre*, December began in horror and descended straightaway into hell.

One midnight, two floors below, Belle heard yelling and slamming doors and sobbing from the penthouse. Curiosity overwhelmed her and she crept to her balcony to hear. Raoul's voice commanded her back to bed. She obeyed, for she knew that the next day Monique would spill everything when they sunned beside the pool. Belle was the closest thing the Canadian girl had to a friend. And spill it she did, a torrent of pain and angry frustration.

How could she have believed Alain Gauthier when he wrote her love letters and telegrams professing his passion and need for her? complained Monique. Why did she leave the security of home and work and family in Canada? Belle nodded; she had heard all of this before. But she was polite enough to listen. Monique seemed on the verge of revealing all the secrets of Apartments 503 and 504. Oh, continued Monique, there were occasional nights, rare as they were, when Alain held her and demonstrated a certain professional capacity for lovemaking. But there had never been two days back-to-back since her arrival in August, when she was certain that the man she loved wanted her for anything more intimate than cooking and ironing his clothes.

But there was more than this familiar catalogue of frustration, all of which Belle had heard regularly. Her intuition suggested another woman. Was May still around? No, in fact May and Charles had recently staged a yelling match, the Thai girl shouting for all to hear one night, "You're a liar! You make promises and break them! You cheat people! Nobody should trust you!" Even though he still saw May, it seemed likely that their relationship was finally what Charles had always deemed it—"business."

"Then what's the problem?" asked Belle.

"He's got a new one," sighed Marie-Andrée, anxious to describe her latest rival. She was even there when the first meeting took place, sensing instantly that Charles had found a new play toy. The girl was a Thai, barely twenty, impossibly beautiful, a student and part-time waitress at a hotel coffee shop. Dining with Marie-Andrée one evening, Charles began paying exceptional attention to the slim young girl whose unpronounceable name was about four inches long and who suggested that customers call her Suzy. She slid among her tables with the grace of a temple dancer, as softly as a fold of silk, shy, a giggler. When Suzy brought the check, Charles introduced himself under the name of "Alain" and presented his companion as "Andrée" and revealed they were newlyweds. Marie-Andrée's mouth flew open, but no one saw it. The other two were busy staring at one another. Suzy was not comfortable in English, but she understood *marriage*, and she found herself envying this Western woman for having caught an attractive and sensuous man with Oriental blood in his veins.

Somehow Charles managed to squeeze Suzy into his life, fitting her neatly between Marie-Andrée, and May, and the sick people, and his travel, and his secrets. Often he dined alone at the coffee shop, always sitting in Suzy's area, bidding her to select his courses, showering her with flattery and gifts. First came flowers, then he began leaving bits of sparkle as a tip. One night Suzy found a gold ring with an amethyst setting, and when she tried to give it back, Charles shushed her. "Before too long," he said, "it will become a diamond." Soon the waitress had a pocket full of semi-precious stones and was thoroughly confused. Was this customer so rich that he could strew jewels in her path, or was he after more? He never made the remotest semblance of a pass. In fact he occasionally returned with Marie-Andrée on his arm, apparently enjoying the icy barrier that he had erected. "He brings his wife in here and keeps flirting with me," said Suzy to a friend. "She must be catching on. I'm afraid."

Quite true. As both Suzy and her predecessor, May, worked in the same hotel, it was not difficult for Marie-Andrée to sneak about and play pathetic detective, watching as Charles swiveled between the two young Thai women. The coffee shop, with convenient large picture windows, could be seen from an entrance road, and there Marie-Andrée melted between a souvenir shop and a collection of tiny Buddhist shrines to spy on the man she loved. When she had seen enough, Marie-Andrée confronted Charles with her discovery. He would not permit an argument, sighing and dismissing her accusations as foolish and misinterpreted. "Suzy is for business," he said, falling back on his favorite excuse.

In the first week of December—and Marie-Andrée would not discover this for some time—Charles asked the waitress to marry him, a routine now as common as sending roses. He confided that Marie-Andrée was not his wife—it was just a little charade they were playing, for fun—but his secretary. "I love you," he told Suzy. "You're the woman I've been searching for all over the world." In understandable confusion, Suzy stammered her appreciation but begged for a breathing spell before she could give an answer. Here was a customer who had demonstrated unusual generosity, who had taken her out for one or two "dates" after the cafe closed and had done nothing but kiss her almost paternally on the cheek. Now he was pressing for marriage! Suzy did what most well-reared Thai girls would do with a situation that was not only difficult but incomprehensible. She giggled and backed away.

Now, sunning with Belle beside the pool, Marie-Andrée broke into angry tears as she spoke of Suzy. The night before, she and Charles had quarreled and screamed at one another for hours. Someone slapped someone. Somebody threw something against the wall. The sick people must have had much to entertain them.

Suddenly Marie-Andrée controlled her crying and reached out for Belle's hand as support. "He wants me to have his baby," she said.

"Well, are you?" asked Belle, wondering if these outbursts of emotion might be tied to the early months of pregnancy.

Marie-Andrée shook her head bitterly. "Not likely," she said. "The baby would be a monster—like its father."

Belle could not resist a quick foray into the coffee shop to behold the wondrous creature who had captured the erratic heart of her upstairs neighbor. All she beheld was a tiny young girl who looked little more than fifteen and who still bore—to Belle's sharp eye—the familiar Oriental scars of acne. The girl was pretty in a wide-eyed, innocent sort of way, but she was certainly not in the social league where Alain Gauthier wanted to play. Suzy was one of a hundred thousand girls in Bangkok who looked exactly the same.

All of this Belle mentioned to her husband, and the little French chef remarked that Friend Gauthier probably didn't like women at all, other than as tools of his trade. Marie-Andrée was kept around to serve as dutiful homemaker and, as she was Western, lent a certain status to a man who despite his tailored clothes and French haircut still looked Oriental. And May? She was, as Gauthier said, valuable for her knowledge of gems and her contacts with customers at the hotel. And she was Thai and knew how to deal with government bureaucracy.

Suzy the waitress was a puzzle. Raoul had no idea how she fitted into Gauthier's life scheme. But there *had* to be a reason. He doubted if it was love. That Suzy was hauntingly reminiscent of a Vietnamese girl named Song was unknown to Raoul and Belle. They could not have realized that Charles had found a woman who was a double for his own mother, the one he felt had rejected him.

Charles' goal to raise $25,000 for establishing a legitimate business was in jeopardy by early December. He

faced an end-of-the-year deadline, else lose an option to
lease a building and purchase equipment for polishing
stones and making jewelry. His income appeared to be
substantial, according to later police investigation, derived
not only from an occasional sale to a customer he met on
the street or in a major hotel lobby, but also from those
unfortunates who were last seen in his company. And
never seen alive again. But his expenses were substantial,
paying rent on two apartments, trying to keep three women
happy by awarding them expensive gifts, feeding a dozen
people each day. Unforeseen calamities also befell him.

One day he was rushing around Bangkok in his brown
Toyota when he ran a red light and struck a Thai youth
on a bicycle. The boy was seriously injured, and a crowd
gathered so quickly that there was nothing for Charles to
do but escort the victim to the hospital, with two policemen in attendance. Once there he realized that he could
not tolerate an investigation of any kind. Telephoning May,
he beseeched her to meet him at the hospital. In hurried
negotiation with the wounded bicyclist, May serving as
interpreter, Charles peeled off 10,000 *bahts* (about $700)
to obtain a release and to avoid further questions.

"The next time I hit a Thai," muttered Charles as he
took May home, "I'll make sure he's dead."

In early December, Charles abruptly left Bangkok alone
and flew to Hong Kong, telling Marie-Andrée only that
he had urgent business. She suspected he was taking either
May or Suzy along as excess baggage and was noticeably
chilly at his leave-taking. Charles pleaded with her to
support him, that he was working night and day to raise
the money needed to start his business. And he promised
to take a few weeks off later for a long holiday, perhaps
on that remote beach in the Philippines.

With $9,000 in his pocket, all the money he had, plus
a few sapphires and rubies, Charles hurried to the airport.
There he had no trouble buying a ticket and clearing customs, even though he was using the name and credentials
of Vitali Hakim—who at this moment was a charred and
unidentified corpse in a closet at Pattaya.

Disappointment was waiting in Hong Kong. His plan

was to hit the casino at Macao, where many years before he had won—and lost—large sums at baccarat while Hélène fretted and wept behind him. But when he checked into the Hyatt Regency Hotel, Charles encountered an old Hong Kong hand, a minor criminal who warned him to stay clear of Macao. Chances were good they would remember him from the decade-old debt that he had skipped out on. And the casino was now using a computerized list —with photographs—of undesirables who would be denied entrance, and whose very visage would summon police.

The risk was substantial, for he knew that Hong Kong's Central Intelligence Division already possessed a substantial dossier on him under his real name. Sooner or later, the various countries he had operated in would piece together the different identities and stolen passports and some computer would belch forth a "WANTED: INTERNATIONAL CRIMINAL" flyer that would be pasted to the desk of every airport immigration officer in Asia and Europe. Charles was smart enough to know that the day was coming; that it was not yet here was testimony to the poor dissemination of police information, and to the brazenness with which he operated.

Hong Kong was his favorite city after Paris, containing all the elements attractive to his life style. The city smelled of money, from the diamonds and gold Rolex watches and expensive Nikons that filled duty-free shopwindows, to the fire-engine-red Rolls-Royces that bore affluent hotel guests to and from the airport. Hong Kong attracts one million tourists a year, and as it is often the first stop for vacationers on a Far East swing, they have money to spend. In 1975, tourists left behind more than *$3 billion* in Hong Kong, astonishing for a territory that could fit comfortably in a remote corner of Philadelphia.

But the other side of this golden coin, and Charles knew it well, was the most sophisticated police force in Asia, with British brain-power and with computers linked to the Scotland Yards and FBIs and Deuxième Bureaux of the world. Immigrations and customs can be tough in Hong Kong, unlike Delhi or Bangkok, where a man in affluent garb and imperious mien could ride an elephant through passport control and not be questioned. In Hong Kong,

sharp-eyed, humorless women paw through luggage gracefully—but thoroughly—and a passport is given Asia's most
thorough examination before entry—or exit.

Beyond these nuisances, Charles was smart enough to
realize that a free-lance drug-and-rob man could not
operate very long here before he attracted the eyes of
Chinese mobsters, men whose tolerance for alien competition is slight.

On this night, Charles elected nonetheless to hunt—
cautiously—and be alert for any tong game wardens in the
forest. He selected, police believe, the area near the Hyatt
Regency, a neon fantasia whose signs promising night club
extravaganzas and massage parlors and live eels and disco
dancing and aphrodisiac powders extend out from buildings to meet signs jutting from the other side. At night
the district is a carnival, like walking beneath a thousand
garish kites that hang and shimmer in the sky.

At the Holiday Inn, a favored hotel of the more affluent
young due to its basement disco and coffee shop, which
produces reasonable approximations of American hamburgers, Charles sat down to watch television in the lounge.
His eyes fell on a young couple who looked bone weary,
a glaze having settled over their faces, as usually happens
to travelers sated with far corners of the globe. The man
was short, a little dumpy, with thick horn-rimmed glasses
and a Vandyke beard. He was about thirty, but in repose
looked older. In his old age, he would no doubt have a
potbelly and garrulously tell his grandchildren of this trip
around half the world. His companion—Charles noted
quickly that the woman did not wear a wedding ring—was
blond, pert, and probably vivacious. She was a little
younger, and deeply devoted from the way she fondly
held her friend's hand. They both watched the television
blankly, probably ignoring the plot and just letting the
images wash over them.

Charles waited for one of them to speak, so he could
pick up on their nationality. At first he thought they were
Americans, and when he ventured a comment to the effect
that the television show was boring, the man answered in
perfect English. But an accent was there, a tiny one, and
Charles knew right away he was dealing with a Dutchman
and his lady friend. Tough customers, the Dutch. Charles

once told his half-brother André that he would avoid them
at all costs, they being inherently suspicious, parsimonious,
and chilly. But at this crisis point in his life, Charles must
have decided to try and hook whatever fish nibbled at his
line.

Henricus "Henk" Bintanja was twenty-nine years old
and the proud possessor of a master's degree in chemistry,
yet it had not opened the doors to a good job, nor to
medical school. He suspected it was somehow due to the
fact that he was of mixed parentage—Dutch and Indonesian, and though it was not his fault that the royal house
of the Netherlands sent out pirate ships to plunder the
long ago world of Bali and its environs, he, like others in
his country, felt the sting of discrimination. His lover was
Cornelia "Cocky" Hemker, twenty-five, a nurse whose
blond hair and blue eyes made her a poster for all things
Dutch—silver skates, good health, cheese, and milk.

They lived happily together in a neat little house near
an unfashionable canal, where their cat dozed beside a
tiled fireplace, where a string quartet played softly on the
stereo, where Henk read his chemistry books and smoked
a pipe. They rode bicycles about the city, and Cocky was
of little help to Henk's continuing war with his girth, for
she made rich cheese pies and even a creditable *rijsttafel*,
the unending feast of Indonesia. On rare occasions they
went out dancing, or smoked marijuana at a friend's house,
but all in all their lives were decorous, unfrilled, and—the
only word is Dutch.

Frustrated by his inability to find work or further education commensurate with his intellect, Henk suggested to
Cocky early in 1975 that they make an uncharacteristic
splurge and "see the world." Cocky agreed at once and
began working extra shifts to earn her travel money. Henk
told his best friend, Benjamin, a lithographer, "We'll probably regret this—but we're going to spend every dime we
have. But if we don't do it now, we never will." Benjamin
saw no financial peril. "Don't look back," he said, "don't
even think that the trip is a *folie*. It's something everybody
would like to do—it will pay itself back in a thousand
unknown ways." If the money held out, Henk hoped to
visit Indonesia, where distant relatives lived. He had a

need to inspect his roots. He also kidded Cocky about finding a grass hut and farming coconuts, to which she raised no objections. Theirs was a solid relationship, two people who respected one another's intelligence, ability, and feelings.

Charles must have dazzled the Dutch. Lunch at the Hyatt Regency and a stroll down the corridor of boutiques where fortunes in gems nestled against red lacquer boxes and pearls as large as eyeballs were fastened to the limbs of a silver and gold weeping willow. An invitation to his room, where uncut movies played from his television, and little bottles of scotch whisky or imported beer could be fetched from a machine that automatically entered the cost on the hotel bill downstairs. Henk was so impressed by the wonders of the room and the man that he wrote a letter home to his family in Amsterdam. It would one day become valuable to the police of half the world.

An investigation would show that Charles led the Dutch couple through the streets of Hong Kong, across the waters of Victoria Harbor on the world's best ferry ride, and into the duty-free shopping district where he escorted Henk and Cocky on a gem-buying expedition. The young nurse had made it known that she wanted to purchase a sapphire ring, and Charles warned her to beware of exorbitant prices and inferior quality. After visits to several stores where they obtained varying prices, Cocky was disappointed at the lack of bargains. That seemed to be precisely the attitude that Charles cultivated.

As a "special favor" to his new friends from Holland, Charles permitted Cocky to buy a sapphire ring from his own "private collection." The Dutch girl paid $1,600 and she must have been nervous. In a letter to her family in the Netherlands, she revealed the purchase, insisting that the price she paid for such a quality ring was about one half what she had encountered in Hong Kong's best shops. "Our new friend's name is Alain Dupuis," she wrote, "and he has invited us to visit him in Bangkok."

"Alain Dupuis," the name that Charles was using in Hong Kong (after gaining admittance to the territory by using Vitali Hakim's passport), offered to send a car and driver to the Bangkok airport when the Dutch couple arrived, plus the offer of free room and board in his "penthouse," where a "French chef" prepared the meals. It must have sounded like an apartment on the Avenue Foch, for Cocky informed her family in a letter that Monsieur Dupuis was fabulously wealthy—in addition to being helpful and generous.

When Cocky and Henk landed in Bangkok and proceeded into the hall where they intended to give Alain Dupuis a telephone call, a young man rushed toward them with welcoming embraces. Alain Dupuis was waiting for them—astonishing, as he had not known their precise flight number. The Dutch must have been a little disappointed when the chauffeured limousine turned out to be a rented brown Toyota, and the French chef a haggard-looking Canadian woman. The guest apartment next door was hardly that of a millionaire, but it was free, and the Dutch were, above all, thrifty.

It was the night of December 10.

A day or two later, Belle rode the lift to the fifth floor and knocked on her friend's door. No answer. She thought she heard Monique's voice coming from next door, from the adjoining flat. Without knocking, Belle opened the door. Inside it was dark, and it took a moment for her eyes to focus on the gloom. On a chair, his bearded face pale and sweating, his eyes swimming wildly in his head, sat a stranger. Beside him, slumped on the floor, was a blond girl, desperately sick, holding her stomach and trembling all over. They looked like figures in a wax museum tableau, and when light from outside streamed through the open door, both moved their lips soundlessly. Her heart went out to the unfortunate pair, but Belle could only shut the door and return the apartment to darkness.

"Who are those poor people?" asked Belle when she caught up with Monique later.

"Some Dutch customers," answered her friend brusquely.

Belle let it go at that, though she was troubled. That night, as she waited for sleep, an image kept running through her mind, an image that could not be discarded. She had only glimpsed the Dutchman for a moment, but it seemed now, in retrospect, that his hands had been tied behind him. He looked like a prisoner.

* * *

As directed, Charmayne Carrou arrived in Bangkok in mid-December and checked into the President Hotel. There she was supposed to wait until Vitali Hakim contacted her. Never an adventuresome girl, Charmayne stayed in her room obediently, fearful that she would miss her lover's call. But when two days passed, she grew worried. Vitali had mentioned the names of two or three hotels where he might register, and she began making telephone calls.

The first hotel had no such person. Nor had the second. The third, the Hotel Malaysia, did not have Vitali on its guest ledger either. Just as she was about to hang up in despair, Charmayne thought to ask if a message had been left for her. Indeed there was one. Charmayne rushed to the hotel and found that Vitali was staying at the residence of one "A. Gauthier, Gem Dealer." She must have sighed with both relief and anticipation at reunion with the man she loved.

Bangkok police believe that Charmayne checked immediately out of her hotel and took a taxi to Kanit House. Her sudden and unexpected intrusion into the grotesque household of Charles Sobhraj must have precipitated concern, for the Dutch couple was ensconced in the guest apartment. It was not, however, to become a major problem. Charmayne was not in residence long. Belle met her briefly, just enough to take note of how nervous the young French girl was, and how much she loved Vitali Hakim, whose whereabouts nobody seemed to know. The question is, thought Belle, how could the portly Turk have entranced such a shy and appealing girl, with a flair for dressing in bright fabrics? The two women spoke of Thai silk, and Belle promised to give Charmayne the name of a shop that sold quality cloth at fair prices.

There would be no time for Belle to get further acquainted, or to deliver the name of a favored silk merchant. The next day, December 15, Charmayne was gone—as abruptly as she had come. And where, wondered Belle, had the girl taken herself? Monique shook her head. She was growing increasingly jumpy, her eyes rarely meeting Belle's. She was thin and pale, despite the Thai sun she sat under.

"I don't know," answered Marie-Andrée. "Who can keep track of hippies?"

The nude body of a young white female was found that very morning sprawled on the bank of a tidal creek near a beach south of Pattaya. The police assumption, as in the case of Jennie Bolliver, was that another tourist had drowned. It would take many months before an investigation was conducted, and an identity made, and an autopsy performed that would reveal Charmayne Carrou had been strangled. The fingers that clamped about her throat were so strong and savage that the neck bones snapped like twigs.

Incredibly, the very next night, the Dutch couple was evicted from the guest apartment. They were half carried, half dragged down the service stairs and shoved into Charles' car. He and Ajay Chowdhury drove away after midnight and did not return until it was almost dawn. They were alone. Their trouser legs were wet and muddy. The first thing Charles did when he entered his apartment was to strip off his pants and call for Dominique to have them cleaned. Dominique smelled the odor of gasoline but asked no questions and did as he was ordered.

The December 18 edition of the Bangkok *Post* carried a front-page article with a particularly grisly photograph. The account was erroneous, for it reported that a young Australian couple had been found murdered:

"The partly-burnt bodies of a young Australian man and woman have been found in a ditch alongside a highway 58 kilometers south of Bangkok . . . An initial autopsy conducted at the Police Hospital . . . showed that they had died before being set ablaze . . ."

Henricus "Henk" Bintanja and his fiancée, Cornelia "Cocky" Hemker, had been strangled. Then she was smashed in the skull with a board. Both were drenched with gasoline and set afire, and in the flames, they writhed and reached out involuntarily for one another.

CHAPTER THIRTY-TWO

Belle and Raoul cut short a fortnight's pre-Christmas holiday on the beaches south of Bangkok. Uncharacteristic winds had spoiled their rest and they returned to the city chilled by a bleak sun. On the night of their homecoming, December 22, a friend called from the diplomatic community to invite them to a holiday party. They accepted with pleasure, and, on their way out, decided to make an impromptu stop on the fifth floor and say hello to Alain and Monique.

The penthouse apartment was eerily silent when Belle knocked. For so many months there had usually been music and the sounds of a yelping dog and a screeching monkey and rooms crowded with houseguests and customers. Tonight it was hushed, dark, forbidding—like a house long ago abandoned and condemned. Nonetheless, the door finally opened, and standing there was Dominique, the first French youth to become ensnared. He greeted the cook and his vivacious wife with a troubled face.

Inside, on a sofa, sat Yannick and Jacques, the former French policemen, now looking like nothing more than children lost in a forest. Had some terrible news devastated these young men? When a car stopped downstairs and a door slammed, Yannick jumped up as if jolted by electrical current and ran to the window. He looked down anxiously to the carport and waited until satisfied that no danger was approaching.

"Where is everybody?" asked Belle cheerfully.

Everybody is in Katmandu, came the answer. Alain and Monique and Ajay Chowdhury left suddenly. They planned to spend Christmas in Nepal. There was talk about a casino that Alain enjoyed patronizing, and he had "business" to conduct.

Belle absorbed the surprising news. "I didn't know they were going," she said. "Monique never told me about a Christmas vacation."

The departure, Yannick said, was abrupt. They packed and left in an hour, leaving the trio of Frenchmen behind to look after things.

Belle studied their faces. They all looked so worried and agitated that she suspected some new illness had felled them. Motherly, she put her hand over Dominique's forehead. It was clammy, but Belle's intuition told her this was the stuff of fear, not disease. "No," confirmed Dominique. He and his friends were not sick. They felt better physically this night than they had in months, since before their lives collided with Alain Gauthier.

Then *what*? Belle's curiosity swelled. "You two go on to your Christmas party and have fun," suggested Dominique. "When you get home, maybe we can tell you what's the matter."

Belle would not have it. She refused to take another step until she learned what was troubling these young men. "No," she insisted, "tell us now." She sat down with resolution and folded her arms, bending forward like a priest expecting full confession.

Yannick fidgeted about the room, as if looking in shadowed corners for alien ears. One dim light glowed against the scarlet wall. Then he stopped and suddenly blurted it all out, pouring terrible *histoires* onto Belle and Raoul, as if by transferring the horror he would no longer be cursed and haunted. Belle would never forget this moment.

"You know your friend, Alain?" began Yannick. "Well, he's a thief. And a robber. And . . . a murderer. He kills people. He'll probably kill us—and maybe you if he finds out that you know what we're telling you."

Belle was confused. "I don't understand," she said. Was this some party game? How was she supposed to respond?

Yannick shook his head to silence her. He did not let

his tale suffer interruption. He hurried on, aided by interjections from Jacques and Dominique, reminding Belle about the sudden disappearance of Jennie, the American girl, and next Vitali Hakim, the Turk, and Charmayne Carrou, who had come looking for her lover. Lastly, there were the Dutch couple—Henk Bintanja and Cocky Hemker. "They found two bodies outside town while you were on holiday," said Yannick. "Burned and unidentifiable. We're sure it's those Dutch kids." From his pocket he withdrew a clipping and handed it to Belle. She glanced at the photograph of two charred corpses and winced. "But it says they are Australians," murmured Belle, reading the account.

"Keep reading," ordered Dominique. Deep in the body of the story was the fact that the girl was wearing a brassiere that said "Made in Holland."

"It's *got* to be those Dutch people," insisted Yannick. He and Dominique then told of seeing Alain and Ajay drag the drugged bodies of Bintanja and Hemker out of the apartment. "They were almost unconscious," said Dominique. Alain and his shadow were also carrying a piece of pipe, and a strip of garden hose. They did not return until dawn, and both men had muddy trousers.

Dominique interrupted here. "Alain told me to take his trousers to the cleaners. I did so and I noticed they smelled of gasoline."

Belle swiveled toward her husband. His face was as stunned as hers. Later the chef would contend that he had been suspicious all along. In retrospect, so was Belle, but she had never imagined the extent of what was going on. She was not yet convinced. Where was the proof? Maybe these youthful travelers had just gotten up and left on their own. They were all nomads, drifting by whim. Visitors had been streaming in and out of the apartments for the entire autumn. Surely not all of them were murdered.

"Perhaps this might convince you," said Dominique. He handed Belle a passport. His own. For more than a month, Dominique had been badgering Alain for the return of his travel documents, those put in "safekeeping" the morning after he first met his host in Chiang Mai. Always Alain had managed some excuse, but just before leaving for Katmandu he had given it back. "Look at it!" dictated

Dominique. Pages were missing. New pages from somebody else's passport had been added. Crudely drawn entrance and exit visas to Thailand had been entered. Apparently someone else had used it.

Did Belle require more? Yannick led the shocked
Frenchwoman and her husband into the bedroom, where
the small safe was kept. Did Belle and Raoul recall that
Yannick's and Jacques' passports were stolen in Pattaya
from the bungalow that Alain Gauthier had rented? Belle
nodded. "I went to the French Embassy and after a big
hassle was finally issued a new passport," said Yannick.
"I told the embassy that my original one had been stolen.
They asked a lot of questions. They wanted to know by
whom? I didn't have an answer. But I know now."

Yannick opened the safe, rummaged inside, and found,
among a dozen others in a paper sack, the familiar red-
bound French passport. *His.* He threw it at Belle. Pages
were missing. False visa stamps were entered. Yannick
took a purple felt marker pen and angrily drew slashes
across every page. "At least he won't be able to use it
anymore," he said bitterly.

There was more to show and tell. In various places
around the two apartments were remnants of dead people
—pieces of lost lives—luggage, travel books, souvenirs,
letters unmailed or half written. The French boys felt
there was enough evidence here to build a solid case of
multiple murder again Alain Gauthier *et al.* But one question burned Belle's senses as she tried to assess the merit
of this tale. Monique. Or Marie-Andrée. Whatever her
name really was. Did *she* know? Did she lie there beside
the pool with tanning oil on her limbs, mooning about an
uncaring lover, when bodies were falling all about her?

In unison, the three French youths nodded. "She knew,"
said Yannick. "She *had* to. Anybody with eyes and ears
could have figured out what was happening in this apartment." It was pointed out to Belle that Marie-Andrée often
played nurse, bringing "medicine" to the ill.

"Then we must go to the police," announced Belle.
Quickly, Raoul disagreed. The police would probably not
believe her. In fact, they might even trump up a conspiracy
and accuse us, agreed the Frenchmen. The best policy for
a foreigner to follow in any strange country, particularly

the East, is to avoid contact with the law. It is too easy to upset the delicate balance and lose a visa.

Yannick spoke up hesitantly. All he and the two other Frenchmen wanted at this point was to clear out of Thailand immediately and return to France. He reminded Belle that, as he and Jacques were both ex-policemen, they still had contacts in law enforcement. Once in Paris, they could go to Interpol and let more qualified investigators go to work. Belle nodded. The plan sounded good to her. There remained only one problem. The boys lacked $250 needed for their air fare home. Belle's eyes sought out Raoul's. He nodded. "We'll loan it to you," said Belle. She looked about the apartment, remembering the nights of wine and music, shuddering now, wanting only to run away and never see the crimson wall or feel the ghosts again.

A flight was not available until the next midnight, but so terrified were the French boys of Alain's returning unexpectedly that they went to the airport immediately, purchased tickets, and waited amid the safety of crowds for almost twenty hours. The last thing Yannick did before he left the apartment was to mutilate the lock to Charles' safe so as to make it difficult to insert a key. Then he took the key he had stolen and threw it into a wastebasket at the airport.

On their way out of Kanit House, the boys stopped by Belle's to thank her for helping. They promised to go to Interpol immediately upon arrival in Paris. "I can pull strings," promised Yannick. "It shouldn't take long to bust this thing wide open."

Belle nodded. So many hundreds of questions were tangled in her head that the moment was a blur. Oddly, at this point, she wondered what had happened to the animals. Where was Frankie, the white spitz, that Monique had adored like a child? "Alain gave it to Suzy, his new girl friend," said one of the youths. And Napoleon, the monkey? Shrugs. Nobody knew.

Actually someone knew. When the garbage collector removed the lid from one of the communal trash receptables for the apartment building, he saw something revolting. In the trash was the fly-infested corpse of a dead monkey. It was wearing diapers and its throat had been cut.

* * *

One can fly from Delhi to Katmandu in little more than an hour, the last stretch of which is a magnificent dash alongside the Himalayas, lined up on the left side of the plane like castles of the gods. Then a plunge down through clouds of whipped cream into the valley of Katmandu, a protected bowl of variegated greens like all the salads in a garden. Farmers cling stubbornly to terraced patches of earth on precipitous slopes, and below, at the bottom, the Baghmati River sleeps like a hibernating serpent. It seems for a few precious moments as if time stopped centuries ago, when priests painted huge polychromatic eyes on temple towers that stare unblinking at all who come.

The alternate route is overland, in a bus that fights its way out of Delhi, along a road congested with bullock carts and sacred cattle who gaze at impatient vehicles with imperious aloofness, through flat stretches of villages baked from clay where the holy river Ganges flows out of the Himalayas on its long journey to the Bay of Bengal. Then, a long and clattering climb up and up, rising to the peak of the world, reaching Katmandu after three days on the road.

It was by bus that thrifty Annabella Tremont chose to venture forth on the last leg of her personal odyssey. In Delhi she had met two Australian girls who persuaded her to join them on a trip to Katmandu and, now that she was on the eternal bus ride, Annabella was glad she had agreed. The ride itself was tedious, the bus fetid with the odors of rural India, but the drivers were nervy and they sat beneath an array of festive posters that represented their individual gods and goddesses. Several other young people were passengers and at every rest stop there was a hash pipe passed around for fortification.

After one of the rest stops, Annabella found her seat occupied by an unbudgeable Moslem woman, and she had to squeeze in next to a friendly Canadian boy whose lap was overflowing with travel books and photographic equipment. Before the next rest stop was reached, Annabella discovered that fate had dealt her a good card. She liked her new companion very much. He was tall, several inches over six feet, and a mite gangly, and boyish, and shy, with a wispy blond beard, but he had a sweet face of considerable peace, as if he had fought all his demons and conquered them. Annabella guessed he was going on a religious pilgrimage, but she was wrong. He was going to see a mountain.

Laddie DuParr was twenty-three and his years had been fuller than most, having taken him from the great flat cereal basket of Manitoba, Canada, to what was soon to be in his reach: a trek up Mount Everest as far as he could hike without professional training. In his shoulder bag were photos and maps of Sagarmatha, the Nepalese word for Everest that means "Mother of the Winds." Every few minutes, once the bus was in sight of the great range, Laddie would run to the driver and ask if Everest was *that* peak, or the one over *there*. Always came a negative shake of the head, for Sagarmatha is a modest woman and hides most of the year behind veils of mist and clouds.

Sir Edmund Hillary and Tenzing Norgay, the Sherpa guide, were Laddie's idols, and for hundreds of miles and dozens of hours he told Annabella tales of courage and challenge. Relationships are formed quickly among travelers, particularly with the young off on exotic larks, and by the time the ancient bus wheezed and rattled into Katmandu, Annabella was attached to the sophisticated farm boy whose excitement over a mountain was genuine and refreshing. The two Australian girls, Mattie and Cora, were gigglers, sitting across the aisle and teasing the new couple, though, in truth, they envied Annabella and Laddie. They all laughed and smoked and sang "Oh, Canada" and "Waltzing Matilda" and "California, Here I Come" and tried to teach the lyrics to a group of Buddhist monks who giggled more than the Australian girls and who tapped spoons against their begging bowls to keep time.

Laddie DuParr was an attractive find for a woman whose emotions were in disrepair. He was a mixture of old-fashioned values and an insatiable curiosity for the unseen and unexperienced that could be contented only by travel—qualities Annabella understood perfectly. One of seven children born to parents who were the descendants of French-Canadian and New England Yankee pioneers, Laddie grew up on a 200-acre farm where his father raised 100,000 Rock Cornish game hens a year. The village nearest the DuParr farm was so minuscule that it was hardly more than a silo and a gas station, and the only paved road around reached a dead end a few miles before the DuParr place, which was accessible only by a dirt road.

Probably he would have been reasonably content to stay on the farm and become part of his father's business had it not been for a high school foreign travel program that extricated Laddie from the house just beyond the dead end and deposited him in a French dairy community where he studied and worked for three months. He flew home from Paris, totally fluent in French, and with the need to see more of a world he barely knew existed. His family was happy that he had enjoyed his sojourn abroad, but now it was time for college and settling down and becoming part of the rich dark soil of Manitoba.

Laddie got through one year of political science and psychology at the University of Winnipeg, then took a job laboring in the silver mines of northern Canada to earn enough money for a six-month tour of the world. As he was not yet twenty, his family agreed to permit him one more indulgence of youthful passion before reining him in.

But once home, life became nothing more than a time to earn more passage to get away, and as he was becoming exceptionally skilled with his camera and spoke of creating travel books and film documentaries of strange places, his parents knew that he would never spend his years getting up at three in the morning to feed game hens and shield them from the bitter winters. In 1974, he worked for three months in the arctic region, on the Beaufort Sea, acting as a mate on a boat that sliced through the iced wilderness with giant suction machines to pull boulders from the bottom of the sea. Artificial islands were constructed of these great rocks, on which were placed drilling rigs. The job was cold and lonely and undemanding of his intelligence, but Laddie made $10,000, enough to stake him on one last circle of the globe. He would be gone a year at maximum, he promised his parents, and after that he would absolutely guarantee to return to Manitoba and complete his college education. He would seal his ears from the sirens.

It happened that Laddie's chronic case of wanderlust had also infected his younger brother, Barry, and when the two set out together, Mrs. DuParr was both relieved—and troubled. "Don't worry about us," insisted Laddie. "I know my way around pretty well by now." Mrs. DuParr, a pretty, blond, sturdy farm woman, had to agree. Her home was already well stocked with travel memoirs—a bust of Napoleon from Paris, statuary from Greece, beads from the Middle East. And her son was a dependable correspondent, sending letters home at least once each week.

The DuParr brothers traveled together in Europe, then separated somewhere in the Middle East, each having routes to explore. They vowed to meet either in Bangkok or New Zealand in early 1976. They would use their mother in Canada as a switchboard, calling in from time to time to check on the other's progress.

In early December, 1975, Laddie telephoned home from New Delhi, even as Annabella had done, and he expressed the same malcontent with the capital of India. The Western people he had met there were "mixed up," he told his mother, and he felt "uncomfortable" in India. On to more exciting news: he was going to Katmandu and at least *look* at Everest. He planned to be in Bangkok by the first week of February and would meet his brother there. Money was holding out well; he had $1,200 of his stake left and that could easily stretch to pay for another two or three months to cap the most spectacular year of his life. His travel bags were filled with exposed film, and he felt there were the makings of a picture book. One chapter might have included photographs of a new friend named Annabella, posing on the shore of a lake called Phewa Tal, as blue and as cold as a frozen sapphire, in a Nepalese town where, it is believed, the Hindu gods reveled and made love. He shot a roll of Annabella striking absurd poses beside the lake and of her futile attempts to catch a white-spotted deer who seemed fascinated by the clicks of the camera. Then Laddie handed it to Mattie, who giggled and took a shot of a Canadian boy and a California girl, newly met, holding hands and looking adolescent, with the deer pawing the earth in mischief behind them.

* * *

Freak Street is the name bestowed by the young to a district of tiny streets leading like drunken insect trails off Durbar Square in the center of Katmandu. The stuff of fantasy and fairy tale, Freak Street has cheap hotels with staircases built for people no more than four and one-half feet tall, grocery stalls that sell cabbages as large as soccer balls, and cafes with whimsical names like Don't Pass Me By Restaurant and the Hungry Eye. There are improbable pastry shops where hand-hewn tables are spread with what looks like Thanksgiving Day at Grandma's—mince, pecan, chocolate meringue, and lemon chiffon pies, initally demanded by the earliest Western visitors who indulged hash-induced craving for sweets and taught tiny Nepalese women how to bake. Nearby is the Pleasure Room, where the customer must bend over double to inch through a dark maze of dungeonesque corridors leading to a main room where pillows are strewn about and where candles dance eerily against the stone walls. Hashish, smoked openly, is the principle refreshment, with scant regard paid to new drug laws installed in the early 1970s, due chiefly to pressure from the Nixon administration. The local story goes that the United States Government grew alarmed over its traveling young being able to purchase legal hashish in Nepal. It was a commodity for sale, like turnips and straw baskets, and a customer was allowed to sit down at a lunch counter and sample the various wares of the hash merchant, not having to pay until he found some to his liking, providing he was able to find his money and reel out of the shop without assistance. Supposedly the Nixon administration, guardian of its citizens' morals worldwide, promised a grant of a few million dollars to help finance a badly needed sewer system for Katmandu, the *quid pro quo* being that Nepal outlaw drug sales. A deal was struck, new laws published, the money delivered. But it apparently got "redirected" somewhere in the royal bureaucracy, for the sewer system has yet to be constructed.

On Freak Street, Annabella and Laddie, like most youthful tourists, were besieged by children no more than ten years old with hair shaved to the scalp to prevent lice nests. They were drug sellers, offering "hash, coke, acid, speed, or smack" in phonetic patter, and if a customer showed interest, he was led by the child into a dark doorway, up a fearful staircase, into a "souvenir" shop where the proprietor offered sweet tea, then reached into a huge roll of fabric and located chunks of powerful hashish as big as bananas. If the customer were shrewd, he could negotiate a buy for around $10, for what might cost $5,000 in the U.S.

Laddie and Annabella took a room directly on Freak Street in a dump called the Oriental Lodge, whose clientele was principally the young and the drugged and the adventuresome. For a dollar fifty a night, they were given a room of minuscule dimension, whose thin pallets were hardly more comfortable than the floor, whose walls were splashed with the psychedelic fantasies of a vivid but not very talented artist, whose ceiling beams were painted to resemble a golden serpent with a sexy pink tongue. Somewhere nearby a flute was usually playing, and soft breezes floated through windows draped with yellow and red shades. Annabella loved it all, the Oriental being a hidden place where no one dictated form or rules. And beyond the threshold was the street itself, an enduring carnival of monks in orange robes walking with bamboo staves, and Tibetan women huddled in clumps and sharing secrets, and oxen dozing, and native artists whose quick strokes brought forth dragons and deities and cobras and tigers on parchment paper. Wherever there had been a dull stretch of wall, someone tied banners of brilliantly colored cloth. To be here, with a man she liked—confided Annabella to her Australian girl friends—was a far better conclusion to 1975 than she had imagined.

Conversely, Laddie was disappointed, for on his first morning in Katmandu he discovered that an organized trek into the foothills of the Himalayas that he hoped to join had already left. Another was not scheduled for ten days, capricious weather permitting. Laddie considered striking out alone, but he was warned off by a tourist official. The morning fogs were thick, and trails were dangerous to a novice. The year before, an American boy had left Katmandu to camp out alone, sought refuge for the night in a farmer's field, and was discovered the next morning with his head neatly severed from his body.

Another couple had simply disappeared, never to be found, somewhere in the awesome reaches of the Himalayas. Nepal, on the whole, is a lawful and safe country whose people are peaceful. But once the city is left behind, another code exists among the mountain people, one that holds less obedience to laws.

Annabella sought to cheer Laddie. Ten days would pass quickly, she insisted, and if ever there was a place in which a fortnight could be wasted gloriously, it was Katmandu, capital of a kingdom so unique that it sets clocks ten minutes ahead of India, to demonstrate a modest amount of independence from Nepal's chief trading partner and access to the outer world.

One day they took a bus almost to the Tibetan border, close enough to see the Chinese guards at "Friendship Bridge." Along the way, Laddie thought he spotted a sliver of Everest beckoning through a brief parting of the clouds. But when he asked the bus driver for confirmation, the answer was, "That's a baby. You'll know when you see the mother."

Sometimes they went their separate ways, Laddie having small tolerance for monuments. After years of foreign travel, he preferred to spend his afternoons sipping excellent tea at the Cafe Govin, where the serious mountain climbers swapped stories and Everest lore. Some days he went to the Yak and Yeti, a restaurant once part of a royal palace and now operated by a flamboyant white Russian named Boris Lissanevitch, who, some claimed, promoted the legend of the Abominable Snowman to boost tourism. "I had rather stand on the top of Mount Everest than walk on the moon," wrote Laddie to a college friend in Winnipeg. "Of course, the problem is once you've reached the top of the world, then everything must be down hill after that . . . It doesn't look like I'll get very far up the old girl this time, but maybe I can make her acquaintance . . ."

Annabella enjoyed sleeping late, taking breakfast at Aunt Jane's, a home-style restaurant started by a U.S. Peace Corps member, then drifting over to Durbar Square, the heart of Katmandu, where young people sit in the sun and drape themselves against the steps of temples and pagodas, often having to shoo away goats and monkeys. One day she insisted on taking Laddie to a nearby temple void of architectural interest save ornate window frames and grilles, but fascinating to Annabella because of its principal tenant —a genuine, bona fide "living goddess." Centuries before, in a dark time, the king seduced a beautiful young girl— *really* young, less than twelve years old—and she died of shame. Misfortunes rained on the king, directed, he believed, by angry gods to punish his sexual rapaciousness. The king therefore decreed that a nationwide search be conducted to discover the one perfect little girl in the kingdom. Once located, she would be called the "living goddess" and would be worshiped as long as she was pure, i.e., until first menstruation.

To this day, a "living goddess" reigns, replaced only after an exhaustive search throughout the kingdom for a child who is usually around four or five, who is beautiful, unmarked by a single scar, and possessed of ususual composure. The last is necessary because one of the crucial tests has priests in fierce masks leaping out from behind pillars to scream at the finalist. Only that rare child who remains calm is selected. Once installed in office, the goddess lives in secrecy and seclusion, within the walls of the Kumari Ghar temple, tutored and fed by holy men, hidden from view until the one day a year when she is borne through the streets of Katmandu in spectacular procession, her tiny body smothered in silks and gems and blossoms.

The tourist who wishes to see the goddess is admitted to an inner courtyard; if a few rupees are placed in the correct palm, the "living goddess" will occasionally come to a heavily grilled window and peer out blankly for a moment or two. Only part of her face is visible, her eyes ringed with kohl and an aura of the forbidden.

Annabella went three times to view the child and was saddened and irritated to learn that the goddess's future, postpuberty, was enforced eviction from office, followed by bleakness. Ex-goddesses never marry, legend cursing their prospects by claiming that any man who takes one to bed will die immediately. The small alumnae association thus consists of old maids, prostitutes, and desperately lonely women.

All of this Annabella found fascinating, in a world of jets and computerized data banks. One night at dinner she told her friends, "I suppose we're all living goddesses in a way. What happens to those little girls is not far off from what happens to any American girl." The remark was cryptic and needed elaboration, but Annabella changed the subject, not choosing to reach into those places within her that still contained pain.

Katmandu held continuing fascination for Annabella and Laddie, the perfect setting for a relationship to flower. Shy around girls, as many tall and gawky men are, the blond-bearded farm boy was not adroit in casual conversation. But as he and his new friend strolled about the ancient city, there was always something to remark on—be it a fountain with sixteen foreign languages inscribed on a slab with an attendant legend that whoever translates them all will cause milk to flow eternally from the tap. Or the processions of carved elephants and dragons and monkeys that guard the steps to temples, as fanciful as a linear carousel. Or the water gardens of Balaju, whose sleeping statue of Vishnu appears to float on lotus pads, guarded by stone serpents who, legend says, will spring into ferocious life if the idol is threatened.

Each day Laddie went to the tourist office for weather information to determine when Everest might reveal herself. One morning, he awoke Annabella at 3 A.M. with an invitation to join a group of young people who were driving east from the city, where it is often possible to obtain a ravishing view of the greatest mountain in first light of sunrise. By 6 A.M., the couple was standing huddled and chilled on a lookout 7,000 feet up, waiting impatiently for the new sun to illumine and reveal Laddie's passion. Only a few clouds molested the mauve horizon. Surely this would be the moment. Annabella clutched his hand tightly and prayed for his dream. On the serpentine climb to the lookout, Laddie had read from a magazine article concerning Tenzing Norgay, the Sherpa guide who failed seven times before he led Hillary to the summit in 1953 during the very week that Elizabeth II was crowned. "I have come back and tried again," said Norgay in the article, "not with pride or force, not as soldier to an enemy, but with love, as a child climbs into the lap of his mother."

They waited an hour, the troubled girl from California and the excited boy from the flat Canadian plains, waiting until the sun chased away every dark corner of the night.

But Everest draped a new shroud of fog around her—as if putting on a hooded robe—and remained hidden. Laddie was able to see only a part, lower down. The pinnacle was wrapped in cold grayness. On the ride home he insisted that he was not overly disappointed, for this was as close as he had come and he could "feel" Everest if not exactly see her. But Annabella shared his frustration. She began planning a Christmas party for the various Western kids they had met in Katmandu, hoping it would cheer Laddie and for a few hours push away the annoying mountain.

A mile or so away from Freak Street, on a road guarded by toy soldier sentries, stands the Hotel Soaltee-Oberoi, at the other end of the tourist scale from he Oriental Lodge. The Soaltee in 1975 was the closest thing Katmandu had to a luxury hotel, housing dignitaries from Lowell Thomas to the random visiting prime minister. Beginning on the night of December 18, the hotel welcomed a well-dressed young man with Oriental visage which was apparently Indonesian in heritage. The guest signed the register as Henricus Bintanja, citizen of the Netherlands. His companion, a stylish and thin brunette woman who did not look the least bit Dutch, signed in as Cornelia Hemker, of Amsterdam. Both presented genuine passports which easily passed muster. The couple was attractive and obviously well traveled, and they blended well with the clientele of the Soaltee, many of whom were industrial tycoons from the U.S. and Europe bent on ravaging the ancient city and erecting high-rise hotels and shopping centers.

It was not known to the hotel that the real Henricus Bintanja and Cornelia Hemker were at this moment quite dead, burned beyond recognition, and stuffed in a locker at the Bangkok morgue.

CHAPTER THIRTY-THREE

On the steps of a temple built before the pilgrims found America, lovers were playing flutes purchased for less than a dime, carved from a rhododendron tree, when a striking couple appeared in their laid-back midst, rather like the rich on a charity tour of the impoverished. At any given daylight moment in Katmandu, there are hundreds of young people clustered around this temple, mingling with the goats and chickens that share temporary tenancy, sitting on worn stone ledges that once drained the blood from royal sacrifices, feeling like characters on the stage of ancient history. But destiny's script for this December afternoon called for Charles Sobhraj and Marie-Andrée Leclerc to survey the colorful pageant and to sit down beside Annabella and Laddie.

Speculation must enter the tale again at this juncture—there are puzzling gaps still unbridged—and matters grow exceedingly complex. Careful attention is needed, for there are shifting identities, unknown motivations, and the exact means to the end can only be surmised.

The end itself, however, is very clear.

An investigation and the testimony of witnesses would reveal that Charles and Marie-Andrée spent a few days principally within the guarded environs of the Hotel Soaltee-Oberoi. In the casino that is an appendix of the inn, the only legal albeit small-time gambling house for thousands of miles in any direction, Charles lost heavily at *vingt et un* and roulette, while his woman pulled the slot

machine handles in boredom. Around them Pakistani
tribesmen and wealthy Indians from Delhi gambled dis-
passionately. The casino is usually as quiet as a church, as
if crying out over win or loss is unmannerly. From the
pattern of his life, Charles probably cruised about the
hotel, trying to strike rapport with affluent guests. Obviously he was unsuccessful, else he would not have invaded the Freak Street territory of the young and frugal.
He was a hunter whose shots went wide of the tiger and
had to settle for a sitting duck.

Ajay Chowdhury was also present in Katmandu, but
was staying at another hotel. He was, however, usually in
attendance, a step or two behind his mentor, waiting for
instructions, totally committed to the destructive and
deadly force that was Charles Sobhraj.

From the moment they first met the well-dressed couple
on the steps of the temple, Annabella and Laddie were
elevated into fast company, caught up in what might pass
for a social whirl in Katmandu. Their affluent new friends
took them to dine at the Hotel Soaltee-Oberoi, an accomplishment out of financial range for their Freak Street
peers, and they rode about town in the rich man's rented
Toyota, a further piece of fortune among those who
haggle fiercely to save pennies before engaging a bicycle
rickshaw. Annabella returned from her first evening flushed
with excitement. She told the two Australian girls, Mattie
and Cora, that their new friends were a "Vietnamese-
looking jewel dealer and his French wife." She said the
couple was "rich, friendly, and expert in buying gems."
Perhaps this was a principal weld that forged the instant
friendship, for both Laddie and Annabella had purchased
gems in Delhi and were known to be concerned about
their quality.

The next day, Annabella told the Australian girls that
her new friend had pronounced the gems to be inferior,
that they had been swindled in Delhi. The small ruby that
Laddie owned and carried wrapped in a soft cloth, pinned
to his underclothes, was inferior and blemished. And so
were the topazes and amethysts that Annabella had
bought. "He told us it is easy to get taken," complained
Annabella to the Australians. So angry was Annabella
that she vowed to return to the crooked merchant in

Delhi and demand a refund. Charles promised to help her. He is an "extraordinary" man, Annabella told a group of young people on the night of December 20, as she ate a piece of pecan pie at one of the pastry shops. Beside her, Laddie was simmering over his imperfect ruby, morose and angry. Then someone brought the cheering news that the weather was improving, that the forecast was that Everest would reveal herself by Christmas. Only five days away! Laddie put aside his anguish over the ruby and bade Annabella to finish her pie quickly. One of the cafes that catered to young people was showing a film of an Everest expedition, provided the city's erratic electricity would stay working long enough to power the projector. Annabella smiled and grasped Laddie's hand and did as he asked. She admired her friend's priorities. A mountain, *the* mountain, was more important than a ruby. Annabella understood that.

On the morning of December 22, in a terraced cornfield a few kilometers outside Katmandu, alongside the Chinese Highway just where the excellent road financed and built by Peking begins to climb and twist upward into a range of foothills leading to the Tibetan border, a Nepalese child ran after his errant dog. The little boy laughed and stumbled and threw small sticks at his pup, who was playing a frustrating game of running several yards, stopping to cock an attentive ear at his young master's commands, then bursting out of the child's grasp and dashing forth another fifty feet. Then the dog suddenly stopped and began to sniff at something odd. Smoke rose in curls from a blackened mass. At first the child thought his dog had discovered a dead cow. Then realization hit both boy and pet—the mass was a burning body—and, howling, they ran for help.

Quickly villagers gathered to view the gruesome sight; someone brought a brace of oxen and a bamboo sled to drag the corpse hurriedly from the field. Someone else ran to fetch a holy man who lived in nearby mountains, the worry being that murder by fire might curse the field and spoil the crop. But when the priest came and pronounced the body to be that of a Westerner (no Nepalese is more than six feet tall, as were the remains smoldering in the cornfield), he decreed that the omen was of no harm. It did not defile the crop. Besides, the first sun of the morning had broken through in a period when the valley was traditionally smothered in gray fog. The holy man stretched out his arm and pointed toward the Himalayas. Look! The Mother of the Winds was revealed in all her awesome glory. The holy man began to pray and the people joined him as oxen dragged the body of Laddie DuParr away.

The U.S. Consul in Nepal was fresh on the job, having been installed but a few weeks earlier. He was Al Eastham, a burly, red-bearded boy from Arkansas, seemingly plucked from the defensive line of a football team. He realized that Katmandu was not exactly the Court of St. James's, but he hoped the post would be interesting. His were chores of diplomatic mundaneness—passport and visa processing, advice to American businessmen, an eye on the activities and pronouncements of the King (one of the few absolute monarchs in the world who controls everything in his country, from the airline to the choicest property), extricating the occasional American youngster who got in a legal jam. On this morning of December 22, toward noon, a group of youngsters came into the modest consulate and brought a disturbing rumor: word was going around that the body of an American had been found just outside the city. Eastham groaned.

When an American citizen dies abroad, it is the responsibility of the consul to protect the remains, make identfication, determine cause of death, notify relatives, and arrange for the deceased to be shipped home, or buried locally, whatever is desired by the family. In a country like Nepal, the process has a certain urgency, for there are no morticians as known in Western society, no embalming, not even a cemetery. The country is 85 per cent Hindu and thus cremation is the custom. As he drove to the rural hospital where the corpse had been taken, Eastham told himself that *if* the body was indeed that of an American, please let there be adequate identification, and, God willing, a family somewhere easily located who would agree to local cremation.

* * *

The body lay on a wooden table in the autopsy room. Eastham could hold his gazes steady only long enough to see that fire had destroyed what life had once been within the mass of blackened flesh. Only one patch of white skin was uncharred, on the back below the shoulders, sufficient to establish that the corpse was indeed Western. No further identification was available—no papers, no passport. Fingerprints were taken, although the digits crumbled as they were dressed with ink and pressed to paper.

The next day Eastham returned to the hospital with a Polaroid camera, reasoning that, as identification would probably take weeks if not months, best he have a photograph should the need arise. He shot a full roll, wincing at the grisly task, then ordered his driver to return hastily to Katmandu. Eastham slumped in the back seat and closed his eyes, trying to erase the awful sight that had spoiled his morning.

Once again the fog was heavy and thick, and when the driver slowed the car, Eastham assumed that visibility was impaired. Then the driver spoke. "What's that?" he wondered. "Over there." He pointed to a group of villagers, gathered in a clump near the road, their figures looming eerily in the gray and mauve of the early morning. Nearby some Chinese Communist workers were building a brick plant and they were scurrying across plowed fields to look. Curious, Eastham got out of the car and stepped between a row of saplings, metal girdles about their trunks to keep the cows away. He walked thirty feet or so into the oozing marsh of a rice paddy. Steam and fog were rising from the wet earth, as if the field were a cauldron. Everything was in misted silhouette, like the painting of a French impressionist.

Politely, Eastham pushed his way through the Nepalese and came to the object of their attention. When he looked down, his stomach churned. Before him, on the rice field, lay still another corpse, also burned, blackened to such extreme that little could be told save the fact that it appeared to be a woman. Her eyes remained open in death and stared in horror at all those who approached. That night, Al Eastham, a strong man, could not sleep, nor think clearly. In office less than three weeks, already he had two unidentifiable corpses on his hands. He would say later, "I almost went bonzo."

Police of His Majesty's Government of Nepal fanned out in Freak Street to ask questions, for the pathologist's initial findings suggested that both bodies were of young Westerners. The male's throat had been cut, "not only cut, but cut away, almost to the point of decapitation," said the pathologist. The female had been stabbed four times just below the left breast, the blade piercing the aorta and causing a fountain of blood to erupt. Then gasoline was poured over the bodies and set on fire. "These are the most terrible killings I have ever seen," said the doctor, who in autopsies past had examined the remains of climbers mutilated from falls down mountains, and adulterous mates slain savagely in remote Himalayan villages.

Detectives stopped young people on the streets, interrupted meditations on the steps of pagodas, bent over to creep through passages leading to the Pleasure Room, questioned room clerks at those hotels—the Unity, the Monumental Lodge—that cater to the counterculture. At the Oriental, the desk clerk reported that two of the hotel's guests who had shared Room 9 were missing. One was a Canadian youngster named Laddie DuParr, the other an American girl named Annabella Tremont. They were friends, probably lovers, and their mutual acquaintances were worried. The two had not been seen for forty-eight hours. The clerk suggested the police talk to the Australian girls who seemed to know the missing couple well.

Mattie and Cora tried to be helpful, but they knew very little. Laddie had vanished first, inexplicably, and was gone at least a full day before Annabella grew concerned enough to go in search of him. Then *she* never returned. The only lead they could offer was that their friends had been spending a lot of time with "a Vietnamese-looking jewel dealer and his French wife" who drove a white rental car and who stayed in "some fancy hotel." That narrowed matters down considerably. As the investigators began checking registries at the few "fancy" hotels in

Katmandu, Al Eastham asked the Australian girls if they would accompany him to the hospital and view the corpses.

The remains of the male were sufficient for the girls to make a positive identification. "Possibly" it was Laddie, they agreed, but they could not be sure. How could they connect the Laddie they knew, a vertical six-foot-plus gentle giant of a man, with the horizontal lump of charcoal on the pathologist's table? Satisfied that they were telling the truth, Eastham led them to another room to see the second victim. While they waited outside in the corridor for the body to be brought out, the Australians began speaking of Annabella, of the sadness in her life, the unhappy love affair in Delhi, the affection she felt for Laddie. Annabella had shared much of her life story with them. One of the girls recalled a quite beautiful serpentine ring from a peddler's tray in Delhi, buried in a glut of junk sparkle.

When they entered the examining room, Mattie took but one drawn-breath look at the awful sight before she turned quickly away and said, "It's Annabella. I'm sure. Look! She's still wearing the ring—the one I was just telling you about." Eastham looked at the victim's hand. Though the gold was darkened by the fire, and though there was little left of the finger itself, the serpentine ring was intact. The Australian girls also recognized part of a sandal Annabella often wore, a shred of blouse, and a piece of brassiere that had escaped incineration. Then they grew faint and had to be helped out of the room where hysteria engulfed them.

It now seemed to Eastham and the Nepalese police that Annabella and Laddie were murder victims, and thus it stood for a day or two. Then a startling piece of news was developed by the investigators, one which would throw them off the track for several weeks. In a routine check of airport entrance and exit records, a card was discovered among the departure documents. It had been filled in by one Laddie DuParr of Canada, and it showed that he flew out of Katmandu headed for Bangkok on the night of December 23, the same day that Annabella's body was discovered. Two and two makes four in every language, and Nepalese police reasoned that DuParr murdered his girl friend and grabbed the first flight out of town. Thus was a "Wanted for Questioning" cable dispatched immediately to Interpol in Paris and thence to the capitals of Asia.

When he digested the news, Al Eastham accepted it, but he was nonetheless confused. If Laddie killed Annabella and skipped the country, then who was the first body found the day *before* the California woman was killed?

On the day after Christmas. in the California home of Annabella's parents, her mother, Jane, was cleaning house, a little concerned that her wandering daughter had not called home on the holiday. It was not like Annabella to miss an important occasion like Christmas. Her parents had spent the entire day watching and waiting for the phone to ring. Now, as Jane vacuumed the rug, the telephone interrupted. A Western Union operator identified herself and asked, gently, "Are you alone? Is there someone with you?" Jane said that she was indeed alone, but what did it matter to Western Union? "I'm so sorry," said the operator, "I wish to God I didn't have to read this, but it's my job. It's from Katmandu, Nepal. Quote: "A PERSON TENTATIVELY IDENTIFIED AS YOUR DAUGHTER, ANNABELLA TREMONT, HAS DIED IN KATMANDU.' " It was signed Alan Eastham, U.S. Consul.

And thus was the first message of death delivered, the first of many to devastate families across the world.

Teku is a burial place beside the Baghmati River in Katmandu, whose waters begin as melting snow in the great mountains. Three small temples, called *stupas,* surround a brick floor approximately ten feet square. They look like wedding cakes or beehives and are not as tall as a man. They are very holy. Like thousands of the dead that came before her, Annabella was brought to Teku wrapped in a coarse gray cotton shroud and placed on a bier of sandalwood and camphor and straw. After brief prayers from the one Protestant clergyman in the country, the straw was set ablaze and quickly the sticks turned into fire. For five hours the body burned; the ashes that remained were put into a bronze box that Al had bought in the bazaar. Had Annabella been Hindu, a bone would have been saved to throw into the Ganges, which dissolves all and helps speed reincarnation.

It occurred to Eastham, the only mourner, as he watched the service and prepared to ship the bronze box home, per Annabella's parents' instructions, that the service was simple, appropriate, and, in its way, exceptionally beautiful.

Not until May of the following year, 1976, would the police of Nepal amass enough information about the confounding murders to issue arrest warrants and formally charge Charles Sobhraj, Marie-Andrée Leclerc, and Ajay Chowdhury with double murder. The investigators should not be blamed for their delay and confusion. Charles had performed with Machiavellian intrigue.

On the fateful evening of December 23, 1975, he did indeed fly hurriedly out of Katmandu for Bangkok, using the passport of Laddie DuParr, who was at that moment in the autopsy room of a country hospital. Now, follow this closely: Charles spent only one night in Bangkok, *then turned around and returned to Katmandu,* this time again using the passport of Henricus Bintanja, the murdered Dutchman, also still unidentified. Why did he flee Katmandu successfully, Marie-Andrée beside him, only to return in twenty-four hours? "It was extremely bold and clever," said one of the Nepalese police officials many months later. "We think he left Katmandu in order to throw suspicion on Laddie DuParr. Another reason may be that he went to Bangkok to sell the ruby and other gemstones that the two victims owned. They were apparently worth about $2,000 combined. Then again, he may have wanted to make a quick check of the situation at home in Bangkok to determine if he had been linked to any of the murders there. Or, one further possibility, he might have gone to Bangkok and then started worrying about the murders in Katmandu. Some little detail might have started nagging him. The criminal, they say, always returns to the scene of the crime. . . . Whatever, the man left—and then he came back. It really takes your breath away."

On the night he spent in Bangkok, Charles hurried to

Kanit House and was stunned when he found his apartment dark and silent. The three French youths whom he had entrusted to be caretakers were in Paris, no doubt kissing the soil of France. Racing through the flat and finding no one, he picked up the phone and called Belle downstairs.

When she heard the familiar, sensuous voice and learned that he was back, just two floors above her, Belle's hand began to tremble and she feared her voice would break and betray her. She tried to remain calm and natural sounding. How was Katmandu? Weather nice? Empty questions rained from her mouth. Did Marie-Andrée buy any nice souvenirs? Perhaps the two of them would like to drop by several days hence once the Christmas social madness was over.

"Where are they?" cut through Charles. "Where did Dominique and the others go?" His voice was cold suddenly, and dangerous.

Belle had a story all prepared in case the need arose. Now she wondered if her voice would remain steady. "They said they received a cable saying to meet you in Hong Kong," answered Belle. Oh God, let me sound routine, she prayed. "They left suddenly. A day or two ago."

Charles did not seem convinced. "That can't be," he said. "They had no passports, no money."

"Maybe their families sent them some, or maybe they did some business," suggested Belle.

A low moan escaped from Charles. He was distraught. "But they *needed* me!" he cried. "They *loved* me! They were my *family!*" While Belle pondered the pathetic interpretation Charles was putting on his "betrayal" by his children, his voice abruptly turned ominous. "I will find them," he said. "I will find them and learn the truth."

That night Belle lay terrified in her bed. It was 11 P.M. Raoul would not be home until after midnight. She propped a chair against the door. Her hands held the telephone, ready to dial Raoul or the police if *anything* happened. Then, out of the silence, footsteps approached her door. Soft ones. Like someone creeping on cat feet. Past her front door they moved, died away, then returned. Suddenly a knock at her door! Quietly at first, then urgently.

Someone was pounding a fist, demanding entrance. She
was too terrified to dial the telephone, fearful it would
signal the person outside and confirm that she was within.
Belle threw her knuckles into her mouth. Paralyzing moments. Not until the footsteps finally went away and the
night returned to silence did she dare find a pillow and
scream into it, praying that her terror was muffled.

In Katmandu, police methodically questioned the
managements of the city's best hotels, and of car rental
agencies. A few interesting facts were emerging. One of
the villagers who lived near the place where the two bodies
were found told police he had seen a white car in the area
and one number on the license plate was "5." The Ghorka
Travel Agency reported that a white Toyota was turned
back in on December 23 by a slim white woman with a
French accent. The license number was 5001 and the
records showed it had been rented by a tourist named
"Henricus Bintanja," who was staying at the Hotel-Oberoi.
In a routine search of the car, police found several items
in the trunk: a pair of jeans, dark glasses, a cap, and a
lens cover for a camera. That was enough to send officers
hurrying to the hotel where Henricus Bintanja was supposedly in residence.

Charles opened his hotel door warmly, courteously, a
little annoyed at the intrusion to his holiday, but willing to
answer any questions. He identified himself as Mr. Bintanja, of Amsterdam, and introduced his companion,
"Cocky Hemker."

They were taken to the central police station, not far
from a statue of Bhairab, god of terror. In olden days,
suspected criminals were brought before the grotesque
figure and questioned. If the suspect was lying, legend had
it, he dropped dead immediately. As it would soon turn
out, modern police could have used the help of Bhairab or
any indicator of truth-telling to deal with Charles Sobhraj.

He treated them as superior to inferior. He fell back on
a favorite disguise, professor of "social sciences" at a
European university, on sabbatical in the Far East. His
lady, Cocky was a genteel scholar and research assistant.
Yes, he said, they had rented a white Toyota to view the
shrines. No, he insisted, neither of them had ever met or

heard of Laddie DuParr or Annabella Tremont. His face
was haughty, like a social lion falsely accused of consorting
with *clochards*. It was unlikely that they would encounter
two hippies from Freak Street, as their frame of reference was the Hotel Soaltee-Oberoi. They produced
restaurant receipts and documents from the casino showing
currency exchanges for the time when police believed the
two murders occurred.

To all questions, Charles responded patiently. He was in
complete control, as unruffled as a fat hen in a favorite
coop. Only when one of the investigators started to take
Marie-Andrée into another room for private questioning
did Charles turn testy. Hadn't the police bothered them
enough? Hadn't they answered every question? It was,
after all, Christmas, and though the holiday was not
celebrated in Nepal, *they* were Christians and entitled to
be left alone on the sacred day of Jesus Christ's birth.
Enough! "My companion is a scholar," protested Charles.
"She has never had contact with the police before." It
worked. Police released them with appreciation for their
answers, but warned of further questioning should the
need arise.

For two days, the couple was kept under casual surveillance by the hotel management, by police instruction.
Neither "Bintanja" nor his companion seemed the least bit
concerned. They feasted on Christmas Day and gambled
enthusiastically in the casino. The police were about ready
to dismiss the couple, when a detective named Preman
Bizra found himself troubled. He thought it necessary to
ask further questions concerning the articles found in the
trunk of the rented white Toyota. The jeans were for a
very tall man, six feet or more, and Henricus Bintanja was
short, more like a Nepalese.

Collecting a sputtering Charles Sobhraj at the hotel,
Bizra drove him downtown for another round of questioning. Marie-Andrée was ill, "feminine problems," and she
was permitted to stay in her room. Charles endured
another solid hour or two of questions, brushing off every
query. The jeans in the car trunk? "They're not mine and
I have no idea how they got in there," he snapped. "It is a
rental car, and the jeans probably belonged to the previous

renter. As for me, I never opened the trunk. Not a single time." Nor did he know anything about the spectacles or the cap or the lens cover. His attitude changed from helpful to surly, and at nightfall officer Bizra thanked him and gave him a ride back to the hotel on his motor-cycle.

During the night, the young police officer slept poorly. A replay of the afternoon's questioning tormented his peace. In the darkness and silence of his bed, it occurred to him that this man Henricus Bintanja was a bit *too* un-ruffled, *too* glib, *too* quick with his answers. Any man should be nervous when being questioned by police over two murders, at least a *little bit* nervous. This man seemed less concerned than he would have been if a waiter brought tea instead of coffee. And the woman! Why was she tense, and pale, and why was she *twice* as nervous as the man? Just as the young policeman drifted off, he decided to pick up the couple in the morning for one more round of questions. No doubt it would be futile, but Bizra was not yet totally convinced he had learned the whole truth from "Henricus Bintanja."

The next morning, when Bizra knocked at the door of Room 415 in the Hotel Soaltee-Oberoi, there was no answer. He knocked again. The room clerk and the door-man had just assured the officer that neither Bintanja nor his girl friend had left the hotel. They were still registered. Hurriedly Bizra swept through the lobby and public rooms and failed to find them. He found the manager and ordered him to open the locked door. "Curious," mur-mured the manager. "It's locked from the inside. They must be asleep. I can't waken them."

The cop did not hesitate. Break down the door, he directed. The manager blanched. Would the police accept responsibility? Bizra nodded.

The room was empty. The occupants had left their luggage behind and had escaped during the night. It was reasoned that the woman left routinely via the door and waited downstairs, while the man locked the room from the inside, slipped out the window, and in a breathtaking acrobatic feat somehow descended four flights by clinging to windowsills and jutting bricks. Bizra stared at the wall of the hotel and cursed, angry that he had not entertained his suspicions earlier.

Immediately word was sent to the airport to watch all departing passengers; the roads in and around Katmandu filled with police looking for an alleged Dutchman and his girl friend. But at this moment, the quarry was far away. Charles and Marie-Andrée and Ajay Chowdhury were somewhere between Katmandu and the border of India, whipping a hapless taxi driver like a balky camel to deliver them out of the kingdom of Nepal.

Behind them, in the hotel room, they had abandoned three suitcases with at least $2,000 worth of clothing, scores of paperback books including *Palmistry Made Easy*, and several oddments—a portable fire extinguisher ("a very good weapon," mused Bizra), four pairs of men's gloves (an unusual item for travelers in the tropical East and which police believed were used to avoid fingerprints), and a large world map on which someone had traced journeys. Lines crisscrossed the globe from Paris to Hong Kong, indicating hundreds of thousands of miles of travel, zigzagging back and forth, east to west, up and down the world, journeys beyond the imagination and endurance of a hundred Marco Polos.

At the Oriental Lodge on Freak Street, investigators found very little in the room that had been occupied by Laddie DuParr and Annabella. In the boy's address book was a new entry for someone named "A. Gauthier" with a Bangkok address, and among Annabella's belongings was a piece of paper with the same name and address. A map was found that belonged to DuParr, showing his travel routes, and directly in the middle of the blue Indian Ocean was written the cryptic phrase "A. Gauthier is called Bintanja, Henk. Soaltee Hotel." But at this moment in the macabre mess, the Nepalese police did not notice it nor make the connection. After several more days, when no identification was made for the male body that had been burned beyond recognition, it was cremated at Teku and the ashes put in a jar and stored on a shelf. Laddie DuParr would have to wait quite a long time before he was returned to the farm in Canada, just beyond the end of the road.

*　*　*

For twenty-four hours they exhorted the taxi driver to hurry, ignoring his pleas that the road was poor and the route dangerous in the middle of a December night. A light snow fell as the taxi left the mountains and descended into a forest of acacia, thence to the flat savannah belt that is the bottom of Nepal and home to tiger, leopard, white rhino, and packs of wolves. Several times the taxi spun out, almost plunging off the road at hairpin curves. Marie-Andrée screamed, but Charles slapped her. She finally found the thinnest of sleep. Beside them, Ajay Chowdhury sat silently.

When the border town of Birganj was reached, Charles paid the taxi and directed his companions to cross the checkpoint on foot. It was December 29. Each crossed separately, each presenting a false passport, explaining to the Nepalese guards that they were naturalists, on a wild-life trek, photographing flora and fauna. Once safely across and on Indian soil, Charles hired three horses from a farmer with the promise to return them in an hour. Half a day later, when the exhausted animals began to foam and convulse, they were abandoned. Indefatigable, Charles led his companions onto a highway where he flagged another taxi, thrusting rupees by the handfuls at the driver, insisting that he take them deeper into India. Somewhere was a ferry that took two hours to creep across a swift river. Then another taxi. And another. They reached Patna, where five centuries before Christ a civilization of gasping opulence existed and where epic poetry was read in pavilions of gold and pink pearl. There they stumbled onto a DC-3 of Air India and were deposited quickly thereafter, on the last night of 1975, in Calcutta.

Here it was cold. Strong winds drove the beggars and untouchables to press their bodies against the sides of buildings, hoping for warmth. The wretched wrapped themselves and their children in thin gray blankets and huddled together.

Charles found a cheap hotel and helped Marie-Andrée into a room. She fell across an iron cot whose sheets were coarse. Her face was burning with fever, and when she tried to stand the room spun dizzily about her. Surely she was rueful. She had nothing left but the filthy clothes on her back, a purse with no money, a passport that was not hers. Charles had even robbed her of an identity, had lured her with the promise of love to the state of nothingness where he had for most of his life been a citizen.

At midnight, the man who had promised her a palace but who at this changing of the years could deliver only a cubicle that reeked with the stench of lower-class India, this man kissed her and whispered *"Bonne année, chérie."*

Sometime before the first light of the new year, she wrote in her diary: "I think I am going crazy . . . I am sick . . . I will die with pain. I am dying, drowning, crushed. Nobody can take me out of this . . . I cannot trust me anymore. For I am nothing. Nothing . . ."

CHAPTER THIRTY-FOUR

The river Ganges, Mother of Life, Mother of Death, Mother of India, flows from north to south, save for a few puzzling miles at Varanasi where, curiously, it changes directions. Some contend this is tribute from the gods to the holiness of a city as old as Babylon, the only place on earth where the most celebrated industry is death and transfiguration. The Western eye newly affixed on Varanasi is assaulted by a spectacle beyond imagination and comprehension, a carnival of ochers and rusts veined by the shock of yellow smoke rising from the biers of the burning dead, where the old come to wait for the end and the beginning. To die in Varanasi, they say, is to be closer to heaven, insurance of a higher status in the next life. Each dawn the Ganges performs two duties—dissolution of ashes and bones scattered by the mourners, and caressing and cleansing the living who bathe in the very same flow.

Here widows wear white saris and sit in open-air pavilions beside the river, singing monotonous hymns of grief and loss. Here one of the most distinguished jobs is "caretaker in charge of burning." At the principal crematorium, he and he alone ignites the holy wood that reduces a corpse to nothing but ashes. But the power of Hindu is that, even as the flames destroy, a new incarnation begins. Above the crematorium, guarding the roof of the house of the dead, carved tigers prowl in ferocious relief, metaphorically reminding that death is waiting for all.

In the first week of January 1976, Charles Sobhraj es-

corted Marie-Andrée, Ajay, and a new acquaintance down
the steep, slippery steps of a *ghat*, a stone porch beside
the river, where hundreds of pilgrims, mostly women,
were cautiously and modestly lowering their bodies into the
cold and sulfurous-smelling waters. The new man, police
would soon learn, was a young Israeli named Avoni Jacob,
thin, bearded, a student in his mid-twenties who was interested in Eastern religions and nursed vague intentions of
writing a book that contrasted them with Judaism. Note
pads spilled from his pockets, filled with thousands of
words each day. He was quiet and rarely spoke to anyone,
but on New Year's Day in Calcutta, Jacob had met a
friendly and helpful Eurasian named "Alain Ponant."
When they discovered that *both* planned journeys to
Varanasi, it was decided to travel together.

Marie-Andrée had protested feebly that she could not
possibly rise from her iron cot and accompany Charles
and a "Jew man," as Jacob was described, on yet another
journey across India. But when Charles threatened to
abandon her in Calcutta, she rose quickly enough and
packed a few new clothes purchased to replace the wardrobe abandoned in Katmandu.

Undoubtedly, Charles held the Israeli spellbound as he
pointed out the sights and shocks of Varanasi. He always
knew his territory. Here was where Buddha preached his
first sermon, and over there the Emperor Ashoka built a
temple in the third century, B.C., that contained a spectacular sandstone pillar supporting a carved lion holding the
dharama-chakra, "wheel of law," which is to this day part
of India's national flag. During their morning tour of the
city, Charles suggested to Marie-Andrée that all bathe in
the river. The devout believed it washed away illness and
sin. Marie-Andrée frowned and shook her head. The river
stank. It filled her with revulsion. Jacob, however, purchased a small clay jug and descended to the Ganges and
filled it. The water he brought back smelled clean. It would
stay sweet and fresh, legend said, for as long as it was
possessed.

They walked farther along the Ganges, whose banks
contain seventy-four *ghats*, each crowded with pilgrims, so
many that it becomes difficult to see the rites. A boat was
engaged and it bore Charles and his friends along the river

for a better view of the spectacle. Jacob wrote in one of his notebooks: "The owner of the boat would not take us close enough to shore to see the bodies burning, but we could see the smoke from the pyres rising and drifting over the Ganges . . . Later we saw mourners bringing a dead man to the crematorium. A hundred men were packed tightly together, and their shoulders carried a wooden pallet on which the corpse rested . . . An air of celebration! Chanting, singing, shouting, it is a festival of death."

On the morning of January 6, 1976, a cleaning woman entered the hotel room where Avoni Jacob was an occupant. She screamed. Sprawled naked across his cot, the Israeli's neck bore ugly purple marks. He had been drugged and strangled. His credentials and valuables were missing. Little was left save a few pages of his notebooks, one of which contained a final entry: "I would like to stay in Varanasi until I understand more. Every exit is an entrance. If one believes strongly enough, life can be lived without fear of death. Here one can almost touch what is hidden, what is beyond . . ."

Police would quickly learn that Jacob's killer had stolen his traveler's checks and cashed two of them, worth $150, at a nearby hotel. The killer had no trouble with the transaction; he used Avoni Jacob's passport. It was also determined that the Israeli had but a few hundred dollars to his name. "Not very much to die for," said a detective, who would one day accuse Charles Sobhraj, Marie-Andrée Leclerc, and Ajay Chowdhury of the murder.

In their wake, the number of dead was now eight.

Avoni Jacob was cremated and his ashes thrown into the river beside which he had walked in awe a few hours before his death.

In Bangkok, Belle and Raoul waited each day with the expectation that police would burst into their apartment building in search of the suspected killers. Surely the three French boys—Dominique, Yannick, and Jacques—were safely in Paris and had reported the ghastly tale of torture and death to Interpol. But New Year's Day came and went, and January slipped by. Belle began to realize, sadly, that help was not over the next hill. The fact was that the

three youths were so frightened that they did not want to
risk further involvement. Alain Gauthier often said that
his arm stretched across continents. And Dominique
learned from a doctor in Paris that his blood contained
strychnine.

Courage is a rare commodity, conceived now and then
in unlikely wombs. With her apartment securely locked,
Belle stayed inside, alternating as the prisoner of fear and
rage. Raoul continued to counsel his wife that the best
avenue to travel was one that steered far away from whatever did or did not happen two flights above them. And
though her head told her that Raoul was right, her heart
disagreed.

One morning she rose and drank coffee and stared out
her window and decided to break open the chamber of
horrors. She could not live with her conscience, otherwise
the memories would torment her the rest of her days. The
way to start, she reasoned, was to wangle entrance to
Alain Gauthier's apartment. At that very moment, destiny
sent the housemaid to walk along the corridor outside her
apartment. The maid had a passkey. She was Belle's
friend.

Quickly Belle prepared a story about how she needed
to get into her friend's apartment because she had left
an important document there. The maid, smiling conspiratorially, agreed. Later it would be revealed that the
cleaning woman, as is the custom of those in her business,
had sized up the situation inside Alain Gauthier's apartment long ago—but was afraid to speak out for fear of
losing her job.

With her heart in her throat, Belle entered the apartment. She felt like a deep sea diver, prowling the wreckage
of a party ship. Everything was dark, everything was
shadows. Yet she felt the powerful presence of Gauthier.
She fully expected him to step out of the closet and pour
poison down her mouth. Hurriedly she crept about, daring only five minutes, but that was enough to locate the
diary of Cocky Hemker, the Dutch girl, her handbag,
shoes, and souvenirs purchased in Hong Kong. Belle carefully tore out one page of the journal and slipped it inside
her blouse. In a large cardboard box she found a blizzard

of documents—receipts, boarding passes, hotel bills—some bearing the names of people who had been grief guests in this room and who were now missing, presumed—by the three French youths—to be dead.

A noise outside the apartment sent panic washing over the plucky French housewife and she made a hasty exit, not daring to grab documents from the cardboard box. It took the rest of the day for her heart to stop pounding.

Now Belle was convinced. No doubt remained in her mind that her friends were killers. But what could she do about it? One of the people in Bangkok whose opinion she respected was a French businessman and she told him the story, worried that he would think she was going insane. "I believe you," he said quietly. "But I don't think the Thai police will." His recommendation was to seek pressure from the diplomatic community, the only foreigners who could exert influence on the police force. An appointment was arranged with a British diplomat who agreed to hear Belle's story.

The Englishman listened attentively with trademarked politeness, but as Belle's dark tale poured out, skepticism and disbelief marched visibly across his face—the attitude officials have when dealing with nuts. True, he did make a few cursory notes, but he seemed anxious to usher Belle out of his office. Perhaps later the diplomat had second thoughts, for he did send a report to the Thai police. But nothing came of it. Either the report was not believed, or it was couched in disclaimers, or it got lost. It did contain one long and convoluted sentence that should have snared *somebody's* attention at the police station: "Allegedly, Gauthier in the course of his jewel business would frequent the lesser known hotels in Bangkok, picking up young persons whom he would discover had traveler's cheques, befriend them on the pretext of helping them buy gemstones, take them back to his flat where he would wine and dine them, invite them to stay, and ultimately extract their monies and valuables, disposing of them in the manner of the Dutch couple . . ."

Even with this shocking accusation, nothing was done. Incredibly, the Thai police did not even send a patrolman over to Belle's apartment for amplification. "I told you so," said Raoul, when Belle finally confided in her husband.

He complimented her on her moral courage, but suggested it was now time to stop playing Inspector Maigret. Visa renewal time was approaching for both of them, and it would not be wise to have their names listed on police reports. "Now forget about them," pressed Raoul. "They'll never come back here." She agreed, but forgetting was not easy, particularly in the nights when she waited for her husband to return from the hotel kitchens, suspecting somehow that she had not seen the last of the tenant in Apartment 503.

The subjects of Belle's concern next turned up in Goa, the former Portuguese colony on the lower Western coast of India. When Charles and his companions arrived in the city of Panaji around January 7, 1976, the area was crowded with tourists—mostly young, mostly naïve, exquisitely ripe.

How absurdly easy it had become. Within hours, Charles zeroed in on three young Frenchmen whom, police would learn, he encountered shopping in the Brick Market, where everything from pineapples picked an hour ago to antique statues of Catholic saints is sold. Goa was rich in religious artifacts as the first Christian colony in the East. All in their early twenties, the three youths were traveling in a van of recent vintage and seemed more affluent than Goa's run-of-the-mill dropouts. They were the kind of Frenchmen encountered on the Boulevard St.-Michel in Paris, lean, stylish, attractive, flirtatious, and appreciative of all women. They kissed Marie-Andrée's hand on first meeting, a touch of gallantry that must have been welcome after the frenetic events of the past fortnight that had begun on the night she fled Katmandu.

By nightfall, they were fast friends, Ajay having materialized from the shadows to join the party, thus evening up the sides. The next day, a glorious interlude on the beach! Lunch was taken at a thatched hut cafe where great platters of cold lobster and crayfish almost spilled into their laps. Then, a siesta under coconut palms, and by nightfall, a hash pipe going around with Charles pretending to make liberal intake. None of the others knew that he would not risk consuming a drop of alcohol or a mouthful of consciousness-altering smoke. He faked being stoned, and no one knew how brilliant was his acting.

The next morning, the French youths announced they were going to a remote beach near the coastal town of Karwar, further south, below Goa. Was there room for his party, wondered Charles? *"Bien sûr,"* answered Eric d'Amour, owner of the van. Just before departure, Charles slipped away and bought a quart of scotch whisky, an expensive indulgence in India that can cost forty dollars or more.

The van stopped for the night on an empty beach beside the Arabian Sea, a place where it was possible to believe no one had ever set foot before. Marie-Andrée busied herself about the campfire, grilling two freshly killed chickens. A radio picked up a faraway station that played something akin to rock. Fueled by the whisky that Charles produced, and hash pipes, and the warm and sensuous breezes from the sea, everyone felt perfect. They danced and gnawed at the chicken and reveled in being young, unencumbered, occupants of a piece of earth so remote that no one could have conjured it in wildest fantasy.

But sometime later, one of the French boys murmured with a thick tongue, "Alain, your whisky is very good. And strong." One of the others stumbled and fell in the sand, giggling. Then all three dropped in their tracks. Thirty-six hours later they awoke in a hospital somewhere in the south of India, frightened, confused, their heads aching and empty. Their van, they would soon learn, was totally destroyed, and all of their personal belongings—luggage, camera, radios, passport, money—gone. So were the nice French couple and the Indian man whom they had met three days earlier in the Brick Market. What happened was not hard for police to reconstruct. The theory was that the scotch whisky was heavily laced with a tranquilizer, probably Valium, and when the French trio fell asleep, they were administered injections of a powerful sleeping powder. Empty packages of the drug were found in the wreck of the van.

It was further believed that the three unconscious youths were tossed in the back of the van and their belongings removed. Then someone started the vehicle, reached a speed of 60 mph, placed a rock on the accelerator, and leaped out. The van was headed for a cliff that would send it tumbling into the sea. But the driverless vehicle swerved and smashed into a palm tree, a violent collision that the drugged Frenchmen did not even hear or feel. Nearby villagers heard and ran to the scene, pulled the unconscious victims from the van, thinking that they had been knocked out in the accident. "We were supposed to die," said Eric d'Amour months later, "but fate gave us a second chance."

In Bangkok, Belle wrestled with her conscience—and lost. She decided to make one more try at getting someone in authority to believe her. This time she chose the French Embassy—her own government—where a lower echelon officer listened to the incredible story. Not only did he disbelieve, he delivered a stern lecture to Belle on the danger of becoming involved with a Thai police matter. He cautioned her that if she kept spreading this tale the police might arrest her as a co-conspirator. "Then and there I decided to stop being a detective," said Belle. And then and there humiliation replaced courage.

Charles led his followers across India, through Bangalore, the city whose name translates "baked beans," down to Madras, then, apparently in search of new territory, to Singapore. Here Charles passed through airport control by using the passport of Avoni Jacob, the Israeli strangled in the holy city of Varanasi. He took the precaution of removing Jacob's photograph and replacing it with his favorite pose—the portrait of himself he wanted the world to see. He was wearing a beautifully tailored jacket, tie, carefully combed hair, and a benign, somewhat mocking smile. He looked dignified and prosperous.

On his arm Marie-Andrée entered Singapore using the passport of a man, Eric d'Amour, the unfortunate Frenchman whose van was wrecked south of Goa. She protested to Charles on the flight from Madras to Singapore that surely the authorities would note the discrepancy between her newly pasted photograph and a masculine name on the document. "Don't be silly, *chérie*," he answered. "In the East, they don't understand Western names." She was admitted to Singapore without a second glance, with no more trouble than when she used to take the ferryboat from Lévis to Quebec City a thousand years ago.

They quarreled bitterly in Singapore, in a bleak room at the YMCA Hotel. If Charles did not let her go, if he did not buy her an airplane ticket for Canada, for home, then surely she would go insane. Of course his response was to put on his soothing, healing, reassurance act, which must have been remarkable. While he whispered his devotion to Marie-Andrée and thanked her for loyalty and strength, he slipped a lovely gold Omega watch on her thin arm and took her to bed. Afterwards, while she slept, Charles slipped out of Singapore with Ajay and was gone for a week, on "business."

Marie-Andrée was left alone for the week. How easy it would have been for her to go to the Canadian Consul and report her passport stolen and cable her family for passage money home. But she did not. She had the opportunity to escape and she did not take it. Later, she would contend that she was frightened, that Charles had warned her that she was under constant surveillance by one of his Singapore colleagues. But the sorrowful truth seemed to be something else. One night in Charles' arms was enough to reignite her passion and her hope that the day would come when she could claim his full devotion. The last entry in her diary, undated but probably written about this time, reflects the strange power of love:

> Day after day, a small piece of myself was taken out of me . . . Day after day I was hurt, I was destroyed little by little. But I'm still on my way, even though I fell in a ditch. I still have hope, and this hope is the only thing I have, and I must hold to it tightly.
>
> If Charles succeeds in taking me out of this ditch and puts me again on the road, I shall live.
>
> If Charles walks on my side and helps me to stay on the road, then I shall go very far, and I shall regain my happiness.
>
> He is the only man who can help me, for I love

him so much that I can make only one being with
him. I can only exist because of him. I can only
breathe because of him. And, my love is increasing . . .

A point of emphasis: according to the passport in her
purse, Marie-Andrée Leclerc had become a Frenchman
named Eric d'Amour. She was abandoned in a hotel in
Singapore. The police of half the world would soon be
seeking her. But her love for the man who had brought
her to this desperate place was "increasing."

If only she had known that at this moment, the "business" that took Charles out of Singapore was a flight to
Bangkok, where he spent an indolent and gratifying week
with Suzy the waitress in the luxury of a deluxe hotel
suite.

In Amsterdam, and Paris, and Los Angeles, and Winnipeg, alarms were at last being sounded by families who
were coming to the reluctant decision that their children
were lost, or in trouble. The pattern was generally the
same. Parents fretted for a few weeks over the absence of
mail or telephone calls from their wandering young. Then
denial set in, whistling-in-the-dark reassurances that mail
from the East was undependable and slow. Worry re-
asserted itself. Sleepless nights multiplied. Finally, concern
grew until they beseeched authorities for help.

The parents of Laddie DuParr asked the Canadian Red
Cross, the Department of External Affairs, and even the
Royal Canadian Mounties to search for their son, unheard
from for two months. Laddie's last letter was postmarked
Katmandu—dated mid-December—and in it he said he
would rendezvous with his brother in Bangkok by February. The Canadian Government promptly sent cables to
their diplomatic representatives in Nepal and Thailand.
Back came the shocking news that Laddie DuParr was
being sought for double murder, a ghoulish prank of fate
that would not be cleared up until blame was affixed on
the elusive shoulders of Charles Sobhraj.

South of Los Angeles, Maggie's fears for her granddaughter mounted. She first began to worry on Thanksgiving Day, 1975, when Jennie neither sent greetings by
mail nor telephoned. "Jennie always keeps in touch,"

fretted Maggie to Cap. He pacified her. Jennie was probably halfway up some Himalayan peak, meditating and
drinking yak milk. Not to worry. "But she didn't even
write and let us know she reached the monastery safely
in Katmandu," countered Maggie. It was uncharacteristic
of her granddaughter to be so thoughtless. As autumn
deepened, Maggie wrote three letters to the Kopan Monastery. The first two were not answered. The third was returned marked "undeliverable." By Christmas Day, Maggie was certain that something had happened to the child
that she had raised.

In early January, her fears were confirmed. One of
Jennie's Buddhist friends in Los Angeles telephoned to report that Lama Yeshe in Katmandu had written a disturbing letter. Jennie never reached the monastery. The monks
and nuns had been expecting her and were concerned.
Had Jennie abandoned her plan? "Dear God," whispered
Maggie. She rushed to the church and fell to her knees
and prayed to St. Jude.

Immediately, Maggie telephoned Seattle, looking for
Christopher, and discovered that he, too, was off on another world journey and perhaps would meet Jennie at
the monastery. *That* lifted the old woman's spirits, for she
trusted Jennie's former boy friend and believed that he
would let her know if anything was wrong. Then she rang
the office of U.S. Senator Alan Cranston, got a brush-off,
followed up with letters and telephone calls all over official Washington. At one point, caught in a frustrating trap
of buck-passings and bureaucratic arrogance, Maggie lost
her temper and yelled at a rude woman in the State Department, "I don't give a damn what you can or cannot do!
I'm a taxpayer and my granddaughter is missing!" Later,
reflecting, Maggie would recall the moment: "I felt so
helpless. Everybody was brushing me away like a crazy
woman. I couldn't even get the name of one single person
to call in Hong Kong or Katmandu or Bangkok. Was I
asking too much? All I wanted was *somebody* with sense
who worked for my own government in Asia to help me.
Isn't that what we pay them to do?"

And in Seattle, Jennie's friends received the news of her
disappearance with no great alarm. Margret and Cybilla
both assumed that Jennie had met a man and was having

"one last fling" before she cloistered herself in the monastery. Then both young women experienced strange dreams in which Jennie appeared to them in distress. Cybilla found her encounter with Jennie to be so vivid that it "was not a dream," rather a meeting between the two girls "on the astral plane." She "saw" her friend inside some sort of warehouse, surrounded by cardboard boxes, trying to struggle free, crying out, "Help me!"

It must be remembered that Jennie's friends in Seattle were mostly young women who had experimented liberally with drugs, and mysticism, and assorted exotic and esoteric philosophies. Perhaps their "dreams" and "astral encounters" should be gently put in the same category as séances. But one other curious occurrence in Seattle cannot be so easily explained. A group of feminists with whom Jennie had been associated held a weekend retreat in the woods during the time that she was missing. After a day of speeches and discussion and sisterhood, the women built a campfire and danced around it, linking arms. One of the women present, older, in her fifties, was known to be shy and preferred to go unnoticed. Someone asked her to join the circle, but she declined, saying that she did not dance well and was, in truth, clumsy. Her feet would probably trip her neighbor and cause the circle to tumble. But in mid-dance the woman suddenly rose and entered the dancing. She danced with passion, with enormous energy, with skill, with such abandon that the others stopped to watch, in wonder. It was as if a force had briefly taken command of her body. Later, Cybilla knew the reason. "Jennie came to us that night," she would say. "Jennie entered this woman's body and became part of us again."

When the dance was over, the woman had no recollection of what she had done.

On the night of February 18, 1976, a date Maggie remembers well, for she is a no-nonsense person who lives an ordered life, an eerie experience gave her the information she needed. It cannot be explained, nor, on the other hand, can it be dismissed as the hallucination of a desperate, distraught old woman.

Maggie was asleep, in her bed beside Cap, when she bolted awake. Or thought she did. Something was in the room. Some *presence* was pulling her out of sleep. Obediently, Maggie rose and went to the hallway and saw a light burning in the breakfast room. Strange, she thought. Never did Maggie leave this light on overnight, and indeed she well remembered turning it off in a sweep of the house before retiring. Electricity is expensive. Better turn it off, she muttered to herself. But when she reached the threshold of the breakfast room, her hand flew to her mouth. Someone was sitting calmly at the table. It was Jennie. The old Jennie, from years earlier, when she was young and fresh and radiant, the Jennie who danced on the sand, the Jennie whose face was unclouded by darkness, looking exactly as she did on the miniature portrait that dangled from Maggie's family tree in the living room. Rushing to her, Maggie exclaimed, "Where have you been, honey? The whole world's looking for you?"

Jennie held out her hand in a command to stop. She spoke softly. "I was waiting for you to bring me home, Grandma. You promised. Remember how you promised?" Then she smiled, serenely, and laughed, laughed until a line of red rose from her throat to fill her face. It was as if she had washed in blood.

In her bed, Maggie woke up screaming. Thank God, she reassured herself. Only a nightmare. But she glanced into the hallway and saw a light coming from the breakfast room. This time, fully awake and rational, Maggie crept fearfully down the hall. The breakfast room was empty. But the window was open. It had been stuck for more than a year after a painting and neither Maggie nor Cap even bothered to try budging it anymore. A cold wind blew against her face.   —

At that moment Maggie knew, in a heart suddenly iced, that Jennie was dead.

In Amsterdam, the families of Henricus Bintanja and Cornelia Hemker did not wait as long before asking The Hague's foreign office to locate their out-of-touch children. When Christmas, 1975, passed, as well as another important family occasion, the Dutch parents sought help quickly. Last word received from the missing young couple was in early December, in letters written from Hong Kong. Cocky Hemker wrote ebulliently of their stay, of various souvenirs purchased there—a fan, black clogs, posters, the $1,600 sapphire ring—and she devoted several paragraphs to the attractive man they had encountered. His name was Alain Dupuis, a resident of Bangkok, a gem dealer.

Enter now a key figure in the case, and an unlikely one at that. His name was Herman Knippenberg, second secretary of the Netherlands Embassy in Thailand, possessor of a boyish face with hair slicked down diplomatically, chipmunk teeth, and a sensual, fleshy caste. He looked rather like one of the younger town guilders in Rembrandt's *Night Watch,* and had he lived in the seventeenth century, surely he would have been guardian of the strongbox. Not only was Herman honest, he was dogged to the point of nuisance. His intellectual credentials were strong: fluent in several languages, working in 1976 on a long-distance PhD from Johns Hopkins University in political science. The problem wth Herman, his detractors said, was that he was querulous and abrasive, two qualities not calculated for diplomatic giant steps. Usually Herman said just what he wanted to say, and from time to time was reprimanded for bullheadedness.

Why destiny chose to weave him into the tapestry of Charles Sobhraj was a question he did not explore. But before his involvement with the case was over, Herman found his marriage to a lovely and equally brilliant young woman named Angela severely shaken, his career in crisis, and his life in danger. It is fair to say that Herman was one of the good guys—and high time that one showed up.

A routine request from The Hague to locate Henricus Bintanja and Cocky Hemker landed on Herman's desk in early February, the kind of unimportant, pain-in-the-ass chore passed down to second secretaries. But Herman did not kiss it off; indeed he approached it with the approximate zeal he would have put into representing his government at a summit meeting. Within ten days, Herman had assembled three disturbing pieces of information:

1. The missing young couple definitely entered Thailand, in early December, according to landing cards found in the immigration files at the Bangkok airport.

2. Mail from home was waiting for the couple at the *poste restante* in Bangkok. It was never picked up. Strange.

3. The passports of both Bintanja and Hemker were close to expiration. They should have come to the Dutch Embassy for renewal. They did not.

All of this struck one practical Dutchman as being unusual behavior for two of his methodical countrymen. He then turned to the file of unidentified dead bodies that every foreign embassy keeps, news clippings and the like, in case something like this mystery turns up. At any given moment there are more than six hundred unidentified corpses in the Bangkok morgue, and it would be difficult not to mention gruesome to inspect them. But as Herman perused the clip file, he kept returning to the photograph and article concerning two charred corpses found outside Bangkok on December 16, roughly the time period when Bintanja and Hemker were supposed to be in Thailand. He telephoned the morgue and determined that the original belief that these remains were of an Australian couple was incorrect. The Australians had surfaced somewhere in the East, and the two burned bodies in Bangkok were still unidentified. On a hunch, Herman asked The Hague to forward dental records of Bintanja and Hemker. Then he located a Dutch woman dentist in Bangkok who was a Seventh-Day Adventist missionary. She agreed to undertake a grisly task. The Thai police dispatched a strong young officer to escort Herman and the woman dentist to the morgue, warning that the experience would be unpleasant.

An understatement. When they entered the examining room of the police hospital morgue, the two bodies were laid out on tables. An overwhelming smell rushed at them in waves, mingling the sticky heat of Bangkok and the powerful fumes of Lysol and preservative. The corpses were scarcely more than chunks of charcoal hanging from exposed bones; with the passage of time, everything had shrunk and decomposed. The policeman assigned to assist Herman and the woman dentist promptly fainted, keeling over on the tile floor. Herman was almost grateful, for it gave him a reason to turn away from the horror spread before his eyes. The dentist went about her job with cool precision, so efficiently that it took her but a few minutes to make positive identification. Yes, she nodded. In her strong face was a sudden sadness. The bodies were definitely those of Henricus Bintanja, who wanted to be a doctor, and his lover, Cornelia Hemker, a very good nurse.

Anger, not sorrow, filled Herman, and from that plateau his rage would grow. When he returned to the embassy and made his report that would be cabled home to The Hague and thence to the families, Herman received a nod for his detective work. "Too bad about the kids" was the attitude. They must have encountered some native Thai bandits. Case closed. Now Herman could return to economic indicators and visa applications. Obediently Herman returned to his desk, but the stack of Indonesian newspapers he was required to cull somehow seemed unimportant. He suspected that unless somebody applied sufficient pressure to the Thai police, then the killer(s) of his two countrymen would go uncaught, unpunished.

Nothing impulsive is appropriate in the diplomatic business, certainly not among the Dutch. Nonetheless Herman defied the protocol of his position and charged over to the Thai police Crime Suppression Bureau. Having no trouble sounding very official and ambassadorial, Herman presented his case. Two Dutch citizens had been brutally murdered in Thailand. Surely the Thai police would want to launch an immediate and massive search for the maniac who did this. In response, Herman received polite smiles—the patented kind Orientals give to Westerners—and nothing else. Although the officer indicated the matter would be studied, Herman left Crime Suppression Division knowing full well that he had not lit a fire.

Any diplomatic officer worth his pinstripes would have let the matter drop at this time. A dossier would not be enriched by the notation that a representative of Queen Juliana was pressuring a foreign government's police department. But Herman had no room for graceful withdrawal in his makeup. He decided to be his own detective, to build a case so compelling that the Thai police would be forced to act. But where to begin?

He reread Cocky Hemker's letter to her family, mailed from Hong Kong. The name "Alain Dupuis" leaped out at him. If indeed the murdered couple had kept their rendezvous with the gem dealer in Bangkok, perhaps he could provide leads as to their activities in the city. It shouldn't be hard to locate "Alain Dupuis," Herman reasoned. There couldn't be many French gem dealers in Bangkok. But after checking with police, immigration authorities, the gem dealers' association, and the French community, Herman came up zero. Puzzled, he sent a query to the Dutch Embassy in Hong Kong to check the guest ledger of the Hyatt Regency Hotel during the December period when he was supposedly in residence and entertaining the Dutch people. Back came an answer: Nobody named "Alain Dupuis" stayed in the Hyatt Regency during December. Now Herman's curiosity was whetted. Did "Alain Dupuis" really exist? Or was he a fake man?

Then, a break. Or a tease of fate. Whatever its origin, Herman was given a piece of interesting, albeit convoluted good fortune. One night he joined a friend named Armand from the Belgian Embassy for drinks. The colleague had a bit of delicious gossip to share. It seemed that one of the low-level diplomats in the Western community of Bangkok was caught up in a silly little *scandale,* the kind that sends shudders through the people of protocol. This young diplomat, according to Armand's gleeful telling, was in a Bangkok hotel noted for its bar girls, lifting glasses with a tempestuous French businessman named Artur Gabreaux. The diplomat was a few sheets to the wind by curfew and made a lavish proposition to one of the bar girls, suggesting a fee far above market value for such services. Artur Gabreaux, quite drunk, criticized his companion for spoiling the market with such lavish payment. Hot words broke out. Soft punches missed. Soon thereafter an advertisement appeared in a Bangkok newspaper. Placed by the Frenchman, it stated that he had been insulted and he wished an apology. All it lacked was the name of his second and a choice of weapons.

Hearing the tale, Herman laughed. Then, casually, he asked: What did this Artur Gabreaux do for a living? "Oil, exports, gems," came the answer.

"Gems?" echoed Herman. He wrote down two names on his cocktail napkin: "Alain Dupuis" and "Artur Gabreaux." Both French. Both gem dealers. Curious.

Quickly Herman ran a discreet background check on Gabreaux, and for a few heady days he felt he had a promising suspect. In December, Gabreaux had been in Tokyo on business. Perhaps, theorized Herman, he stopped off in Hong Kong on his way back to Bangkok. Perhaps he met the Dutch people there. One more intriguing fact tantalized Herman: Artur Gabreaux reported his passport missing or stolen to the French Embassy in Bangkok, about the same time that the murders occurred.

With that, Herman felt close to cracking the mystery. The way he interpreted it, this Gabreaux person was in Hong Kong, met Bintanja and Hemker, invited them to stay with him in Bangkok, murdered them, got nervous, reported his passport stolen so he could claim someone was impersonating him. Unfortunately, it was only conjecture. Word came down from indisputable sources that Artur Gabreaux was legitimate, well connected, had no police record, and aside from occasional emotional outbursts when too oiled with good whisky, was a solid citizen. Moreover, he had not been in Hong Kong during the critical period. He had flown directly from Tokyo to Bangkok.

Up to this disappointment, Herman's superiors at the embassy had tolerated their second secretary's zestful detective work. But now that he was becoming troublesome, suspecting a prominent French citizen of double murder, he stood on the threshold of diplomatic embarrassment. Herman was summoned to a superior's office and told, in stern language, to cease and desist. Herman's response was characteristic of his nature:

"Goddamnit, with all due respect, *somebody's* got to do something. Two good kids—Dutch citizens—were brutally murdered. I want the bastard who did it. I want him hung—or shot."

Once more Herman was told to leave police matters to the police. And return posthaste to the duties for which his government employed him.

Perhaps Herman would have bowed to his superior after this meeting, for he realized that his patience was very thin. But then he received a telephone call from an informant, one of the many tipsters he had all over the diplomatic community. The caller wanted to tell Herman that during the investigation of Artur Gabreaux another name had risen once or twice. And the funny thing about this other name was that it also was French, and also bore the initials "A.G."

"And who is this man?" asked Herman.

"Somebody named Alain Gauthier," was the answer.

"And what does Alain Gauthier do for a living?" asked Herman.

"Gem dealer."

Herman gripped the telephone tightly. "Do you have an address?" he asked, a current of excitement building within him.

"Yes."

With that, Herman would one day recall, "I almost jumped through the ceiling. Somehow I knew we had our man."

CHAPTER THIRTY-FIVE

"Belle! *Comment vas-tu?*"

She froze. The voice behind her was as unmistakable as the edge of a sharpened knife. She was sitting in the lobby of the Indra Hotel in Bangkok, waiting for a luncheon companion on the midday of February 13, 1976. There was nothing for her to do but turn around and smile and pray that her panic did not bleed through her false mask of friendship.

Charles and Marie-Andrée greeted her warmly with abundant kisses and embraces. They seemed completely normal. No menace hid in their eyes; no blood dripped from their hands. They had returned to Bangkok after several weeks of travel and had decided to take a room in the hotel for a few days before returning to their apartment. This struck Belle as strange—Kanit House was not far away—but she gathered that Charles wanted to sample the climate before venturing back to his home turf.

"Well, be sure and call when you get back to Kanit House," murmured Belle, making fast excuse to leave their company. Charles stopped her. He gripped her arm. What was the hurry? They could all go home together.

"But . . . but I have a lunch date," stammered Belle.

Charles said he and Marie-Andrée would be glad to wait.

Later in the afternoon, sharing a taxi, Belle kept her hand on the door handle, prepared to leap out if necessary. And in the elevator rising to their apartments, her body wedged against Charles, her heart beat so loudly that it threatened to reveal her terror. But aside from a few more questions about the mysteriously vanished French boys— Dominique *et al*—Charles did not seem concerned. In fact, he invited Belle and Raoul for dinner that night. She declined, but she knew that the choice was either to resume her friendship with these people or else cut them off and arouse their suspicions. Each night thereafter she slept with a heavy chair propped against the door and a stomach heavily sedated with Valiums. Otherwise, she would have awakened a hundred times before dawn.

Charles and Marie-Andrée had just come from Hong Kong, where, it would later be discovered, one of their more successful accomplishments was achieved. The victim was an American schoolteacher in his mid-thirties, a man from Iowa named Robert Paul Grainer. For years he had saved money for a trip around the world and was happy to be in Hong Kong for the Chinese New Year in January 1976. Grainer's only misfortune was to push his way into a street crowd watching a lion dance. He found himself standing next to a friendly and helpful French-speaking couple who invited him to join them for a tour of the festive city, its skies erupting with Roman candles and exploding stars.

The last thing Robert Grainer remembered was being in the couple's room at the Sheraton and watching an American movie on television. Two days later he awoke. Wearing only his underwear, he staggered in shock along a corridor of the hotel, fell into a chambermaid's arms, so disoriented that for several hours he could not remember his name or his citizenship. His own room, in another hotel, had been ransacked. Everything was gone—luggage, clothes, money, a letter of credit for $4,000, a valid round-the-world air ticket.

"They were so nice," Grainer told Hong Kong police. "Especially the woman. She was Canadian, and she spoke so longingly of going home . . ."

In the dead of an early March midnight, a knock shattered Belle's shallow sleep. She sat up in fear. The knock came again. It was time for Raoul to be home. Perhaps he had forgotten his key. Cautiously she opened the door, se-

cured by a chain. A strange man stood on her threshold.
A scream rose within her. The man smiled and quickly
flashed his identification. He was from the Belgian Embassy and in his face were strength and legitimacy. "Don't
worry," said the man. "I'm here to help you. Get ready in
five minutes. We're taking you and your husband to a safe
house."

Belle began to stammer. The man bade her to obey. "We
believe you," he said. "It's time to stop these killings."

Outside Kanit House, on a side street, a black Mercedes
waited to speed the housewife and her husband to a secluded home in a remote section of Bangkok. Once there, a
young, boyish man with a toothy smile opened the door in
welcome. "My name is Herman Knippenberg," he said,
presenting his credentials. One of his tipsters had put him
onto Belle and Raoul as being possible sources of information. Herman introduced a half-dozen other men in
the room. They were all junior men from various Western
embassies in Bangkok, a gutsy and risk-taking group who
would soon call themselves the "Action Committee."

For the better part of two days and nights, Belle and
her husband were "debriefed." They told their story a hundred times, with Beethoven playing loudly from a stereo
to confound bugs or eavesdroppers. Belle knew more than
Raoul, and she told it well, a catharsis for her fear. She
spoke of the young people who came and got sick and vanished, of the Dutch couple seemingly imprisoned, perhaps
bound, of the passports she had glimpsed in Alain Gauthier's portable safe. Herman was an excellent interrogator,
dredging up bits and pieces of what seemed trivial—Marie-
Andrée's affection for her white fluffy dog, Frankie, for
example. But later on, this would become a vital clue that
would help connect the gem dealer and his girl friend to
the drugging and robbing of the newly-wed Lapthorne
couple from Australia.

When Belle mentioned Alain's sudden pre-Christmas
trip to Katmandu, Herman snapped his fingers. His embassy duties included reading most English-language newspapers in Asia, and he instantly recalled an account of the
two December murders in the Nepalese capital.

At the end of the marathon, Herman thanked Belle for
her courage. One of the other committee members asked

her why she had not come forward with this horrible
story earlier. "But I did," said Belle. "In January I went
to the British Embassy and they didn't believe me. Neither
did the French. I showed the Englishman a page from Cornelia Hemker's diary." Herman was furious. The next day
he reported the cavalier attitude of the British to one of
his superiors, who promptly rang an English counterpart
to complain. "This is unbelievable," said the Dutchman.
"Don't you people communicate with Common Market
members?"

Belle's testimony was helpful and illuminating, but Herman knew that he needed much more before the Thai
police could be persuaded to make arrests. "We've got to
have photographs of these people, and a day-by-day account of what goes on up there," he told Belle. "I know
this is a lot to ask anybody, but you're the only one who
can do it." Anxiously Belle looked toward her husband.
Prudently he demanded to know what protection could the
Action Committee offer?

"I promise never to be more than five minutes away,"
said Herman. "Everybody in this room will either come to
your assistance instantly, or send security people from
their embassies." Raoul asked for a moment of privacy.
He and Belle went to a corner and spoke in whispers.
Watching them, Herman did not envy these people. Their
lives had collided with what he believed to be a fiend—
there was no other word in Herman's vocabulary—and
now their options were between slim and none. They were
decent and lawful citizens, the chef and his wife, and now
they were in jeopardy no matter what they did. Or did
not do.

Belle agreed to become a spy. Over the next several days,
she kept a journal of everyone who rode the creaking elevator up to the fifth floor, of the tenants' every exit and
entrance. She visited Marie-Andrée often, using the pretense of girl talk or the need to borrow something, but in
truth making mental notes of the apartment's floor plan.
Thus was Belle able to draw elaborate diagrams of the
two apartments leased by Gauthier, with arrows marking
strategic places such as where the safe was kept, where she
had seen the big cardboard box that seemed to contain

documents of the dead people. On secluded balconies of the apartment house Belle hid and snapped long-lens photographs. Marie-Andrée was easy to capture, lying as she so often did beside the pool. She caught Ajay Chowdhury emerging from the garage. But Charles eluded her lens, save for a blurred and half-figure image, as if he could sense and confound the offending instrument aimed at him.

Each night Belle reported to the Action Committee, now meeting at Herman's own home, delivering whatever she had learned. At every session, Belle was asked if Alain was catching on. Not that she knew of, answered Belle, who, in truth, was enjoying the danger and intrigue of her adventure. Both Alain and Marie-Andrée seemed *normaux* to Belle, save a distinctive hardening in the Canadian girl's manner. She was growing, in Belle's eyes, tough and cynical. One afternoon Belle was witness to a flash quarrel between the couple in which Alain accused Marie-Andrée of stealing a few gems from his strongbox. Readily, almost eagerly, she admitted it. Belle told the committee that Marie-Andrée snapped angrily at Charles: "Yes! Absolutely! I've been with you almost a year and what do I have to show for it? If I'd stayed in Canada, I would have made a salary. Here I work harder—I'm the perfect slave! —and I get nothing. You're damn right I took them. I'll take whatever I can get."

Belle next reported the arrival of a new man who seemed neither potential customer nor victim. In fact, he appeared miscast, completely out of his element. He was a French businessman named Jean Dhuisme, about thirty by Belle's guess, with a prissy mustache and a weary expression and eyes as sad as a basset hound's. In brief conversation, Belle discovered him to be quiet, shy, a well-educated architect who had made substantial money by purchasing old houses outside Paris and remodeling them. He had a wife and a child in Paris and did not appear to have a larcenous or murderous bone in his body. Yet he seemed to be a valued addition to the entourage who ate and slept in the apartment and often left with Alain on "business." Ajay Chowdhury, noted Belle, was not overjoyed at the arrival of Jean Dhuisme. His stature was lessened, his role as second-in-command to Alain seemed usurped. Dhuisme had come to the Far East to buy fabrics and *objets d'art* for his remodeling business, and at a hotel bar in Bangkok encountered Charles Sobhraj. Obviously he succumbed to oft-sung songs of glitter and wealth, for he abandoned plans to return to Paris and moved into Kanit House. He also loaned enough money to Charles to lease office space at a respectable Bangkok building. In early March, Belle heard continuing talk in the apartment about a planned "grand opening" of Gauthier's long-dreamed-of jewelry store.

"I don't understand why a man like Jean Dhuisme is attracted to Gauthier," said Belle to her husband. "He seems too sensible to fall for his sales pitch."

Raoul did not find it unusual. Not at all. "It's the lure of a fast buck," he suggested. "Nobody is immune to that disease."

Herman hardly slept, his juices at full flow. He was consumed with the case, so much so that he usually reported for work at the embassy with flaming eyes from lack of rest. Pleased with Belle's sneak photography, he asked if she dared slip a small 35-mm camera into her purse and attempt to take pictures *inside* Gauthier's lair. "Don't try it if there's the slightest bit of danger," counseled Herman. Belle answered sensibly, "Of course there's danger, but I'll see if it's possible some morning when Alain is gone."

The next day Belle waited at her window until she saw Gauthier and his new adjutant, Jean Dhuisme, leave Kanit House. Then she hurried upstairs unannounced to take coffee with Marie-Andrée. While there she slipped into the bedroom on the pretense of using the toilet. With trembling hands she hurriedly snapped photos of a pile of odds and ends in a corner. Clearly visible in the developed picture was what appeared to be Cornelia Hemker's brown leather shoulder bag. That might be a valuable piece of hard physical evidence, mused Herman after congratulating Belle. He asked if she could steal it on her next visit. "It's too risky," she said. "I think they may be watching me. When I came out of the toilet after taking the pictures, Marie-Andrée was looking at me curiously. Maybe I'm imagining it."

* * *

On March 10, Belle dropped by the apartment for morning coffee and encountered Charles hurrying out. She overheard him murmur something to Marie-Andrée about packing and reservations. When he was gone on his morning prowl of the city, Belle casually asked Marie-Andrée if the couple were going away. "Who knows?" answered the Canadian girl testily. "He changes his mind ten times between breakfast and lunch." Yes, they had been discussing a trip to Malaysia. But she would not believe it until the airplane left the ground.

Belle fidgeted a few moments, then "remembered" an important appointment. Fairly flying out of Kanit House, she raced on foot to the Dutch Embassy to tell Herman. He was stunned at the news. Their case was growing, promising, but not yet strong enough to throw a rope around anybody's neck. Nonetheless he had no other choice. He had to move now, this instant, or else risk losing the suspects. Cursing, he dialed the Crime Suppression Bureau, got through to a General Suwit, and put on a voice equivalent to that used by United Nations delegates outraged by territorial encroachment. A gang of killers was operating brazenly in Thailand, revealed Herman, knocking off visitors and threatening to destroy the valuable tourist trade. The general was impressed enough by Herman's story to send over a pair of junior officers. They listened attentively to the story, read Herman's meticulous almost hour-by-hour report of his investigation, looked at Belle's photographs, perused autopsy reports and diagrams. When they were done, they looked up, impressed. Herman said, softly, "Raid the bastards."

They made plans until late in the night, Herman and his committee and the Thai police. It was a time of supreme excitement.

The next afternoon, at the stroke of four, seven Thai policemen rode the elevator to the fifth floor of Kanit House. One was wearing a paratrooper's uniform and on his feet were thick-soled shoes capable of kicking down a door, if necessary. A few blocks away, in his office at the Dutch Embassy, Herman waited, staring at the telephone. The strategy had been rehearsed a dozen times. As soon as police broke into the apartment and arrested the suspects and took them away, one of the officers would call Herman and put Act Two in effect. At that moment, Herman, his wife Angela, and Belle would enter the apartment and fine-tooth-comb the rooms, searching for evidence. They were more familiar with what might be found than the police. The legality of such a joint undertaking might be arguable, but Herman cared only that the objects of his fanatic attention did not manage to squeeze out of custody for lack of proof.

As Herman watched his telephone, and waited, he fingered the small weapon that he would carry in his pocket. It was a gun called "Cobra," so named for its three-holed shaft, like the mouth and fangs of Asia's most deadly serpent.

It was not necessary for the paratrooper to kick down the door of Charles Sobhraj. It was standing wide open. When the seven officers rushed in with drawn guns, they encountered a scene of domestic tranquillity. In a chair, Marie-Andrée was reading philosophy. Nearby Charles was sitting at the kitchen counter, working on his gems, holding up stones to a work light and examining their character. At first sight of the police, Charles thought it was a robbery and leaped up in a karate stance to fight. But when the invading force yelled, "Police!" Charles simply turned and murmured to Marie-Andrée, "Call me *Robert*." Apparently he made a snap decision to try and pass himself off as Robert Grainer, the American whose passport he had stolen in Hong Kong.

For three hours the raiding party turned Charles' apartment upside down, scattering papers, stripping bed linens, pulling pots from the kitchen shelves. Marie-Andrée was sobbing, Charles protesting bitterly the "barbaric" and "illegal" raid, demanding to see a search warrant. Didn't the police realize he was a responsible American citizen, in Bangkok to do "business" and enrich Thailand's economy? Shortly after 7 P.M., the police took the suspects and the portable safe to headquarters. The safe resisted their attempts to open it on the spot. And no one thought to telephone Herman until 10 P.M. For six hours he sat in his office stewing, pacing, fingering the gun, resisting the impulse to rush over and see what in hell was going on.

Finally, his phone rang. Herman snatched it eagerly. On

the line was a member of the Thai police posse. His English was broken, but his message was clear. And shocking. The conversation, as Herman would remember it, went like this:

"Have you got them?" asked Herman excitedly.

"Yes, they're here now," said the officer. "Two men and a woman."

"Well, what's happening to them?"

"There's a mixup, I'm afraid," said the officer. "The man you said was Alain Gauthier turns out to be an American named Robert Paul Grainer."

"An American!" Herman's voice was incredulous.

"Yes, an American." The Thai cop said he was looking at the passport that very moment, and it was genuine and it showed that Grainer had been in Sri Lanka at the time of the Dutch murders in December.

"What did you find in the apartment?" begged Herman.

"Nothing of interest."

Herman began to stammer. "How do you know the passport is real?" In times of stress, his words stuck together and now his anger was mounting.

"Because we checked it."

Herman felt reeling disappointment. This couldn't be! Too much work had gone into building a house of brick only to have it come crashing down like a thatched hut at the first stirring of a new wind. "This man *deals* in stolen passports," he fairly yelled. "He changes his identity like I change shirts. I urge you, I *beg* you—check him out further. Get somebody from the United States Embassy over there!"

The officer responded politely. "We *have* checked the passport. The decision has been made to send these people home until tomorrow."

Herman almost dropped the phone. "Send them home! My God, that's the *last* you'll ever see of them!"

The officer hastened to explain. No one had been able to open the safe (presumably due to the mutilation of the lock committed by Yannick on the December night when he first told Belle of his suspicions). It was agreed that everyone would reassemble the next morning at ten-thirty when a police safe expert would be available.

"What if there's forty-five pounds of heroin in that safe

right now?" demanded Herman. "Do you really think they'll be back tomorrow? What if there are two dozen stolen passports belonging to corpses?"

"They'll be back," said the Thai. "They promised. We confiscated their passports. They can't go anywhere."

Herman made one last plea. At least keep "Robert Grainer" and his friends in custody until someone from the U.S. Embassy could be found to determine the validity of the passport. The officer refused. "The general has personally ordered their release," he said. "We cannot do anything else."

The line went dead. Herman stared at the telephone dully. But he was not yet ready to give up. For two hours he searched the city by phone trying to locate Bob Jacobs, a consular officer that the American Embassy who had been an occasional member of the Action Committee. Jacobs was working on the disappearance and death of Jennie Bolliver. He had been interested in Herman's snooping, but he was not as consumed by the case as his Dutch colleague. Near midnight Herman reached Jacobs and said, "The man they arrested carries an American passport in the name of Robert Paul Grainer. Either Alain Gauthier stole his passport and is using it, or else Robert Paul Grainer is murdering people." The development was interesting enough for Jacobs to promise and dispatch someone from his office to Thai police headquarters on the morn.

Then Herman called Belle and told her of the bizarre developments. She already knew. She had heard the suspects return to Kanit House. Lights burned even now in their apartment. "They're probably destroying evidence," said Herman morosely. Belle did not care about evidence. She was terrified. Half of her furniture was piled against the front door. It was her intention to drink coffee until sunrise, and then, if push came to shove, flee Bangkok on the first flight.

With composure and an attitude of substantial annoyance, Charles appeared as ordered the next morning at police headquarters. Marie-Andrée and Ajay were at his side. The police locksmith broke open the small safe. It yawned empty. Nothing was inside. Charles nodded and rose. Could he go now? An important luncheon meeting must be attended. Impatiently he tapped on his gold watch. Then an American strolled into the Crime Suppression Bureau. He was Sam Anson, from the U.S. Drug Enforcement Agency, one of thirty agents on continual duty in Bangkok, headwaters for a river of heroin that flowed from Asia to Europe and America. Anson scrutinized the U.S. passport—Charles had substituted his own photograph—and eyed its owner, "Robert Paul Grainer." Casually, Anson asked several questions, all of which Sobhraj/Gauthier/Grainer answered helpfully. He offered himself as a language teacher; he had emigrated from Asia to the United States as a small child; he now lived in Iowa. He had no idea why the Thai cops were hassling him, but he was delighted to encounter a representative of his own government. Surely this unpleasant mess was now straightened out.

But Sam Anson had one more question. Where was Grainer's home town? Quickly Charles replied, "Oak Park." *That* was a blunder. In his homework, Charles had correctly memorized the street address in Grainer's home town, but at this tense moment he had mistakenly given it as the city where he lived.

"I think something fishy's going on here," said Anson to the Thai chief investigator. "The passport looks funny, but I can't be sure. It's not my department. Keep this guy on ice until somebody from Consular can get over and check him out."

An hour later, when a U.S. consular representative arrived to examine the passport, the three suspects were nowhere to be found. Charles and his companions had been instructed to sit quietly on a bench in the corridor outside the Crime Suppression Bureau. Nobody watched them. The hallway was busy, with police and clerks and complaining citizens bustling to and fro. To request Charles Sobhraj to sit on a bench and await further investigation was like ordering a bird to stop flying. When the suspects were discovered suddenly missing from their bench, the not-overly-chagrined police theorized they simply got up and strolled out—against orders. And by nightfall, the gang, not unexpectedly, was fleeing the country.

When Herman received the incredible news, he crashed

his fist onto the desk. "I can't believe the Thais let these people get away," he told his wife. "I wonder how many more people are going to die!"

Angela Knippenberg shared her husband's crushing disappointment, yet she was also relieved. For weeks her marriage had been dominated by talk of death. Pictures of corpses littered her table. Ghosts of the murdered young haunted her rooms. She told Belle in a private moment that even her tears had to be hidden from Herman because she believed in what he was trying to do and did not want her pain to inhibit his cause. Rumbles were being picked up that Herman was the subject of derisive cocktail party talk. And now that he had pointed an accusing finger at someone who Thai police said was the wrong man, and an American at that, Herman's career was in jeopardy. An erroneous rumor had even leaked out that the Action Committee had discussed hiring a hit man to assassinate Alain Gauthier. Indeed one of the junior diplomats had mentioned such a possibility, but the idea was flip, made in jest. Never before in their marriage had Herman and Angela quarreled, but lately they had begun snapping at one another, weary and exhausted from his obsession with murder.

Herman was summoned to the decorous office of the Netherlands Ambassador to Thailand. The dressing down was elegant, but its intent clear: Herman was tired, Herman was overworked. It would be appropriate for Herman to take a brief "leave of absence," get out of town for a while, find some sun, catch some fish. This Herman translated correctly to mean: Stop Playing Detective and Stop Making a Fool of Yourself.

At that moment, Herman's temptation was to resign. The thought had occurred to him before. Frustration had been his reward for trying to solve the murders of two Dutch citizens. He told his boss, "We are supposed to look after the interests of our people abroad . . . How can we stand by and let our citizens get popped off without doing something? Those kids were valuable. One was going to be a doctor. The other was a nurse. They weren't hippies. We educated them, maybe they would have made a contribution to our world . . . I'm not a moralist, but this is too much for me to stomach . . ."

Nonetheless, directed the senior man, Dutch interests would best be served by Herman's discreet withdrawal from Bangkok for a while. That night, very upset, Herman typed up a thirty-page report documenting his committee's efforts and dispatched it around to the Western embassies. He had the notion that other bodies were probably buried in Southeast Asia, the remains of people whose last moments were spent in the company of the man he knew as Alain Gauthier. Then Herman left town, as directed, feeling his ears burning, like a child sent to his room.

During Herman's enforced holiday, the question that tormented him most was: How did Charles Sobhraj and the others manage to stroll casually out of police headquarters? A few days later Belle learned the answer.

Her telephone rang one afternoon and on the line was Charles. His voice was calm, he spoke warmly. He revealed that his group was in Malaysia, lying low until the heat cooled in Bangkok. Belle listened in astonishment and later told Herman what was said. Her recollection of Charles' version:

"The Bangkok police are crazy. They accused me of robbing and drugging people. If only they knew how many people I nursed back to health! . . . Somebody must have made a false complaint. It might have been a customer who lost $18,000 worth of sapphires. A massage girl probably robbed him . . . Well, don't worry about us. We'll be back soon . . . I gave the *grand chef* some money to weaken his memory . . . Soon everything will be just as it was . . ."

The *"grand chef,"* Belle gathered, was a high-ranking police official. Charles hinted broadly that he had paid $15,000 to "weaken his memory." Later, Bangkok police would denounce this suggestion of bribery in high places. But it was decidedly curious that a suspected multiple killer —soon to be the most wanted man in Asia—would dance so easily out of custody and into flight. This time Charles did not even have to betray his wife or his half-brother, or dig a tunnel, or break a bottle of perfume and set it afire.

CHAPTER THIRTY-SIX

Dark and sour and a horrendous mess, the two apartments leased by Charles at Kanit House were now under police seal. No one had been inside since the day he rose from the police bench and skipped out of the country. Belle learned that the building's owner was demanding that police release her property so that the rooms could be cleaned and prepared for new tenants. The moment Herman returned from his enforced vacation, Belle passed along the disturbing news.

"If that happens," warned Herman, "then a lot of vital evidence will wind up on a garbage dump somewhere." Despite the ambassadorial scoldings, Herman decided to undertake one more mission. He went to the Thai police and said, in effect: Someday it is going to be revealed that a mass murderer was arrested by you people, but you let him slip through your hands. He's probably off killing others because he is a homicidal maniac. And you blew the opportunity to stop him.

Whether the argument was persuasive, or whether some cop simply sighed and realized the only way to get this bulldog of a Dutchman out of his office was to agree, Herman was granted permission to search the two apartments. With two policemen as escorts, remnants of the Action Committee reassembled in April and entered the house of darkest fantasies. When the door was opened, they beheld a disaster, as if a tropical storm had raged within, and rather than clean up the damage, the occupants had simply abandoned the flotsam and jetsam of their lives. Papers were scattered everywhere, clothing was strewn about, chairs and tables lay on their backs with legs pointed to the ceiling, like dead dogs. The blood red wall cast an eerie glow.

"Once it was nice in here," remembered Belle. "There was music playing, always music. And there was wine and good food and people laughing. Charles used to sit over there and watch. He was always watching, studying, like an anthropologist. I don't think he ever had any fun, though. He wouldn't permit himself."

They searched through the rubble for hours, until their hands were black with dirt, pouring over the wreckage and feeling the chill of the dead at their necks. In the end, a formidable mass of evidence was accumulated, all of which Thai police had "overlooked" in their initial raid.

In the bathroom and bedroom, Herman found an astonishing *fifteen kilos* of various medicines, pills, potions, ampules, suppositories, most of which tested out to be of a sedative or barbiturate nature. Among these was a bottle marked "Kaopectate" that was a potion to *increase* diarrhea and stomach trouble, rather than diminish them.

Among other discoveries:

—A pair of handcuffs that had been used frequently. Herman theorized that the Dutch couple had been handcuffed to the brass slats of the guest bed in their final hours. There were similar metal scratches on both cuffs and slats.

—A handkerchief still bearing the faint aroma of gasoline.

—Half-finished letters in Dutch, apparently in the hand of Cornelia Hemker.

—The leather shoulder bag owned by Miss Hemker, and a fan and poster she purchased in Hong Kong, mentioned in her letter to her family.

—A plastic cosmetics bag of floral design owned by Jennie Bolliver. It contained such exotica as seaweed toothpaste and had been given to her as a farewell present by her girl friends in Seattle. Also, the book on Buddhist practice that Jennie had been reading on the flight from Seattle to the Far East. Inside, on the flyleaf, was her name.

—Used hypodermic needles, along with a four-page handwritten document that told how to administer injections, plus a drawing of the human body with the best sites for sticking needles. It was believed that Marie-Andrée wrote the document, and one of the committee members commented, "This will be valuable in case she pleads that she had nothing to do with what was going on in here."

—Transactions of gem sales to customers, including prominent names in Bangkok, and several members of the diplomatic community!

—Hundreds of hotel bills, used airplane tickets, money exchange receipts, and car rental papers. Among them was discovered an automobile insurance paper from Spain and a bank statement both owned by Vitali Hakim. His silver necklace was also found.

—Driver's licenses belonging to twenty different people.

"Why on earth did he keep all this stuff?" wondered Angela Knippenberg as she sifted through the incriminating papers.

"He thought he was God," answered Herman, who had formed an accurate picture of the man he had never met. "He thought he could bluff his way out of any predicament."

"And indeed he has," put in Belle.

"Was he attractive?" wondered Angela. The few pictures that Belle had snapped were of poor quality. Belle chewed on the question. "In a sensuous way, yes," she said. "He didn't do anything for me, but I can see how women might be turned on. He was intelligent and quick and mysterious. He had strength. His voice was very soft, romantic, very macho. He always paraded his masculinity as if he were afraid it might go away."

Then Angela discovered a cache of photographs amid a box that contained hundreds of paperback mysteries. One showed Charles and Marie-Andrée posing in a bar somewhere—appearing very rich, bored, like celebrities snared by *paparazzi*. In the foreground, Charles was dominant, dressed in a casual but well-tailored suit, looking a trifle like the French actor Alain Delon. Slightly behind him sat Marie-Andrée, on a barstool, sultry, faking a woman secure in her sexuality, in her hold on this man.

They also found, among Marie-Andrée's possessions, a

snapshot of Charles in bed, on rumpled sheets. Naked, he stared insolently, a teasing smile on his face. His hand cupped his penis. It was spectacularly erect. "At least," murmured Belle, "she had this picture every night."

But where *were* they? The assumption was that Charles was hiding out in the Far East, waiting until it was safe to return to Bangkok. Every night Belle tried to sleep, with the thought of Gauthier's reappearance tormenting her. Then the mail brought a postcard from, of all places, Switzerland. From the man himself, it informed that all was well, that he was conducting business in Europe, that he would see her "soon."

Upon reading the postcard, Herman was elated. If he was right, fate was giving them one more opportunity to catch their quarry. Among the storm of papers found in the apartments, Herman had discovered the address of Jean Dhuisme's family outside Paris, as well as the address of Song, Charles' mother, still living in Marseilles with her invalid husband. "I'd bet everything I own that they're headed for France," said Herman. Belle agreed. Once Charles had told her that France was an easy country to enter without proper documents. The trick was to rent a car in Geneva—from whence the postcard had been mailed—then arrive at the French border after 8 P.M., when traffic is heavy with people going to and from the casino at Divonne les Bains. The *douaniers* wave everybody through without checking, he had told her.

But Herman was loath to entrust the notion of Gauthier's whereabouts to Bangkok police, doubting if it would be cabled to Paris. Fortunately, a Catholic priest whom Belle knew was at that moment preparing a return to France. He agreed to carry a packet containing a summation of the case, and the addresses of Dhuisme's family and Song. The priest delivered the packet to the Perfecture of Police in Paris with a plea that it required immediate action. But his effort was in vain. The French police did not investigate, nor did they even telephone the places mentioned. What was alleged to have happened half a world away apparently did not whet Gallic interest. Which was too bad, because Herman's theory was one hundred per cent correct. Charles and Marie-Andrée and

Jean Dhuisme were indeed in France and passed several unmolested days exactly where Herman had suspected they would.

"The French behaved very poorly in this matter," said Herman later. "But then, so did the British, and a lot of other people. They thought we were nuts."

Later in 1976, Belle and Raoul left Bangkok and moved home to France. Fear was not the major determinant, although it contributed its share. Belle had reached the position where she could no longer live in a house where so many dreams had died, or in a country that held little reverence for human life. When she arrived in Paris, Belle played one more scene. She had brought with her a book on palmistry that had been found in Charles' apartment. Once he had mentioned that it was a favorite volume, that it had been purchased in India, that he had memorized most of it, that he had encouraged Marie-Andrée to study it. Belle telephoned a noted Paris psychic and made an appointment. She handed over the book and said, "Please tell me what you feel about the person who owns this book." She did not give the psychic any further information.

The psychic examined the book, closed her eyes, meditated, then dropped it suddenly on the floor, as if the pages had become poisoned. On her face were disgust and fear. She ordered Belle to throw the book away, or burn it, or keep it wrapped in black cloth. It was a "*porte malheur.*"

"But what do you see?" pressed Belle.

"Chains," answered the psychic. "Chains . . . and prison . . . and high trees."

"What is the future for the person who owns this book?"

The psychic terminated the appointment and pushed Belle to the door. Just as she shut it, she hissed, "Death."

Next Belle went to a respected handwriting expert and presented samples of Charles' and Marie-Andrée's penmanship. Of Charles, the expert said, "He was hurt as a young person. He experienced great trouble. And he wants revenge on the world."

And Marie-Andrée? The analyst answered, "This one is easier. It is the hand of a woman. She has no moral sense whatsoever."

＊ ＊ ＊

Now the families began journeys to the East to claim
their children, what was left of them. In Istanbul, Leon
Hakim was in his clothing shop at the Spice Market when
a call from the local police delivered the sorrowful news.
Vitali, his son, was believed dead in faraway Thailand.

When he was unable to learn more from either Turkish
police or from maddening transcontinental telephone calls
that seemed to drop into a void, the aging and portly
merchant flew to the East alone. He had not seen his son
for years, not since the one night that Vitali had suddenly appeared at his door with hair longer than a woman's
and with silver necklaces about his chest. When he reached
Bangkok, Leon Hakim wandered frustratingly about the
city, knocking on police doors, encountering smiling little
men who could not speak his language. One afternoon
Leon sat in the lobby of his hotel, his head buried in his
hands, weeping. When the concierge asked what was the
matter, Leon wept, "It's my son. I can't find him. He's
dead—and I can't even find him."

Finally the right police door opened, and Leon was
given the particulars of his son's drugging and death by
fire. He had not been told the grisly details, and when he
was shown a photograph of the young man whose name
meant "life" but whose last image was a blackened body
and a face whose tongue protruded grotesquely, Leon
Hakim collapsed in a dead faint.

When he was revived, Leon asked, "May I take my son
home?"

No. The body could not be released until the trial.

"*What* trial? *Who* killed him?"

The police did not answer. Someday there would be a
trial, presumably, when the person who committed this
murder was apprehended.

Not until the following autumn, almost a year after the
murder, were the remains of Vitali Hakim mailed home
to Turkey. His father put the small container of ashes and
bone into a refrigerator at his synagogue and asked the
rabbis for permission to bury his son in sanctified ground.
Under Jewish law, adequate remains of a corpse must be
available to establish positive identification. The rabbis met

for three days to study the matter, while Leon and Rachel Hakim waited in agonizing suspense.

Their decision was favorable, perhaps bending custom in deference to the Hakims' stature and respect in the community.

The funeral was held on a hot Sunday in Istanbul's major synagogue, Neve Shalom, and the family were flattered that the ancient house of worship was full. Istanbul's affluent Jews usually go away for weekends. The remains were transferred to a coffin that, it was said, cost 100,000 Turkish lira. The funeral was elaborate and comforting to the family.

"Do not mourn too much," said Leon to his relatives. "I lost my son a long time ago, even before he was killed."

He heard someone murmur the word "hippie" and Leon whirled in modest anger. "If Vitali was a hippie, then God made him a hippie."

At the burial in Arnavut-Koy, in the separate section for Sephardic Jews, Leon stood for a long time over his son's grave. Beside him was Israel, the eldest, more than ever a prosperous and prominent citizen, the antithesis of his kid brother.

"How sad this is," mourned Israel. "Vitali was looking for freedom, but he found death."

And in Katmandu, Christopher took Francine's hand and led her delightedly through the crowds of giggling Tibetan women and worshipers spinning prayer wheels beside the Temple of Bouddhanath. They must hurry. The arduous climb to the Kopan Monastery was just ahead. How pleased Jennie would be to see them! Christopher suspected that she knew he was coming, even though the postcard he had mailed from somewhere on the road had been indefinite as to day or even month. If Jennie were standing at the entrance in welcome, he would not be surprised.

As the couple trudged up the ruts to Kopan, their eyes dazzled by the heavy blankets of rhododendron in bloom, showering the valley with reds and pinks, Christopher wondered what changes had taken place in the young woman he had once loved, and who had once walked beside him on this same path. Surely she had located peace and serenity; surely she would understand that his love for Francine had deepened. Francine had been a good traveling companion, not as adventuresome as Jennie, but usually game for whatever righthand turn Christopher decided to make. After a few days in Katmandu, it was their intention to return to Seattle. Get married. Settle down. Perhaps open a business. Plants. Spices. Handicrafts. Christopher counted on his fingers; Jennie had been in residence at the monastery for almost half a year. Surely the wounds of their broken love affair were healed by now.

Near the end of the long climb, Christopher heard the laughter of the Tibetan children from the monastery school. He suspected that Jennie would be found amid them, probably leader of a game of tag. She had always adored the youngsters. Once Jennie told Christopher that upon her death she hoped to be reincarnated as a child who would attend the Kopan school.

Engulfed by a group of little boys in bright purple robes and red clogs on their feet, Christopher knelt among the monks-to-be and tried to remember the few words of Nepali that he once knew. "Jennie?" he asked, drawing blank looks in response. Then he saw a blackboard propped up against a great pipal tree whose massive trunk contained a lovely shrine to Buddha and which was the heart of the monastery. On it was written "Meditation for Jennie. 4 P.M." A surge of happiness filled Christopher and he hurried to the main hall, where monks and nuns were emerging from an afternoon study course. Christopher found a Western nun and inquired about Jennie. Would she be coming out soon? Could he visit with her before the meditation began?

The nun shook her head sadly. "Jennie died in Bangkok last October," she said. "We've only just gotten confirmation."

He did not weep until he reached the little hill above Kopan, where once they had pitched their tent and slept beneath the Himalayas. Standing there now, he was unable to summon emotional strength from the teachings of Buddha, from the promise of a renewed life after death. All he could feel at this moment was loss—irrevocable, maddening, incomprehensible loss. Crying, he sat alone on their hilltop, until the sun fell behind the great mountains and the world turned dark.

It took a complex and exhausting three weeks for Charles to lead his loyal companions from the bench in the corridor of the Bangkok police building to the boulevards of Paris. By rented car they drove down the long elephant trunk of southern Thailand to where it empties into Malaysia. At the border the car was abandoned and Charles instructed Marie-Andrée and Jean Dhuisme to stroll casually across on foot. Then, using a series of taxis and buses,. the suspected killers threaded their way to Pinang, the drowsy colonial city founded by the British East India Company in the eighteenth century. A week passed while they hid in a cheap hotel under false names.

Marie-Andrée and Jean Dhuisme slept most of the first days in Pinang, trying to repair nerves shattered by the grueling dash. But in midweek Charles, displaying an astonishing insensitivity, imported Suzy, the Bangkok waitress, to join his group. She turned up looking happy, fresh, lovely, and even younger than her twenty years. It seemed a deliberate act of cruelty toward Marie-Andrée and she exploded in fury. "You've dragged me into hell," she screamed, "and now you bring on my replacement." She hurled an ultimatum: me or her, take your pick.

This time Charles was unable to douse the jealous fire with whispers and promises and an insistence that Suzy was present only to help his "business." He sent the bewildered waitress back home again, although once out of Marie-Andrée's sight Charles rewarded Suzy with a radio, a camera, a gem, and a promise of reunion. "I still want to marry you," he insisted, promising to join her in Bangkok in a few days.

Then Ajay Chowdhury materialized, having been dispatched on a business errand by Charles to the jewel mines of Chanthaburi. Somehow Ajay had managed to accumulate a packet containing a few hundred carats of rubies and sapphires. Of middling quality, they nonetheless gave Charles the notion for a new venture—one that would reap substantial profit and at the same time allow the group to remove themselves from the attention of Asian police.

They would all fly to Europe, explained Charles, where the stones could be sold for perhaps as much as $40,000. And once there, Charles promised, Marie-Andrée could obtain a new passport from the Canadian Embassy. "If you really want to," he told her, "you can fly home to Canada." The promise was so seductive that Marie-Andrée forgot about Suzy.

As they flew out of Asia, Marie-Andrée noticed that Ajay Chowdhury was not present. She knew that Jean Dhuisme had taken a separate flight, with instructions to rendezvous in Geneva. But what happened to the handsome Indian who had been so devoted to Charles—and to her—since he became part of their lives the previous autumn? Would he meet them in Geneva? Or Paris? Charles brushed off the question, ignoring Marie-Andrée, burying his nose in a paperback mystery. "Where *is* Ajay?" pressed Marie-Andrée. The night before their departure, the two men were overheard speaking hotly about money and precious stones, but it had not seemed overly serious.

Lifting his attention from his book, Charles silenced Marie-Andrée. His eyes told her not to ask those questions again. Marie-Andrée shut up. She assumed the Indian had fallen from grace. Several months later, when police were assembling the tale and its characters, the theory was that Ajay had filled his purpose, that he was dead, that he was buried in a Malaysian jungle. Whatever his destiny, he was not heard from, nor seen, again.

Enroute to Paris, Charles elected to stop over briefly in Karachi, the port city of Pakistan. The unexpected delay irked Marie-Andrée, but she was so thrilled to be on the final leg of her bizarre odyssey that she did not protest. At least their direction was west.

Karachi has a spectacular beach at Banks Bay with a colony of foreigners living in cheap huts and bathing in the Arabian Sea. Mostly young and frugal travelers, they were under frequent scrutiny by fanatically puritanical Moslem authorities. One morning Charles took Marie-Andrée to Banks Bay, where they strolled and sunned. There Charles discovered a promising young woman stretched out on the sand. Blond and robust, she wore a tiny gem in her nostril and was possessed of an earthy sensuality. Her name was Mary Ellen Eather, a dropout nurse from Australia, running away from a broken love affair.

Sensing Marie-Andrée's hostility, Charles insisted that he had no interest in the girl save as a possible employee when and if he returned to Asia from Europe. If she were bathed, and coiffed, dressed and bejeweled, mused Charles, she could turn the head of a maharaja. Quickly Charles introduced himself, went to Mary Ellen's hut for tea, made his basic "courier" pitch, received mild interest in return. "We are on our way to Europe for business," said Charles. "We will be back through here in a few weeks. Can you be ready to leave—quickly?"

Mary Ellen nodded. She needed work. She was broke. "I'll wait for you," she said, not really expecting more to come of it.

As the plane lifted out of Karachi and headed across the great body of Asia, bound for Switzerland, Charles was in fine spirits. In his pockets were gems worth $40,000, and waiting for him in Karachi was a ripe young woman of immense potential.

Alas, he had also, as time would tell, made a grave misjudgment of a woman's character.

Resembling more an affluent couple on a grand tour of Europe than a man and woman suspected of multiple murder, Charles and Marie-Andrée flew to Geneva using stolen passports and credit cards and were met by Jean Dhuisme in a terribly expensive new Citroën—silver and gleaming like the Swiss franc. Using the method he had once mentioned to Belle, Charles guided his associates across the border into France, then across the awakening greenness to Paris.

His first call was to Félix d'Escogne. His patron, ex-prison *visiteur* and "best friend," was startled to hear the voice that had plagued him for a decade. What was Charles doing in Paris? Unspoken was the reminder that Charles had been officially thrown out of France years ago, with his citizenship revoked. And he was still wanted on old criminal charges. Nonetheless, Félix invited Charles to his apartment and greeted him warmly. Immediately Félix observed that Charles was neither attentive nor particularly proud of his "bride." Marie-Andrée was left to fend for herself in a corner chair—like a senile old aunt—and not brought into the conversation unless Félix asked her something. Quietly, shy, and in some sort of anguish, she made scant impression at all on d'Escogne. Rather rudely, thought Félix, Charles asked if there was news of Hélène and his daughter, now nearing six. "None," answered Félix. "That chapter is closed, Charles."

Was there news from the rest of Charles' family? "I really haven't kept up," answered Félix. But he did possess one piece of good information. The half-brother, André, had been freed from the Turkish prison in what he called a "miracle." After serving only a few months of the eighteen year sentence, for the Istanbul Hilton crimes, André was pardoned as the first act of a new government that ordered a general amnesty.

Charles was delighted. Where was his little brother?

"I don't know," answered Félix, fudging. In truth he knew well that André was in Paris, looking for work, trying to shape a new life, apparently chastened by his swim in murky waters beside Charles. Félix prayed the younger man would not encounter the half-brother who almost destroyed him.

The next day, Marie-Andrée went to the Canadian Embassy and stood outside for a long while. Had she summoned the courage to cross the threshold and tell a clever lie, or even confess the truth and beg for mercy, perhaps destiny would have permitted a return to the healing of anonymous life in the little town on the wrong bank of the St. Lawrence. But at this crisis point she could not locate the will to act. Perhaps another day. She found a taxi and bade the driver to hurry her back to Charles.

During her absence, Charles was alone with Félix. Privacy did not ease the discomfort felt by both men. Félix had quickly grown weary of trying to smoke Charles' pipe dreams. He suspected that something was gravely wrong. "How is your life, Charles?" he asked. "I mean, let's have the truth. How is it *really?*"

"My life is very complicated," answered Charles. "Many people depend on me. Many people *need* me." Then, as if to blunt further intrusions, Charles telephoned Jean Dhuisme and instructed him to bring the silver Citroën.

They must be leaving. A chasm had developed between Charles and Félix. It could not be bridged.

When they left, Félix d'Escogne stood at the window of his flat and watched the expensive car hurry away. *Plus ça change, plus c'est la même chose.* The dark forces still raged within his nemesis. *"Adieu,"* he murmured. *"Adieu, Charlot."* And he made a mental note to change the locks on his doors.

In a Paris suburb, Hélène's mother was dying. Her family gathered to attend her last hours. Exhausted after the long flight from her new home in the United States, Hélène sat beside her mother's bed until the others insisted she slip away for a little sleep. As she left the hospital she heard the familiar voice behind her *"Chérie,"* said Charles, "I've been waiting for you."

Hélène whirled and tried to be composed. How had he found her? She tried to run for help, but Charles gripped her arms and led her toward a cafe. They ordered apéritifs, spoke routinely for a few minutes. Hélène told Charles of her new life. She was remarried. To an American. Nice man. Good to Shubra. A kind, lawful, hard-working, legitimate businessman.

Hélène begged him to forget her. She had a new name, a new world, no one knew of her past. "What of my daughter?" demanded Charles. Hélène nodded. He had a right to know of Shubra. She produced a recent snapshot, the child now radiantly beautiful, brunette, a coquettish smile, a face of elegance and cheer.

"Does she remember me?" asked Charles.

Hélène shook her head. "I have another child, too," she informed him. Both of her daughters recognized only their American father.

She rose to leave; a taxi stood empty outside the cafe. Perhaps she could escape. Charles spoke quietly, but his words contained a threat. Someday, he warned, his daughter would know her real father, acknowledge her real blood.

Hélène cried out, "If you love her, leave us alone!"

"I think you still love *me*," he taunted. "Isn't that so?"

She freed herself and ran to the taxi. Charles did not follow.

She was crying; Charles took heart in that.

"Mama?"

"Who is this?" Song did not recognize the voice on the telephone that had summoned her from her garden on a fine spring morning in Marseilles. She had been pruning her lemon trees when the call came; she rushed inside so that the noise would not awaken her husband and set off a tirade.

"It's Charles, Mama."

Charles! What was he doing in Marseilles? Song had not heard from, or in truth barely thought of her firstborn son, in years. Her assumption was that he was in jail—somewhere.

Just beyond the half-century mark, Song was an alluring woman, still given to tight dresses with slits and brightly painted toenails and large quantities of jewelry that filled her arms and neck. A few crinkles marked her dark eyes, but her almond skin was clear and soft, and when she wore pedal pushers and a peasant blouse to the outdoor market, men turned in approval. Now, hurriedly, she dressed in a red silk gown and splashed perfume on her shoulders and put a fresh yellow rose in her hair. She stood at her window and watched a long silver Citroën stop outside her tiny house. Out of it bounded Charles, dressed like a model in a Paris fashion magazine, carrying an attaché case and looking like a man whose life careened from private jet to corporate boardrooms.

Song rushed to kiss her son and he held her tightly. He whispered in her ear, "My friends are coming in. I want you to tell them you are my *wife,* not my mother."

"Your *wife?*"

"Please do as I say, Mama."

But once Marie-Andrée and Jean Dhuisme were inside and accepting drinks from Song, the strange order never was mentioned again. Whether Charles was playing some cruel trick on Marie-Andrée or else giving vent to a chronic fantasy, Song never knew. It simply became another entry in the troubling book of memories she had for her firstborn child.

The visitors stayed for three days, three unpleasant days. Song disliked Marie-Andrée intensely, found her rude, lazy, and given to lying on the daybed in the living room and dispensing orders. Get me a Coke. Get me a tissue. Get me a pillow. Get me breakfast. The house was filled with conspiratorial whispers. Song would enter a room and find Charles and Marie-Andrée in the midst of an animated conversation which would immediately cease and be replaced by false smiles. "Charles was constantly on the telephone," Song remembered later on. "There was always talk of money—and gems—and airplane-schedules." The third member of the group, Jean Dhuisme, was very polite and flattering to Song, but she wondered why a solid, educated family man would be clinging to the dangerous coattails of her son.

Alphonse Darreau could not tolerate all the commotion in his home. The sound of a bird singing could drive him into intense pain and anger. Three visitors who were constantly on the telephone and slamming doors brought him to the brink of total collapse. On the fourth day, Song went to her son and told him to leave. Hotels were nearby—and inexpensive. She gathered that despite the rich clothes and fancy automobile parked outside Charles was in need of money. Marie-Andrée had even asked to borrow twenty francs to buy cosmetics.

The eviction notice broke the dam of hurt and anger pent up in Charles. His mother, he charged, had rejected him all his life. "You never loved me," he accused. "I could feel it as a child."

Song shook her head. "I loved you the most of all," she countered. "But I never knew how to show it." Once, she pointed out, she had bribed a newspaper reporter to keep his name out of the paper. "That wasn't to help me," said Charles bitterly. "That was to protect *your* name."

A lifetime of grievances spilled out of Charles, lashing his mother like strokes from a whip. She had abandoned him in Saigon, she made him feel the "outsider," she exiled him to boarding school, she locked him in his room, she tied him up with rope, she threw him across half the world. "Whenever I needed you, Mama, you were not there. That is my legacy from you."

Song would not accept any of it. "Leave this house and get out of my sight," she ordered. "The reason I have such a tiny house is that I had to pay so many lawyer bills and stowaway fares for you."

Marie-Andrée tried to be peacemaker. She suggested they take leave. Song watched her son hurry toward the Citroën and she cried, "Don't come here again! Forget that you have a mother!"

"What is there to remember?" Charles shot back. The silver car dug its tires into the dirt road and disappeared in a cloud of reddish dust.

Sometime later, Song received an officious letter from a Marseilles lawyer. It stated that one Charles Sobhraj had swindled a woman in a jewelry deal recently in the city, and he was now being sought. Unless he presented himself, charges of grand theft would be filed with the police.

Song read the letter many times and carried it inside her blouse so that no one could find it. Then she wrote back a simple reply. "The name Charles Sobhraj is not known to me. He is not a member of my family."

Thus rejected, in his view, by his best friend, his first love, and his mother, Charles ordered Jean Dhuisme to turn the Citroën toward the East. And Marie-Andrée, out of wasted love, or fear, or sympathy, or perhaps the promise of more adventure and money, took her seat beside him. Once again she would forget about Canada.

CHAPTER THIRTY-SEVEN

As ostentatious a choice of chariots as Hannibal's elephant, the silver Citroën flashed across half the world, through villages in Turkey and Iraq and Pakistan so primitive that a bicycle would bring people running from their huts to look. The journey must have been tense. All three passengers must have panicked at the sight of a policeman or border guard, wondering if just beyond the next curve in the road was a barricade. But this was not true. Later investigation revealed that the trip was quick—three weeks —and comfortable, the Citroën being celebrated for the soft embrace of its cushions, with French disco music serenading the soon-to-be accused killer, his lovesick woman, and the foolish designer.

By early June, the trio reached Karachi, where, surprisingly, Mary Ellen Eather was still stretched out on the sand, stoned but ready and willing to find a seat in the Citroën. And thus they were off, a handsome quartet on holiday, bound for Thailand.

Just outside of Karachi they finally encountered a roadblock—of sorts. Marie-Andrée was browsing through a stack of magazines and newspapers that Charles had purchased. Thumbing idly through *Asia Week*, she came across an article that made her blood turn cold. There, in black and white, the horrors were made real, for all the world to see, like a deadly spider suspended in a transparent cube. It was complete—names, dates, deaths, and the stomach-churning news that Thai police were preparing murder warrants for the arrests of "Alain Gauthier" and his girl friend, "Monique," believed to be a Canadian nurse. She threw the article into Charles' lap and he perused it while driving. No sign of concern, not the barest trace, came to his face. All he did was shrug and whisper, so that the others in the back seat could not hear, "It's a bunch of lies. They just make this stuff up to sell newspapers."

"But what are we going to do?" whined Marie-Andrée.

Charles smiled. His name was not really Alain Gauthier, nor was hers Monique. Why worry, then? Police were looking for other people. But there were photographs of Charles and Marie-Andrée! How could they avoid getting arrested by some ambitious and alert border guard? "Trust me," said Charles. "This is Asia. I know how to operate in the Asian way." He dictated an immediate change of itinerary. Instead of Thailand, they would go to India. Rest. Take stock. Make some money. It seemed of no more importance to Charles than a rock that had tumbled into his path, easily stepped around. After India, they would either return to Bangkok if the heat cooled, or proceed to Taiwan. Or the Philippines. Marie-Andrée begged Charles not to re-enter India. She had a premonition that trouble was waiting there.

"Go to sleep," he countersuggested. He threw the article out the window, somewhere near the Pakistani-Indian border.

Looking back, and applying the standards of American journalism, it seems incredible that not a word concerning the suspected killers reached public print until well over half a year following the Thailand murders. In May 1976, Herman Knippenberg received a call from a Bangkok *Post* reporter who had heard rumors of the Action Committee and its sleuthing. He wanted an interview. Cautious now, several times burned, Herman declined, trying to throw the reporter off the track. He was well aware that foreign service officers are not supposed to get their names in the paper unless they have completed a treaty for cotton tariffs or have thrown an especially good party for the birthday of Queen Juliana. But then he began to chew on the matter and decided that if nothing else, a newspaper account might give warning to Gauthier & Company, and perhaps to potential victims.

On May 7, the following headline stretched in sensation across eight columns of the Bangkok *Post:*

VICIOUS FOREIGN KILLERS MAY BE INVOLVED
YOUNG DUTCH COUPLE WERE BURNED ALIVE

English language newspapers in the Far East are rarely more than sycophants for their governments, but the *Post* showed remarkable courage, going out on a very slender limb. The article told of "horrific evidence" that had been uncovered in the mysterious adjoining apartments in Kanit House, and that after the deaths of the two Dutch young people, "Gauthier was seen returning to the apartment carrying a gasoline can."

A day or two later, the *Post* followed up with an even bigger splash that tied in the murder of Vitali Hakim, Charmayne Carrou, and Jennie Bolliver. Grisly photographs made the words almost impossible to read. And quickly a climate of fear fell over the tourist business in Bangkok. Meetings were called at the highest levels of government. Police Chief Lieutenant General Montchai announced that the case was "the most shocking that has ever occurred in Thailand." He was launching an "immediate investigation."

All of this Herman found satisfying, shaded as it was by irony, since the Thai police could have arrested the suspects at any time prior to March, and indeed had them in custody only to let them go. Not until Thailand's vital tourist economy was threatened by printed accounts of death and torture did the police elect to launch their "immediate investigation."

Colonel Sompol Suthimai was on holiday in the northern Thailand city of Chiang Mai when he received a cable from the general. It was a "rocket," a drop-everything order to return to Bangkok and take over investigation of what was becoming known as the "tourist murders," or, more luridly, the "bikini killings," so called because Jennie's corpse had been discovered wearing a bathing suit. The selection of Sompol Suthimai was fortunate. In a country where corruption begins in the rice paddies and rises to the most exalted suites of government, where one study suggested that between 15 and 20 per cent of Thailand's entire national budget was drained into sticky hands, Sompol was honest. A good cop, smart, sophisticated, the kind of modern Thai who might have made a good prime minister, Sompol lacked the devious bent required for political advancement in the Orient. Instead he was content to boss Thailand's Interpol division, an elite group containing the classiest cops on the national force. At forty-five, Sompol looked barely half that, with a sweet, unlined, and boyish face. He was a very appealing man with the kind of eyes that veteran cops the world over often develop, rather sad, melancholy, as if the years of witnessing tragedy and the darkest corners of the human conditions created a glaze of sorrow. Sompol did not smoke, nor drink, nor had he ever been to a massage parlor even in the line of duty, a feat in Thailand somewhat comparable to an Englishman never setting foot in a pub. He spoke several languages, including good English and French, and had studied in both London and New York, with Scotland Yard and the FBI, specializing in narcotics traffic and international fraud. Had Sompol been present on the day when Charles and Marie-Andrée were hauled into police headquarters for questioning, perhaps they might not have strolled out with the ease of paying a restaurant check and calling a taxi. But fate on that day placed him in an office across the street from the pair that would soon dominate and consume his every waking moment.

The report that tourists were being murdered in Thailand was not altogether new to Colonel Sompol. His French wife, Nicole, had brought the dark rumor to their dinner table earlier in the year. One of her friends in the international community had asked Nicole to inquire of her husband if it was true that killings were going on, and that the police were hushing them up. "Is this possible?" demanded Nicole.

Sompol's reply had been that such was not possible. The police did have limitations and were often inefficient, but he could not conceive of mass murder being concealed in an official closet.

* * *

He began by calling on Herman Knippenberg, who was testy and officious, in no mood to waste further time dealing with a Thai cop. "We made a case," said Herman, "and we gave it to you people. All you did was arrest them and let them go." Herman had it on good authority— Belle's—that a bribe of 300,000 *bahts* had been paid.

"I have no faith whatsoever left in the efficiency of the Thailand police," said Herman bluntly. He rose to dismiss Sompol.

"Please," countered the young colonel. His voice was soft. "I can't say that I believe you, because I'm just beginning my investigation. But I promise you this: you won't be wasting your time if you tell *me* the story."

"How can I believe that?" snapped Herman. Then he stared at the gentle face of Sompol Suthimai and found trust there. Reluctantly he sighed and agreed to plow the field one more time.

After a few days of studying Herman's massive files— they now contained hundreds of pages and were several inches thick—Sompol went to his superior, General Montchai. "It's bizarre," he said, in effect, "but I believe this Dutchman. I think we'd better move—and move fast."

"What do you need?" asked the general.

"A task force of eight men," answered Sompol. The best on the force. He would pick them. No interference from anybody. *Carte blanche.*

Montchai agreed. He was under intense pressure from the military men who stood behind the King's ceremonial throne and ran the booming country. Montchai wanted "Alain Gauthier" and "Monique" and "Ajay" arrested posthaste. If they had fled the country, then he wanted them extradited back to Bangkok. Thailand has a very convenient means of dealing with major criminals, a clause that allows instant execution, without trial, of those people deemed dangerous to society. They can be stood against the wall and shot.

The silver Citroën crossed the frontier of India and stopped in Amritsar, principal city of the Punjab and spiritual home for the Sikhs, those men who embody the poster image of India. Their hair, uncut since birth, is

stuffed into a turban and thus makes the skull so insulated
that, legend dictates, no enemy's sword can slice into the
brain. Amritsar's streets and bazaars swarm with Sikhs,
most on pilgrimage to the Golden Temple, where three
centuries earlier a courageous Sikh named Baba Dip led
a raiding expedition in an attempt at wresting the holy
shrine from Moghul hands. In mid-battle, Baba Dip had
the misfortune to encounter a Moghul warrior who de-
capitated him, but the Sikh, undaunted, placed his severed
skull back onto its bleeding neck and fought bravely until
the temple was liberated. Today the grisly portrait of
Baba Dip, head in hands, hangs everywhere in Amritsar.

While Charles led the others to view the temple, Marie-
Andrée feigned illness and instead found the international
telephone office. She placed an urgent call to her sister in
Canada, awakening Denise in the middle of a Quebec
night. Though her words were guarded, maneuvering
around the sword over *her* head, Marie-Andrée sounded
so grave and distraught that Denise immediately knew
something was wrong. The connection was poor and the
two sisters shouted at one another across the globe. Marie-
Andrée kept wanting to know if anyone had been asking
questions about her in Canada. Had the Canadian Government been bothering her parents? Was her name in the
newspapers? Confused, Denise pleaded for more information. She did not understand what her sister was
saying. Then, in mid-question, the line went dead. In
Quebec, Denise stared in annoyance at the telephone. In
India, Charles lifted his hand from the depress button. He
warned her not to try that again. His voice was cold. He
grabbed her by the hair and yanked her from the booth.

In mid-June the gang paused briefly in Delhi, where
Mary Ellen Eather made her debut. As police would later
charge, the Australian girl was sent forth with newly
coiffed hair and seductive clothes to sit in the lobby of the
YMCA Hotel, one of the better middle-class inns in the
capital. There she encountered three young French tourists.
Quickly they fell ill, worsening after taking medication
recommended by their new friend. Next came unconsciousness. When they awoke, their salable possessions were
gone. Proceeds: a few hundred dollars.

Surfacing next in Bombay, Charles installed his associates in a cheap hotel while he hit the familiar streets,
looking no doubt for a riper plum, one that would bring
more substantial nourishment. He had many mouths to
feed. At a cafe favored by would-be actors and peripheral
people pretending to be in the motion picture business—
its counterpart in Hollywood would be Schwab's Drug
Store—Charles examined the customers, idling and waiting
to be discovered. His eye fell on an interesting girl. Smoky,
dark-haired, she was obviously English, for her cheeks
were as soft and as clear as a cream-colored rose. Although
her clothes were grimy, Charles thought she might be
transformed into a spectacular counterpoint for Mary
Ellen, one dark, the other light—together an irresistible
promise. The new girl's name was Barbara Smith, barely
twenty. And when Charles sat down at her table he immediately discerned that she was a trifle eccentric. When she
spoke, her sentences had gaps in them, like clouds, crossing the sun and blocking the warmth. But when she
kept her mouth shut, Barbara Smith was enchanting. He
could use her.

Coincidentally, Barbara was in the company of a dolt
whom Charles knew vaguely, from some long ago moment in India. He was a Belgian named Hugey Courage,
a hulking giant well over two meters tall, with cheeks
sunken from chewing opium balls, and a face almost
handsome save those unfortunate moments when he
laughed, for the few teeth he had left were mostly jagged
stumps.

Hugey Courage was a classic character from a Joseph
Conrad novel, the European degraded by the East, too
mired to pry himself free. Mercenary, construction worker,
cook, brawler, petty crook, the Belgian had migrated to
India a decade before and married a stout, shrewish Portuguese woman in Goa. Together they ran a beach shack
cafe that sold omelets and fiery sausages to the youth who
frolicked on the sand, but Hugey relished every opportunity that permitted him escape to Bombay, where his
wife's curses did not assault his ears from dawn to midnight. In Bombay, Hugey occasionally got a walk-on in a
film, since his face was Western, albeit ravaged.

Charles spoke mundanely of this and that, but he was

in truth forming a new plan, a drama for his stock
company to enact that, if successful, would break box
office records. Quickly he recruited both Hugey and
Barbara as employees, neither inclined to press for details
as to what the job entailed.

When Charles installed yet another comely young woman in their hotel room, Marie-Andrée watched with silent anguish as the man she loved dressed Barbara Smith
with new clothes and arranged her hair and cleaned her
face. In a chair sat Mary Ellen Eather, saucy, beautiful,
and very very young. Marie-Andrée had almost stopped
looking at her own face in the mirror. Each time she did,
back came a woman whose hair was shiny with black
dye, a shade achieved by the vain and elderly, and a face
pinched, like a pouch containing secrets. She was thirty-
one and in this competition she probably felt a hundred.

In Bangkok, Sompol Suthimai assembled his squad and
told them that the reputation of the Thai police force was
at stake. "We cannot rest until these people are in our
custody," he said. They must answer for the lives destroyed
and burned and tossed into ditches. Sompol had personally
supervised the identification of Charmayne Carrou by
means of dental charts. He had shuddered when the
remains were removed from a deep freeze and dropped
onto an examining table. "These killings were merciless,"
Sompol told his team. "They were the work of a savage.
The Dutch people were set afire and burned while they
were still breathing. The Turk—the same. The American
girl was drowned by forcing her head into the sea and
holding it there until her lungs literally burst. We cannot
call ourselves a civilized nation when atrocities like this
go unpunished."

Over the next few weeks, Sompol and his men covered
familiar territory, that already developed by Herman
and his dogged diplomats. But with the force of police
credentials, Sompol was able to build a more thorough
indictment. Belle and Raoul told their stories once more,
and then again, and the maid and concierge of Kanit
House were interviewed. May and Suzy, the two Thai
girls romanced by Charles, gave detailed statements. In
Australia, Sompol interviewed the Lapthorne couple,

whose honeymoon ended in their being drugged and robbed in Hua Hin. When the couple was shown photographs of the suspects—those taken by Belle with her long lens camera—they immediately identified Charles and Marie-Andrée as the charming couple who had used the false names "Mr. and Mrs. Belmont" while dispensing chocolate milk laced with sleeping potion.

Working around the clock and grabbing brief naps on the floor of Sompol's office, the investigators poured through hotel registers, airport landing and departure cards, money exchanges, the spoor left behind by tourists in any country. By mid-May, Sompol was able to report to General Montchai: "We have five dead bodies positively identified. We can place each of them in Alain Gauthier's apartment just before death, and we have personal belongings of the victims that were found in the apartment. We have eyewitness testimony from others in the building, and statements from employees which tell how some of the victims were carried out in a drugged state. One witness can testify the killers returned smelling of gasoline, with mud on their trousers."

Interesting and grotesque stones were turned up by Sompol's digging. "To dispose of the Dutch youngsters, Gauthier rented a car," said the detective. "He paid for the rental with traveler's checks stolen from Mr. Bintanja, the victim." And Gauthier also asked May, the Thai girl who worked in the hotel jewelry shop, to cash traveler's checks for him. "These were stolen and the signatures a forgery," remarked Sompol. "When some of them were kicked back by banks as being fraudulent, May was unable to collect from Gauthier . . . Thus did she fulfill her role. She thought she was his lover. What she was was a dupe."

Toward the end of May 1976, arrest warrants were issued by the Thai Government charging "Alain Gauthier," Marie-Andrée Leclerc, alias "Monique," and Ajay Chowdhury with (1) conspiring to murder other persons by premeditation, (2) forging and using forged documents, and (3) receiving stolen goods. The warrants were specifically stated to be valid for twenty years. At the same time, Sompol prepared dossiers on the three suspects and cabled Interpol headquarters in Paris, requesting that the news be flashed immediately to police departments throughout the world.

To INTERPOL PARIS—INPOL 270658

We wish to inform you that a number of foreign tourists have been murdered in Thailand . . . by the group of persons named as follows: Mr. Gauthier, Alain—French national, Miss Leclerc, Marie-Andrée Lucie, Canadian national, and Mr. Chowdhury, Ajay, Indian national. Stop. These three persons fled Thailand. Stop. They are being sought by our police authorities for questioning concerning five murder cases. Stop. The victims were drugged and later murdered. Stop. According to the post-mortem report, death for two Dutch victims was caused by being hit over the head with a hard object that caused cerebral hemorrhage. They were then set on fire with gasoline when they were still breathing. Stop. The French girl victim was strangled to death. Stop.

Alain Gauthier is believed to have many passports belonging to his victims. Stop. Miss Leclerc may have obtained new passport recently in Europe. Stop. Suspects are now believed in France. We have requested Interpol Paris to keep the suspects under close surveillance. Stop. Extradition will be requested.

As the cables sped to the designated world capitals, Sompol rang up Herman Knippenberg to share the satisfying news. "We'll get them," he said. "I want them as bad as you do." But for now, all Sompol could do was wait. Impatiently he sat in his small office with color portraits of Thailand's king and queen on the wall beside him, and a painting of two dragons guarding a temple, and, in a corner, the small mountain of paper sacks, cardboard boxes, and junk. A pathetic pile, it was the sum of all the dead, the young people now being mailed home in metal urns.

The two new young women working for Charles had personalities contradictory to their looks. Mary Ellen, the blond Australian, seemed as vibrant as the sun. But she

was more often than not quiet, morose over the breakup
of a love affair, shy, sullen. She enjoyed burying herself
in philosophy and poetry. Conversely, Barbara Smith,
the brunette English girl, would be taken on first glimpse
as an introverted, naïve, and dim-witted child. Her reading
tastes leaned more to the Sunday matrimonial ads in
India's newspapers, those astonishing and anachronistic
listings of men and women who sought specific marriage
partners.

Barbara turned out to be far the more interesting—and
troublesome—of the two. She had been born in Pakistan
to an English mother who would die soon thereafter and
a father who had "something to do with radar." He was
not the kind of man who communicated much about his
life, or his feelings, or his work. All Barbara could remember from her early years was being yanked about
from place to place, from country to country, landing in
England at age three, and moving continually through
small towns south of London. When Barbara reached the
teen-age years, her father remarried, to a woman who
became The Classic Stepmother. "I hated her, and vice
versa," Barbara would recall. "Our house was constant
fighting, continuing anger, endless screaming. It grew
so hostile that Daddy put me in a house for wayward
girls . . . a place right out of old *Oliver Twist*." Mainly the
shelter contained very young children, and the few girls
of Barbara's age were expected to perform hard labor—
washing, cleaning, peeling potatoes. At sixteen, Barbara
was transferred to an "Assessment Center," where it was
assessed that she was not yet rehabilitated. Another two
and a half years were dictated in various institutions. Part-
time work allowed her to save up $800 and in June of
1975, Barbara fled England with no purpose in mind other
than to search and to wander. She took the ferry to France,
and there met a boy named Clifford. They decided to go
wherever the winds blew. Here and there they worked a
little, hitchhiked around Europe, maneuvered through the
Middle East, into Afghanistan, and broke up. Clifford
experienced some mystical and religious stirrings—he
later became a Jesus freak—and the couple parted in
Kabul. "We couldn't identify any longer," said Barbara.

She decided to venture into India. Perhaps settle down.

Later someone asked *why,* and she answered, "I just couldn't see any point of pretending to live in the English society. All it did was punish me. Nobody cared about me. Nobody wanted me. So perhaps India would adopt me."

Barbara headed immediately for the beach community of Goa. She rented a shack and shared it with other free spirits. "For the first time in my life I really enjoyed myself. Total freedom! I ran naked on the sand, I ate fresh fish just pulled out of the sea, I climbed palms and fetched coconuts, I found friends from England who built a huge tent out of palm fronds. There were times that eighteen people lived in the tent and on top we flew a banner that read, 'Royal Rock and Roll Hut.' "

Occasionally, police came by and arrested someone for being naked, or for smoking hash openly in the town. But these unpleasantries were washed away by such events as Christmas 1975, when the Royal Rock and Roll Hut contained two thousand young people, crowded around a Christmas tree built from bamboo, with a gigantic cloud of hashish smoke hovering overhead like fallout from a bomb. The party went on for days, warm days, golden days, with crisp nights perfect for campfires and lovers on the soft sand.

Later, there came an ugly period, a drug war. "The vibes turned evil," remembered Barbara. She hitchhiked to Bombay, intending to find work sufficient to finance a venture into Thailand and Malaysia. Two minor tragedies befell her in quick order. The first came when she foolishly left her remaining money, $300, in her rucksack at a student hostel. She only went down the hall for a wash, but when she returned, every penny she had was stolen. Then, while walking outside in heavy grief over her loss, a monsoon broke from the skies and drenched her, and her passport. Barbara took the wilted, sopping document to the British Embassy and asked for a replacement. She was told it would cost 250 rupees, an impossible sum. Could she pay it later? No. Could she sweep floors or clean toilets to earn the fee? No. Barbara stumbled out onto the streets of Bombay, frightened and desperate. "There is nothing more scary than being alone in India, without a penny, and with a mutilated passport." On this very day she met Hugey Courage, who took her to the cafe for tea, and there she collided with Charles Sobhraj.

Charles' new plan was, as police would one day charge, audacious—the making of a silk purse from a sow's ear, the transformation of Hugey Courage from a beach rat with crumbling teeth and opium-shrunken cheeks into a sleek and affluent diplomat. It would be both a variation on Pygmalion and on the Ashoka Hotel jewel theft in which La Passionara was an unwilling star.

This one would take some doing.

First Hugey soaked in a steaming bathtub for a solid hour until he emerged pink and glowing—and wrinkled as a mummy. Then Barbara cut his hair short and dignified. Two suits of clothes appropriate for a diplomat were commissioned at a good Bombay tailor. One was gray pinstripe, the other funereal black. Jean Dhuisme, the most cultured member of the group, was ordered to teach Hugey how to speak—no simple task since the Belgian conversed normally in a weird mélange of Flemish, French, Portuguese, and Hindi, often employing all four in one sentence. For days, Dhuisme patiently drilled Hugey on how to speak certain basic sentences, "How much is that necklace?" or "The price is too high." Finally Henry Higgins announced, wearily, that his Liza Doolittle had broken through the language barrier.

In a fortnight, a dress rehearsal was staged. Charles went out into the corridor of their hotel and knocked. Presently Barbara Smith, astonishingly lovely in a crimson hostess gown, opened the door imperiously and summoned Hugey. The new diplomat shuffled awkwardly into the room wearing his pinstripes and attempted a look of hauteur. So far Charles was pleased. But then Hugey attempted a line of dialogue and, fumbling, broke into a clownish grin. He had forgotten his speech, it being no more challenging than "Hello, how are you? . . . Thanks for coming." Charles cursed. Not only was Hugey the worst actor east of Paris, each time he opened his mouth the shortage of teeth made him look like a boxer who had hit the canvas face first in every bout.

A cut-rate dentist was located who in a few moments fashioned a cheap set of wooden teeth that fitted over

Hugey's stumps precariously. "That hurt, man," complained Hugey, whose words now came out coated in mush.

Charles ordered him to speak rarely, softly, and avoid smiles. As long as Hugey kept his mouth shut, he at least *looked* like a diplomat. The girls laughed and applauded and could not wait for opening night of this novel playlet.

The logical place to pull the job in Bombay was the Taj Mahal Hotel, for almost a century the citadel of the rich and celebrated traveler. But one day when Charles slipped cautiously into the lobby to check out the potential jewelry store, a man who was obviously a house detective eyed him with more than casual interest. Quickly Charles made an exit. Due to his previous sojourns in Bombay— there were periods when he had made the Taj a semi-permanent base of operations—his visage and methods were too well known.

Incredibly he ordered his group to move to New Delhi— the city where he was already wanted for the Ashoka Hotel gem theft in 1971, and for escape from the hospital following that, and—though the connections had not yet been made—for the theft of money and valuables from three French tourists in the YMCA Hotel only a few weeks earlier. In retrospect it was a foolish decision. But as one Delhi cop would later say, "Sobhraj needed money. Desperately. He was spending it fast. He had a big family to support. Charles decided to try Delhi. Delhi was the place where the action was."

Mary Ellen and Barbara were sent ahead via Air India with instructions to check into the three-star Lodhi Hotel. Then they were to study jewelry shops in the city's better hotels and at the same time look for tourists who might be suitable for Charles' needs. In a merry mood the girls flew out of Bombay, caught up in the heady excitement of the charade.

The silver Citroën bore Charles and Marie-Andrée and Jean Dhuisme and Hugey Courage up the face of the subcontinent, a grueling journey of two days broken when they reached Agra and collapsed for a few hours sleep in a cheap motel near the Taj Mahal. Marie-Andrée was ill, her stomach churning at every rut in the road.

In Delhi, Barbara and Mary Ellen had a little good

news to report. They had not been able to discover a wealthy tourist who might enjoy the hospitality of Charles Sobhraj, but they had found what seemed a promising jewelry store in the Imperial Hotel, an old and gracious white Colonial relic with elegant lawns where dowagers still took tea at a quarter to five. Already the girls had been in the shop, browsing over trays of rubies and sapphires and mentioning that a diplomat friend of great wealth might possibly be journeying to Delhi and probably would want to make a major gem purchase. Discretion was necessary, they had whispered to the merchant, for the diplomat demanded exceptional secrecy and protocol.

Upon hearing this, Charles was moderately pleased. So far, so good. The plan *had* to work, for he was nearly broke. It was nearing the end of June and Delhi reeled under the scorching heat that is prelude to monsoon season. One day the thermometer reached 114 and forty people dropped dead on the capital's streets. Marie-Andrée told Charles she could not endure more than a few days in the city, for she teetered on the edge of collapse. "Then take a nap," he snapped. "You're not much good for anything anymore."

Hugey Courage was also complaining. In Bombay, a city he knew well, the Belgian was reasonably comfortable playacting the role of diplomat. But in Delhi, he was developing the coldest of feet. He confessed his fear to the new girls. Nobody was going to buy his performance, and, besides, he knew nothing about jewelry. He could be presented with a pearl made from putty and he might pronounce it perfect. Overhearing this, Charles erupted. His patience was thin; he had spent too much already. All Hugey had to do was stand there in a pinstripe suit, keep his mouth shut, look rich, and wait for Charles to step out of the bathroom. Any *idiot* could do it. Hugey's face turned dark with worry and he muttered something about needing a drink.

Something else was troubling Hugey, something that Charles did not know. Hugey had telephoned his wife in Goa and she had screamed at him like a woman buried alive in a collapsed building. The children were hungry, the beach cafe was falling apart, bill collectors were leaping out from every tree. If Hugey did not hurry home to Goa, she would notify the police, the Belgian Consulate, and Indira Gandhi if necessary. Between a rock and a hard place, Hugey agonized for another day or so, donning the diplomatic clothes and standing in front of the mirror and trying to smile feebly. Each time he rehearsed he felt worse.

One morning Marie-Andrée told Charles she *had* to telephone her family in Canada because her father had a heart condition and she was anxious to hear how he was doing. At that moment Charles was occupied with something else and could not escort her to the telephone office. He had forbidden her to speak with anyone unless he could monitor the conversation. But she pleaded and wept and finally Charles agreed, ordering Hugey to go along and make sure the woman did not say something unfortunate.

While Marie-Andrée was inside the telephone *cabine*, struggling to communicate with an overseas operator, Hugey waited outside, wondering if he should also call home. Then he noticed Marie-Andrée's purse, which she had left on the counter with a request that Hugey watch over it. At that moment Hugey made his decision. He could not continue in the role of diplomat or partake in a jewel robbery. But he needed funds to get back to Goa. Snatching up Marie-Andrée's purse, which contained $150 in cash, four passports, a gold chain, and a watch, he ran out. Suspecting that the others were probably out in the city by now looking for tourists, Hugey dared to go to their room in the Lodhi Hotel. Finding it empty, he scooped up everything he could stuff in a suitcase—a few hundred dollars, a camera, a radio, assorted valuables—and fled Delhi.

Home by nightfall, two thousand miles away, Hugey embraced his wife, whereupon she withdrew and slapped him. At that, his wooden teeth fell onto the floor with a clatter, and for the first time in a long while, Mr. and Mrs. Hugey Courage laughed together.

CHAPTER THIRTY-EIGHT

Rooted not so much in loss but in betrayal, Charles' anger
was awesome. "But he *needed* me!" cried Charles, slamming the butt of his palm into the hotel room wall. He
cursed Hugey Courage in several languages. Summoning
Jean Dhuisme, the two men flew immediately to Goa and
spent two frustrating days searching for the traitor. Wisely
Hugey had never revealed exactly where he lived. When
they could not find him, Charles, furious, ordered a
return to Delhi. His situation was bleak. He had spent
more than $3,000 in custom-tailored suits, false teeth, and
travel expenses. There was little left.

Hardly had Charles left Goa when word reached Hugey
that someone had been in town looking for him. Hugey
knew that he could not hide forever. Someday Charles
would return and be waiting for him in the darkness.
Frightened, Hugey brooded for a few days, then he went
to a favored private place next to the sea and sat down on
a jagged rock and wrote a painful letter. Crossing his
fingers, he mailed it to Delhi.

Interpol is a name that conjures much more than its
franchise. True, it is the world's only organization of
international police, but Interpol is little more than a
post office. Headquarters in St. Cloud, an affluent suburb
of Paris, is an anonymous-looking gray cement building
of no architectural interest, save gardens and terraces
planted with tulips and azaleas, and a fine view of Paris

with the Longchamps racetrack close enough to view the
horses through binoculars. The only element that marks
the building as something more than an insurance office
is a forest of antennae on the roof, the hub of a sophisticated communications network that can receive and
transmit information anywhere in the world within seconds. Interpol, surprisingly, has no power. It cannot make
arrests or question suspects, nor does it have agents in
trench coats to prowl the subterranean world of espionage
and international danger. But it does have several able
detectives on the payroll, one of whom found several
cables from Bangkok on his desk on a late May afternoon in 1976.

Paul Delsart is a veteran French homicide cop and he
suits the image well. An excitable little man, he has a
face that flushes easily and animated hands that gesticulate
theatrically when recalling a particularly choice murder.
He is the possessor of an analytical mind to rival the
detectives of literature. If Hercule Poirot and Inspector Maigret were seated at a bistro table, Delsart would
fit neatly beside them.

The first thing that Paul Delsart did was to expedite
Bangkok's murder warrants and descriptions of the suspects to police departments from Paris to the Philippines.
And he asked each country if it had unsolved crimes
similar to the ones being investigated in Thailand. Then
he ran the name "Alain Gauthier" through the Interpol
identification computer, repository of the world's recognized criminals. The computer obediently belched
forth two or three men by that name in the world, but none
remotely resembled either in physical characteristics, age,
nationality, or modus operandi the man wanted by Thailand's police.

In the next several days, cables and telexes poured in
from Hong Kong, Katmandu, New Delhi, and Karachi, so
many that Delsart was stunned. "There seemed to be a
new murder every day when I got to work," he would later
recall. "The case was maddening—incredibly complex.
We didn't know if we were looking for Alain Gauthier, or
Henricus Bintanja, or Laddie DuParr, or Robert Paul
Grainer, or Eric d'Amour, or all of them. It seemed a
United Nations of murder."

Inspector Delsart considered his mental card file to be as dependable as, if not more so than, the computer. After a quarter of a century dealing with criminals and their methods, he owned a substantial index in his head. Putting his feet up on his desk, he took a large yellow note pad and began scribbling, listing several names that he personally knew of, names of criminals who specialized in the general category of "drug and rob." Then, if the name did not belong to an Asian face, he crossed it off. If a name did not deal in false passports, it was eliminated. Finally but a half-dozen names remained on the pad. He studied the list for the better part of a day. One name and one name only seemed to fit all the specifications of the "Alain Gauthier" wanted so badly in Bangkok. Delsart called for a certain dossier and when the folder hit his in-basket he suspected strongly that his hunch was accurate.

When he read the file, he was almost certain. Interpol had sent out a "WANTED" flyer on the man in 1973. The suspect was known to have used at least a score of names, often those of his victims. He had an Oriental face. He operated mainly in Asia. And his real name was Hotchand Bhawnani Gurmukh Sobhraj. Unfortunately, the inspector was not confident enough to flash a worldwide alert. He decided instead to let his hunch ferment for another day or two. It was July 1, 1976.

While Charles and Jean Dhuisme were searching in vain for Hugey Courage, the girls cased Delhi. As directed, they lounged about the airport lobby, looking for tourists, specifically French tourists. At a tourist information center, they picked up the interesting rumor that a large tour group from France was en route to Delhi, estimated to arrive around July 1. Perhaps as many as sixty French men and women were due. When Charles received the news—Barbara Smith would remember—his face "lit up like a Roman candle."

To a man in need of funds, this seemed as opportune as finding the keys to a bank vault. But alas, even in Charles' line of work, it takes money to make money. The group needed new clothes, a new collection of gemstones to sell. There would be hotel bills and bar tabs and restaurant checks to pay. An affluent façade would have to be presented to the French tourists, else they might dismiss Charles as just another street hustler trying to sell brightly colored bits of glass. The cash flow in Charles' camp must have been at crisis point. Marie-Andrée asked him for a hundred rupees (about twelve dollars) to make another call to Canada, but he said there was not enough money for breakfast. The turndown lit a flash fire in Marie-Andrée that raged for most of a day, she contending that he had stolen her $2,000 nest egg, he countering that her constant demands for jewels and high living had drained his coffers. "Did you ever give me something that I was allowed to keep for more than two weeks before you took it back and sold it?" she shrieked.

The group had been changing hotels almost daily, and at the end of June took rooms at the respectable, three-star pink- and cream-colored Ranjit Hotel. All used fake names. Police would theorize that Charles needed to accomplish one more robbery before moving in on the sixty-person French tour group. The ill-fated subject for his maneuver turned out to be a lone young Frenchman named Jean-Luc Solomon, a thin, bearded man in his mid-twenties. Testimony would later reveal that Charles dispatched his twin sirens, Mary Ellen and Barbara, to meet Solomon at the bar of the hotel. On the last night of June, the Frenchman was delighted to take dinner at a restaurant near Connaught Circle with a brunette on one arm, a blonde on the other, with Charles as charming and gracious host. Charles recommended chicken curry, and when it came he deftly poured a vial of clear liquid onto Solomon's portion. The Frenchman's night began to blur. Groggy and stumbling, he was helped back to the hotel, where he had expected to pass the postmidnight hours in the arms of Barbara Smith.

Instead, Jean-Luc Solomon was discovered two mornings later by a room service waiter. Naked, sprawled on the balcony of his room, an arm outstretched in vain for help, he was clinging to life by a thread. Taken to a hospital, he was dead by sundown.

And Charles now had the funds to finance what would be his *coup de foudre*. He directed his companions to pack quickly and hurry into the silver Citroën for the three-hour drive to Agra. Sixty French tourists were soon to be standing in front of the Taj Mahal. None of them could know that destiny had put them on a collision course.

The telephone rang in the office of N. Tuli, a policeman of legendary stature in India. He was head of Delhi's Crime Branch, an elite group of police who specialized in difficult and important criminal cases. On the line was a diplomat friend from the Canadian Embassy. He had just received the most curious letter. From Goa. "I can't make the damn thing out," said the Canadian official, "but I think you people might want to take a look at it."

"By all means send it over," said Tuli.

Hugey Courage had written in his mélange of Flemish, Hindi, Portuguese, and French, but the tenor was disturbing. Obviously seeking to extricate himself from Charles & Company, Hugey was informing the Canadian Embassy that an international gang of thieves was planning a major robbery of a Delhi jewelry store or, failing that, a bank. Why Hugey chose the Canadian Embassy to receive his letter is something he never revealed. But his words accomplished his purposes—and more. Police everywhere receive crank letters like Hugey's seemed to be, and they usually are filed in the nut drawer. But fate stepped in once more and routed the warning to N. Tuli, a cop with an extraordinary sixth sense. Something in the back of his head told him to find the writer of this letter. The cables from Interpol describing the murders in Thailand had reached his desk, but at this point he did not make a connection. At least consciously.

Clearing out his schedule, Tuli caught the next flight for Goa. He was not a man to squander time. He could not have achieved the nickname "Sherlock Holmes of India" by taking afternoon naps.

In any country, in any language, Tuli would be taken immediately for a cop. He looked like one, talked like one, acted like one. In a country where men wore turbans or hair that tumbled to shoulders, Tuli had a silvery crew cut. In a city where men wore pajamas on the streets, Tuli favored bright plaid sport coats. He would have been home in the Houston, Texas, homicide office. He was lean, tough, fifty years old, and good-humored. The trouble was that his smile did not convince. It clashed with his eyes, dark brown and cold, the eyes of all veteran cops, like a faith healer who takes on the disease of his patient. His ego was as substantial as a film star's, justifiable considering his track record.

Tuli was born in Lahore, then a city in India, later to become after the 1947 partition a major metropolis of the new nation of Pakistan. His father was a postal superintendent. There were four brothers and three sisters, all to become professional people including one a leading doctor, another a general in the Army. Tuli had completed four years of pre-med study when the world that he knew suddenly split and caught on fire. It was 1946 and he remembers it well:

"We were Hindus and we lived next door to Moslems. There was never any trouble. We partook of one another's marriages, sorrows, deaths, and triumphs. We worshipped different gods, but we had no grievance for that. Then some fool in London proposed a Pakistani nation and the blood started to flow." After six thousand people were massacred in Calcutta in 1946, riots broke out all over the subcontinent. In Tuli's quiet neigborhood neighbors turned against neighbors and corpses fell to the street where they bloated in the sun. Tuli's father, sensing that millions of Hindus would be fleeing Pakistan and seeking refuge in India, arranged a transfer in the postal service and moved his family to Delhi in 1947. They traveled by plane, train, and bullock cart, able to take but a few possessions from a fine house and a lifetime in Lahore. As they fled the city, the house was burned by Moslem fanatics, some of whom had once drunk tea in the Tuli garden.

Although Tuli had been an exceptional student in Lahore, he was unable to enroll in a medical school in Delhi, as the city and all of its institutions were overwhelmed by the chaos of war, national rebirth, and millions of refugees. At the age of twenty-two, Tuli could not wait for a second chance. He was an impatient young man, eager to make his mark. If he could not be a doctor, then he decided to be a policeman. His father was appalled. The police he knew were creatures of bureaucracy, often corrupt, usually ignorant, and scarcely removed from brutes. Nonetheless, Tuli was one of a thousand applicants for eighteen positions on the Delhi force. The entrance exam was grueling. Not only did it require two days of written tests, but the physical examination required prowess in karate, hurdle jumping, rope climbing, calisthenics, and running—nine miles had to be covered in one hour. Tuli passed with ease, spent a year at the police academy, and began his career as an assistant subinspector in the Paharganj district, a thickly populated chunk of Old Delhi. There his work was routine, mainly catching bicycle thieves with an occasional opium arrest to spice an otherwise bland cake. He earned 150 rupees a month, less than twenty dollars, for working seven days a week.

Strange how reputations are built. In this first year, Tuli was offered a bribe of 1,000 rupees from a prominent contractor under investigation for receiving stolen goods. He refused. The contractor doubled his offer. Two thousand rupees was more than the young cop made in a year. But Tuli not only said no to temptation, he arrested the contractor, an act of notable integrity in a country where *baksheesh* (a bribe) is as common as grains of rice. Thus did a young police officer earn the reputation of being honest.

Over the next decade, Tuli moved quickly up the police hierarchy, serving in the Criminal Bureau of Investigation (India's FBI), then earning an appointment as Deputy Superintendent of Police and head of the Crime Branch, the cream job in law enforcement. India's press picked up on him, affixing labels such as "ace" and "supersleuth." Delhi usually has about four hundred murders a year, but few qualify as interesting enough for a Tuli investigation. These are the routine killings—neighbors quarreling, tenants falling out with landlords, marital violence. In a rare interview, Tuli said he chose his cases carefully. Before he would personally undertake investigation of a crime, it had to (1) involve important people, (2) have considerable mystery, and (3) contain an element of sensationalism.

Hugey Courage opened his door and was not delighted to encounter India's most celebrated cop on his hearth. At first Hugey denied his identity, he denied authorship of the letter, he feigned illness, he put forth a score of hastily improvised excuses to shoo away the unwanted intruder.

"Don't be afraid," said Tuli gently. "You did a very good thing, writing that letter . . . Come, let's take a walk. We can at least stroll on the beach together." The hulking blond Belgian agreed. The monsoons were beginning, it was off-season, the day was gray and sticky, the ocean and the shore were beautiful and deserted. For two days Tuli and Hugey strolled, gradually building trust. Tuli discerned that Hugey was most concerned about being charged with robbery, for stealing Marie-Andrée's purse and the money from the group's hotel room.

"You didn't do anything wrong except steal from a thief," said Tuli. "I don't really blame you."

Hugey looked incredulous. Was this sharpie cop from Delhi conning him? "You didn't know what you were getting into," suggested Tuli. "And you did the right thing by breaking away and writing that letter. Now. Why don't you tell me about these people?"

There was one more thorn in Hugey's side. He was afraid for his wife and children. He suspected that "Alain Gauthier" would return to Goa and kill him, perhaps his family as well. Tuli offered quick assurance that police would keep a continual eye on the Courage household until the danger had passed. "I ask you to believe me," said Tuli. "And trust me. There comes a time in every man's life when he must decide to put his trust in something."

The story spilled out of Hugey in great torrents. He told everything, how he was to be transformed from a beach bum to a pinstriped diplomat, how the girls were used to entice customers, how "Alain Gauthier" was a strange sort of father to a brood of lost children. "He wants everybody to love him," said Hugey. "When I found out he also wanted to hurt them—I had to leave."

From Hugey, Tuli obtained a few snapshots of the group, including those of Charles and Marie-Andrée. He flew to Bombay, had them enlarged, and distributed them to security officers of the major hotels. "If one of these people shows up," he ordered, "call me day or night." And once back at his office in Delhi, he sent copies of the photos to every major hotel in India. Tuli did not know that his targets were at that moment just a few blocks away from his office, in the countdown for a caper that, if it came off successfully, would be one of the most brazen ever committed. With Hindu fatalism, all Tuli knew was that quite soon his life would collide with these people. It was karma, just a matter of time.

The Vikram Hotel in Delhi has an air of North Africa —bamboo blinds, rattan chairs, lazy ceiling fans, riotously colored blossoms. Catering to tour groups and not considered one of the city's deluxe inns, the Vikram has a certain charm based on cleanliness, bathrooms that work, and an aura of hygienic exotic. On the afternoon of July 5, 1976, the hotel's public rooms were crowded with French men and women, sixty ebullient members of a tour that was crossing the face of Asia. Many of them were engineering students doing postgraduate study. They were intelligent, middle-class, hard-working, and at last embarked on a trip for which they had saved and scrimped. They were also indefatigable, save for a few who were enduring mild cases of Delhi belly, refusing to let the torrential storm of this day spoil their last hours in India. Some of them stood on the hotel steps, watching the awesome sheets of driving rain sweep even oxcarts from the streets; others stayed inside sipping the last drops of luncheon wine, playing cards, writing letters home that told of the Taj Mahal, where they had just spent two days examining the tomb with both the passion of Frenchmen and with the professional respect of engineers.

Amid them, very much the center of attention, was a helpful young man the group had encountered in the gardens of the Taj Mahal. He had suddenly appeared beside them, had struck up a conversation, had led them to the best restaurant in Agra, to a souvenir shop that had low prices, chattering all the while about his happiness over encountering a busload of his countrymen in this faraway place. His name, he said, was "Daniel Chaumet" and his mission, he said, was to make their stay in India a memorable one.

Certainly he was helpful. When "Daniel Chaumet"

learned that several of the French had already purchased gemstones in Agra, he asked to see them and frowned at both the quality and the price. Cursing thieves who took advantage of tourists, he escorted his new friends back to the shops in question and with menace demanded—and obtained—refunds. "Seeing the Taj Mahal and meeting Daniel Chaumet are the two best things that have happened so far," remarked one of the engineering students.

He stuck to them like epoxy. And the discovery that Daniel Chaumet had two stunning girl friends, one brunette, the other blond with a diamond in her nostril, enhanced his stature. The girls were flirtatious and seemed receptive to romantic suggestions by the students. After two days, it was as if they had all known each other for lifetimes.

Now, in Delhi, their last day in India would soon be ended. At 2 A.M. the tour would fly to Bangkok. No one wanted to sleep and the Vikram Hotel churned with festive Frenchmen. During the long, rainy afternoon, Chaumet began talking to a cluster of his new friends. The subject was the danger of disease in the Far East, specifically how tender French stomachs can easily fall victim to exotic bacteria. Any Frenchman relishes conversation about his *foie*, and the tourists were rapt. Horror stories fell from Chaumet's lips, grim tales concerning Europeans he had known in Asia who were doomed to suffer forever from chronic amebic dysentery. Beside him, Chaumet's friend and associate, another Frenchman, who said his name was Jean Mare, nodded knowingly. Jean Mare had sad eyes and a pencil-thin mustache and drove a silver Citroën.

At day's end, as the group assembled in the Vikram's private dining room for the "Farewell Cocktail Party and Traditional Indian Dinner," Daniel Chaumet drew the tour director, a man named Ribaud, into private conversation. Had Ribaud heard about the severe outbreak of dysentery in Thailand? No, answered the tour director, but he believed that every member of the group was well fortified with both prudent information and various medications prescribed by doctors in France. And Ribaud was constantly warning his charges not to drink tap water, or eat unpeeled, uncooked vegetables, that sort of thing.

"That's not safe enough," warned Chaumet. He presented himself as a veteran of Eastern travel whose experience had taught that simple precautions were not sufficient to defeat the legions of bugs waiting to invade French stomachs. He asked Ribaud if there were objections to his offering medication to his friends that was "guaranteed" to forestall intestinal agonies. Chaumet was carrying a black bag and from it he produced a handful of tablets and capsules.

The tour director declined the offer for himself, as he, too, had traveled often in Asia and had never gotten sick. But he did not object if the helpful friend gave his pills to the others. Thus did Chaumet find, incredibly, twenty French tourists who were pleased to accept his pills. They popped them into their mouths on the spot, perverse tribute to the charms of Charles Sobhraj, who passed among the celebrants as a priest dispensing communion wafers. Jean Mare, alias Jean Dhuisme, was beside him as altar boy.

Now it was night. Dinner was over. Charles began to glance nervously about the dining salon. Tour director Ribaud suggested that everyone return to his room and ensure that baggage was properly packed and tagged and ready for the postmidnight flight. With urgency, Charles seconded the suggestion. He recommended to those sitting near him that a quick nap would be appropriate, as clearing Indian customs was often chaotic and harrowing.

But no one wanted to go to bed. Charles' words were drowned out by laughter, and wine splashing into glasses, and someone's guitar. One of the women in the group tried unsuccessfully to show off a peacock-blue sari she had purchased; one of the students hurried over to wind it enthusiastically about his middle.

In his place, Charles must have felt panic swelling. He knew when the pills would take effect. He *had* to convince the twenty who had taken his "medicine" to be out of the dining salon and upstairs, where they would pass out in their rooms. Then Charles could pay each of them a private farewell. He stood up and yawned. "Everybody ought to get some sleep," he said, trying to steer the intended victims toward the elevator.

"It's early," answered one of the students. "The night has just begun!"

A few moments of agonizing suspense crept by. And then a woman screamed. Beside her, a student had pitched forward into his wineglass. Another suddenly slumped in his chair, sliding out and onto the floor like a blob of gelatin. People began to vomit. For a stunning few seconds, no one grasped what was happening. Bodies fell. A man grabbed the tablecloth as he lost consciousness; plates crashed around him. "They're all dying!" cried someone. "Get the manager," cried somebody else.

The wife of the tour director fell to her knees and began to minister to the fallen. "Poison!" she screamed. "Assassins!" When the manager ran into the room, he threw his hands to his face in horror. A plump little man with a twitching mustache, he was in the unenviable position of having to witness his guests drop like flies. A woman crawled toward the manager and bit him on the leg. Disengaging her teeth from his flesh, he hobbled into the kitchen, fearful that mass food poisoning had occurred. Then someone yelled for him. He ran back into the dining room.

Someone had been smart enough to discern that only those people who had taken Daniel Chaumet's pills were passing out. Several men had grabbed Chaumet and were trying to tie him up. He broke loose and ran madly about the room, stopping to threaten his pursuers with karate chops, then hurrying on, trying to find the exit. Three French students made a flying tackle and grabbed his legs; others jumped in and sat on him. In the farcical pandemonium, Jean Dhuisme prudently fled, leaping into his Citroën and screeching away at high speed.

When the police arrived, they discovered Charles Sobhraj pinned to a chair by several strong young students. With enormous indignation he was sputtering, cursing, threatening—and left literally holding the bag.

CHAPTER THIRTY-NINE

Tuli was rousted out of bed by a telephone call from the Crime Branch night duty officer. "Sorry to disturb you, sir," said the policeman, "but something funny is going on at the Vikram Hotel." A large number of French tourists passed out in the dining room after the evening meal. Ambulances had been dispatched to rush them to a hospital. The hotel management was holding a suspicious-acting Frenchman in an office off the dining room. Could this be something connected to the people Tuli was looking for?" "It just might be that," said Tuli, rubbing the sleep from his eyes.

At the Vikram Hotel, Tuli discovered quiet after the storm. The sick people were all gone, their stomachs being pumped out. It appeared that none would die. Fortunately they had collapsed in public view, rather than in their rooms. The others stood around the lobby in small clusters, dazed, like survivors of a plane crash, still not sure just what had happened. The distraught manager led Tuli into a small anteroom and on the way warned that the suspect was in a steaming rage.

An understatement.

Daniel Chaumet was purple with anger. "This is a terrible mistake," he snapped when Tuli introduced himself. His voice was broken English, heavily accented with French. It was difficult to understand him. One of the tourists was summoned to be translator. "I demand that you release me immediately," insisted Chaumet, "or else you will face severe consequences . . . I am a French citizen . . . I am a prominent businessman . . . And my embassy will not think well of this . . . I will file damage suits against this hotel and the New Delhi police . . ."

Tuli nodded to indicate that he understood the threat—but he did not respond for a time. Instead he studied the young man carefully, seeing before him a fellow in his early thirties, dressed handsomely in well-tailored slacks and a fine cotton shirt. His eyes hid behind tinted glasses. His wristwatch was Swiss, gold, and expensive. Around his neck was a thin gold chain. He seemed authentically upper class, particularly in the imperious way he carried himself and addressed inferiors, i.e., hotel managers and cops.

"Can you tell me what happened here tonight?" asked Tuli politely.

"Who knows? Probably the hotel chef served poisoned food. Many of my friends got sick and fainted."

Tuli drew the manager outside to answer an odd question. Were there any attractive young women accompanying this man? The manager shook his head. He did not know. Then Tuli asked the same of those tourists who had not fallen ill. Yes, came the answer, there had been girls. Three of them. They had been with Chaumet in Agra. They were "vivacious" and "friendly." But they had not been present on this night of falling bodies.

"Oh," said Tuli. "You only met this man in Agra? He is not part of your group?"

"No," said the tour director. "Monsieur Chaumet just suddenly appeared in our midst. Everybody liked him. He helped several members in our party to buy gemstones."

Gemstones! Tuli whirled and returned to the anteroom. He informed Daniel Chaumet that it would be necessary to accompany police crosstown for further questioning.

"I refuse," said the custom-tailored Frenchman. His eyes glared.

Shrugging, Tuli gestured to a pair of quite large Indian police who picked the pseudo-Frenchman up by the armpits and dragged him yelling out of the hotel.

Jean Dhuisme parked the Citroën in a hidden back-street garage and worked his way on foot to the hotel where the girls were staying. It was midnight. He told the tale of the black comedy at the Vikram and in telling it grew funny, particularly at the point when Charles was trying in vain to persuade the drugged tourists to go upstairs so they would pass out in private. Barbara and Mary Ellen began to giggle, but Marie-Andrée was stricken.

"Where is he?" she begged.

Dhuisme did not know. He had not stayed around long enough to find out, and it did not seem appropriate that he return to the Vikram and learn the dénouement. Nor did he seem particularly worried, Charles having wriggled out of tight places before.

"What are we going to do?" said Marie-Andrée. The group had less than ten dollars between them. The branch to which she had clung had suddenly snapped, and now she was falling. She began to weep. Mary Ellen shook her by the shoulder and spoke sternly. She was strong and tough. "You're going to shut up," she ordered. "We'll sleep and figure out a plan temorrow."

Daniel Chaumet was brought to Tuli's office, where the veteran cop bade him sit down. A bearer brought in glasses of hot sweet tea. Charles took one look, sneered, and swept it off the table as if presented with a goblet of sour wine. The glass crashed on the floor, spilling tea over the cold speckled tiles.

In a quarter century of police work, Tuli had never encountered anyone like the seething man who sat before him. The performance, which endured this first night from midnight until past sunrise, was spectacular. More than once the cop felt the dreaded fingers of A Major Mistake creep about his neck. Perhaps he had arrested the wrong man, perhaps the French Embassy would be banging on his desk tomorrow morning in diplomatic protest. Charles' act was most convincing. For the first few hours, he simply sat mute, his face contorted by rage. Then he exploded in French, demanding that the embassy send over an interpreter to sort out this grave misunderstanding.

Tuli wasn't buying *that*. "I think you speak English as well as I do, Mr. Chaumet," he said sharply. "If not, it might take several days to find an adequate interpreter."

"Yes, I speak English," said Charles, appreciating the threat. "A little." He almost smiled, thought Tuli. Here was a man who appreciated the game of cat and mouse.

Throughout the long night, Charles continued his harangue. He demanded that a cable be sent to Paris to confirm his identity. He insisted that he was a prominent importer-exporter who was exceedingly well known in the Parisian business community. He was in India to establish a major branch of his business, one that would enrich the economy and provide jobs. And now, here he was at the hands of barbarians. He threw out the name of a woman magazine editor in Paris. "Just call her," he pleaded. "I will pay the charges." He demanded a lawyer.

"All in good time," said Tuli. Where was Chaumet's passport?

He almost flinched. But he quickly recovered. It must have been lost during the scuffle at the Vikram Hotel. Ask the stupid manager, suggested Charles.

Then where was Daniel Chaumet staying? In what hotel?

"I refuse to answer any more of these insolent questions," said the suspect. He folded his hands and shut his eyes. He held his body rigid, as if in a trance.

Three other detectives rotated in and out of the room, reinforcing Tuli, dropping new pieces of information as they became available. Most of the tourists had been treated at the hospital and released. Three or four were serious enough to be kept under observation. Nobody was dead.

"Why would I want to hurt these people?" asked Charles during the night. "These people are French. They are my friends. French people stick together."

Tuli pawed through Charles' black crocodile bag. In it were several pills of various hues and shapes. "What are these?" the deputy chief asked.

"Medicine. A man would be a fool to travel in India without medicine."

"Who is Monique?" asked Tuli quickly.

Charles looked blank. He had no idea.

"There was a girl named Monique with you in Agra. We know that. And two other girls."

"I have known many girls," said Charles. "I can't remember all their names."

To every query, Charles had a quick retort. Had he ever been arrested? "Of course not. I told you I am a respectable businessman. The only mistake I ever made was in coming to this country of savages. I assure you that the Delhi police force will regret this. I intend to take it all the way to Indira Gandhi."

Toward dawn, Tuli sent out for food. When it arrived, Charles stared at the plate of spiced vegetable patties and rice and *nan,* the thin circle of bread. He swept this onto the floor as well. He demanded that food be sent over from the Oberoi Hotel or the French Embassy. He did not eat "garbage."

At 7 A.M., Tuli waved his hands in disgust and Charles was taken away to a lockup cell. He could stew there awhile. Tuli wanted time to study the Interpol cables. He could have cleared the water immediately had he been permitted to take the suspect's fingerprints and cable them to Paris for identification. But this was impossible. In India, fingerprints cannot be taken until *after* a conviction—and Charles, incredibly, had never been convicted of anything in India. Nor was the photograph which Hugey Courage provided of good enough quality to identify Charles positively. Similar, but not dead on.

While Tuli read the cables, police were dispatched to every hotel in Delhi, trying to locate any European girls who fitted the description of those in the company of Daniel Chaumet at Agra. The task would take several days, there being hundreds of hotels, student hostels, and guest lodges. Airports and train stations were suddenly swarming with plainclothesmen, watching every departing tourist.

Mary Ellen took charge and moved the group to a third-class dump near Connaught Circle. The Australian girl insisted that everyone stay put, that Charles would somehow send word. Marie-Andrée protested, pleading that she had to go to the international telephone office and call Canada. Her father was dying. "Not bloody likely," threatened Mary Ellen. "You're not going anywhere."

"Then you'll have to kill me," said Marie-Andrée, walking out of the room with false bravado. Mary Ellen was all bluff as well. In both women was a mounting wave of desperation. At the telephone office, Marie-Andrée placed a collect call to her sister, Denise, in Quebec and waited all day before it went through. She tried to keep her voice steady. She told Denise that she was in trouble, serious trouble, but innocent of everything. She implored Denise to help her get out of India. Denise knew more than she let on. A story had broken in the Canadian newspapers a few days earlier stating that a Quebec nurse named "Monique Leclerc" was wanted in Asia on charges of multiple murder. Denise had rushed home the day the story appeared, hoping to steal the newspaper before her father read it. The worry was that his failing heart would stop. But Augustin already knew. The phone in his house had scarcely stopped ringing. Even the Royal Canadian Mounted Police had called. What in God's name was going on? Marie-Andrée was his most dutiful daughter. She had never even stepped on an ant. She had gone to mass six times a week since she was old enough to stand alone.

On the transoceanic phone, Marie-Andrée beseeched her sister to send Bernard, her old boy friend, to extricate her from the mess. Denise had a better idea. Why not just go to the Canadian Embassy in Delhi, tell them the truth, ask for asylum, and obtain the justice to which Canadians were entitled?

"I can't," said Marie-Andrée. "I'm too afraid. Please send Bernard." It was in her mind that the balding accountant who had accompanied her on her first trip to the East—could it have been only fifteen months ago?—would ride to her rescue. Denise promised to try, just as the connection became so poor that neither party could hear. Marie-Andrée hung up in despair.

The next day, the girls and Jean Dhuisme fanned out to sell whatever they could. Money had to be raised. In Charles' suitcase, they found several cameras and radios. They sold these. Their clothes. A hair dryer. Shoes. But the proceeds were only 800 rupees, less than $100. Then Mary Ellen ordered the group to the Oberoi Hotel to wait around the swimming pool. She said Charles had always told her to do this in case of emergency.

At Delhi's most deluxe hotel, the three young women and the sad-eyed Frenchman sat around the pool nervously, trying to blend in with the stewardesses and flight crews broiling in the sun. Marie-Andrée watched each new face that appeared, anxiously trying to read intent. She ordered a sandwich but could not swallow. While she stared at the food, resting on the table beside her chaise, wondering how she could wrap it up for later on, two ravens swooped down and seized the bread, fighting over it, shrieking, their razor beaks tearing at one another. She ran out of the hotel.

The next day, after waiting ten hours, Marie-Andrée spoke again with Denise. Her sister had cheering news. Bernard had agreed to fly to India and help her. He was trying to book a flight that would arrive on July 7. Tomorrow! He would send a cable to *poste restante* informing her of his flight. Marie-Andrée hung up this time with tears of cautious happiness, feeling that her ordeal would soon be over.

But tomorrow, as is its habit, never came. Nor did a cable from Bernard. After spending the day haunting both the *poste restante* and the airport, waiting with stretched nerves for every incoming flight, she returned to the cheap hotel in despair. At the desk she identified herself and asked if there was a message. And as she walked toward the stairs, two men blocked her path. "Monique?" asked one of them. She shook her head and tried to pass. The other presented his credentials. They were Tuli's men. Handcuffs bit into her wrists. A few minutes later, Mary Ellen entered the hotel and was arrested. Both girls feigned indignation and anger, but their cries were for naught. By midafternoon on July 7, 1976, they were under arrest and taken to the same police building where Charles had been undergoing questioning—without breaking.

That night police captured Jean Dhuisme when he foolishly went to check on his Citroën. And a few minutes after midnight, Barbara Smith, the brunette English girl, returned from the powder room at Wheels Discotheque

and found two policemen sitting at her table, like new-
found admirers. They were polite and pleasant, and when
Barbara found out their mission, she laughed. She had
smoked a very potent chunk of hash in the toilet and for
a mistaken moment, she thought she was being arrested
for drug use—not on suspicion of robbery, drugging, and
murder.

"We've arrested your accomplices," announced Tuli on
his sixth day of interrogating Charles.

"I have no accomplices," shot back the suspect. His
composure was unruffled. He was as calm as a mirrored
lake in Kashmir. He still wore the same clothes and Tuli
marveled how he could look so tailored after almost a
week of intense pressure, days when the thermometer
stayed resolutely over a hundred degrees. And his manner
remained regal. He refused to eat jail food, insisting that
he could not tolerate the nourishment slopped for prisoners. At times he grew so indignant that he banged his
head against Tuli's wall, or cracked his handcuffs against
his face. Like no actor Tuli had ever seen, Charles summoned anger, tears, rage, sardonic humor, menace, and
Gallic fatalism. The experience was mesmerizing.

And troubling.

All the basic police interrogation procedures Tuli tried.
One hour he was sweet, the next sour. He worked alone.
He worked in tandem. He informed Charles, still clinging
to the name Daniel Chaumet, that his friends were making
statements implicating him. Charles glared in disbelief.
"Then bring them in and let them accuse me to my face,"
he demanded. Quickly Tuli backed off that bluff, suspecting that his prisoner would probably be able, through
gestures or looks, to silence the girls.

The quintet of suspects was stashed in various offices
around the Crime Branch, Tuli visiting them each daily,
like a doctor making hospital rounds. He discovered
immediately that Marie-Andrée was as adamant as
Charles. After the first few hours of fright and panic,
she turned hard and testy. Demanding that the Canadian
Embassy be notified to send an attorney, she was brusquely
informed that in India a suspect is not entitled to legal
counsel during police questioning. "That's about what I

would expect in a country as primitive as this," she said. "I assure you that someone will pay dearly for this mistake."

Jean Dhuisme was also silent, mostly, but also a void. Tuli reasoned early on that the melancholy Frenchman was neither a veteran criminal nor even an important member of the group. The two other girls, Barbara and Mary Ellen, were the most vulnerable. Both began to weep the moment they were jailed, continuing to vomit and tremble during interrogations.

Like any cop anywhere, Tuli was looking for the one brick loose enough to extricate, knowing that the wall would then collapse. He suspected that these young women were breakable. Purposefully, Tuli ordered that Barbara and Mary Ellen be placed in the same holding cell and he began to question them together. On the fifth day, Tuli was speaking in general of the special consideration that might be given to an "approver," that being the Indian term for state's witness. The Australian girl, who Tuli felt was the stronger of the two, began to weaken. Spasms shook her body, tears welled in her eyes. The detective asked courteously—and paternally—if she was unwell. She shook her head and laid in on the cop's desk. Tuli placed a gentle hand on her shoulder. "Why don't you tell me about it?" he suggested. "You'll feel better." Finally Mary Ellen nodded. She raised her head and looked at Tuli in surrender. "All right," she said. "I'm one of them. We're the people you've been looking for . . ."

Tuli shifted his attention to Barbara. She nodded almost cheerfully. "Do you want me to dictate a statement?" she asked. His elation growing, Tuli nodded. And called for a stenographer.

The news was delivered to Marie-Andrée. Her two female companions had confessed—everything—from the robberies in Delhi, to the entrapment, drugging, and death of Jean-Luc Solomon, the French boy found dying on the balcony of his Ranjit Hotel room.

"Absurd," snapped Marie-Andrée. If the police believed that, they would believe anything. She launched into an oft-heard tirade about her innocence and her desire to remain silent until a Canadian lawyer was brought to her side. Then she stopped and looked away, far away, out Tuli's window to the awakening city of Delhi, to the thickening gray clouds that would bring the summer morning's dependable storm. "Yes," she finally said.

"I beg your pardon?" responded Tuli.

"I'm so glad it's over," said Marie-Andrée. "I'm so tired of running." She then signed a thirty-two-page detailed statement that began with her life in Canada, continued through her fateful meeting with Charles Sobhraj on the romantic lakes of Kashmir, telling in a rambling, confusing narrative how the two of them crisscrossed Asia and Europe, but not confessing to any part in the crimes save that of companion and prisoner—unable to leave due to lack of money and credentials.

But in another room was Daniel Chaumet. He did not even blink nervously when the three girls were paraded before him and pointed accusatory fingers at their leader. Tuli was exhausted. The insolent man sitting calmly on the other side of his desk had withstood questioning—*hard* questioning—for ten eternal days and was no closer to cracking than on the night he was seized. The walls of brick stood firm. "Surely if I was the man you were looking for," insisted Charles, "I would have confessed by now." No guilty man, he went on, could withstand the torture he was undergoing. Charles contended that once out of Tuli's presence he was savagely beaten in the holding cell by police skilled in striking people on parts of the body that did not bruise.

At the end of the tenth day, Tuli was distraught. He was pleased to have the statements of the others—Jean Dhuisme had by now capitulated—but it was like catching a handful of guppies when the shark swam on unmolested in the tank. Then, in early evening while taking a catnap on an old couch, Tuli bolted upright. An old crime lodged in the back of his head like a bone in the throat suddenly came back in his memory. And while he had not personally investigated the case, he had studied it over the years and had always marveled at the brazenness and absurdity with which it had been staged. Police *do* admire professional work on the other side.

He called to an aide. Bring the yellowing file on that long ago jewel robbery at the Ashoka Hotel, the one in which the American dancer had been held hostage in her

room. For an hour Tuli studied the file, relishing the tale.
Then he fairly flew back to his desk, first telephoned
Wellington Hospital, then ordered that Daniel Chaumet
be brought back for one last go-round.

"Does the Ashoka Hotel mean anything to you?"
casually asked Tuli.

Charles shrugged. Everybody knew the Ashoka Hotel.
It was like asking a Parisian if he knew the Ritz.

"Were you ever at the Ashoka Hotel?" asked Tuli.

A negative shake of the suspect's head.

"Have you heard, perhaps, of a jewelry robbery at the
Ashoka Hotel in the autumn of 1971?"

"Of course not."

Tuli nodded. "Then I will tell you the story of that
crime. It is a very interesting story, and if nothing else,
it will entertain you."

He told the story well, how La Passionara was enticed
to open her door, how she was kept prisoner while two
French-speaking men tried in vain to drill a hole from the
floor of her bedroom to the jewelry store below, how the
principal thief, "Lobo," managed to escape police at the
airport, only to be rearrested at the train station. Then,
pausing in his narrative, Tuli looked sternly at Daniel
Chaumet. He said, of all things, "Drop your pants, please."

"What?"

"Drop your pants. Now."

"Are you going to beat me?" asked Charles.

"I repeat. *Now.*"

Charles opened his buckle and let his expensive trousers
slip down his coppery, hard-muscled legs. Tuli directed
his gaze directly at the suspect's belly. And he saw what
he had expected to see. "When were you operated on for
appendicitis? I notice that you have a scar."

"That's not for appendicitis," lied Charles quickly and
smoothly. "I fell out of a tree . . . You can verify it with
my family physician in France."

Tuli smiled, the smile of a hunter who has found game
in his trap. A call to France would not be necessary. He
clapped his hands and the door opened. A doctor entered
the room, a surgeon from Wellington Hospital. He bent
over the scar and examined it and confirmed that it was

the memoir of an appendicitis operation. Tuli led the
doctor outside.

"Did you perform the operation in 1971 on this man?"
asked Tuli.

The doctor could not be sure. The work looked very
much like his own, the patient seemed familiar, but he
had done hundreds of the operations in the past five years.

Tuli pressed him. Could the doctor testify in court that
this was the man he operated on in 1971 in the prison
ward of the hospital? The surgeon shook his head slowly.
No. Not positively. Not under oath. Not if his testimony
might send a man to prison—or the gallows.

Disappointed—for he *knew* he was right—angry to the
edge of eruption, Tuli went back in and tried once more.
This time he was tough. He grabbed the dossier that Interpol had cabled concerning "Hotchand Bhawnani Gurmukh Sobhraj" and spat out the contents, dropping details of the horrible murders in Thailand and Nepal like
pellets of acid, warning that unless the suspect made a
clean breast the government of India would fly in police
from the countries involved and let them join the questioning of "Daniel Chaumet."

"Then do it," snapped Charles, smugly, smiling. "If
that's what it takes to clear me, bring in anybody."

Numb with fatigue, Tuli took a break to clear his head.
In the wash room he stared at his face in the mirror, and
the shadow circles under his eyes and the new lines in his
forehead were testimony that he was suffering more than
his prisoner. The temptation was to book the exasperating
young man on some technicality and let him stew for a
while in Tihar Prison. Nearly two weeks of intense questioning had brought forth less fruit than a banana tree in
the desert.

That night he returned to his office with very little zest
for another session. Hoarse, feeling a cold coming on, he
spoke quietly to the suspect. His voice was soft. He had
sent out for a tray of deluxe food from a good hotel and
he sat quietly while Charles ate with approval. Then Tuli
complimented him on his strength and endurance. He was
paying respect, and Charles was touched, so much so that
a new notion dawned on the cop. The one thing he had

not tried was *flattery.* Would praise and honeyed words accomplish what everything else had failed? The two men began to speak easily. Tuli asked if he had children. Charles brightened and pulled a snapshot of Shubra from his pocket. "She's very beautiful," said the cop, truthfully. "She looks like her father." Tuli spoke of his wife, whose name means "gold" because she came into the world after five brothers. Within an hour or two, Tuli had become, in some bizarre, unforeseen, upside-down way, a father figure.

And *that* did it.

When Tuli crossed the barrier and placed his arm around Charles as if he were a prodigal son welcomed home, he became the father that Charles had always wanted. He became someone to trust. Someone to obey. Charles looked up at India's most celebrated cop, and he broke.

"My compliments," he said. "I never thought I would get arrested in India. I didn't think you had the brains."

"Tell me about it, son," murmured Tuli softly, afraid he would shatter the alliance. "You'll feel much better."

Charles nodded, grasping the outstretched hand.

CHAPTER FORTY

An urgent cable was sent by Tuli to Interpol in Paris, which in turn flashed the news to police around the world. In Bangkok, Herman Knippenberg had just returned from a fishing trip and was heady over winning a prize for landing the largest mackerel of the day. He stepped out of the shower to discover the phone ringing with news of a more exciting catch.

"Hooray!" cabled Herman to his wife Angela, visiting her parents in Germany. "Caught them all in Delhi. Hooray! Hooray!" Then Herman got uncharacteristically and gloriously ripped. He and the members of his Action Committee lost count after the third bottle of French champagne.

In Paris, Félix d'Escogne read the headline and with great sadness clipped it out, slipping another entry into the thick file that began the day ten years earlier when he first encountered a skinny, frightened, big-eared youngster in Poissy Prison. He felt an enormous sense of waste and loss. And he remembered what a consular official for the Indian Government in Paris had prophesied so long ago: "This man will meet his destiny in India."

And in Marseilles, where the newspaper said that Charles Sobhraj was accused of at least twelve murders, Song wept in bewilderment. She told her husband that she must go on a pilgrimage. By bus she crossed France and journeyed to Lourdes. At the grotto where Bernadette

Soubirous saw visions of a lady in white which were judged authentic by the Vatican in 1862, Song crawled on her knees amid the broken bodies and wheelchairs and crutches, stopping finally at the edge of the icy waters where miracles have occurred. But Song sought no deliverance from physical pain or twisted limb.

"Seigneur," she prayed, "if my son is truly guilty of these terrible deaths, then You judge him. If You find him guilty, take him to Paradise now. Don't let the hangman take his life . . ."

Once the prisoners completed their statements, Tuli sent them in an ancient, wheezing black bus to Tihar Prison. Charles was in chains and heavily guarded. Now Tuli was once again a national hero, his telephone ringing day and night with calls from Paris and Bangkok and New York. The reporters' questions were usually along these lines:

Q. Has Charles Sobhraj confessed?

A. He has made a statement admitting the drugging of several victims. But he denies killing anybody. He says that no one ever died from his medications. If there were murders, he says, blame them on Ajay Chowdhury.

Q. Where is Ajay Chowdhury?

A. We do not know. Marie-Andrée Leclerc, in her statement, suggests that Charles killed him in Malaysia and buried him.

Q. After the gang's arrest in Bangkok and subsequent flight to Europe, why did they return to Asia?

A. He had a lust. Something within him snapped and turned him into a killer. Once you taste blood, you must go back and have some more. And, of course, Charles Sobhraj was a hunter. A hunter is always stalking his game. His favorite place to hunt was Asia.

Q. *How could this man have operated so long without getting caught?*

A. He *was* caught, and often. But he always got out of his predicament some way. He is brilliant, and clever and dynamic—and always believable. He never traveled under his own identity. He always had a false passport, and he was able like no other man to change his appearance so that it would match the passport photograph. And if the picture were too far off, he would substitute his own photograph. He muddied the water better than any man I ever encountered. He is an astonishing criminal.

It was the worst of times to be arrested in India.

Indira Gandhi, annoyed by the political opposition's attempt to invalidate her election as Prime Minister, took the unprecedented step of turning the world's largest democracy into a dictatorship. Invoking emergency rule, her draconian measures were supposedly to thwart what she termed "subversive and disruptive" forces. That more or less translated to mean her political enemies, specifically a group of judges, lawyers, and rival politicians. But her wrath spread far afield. Her government suspended freedom of the press, ordered mass arrests of those unfriendly to the Prime Minister, decreed that those suspected of being "subversive" or "disruptive" could be grabbed without regard for habeas corpus, thrown into prison, and held there indefinitely—without bail, with little or no civil liberties. A climate of fear swept over the nation; police knocked on doors in the middle of the night and took prominent men and women to jail in their nightgowns, thousands upon thousands. The prisons were quickly jammed. All of these dictates came under what was known as MISA (Maintenance of Internal Security Act).

MISA applied to all prisoners, even those without a political thought in their heads—like Charles and his associates. It meant that the five men and women accused of murder could be held up to two years without bail, without going to trial, under the most harrowing conditions.

Dubbed the "international killers" by India's press, the five caused a stir within the thick and ugly walls of Tihar Prison, even though it was newly home to many prominent Indians. One of the prisoners was the Maharanee of Jaipur, a celebrated woman of beauty and enormous wealth. Theoretically she had been jailed because her family had hidden unlawful gold in its palace, but it was well known that the Maharanee was an outspoken opponent of Indira Gandhi. Nonetheless, in India caste is caste, and the Maharanee did not suffer quite as much as

others. Her meals in Tihar were brought to her by a
liveried waiter on a tray from the kitchens of the Oberoi
Hotel.

Marie-Andrée was led to the cell that would be her
home. Now she was at the nadir. Classified as a "C"
prisoner under MISA, the severest and lowest category,
she was entitled to nothing save a food ration barely
sufficient to sustain human life. Her entire daily allotment
was one *chapati* (a thin bread patty), one half cup of
milk that soured quickly in the blazing August sun, and a
cup of *dal,* a mashed bean soup. She was denied a radio,
a bed, writing material, cooking pots, and, most important, visitors. One thin blanket was issued, its threads
containing colonies of fleas and ticks. Her mail from
Canada was often withheld for weeks after its arrival,
more often than not thrown away. The cell was infested
with insects of wide and exotic variety, most of which bit
and stung. Bold rats waltzed by, stopping to examine the
new resident. On her first day there, the Canadian Consul
in Delhi, John Church, paid a visit, after first obtaining a
pass from a magistrate. He said there was very little the
government of Canada could do, other than make sure she
was provided with counsel.

"Can't you get me out of this hell?" she begged.

Church shook his head. It would not be much better
in the jails of Canada.

"I wouldn't know," she said. "I've no basis for comparison. I've never been in jail before."

Church promised to try and get her classification raised
from "C" to "B," which would entitle her to more food
and privileges. But he warned that it would be difficult
under Mrs. Gandhi's MISA. When he left, taking with
him a fragile link to her homeland, Marie-Andrée sank
into a corner of the cell and hunched on the dirty floor.
The room swam around her, spinning like a carousel of
the doomed. Two lesbians entered and squatted beside
her and tried to touch her arm. Naked children, crying and
hungry, beseeched her for food. Their mothers laughed
and whispered, thrusting mahogany arms at the "white
woman," inspecting her as if she were a new animal in
the zoo. Only five Western women were in residence out
of three hundred female prisoners. And on the first night,

tossing sleeplessly in the thick heat, she heard the babble
and screams of the madwomen—condemned to the most
grotesque Tihar chamber that housed the criminally
insane. She wondered how soon she would become one
of them.

Conversely, Charles adjusted quickly and smoothly,
not surprising for a man who had spent the majority of
his adult life behind bars. Placed initially in solitary
confinement, he managed to talk—or bribe—his way into a
"C" cell with two Pakistanis. Then, through the prison
grapevine, Charles heard that a Vietnamese criminal
named Tete was in Tihar, and Charles persuaded a guard
to transfer him there. The two men, Charles and Tete, had
an emotional reunion. They had known each other for
years, having common roots, having operated in the
underworlds of Paris and Hong Kong. Tete was a fearsome sight. His face was thin, bony, with crumbling teeth
and cold slits for eyes. An ancestor must have been in the
shanghai business, for Tete looked like the kind of man
most often encountered in dark alleys. He was in Tihar
because of a faint resemblance to Charles Sobhraj. A few
weeks before Charles was arrested at the Vikram Hotel,
Delhi police had snatched Tete off the street, convinced
that he was the man of the hour. For several days, Tete
denied that he was the most wanted man in Asia, even
though he had engaged in similar lines of endeavor. Finally, exasperated, police charged him with possessing fraudulent passports and flung him into Tihar.

When Tete saw Charles Sobhraj being led, chained, into
his cell, the first reaction was glowering anger. "You
bastard," hissed Tete, "you're the reason I'm in here. They
thought I was you." But after a while they were laughing
and pounding one another on the back and vowing to
make the most of it.

When two Canadian boys were transferred to the cell,
it quickly became the most remarkable in Tihar. Within
days, Charles had arranged a network of flunkies, both
within the prison and out, who brought him food, ran his
errands, contacted lawyers, and smuggled in accouterments
not normally allowed to the lowest-class inmate. Radios,
as Marie-Andrée learned, were forbidden. Absolutely.

Charles had three. And a stereo tape deck. Each day he received several eggs, numerous containers of milk, onions, potatoes, even freshly killed chickens and roasts of beef, incredible in a vegetarian country and unbelievable in Tihar Prison. He obtained writing paper and pens. And books on the Indian judicial system. And paperback mysteries. And Carl Gustav Jung, whom he read every night by an oil lamp, which was, of course, also forbidden.

One of the Canadian youngsters, Pierre, a stocky farm boy with a Fu Manchu mustache, was amazed at his cellmate's ability to get what he wanted. Pierre and his buddy, Rob, had been caught at the Delhi airport trying to smuggle out $500 worth of morphine powder. "This is India," said Charles. "Everything can be bought with money . . . That's why the country will never amount to anything. Corruption begins in the villages and goes to the very top."

But how, wondered Pierre, how did Charles get money? He was stripped of his valuables upon entering prison and so was every other inmate he knew.

Charles smiled but did not answer. Only Tete knew. He had seen his old *copain* reach into his mouth one morning and extract a tiny, sparkling blue stone. A sapphire. Charles confided that he had sixty-eight carats of sapphires and rubies concealed in his mouth. If danger or an unexpected search arose, he simply swallowed the cache and extricated them later from his waste. Charles managed to smuggle tea, eggs, and an occasional chicken leg over to the woman's barracks, where they were delivered to Marie-Andrée. At one of the first court hearings in the case—the first of literally hundreds yet to come—Charles told the magistrate that Marie-Andrée was not guilty of anything. "She is a victim of love," he said. "She should not be accused of anything else." The judge, it was noted, showed little interest in this novel defense.

One morning, Charles was meditating as was his custom—he began each day with at least an hour of silent introspection—and the others knew better than to even breathe heavily during these moments. The guards, however, interrupted at will. On this day they had another prisoner for the star cell. Charles looked up in annoyance, then the puzzle of trying to recollect crossed his face. The new man was tall, and rail-thin, and American, and his eyes were rimmed in crimson. "Red Eye!" cried Charles, recognizing the stringy Yank who had shared the abortive prison escape in Kabul, Afghanistan.

Red Eye had gone from bad to worse. He looked terrible, his pasty skin as white as ivory. Finally released from jail in Kabul, he had waited for the snows to subside in the Khyber Pass and then wandered into India. In Bombay, he became enamored of a Swedish girl who took his money and was later arrested by the police as a smuggler. Then his passport expired in Delhi. Afraid to present himself to the American Embassy, he instead bought a British passport on the street. On his supposed last night in Delhi he attended a party at a student hostel and by midnight the air was rich with hashish smoke. Police raided the party and Red Eye was accused of several minor offenses including passport fraud. He drew a year in Tihar Prison.

"My karma is rotten," he announced, grasping Charles' arm and shaking as he sat down. The cell was growing more cozy each day. Charles had obtained two rope-sling hammocks, not only comfortable for sleeping but valuable for keeping one's body off the floor and away from the armies of insects. French music played from the tape deck. One of the Canadian boys made Red Eye a welcoming sandwich of cold chicken with slices of potatoes. A pot of soup was simmering over a fire. Red Eye's mood instantly lifted. "I thought Kabul was the worst," he said. "I thought it was the ultimate in human suffering. But the Indians beat them all to hell. This place is incredible. You don't get anything unless you pay for it. I tried to buy a book of matches yesterday and the guard wanted eight rupees."

"This is the jungle," lectured Charles. "And only the strong survive." Tihar Prison was a metaphor for India.

Charles asked Red Eye if he had a good lawyer. The question brought a snort and a spit against the wall. "My parents sent me five hundred dollars and I gave it to the lawyer to make bail," he said. "He took the money and didn't get any bail. Then I got convicted of passport fraud, and the bastard wanted another five hundred dollars for appeal. My parents sent that, and the appeal was rejected." Red Eye took a stick and wrote the lawyer's name in the dirt. Then he rubbed it out viciously. "He's a ghoul who preys on Western kids in trouble. He has cops at the airport on his payroll."

"You should have come to me," said Charles. "I know all the lawyers in Delhi."

"No offense," Red Eye would remember saying, "but if you're all that well connected, what are you doing in Tihar?"

"The question should be," answered Charles, "how long will I stay? And the answer is, until I decide to leave."

Deeply stoned on hashish one night, Tete let slip to Red Eye that Charles had already negotiated the price for his escape. One million rupees. It would be difficult to raise, confided Tete, but he had no doubt that Charles would.

The two other girls, Barbara and Mary Ellen, were awarded "B" classifications because they were "approvers," state's witnesses, having agreed to testify against Charles and Marie-Andrée. Theirs was a far better existence, and even though they were imprisoned several yards away from the Canadian woman and forbidden to speak with her, occasional visits were easily accomplished.

At first there was a certain linkage, as all three of the young women were in the same awful predicament. But then, as the days and weeks and months passed, and autumn came, and their cases became ensnarled both in the snail's pace of Indian justice and the MISA restrictions, a bitter falling out developed. Marie-Andrée made complaint that Mary Ellen Eather, "who is two times stronger than me and very tall," came into the cell and beat her up, accusing the Canadian of helping bring on their arrest and imprisonment. "She banged my head against the wall," wrote Marie-Andrée to a prison official, "and she told me that next time she would scratch my 'horrible face.' I was lucky there was a guard in the section and she came in time. They had to fight to get Mary out. I'm so very afraid. I always have a tear at the corner of my eye. And I feel so lonely . . ."

Then, according to her complaint, the two girls tried
to turn the entire women's section against Marie-Andrée,
insisting she was a mass murderess and thus dangerous.
"Everyone looks at me like I was an enemy," complained
Marie-Andrée. "I am afraid to sleep for fear someone will
kill me."

Questioned by prison officials, Mary Ellen and Barbara
denied the accusation. "She's loony," said Barbara in
dismissal. "We've got enough to worry about without trying to do her in." When word reached Tuli about the fric-
tion, he ordered that special attention be paid to the wom-
en. His case rested heavily on the shoulders of the two
prosecution witnesses.

In Quebec, Marie-Andrée's family engaged a criminal
attorney who shrewdly realized that there was very little he could do from his end. But he could try and inject
the case with the memory of Dreyfus, falsely accused. The
lawyer's name was Raymond d'Aoust, one of Canada's
most celebrated and flamboyant, a man who recognized a
headline case if ever there was one. And, as it happened,
he was in a position to more or less write his own copy.
D'Aoust was part owner of a lurid tabloid called *Photo
Police,* which leaped onto *l'affaire Leclerc* like a starving
lion presented with a plump impala.

Every week, in every issue, in headlines printed in blood
red, there was a new scream:

LE VRAI VISAGE DU MONSTRE SÉDUCTEUR
  QUI A IMPLIQUÉ MARIE-ANDRÉE LECLERC DANS 12
MEUTRES

This one featured a sullen photograph of Charles at the
top of the page, with an angelic, retouched picture of
Marie-Andrée beneath, looking like a maiden about to be
sacrificed.

Then came:

MARIE-ANDRÉE LECLERC EST DÉSESPÉRÉE: "Je n'en peux
plus, je vais mourir."

And, in one of the most ghastly front pages ever printed
anywhere, on September 11, 1976, *Photo Police* featured

a full page photo of their heroine wearing a bikini and looking as tough as an aging tart, next to which were the burned and bloated faces of the Dutch murder victims in Bangkok. The headline announced "*Quatre Nouveaux Cadavres—Marie-Andrée* Détenue pour 16 Meutres." *Photo Police's* arithmetic was difficult to follow, as only twelve killings had been tied to the gang by Asian police departments. If the story were read carefully, it would turn out that India's police were trying to link Sobhraj and Leclerc to four more. Tuli often said that there were "probably" more bodies buried in the vastness of Asia. But he had made no further official charges. Inside the newspaper, a disconsolate Marie-Andrée was pictured sitting in her cell, looking painfully thin, beggar-like, with a headline that screamed she was under attack from rats and was dying of hunger. It would have taken a brave stomach to get past the front page, however.

L'affaire Leclerc decorated the front pages of *Photo Police* for months, and indeed it did accomplish what d'Aoust had desired; the French-speaking citizens of Canada were stirred to protest. If one read only the accounts in this newspaper, it appeared that the young churchgoing woman from outside Quebec had been captured and enslaved by barbarians. Biographies were printed in great detail, attesting to Marie-Andrée's religiosity, her family devotion, her diligence at work, her quiet and respectable life before she answered the siren call of the "*monstre séducteur.*" Hundreds of letters poured into Prime Minister Pierre Trudeau's office in Ottawa, to Indira Gandhi in Delhi, to the United Nations, and to the heroine herself, whose plight and photographs in *Photo Police* wrenched the hearts of Canadian mothers. Marie-Andrée fanned the flames of public opinion by writing long letters herself and smuggling them out of prison. In each she swore her innocence and wrote dramatically of her torment.

On September 17, 1976, approximately two months after their arrest, Charles, Marie-Andrée, and Jean Dhuisme were taken before a magistrate in Delhi and granted bonds of approximately $3,000 each. But the announcement was academic. Only a formality. As long as Indira Gandhi had the country under emergency rule, prisoners were not being released on bail. And the Indians were proud of having caught the suspects; they were not about to grant bond and risk having them skip across some border while the world press snickered.

The most interesting event at the brief hearing was an outburst from Marie-Andrée, who was confronted with Charles for the first time in weeks. He was wearing not only handcuffs but chains that linked his arms, and on his legs were shackles. He had grown a beard, and his couturier suit was dusty and wrinkled. Charles smiled at Marie-Andrée and began an impetuous speech to the court pleading for better conditions. But she interrupted him with an outburst, drenched in tears, "I never want to speak to him again. He's brought me nothing but problems for the past year. I never imagined I could get involved in anything like this . . . The year I spent with him was worse than my prison cell in Tihar."

A reporter for a Bangkok newspaper asked Marie-Andrée if she had anything to say against the accusations that she had committed murder. "All they can say against me is that I was there," she said. "Nothing else."

But there was a public Marie-Andrée and a private one. In the loneliness of her cell, she wrote a long dozen-page letter and smuggled it to Charles in the men's section. The document was exceptionally revealing, both of her character and emotions, and how she viewed her lover. And indeed she still loved him:

Hello, my darling:

I read your long letter over and over again . . . On many points I agree with you. As to your complaint that I "scream and cry" all the time, I am conscious of it. But if I had screamed louder before, maybe I wouldn't be where I am. You understand that my nerves are raw. I must stay in jail for I don't know how long—for doing nothing . . .

You say I have a "tendency to conquest" . . . Yes, it is strong inside me, like most women, to be liked by people I meet . . . But you are not satisfied unless all the women are in love with you . . . Remember the women clients in Bangkok? You tried very hard to seduce them. Any woman that we have known together, you have tried to seduce. It's known that you have women in all the countries of the Orient. And that's not something I invented! . . .

I am not a criminal, that you know very well . . . You may understand psychological principals, but to know them and to live them are two different matters. You do not respect the human being. For you, the human being is a thing at your service, to utilize at will . . . You obey your own desires and nothing else . . . Remember your behavior in the first week that we lived together? No understanding, no comprehension of what I wanted or needed . . . No delicate attention, only reproaches, only complaints about my "lack of manners," my lack of knowledge, my inferiority . . . You live your "psychology" like Catholics live their religion. They know all the principles by heart, but they do not live them in every day life . . .

. . . you say you never slept with married women. Maybe so. I can't verify it. But in one year, you broke and tore apart the hearts of three women—May, Suzy, and myself . . . you didn't make anyone happy. All you gave was suffering. You played with love. And then you reject us like an old rag you don't need anymore . . .

I am stopping now. If you are hurting, I am hurting even more. It is true that I once loved you, and it is still true. But my eyes are more open than before . . .

You frighten me . . . I don't know if I'll have the courage to give you this letter. I may tear it up . . . You talk about "change." . . . The one of us who "must change" is not me . . . You must change yourself totally, change your mentality completely, learn to respect the human being. The day you understand that is the day you will become good . . . There must be a housecleaning inside your soul. Destroy everything that is old, only keep the beautiful and the new . . .

I love you darling. But I must have the courage to speak to you this way . . .

Your "little girl."

CHAPTER FORTY-ONE

For a full year the prisoners waited in Tihar Prison for their trials, the monotony broken only by regular trips into the very heart of Delhi for preliminary hearings at the Parliament Street Courts—a curious place that resembled both a legal bazaar and a minor Asian ruin. The courthouse itself is a U-shaped one-story building with a corrugated tin roof and tiny hearing rooms facing onto a courtyard where beggars importune, old men roast peanuts over smoky braziers, and the relatives of defendants sleep, cook, defecate, and wail at attorneys stalking about in starched black frock coats.

Most of the real action, however, takes place next door in the rubble of what was once a multistory building occupied by lawyers. The building did not fall down from earthquake or poor construction. One morning when the lawyers arrived routinely to begin their day, bulldozers were preparing to level their building. The lawyers had but a few hours to frantically remove files and books from their chambers before the structure was smashed into gravel. Nobody could find out precisely why the lawyers' office building was so suddenly condemned and toppled, other than some vague muttering by authorities that it violated the building code. A more likely reason, the lawyers came to believe, was the wrath of Indira Gandhi. Lawyers had been bedeviling her; they had led the campaign to have her election as Prime Minister invalidated.

"Our mother decided to punish her children," said one prominent attorney, "so she knocked our house down and forced us to set up shop outside. I'm sure she is delighted each time it rains."

Deprived of shelter, lawyers were forced to find space in and around an enormous pipal tree whose branches offered shade to those sweltering below, and a home to hundreds of screeching bluebirds and ravens who from time to time dropped mementos onto both attorneys and their documents.

Each morning, some of Delhi's most prominent members of the legal profession brought portable tables and chairs and signs advertising their specialties: "K. L. Vacher, Advocate. Oath Commissioner. Attested Here." Or, "C. S. Ashwalia, B.A., LLB, Advocate, High Court. Ex-Prosecuting Deputy Supt. Police. Decorations: President's Medal, Police & Fire Services Medal." Around these alfresco offices worked stenographers in brilliantly colored saris, clacking away at ancient typewriters, and servants who ran errands, fetched tea, and occasionally carried their masters piggyback across swampy, oozing ground to the courthouse. "It's a flea market of the law," remarked a startled French reporter who had come to write of Charles Sobhraj. "But somehow it's wonderful to anyone who ever got screwed by a lawyer."

The prisoners were delivered in the black bus with thick steel mesh at the windows and were placed in an adjoining police lockup that had once been a military barracks. Ordinarily Marie-Andrée sat quietly in a corner of the yard in the company of two stout prison matrons, both of whom she called "Mommy" and both of whom seemed both tolerant and kind to the Canadian. Charles, however, was always the center of a carnival. Squatting on his haunches because the chains made it painful to sit down, he was surrounded by a forest of guards and rifles, yet somehow he managed to conduct business. Activity swirled about him. His minions eluded the security precautions and danced attendance, receiving orders to buy this lawbook or that little necessity. His lawyers often encountered difficulty in obtaining permission for a conference with Charles, but either through bribes or exceptionally eloquent

persuasions, the famous prisoner rarely lacked the opportunity of speaking with his flunkies, some of whom were
out on bail themselves.

They were stars. *Celebrities.* India's newspapers, subdued
and fearful under Indira Gandhi's dictatorial powers, relished a story that had no political overtones. The "notorious gang" and "international killers" were profiled endless-
ly, mug shots decorating Sunday feature pages. And both in
and out of Tihar Prison, a curious and motley array of
people danced about them.

In December 1976, Marie-Andrée passed Christmas in
predictable despair. She weighed less than ninety pounds.
On her back were festering sores from insect bites. Her
eyes were weak and she feared she was going blind. Her
sister Denise had brought happiness and love from Canada
on a brief visit, but now she was gone. For a time it had
seemed that the authorities would not permit Denise to
visit, but Marie-Andrée threw a hysterical tantrum in her
cell that so worried the prison administration that two
meetings were allowed, both with guards in attendance,
the rule being that the sisters had to speak in English.

Denise had been shocked at her sister's appearance.
Marie-Andrée was not only thin, her face was as pale as
a wintry Quebec sun, her hair chopped off to keep the
bugs from nesting. Her old limp had returned and she
fell awkwardly into Denise's embrace. They wept together.
"Why did you come?" asked Marie-Andrée with a note of
sternness. "You don't have that kind of money."

"I'm here because you are my sister and I love you,"
answered Denise. She was young and pert and so resembled her older sister that Inspector Tuli had done a double
take when introduced. "I told the bank I had to have
$2,500 and I wouldn't take no for an answer. If you need
me to come back, I'll borrow $2,500 more." She assured
her sister that the family supported Marie-Andrée one
hundred per cent. "Daddy has given up wine until the
day you come home," she said.

Denise was permitted to attend one of the hearings in
the Parliament Street Courts at which both Marie-Andrée
and Charles were present. The courtroom was a tiny
place, scarcely twelve feet square, with whitewashed
stucco walls, an armoire atop which rested buckets and

bottles, and several cane-backed chairs scattered about at random. Had a waitress appeared with a tray of beer, the chamber would have made an exellent Mexican cantina. A young judge sat in another cane chair and before him was a long shelf, where lawyers rested their elbows and books and about which formed 'a jumble of those involved —counsel, defendants, guards, press, and relatives. It was Denise's first glimpse of the man who had wrecked her sister's life, and she looked at Charles Sobhraj with both fury and fascination. She found him menacing, yet "cute," "childish," and "chic" even in irons and chains. His allure remained. After the hearing, Charles edged close to Denise and he bowed and said, in whispered French, "I regret that Marie-Andrée has these problems. I will try and help her out of this. Believe me."

Denise nodded. "I should hope so," she said, with unhidden sarcasm.

But then Denise returned to Canada, and the year ended, and the emotional nourishment of her sister's visit was gone. Marie-Andrée was left to her dwindling resources. From childhood, she resurrected the fancy of being a Carmelite nun, and now she once again pretended, spending the days in prayer and deprivation. "This must have a purpose," she said. "It was meant to be, and I cannot question the will of God."

"What a dump!" brayed a raucous voice in best Bette Davis impersonation. Marie-Andrée looked up to encounter a young woman being escorted into her cell. The new arrival was tiny, barely five feet tall, but so bursting with energy and vivacity as to resemble an overpacked suitcase. She shook herself free of the matrons' arms. "Okay, end of the line," she snapped. "I know my way from here. Beat it." The guards giggled and turned her loose, rather gratefully.

"I'm Checkers," announced the new prisoner, who, upon hearing Marie-Andrée's response in accented English, switched immediately to French. Marie-Andrée's mood lifted, this being the first cellmate she had encountered who spoke her language.

"You've been here before?" ventured Marie-Andrée.

"Oh, hell yes, honey," said Checkers, already busily

stepping off the cell's dimensions. It was eight feet by ten, with a dirt floor, a hole cut in the earth for a toilet, and a rusty pipe that on infrequent occasions belched forth dirty water that was valued more highly than food. The prisoners had to be ready to rush to the pipe and catch the water, no matter what time of day or night it abruptly sprang into life. In one corner of the tiny room sat the crumpled figure of a third young prisoner. Her name was Dharma, a girl from North Africa who had been arrested on a currency violation. Already in Tihar for a year, she had apparently fallen through a legal crack. Nobody seemed to know the status of her case—or care—and no one spoke her language. Dharma was going insane. She spent her waking hours either moaning an eerie chant that was driving Marie-Andrée up the wall, or else she sat blankly, staring at nothing with dead eyes, fondling her breasts and allowing flies to congregate on her body without bothering to brush them away. Kneeling before her, Checkers smiled tenderly and made as if to stroke her forehead in friendship. But Dharma drew back and snarled like a trapped dog. "Excuse me," said Checkers. "If you want anything, just rattle your cage."

Checkers felt it important that she deliver her biography to the others—and an astonishing one it was. Though barely twenty years old, Checkers had lived what seemed to be a hundred lives. If one tenth of it was true, Checkers had already accomplished more than Zelda Fitzgerald, the Empress Josephine, and Bonnie Parker.

By her telling, she was the daughter of a multimillion-aire Virginia family whose fortune was rooted in tobacco, horses, and land. Her father, a dour man who often slept in his office and rose during the night to study his balance sheets, owned a breeding farm in Virginia, a private island in Maine, an apartment in Manhattan, and a condominium in Key West. Checkers' mother, a mid-European beauty with a few drops of distantly royal blood in her veins, bore six children between trips to Paris, where she was a valued customer at the salons of *haute couture*. When Checkers was ten, her parents divorced and she was exiled to a series of private schools. "I was kicked out of six before I was fifteen," she told Marie-Andrée, proudly.

Checkers claimed to have begun a flourishing career as

occasional prostitute at the age of fourteen, working both the locker rooms of her father's country clubs and the streets of New York. By seventeen, she had funds sufficient for an escape to Europe, where the intent was to reclaim the attention and affection of her mother, then on a fourth marriage, to a wine baron. "My dear mother told me to kiss off," remembered Checkers, "so I said to hell with everybody. I've been on my own ever since and never regretted a minute of it."

But how did Checkers happen to be a repeating resident of Tihar Prison? "I'm a smuggler, honey," she told Marie-Andrée. Checkers had been arrested several days before at Delhi Airport with seven kilos of hashish hidden in her brassiere, giving her the appearance of an exceptionally well-endowed stripper, plus a vial of morphine powder, plus a flight bag that contained $30,000 in crisp Canadian hundred-dollar bills. "They took me to the tax office and beat me for five days until they saw it wasn't going to get them anywhere," contended Checkers. "So they decided to dump me into Tihar for a while—Tihar, beloved Tihar. I asked if any Western women were around and Marie-Andrée Leclerc was the star attraction."

Quickly Checkers proved that she knew how to operate —and survive. Her face still as fresh as an ingénue's, her eyes always sparkling save when their lids were heavy with hashish smoke, Checkers refused to permit melancholy to visit her. Even if her tales had to be reduced by three quarters before they could be believed, the girl had spunk and warmth and was as welcome in the cell as a splash of French cologne. Within a half day of her arrival, Checkers returned from a "scavenger hunt" about the prison, bearing an armload of bananas, onions, garlic, potatoes, a chunk of suspicious-smelling meat, and a squawking live green parrot. The last she took to the next door cell, where an old Indian woman obediently strangled the bird and plucked it for roasting. That night the three young women, Marie-Andrée, Checkers, and the deranged Dharma dined well. Checkers had even bargained for the stub of a candle that threw a soft glow over the hideous chamber. Long ago Marie-Andrée had surrendered her interest in food, but Checkers threatened to force-feed her if she did not eat every morsel of the stringy parrot.

"This noble bird died for us," she said. "The least you can do is show your appreciation."

Marie-Andrée smiled and ate with reasonable enthusiasm.

"Did you kill all those people?" asked Checkers.

Marie-Andrée shook her head. "Of course not."

"Good," announced Checkers. "I believe you."

Each night Checkers smoked hashish or, if she had been lucky, a bit of opium, pulling on the pipe until she was drugged enough to find sleep. Most of the women in Tihar did the same, else they could not have survived the night with its screams from the insane asylum, or the cries of babies who were condemned along with their mothers. In India, when a mother is sent to prison and there is no one to care for her child, then both are locked up. One day Checkers returned to the cell with a revolting piece of news. She had seen an enormous rat crawling over the taut skin of a malnourished infant nearby who was apparently asleep. When Checkers rushed in to shoo the rat away, she discovered that the baby was dead. "They die in here every week," she said. "This is the bottom circle of hell."

Somehow Checkers managed entree to most every part of the sprawling prison, accomplishing such freedom of movement by a show of bravado whenever confronted by authority. "They think I'm crazy," said Checkers. "If any guard gives me trouble, I explode and curse the son of a bitch. Most Indian men are afraid of Western women."

There came a morning when Checkers broke and sobbed like the youngster she truly was. On this day she returned from a tour of the prison, her face a rare slash of despair. She fell onto her blanket and wept. Marie-Andrée pleaded to know the cause of her pain. "Bastards," said Checkers. "They killed her. I saw them." When she turned her cheek to Marie-Andrée, an angry red bruise was newly present.

"Who?" asked her cellmate. "Who did they kill?"

Checkers told of a young country girl in prison on a minor robbery. She had progressed from tears to blankness to attempted suicide. A broken light bulb. Jagged edge across her jugular. Unsuccessful, she tried to hang herself with her blanket. "The guards found her and cut her down and beat her up as punishment—and she finally died." Checkers said she rushed into the prison office and was informed by someone in authority that the girl died of dysentery. "I went berserk . . . I started kicking chairs and trying to get at the guy's face with my fingernails. I said, 'How can you permit a woman, a *human being,* to be beaten to death?' And you know what he said? He said, 'She's not a woman, she's a criminal. And she's not a criminal anymore because she's dead. One less case to tangle the court.' "

When a guard was summoned to escort Checkers back to the cell, she struggled. He slapped her. "I'll kill the bastard someday," she vowed. "He's going on my list."

In January, an unusual cold settled over Delhi. In Tihar, the thick walls drank up the chill and prisoners went about huddled in thin blankets. Each cell was a crypt, the sun hid, and Checkers said the smell of death was in the air. She won permission to keep a fire going in the cell, but as there was no ventilation, the flames could not burn for more than a few minutes before smoke overwhelmed. Each morning, one of the girls rose before the sun and hurried to a communal woodpile where the guards tossed out a few sticks and laughed while the women fought over them like starved cats. If a woman arrived too late, it was either endure the cold until the next dawn or barter with chits that were the unit of currency inside the walls. Chits could purchase food or drugs, or bribe a guard to smuggle out a letter, or to keep a lesbian from making unwelcome advances. Adroit in such negotiation, Checkers was late one morning to the woodpile and returned instead with an armload of hard, round loaves of bread. Marie-Andrée caught one as Checkers tossed them about the room. She grimaced. The bread was inedible. "Of course," said Checkers. "It's our firewood today." And until the bread was gone, their cell smoked with a pungent aroma that delivered a modest amount of heat.

On occasion, Checkers even maneuvered her way to the men's side, where "all the best drugs" were available, and where she renewed an old acquaintance—Charles Sobhraj. "I knew him once under a different name," she said. Marie-Andrée was hungry for news. She had not seen him in several days. Was he well? Did he speak of her? Had he managed to remove his leg irons? The last time they met at the Parliament Street Courts, his legs were raw from steel scraping flesh.

"He said to give you his love," answered Checkers, "and not to worry." Later, Checkers described Charles more fully to another friend: "He's sitting over there like the Godfather, trying to run the criminal business of the entire continent of Asia . . . He says he has 'people' working for him on the outside, but from what I gather they consist of three or four French junkies who are stupid enough to run errands for him."

Checkers told Marie-Andrée that if MISA were not in effect she might have been released on bail long ago. "Who would have thought a nice woman like Indira Gandhi would turn out to be Franco?"

Presently, Checkers heard an interesting rumor that she brought to Marie-Andrée. Several hundred letters from Canadian supporters were piled up in the prison office. Somebody had decreed that an MISA prisoner was not entitled to read the avalanche of mail. Marie-Andrée burst into angry tears, begging Checkers for a scheme to pry them loose.

Checkers nodded and begged for quiet. She was thinking. "It's simple," she finally said. "A hunger strike."

"What good would that do?" wondered Marie-Andrée.

"Oh, cause a little drama, shake the bastards up. I can see that it gets leaked to the press. The Indians are terrified of hunger strikes. They're a famous weapon in India; remember Gandhi? If that old man could bring down the British Raj by the simple act of refusing to eat, then you ought to get your mail."

Marie-Andrée agreed enthusiastically, informing the female guard the next morning that she was refusing to eat until (1) all of her mail was given to her, (2) she was removed from the MISA category, as her alleged crimes had nothing to do with politics, and (3) she was allowed certain privileges such as a writing table, stationery, and a large ration of lye soap to wash down the cell and keep the insects under modest control. The guard shrugged and went to get a superior who in turn fetched an assistant warden who then persuaded the top man himself, a stocky, muscular, mustard-faced man in his late thirties, named Ranawanda, to visit the troublesome Canadian girl.

Their meeting was brief and inconclusive. Marie-Andrée presented her demands, Ranawanda warned her that she was risking her health, then he stalked out.

"It worked," said Checkers excitedly. "He's already worried about this getting into the papers."

It was not difficult for a Tihar prisoner to go on a hunger strike. Her stomach already shrunken, Marie-Andrée suffered no pangs after the first day. The prison countered by increasing her food ration, adding tempting dishes like fresh fruit and a piece of broiled chicken. But she refused steadfastly to eat. At mealtimes, when the guards came, she stretched out on the floor and looked—under Checkers' careful stage directions—in the throes of terminal starvation. "Wait'll the press gets a hold of this," taunted Checkers. "I can see the headline now: 'Canadian Woman Dies of Starvation in Indian Prison.'" Checkers embellished the act by locating some white powder somewhere in the prison with which she transformed Marie-Andrée's face into a ghastly death mask.

At the end of a week, prison authorities were in and out of the cell several times daily, coaxing, threatening, promising a beating or solitary confinement. But the striker refused to even look at the food in their arms. On the twelfth day, taken to the prison hospital, Marie-Andrée was warned that death was imminent. Marie-Andrée nodded. She had heard that a Western woman is lucky to survive a year in an Indian prison under optimum conditions. It did not matter. The way she saw her situation, death would be little more than a lateral move.

"Will you just eat one bite?" begged a female matron, holding forth a plate of newly baked biscuits. Marie-Andrée stared at the food. It was indeed tempting. She picked up a biscuit, examined it, took a tiny bite, dropped it back onto the plate. "All right," she said, "I took one bite. Now can I go back to my cell and die in peace?"

Finally the warden was smart enough to produce Charles, who was shocked at Marie-Andrée's appearance. He asked for a few moments of privacy. They were granted. He urged her to break the hunger strike. Her body clearly could not tolerate more. To commit ritualistic suicide was abhorrent to Charles' philosophy. Assuring her of his love, he negotiated a compromise. If the prison would release her mail, and allow her to have paper and pen, then she would call off the strike. With relief, permission was granted.

Marie-Andrée spent the next several weeks happily reading letters from Canada, many of which viewed her predicament as the fate of a French-speaking citizen abandoned by Ottawa. "If you were an English-speaking Canadian," wrote one woman, "Pierre Trudeau would have invaded India to get you out."

Soon thereafter, Checkers won release on bail, the money put up by a relative and a friend on the outside. But her passport was not returned. On the day of her release, she checked into the deluxe Imperial Hotel, ordered six Coca-Colas, a double cheeseburger, and "all the French fries in your kitchen," then began to think about ways to get Marie-Andrée out of prison. She loathed Charles Sobhraj, she knew others whose lives have been ruined by him. Her heart went out to the foolish Canadian girl. And Checkers knew it was a race against time. If Marie-Andrée did not get stabbed by a spiteful prisoner, or beaten to death by guards, or succumb to blood poisoning from insect bites, then her innards would twist and shrivel into necrosis from malnutrition.

Remaining in Delhi several weeks, Checkers raised money by an occasional sale of her sexual favors to a wealthy businessman from Madras, who paid well to chew on her toes and stroke her elbows, nothing else. And she always had a little hashish in a jeweled compact to sell, but the drug was so plentiful and cheap in India that scant profit could be made. A telegram to her mother, holidaying in Lisbon, asking for an advance against her someday-family inheritance did not even produce a reply.

At least once a week, Checkers went to the teeming, scheming street fair that was the Parliament Street Courts, where she usually managed to steal a moment or two with Marie-Andrée and serve as postman or messenger girl. She avoided Charles, for he never lacked attention. His minions shared common characteristics: none was very bright, but each moth was passionately attracted by the flame of Charles Sobhraj.

One night in the Cellar night club, Checkers searched the murk for a table and was invited to squeeze into a group of youngsters. She found herself sitting next to an extremely tall, very thin American whose most distinguishable feature, even by candlelight, was eyes the color of scarlet. Red Eye had been sprung from Tihar that afternoon, and the American Embassy had indicated that a new passport would be issued to him. Merry, celebrating, and anxious to make a final exit from the East, Red Eye announced that fate had finally blessed him. "I'm on the way home," he told Checkers, "and if I ever get there, whatever is square, and normal, and double-knit, I'll be all for it."

Checkers nodded, understanding how the values of home that had seemed so tarnished took on the luster of gold once they were remembered in the hell of an Indian prison. Quickly the two young people made the connection that both had been recent residents of Tihar, and that their friends had been Charles and Marie-Andrée. "Have you seen Charles operating at the courthouse?" asked Checkers, answering her own question. "It's madness. In the kingdom of the blind, the one-eyed man will rule. I really believe Charles is enjoying it. He's on the front page of every newspaper, and he has a bunch of stupid courtiers to dance in attendance."

Red Eye was convinced that Charles was planning an escape. "He has six sets of blueprints and he knows Tihar better than the men who built it," said Red Eye. It would not be easy. Not only was Charles under exceptional surveillance, the prison staff was nervous and quick-triggered. In recent months, probably due to the confusion and overcrowding from the MISA emergency rules, Tihar was unusually restless. One prisoner, a minor robber who protested that he had been sentenced unfairly, attempted a Herculean escape. The man, whose name was Galwar, dug a tunnel with a tin cup, burrowing beneath the wall of a house within Tihar where lepers were kept, across several hundred feet of earth, then down under a street. Galwar knew that only a moat and an eight-foot-thick final wall

stood between him and freedom. But on his hundred and
thirteenth day of labor, as he dug toward the moat and
wondered how he could avoid potential drowning, a prison
truck drove over his tunnel and encountered the new
weakness of the street's underpinnings. The truck sank, destroying the road, Galwar's dream, and Galwar.

Sometime later, ten quite dangerous prisoners united to
dig a new tunnel, profiting from Galwar's mistake. For six
months the ten dug, this time in a zigzag pattern, calculated to put less strain on the surface. Beginning near a
wrestling pit in the exercise yard, which served as a place
to dump the dirt and rocks dredged up by their digging,
they proceeded without discovery. One night when the
prison staff was watching a film, the ten calmly crawled
to freedom. Alas, the story ended sadly. The escapees,
once in the arms of freedom, split up, stole guns, got
drunk, threatened to shoot up the interior of a restaurant.
The other customers made citizens' arrests, and seven of
the ten were promptly returned with hangovers to Tihar.
The three others were reportedly slain.

After these embarrassing flights, fifteen members of the
prison staff were fired, and rumor had it that Indira
Gandhi herself scolded the chief administrator and warned
him to tighten security within the huge institution.

There had also been the horrible story of a convicted
murderer who was waiting in Tihar for his execution.
Deranged, he warned the guards daily that the government
of India would never take his life, and the guards responded with taunts and promises. One night the prisoner
poured kerosene on his blankets, wrapped them about his
body, and set himself afire. He rushed down a corridor in
flames, screaming for the guards to try and kill him.
Someone threw a bucket of water over the wretch; another
guard tackled him; enough of him was left breathing to be
taken to the prison hospital for intensive treatment. After
a week, the doomed man was pronounced well enough to
be hanged, which he was, on the ancient gallows, in the
chill of an autumn dawn.

Checkers did not believe Charles would try and escape
from within the prison. More likely he would engineer
some spectacular drama either on the bus that bore him
from jail to courthouse, or in the courtyard where he

waited for court appearances. "One thing is certain," she predicted, "Charles will either bust out or he will kill himself. He simply cannot allow authority to hang him, for that would be the ultimate negation, his final defeat. He will either escape in some grandiose flash that will be written about for years—or else he will execute himself and rig it so that he will take an awful lot of people to death with him. Charles wants his name writ large in history."

Red Eye agreed. Charles was just "strange" enough to do that.

"Strange?" echoed Checkers. "He's *mad*. Face it. The exterior Charles Sobhraj is personable, intelligent, charming, handsome. Only when he feels threatened does his trigger mechanism engage and he retreats 'inside.' And there lives a deadly sociopath. When he is threatened, he kills."

"He told me he didn't kill anybody," said Red Eye. "He said if anybody died, it was by Ajay Chowdhury's hands."

"But where is Ajay?" teased Checkers. "The cops have turned every inch of Asia upside down looking for him. Poor Ajay is enriching the sod somewhere. And I don't think he killed himself."

Checkers turned the conversation to Marie-Andreé. She was convinced that the Canadian girl had not participated in the killings. "Maybe she knew about them, but she was too scared to get out."

"Maybe," said Red Eye. "The thing I don't understand is why Charles fell for her in the first place. She's not going to win any beauty prizes."

Checkers laughed. "That's not the point . . . Don't you understand that Charles Sobhraj is bonkers? Psycho? Marie-Andrée appealed to him because she is his total opposite. Resolutely small-town. Never did anything wrong. She represents home, family, roots, permanence— all the things he never had. And when he introduced her as his 'wife,' to customers, they must have had confidence in a man with a woman so foursquare."

Red Eye looked about the room and saw Tete, the creepy Vietnamese, sitting in a particularly dark corner with a few other denizens who looked like they would stab a man for bus fare. Tete had also won conditional release from Tihar. Checkers shuddered. "They're all sick," she whispered. "They've all got holes in their lives, unfulfilled aspirations, gaps, missing pieces of the puzzle, and Charles is smart enough to spot those weaknesses and use them. Any form of madness generates a higher energy level."

Checkers rose to leave. She had a midnight date with a Pakistani friend who supposedly could get her a Swedish passport for only a thousand rupees. But she had one more thing to say: "Charles makes the others feel that by clinging to him they can realize their fantasies. He is carrying the dream. He says there *is* a pot of gold at the end of the rainbow, but he is the only one with a map."

They kissed affectionately and vowed to meet again, someday, on Fifth Avenue or Wilshire Boulevard. "I'll bring Marie-Andrée with me," said Checkers, "if Charles doesn't kill her first."

Red Eye shook his head. "He won't kill her. He feels guilty."

"Bullshit," said Checkers. "He's going to escape and leave her in jail to rot . . . She's just another notch on his gun belt."

CHAPTER FORTY-TWO

A rumor wriggled out of Tihar and reached Tuli that his two star witnesses, Barbara Smith and Mary Ellen Eather, were feeling pressure from Charles. An informant passed along the news that the baby-faced British girl and her Australian friend were being squeezed to recant their confessions. If they refused and went to court as hostile witnesses against Charles, the informant said, the girls had been told they were signing their death warrants.

Gravely concerned, Tuli hurried to the prison and asked to see the young women. He encountered difficulty in obtaining an interview, for MISA forbad anybody, *anybody*, from speaking to a prisoner without a signed authorization from a magistrate. Tuli permitted himself a rare flash of anger at bureaucratic nonsense. Two guards ran to fetch the girls.

Barbara and Mary Ellen relished the opportunity to get out of their cell, even briefly. They were housed in a chamber for the "condemned," though the assurance was that it was chosen only for security, not as prophecy. On their first night in residence, Barbara was attacked by a religious fanatic who screamed that the new girl was a reincarnation of an evil serpent. When they were brought before him, Tuli saw immediately that their nerves were frayed. He wondered if either or both could endure several more months of waiting, then hold up under what was certain to be savage cross-examination from attorneys for Charles and Marie-Andrée. The defense was clearly going to attack

both young women as self-serving prostitutes and drug
users who were co-operating with the state only to save
their skins.

"Has Charles Sobhraj threatened you?" demanded Tuli.

The two girls looked at one another. Barbara, the dark-
haired English girl with a complexion that somehow remained soft and creamy even in the hell of Tihar, answered
with a giggle. She usually giggled.

"I hear Charles is *interested* in what we're going to say,"
she answered. Beside her, Mary Ellen nodded cautiously.
Both were afraid of Tuli, even though he had behaved
courteously toward them. They were afraid of all police.
It would not do their plight any good to tell the inspector
that anonymous notes and whispered messages were warning them almost daily not to speak ill of Charles Sobhraj.

"I hope you're still going to testify," said Tuli. He
praised the two young women for their moral courage.

Barbara giggled again. "I still am," she said, "unless I
die from the waiting . . ."

From Bangkok, Colonel Sompol Suthimai wrote and
telephoned Tuli to request that the accused killers be turned
over to Thailand, which, unfortunately, had no extradition
treaty with India. He wanted them badly. Finally the young
officer's patience and curiosity—he had never seen the
subjects of his concern in the flesh—overwhelmed him
and he flew to Delhi. There, Tuli received him warmly.
The court proceedings were slowed by MISA, he explained. It was now ten months after the arrests, and trial
had not begun. "We would like very much to try them in
my country," said Sompol.

Tuli nodded. "And if they were found innocent in
India," he said, pausing, for he did not think the likelihood
was substantial, "I would recommend that you get them
next."

An interview was set up at Tihar with Charles, but the
celebrated criminal sat stonily for half an hour, denying
everything, scoffing at Sompol. "I didn't kill anybody,"
he insisted. He denied even *knowing* the people who were
murdered. But, wondered Sompol casually, not wanting to
give away the mass of evidence he had stored in the

corner of his office, how did some of the victims' belongings get into his apartment in Bangkok?

Charles did not raise a concerned eyebrow. "I have no idea," he said. "Perhaps someone planted them there."

Sompol asked the same questions over and over, but he did not receive an answer worth committing to a report. "He's the coolest killer I ever encountered," Sompol later said. "He is very sure of himself, and he is afraid of nothing."

Marie-Andrée was not at all happy to be yanked before the visitor from Thailand. She arrived for her talk with Colonel Suthimai, flashing fire in her eyes. Wasn't it enough to cope with Indian police? Did she have to receive delegates from other nations as well? For several minutes, she stared mutely at the boyish and polite cop from Bangkok.

"See my lawyer," she muttered to every question. Sompol fell silent and they studied one another. "There's no law that says I have to talk to you," she finally said. "I'm so tired of everything."

Sompol nodded. In his kind face were understanding and a spot of sympathy. He tried another approach. "How do you feel?" he asked. "Is your health holding up?"

Marie-Andrée was startled. Never had a policeman in Asia asked after her well-being. "All right," she answered, "as well as could be expected . . . It's just that the rats are driving me insane. They come out at night and crawl over me when I sleep. And the bugs. Every day, three times a day, I wash everything down with lye soap, but they thrive on it." She held out her arms and legs for Sompol to see the clusters of red bites, standing out on her pale, colorless skin like stamps on an envelope.

If, suggested Sompol, if a deal could be struck with the Indian Government, if they would release the two prisoners and turn them over to Thailand, if that could be arranged, would Marie-Andrée turn state's evidence?

"Would I go free?" she asked.

"I don't know," answered Sompol honestly. "I'd have to speak with my superiors. But I do think a deal could be discussed."

It was time, said Marie-Andrée, for her to start looking after Number One. She felt slim allegiance to Charles, and if she did not get out of Tihar soon, nothing would matter. Nothing would be left to bury after the bugs and rats destroyed her. It was now late spring in Delhi, and the cruelest heat was beginning. There would be no respite for months, until the monsoons came and went away.

"The Indians tricked me, you know," she went on. "I was so tired and so sick when they arrested me. They told me if I would make a statement and implicate Charles, then I would go free. And they wrote it in English, a language I didn't understand at the time."

Sompol flew home to Bangkok and reported to General Montchai that Marie-Andrée seemed to be weakening. "The girl wants out," he said. "I think she wants a deal." The general doubted if the Indians would turn loose their famous prisoners anytime soon. Things go slow in India, he said. "They've got the prize and they're not going to share it," he said.

The plan was ingenious in its simplicity. And it might well have worked if an informant had not tipped off Tihar authorities that Charles Sobhraj was preparing to escape. One morning a squad of guards burst into his cell. They seemed to know exactly what they were looking for. Charles rose in protest, but a guard seized his arms and pinned them behind his back. Another cocked a rifle and held it at his neck.

On a nail in the wall, a khaki shirt hung, seemingly innocently. A guard ripped it down. In another corner of the cell, guards found a pair of khaki pants to match. An ordinary piece of rope was loosely tied around a cardboard box. The guards took that, too. In a niche in the wall, they located various regulation military insignia, even a medal for valor. In another hiding place were a wig, a beard, and a mustache. If all of these were put together— the pants, the shirt, the rope to serve as decorative braid, the wig and facial hair, even a turban—a very good approximation of an army uniform could be assembled. Charles Sobhraj, it was charged, had planned to dress himself as an officer and walk quietly out of greased doors to freedom. The guards also found the grease—8,000 crisp,

brand new rupees, carefully concealed within the corrugated layers of the cardboard box. "I never saw a search
like that in my life," commented one of the prisoners who
watched. "Had they been looking for a particular ant, they
would have found it."

The theory was that Charles had arranged for his "contacts" on the outside to smuggle the clothing and other
articles into Tihar. Of course he denied it, passionately,
but his protests did not prevent the prison authorities from
throwing him into a solitary cell for a few weeks. After
that he was denied companionship and forced to change
cells every few days. When Tuli heard of the clever plan,
he had to smile. In fact he would have enjoyed seeing
Charles gussied up in a military uniform with the beard
of a Sikh. But then he shuddered. If Charles had succeeded, heads would have rolled, from the lowest guard to
the minister of justice.

The heat crushed everyone within Tihar. For a week in
May the thermometer climbed to 110° every noon. Wet,
sticky, exhausting, punishing, the intensity of the sun was
paralyzing. In their cell, the two star witnesses, or "approvers," lay limp and dehydrated. Barbara Smith had
nothing left to giggle about. "I'm only twenty years old,"
she said. "I never thought it would end like this." Mary
Ellen nodded weakly. She was a nurse in her native Australia, and now she was trying to remember the symptoms
of sunstroke. She wondered how much heat the human
body could take before all the circuits blew.

"I can't go on much longer," said Mary Ellen.

"Neither can I," gasped Barbara. She spoke of the irony
of their predicament. They had agreed to become state's
witnesses because the implication was that as soon as they
had their day in court the prison doors would swing open.
Now almost a year had passed, and there might well be
another—and another. God knew how long they would
rot in Tihar while waiting to co-operate with the government of India.

For another day or two they endured the torment of
the sun and the hell of their lives. Barbara had received
a few letters from her father in England, but they were
hardly comforting. "My dear old dad writes variations on

the theme of 'I told you so, I told you that you were no good.' That's just what I want to hear from my family—loyalty and support," she told Mary Ellen.

They began to discuss suicide. At first it was more of a game, something to pass the time. One girl suggested cutting wrists with a razor blade. Neither prisoner had one, but with enough money, anything could be bought. They had a few hundred rupees hidden for an emergency. The other girl countered with hanging, or strangling, somehow breaking the neck with a knotted blanket. Mary Ellen dismissed that; it would be painful, perhaps unsuccessful. "When you set out deliberately to break your neck," she said, "it's hard to do it correctly." Next Barbara had a fanciful idea. "What if we went out into the yard and ate all the leaves we could find? Surely some of them would be poisonous."

Perhaps, agreed Mary Ellen. But on the other hand, the leaves might only make them violently ill.

Up to this point it was only a game. But the two had now spoken of the sweetness of death for too long. Without really acknowledging it, their fantasies had come into focus. They began to plot their suicides in earnest.

Mary Ellen was permiitted to work now and then in the prison hospital, as nurses were at a shortage. She was a good nurse, and the hours she spent on duty reminded her that she really liked the work, found purpose in it. She wished she had never abandoned it to lie on the beach in Pakistan where Charles Sobhraj rode into her life in a silver Citroën. But now it was too late.

One afternoon, Mary Ellen returned to her cell from the hospital and she beckoned Barbara into a corner. She spoke in whispers. The lock on the hospital's medicine cabinet had been broken by another inmate, looking for morphine. The inmate had heard footsteps approaching and ran away, not knowing that the steps belonged to Mary Ellen. The Australian girl stared at the broken lock and put it back in place, so that it would seem unmolested.

"So?" asked Barbara.

"So there's enough sleeping pills in that cabinet to put away half of Tihar. Are you game?"

Barbara sucked in her breath. She could back out now.

She could laugh. She could stop the game. But all she did was nod, slowly, wondering why no tears came to her eyes, or protest to her lips. That evening the two girls made their way to the infirmary. Mary Ellen told Barbara to stand outside as lookout. The plan was to steal a handful of barbiturates, take them to the cell, swallow them immediately, wave "night-night" to the guard who came around at 7 P.M. to lock the cells for the evening and count noses. At dawn, when the cell doors were unlocked, they would be discovered stiff and dead.

With enormous caution, Mary Ellen grasped the doorknob to the medicine room and tried to open it. Locked! She swore silently! Ordinarily the room would be open at this hour, for nurses would soon be coming by to pick up evening medication for patients. Then she had an idea. Not a good idea, but an idea. Mary Ellen went to the head nurse and nonchalantly asked for the key to the medicine room. Her excuse was that she needed cotton wool to swab out the ears of a woman prisoner housed near her cell. The ears were infected from insect bites, a common complaint. The nurse looked suspicious. Mary Ellen tried to stay calm. She said she didn't give a damn one way or the other, but if she handled the prisoner's complaint in her cell, then the inmate would not take up space and time tomorrow in the overcrowded hospital. The nurse agreed. It made sense, putting the request that way. She gave Mary Ellen the key.

Once inside the medicine room, everything went smoothly. The lock on the drug cabinet was still broken. No one had discovered it. Mary Ellen reached inside, found a large container of barbiturates, shook out almost two hundred into her hand, then hid them inside a pair of nursing gloves. She took a deep breath; she tried to stop trembling. It was over. She had found a way to die.

But as she made an exit, the door abruptly opened and the night Resident Medical Officer bumped into her. He recognized Mary Ellen and was not immediately suspicious. But he did ask *why* she was in the medicine room. Quickly she told her cotton wool story. The doctor accepted it. Mary Ellen went further. Did the RMO need assistance on a patient matter? He shook his head. No. He had just learned that the lock on the narcotics cabinet was broken. He had to check and determine if any medications were missing.

"I just did," blurted Mary Ellen in hasty improvisation. "I counted all the pills and nothing is gone." The RMO looked at the slender blond prisoner carefully. The logical question would have been: How did you know about the lock? But he did not ask it. Instead he only nodded, giving her permission to leave.

Barbara was lurking around the corner. "I've got them," the Australian girl told her cellmate. "But the RMO may be onto me. Hurry!"

Without interference they returned to their cell and endured a few breathless moments until darkness gave them a shield. The cell door stood open, and neighboring prisoners wandered in and out. Normally the two girls were hospitable, but on this night they turned every caller away. Then the noise of doors slamming and locks turning began to fill their area. When their own door clanged shut, they nodded good night to the guards. Then, left alone, Mary Ellen handed over a fistful of sleeping pills. "Sorry there's nothing to wash 'em down with," she said.

Barbara stared at the pills. "Should we say anything to one another?" she asked.

"I dunno," answered Mary Ellen. "How about, 'Sorry for everything. See you later.'" She ate one pill slowly. Then another. She threw a handful into her mouth, like candy. The taste was awful, but what did it matter? Barbara sat squat-legged beside the nurse and began her own rite of passage. She encountered trouble swallowing, but after a few minutes worked at least eighty down her slender throat.

Mary Ellen had a *coup de grâce*. She held up a can of insect repellent also smuggled out of the prison hospital. Its name, appropriately, was Finit. They drank the foul liquid.

"I never hurt anyone," murmured Barbara.

"I know," whispered Mary Ellen. She smiled and held out her hand to the English girl.

"God have mercy on us," gasped Barbara.

"He will," promised Mary Ellen. Her eyes were heavy. She forced them open. They needed to be awake in case a bed check was made. Oh hurry, she begged. Please hurry. Come and see us and go away and leave us to die.

Both women had written farewell notes, chiefly complaints about the inhumane conditions of the prison and proclaiming their innocence. And now, at one figurative minute to midnight, Barbara remembered something she wanted to add. Lurching across the cell to where the notes rested, she found a pen. At the bottom of her letter she scrawled, "P.S. Charles Sobhraj is a goddamned ass hole."

Then she fell, and the cries of a hungry baby somewhere down the line and the screams of the lunatic women in the insane asylum were her serenade.

She felt warm. It was as if her mother had at last found her, cleansed her, hugged her to her breasts.

Surrender.

CHAPTER FORTY-THREE

On July 4, 1977, children rode a great elephant around the parking lot of the United States Embassy. A Ferris wheel turned slowly, propelled not by a motor but by the nimble feet of Indian servant boys. A man dressed as Uncle Sam strutted about a playing field, and on the sidelines, an orchestra fit for Queen Victoria played stiff marches. Hot dogs sold for one rupee (ten cents) and the crowd was huge, swelled by legions of the backpack set who came running for the cheap food and the fellowship of home. At dusk, an awesome and ear-shattering display of fireworks filled the skies with smoke and color, and at least one American remarked that it seemed improper for the wealthiest country on earth to spend thousands of dollars on pyrotechnics when citizens of India dropped dead each day from starvation.

But the conversation was not of hungry people, nor the surprising defeat of Indira Gandhi and the rumor that she would soon be charged with corruption. It was of the murder trial of Charles Sobhraj, which had finally begun on this American holiday, and which promised tempting revelations of sex and murder. One American woman was heard to say, "I hear the man looks rather like Sabu, the Elephant Boy. Remember him?" But her companion disagreed. "The picture I saw he looked like Alain Delon. Yum."

* * *

After a year of dribbles and drabs, of coming into court, and going back out again after five minutes, of pleadings, shouts, anger, hysteria, and so much confusion that no one seemed to know the precise status of anybody's case, Charles Sobhraj, Marie-Andrée Leclerc, and Jean Dhuisme finally went on trial for the murder of French tourist Jean-Luc Solomon. The original estimate by the bench was that the case would take a month, perhaps six weeks. A long twelve months later, the judge was making the same prediction. The trial would become one of the longest and most tempestuous in modern Indian history, though it would hardly compete with others down through the centuries. One case has been pending in the Indian courts for—incredibly!—almost one thousand years, having been initiated in the tenth century.

When the British left India in 1948, the founders of the new nation moved quickly to make their country their own again. Much of the British system of common law was kept, but the tradition of a jury trial was thrown out. "Twelve men are too susceptible to bribery and corruption," explained one of the framers of the new code of law. Responsibility was shifted to one judge. "Of course it is impossible to bribe a single judge," muttered one of India's leading advocates, the wryness in his voice unhidden.

Proceedings in the Charles Sobhraj matter were transferred to the Tis Hazari Courts of Old Delhi, a temple of pandemonium, to the Western eye the most crowded, confusing hall of justice extant. An old, huge, rambling stone barracks of a building, its corridors were dark in the full blaze of noon and swarming with tens of thousands of defendants and their families and lawyers and the curious jostling through the halls in search of their appointed rooms. Beggars slept on benches or the cement floor, naked babies laughed or wailed while waiting for their fathers (or mothers) to be condemned, or returned. Men on the precipice of madness—and many in the gorge below—clutched sheaves of documents that contained tortured life histories and bureaucratic assaults, begging attention from anyone who would listen. Men with no legs dragged themselves through the mobs selling orange soda, and an occasional raven flew mistakenly in an open window and—like a condemned prisoner—flapped in terror to escape.

"And now we begin," murmured an attorney named S. N. Chowdhury, one of two locally engaged by the Canadian lawyer d'Aoust to represent Marie-Andrée. Young, appealing, with a kind face that would well suit a priest, Chowdhury was apprehensive over what he suspected would become a carnival. "I hope the world is not watching us today," he said, "for no one else could possibly understand the confusion and tumult of our system of justice. Particularly since Charles Sobhraj is bent upon turning this room into a stage for his performance. The Indian Government has never cared too much about the dispensing of justice. It is society's stepchild. Parliament has always been far more important in the view of government."

A stir outside the courtroom caused Chowdhury to stop talking and defer to a dominant figure making grand entrance. "The star has come," he said, speaking not of the defendant but of a celebrated lawyer named Frank Anthony, his co-counsel in the defense of Marie-Andrée. One of the most vivid and imperious men in India, Anthony was slim, silvery, and articulate, with dark circles about his eyes like the kohl of a heavily made-up woman. Anthony had not bothered very much with the case during the year of pretrial hearings; indeed he was scantly familiar with the details. But it did not matter if he had only read the case file in the taxi on the way to court. Anthony's brilliance was beyond argument. He was a slasher, a specialist in ripping, savage cross-examination, in picking out tiny flaws in the state's case that might be exploited or, better yet, ridiculed. Few if any surprises are to be found in an Indian murder trial. When a major crime has been committed and an arrest made, the police and prosecutor's office prepare what is known as a First Information Report, or FIR. It contains everything presumably discovered in the matter and often runs on for hundreds of pages. The FIR has statements from the accused, from witnesses, pathologists, police, a list of evidence, trivia, even unsubstantiated gossip—all bound in a ragged bundle and tied with string like a manuscript that an author has been trying for years—unsuccessfully—to get published. If a lower court magistrate decides that enough evidence exists in the FIR to establish a *prima facie* case, then what corresponds to an indictment is delivered by the bench. And by the time trial begins, everybody and his brother have read the FIR—lawyers on both sides, the press, even the defendants. Charles Sobhraj of course obtained an early copy and studied it so ardently that it was almost in shreds, vividly marked in red ink where he discovered passages that might be turned to his advantage.

The defense does very little research. Rarely are private investigators engaged to run about looking for surprise witnesses or new pieces of evidence. Rather, the accused's lawyers concentrate on attempting to devastate the prosecution's case as detailed in the FIR. *That* was Frank Anthony's forte, and everyone assembling in the small, fetid courtroom anticipated a crackling good show. "The court has three heads," commented Rupinder Singh, lawyer for Charles and the man who once went to Saigon in search of Sobhraj the Tailor and found the old man rich and dying. "They are the judge, the prosecution, and the defense. All three heads study the case, the precedents, the evidence—and all three heads reach a conclusion. Three brains are at work here, so it is not the burden of one man. Theoretically, that is."

Rupinder, or Rupi as he was known by everyone around the courthouse, had been fired by Charles on several occasions, but he refused to accept his termination. Standing rail thin in his dusty French-cut blazer and peacock blue turban, his eyes both hidden and amplified behind thick magenta-hued glasses, Rupi looked like a magician in search of a booking. He knew that this was a major case that would shower publicity on all the participants. He also sensed that there was money to be made, and if gold fell on the courtroom floor, he was going to be there scrambling. As it would turn out, Charles used attorneys like ventriloquists used dummies.

The defendants entered to the music of clanking chains, boots, and guns. The first was Jean Dhuisme, blinking and bewildered, looking like an owl awakened at midday. Those near the case had a modicum of sympathy for the

Frenchman with the melancholy face and the floorwalker's mustache. Even Inspector Tuli commented to a newsman that Dhuisme's role was minor. But Dhuisme was misfortunate enough to have been around when Jean-Luc Solomon died, and now he had to pay the check. When a lawyer asked during these opening moments if he was ill with influenza, for he appeared pale and clammy, Dhuisme shook his head. "No," he said. "I have a disease called 'being tried for murder.' There is no pill you can take to feel better."

Marie-Andrée's appearance disappointed those who anticipated a *femme fatale* of romantic dimension. Small, bird-like, she seemed to have wandered mistakenly away from a tour group of spinsters. Her hair was freshly dyed an unconvincing shiny black (perhaps due to the bitchy comment of a Canadian woman journalist who wrote that 'Mademoiselle Leclerc is 31 but looks 50 and acts 16.'). Unlike the other defendants, she was not handcuffed or chained. From a distance, she seemed fresh, wholesome if not pretty, but face to face, the former medical secretary was hard. Aging. Once again the wallflower. No more was she the glowing youth on her passport, the one that smiled contentedly when so long ago she had flown to Asia on a first fling at impulsive adventure. On this crucial morning, she fingered a dangling ivory cross about her neck and carried a book by Billy Graham. Her face was grave and lined, in contrast to the festive green and yellow long skirt and skinny-ribbed yellow sweater that was stretched across breasts of modest proportion. Hovering ever behind her were two motherly matrons in military saris on which were sewn the red insignia of sergeants. They permitted the prisoner to roam freely about the room, but they were never more than an elbow away.

Then came Charles.

He could not be glimpsed until the phalanx of guards parted and funneled him toward a chair. With chains and manacles draped about his limbs, he looked like a monkey on a leash. Small, haggard, his French clothes having become shredded or torn by guards, he faced the bench on this day in jeans and a polo shirt, hugely embarrassed to be so commonly garbed. The night before, he had written his last will and testament and mailed it to Félix d'Escogne in Paris. Was the man at last fatalistic? Was he resigned to doom? Or was this a new charade? Probably the last, for he calculatedly slipped the news to a reporter, perhaps hoping for a gift of sympathy.

Charles looked quickly about the room and sized it up. Small, barely thirty paces from one wall to another, an elevated section at one end was dominant where the judge and his clerk would sit.

The presiding judge, Joginder Nath, a stocky man with a wide, coppery face who resembled the actor Ed Asner, took his seat with an attitude of bewilderment over the commotion in his chambers. At this moment he did not realize the magnitude of the case, but he would soon learn. Judge Nath was not celebrated for the brilliance of his legal mind—no one would accuse him of being a scholar —but he was at least respected for honesty. "That's something in a country where the magistrate judge is paid forty-five dollars a month and the sessions court judge— like Nath—gets a hundred fifty," remarked attorney Chowdhury during the first recess. Many of India's judges are little more than a joke to competent lawyers. The pay is so low that few men of excellent capacities accept an appointment. The positions are supposedly plums, but the government usually has to scout around looking for some lawyer willing, or badly off enough, to accept the fruit.

The trial lurched into life. No rap of a gavel. No clearing of an official throat. The judge simply nodded casually at the public prosecutor, a man who, no matter what his real name, would be referred to by his job's initials, "P.P." The P.P. bowed in respect and in a small, metallic voice announced his first witness.

It was a shock.

Into the courtroom strolled Barbara Smith. She had not died from her intended last meal of sleeping pills and insect repellent. In fact, she looked terrific.

On that fateful night in May when the two girls attempted suicide, a night guard had routinely strolled past their cell. The guard liked the two approvers and called out to them, as was her custom. When she received no response, the guard quickly unlocked the cell and hurried to the crumpled forms. They seemed quite dead, and the Resident Medical Officer at the prison hospital doubted if there was the slightest ember of life worth fanning. But he rammed a nasogastric tube down their nostrils and into the esophagus, then washed out stomachs with saline solution. "Five minutes later and it wouldn't have mattered," he said, pleased and surprised as signs of life crept slowly back—and annoyed that he had not suspected Mary Ellen when he caught her redhanded coming out of the medicine room. By the next morning, both girls were alive. On the second day they were out of danger, and on the third fully conscious but disappointed that death had been stolen from them.

Within a week, both were returned to the cell and warned that the government might lodge charges of attempted murder, *of themselves*. "That's justice!" snapped Barbara. "Here we promise to help convict the most notorious criminal in Asia, and we may wind up getting ten years in Tihar for trying to do our bloody selves in." As the girls recovered, an investigation was conducted. Naturally the initial reaction was that someone else had poisoned the approvers. When Tuli heard the news, he swore and slammed his fist against his desk. "Somehow Charles got to them," he told an associate. "We should have had somebody watching those women twenty-four hours a day." Even when the revelation came that the would-be suicides had been just that, Tuli was not altogether convinced that the seed of the poison flower had not been planted by a gardener named Sobhraj.

The waltz with death had a profound albeit varying effect on Mary Ellen and Barbara. During the next several weeks, Barbara hardened her resolve to testify against Charles *et al*. But Mary Ellen was having second thoughts. A few days before the murder trial began, the Australian nurse attended a pretrial hearing and informed the bench that her statement had been "coerced" and contained errors. As she spoke, she suddenly began to shake as if in the grip of palsy. She began to scream. "I can't take this much longer!" She continued screaming until she was led in collapse from the courtroom. Tuli was present, and he wondered if the chaotic events of the girl's life had so rattled her that she could no longer distinguish fact and fantasy. And would she affect Barbara's resolve?

"What is your name?" asked P.P., whose name was Daljit Singh. He was gnome-like, with a plodding, unspectacular personality.

"Barbara Smith." The witness stood in the center of a football huddle. Before the judge she was the core of a crescent moon that contained all the lawyers, leaning in, trying to hear over the hum of ceiling fans that simply moved hot sticky air around a little, while at the same time drowning out speech. The decorum associated with Western courtrooms was totally absent. In its place was a legal free-for-all, lawyers squabbling, the witness trying to be heard, the defendants standing directly beside her, close enough to touch, clearly able to cajole or whisper. Above them sat the judge, at this point more of a referee than a Solomon, trying with courtesy and a pained expression to listen to everybody.

Most curious, testimony was *not* taken down in a fashion remotely approaching verbatim. Instead, the judge's custom was to listen to the witness's answer, then he repeated it by dictation to the court clerk, a Sikh in a scarlet and gold turban and with a fierce-looking pocked face. The clerk then pounded out the judge's version on an ancient typewriter that added to the clamor. Often what the witness actually said and what eventually filtered through the babble and the judge and the ancient typewriter were not only different but *substantially* different. The judge considered it his franchise to edit, censor if the testimony was too spicy for his prudish ears, and to paraphrase. The Western observers at the trial were flabbergasted by the cavalier handling of the official record. But it is the Indian way. And it *is* their country. "In America, a case might be overturned because of a misplaced comma," said a visiting attorney from New York. "Here the witness is fortunate if seventy-five per cent of the testimony is taken down exactly as it is uttered."

The P.P. led Barbara through a brisk series of biographical questions before the judge announced, not surprisingly, that he could not hear. Would the witness please move closer to the bench and take it all again, from the top? Nodding, Barbara moved sideways and forward, standing now in a puddle of water, close enough for Charles Sobhraj to reach out and pinch. He was half an arm away. His eyes bore meanly at her and she must have felt their heat. But she did not look at him; she appeared unafraid. More than one reporter marveled at her spunk.

"When did you first meet Charles Sobhraj?" asked P.P., wiping a film of sweat from his brow. The social and economic dichotomy between the government counsel and the defense lawyers was delineated by what they wore. The P.P. had on baggy white trousers that threatened to fall to his knees, a black cotton coat with perspiration marks striping his back, and a blue turban mottled with dampness. The other side, to a man, wore splendidly tailored gray striped trousers, black coats, and white flapping choirboy collars. And they managed to look cool, as if their caste did not tolerate public perspiration. In particular Frank Anthony looked elegant enough for presentation to the Queen. In his early sixties, he was exceptionally fair, unlike the darker faces around him. As the prosecutor worked with Barbara, the waspish Mr. Anthony sat sidesaddle below the judge, on a long shelf, and delivered a running barrage of acidulous remarks—sarcastic, often condescending, all directed at no one in particular save some legal god to whom he regularly raised his eyes. They were decidedly intrusive, but the judge did not tell him to shut up. Anthony was, after all, a founding father of the new India and an author of the constitution. He was a man to whom respect was paid.

"I first met Charles in June 1976, in Bombay," answered Barbara.

"Who introduced you?"

"A Belgian." She did not reveal Hugey Courage's name, nor did the defense press her on later cross-examination.

"What did Charles Sobhraj tell you about himself?"

"He told me he was a big businessman." Barbara spoke now in the tone of a tape-recorded announcement, like witnesses do when they are hewing carefully to a rehearsed script.

"What did he ask you to do?"

"He asked me to accompany him to Japan."

"Was Marie-Andrée Leclerc also known as Monique?"
Barbara nodded cheerfully. "Yes, that was her alias."

The P.P. paused, half expecting an objection from
Frank Anthony. But none came. Pleased to have slipped a
strong word like "alias" into the record, the prosecutor
hurried along. He was a competent lawyer, time would
tell, but void of color or flair. His questioning was as dry
as November leaves.

"When did you come to Delhi?" he asked.

"On June 18, 1976. I came with Mary Ellen Eather."

"Who paid the fare?"

"Alain. I knew Charles Sobhraj as Alain."

"What were your instructions?"

"Alain told us to stay in the Lodhi Hotel and to visit
the Oberoi and Imperial Hotel jewelry shops and check
out ornaments and other valuables."

"What for?"

"He did not tell us the purpose," answered Barbara. She
went on to tell how Hugey Courage disappeared from their
midst and fled to Goa, and how Charles and Jean Dhuisme
raced off in pursuit of him.

"What happened when Alain returned to Delhi?"

"He ordered me to go to the Ranjit Hotel and book two
rooms . . . we got Rooms 125 and 315. Everybody had
lunch at the hotel restaurant. After lunch, Alain instructed me and Mary Ellen to 'have an acquaintance' with
a French tourist we saw sitting in the lobby. His name,
later on, came to be known as Jean-Luc Solomon."

From a worn and shabby folder, the P.P. promptly
withdrew two tiny, postage-stamp-size photographs of the
dead tourist and passed them around. Everybody, including Charles and Marie-Andrée, strained to peer at the
thin, bearded, intelligent-looking young Frenchman. It was
the only moment of the trial when the victim became
more than an abstract name tossed about from time to
time. Nothing else about him was revealed, neither his
work, nor his age, nor his purpose in being in India, nor
his dreams. He could have been given a number and referred to by that, for all the form his life and death took
in this courtroom.

"Then what happened?"

"After some talk, I and Mary Ellen went to the bar of

the hotel with Mr. Solomon. Alain and Jean Dhuisme also came. They had a conversation with Mr. Solomon in French which I could not understand. Then Alain suggested we all have dinner. We went to the United Coffee House at seven-thirty."

The P.P. nodded contentedly. His witness was under control. She was testifying calmly and forthrightly, sticking resolutely to the story. "What happened at dinner,"

"Alain suggested we all have chicken curry . . . Alain took out from his pocket a small plastic bottle and placed it on the table. Solomon inquired about the contents of the bottle. Alain told him it was for stomach problems . . ."

"Then what did Alain do?"

As she prepared to answer, Charles edged closer, close enough for Barbara to feel his breath. Reporters saw him mutter something which she obviously heard. But she did not falter.

"Alain mixed the contents of the plastic bottle with the curry meant for Solomon," answered Barbara. Beside her, Charles shook his head in theatrical negation. The judge saw him and frowned, but said nothing.

"Were you aware of the effects of the contents of this colorless liquid?" asked the P.P.

Barbara nodded. "I knew that the contents would make a person tired. Or dead."

Judge Nath interrupted. He had not heard clearly the witness's last remark, damning as it was. "Make a person *what?*" he echoed.

Barbara shrugged. "Go to sleep," she said.

Charles smiled and hurriedly repeated what Barbara said. "She said, 'Go to sleep . . .'"

The judge nodded and dictated the altered statement to his clerk: "I knew that the contents would make a person go to sleep." Somehow the original words "Or dead . . ." that had come out of Barbara's mouth did not make it into the record. It was an important bit of sleight-of-mouth from the defendant, who, of course, had no right whatsoever to butt in.

"Please continue," said the prosecutor, who did not object. Perhaps he had not heard Barbara either.

"While taking dinner," she went on, "Alain found out

that Solomon intended to take a train that evening out of Delhi. Alain said it was too bad, because if Solomon did not leave Delhi, he could sleep with me."

With classic Indian modesty, Judge Nath altered this testimony and dictated it to read instead: ". . . if Solomon did not leave Delhi, he could *stay* with me." Barbara permitted herself a look of humorous disbelief.

Now the P.P. eased his witness gently to the moment after dinner when she and the soon-to-be-dead French tourist were in Room 125 together—alone. Barbara testified that Alain appeared with more pills in hand.

"Alain gave one capsule to me and one to Solomon . . . I did not take mine because I knew it would induce sleep . . . Solomon was feeling tired, so he lay down on the bed. He was already under the influence of the contents of the plastic bottle . . .

At this, Charles glowered and tried to nudge Rupi in the ribs to make an objection. The witness was dropping expert medical testimony into the record, and she was not qualified as an authority on pills. But Rupi did not object, nor did Marie-Andrée's lawyers, and all Charles could do was squirm uncomfortably and mouth, silently, "Objection."

Barbara continued briskly: "Alain said he was leaving, but in fact he remained on the hotel room balcony . . . After a while, Solomon got up and went to the bathroom for a shower. While he was in the shower, Alain called me to the balcony and gave me some more white tablets, which he instructed me to administer to Solomon."

The prosecutor nodded. The dark story was coming across powerfully. The judge was rapt, sometimes shaking his head as he repeated more or less what Barbara was saying and watched the clerk hammer at the old typewriter.

"Did you administer these tablets?" asked the P.P.

"No."

"Why not?"

"Because I felt he was *already* sleepy . . . Solomon came out of the bathroom and lay down on the bed. Alain came in from the balcony and asked if I had administered the tablets to Solomon. I told him that I had. Alain then gave

some more tablets to Solomon and he went to sleep . . ."
Reading between the lines, Solomon was apparently groggy
and staggering.

"And?"

"Alain opened Solomon's bag and found two hundred
rupees and six hundred dollars in traveler's checks . . .
Alain then left with Solomon's bag and said he would
return early the next morning."

The next morning, Barbara testified, Charles scurried
around the hotel rounding up his entourage. He was anxious to be on the road for Agra, where the sixty French
tourists were in brief residence. After a hurried breakfast,
said Barbara, she returned to Room 125 and was shocked
to find that Solomon was gone! She summoned Charles,
who appeared quickly. He did not believe that Solomon
could have possibly left Room 125. And he was correct.
"We found Solomon on the bathroom floor, slumped beside the toilet, semiconscious," testified Barbara. "We put
him on the bed under the ceiling fan and gave him water
to drink and put a damp sheet over him."

The prosecutor intruded, as if he had forgotten someone. "Where was Monique?" he asked. The name of Marie-
Andrée Leclerc had not yet become part of the tale and
the state needed to link her to the death.

The question roused Frank Anthony like a rock thrown
at a sleeping lion.

"Monique has not been introduced in this tale, not even
remotely suggested," he said, his voice crackling like a
whip over the babble in the room.

Barbara was not afraid of the imperious lawyer. "I believe I saw her in the coffee shop," she said.

Anthony frowned and addressed the bench. "I object
to this witness saying she 'believes' she saw somebody.
She's being coached. They're trying to get her to say
something. I'm sorry."

The P.P. got testy, too. "You may be sorry, Mr. Anthony, but I'm not."

Anthony drew himself up, haughtily, and gazed at the
P.P. as if encountering an arrogant beggar. "Shame," he
said. "Tsk, tsk." He really said, "Tsk, tsk."

The judge separated the scuffers. "Let's get on. Then
what happened?"

Barbara continued her account. The group—herself, Mary Ellen, Jean Dhuisme, "Monique" and "Alain"—assembled in front of the hotel and prepared to leave in the Citroën for Agra. Alain was the last to arrive.

"Why?" asked the prosecutor. He was carefully trying to get Marie-Andrée's name into the story as often as possible.

"I asked Monique and she said Alain had gone back to Room 125," answered Barbara. The sweat was pouring down her face and her skin was flushed, as if she had just emerged from a steam bath.

Frank Anthony jumped off his sidesaddle seat and was angry. "Objection, sir. *Objection!* I say this with regret, but I *must* object. This is a deliberate fabrication. This so-called story has already reached the stage where the accused and others are leaving for Agra. Now the public prosecutor is suddenly putting us back in the Ranjit Hotel, trying to get an answer to falsely implicate Miss Leclerc."

The judge did not rule on the objection, but dictated it into the record. As he waited, Anthony muttered loudly, "This witness is lying. I will deal with her later."

The prosecutor asked Judge Nath for permission to back up in Barbara's story. Apparently he had forgotten to elict an important point from his witness.

"Did you ever see Monique, Miss Leclerc, in Room 315 at the Ranjit Hotel?"

Barbara nodded vigorously. "Yes. They were sitting on the bed sorting out drugs."

At this, Frank Anthony slammed his hand down on the bench with force enough to lift the judge's papers and he leaned angrily across at the witness. "How many of these lies must we hear? This witness never said anything about Miss Leclerc sitting on a bed sorting out drugs in her first statement to police. She put it in later after they forced her to."

Charles and Marie-Andrée, standing next to one another, nodded in unison, cheering on their lawyer. "Lies, lies, lies," muttered Marie-Andrée, fingering her cross and rubbing it against her cheek, as if attempting to expel evil.

The judge held up his hands for order and asked Barbara with soft courtesy, "Have you made this particular statement before?"

"Yes," answered Barbara matter-of-factly. "I made this statement to police and to the other magistrate."

Anthony harrumphed. "Yes, and she adds lies each time." He thrust out a long finger at the English girl and shook it, like a schoolmaster warning a truant that punishment was due.

The prosecutor had but a few more items to cover. "Where were you arrested?" he asked the witness.

"At Wheels," she answered.

The judge raised his eyebrows. "What is Wheels?"

"A discotheque," explained Barbara. The night she was arrested, she had emerged from the powder room to find plainclothes detectives sitting at her table, waiting to bust her.

Judge Nath did not know what the word "discotheque" meant, nor did his clerk, who looked up from his ancient typewriter in confusion. "Just write down 'Wheels,'" suggested the judge.

Frank Anthony cut in sarcastically. "You'd better write down that it is a night club where young people dance. Some high court judge might think it is a garage."

The P.P. snapped his fingers and at the doorway to the courtroom, a small stir occurred as a burly, unshaven cop in slacks and a seldom washed sport shirt pushed through the crowd of guards. In his cupped hands, held before him like a priest approaching the altar, could be seen a small white cloth bag, tied at the neck with a red string. When he reached the bench, the policeman opened the little bag with great ceremony and care, while all the lawyers and defendants and even the judge and clerk leaned in with curiosity. Inside the white bag was another, smaller sack, this one green, and when it was opened, the contents were revealed—several pills of bluish, white and yellow hues, some crumbling, some broken in halves.

These pills, announced the prosecutor, were taken from the witness Barbara Smith at the moment of her arrest and were the ones which Charles Sobhraj had given her to feed to Jean-Luc Solomon.

"Do you remember the number of tablets taken from you by the police?" asked the prosecutor. Barbara shook her head. "Not the exact number," she answered.

Everyone peered at the tablets, their faces so close to the cloth that a sneeze might have blown the state's case out the window.

"Some of them were these?" asked the P.P.

"Yes," said Barbara with a positive tone. "I recognize them."

From his place, Charles Sobhraj snorted derisively. All morning long he had been making grandiose noises of disbelief and the judge either did not hear them or ignored them. But this time, Judge Nath whirled in his chair and dispatched a look of severe impatience. Charles elected to smile, boyishly, innocently.

On cross-examination, Frank Anthony tried to score a minor point but he was defeated by Barbara. Waving a list of the belongings seized by police when the girl was arrested, Anthony noted that it contained mention of "some pills" but that the list was not signed by Barbara or notarized. His implication was that the police had substituted a new list of personal effects.

The judge ordered Barbara to peruse the list and she did so, nodding. "This is a very faint carbon copy," she said. "My signature doesn't show, but this is definitely the list I signed." She thus deftly shot down *that* defense ploy.

At the end of the first day, Marie-Andrée begged the prison matrons for a moment alone with her co-counsel, S. N. Chowdhury. He had been overshadowed by the flamboyance of Frank Anthony, but he knew the case as well as anyone in the courtroom. Now he was in the position of a junior surgeon who opens the patient's chest, then must step aside while the celebrated senior man appears wreathed in glory and dips his hands into the open heart.

"How did it go for me?" asked Marie-Andrée. "You don't believe Barbara, do you? She's lying."

"What I believe is not very important," answered Chowdhury. "What the judge believes will determine your fate."

"You must make the judge understand she's lying," dictated Marie-Andrée. "I was never in Room 315 sorting out drugs. Don't think I'm stupid. I'm clever."

Chowdhury shook his head slowly, patiently. His client

obviously did not recognize the gravity of Barbara Smith's accusations.

"No, my dear, you are not clever," said Chowdhury. "Or else you would not have wrecked your life and so many others."

CHAPTER FORTY-FOUR

On the second day, Frank Anthony swept into the court-room like a maharaja en route to a great battle, trailing reporters, assistants, and sycophants. He was the kind of man for whom a path cleared automatically. He nodded brusquely at the P.P. and received, in reply, a chilled glance. The two lawyers were more than society's oppo-sites, they were symbols of the polarity of India. Anthony was the relic of Kipling's Raj, sleek as a wolfhound, a man accustomed to money and power. His opponent could have been Mahatma Gandhi's child—homely, untidy, a stubborn village cur. Theirs was a clash of castes, a prince dueling a gnome, the haves vs. the have-nots. Anthony's every moment in this dreadful courtroom registered on his face as offensive to his manner. Conversely the P.P. was at home, amid the fetid smells of dacoits and murder-ers. The hostility between the lawyers was evident. It would grow.

"Why are you in this case, Mr. Anthony?" asked a re-porter for a Delhi newspaper.

"Well, certainly not for the money," he answered. "Thus far I haven't earned taxi fare . . . I rarely do this kind of thing anymore." He sat down in a cane-backed chair and newsmen squatted beside him, like supplicants before the throne. He went on: "Fights like these are for the younger men. But these accused prisoners have been abused by the state. They were arrested under MISA, which should not have applied to them, and the state did not comply with mandatory procedures. The police have behaved disgracefully. Have you seen the police report? More than one half of it is letters, sheaves of letters, from foreign police and Interpol. What does this have to do with the case at hand? Does it matter if Charles Sobhraj is wanted in Turkey or Timbuktu? The state has tried to make their flimsy case seem more substantial by weighting it down with extraneous foreign matter. Now, if you will excuse me, I must prepare to cross-examine these young women who change their stories and attempt suicide on alternating days."

A few feet away the P.P., his turban soaked with sweat and slightly awry on his head, overheard Anthony's oration. He muttered to his assistant, a thin, gangling fellow with one eye out of control and the air of a mystic, "Mr. Anthony is upset . . . I should imagine that the families of these unfortunate murder victims do not share his feelings."

The prisoners were led into the room and instructed to wait quietly while the judge finished some paper work in his office. Charles was grateful for the delay. He had signed a contract with a Bangkok firm to merchandise his life story in a book or a film or both, and now he was dictating choice anecdotes from his career to an English writer. Marie-Andrée saw what was going on and approached Charles, but he shooed her away. A little hurt, she retreated to a chair and began reading the Bible, looking up from time to time to observe Charles whispering to his biographer. She was probably annoyed that he might reap substantial reward and nothing would go to her. Other reporters hovered near Charles, hoping to embezzle a quote, but he was aware of them and spoke so softly that only his authorized biographer could hear. The scene was insane, but then it fitted right in with the larger event.

Just before the session began, a reporter hurried in with dramatic news. A coup was taking place in Pakistan, the government of Bhutto was falling. "Good," snapped Frank Anthony. "We need one here."

* * *

Mary Ellen Eather caught the eye of every man when she entered the courtroom. The former Australian nurse wore hot pink Bengali pants and a filmy blouse embroidered with mock emeralds and rubies. In her nose a gold pin glittered. She approached the bench gracefully and bowed, making the hands-folded sign of respect to the judge. Six weeks earlier she had swallowed one hundred sleeping pills and was not expected to live. Today she looked like a model, set down in a bizarre showcase to please the whim of a fashion editor.

The P.P. studied her cautiously, like a man standing before a door that led to an unknown room. The prosecutor well knew that his witness was emotional and unpredictable. She had hinted that she might recant certain portions of her original statement to police. But the P.P. had to use her nonetheless. He picked up his file and prepared to begin. All the participants promptly squeezed around Mary Ellen, at least thirty people pushing ears as close as possible to hear the singsong interchanges. English is the official court language of India. Frank Anthony, who spoke like an Oxford don, was a passionate advocate for retaining the once loathed tongue. But to the Western ear, it often sounds as exotic as the four hundred other dialects spoken in the subcontinent.

"When did you come to India?" asked the P.P.

"I came to India on June 5, 1976," she began.

The P.P. took her through a series of brief biographical questions, trying to keep her within the boundaries of her original statement. But she kept making little changes despite the prosecutor's prompting. Finally Mary Ellen snapped, testily, "May I make my statement on my own without having it dictated for me? It is my life that's at stake here, after all!"

Frowning, the prosecutor nodded. This kind of response is hardly what a government attorney wants to hear from his co-star witness. He thought briefly about stopping his questioning at this point, but it was too late. Frank Anthony would elicit the changes in Mary Ellen's story. The P.P. suspected that Charles had influenced her somehow. His arm reached to the far corners of prison, even to solitary.

She went on to testify that Charles and Marie-Andrée
met her on the beach, at Karachi, Pakistan. Charles was
using the name Alain.

"And what did Alain say to you?"

"He said he wanted to purchase a forged passport. This
was not surprising to me, as I had come to know that
people often did this in the Far East . . ."

The P.P. glanced at the judge, who dictated this sentence
into the record without a show of expression. It was helpful that the early words out of Mary Ellen's mouth
branded Charles as someone who dealt in forged passports.

"They were quite presentable people," continued Mary
Ellen, "so I invited them to come to my house to take
tea . . . There I learned Alain was a gem dealer and had
a part-time business with leather goods. He said he was
on his way to Europe to sell his merchandise. He offered
me a job to courier precious stones from one place to another . . . I said I would consider it, if I was still in Karachi
on his return from Europe . . . In a month, he returned
and I accepted his offer of employment, as he would pay
me a salary, expenses, give me travel opportunities, and
permit me to use my knowledge of stones."

The P.P. guided his witness to the point where Charles
and his entourage were occupying two rooms at the Ranjit
Hotel. In her original statement to police, Mary Ellen
said, "Charles instructed us to mix it up with the French
boy . . . and create intimacy with him." But now, as she
began to tell of her encounter with Jean-Luc Solomon, her
composure shredded. Her face turned as red as a poppy,
then drained of blood to become ashen. She wept, sobbing
loudly. Judge Nath was distressed. He leaned to the witness and said, not unkindly, "Please compose yourself,
Miss Eather."

The prosecutor made a quick decision. He elected to
push on before she collapsed altogether. He might not be
able to get her back on the stand. "So what did Charles
Sobhraj, or Alain as you knew him, tell you to do?"

Mary Ellen found control and answered brokenly.
"There was this Frenchman at the hotel . . . Charles told
us to be nice to him . . . and make friends." The P.P.
stared at his witness like a man betrayed. This new version
of Charles' orders was not nearly as harmful. To "create

intimacy" with an intended victim was one thing, to "make friends" made it sound as if the gang members were Good Samaritans.

Mary Ellen was just getting warmed up. When the P.P. moved her along in testimony to the moment when everyone was having dinner at the United Coffee House, she described the gathering as a pleasant social affair with no hidden undertones of poison and seduction.

"Just what happened at this dinner?" demanded the prosecutor.

"Nothing that I know of," answered Mary Ellen, bringing a scowl to the face of the prosecutor, and a smile of great satisfaction to Charles. More than one spectator in the chamber wondered if they were lovers.

The P.P. began a comment of reproach, designed to suggest that the girl was changing stories from what she had originally told police, but Mary Ellen throttled him. "This is the truth! After all, I'm being judged."

Wisely, the prosecutor did not argue, for the witness's nerves were stretched as tautly as they could go, and the emotional outbursts were in sharp contrast to the cool and unshakable testimony from Barbara Smith.

From this point on, Mary Ellen denied four or five other passages from her sworn statement, the most important being that, to her knowledge, Jean-Luc Solomon was *not* given any drugs. "This is what happened," she said. "Barbara called me to Room 125 and said Luc had fainted in the bathroom. I found him slumped against the wall beside the toilet, not fully conscious. I asked Barbara if he had taken narcotics or drugs, for he seemed to be showing symptoms. Barbara Smith replied, 'Not that I know of.' "

Frank Anthony clapped his hands, as if applauding a beautifully spoken line of dialogue in the theater. "That's important," he said. "The witness said, *'Not that I know of, not that I know of.'* " Beside him, Charles glowed in small triumph.

"I checked the boy," continued Mary Ellen, surely feeling the prosecutor's wrath at her elbow. The P.P. was steaming. "I checked his eye pupils, his pulse, his responses, he was making funny noises. I slapped him on the face and cried, 'Get up' and 'Wake up.' We helped him to bed, put a damp sheet on him, then the two of us left."

With that her tale was done. The P.P. hissed at her loud enough for all to hear, "Why are you lying?" And she shot back, "I'm *not* lying. I *was* lying . . . before . . . Now I am giving this court a true statement." During a brief recess, the P.P. was heard to say, "She got run over in prison. Somebody threatened her and it's not hard to imagine who." He glanced at the back of the room where Charles was once again ensconced and enthusiastically dictating his memoirs. The P.P. must have felt short-changed. He made less than a hundred dollars a month. But a man accused of multiple murder was receiving, rumor had it, a $35,000 down payment and a substantial percentage of future royalties. And not only was the prosecutor's case damaged by the rebellion of Mary Ellen, he was personally embarrassed by having the witness turn on him. The P.P. muttered to his aide that he might well file perjury charges.

Frank Anthony was ebullient. He told a group of reporters during a recess, "It's standard for our police to alter statements. It's shocking and sad—but it's true. These chaps always pad their cases. They will not leave good enough alone. And thank God they cheat. They enable me to go to the High Court and get clients off every other day by showing how their statements have been doctored . . . When the police do this to one of our people, a Hindu man or woman, they would never dare to repudiate it. Only a Western woman would have the courage."

The old legal lion strolled to Mary Ellen and patted her on the arm in compliment for her "honesty." Then, on cross-examination, Anthony introduced a new statement from the witness. Further damning to the state's case, it read, in part: "The police presented me with a statement which was fabricated. I was asked by police to depose this statement in court. I told them I could not make a statement that was false. The police stated that I was under their protection, that I would be granted a pardon, and that I had to state in court what they wanted me to . . . I was told that if I did not cooperate, I could be held under MISA without having counsel, or going before a magistrate, or having access to my embassy . . ."

Next Anthony had but a few gentle questions for Mary

Ellen. He did not want to risk another emotional eruption, and he was anxious to have at Barbara Smith.

"Did Barbara tell you that she was being pressured by the police to become an approver in this case?" he asked, making "approver" sound like Judas Iscariot.

"Yes," answered Mary Ellen.

"Now," continued Anthony, changing gears. "You say that during dinner at the United Coffee House, Alain took out a plastic bottle and put it on the table?"

"Yes."

"Did it have a label on it?"

"No."

"Was there anything to suggest the plastic bottle contained a drug?"

"No. It was like an eyedropper."

Before he asked the next question, Anthony put on a sour face, as if the approaching subject was offensive to him. "Presumably," he said, "Barbara Smith slept in Room 125 all night long?"

Mary Ellen nodded. "Yes."

"Only one bed in the room?"

"Yes."

"Presumably Barbara Smith and . . . what's his name?" Alas, the great advocate could not remember the name of the dead man. An aide rescued him with a whisper, "Jean-Luc Solomon."

". . . and Solomon slept in the same bed?"

Mary Ellen smiled for the first time. "I don't know. I wasn't there." She looked as if the mud on her skirts was suddenly gone.

Outside the courtroom, sitting on a bench between two prison matrons, Barbara watched in fascination as an ancient Moslem woman ate a spiced patty. She was in total black, like a raven, and her face was heavily veiled. It had been Barbara's hope that when the old woman began to eat she would remove her veil and expose her secret features. But no, she broke off tiny pieces and slipped the food up under her veil into her mouth, maintaining her privacy. "How extraordinary," murmured Barbara. It would be nice, she said, to proceed through life with a mask on the face. Then no one could tell precisely how you felt or looked. "I may become a Moslem in my dotage," she said. Then her name was called, and she rose.

"*If* I get there," she added. In the next few hours, she faced an ordeal. Anthony's knives were sharpened.

Once again wedging a place within the mob that congregated before the judge, Barbara looked impossibly young to be cast as the latest in a long line of conniving women that began with Eve. Her clothes were modest, and mannish—a polished-khaki cotton dress with a few bangles about her neck. She looked vacant, neither here nor there. The courtroom feeling was that Anthony would crush her in ten minutes. During his illustrious career he had devastated men of great power and intellect. Barbara Smith, only twenty, who had wanted to dance on the sands of Goa, would be a footnote at best in his autobiography.

The famed advocate went directly to what he considered the heart of the matter. Sex.

"Miss Smith, do you remember saying that Alain told Solomon he could sleep with you, and you agreed?"

"Yes." Barbara nodded, almost sweetly.

"How long had you known Luc Solomon?"

"I met him only on that day."

Anthony's eyebrows rose like flags at sunrise. "You are in the habit of sleeping with men you meet casually?"

"No." She shook her head weakly.

"Why did you agree to sleep with Luc?"

"Because Alain asked me to."

"I see. Did Alain ask you to sleep with him? With Alain, I mean?"

Barbara almost gasped. Across her face hurried disgust and a shudder. "No. Of course not."

"You slept there the whole night, in Room 125 of the Ranjit Hotel?"

"Yes." Judge Nath took a bit of this and a bit of that and dictated into the trial record, "I slept the whole night with Luc in Room 125." Which was not precisely what Barbara said.

"Are you conversant with drugs?" said Anthony abruptly. "Are you a peddler of drugs?"

Barbara gave the first question a half nod, but the second one got a sharp "No." But the judge interpolated and dictated an answer, again his own: "It is correct to say that I am conversant with drugs, but I am not a peddler." At this Barbara bit her lip to stop a giggle. Later she would tell a friend that she felt like Alice taking tea with the Mad Hatter.

"You mentioned this plastic bottle. What kind of a label did it have?"

"It didn't have one."

Anthony nodded as if pleased that the truth, long buried, was finally emerging. "What made you think it would put somebody to sleep?"

"Because Alain told me—just before we went to the coffee shop." Barbara waited impassively. She did not seem concerned over Anthony's intrusions. The perspiration on her face was due more to the aftermath of the morning's rainstorm, and the jumble of lawyers and reporters who pressed around her, than to the heat of cross-examination. If she fainted, she could not possibly fall to the ground. There was no room.

"Are you a special sort of confidante to Alain?"

"No."

"At the dinner table at the United Coffee Shop, you each had a glass of water, didn't you?" Barbara nodded. "And Alain is supposed to have said these drops from the plastic bottle were to purify water?"

Another nod.

"And you testified he poured these drops on the chicken? What for? To *purify* the chicken?" Anthony's voice was rich with sarcasm.

Barbara squirmed a little. "Well, yes, he did . . . but nobody else saw him."

"What was the size of the table?"

"For six people."

"How big?" Anthony tried to rattle her by demanding details. "Three feet by two feet? As wide as this?" He slapped the bench in front of the judge.

"I don't know," said Barbara. "If you provide me with a ruler, perhaps I could answer. I don't normally measure a table size in a restaurant. Do you?"

Anthony scowled, but the judge was laughing. Score one for Barbara.

"Where was everybody sitting?" demanded Anthony.

"Alain and Mary Ellen were on one side. Dhuisme, me, and Luc on the other."

"Was there one portion of chicken curry?"

"One big plate. Five portions."

"So what happened?"

"Alain served Solomon's curry first. Then the rest of us helped ourselves. I saw Alain put in the colorless liquid when he was serving Solomon."

Looking dubious, Anthony threw out his hands as if trying to stop a tower of lies from tumbling onto his head. "Just how did he do this? Demonstrate for us! Tell us, come on!" Barbara was happy to answer, but she could not find an opening between Anthony's machine-gun fire. He shot forth a dozen, each growing in volume and tempo.

"Come on, Miss Smith. We're waiting. Show us. Demonstrate for us. Did he do it near his chest, or in front of Luc's chest, or under the table? Did he take Luc's chicken curry to the toilet? Didn't anybody else see this being done? Mary Ellen Eather was sitting right there and *she* didn't see anything."

Barbara waited patiently. The moment Anthony ran out of breath, she answered, sweetly. "Well, I did. As Alain was putting chicken on Luc's plate, he poured in the colorless liquid."

Putting his hands to his ears, Anthony wisely changed the subject. The girl was not budgeable on the subject of chicken curry.

"Tell me," he asked, his voice newly calm and flat. "You became an approver on what date?"

"I don't remember." Anthony fished among his papers and located a date. August 3, 1976. Barbara agreed this was correct.

"When did the police ask you to become an approver?"

Barbara shook her head negatively. "They did not ask me." Judge Nath dictated her response a little differently: "I decided to become an approver on my own."

Anthony didn't buy this at all. "Didn't you complain to Mary Ellen that you were under intense police pressure to become an approver?"

"No."

The girl was uncrackable on this point.

Frustration was edging into Anthony's voice. The other lawyers, those representing Charles and Jean Dhuisme, tried to whisper suggestions in Anthony's ear, but if he heard them he did not show it. He elected to use an old technique favored by defense lawyers the world over—rattle the witness's memory for small details.

"Do you have a phenomenal memory?" wondered Anthony.

"No," said Barbara. "I've got a normal memory."

"At what age did you leave school?"

"Sixteen. But I took some college courses. Finished fifth form. I passed government exams in English, biology, and chemistry."

Anthony did not seem to believe this. "Give me the name of the person who signed your certificate," he demanded.

"I don't remember," answered Barbara. "Why should I?"

"Give me the address of your last school," pushed Anthony.

"Testwood Secondary School, Totton Near Southampton, Hampshire, England."

Once again failing, Anthony tried a little meanness: "Tell me, Miss Smith, you deliberately *lied* on page 164 of this record . . ."

Barbara shook her head. "What are you referring to?" she asked politely.

Anthony poked around in his papers trying to find where she "deliberately *lied*." It took him several minutes, while everyone waited in modest suspense. "Ah," he said. "You testified that you went up to Room 315 and found Alain and Monique unpacking some drugs. That isn't true, is it?"

"It's not a lie. I stated this before the magistrate."

"But in your original statement it is not there."

"I don't know why," said Barbara. "I said it."

Charles Sobhraj leaned into Anthony's ear and spoke urgently. But the lawyer was so annoyed at the witness that he snapped at the defendant, "Please let me do the questioning, sir!" And beside *his* witness, the P.P. was aglow, like a boxing coach whose challenger was standing up to the most devious punches of the title holder. Now and then he patted Barbara on the back. Judge Nath took exception to none of this.

Anthony changed directions again. Perhaps he could so sully the reputation of the witness that her testimony would smell like tainted meat. Official India does not care much for the hippies who wander through her arteries in search of drugs and mystical revelations.

"How long have you been on the road? Without funds?" he asked.

"I had all my money stolen in June 1976, in Bombay—at the Apollo Guest House."

"Did you make a report to the police?"

"No. It wouldn't have done any good."

"From June 1976, you were living off of Alain?" asked Anthony, making it sound as if Barbara was an expensive concubine.

"I suppose so," she agreed. "I was working for him."

"Before June, who supported you?"

Barbara did not hesitate. "A friend."

"One of those *platonic* friends of yours?" sneered Anthony. "What was his name?"

"Paul."

"Paul? Did he have a surname?"

"I don't know."

Anthony smiled knowingly, glad to have a minor victory, anxious for the judge to understand that here was a girl who lived off men, who took lovers whose last name, she did not bother to learn. Anthony told the judge, "Please put in the record that she does not even know this Paul's surname." The judge nodded. He, too, appeared troubled by a young woman who drifted so hedonistically through his country.

"How much was he giving you a day, this Paul?"

"I don't know. A few rupees to eat."

Again Anthony's eyebrows reached for the ceiling. "How much? My dog costs me fifteen rupees a day." This was an astonishing statement in a country where millions of people—some of whom are magistrates—earn less than that a day.

"You have a very lucky dog," parried Barbara appropriately.

Anthony would not let the question go, even though it drenched him with condescension. "Come on. How much?

How much did this lover with no last name pay you for your favors?"

"Five rupees a day, perhaps."

"Five rupees!" exclaimed Anthony in disbelief. "And you ate on that? Will you be *my* shopper?" He extended his finger and shook it at Barbara once more. "I put it to you that you were living by prostitution in Bombay."

"Rubbish!" Barbara's eyes had newly lit fire.

"Charles told you to 'make up' to the Frenchman, according to your testimony. What was the purpose?"

Barbara shrugged. "I don't know."

"Was the purpose to murder?"

"No. Of course not."

"Was the purpose to drug him? Or rob him?"

"No." Judge Nath rolled these answers around in his head and dictated an answer that was favorable to the defense. The judge told the court clerk to type down: "It is correct to say that there was no purpose to murder him or drug him or rob him." Barbara started to protest. Her answers had been misconstrued. She meant that from her point of view there was no mission of murder. She had *not* meant to clear Charles of intent or deed. But she realized it would take more patience than she possessed at this moment to sort it all out. "I thought to myself, To hell with them all," she would say later.

Anthony asked the witness if she remembered seeing the bits and pieces of pills that had been introduced the day before. Barbara nodded. These were supposedly the ones that Charles gave her to administer to Jean-Luc Solomon.

"Why didn't you return these to Alain?" demanded Anthony.

"Because I had told Alain I gave them to Luc."

"Then you *lied* to Alain?"

"Not really. I just didn't want to give Luc any more pills. He was staggering."

Suddenly Marie-Andrée, who had been silent most of the morning, began to make a whimpering noise. Charles squeezed her arm and she stopped. When he took his arm away, there were angry red marks from his powerful fingers.

"What were those tablets? Barbiturates?"

"I have no idea," said Barbara.

"Do you take Mandrax?" said Anthony, invoking the name of a potent sleeping pill made from mandrake root.

"No." The judge dictated: "It is incorrect to say that I am in the habit of taking Mandrax."

Anthony found the answer unacceptable. "Come on, Miss Smith. I read American magazines. You people on the road get high on many drugs."

Barbara opened her mouth to deny, but Anthony wasn't finished. He needed to establish the girl as a sophisticate in drug use. "What is Mandrax? You would be a great disservice to your tribe if you did not know."

"I know a lot of people take it for insomnia."

"You saw Luc naked, didn't you?"

Barbara nodded. "Yes."

"And you did notice that he had a series of hypodermic needle marks on his arms?"

"No." Barbara looked puzzled. What was Anthony driving at?

"Did you know he was a drug addict? *Hard* drugs?"

"No, I didn't know that."

Anthony was tired. His face showed the wrath of age that had not been present when this day began. He had hammered at Barbara for hours and had, it seemed, accomplished very little. In a quiet and weary voice he made one last attempt to defame her.

"Weren't you traveling on a false passport?" he asked.

"No," said Barbara, laughing merrily. She knew she had won.

"That's all," said Anthony, exhausted, washing his hands of the witness. He slumped in a chair while a junior man hurried out for a glass of sweet tepid tea to revive the greatest lawyer in India.

But Barbara was not quite done. Another lawyer wanted a crack at her. Charles had engaged a new advocate to supplement the indefatigable Rupi Singh, who seemed to have been downgraded to the role of gofer. The new man, S. K. Sharma, was ferociously handsome with a scar curving around one eye like a scimitar. During Barbara's long stay in the witness box, Charles had made notes on his

FIR copy. Now he gave them to his new lawyer and in-structed Sharma to attack.

Barbara returned to the dock, her hair newly festooned with fragrant white blossoms. Someone in the corridor had given them to her with a compliment for her strength. She looked fresh, and very pretty, and proud of standing up to Anthony.

Sharma began softly. "I believe you took some pills in a suicide attempt in May," he said, sympathetically.

"Yes," said Barbara. It was no secret matter. Delhi's papers had been full of it.

"How many?"

"Seventy-five or eighty."

"Where did you obtain them?"

"From the dispensary of the jail. Female department."

Lawyer Sharma launched into a rambling, demeaning little speech about how he did not blame her for trying to end her life. Since she had told "so many lies," obvi-ously her conscience must have been inflamed and fester-ing. Judge Nath tolerated a few minutes of this before he turned uncharacteristically stern. He had let Frank An-thony wander all over the lot. But to Sharma he said brusquely, "Do you have a question, sir? Then ask it."

Sharma asked the obvious, *"Why* did you take seventy-five or eighty barbiturates?"

Barbara was ready. "I took the tablets because I was very depressed . . . I had spent one endless year in jail, and it was horrible."

The judge nodded in understanding. He rearranged her answer for the record: "And as the conditions in jail were unacceptable to me, they brought on depression and I attempted suicide."

Sharma's voice suddenly lashed out, harsh and cold. "I put it to you that you had made so many false state-ments that your conscience was hurting you."

Barbara glared at the menacing new lawyer. "No, sir. That is not true."

"Well, then, after you were arrested by the police at Wheels discotheque, how many days were you kept in the police lockup undergoing interrogation?"

"Mmmm. About a week."

"During that week, how many police officers came into contact with you?"

"Many."

"And did not every police officer ask you to become a witness for the prosecution to save your skin?" Sharma was shouting. Judge Nath held out a steadying hand in suggestion that he turn the volume down.

"No."

"No?" The lawyer echoed the girl's answer in disbelief. Sharma circled around Barbara for almost an hour, attempting to put across a new theory. Charles Sobhraj and Jean-Luc Solomon were speaking in French, weren't they? Then how could Barbara have known what was being discussed during the notorious chicken curry dinner. *Perhaps* they had been talking about stomach problems. *Perhaps* Charles asked the French tourist if he wanted the colorless liquid added to his meal to forestall dysentery. *Perhaps* Charles was performing an act of kindness toward a new friend.

Barbara listened patiently to the lawyer's hymn to fellowship but she finally had to laugh. "Not bloody likely," she said, so softly that no one else picked up on it.

"All right," said Sharma, as Charles purred in his ear. "Miss Smith, if you *knew* the contents of this bottle would make a man sleep, did you warn Mr. Solomon?"

"No."

"During this entire dinner, did you ever mention *anything* to Solomon about this liquid?"

"No."

The next question logically would have been, "Why not?" But Sharma, of course, dared not ask it because the answer might have been, "Because Charles told me not to." Instead Sharma rushed hurriedly to Room 125, where Solomon died. "When you went with Luc to Room 125, did he tell you he was feeling sleepy?"

Barbara said that was correct.

"And at that time, you and Luc were the only persons in the room?" Again, Barbara nodded.

"But you did not tell Luc that he was sleepy due to the effects of a drug?"

"No."

"Luc went to sleep immediately after that?" asked Sharma, as his client nodded behind him.

"Yes," said Barbara, fumbling. "But wait . . ."

She had more to tell, but Sharma stopped her. He wanted to leave it right there, with Luc passing out, not discussing the previous testimony that Charles came into the hotel room with more pills. Barbara got stubborn. She would not permit herself to be extinguished without shedding a little more light.

"My answer, sir," she said quickly, "is that Luc lay down on the bed feeling sleepy, then he got up to take a shower. Charles came in at that point with more pills, and then Luc went to sleep." The words raced out, so pell-mell that the judge asked her to repeat them. They thus had a double impact. Charles' face blazed with irritation. He bent into Sharma's ear again.

"Do you or do you not know that there were some medicines recovered from the baggage of Jean-Luc Solomon?" the lawyer asked.

"I do not know." The question seemed unimportant, as few Western travelers would brave the East without some medication in their toilet kit.

"Do you know that Luc Solomon was addicted to drugs and aphrodisiacs?"

"Aphrodisiacs?" echoed Barbara, trying to keep from breaking up. "No, I did not know."

Sharma frowned and looked at the judge, suggesting that the bench chastise the witness for impudent laughter. "Now, Miss Smith," he finally went on, "I say to you that Mr. Solomon took tablets and aphrodisiacs on his own."

"I did not see him do that. On his own."

Judge Nath, a little nervous in this swamp of sex and drugs, dictated her answer as "I did not see Luc take drugs and aphrodisiacs." At that, the P.P. rocketed out of his place and reminded the judge that he had omitted the key phrase *"on his own."* This was important. Had the record stood without the addition of the three little words, it would have indicated that Barbara had not seen Solomon take *any* "drugs or aphrodisiacs."

Sharma decided to try and paint Barbara as the whore of Babylon, even though Anthony had failed miserably.

"I put it to you that you had sex with Jean-Luc Solomon—for money," he said.

"I did not," said Barbara indignantly. Now *she* was showing streaks of anger.

"Isn't it a fact that in your country and other Western countries, young people consume aphrodisiacs and stimulants to enhance sex?" Sharma sounded as pious as a preacher.

"I don't know," answered Barbara.

"It may be true?" suggested Sharma.

"Perhaps," agreed the witness.

Sharma got down in the dirt. "Isn't it a fact that when Mary Ellen came to wake you up the next morning, you were scantily dressed?"

"No," said Barbara.

"You were naked, weren't you!" thundered the scar-faced lawyer.

"No," said Barbara calmly.

"Half naked?" countered Sharma, sounding like a haggler in the bazaar making a counteroffer.

Barbara smiled rather coquettishly. "I had a few things on."

Judge Nath considered these exchanges and put them through his prudish mill. It came out, as he dictated to the clerk, "It is a fact that when Mary Ellen Eather came to awaken me, I was only half dressed."

Sharma was defeated, but he threw one last weak punch.

"What 'talks' did you have with Solomon when you first met him?" he asked, the question suggesting that their conversation dealt with the price of sex.

"I don't know," answered Barbara. ". . . general conversation." The blossoms in her hair had wilted in the steamy courtroom and they were dropping onto her khaki dress.

Sharma repeated her answer for the judge, pressing him to dictate a distorted version of her answer. Sharma wanted the record to read: "I cannot tell the subjects of our conversation."

Barbara was irritated. "Wait," she said, "I'm thinking."

The P.P. leaped up again and attempted to protect his witness. "She is *thinking,* sir; she is not *refusing* to tell the subjects of this conversation. The record cannot reflect the false statement that she refuses to tell."

Barbara spoke again. "We were just talking about the various countries we had visited. Just general talk." The P.P. nodded happily. Though vague, this was a far better response for the record.

A gloom had clearly settled over the defense. The bombast and legal cunning of Frank Anthony, the meanness of Sharma with Charles at his ear, none of these had tarnished the English girl with the creamy cheeks and enormous brown eyes. They were all silent for a few moments before Charles whispered one final innuendo in his lawyer's weary ear. Sharma nodded.

"Is it not a fact that on the next morning, when Mary Ellen Eather came to Room 125, you would not open the door fully?"

"I opened it halfway," said Barbara.

Sharma nodded as if he knew the reason. "I put it to you that the reason is you and Luc had a very high and hot night together."

"A *what?*" asked Barbara.

"That you had *sex* several times."

At that Barbara could no longer dam up her amusement. "No." she said. "No. No." The last two negations were smothered in laughter.

"That's all," sighed Sharma, as the judge primly dictated: "It is incorrect to say that Luc and I had sex several times."

Outside the chamber, on a wooden bench where two babies slept fitfully while their mother defended herself in another courtroom, Barbara sat down gratefully and reflected on her moment. "I did it," she said. "I put a price on my head, but I don't give a damn . . . I never stood up for anything in my whole life until now . . . I wanted to tell the judge more, but how could he understand what it's like to be twenty years old and a little lost and broke and all caught up in the madness of India?" She rambled on, like an actress unwinding, the matrons beside her listening but not caring, nor understanding all that much. Her thoughts were of the most mysterious and maddening word in the language, *if*. "*If* I hadn't lost all my money in Bombay, and *if* it hadn't rained that day and ruined my passport, and *if* I hadn't gone to the cafe at the very moment that Charles was there . . . I'll never understand why our paths crossed. Did fate really want it to happen this way?"

She accepted a cigarette and lit it gratefully. "Do you want to know what I should have told the judge? I should have said that the whole experience was like a movie. It didn't seem real. I never thought anyone would get hurt. I thought the blood would be catsup. I thought Solomon would only pass out for a while and Charles would 'borrow' his valuables. He told me that the boy could easily get a new passport from his embassy and his traveler's checks would be reimbursed . . . I wouldn't hurt anyone. Pain is abhorrent to me. When I heard that Solomon had died, I was horrified. I wept for him . . ."

The matrons took her by the elbows and began to escort her to the black bus parked below. She would be returned to the prison where Charles and the others lived. "It's Bye-Bye, Barbara, I suppose . . . somebody will kill me now . . . But I did it! I told the truth. I didn't break. Maybe a life is worth something if a person stands up one time and does the right thing."

She looked across the crowded corridor; Charles was departing the courtroom, surrounded again by guards and weapons. Through a crack in the wall of khaki she saw him. And he saw her. He was smiling, the mocking smile of terrible menace.

"I hope the bastard hangs from the highest tree in Asia," she said, but the eternal cries of India drowned her curse.

CHAPTER FORTY-FIVE

Checkers finagled her way into the courtroom, nodding cheerfully at guards she knew from Tihar, and stole a few moments with Marie-Andrée. "You look great," she lied, for in truth the Canadian was still terribly thin with the pasty skin of the malnourished. "I hear the case against you is flimsy," went on Checkers. "The talk is you'll be acquitted."

Marie-Andrée smiled. "I think so, too," she answered. Then a guard came and shooed Checkers away with the butt of his rifle. "Don't worry," cried Checkers. "Things are happening."

Indeed they were.

In Paris, André borrowed money from his friends and purchased an air ticket for New Delhi. When Félix d'Escogne heard, he warned André to stay away from his half-brother. "Hasn't Charles brought you enough grief?" said Félix in dismay. The last time André answered Charles' summons, he was imprisoned in Greece and Turkey. Was he foolish enough to risk more of the same? "Charles is my brother," said André. "I love him. And he needs me." The power of Charlot remained stunning.

In the gloom of the Cave restaurant and discotheque, Checkers found Tete, the Vietnamese-born ally and chief supporter of Charles. She made it seem like a surprise meeting, but in truth she had been looking for him. Rumors were swirling about Delhi's underground—rumors of a "commando force" assembling on behalf of Charles, rumors of weapons being smuggled in from Iran, rumors of moneys being raised to pay an enormous bribe. Was any of this true? she asked Tete. He neither confirmed nor denied. All Tete would say was that Charles had access to six separate sets of blueprints for Tihar, and one of the Tis Hazari courthouse. "Other options" were under consideration.

"Charles will get out of prison when the time is ripe," he told Checkers. "And on the day that this occurs, he will go directly to the airport—but not to an international flight. They'll be watching those. His destination will be someplace in India. It's a big country."

And then, wondered Checkers, what would the great man do?"

"Disappear into the landscape for a few months," said Tete. "Perhaps he will alter his face, perhaps he will become a monk, or a Moslem, or a *saddhu,* or a diplomat, or a pilgrim, or an untouchable." Once his escape died off the front pages, it would not be difficult for Charles to leave India, by car, or by foot across the border. He would proceed east to Pakistan, or west to Burma.

"Whatever," said Tete, "he will go free. We will see to that. Charles will escape from Indian custody and become the most wanted man in the world."

"That appeals to Charles, doesn't it?" suggested Checkers. "Being *wanted.*"

Tete grinned, his broken teeth like jagged rocks in a lagoon, waiting to tear a boat apart.

"What about Marie-Andrée?" demanded Checkers. "Do these wonderful plans include her?"

Tete shrugged. "Charles will do everything in his power to help her. But . . ." His sentence dangled unfinished. There was no need for more anyway. Checkers well understood that in this league, self-preservation did not include anyone else, even a woman who had destroyed her life in poignant response to a madman's importuning.

For several days Checkers smoked hashish and brooded over the injustices of life, expecting each morning to hear the news that Charles had escaped and left Marie-Andrée behind to feed the wolves. It occurred to Checkers that she had never really been *involved* with anything—not a lover, not a cause, not a passion, nothing save the excitement of a life on the edge. She also thought about Barbara Smith, envying the plucky girl's appearance in court, admiring her well-spent courage. Even if Barbara died for her testimony, she had, in the language of karma, put out an exceptionally good "cause." Checkers reasoned it was at last time for her to commit a positive, useful act.

She decided to assassinate Charles Sobhraj. She believed that if the head of the snake were chopped off, then no one would care what happened to the tail. Surely it could wriggle away unnoticed.

Like any cop anywhere, Inspector Tuli possessed a network of snitches whom he regularly leaned on for news and rumor. Very little went on in the swirling intrigue of the Charles Sobhraj murder trial that did not reach Tuli's ears quickly. When André flew in from Paris to see his half-brother, he was hardly through passport control before a plainclothesman was on his tail. And when André went to the court and fell into Charles' chained arms in an emotional reunion, Tuli was watching surreptitiously. "It's uncanny," he said. "They could be taken for twins." By now Tuli was familiar with the nooks and crannies of Charles' remarkable life, and he was aware of the identity switch that the two men had pulled in the Athens prison. He did not think a similar trick could be accomplished in his town, but Tuli nonetheless ordered a few precautions. The police guard around Charles was doubled. Everyone who entered the courtroom would be frisked and made to present satisfactory identification. André was placed under full-time surveillance. And word was sent out that, should any guard or prison employee succumb to the temptation of a fat bribe, then best that man plan to spend the money in paradise. "I won't tolerate that killer escaping," said Tuli.

Checkers put aside her first impulse, which was to buy a jeweled dagger in the bazaar, hone it to jugular-severing sharpness, wait in the courthouse corridor, then rush forward with an avenging cry to plunge the blade into Charles' heart. The theatricality was seductive, but she did not wish at the same time to forfeit her own life. Next she inquired around as to the price of a hit man, learning that under the special circumstances of Charles' confinement, his assassination would cost at least 50,000 rupees. (An interesting comparison of fees here: the rumored price for Charles' freedom was one million, and for his death only one twentieth of that.)

Then Checkers remembered a favor that had once been offered. A year or two before, she had been in Pakistan to negotiate the sale and shipment of hashish oil to the United States. At a trading village near the Khyber Pass, she had met a tribe of Pathans, the fabled nomads whom the British always called the best guerrilla warriors in Asia. The Pathans possessed their own world, beyond the boundaries and laws of Pakistan, and were so feared that no local law authority dared molest them. Checkers had caught the eye of a chief who invited her to go riding on a magnificent black stallion. The ride lasted two months during which Checkers filled the roles of both daughter and lover to the chief, a man well into his seventies but more handsome and daring than the men with one third the years. On the day Checkers left, overwhelmed by the smell of unwashed bodies and smoky campfires of dried dung, the chief had said that the vitality she brought to his household was worthy of any favor.

When Checkers later told the story of her long ride across the northwest frontier of India/Pakistan, no one believed her. But she had a stack of photographs to prove it, and as she looked at them again in the privacy of her Delhi hotel room, the idea was born. *If* she could slip out of India and into Pakistan, and *if* she could find the tribe again and *if* the chief were still alive, and *if* he remembered his promise, then the Pathans would ride to the rescue of Marie-Andrée! They would slice off the head of Charles Sobhraj and drag it through the streets of Delhi. The more hashish she smoked, the more she felt the scheme would work. That the plan was about as substantial as a suspension bridge made of gauze ribbons did not occur to her. That it was the fourth quarter of the twentieth century further escaped her attention.

As if predestined, Checkers promptly met three English

youths who called themselves "the Liverpool Connection." Fortuitously, they were planning a drive to Pakistan, where they hoped to make a major hashish oil purchase. That was *her* territory, exclaimed Checkers. If they would give her a ride, then she would steer them to the proper drug merchant. By the next dawn they were bouncing out of Delhi in an old station wagon, honking at cows on the highway, hurrying toward the troublesome border of India and Pakistan. Checkers did not have a passport, but the Britons assured her it did not matter. Either they would buy one along the way, or they would devise a method of smuggling her across.

The public prosecutor was reasonably content after the first few days of trial. Barbara's testimony was powerful, and even though Mary Ellen had recanted much of her original statement, the Australian girl still bolstered the state's case. She placed Charles and his associates in the hotel where Solomon died, and at the restaurant where the chicken curry was allegedly poisoned. Now he had another forty witnesses on tap, ranging from the waiter who served the food to the room clerk at the Ranjit Hotel. "I am quite confident we will convict Sobhraj," the P.P. told reporters. "And I will seek the death penalty . . . I also believe we will convict Leclerc because all that is necessary is to prove her association with this group."

The state next summoned a young Sikh doctor named K. S. Chaddha, who had been on duty at the hospital where Solomon was taken after being found nude and dying on the balcony of his hotel room.

In a mustard-colored turban and a rich beard tied under his chin like the straps of a flight helmet, Dr. Chaddha routinely testified as to the medical efforts made to save the tourist's life. An autopsy later revealed traces of methaqualone, a barbiturate, in the dead man's stomach, kidney, and liver. Then the doctor roused the courtroom—and cheered Charles no end—by casually mentioning "needle marks" on the dying man's arms.

"Needle marks?" echoed Frank Anthony, like a drowsy man hearing a fire bell.

"Yes," answered the doctor. "There were needle pricks

on both arms, and signs of hematoma also . . ." Then
what, *specifically*, was the cause of Jean-Luc Solomon's
death? asked Frank Anthony.

Dr. Chaddha pursed his lips. "We could not come to
any conclusion about this case," he said. "So it was la-
beled 'death by unknown poisoning.' "

"Were these needle marks fresh?" demanded Anthony.

Dr. Chaddha nodded again. The marks seemed to have
been inflicted within twenty-four hours prior to admission
to the hospital.

"Who treated him when he was admitted?" asked Anthony. Dr. Chaddha glanced at the case sheet. "Well, according to the case sheet, he was given a stomach wash
first, and then intravenous fluids . . . I was not there
then." Chaddha went on to explain that he was only the
hospital registrar on July 1, 1976, when Solomon was
brought in for care.

"Answer my question, Doctor," said Anthony sternly,
"Who treated him upon admission?"

"The intravenous fluids were administered by a lady
doctor," said Chaddha. "It was the principal treatment
given him before the patient died . . ."

Anthony returned to the tantalizing needle marks.
"These marks," he wondered, "were there many on Solomon's arms?"

Dr. Chaddha rolled up his shirt-sleeves a little and
gestured with a pencil. "Three or four marks on both
arms," he said.

At this, Charles buzzed into Frank Anthony's ear. The
lawyer shook him off, obviously not requiring a defendant
to point out a tempting line of questioning. "After having
examined this patient and seeing these marks, were you of
the opinion that the poisoning was done orally—or intra-
venously?"

The doctor shrugged. "It could have been both ways."

Anthony nodded. "I put it to you, Doctor, that people
who are narcotic addicts sometimes die of drug over-
doses."

Dr. Chaddha could not argue with this, but he could not
affix a precise cause of Solomon's death. "I cannot offer
an opinion," he said. "It is impossible." Standing next to
Charles, Marie-Andrée was having difficulty following the

testimony. The young doctor spoke in a rumbling baritone that was muffled by the ceiling fan. And the Canadian girl did not understand English all that well, although she was daily improving. "What did he say?" she whispered to Charles in French.

"Solomon was a junkie," shot back Charles, smiling broadly.

"How much of a dose of methaqualone is considered fatal?" asked Frank Anthony.

"Five grams," answered the doctor. "It is available only in tablets." It was well known in India under the name Mandrax. On the other side, the P.P. nodded knowingly. It was helpful for the judge to learn that Solomon could not have injected himself with the drug whose traces were found in his innards.

"What is Mandrax?" asked Anthony.

"A hypnotic drug," answered Dr. Chaddha.

"It is not a tranquilizer?" pressed Anthony, presumably trying to make the point that the drug was something that women took for nerves.

"No," said the doctor. "It is a powerful hypnotic drug used for insomnia. Methaqualone is an ingredient of Mandrax."

The scar-faced Sharma, Charles' new lawyer, took over and asked a few silly questions about sex, all of which seemed to annoy the judge. Sharma was trying to suggest that Solomon and Barbara Smith were taking downers for sexual kicks on the night in question.

"Don't people in the West use aphrodisiacs for stimulating the sexual urge?" asked Sharma.

"I don't know," exclaimed the doctor, to the prim judge's considerable relief.

The defense posture was evident by the second week. The trio of defendants—Charles, Marie-Andrée, and Jean Dhuisme—would deny that they had ever even met Jean-Luc Solomon. The suggestion would be made that the two witnesses for the prosecution—Barbara and Mary Ellen—were prostitutes and drug users who were actually responsible for the tourist's death, or, failing that, Solomon was an addict who might have died of an overdose.

But there was also serious dissension in the defense

camp. Frank Anthony—as if by divine right—had seized leadership of the several lawyers representing the accused, even though his client, Marie-Andrée, seemed to be in the least peril. The state's case against her was not strong. No testimony was offered that she either participated in the seduction or the drugging or the robbing of Solomon. The best the P.P could do was elicit from Barbara Smith that she had seen Marie-Andrée with Charles "sorting out drugs" in Room 315 of the Ranjit Hotel.

Nonetheless, Anthony was usually the first lawyer on his feet for cross-examination, often exhausting the witness to the point that there was little left for the other attorneys to pick over. "He may get his girl off," said the Delhi reporter, "but he sure isn't doing Charley Boy much good." After one session, the lawyer Chowdhury, who had done scut work for a year leading up to the trial, and who was now forced to endure Anthony's hogging of the spotlight, could not conceal his irritation. "Anthony is putting on a wonderful show—as only he can—but he's just showing off."

A reporter asked, "How has Anthony done so far?"

Chowdhury smiled tolerantly, as if excusing an elderly uncle's social gaffes. "What I think—and what the judge thinks—are, one hopes, two different judgments." Just at that point, Chowdhury's attention was diverted by the police guard escorting Charles out of the courtroom for a rest break. The lawyer's face was an unconcealed study in disgust. "That man is a diseased animal and should be destroyed," he said, a rather unusual comment from a defense lawyer whose client was intimately involved with the agitated little man in chains and manacles. Marie-Andrée trailed after him, busy whispering to Charles in French, as frenetic as a bird newly come on a branch of plump insects.

"She's very strong," mused Chowdhury. "Foolish, yes. Impulsive, yes. Lovesick, yes. But aside from that slight limp she gets when she is very tired, Marie-Andrée is steel. I think it will be hard to convince the judge that she was a helpless willow blown in the wind."

While Charles continued to speak with his biographer during every break in the trial, Marie-Andrée was icy to reporters. She told one that her story was "valuable," and that she would write it herself at some later date. The press had to be content with descriptions of her clothes and hairdos, neither very interesting, and the manner in which she looked at Charles, usually alternating between love and hate. But one afternoon she began speaking candidly to a heavy French-Canadian nun who had spent her entire adult life in India as a missionary, and whose face was as permanently crimson as the sunset. "Of course I was a serious girl," Marie-Andrée said, as if the whole world thought her frivolous. "I knew what I was doing when I returned to the East. Everybody in my family tried to discourage me . . . but I was thirty, my eyes were wide open. I analyzed the trip a long time. I had a round-trip ticket. I had two thousand dollars in cash. I said to myself, 'What could possibly happen to you with two thousand dollars in your pocket? If things go bad, you simply get on a plane and go back home."

The plump nun nodded, agreeable to whatever the girl said. She was, after all, Catholic. "He started taking my money very cleverly," Marie-Andrée went on. "First, it was, 'Let me borrow eight hundred fifty to buy some stones and we will triple it overnight.' Then it was, 'Let me have four hundred dollars just until tomorrow morning, when I collect from a customer. The banks are closed and I forgot to cash a check.' Then it was something else, and something else, and before I knew it all my money was gone, and so was my return ticket, and my visa was expired, and I was totally in his hands."

She glanced across the room at Charles, engrossed in an anecdote.

"The year I spent in jail in Delhi is better than all the time I spent with him before," she said. "He used to tell me, 'Stop worrying, I'm clever.' And I used to answer, 'If you're so clever, why have you spent half your life in jail?'"

And what was his response to that? wondered the Sister.

"Sometimes he would laugh. Sometimes he would hit me."

On another day, the subject of Mary Ellen and Barbara's unsuccessful attempt at suicide was being discussed. Someone asked Marie-Andrée if she had ever considered the possibility. Surprisingly she answered. "I would never

commit suicide," she said. "I am trying to *save* my life
. . ." She thought a few moments, then amplified her remark. "But who can say something with finality? Suicide
is the product of many months, of a whole life. Perhaps
things are building within me that I do not understand."

And what did she mean by *that?*

"I don't know," she said, growing emotional. No one
had seen her weep in the courtroom. "There are forces at
work on me. Sometimes I think I am a prisoner of them.
Karma? Perhaps. All I know is that one cannot really control one's life."

CHAPTER FORTY-SIX

When the Liverpool Connection reached the Indian border safely and prepared for the crossing into Pakistan, Checkers developed an acute case of cold feet. True to their word, the British drug dealers had obtained a passport for her somewhere along the line, but the substitution of Checkers' photograph was sloppily done. She did not think it would fool anyone. And she could not risk a new arrest in India, as she was already out on bond for the charges of smuggling and hashish transport. She did not know the ropes in this corner of India, where most every man wore a turban and a beard and seemed eminently capable of swinging a figurative sword to slice off alien heads.

The youngsters parked the station wagon and walked to a clearing where the hash pipe went round and round. One of the young Englishmen, who called himself Johnny Good Vibes, conceived a novel idea for Checkers' passage into Pakistan.

Thus did three young Britons drive routinely and unquestioned across the border, their passports barely perused, their tailgate door unopened. Had the border guard been more perseverant, he might have poked about the bedrolls and knapsacks and discovered a rolled-up carpet. Inside the carpet—like Cleopatra being smuggled to Caesar—rested Checkers, enormously stoned, trying not to squeal with laughter.

Safely inside Pakistan, the adventurers drove to a town near Lahore where, as she had promised, Checkers arranged for the Liverpool Connection to meet the region's major hashish merchant. A substantial buy was negotiated, enough to merit an anticipated $25,000 in profits, predicted Checkers. Her companions decided to make a U-turn and drive back into India, destination Goa, where a market of the young was waiting to buy their wares. Did Checkers want to go along? She shook her head. Goa was once her paradise, but now it was dangerous. Someone opened the door, she once said, and let the serpent in. Checkers wished her companions well, warned them to be cautious, and with a kiss they parted ways. A few months later, Johnny Good Vibes was murdered near Goa. His body and his head, which were separated from one another, were stuffed into a pile of rotting fish.

Checkers had money in her pocket now, $500 from the Britons as a finder's fee, another $200 under the table from the Pakistani drug merchant. Now she would attend her business. She hailed a taxi and set forth to find the Pathan nomads who, in her fantasy, would rescue Marie-Andrée from the injustices of India and the punishment of unhappy love.

Rumors of the impending "commando raid" on the courthouse to free Charles reached fever pitch by late summer. Already more guards than spectators were in and around the court, and a team of plainclothesmen tried to blend among the rivers of humanity that flowed at storm tide in the dark corridors. Nonetheless, Indian authorities elected to puncture any escape balloon before it attempted takeoff.

It was as if war had been declared.

Another squad of guards, armed not only with rifles but with fixed bayonets, plus a squad of judo experts, appeared at the door of Judge Nath's courtroom. Every person who entered was scrutinized. Heat was applied to Charles' camp followers. Half-brother André was arrested on charges of "passport irregularity" and thrown into the police lockup for a long night. Though released the next day on bail, the younger man was severely shaken. He was not permitted to visit Charles except in the courtroom, and then their moments were brief, stolen during recess. After a few days of enduring the threatening stares of the guards, André skipped town, prudence dictating that he forfeit bond and return hastily to the City of Light.

Then two other men-in-waiting abandoned Charles, not even bothering to explain that they feared arrest. Tete vanished, reportedly moving to Bombay. If Charles felt like the captain of a sinking ship, he did not show it. Instead he cried out his anger and frustration in open court. "What kind of country would deny me the chance to visit with my own flesh and blood in private, without a guard listening in?" he demanded of Judge Nath. "My brother was arrested for nothing! I cannot speak with my family or my friends or even my lawyers in prison without a guard around. If I say anything in confidence, the guard is going to report it to the administrator who then tells the public prosecutor . . . I demand justice! I demand basic human rights!"

To dramatize his plight, Charles invited reporters to gaze upon his thin but heavily muscled legs, where bruises marked the force and pressure of his leg irons. The wounds were indeed ugly and obviously painful, but anyone familiar with Charles' history of inflicting injuries on himself as prelude to escapes might have wondered if he had amplified their intensity.

On September 1, 1977, Charles filed a petition with the High Court seeking a delay in not only the Solomon murder trial, but the Ashoka Hotel jewelry robbery and other crimes charged against him. The petition, carefully written and replete with scholarly legal terminology, asked that the High Court grant him permission for private conferences with lawyers and family members, that he be allowed a typewriter and a tape recorder to help in his defense, and that the "cruel" and "inhuman" leg irons be removed. "Did he ask for afternoon tea as well?" wondered Inspector Tuli, considerably annoyed that the murder trial was being drawn out by stunts. The P.P. was similarly put out, complaining to Judge Nath that "this delay is very irritating . . . I had planned to finish my arguments this week. The case could have been wrapped up by mid-September. Now it will be a miracle if it finishes in October."

* * *

The Supreme Court of India voted to hear the petition of Charles Sobhraj. The decision thrilled the prisoner, repairing some of the ego damage suffered by the attrition in his ranks. "It's the first time in the history of Indian law that a prisoner on trial had been able to get a personal hearing before the Supreme Court," he told one reporter, reveling in the attention.

The Supreme Court of India, built during British rule, remains a gracious, dignified old woman with massive pillars ringing her girth like Victoria's attendants. On the late morning of September 6, 1977, the corridors were thronged with lawyers and students, paying appreciation to Charles' petition. "I heard it was quite brilliantly written," said one advocate with an enormous silver mustache stained briefly red by his digestion of *paan*.

On this important day, Charles was attended not only by his regular guards, but by one weapons expert who carried a bazooka, and another who had a container of hand grenades. There were also lawyers, reporters, beggars, embassy personnel, and legal wives, all jostling for a peek at the notorious prisoner. Marie-Andrée had no business before the court, but she was permitted to attend. And when she entered the chamber, a shock awaited. Next to Charles, hanging on his every word, her face carefully painted and her limbs draped in fine silk, sat Suzy, an exquisite Oriental doll appropriate for the emperor of the hour.

Reporters badgered Charles for the young woman's name, but he refused, insisting she was "just a pen pal." He was more interested in speaking of his petition. And he was annoyed that the leg irons had been removed by prison authorities prior to the hearing. As he drew quick sketches of the fetters and distributed them to reporters, he recited a dramatic scenario:

"They tried to take them off me yesterday . . . But I wouldn't let them. I told the guards I would fight anyone who touched those leg irons. I wanted the Supreme Court justices to see for themselves . . . Then, this morning, when I was walking toward the police bus, several hefty guards grabbed me and threw me to the ground . . . Then three others rushed out with hammers and smashed the leg irons."

"Did you put up a resistance?" asked a young reporter.

"Of course," answered Charles. "But what could I do against all those men? Look at my legs . . ." Charles lifted his trousers to reveal white gauze bandages stained red on his ankles, and similar red marks midway between his ankle and knee.

Another reporter asked if a doctor had been called.

"No," replied Charles. "I bandaged myself. I don't trust the prison doctor. He works for the police. It took at least a dozen hard hammer blows to break the irons, so you can imagine how much pain it caused . . . I have been so harassed by Indian police that I am pessimistic about justice . . ." Suzy nodded in vigorous support and nuzzled as close to Charles as the guards would allow. Nearby, Marie-Andrée sat in familiar humiliation.

High-domed, cooled by fresh breezes, the spacious chamber of the Supreme Court of India was a marked contrast to the squalid and unpleasant room in Tis Hazari Courts where the Solomon murder trial was taking place. Here was the majesty of the law, with sleekly gowned lawyers gliding respectfully on carpeted floors, fine wooden walls gleaming with polish and care. Here the ceiling fans turned noiselessly, as if fearful of disturbing the judges of history whose oil portraits stared sternly over all who came here.

Appearing for the prosecution was no less a person than the Attorney General of India, Mr. S. V. Gupte, a distinguished lawyer with a sharp aquiline face and a posture that bespoke a lifetime of personal discipline. It was soon clear that he did not know a great deal about the case at hand, but he obviously well understood that his government desired Charles Sobhraj to remain under the tightest security. He would argue for the continuance of leg irons and chains.

No one doubted that Charles would have preferred to be his own lawyer, to star in the unusual drama that he had written. Unable to win permission, he engaged a new advocate, a lawyer name Ghattate. He was of substantial reputation and argued persuasively on behalf of his client. "My lords," pleaded Ghattate before the three justices, "my client cannot even answer the call of nature when he is wearing these inhuman fetters on his legs. They are welded in place. He cannot sleep properly. He is in continuing pain and discomfort. He cannot consult his lawyers without a jail official listening to everything and taking notes."

The Attorney General rose, bowed respectfully, and began counter-argument. "My lords, this chap has escaped several times from jails in the past . . . He has also evaded arrest successfully . . . This man is very clever. The court must realize his resourcefulness." From a lengthy document, the Attorney General read a list of the known number of Charles' arrests, the prisons from which he had escaped, and the pending charges of murder brought against him in India, Nepal, Thailand, and Pakistan.

The Chief Justice, his face troubled, agreed that these were "serious charges . . . very serious charges indeed."

"This man is responsible for many murders," continued the Attorney General. It was not only necessary, but *vital* that the prisoner be hobbled by steel.

Ghattate, the new lawyer, introduced a sketch and diagrams of leg fetters. He handed them to the justices.

"Who drew these things?" inquired the Chief Justice.

"We did, my lord," answered the lawyer. He delivered a graphic account of how severely his client's legs were damaged when the guards "smashed" the fetters to remove them this very morning.

In his chair, Charles raised his trousers, hoping that the judges would look at his legs.

The Attorney General rebutted with skepticism, "We feel that he inflicted these injuries on himself."

The Chief Justice looked incredulous. "How could a man do this to himself?"

"My lord," came the answer, "this man is capable of anything . . . The Interpol reports show that he escaped not from one, but from several prisons. He has committed a number of murders. We cannot chase him around Asia if he gets loose. That is why these fetters are necessary."

Charles' lawyer disagreed with passion. "But these bars and fetters are *welded* onto him! This is a very cruel form of punishment."

The Chief Justice leaned forward and addressed the Attorney General. "What can his free legs do?"

"He can attack members of the jail staff and escape," warned the Attorney General.

The Chief Justice gazed out at the throng assembled be-

fore him. "Where is this man, anyway?" he asked. With
elaborate difficulty Charles rose and bowed, lacking only a
spotlight and a clash of cymbals to mark his ascent to this
supreme moment, wretched as it was. Born in torment,
reared without identity, he now commanded the eyes of
India's greatest men. History would record him!

Staring for a long while, perhaps wondering how this
ragged and insignificant-looking little man could have filled
the pages of such an incredible dossier, the Chief Justice
gestured for Charles to sit down. Then, after huddling
briefly with his associates, the jurist presented two choices:
"Will you ask your client whether he would prefer solitary
confinement to fetters?" Charles was stunned. This was
like asking a man if he preferred a cobra or a mamba in
his bed.

The defense lawyer bent over his client's ear and the
two men whispered animatedly.

"My lord," finally answered the lawyer, "this man prefers bar fetters to solitary confinement." Sputtering indignation, his face flooded with an odd crosscurrent of fury
and hauteur, Charles was led from the great hall, Suzy
murmuring comfort on one side, Marie-Andrée ministering
to the other.

That afternoon in Tihar, guards welded on new leg
irons, rather enthusiastically, one would suspect.

Ten months later, ten very long months later, Judge
Nath retired to prepare his verdict in the death of Jean-
Luc Solomon. A collective sigh of relief swept over the
courtroom. The trial had long since become mired in tedium, a play with no end, its performers trapped on a
stage whose wings were sealed. One of the young lawyers
involved likened the experience to a dreadful evening
once spent in a Bombay theater: "We were all waiting for
the star, a great woman singer, but first we had to endure
a magician. Nothing went right for the poor chap. His
rabbit jumped out of the hat before it was supposed to.
His assistant bumped into a table and the supposedly
empty pitcher spilled wine on the floor. The mirror in his
disappearing box fell on his head. But the bloody fool
would not get offstage. He may still be there, for all I
know. He seemed just stubborn enough to keep attempting

tricks, either until the audience succumbed from boredom, or until *something* worked sufficiently well to reward him with applause."

Charles' bag of tricks was similarly abundant.

First came the Disappearing Woman, which Charles tried to present as an epic romance more poignant than *Romeo and Juliet*. Alas, it became more like a modest variation of *The Sting*. After Suzy the waitress's surprise appearance in the Supreme Court chamber, she clung to the defendant like moss on an oak. For several weeks in late 1977 she appeared in Judge Nath's courtroom, rushing to the chained arms of her beloved and smothering him with kisses. Their liaison was a spectacle that could only be called extraordinary, necking and cooing amid clanking chains at odd moments of the trial. Certainly Suzy brightened the drab chamber of khaki guards. She appeared in brilliant silks, fluttering eyelashes, and on occasion sat in the lap of the prisoner while both professed titanic love. The assumption was that Charles paid not only for Suzy's importation, but for her wardrobe and substantial hotel bill as well. He must have parted with a few of the sapphires hidden in his mouth.

Marie-Andrée pretended indifference to the gaudy intruder and told a reporter, "I have known this was coming . . . I wish them well . . . Charles and I are just friends." But the hurt that came to her face could not have been hidden by the veil of a Moslem woman.

Then Charles grandly announced an intention to wed Suzy. The Indian Government reacted with no tolerance for romance, denying the couple permission on numerous grounds, principal of which being the lack of a document to prove that Charles was legally divorced from his first wife. This gave the prisoner an opportunity to protest anew with all the passion he had directed toward the irons that bound his legs. For a time, newspapers covered the new development enthusiastically, thwarted love being a favored subject in any setting. One paper even wrote that Charles was "contrite" and "so in love" that he wanted to turn over a new leaf. During all this, the murder trial managed to continue, but with attention focused less on

the witness box than at the rear of the courtroom where
Charles conducted frequent press conferences, storming
over the cruelty of a bureaucracy that would deny a man
his bride.

What *was* Charles up to?

The romantic might have believed that Charles was
truly the prisoner of love whose heart was committed. The
skeptic might wonder whether Charles was simply attempting a diversionary tactic, seeking to shift the attention of
the press and public—and judge—from murder to matri-
mony. And the cynic might speculate whether Charles was
buying a little flight insurance should the day arise when
he was delivered to the eager lawmen of Thailand. Suzy's
father, it was learned, was a Bangkok policeman.

Whatever, the wedding did not occur. Suzy disappeared
from her lover's lap as abruptly as she had come. Rumors
had reached Charles that his *inamorata* was not exactly
staying in her Delhi hotel room each night, praying for
his well-being. Secretly he engaged a lawyer to investigate
Suzy. The ensuing report, both disturbing and somehow
amusingly appropriate, brought a sudden final curtain to
l'affaire Suzy. The lawyer informed Charles that while his
intended was enjoying his largesse she was also accepting
the romantic attentions of an Indian waiter, a handsome
young man who shared her quarters. Some days the other
man even waited outside the courthouse! The implication
was that Suzy and her boy friend intended to take Charles
for all they could get, then return to Bangkok and live
happily ever after.

So much for love in chains.

Charles fired lawyers and hired lawyers and on one occasion received permission from Judge Nath to represent
himself. It happened because on the day that Charles was
scheduled to enter the witness box and testify on his own
behalf, his newest lawyer did not show up. Judge Nath
stewed impatiently for one hour, then another, finally
summoned the defendant to the bench.

"What is this delay all about?" asked the judge, his tone
indicating that he was growing weary of the defendant's
stunts.

"Sir, I have engaged a new lawyer and I have to consult with him before giving my statement," answered Charles respectfully. "Please, may I wait for him?"

Judge Nath mulled the request. "Your lawyer has nothing to do with your statement," he said. "It is *you* who must answer questions and give a statement." But he granted another few minutes.

The P.P was even more dubious. He had several hundred other pressing criminal matters in his portfolio, and it angered him that, due to Charles' stalls, delays, and sleight-of-hand this murder trial threatened to become a life's work. Standing next to Charles while waiting for the new lawyer to materialize, the P.P. could not resist muttering, "Mr. Sobhraj, since I assume you are going to deny all these things, then why do you need to suffer having to await a lawyer? You can give your statement on your own."

"I am innocent," snapped Charles. "That is why I am going to fight. Why did *you* accept this bloody case? I've lost my money, my lawyers . . . do you actually think I killed this man?"

The P.P. shook his head sadly and moved away. "I am merely going by the evidence," he said. "It is up to the court to decide."

By midafternoon the judge had no patience left and once again summoned the defendant. "I intend to read from the evidence on record from the prosecution witness, Barbara Smith," announced Judge Nath, "I will ask you questions . . . and you can say that the statements are correct, incorrect, or, if you wish, further explain yourself."

Charles agreed, looking not the least upset over having to handle his important appearance without benefit of counsel.

"It is in evidence that you, Jean Dhuisme, Marie-Andrée Leclerc, and Mary Ellen Eather came to India on June 5, 1976, in Dhuisme's car, from Pakistan. Is that correct?" asked Judge Nath.

"It is correct," answered Charles.

"At the time did you have a valid passport?"

"Yes, your honor."

"It is also in evidence against you that on June 8 you,

along with the others previously named, went to Bombay."

"It is correct."

"It is further in evidence against you that you were introduced to Barbara Smith in Bombay . . . and that you represented yourself to her as a 'big businessman' and asked her to accompany you to Japan. What have you to say?"

Charles shook his head in elaborate negation. "It is totally incorrect," he said. And from that moment on, he denied everything. To each of Barbara Smith's sworn statements as read by Judge Nath, Charles replied, "It is totally incorrect." He denied even knowing Barbara, he denied having been inside the Ranjit Hotel, or the coffee-house where the chicken curry was allegedly doctored, or ever having laid eyes on Jean-Luc Solomon. When Judge Nath was done, having dictated each of the defendant's denials into the record, he posed one more interesting question to the man who claimed to be the victim of a young woman's self-serving lies. In the months gone by, a parade of witnesses had come before the judge to identify Charles and link him with Solomon, they being waiters and room clerks and cleaning women and doctors and police. "Why have all these witnesses spoken against you?" asked Judge Nath.

Charles answered quickly, as if punching a button in his head to deliver a programmed response. "Because they are all being tutored by the police," he said hotly. "Because they are testifying at the insistence of the police . . . Barbara Smith was pressured by the police to turn approver and make false statements against me . . . I also want to bring to the notice of this court the fact that the two approvers tried to commit suicide . . ."

Judge Nath interrupted. "What does this have to do with this case?"

". . . They entered into a conspiracy to impress the court and make their statements believed. They made a show of suicide." In modest astonishment, Judge Nath called it quits for the day, probably thinking, as was the press, that if the girls' attempt at suicide was only a show, then it bordered on Grand Guignol. Each ate enough barbiturates to knock out everybody in the courtroom.

The next day Marie-Andrée took the stand, Frank Anthony carefully guiding her though a similar minefield of "It is totally incorrects" and Charles at her elbow murmuring, *"Chérie!* say, 'I do not remember,'" or "'Say it is not within my knowledge as I was not there.'" At one point Charles' prompting grew so intrusive that Frank Anthony whirled and hissed blazingly, "Shut up! Don't interrupt her! Please let me question my witness myself!"

When Marie-Andrée was finished denying everything except her name and age and the fact that she wore a black turtleneck sweater and leather jacket, Judge Nath asked her the same question he had of Charles. *Why* did so many prosecution witnesses testify against her? *Who* should be believed?

Marie-Andrée nodded expectantly, as if she were a schoolchild finally asked the question on which she had done her homework. She pulled out a handwritten statement and received permission to read it to the court. It echoed Charles' declarations of the day before, that in particular Barbara Smith and Mary Ellen Eather had been squeezed by Tuli and his cops. "Barbara told me that she had no choice in the matter . . . She said, 'If I refuse to become an approver, they will charge me in the murder and I will spend many years in jail' . . . On August 4, 1976, Mary Ellen told me that both of them had agreed to become approvers and that the police had given to each of them a typed statement to learn by heart . . ."

Nor could Marie-Andrée resist the temptation to pour black paint over the character of Barbara Smith. She told the judge that Barbara was "a loose type . . . she used to go to bed with anybody who was ready to pay her . . . she was in the habit of taking drugs . . . she lies in everything she says."

On her way out of the courtroom, Marie-Andrée accepted the congratulations of Charles and held her head high. She told a reporter, "No, I was not nervous because I did not do anything . . . I feel at peace now . . . I have confidence I will get out of everything."

Lawyers came and went as quickly as Suzy. Fed up with playing second fiddle to Anthony, the able young Chowdhury quit the defense of Marie-Andrée with the complaint that he had not been paid. Charles fired Rupinder Singh regularly, but always hired him back. Rupi was valuable in looking after the other cases against Charles going on simultaneously in other courtrooms around Delhi. And Frank Anthony was sidetracked in mid-trial by having to defend an even more celebrated client—Indira Gandhi. The fallen Prime Minister engaged her old friend to represent her in charges of corruption and obstruction of justice. The tempo of the Solomon murder trial, already funereal, became a gasping bagpipe.

More than likely Charles was happy, for after the prosecution finished its case and Judge Nath nodded toward the defense to commence, Charles began throwing new wrenches into the wheels of justice. He wanted delays, both to keep himself in the center ring and to afflict the other side with weariness. From his pen flowed new petitions seeking to halt the trial unless his "human rights" were restored, accusing the police and guards of treating him like "an animal" or "a robot" or "a stone" or "a tree." Judge Nath routinely denied the petitions. Then Charles fired what he obviously intended to be a major cannon: he came up with a most curious letter of repentance allegedly written by Barbara Smith. In it, she took back much of her testimony and said she had borne false witness due to fear and the arm-twisting of Tuli's interrogators. The trouble was, the letter was neither signed nor witnessed, and it was printed in a rather anonymous-looking hand. Moreover, the letter was absurd in places, particularly the suggestion that the doctors who tried to save Solomon's life did not give their best efforts. "He [Solomon] was a Jew, so there could be political explanations," said the letter.

Judge Nath refused to admit the document, nor would he allow Barbara Smith to be recalled for another defense examination. "You had adequate opportunity to ask Miss Smith questions when she was a witness before this court," said the judge, tartly adding that the defendant was deliberately trying to delay the outcome of the trial.

Undaunted, Charles withdrew to the lawbooks in his prison cell and with the aid of his newest lawyer, a capable advocate named Batra, drafted still another motion to the High Court. This one demanded that Judge Nath's decision be overruled and that Barbara Smith be yanked back be-

fore the bench. It further contained a steamy and graceless
attack on Judge Nath's capabilities, accusing him of issu-
ing an order that was "wholly illegal," that he had "erred
in law," and that he was "denying justice to the petitioner."
Charles insisted that he had "in no way tried to delay
proceedings to defeat the ends of justice and hence the
judge's order is illegal and immoral." Finally he suggested
that the reason Judge Nath did not admit the letter was
because it would explode the prosecution's case.

The High Court refused to grant Charles' plea and declined to order his requested new delay in the proceedings.
"Matters do not appear to be going very well for the great
man, do they?" mused Inspector Tuli, his delight unhidden. But Charles gave no sign of even a fractional loss
of optimism. Reporters overheard an interesting snatch of
dialogue between the defendant and his lawyer, Batra,
during a recess.

"Isn't the judge getting a bit fed up with these delays?"
asked Batra of his client.

Charles shook his head. "He has listened patiently to
the police. Now he should give us time and listen to us
. . . Do not worry. I will not hang as a result of this
crime."

The months passed. The great cycle of seasons pushed
India from her vibrant winter greens to the parched mus-
tards of April. Matters of greater importance shoved
Charles to the back of the newspapers, and then out altogether. A cyclone killed forty people. A tiger ate two
children. Riots broke out both for and against Indira
Gandhi as she attempted a comeback. The political landscape turned violent and bloody. When the monsoons
broke the paralyzing heat of June, the rivers overflowed.
Hundreds died. The new Prime Minister, an ancient ascetic
named Morarji Desai, who attributed part of his longevity
to the practice of drinking a glass of his own urine each
day, refused to withdraw India from membership among
nations possessing nuclear bombs. Another thirteen million
people were born in the year of the trial. The saga of
Charles Sobhraj shriveled to a significance less than that
of graffiti scrawled on a wall, washed away by the rains
of time.

* * *

At last came the closing arguments.

As the lawyers assembled for their final sermons, observers in the courtroom measured the two sides. It was agreed that the doughty little P.P. had performed commendably. The state's case was well presented, all bases touched, all witnesses save Mary Ellen Eather standing up to the winds and wrath of the defense.

Conversely, the defense to this point seemed all flash and dash, with precious little underpinnings. For months, Charles and his several lawyers had been yelling that Barbara Smith was a liar, a user of drugs, and a prostitute. Yet the defense offered no testimony to substantiate any of this except accusations made by the defendants themselves. Importantly, her account of the poisoned chicken curry and the fatal aftermath in the Ranjit Hotel was not discredited at all, *not a syllable*, save those denials uttered by other members of the entourage. The defense further tried to establish that Jean-Luc Solomon was a drug addict, emphasizing that almost two full days passed between the time that Charles & Company left the Ranjit Hotel and the French tourist was found unconscious on his balcony. But no testimony was presented that would confirm Solomon used drugs, nor was any witness summoned who could shed light on what happened during the last forty-eight hours of his life.

The defense posture boiled down to one favored by criminal lawyers all over the world: (1) smear the state's star witness, (2) smear the reputation of the victim, (3) smear the police and their strongarm tactics, and (4) pray that everything was sufficiently confused so that the judge would give the defendants benefit of the doubt.

"My client is innocent, my lord," said the lawyer Ghattate, who had represented Charles during his appearance before the Supreme Court of India. "There is no evidence against Charles Sobhraj which can stand the scrutiny of this court . . . There is only the evidence of Barbara Smith, the approver, and without substantial corroboration on each point it cannot stand . . . Sobhraj is supposed to have given tranquilizers in the chicken curry to Jean-Luc Solomon. But even the prosecution does not contend he gave any tranquilizers after the night of June twenty-eighth. For more than forty-eight hours—between the twenty-ninth of June and the first of July—nothing was known of Solomon. What is known is that there were injection marks on his arms which doctors have testified were recent. . . . I say it was a case of attempted suicide . . . The police want to keep Sobhraj 'in.' They have foisted this case. They concocted his arrest and they concocted this trial, saying he was a notorious criminal . . . Now I come to the fateful night when my client is accused of drugging Solomon's dinner. Sobhraj was serving the chicken curry with one hand, holding the plate with the other. My lord, where did the third hand come from to drug the food? . . . This theory of the plastic bottle is a figment of the imagination! . . . I repeat, my lord, that the charges are false and fabricated. My client is innocent . . ."

On behalf of Marie-Andrée, Frank Anthony submitted his final argument in writing. Long, scholarly in parts, scalding in others, it was principally a slashing attack on Barbara Smith. Reminding the judge that the witness was unable to remember the name of the school administrator back in England who signed her graduation diploma, Anthony construed this gap to illustrate how everything Barbara said was "a tissue of lies."

To all of this, the P.P. listened quietly, standing in his usual place before the bench, a solemn, dour little man whose face was void of the theatrical emotions favored by the defense. The P.P. had less money in his pocket than the opposition, and less prestige. He was not even given the courtesy of being addressed by his name, Daljit Singh. But the P.P. had, at this moment, something that to his thinking was far more valuable: a better case. When it was his turn, he defended the state's evidence calmly, then turned to look at Charles Sobhraj. Behind his thick glasses burned strength and determination, like a man who refused to be shoved around by bullies a moment more.

"The prosecution case has been fully proved, beyond reasonable doubt," he said calmly. "The accused, Sobhraj, *must* receive the maximum penalty for his heinous crimes. We demand the penalty of death . . . death by hanging."

* * *

During the next few weeks, while Judge Nath secluded himself to prepare the verdict, Charles remained at center stage. He had a few more cards to play. On the night of July 25, allegedly morose and despondent, he tried to hang himself in Tihar Prison. At least he said he did, but guards found him only a moment or two after he draped a not very taut piece of blanket strip about his neck.

Then he began a hunger strike in protest against his treatment in prison and as melodramatic illustration of his pessimism concerning his fate in the courts of India. "This is a fast unto the death," he sent word to reporters. ". . . I cannot bear any more mental and physical torture . . . I feel I am going mad . . . I am advising my lawyer to inform my family in France and the French Embassy . . . Once I thought there was justice in India . . . Now I realize there is none . . . I will die by fasting . . ."

On August 8, 1978, Judge Nath beheld a strange scene as he prepared to pronounce his decision. Charles Sobhraj was brought into the courtroom on a stretcher, one wrist handcuffed to an attending guard. He was almost lost within the folds of a dirty gray blanket. He looked ghastly. Rumors circulated through the courtroom that his fast, three weeks old at this point, was truly killing him. Doctors had found a blood clot near his heart, the rumors went.

The distinct possibility existed that this thin, wretched, shocking little man would die before Judge Nath could intone his fate.

"I do not care what this judge does to me," gasped Charles, his voice a death rattle. He clutched his throat with the free hand, as if feeling the place where the noose would be draped. "I am . . . my own judge . . . and I judge myself . . . *innocent* . . ." With that his hand fell to the stretcher and his head rolled about as if it were no longer attached to his spine.

Marie-Andrée went to him and nuzzled him and wept— for herself, for Charles, for what never was, for what never would be. As Judge Nath took his seat, the prisoner did not even pay him the courtesy of attention. With supreme indifference to the business of the morning, Charles had roused himself and was reading the financial page of the Hindustan *Times* as his sentence was pronounced.

Book Five

DESTINIES

EPILOGUE

When the sky turns green,
And the earth spins gold,
When the elephant climbs tree,
And the fires of sun are cold,
Then look sharp! A man can change his destiny.

Nineteenth-century sailing chant

—Checkers was not seen again in Delhi. Friends in India shared several rumors. One had her living in Paris, where she became a successful prostitute in the 16th Arrondissement. Another insisted that she had married a wealthy Pakistani businessman and was mistress of a great household in Karachi. And yet another suggested that hers were the unidentified bones of a Western woman found stripped clean by wolves and vultures, in a remote, savage gorge within the Khyber Pass.

—Red Eye obtained a valid American passport and returned to the United States.

—Barbara Smith was released from Tihar Prison and pardoned for any offenses connected with the death of Jean-Luc Solomon. Several months later, she was still in Delhi, seen often in the company of well-to-do Indian businessmen.

—Mary Ellen Eather was returned to Tihar and faced charges in the drugging and robbing of three French tourists at the YMCA Hotel. The P.P. was studying the possibility of charging the Australian woman with perjury in the Solomon death.

—Jean Dhuisme was acquitted in the Solomon case,

but pleaded guilty in the YMCA crimes and was given three more months in Tihar.

—Marie-Andrée Leclerc was found not guilty in the Solomon murder. But she did not savor a moment of freedom. After a brief interlude of rejoicing in Judge Nath's courtroom, she was led once again to the black prison bus and returned to Tihar. She faced charges in the YMCA case and in other crimes. Inspector Tuli, annoyed at her acquittal, talked of handing her over to Thailand authorities to answer for the five murders committed there. And after that, to Nepal. Whatever, it was not believed that she would ever sit beside the St. Lawrence River again.

Charles Sobhraj was found guilty of three lesser counts in the death of Jean-Luc Solomon: (1) culpable homicide not amounting to murder, (2) drugging and administering stupefying drugs for the purpose of robbery, (3) voluntarily causing hurt to commit robbery.

His attorney, Ghattate, pleaded for leniency. "My client has suffered enough because of barbaric and inhuman treatment in jail," said the lawyer. "Mr. Sobhraj is away from his family and in a foreign country and atmosphere. The two years he has suffered in Tihar are equal to life imprisonment. Therefore, my lord, he should receive minimum punishment. Your lordship could order his deportation and a fine; these would meet the ends of justice." From his stretcher, Charles croaked a warning, "I will not break my fast . . . I am not afraid to die."

Judge Nath considered all of this and he announced his decision:

"No evidence was advanced before me to show that the accused met inhuman treatment at the hands of jail authorities during the trial. The sentence of a fine as suggested would not be enough. The sentence has to be commensurate with the nefarious acts of the accused. Due to the callous and preplanned act of drugging, an innocent foreign national lost his life. This act was visited with robbery. Sobhraj's coming to India, far away from home and family members, was for the commission of a criminal act, of his own choosing. This can hardly be reason for any consideration of a sentence which has to be adequate under the circumstances of the crime."

But after rolling these drums of doom, Judge Nath sentenced Charles Sobhraj to seven years at hard labor. Seven lousy years—a penalty so trivial that both Inspector Tuli and the P.P. stared at the bench in shocked disbelief.

Charles, of course, moaned over the injustice of it all, but he returned from the embrace of death quicker than Lazarus. No more than a day or two passed before the old currents began to flow. He broke his fast. He rose from his stretcher. He wrote a new petition of complaint against prison guards. He sent word to Marie-Andrée in the woman's section to lose neither heart nor her trust in him. He seemed eminently capable of vaulting a fence. "This man knows exactly how far to push his body," said Tuli, who had never believed in Charles' attempted hanging or hunger strike. "What a perverse character!"

And although Tuli was moderately happy to slam the prison doors on Charles for seven years, he wondered just how long he could keep him. It would have been hard to find a man in Delhi to bet on the full term.

Certainly not Charles. Amid his busy schedule in Tihar, he found time to consider a new place on the map for the next installment in his life. Several criteria had to be met. He required a country in which he was neither known nor wanted by police, one in which riches abounded, one whose borders were easy to traverse illegally, one whose residents were generous with attention—and applause.

At last report, the serpentine roads of destiny—he believed—would lead him to the United States.